W9-BWN-378

Convenor

CHRISTIANE BRUSSELMANS

Co-Convenor

JAMES A. O'DONOHOE

Senior Authors

JAMES W. FOWLER

ANTOINE VERGOTE

AUTHORS

CHRISTIANE BRUSSELMANS

JEF BULCKENS

JAMES W. FOWLER

CAROL GILLIGAN

STANLEY HAUERWAS

DIRK HUTSEBAUT

JEAN-MARIE JASPARD

ROBERT G. KEGAN

LAWRENCE KOHLBERG

THOMAS LICKONA

JAMES E. LODER

HERMAN LOMBAERTS

ENDA McDONAGH

JAMES A. O'DONOHOE

FRITZ OSER

F. CLARK POWER

ANA-MARIA RIZZUTO

WILLIAM R. ROGERS

EDMUND V. SULLIVAN

ANTOINE VERGOTE

TOWARD MORAL AND RELIGIOUS MATURITY

The First International Conference on Moral and Religious Development

SILVER BURDETT COMPANY
Morristown, New Jersey
Glenview, Illinois • Palo Alto • Dallas • Atlanta

Cover and Frontispiece: *Photos by Lescuyer-Lyon*

RELIGION CENTER
ST. MARY, KENOSHA

TOWARD MORAL AND RELIGIOUS MATURITY

© 1980 SILVER BURDETT COMPANY.

All Rights Reserved.

Printed in the United States of America.

Published simultaneously in Canada.

This publication, or parts thereof, may not be reproduced in any form
by photographic, electrostatic, mechanical, or any other method,
for any use, including information storage and retrieval,
without written permission from the publisher.

ISBN 0–382–00286–5

Library of Congress Catalog Card Number 79-67161

Psy
2068
Brio

CONTENTS

Contents

II

PROCESSES IN RELIGIOUS AND MORAL DEVELOPMENT

Contents

III

THEOLOGY AND PSYCHOLOGY IN DIALOGUE

IV

MORAL AND RELIGIOUS EDUCATION

Foreword

DR. CHRISTIANE BRUSSELMANS

From May 27 to June 2, 1979, twenty European, Canadian, and American scholars gathered at the Abbey of Senanque in southern France. During the week-long international symposium these men and women shared the results of their research in moral and religious development and probed the educational implications of that research.

For the past fifteen years, I have been involved in the field of religious and moral education both in the United States and in Europe. I heard of the work of Lawrence Kohlberg in the area of moral development as early as 1972, while teaching at Fordham University and at Union Theological Seminary in New York. That same year, I had the pleasure of being introduced to him by his colleague James Fowler, who was then in the early stages of his research on faith development. I gained deeper insights into Kohlberg's and Fowler's research when it was my privilege to serve as a visiting lecturer at the Harvard Divinity School in 1974.

I brought to that work a familiarity with the research being done at the Catholic Universities of Leuven and Louvain in Belgium by the Center for Religious Psychology. The Center was founded by Antoine Vergote and has been under his direction for the past twenty years.

As I reflected on my American experience with Kohlberg and Fowler, I could see how their work complemented the research being done by European scholars, and especially that of Vergote and his colleagues. The North American scholars were more interested in the cognitive theories on moral and religious development. The European scholars gave greater emphasis to the relational and affective dimensions of moral and religious development and, as a consequence, were more interested in psychoanalytic theories.

The North Americans impressed me with their remarkable theoretical frameworks embodying the structural-developmental approach. I must say, however, that I was equally impressed by the Europeans with their penchant for empirical investigations into such areas as the role of the parental figures and the formation of the representation of God in children and adolescents, the identification processes relative to sex differences in children, and the role of symbol and worship and their connection to moral commitment to social change.

As time went on, I began to think that it would be a very good thing indeed if representative scholars of both the North American approach and the European approach could be brought together to exchange and discuss the things that unite and differentiate them. To be a bridge builder—that was my dream.

And this dream began to take on concrete form at Easter time in 1976. I was traveling in the south of France and came upon the splendid twelfth-century Cistercian Abbey of Senanque. (Today it is a conference center for those concerned with cultural and religious matters.) Nestled in the depths of an impressive gorge, serenaded by nightingales, and perfumed by the lush fields of lavender surrounding it, the Abbey of Senanque has amazingly survived eight hundred years of sometimes violent history. Around the bell tower are grouped the traditional elements of a monastery—chapter room, refectory, kitchen, dormitory, study room, and church. Generations of master builders and masons have dedicated themselves to creating beauty and unity: perfect simplicity, the search for truth, and a humble and very great skill permitted them to realize the equilibrium of mass and line. On the pillars of the church and on the stones of the walls, one finds the identification marks of the stonecutters. These men succeeded in imparting unity to the variety of forms, volumes, and distributions of light that cannot fail to captivate. Those who lived here found the divine measure and rhythm of all things.

This, obviously, was the perfect place to realize my dream of bringing together those scholars from North America and from Europe who represented such divergent traditions of moral and religious research. And the men and women who finally gathered there reminded me of those who built and created the Abbey of Senanque. Like the architects and masons of the Middle Ages, they succeeded in finding unity in the diversity of tasks and talents they represented.

Many, of course, collaborated in the realization of this dream, and I must mention here first of all the men and women who gave so freely of their time and their learning to the symposium. Their papers represent an immense amount of work and a genuine concern for moral and religious education.

And I must acknowledge in particular the selfless preparatory work done by James Fowler of the Candler School of

Theology at Emory University, Antoine Vergote of the Catholic University of Leuven, William Rogers of the Harvard Divinity School, and James A. O'Donohoe of Boston College. Thanks to their untiring efforts, the International Conference on Moral and Religious Development was brought to a most exciting conclusion.

Finally, I also wish to express my sincere gratitude to Mrs. Barbara Thompson Howell, Senior Vice President and Editor-in-Chief of Silver Burdett Publishing Company. Because of her faith in my dream, her constant support, and her presence at the Senanque Symposium, the Senanque Papers will become a published reality. By underwriting this symposium, the Silver Burdett Publishing Company has once again manifested its deep and abiding concern for excellence in education.

ABOUT THE AUTHOR

Dr. Christiane Brusselmans *completed her theological studies at the Catholic University of Leuven, Belgium. She received a master's degree in pastoral catechetics at the Institut Catholique in Paris and her doctorate in religious education at the Catholic University of America in Washington, D.C. Since 1966, Dr. Brusselmans has been commuting between Belgium, where she teaches in the Theology Department of the Catholic University of Leuven, and the United States, where she has served as a visiting professor at several institutions including Fordham University, Union Theological Seminary, Harvard Divinity School, and Boston College.*

Dr. Brusselmans has authored a number of books and articles, most of which deal with the Christian initiation of children. Her most successful series is We Celebrate the Eucharist, *published by Silver Burdett Company and translated and adapted for use in Spanish, French, German, and Dutch. Another series,* We Celebrate Reconciliation, *is also published by Silver Burdett.*

Before beginning her study of theology, Dr. Brusselmans was a poultry farmer and a folksinger. In 1955, she started a Sunday school for her 24 nephews and nieces, who now number 50. Among her hobbies are gardening, flower arranging, and watercolor painting.

Introduction

An Overview

{2} Virtually no one in our time who looks seriously at the events of the world can escape the uneasy apprehension that values are in flux, that moral convictions have eroded, that a sense of unifying purpose in life and history has all but disappeared. Crimes, from the simplest vandalism through senseless homicides to systematic economic and political oppression, seem to be flagrant and increasing. Even attempts at peace and increased understanding, as in the SALT talks or Mideast accords, are fraught with areas of suspicion, guardedness, and profound value conflict. There appears to be a new wave of narcissism. Both individuals and nations seem to have retreated to a principle of self-interest—the protecting of one's own pleasure and material security amidst a rampant fear that everything, including one's own life, is increasingly threatened: threatened by nuclear explosion, by political and financial decisions outside our grasp, by the diminishing of resources. In short, things feel out of control.

This is a crisis of psychological and theological consequence. People yearn for a way of understanding what is happening to them; a way to recover something of the reassurance that religion offers when it is intact; a way of inspiration and motivation for cooperative responsibility with one another in conserving resources and sharing the possibilities of a better life with all people. There is a yearning for the depth and security of faith, for the sense of God's presence, and for a healing of our malaise, our selfishness, our confusion.

With such yearning it is natural to turn to leaders who are knowledgeable in moral and religious education, to persons of stature and seriousness who have made a careful study of the ways in which individuals and communities become more moral, more significantly religious. Such a group of leaders was selected to work together at the Abbey of Senanque with the specific task of writing the essays that appear in this volume.

Yet to some readers the research, insights, and theory that appear here may seem somewhat distant from those commonplace but universal anxieties about moral violations, the privatism of values, and powerful forces of injustice. No ready answers are given to the pressing problems of how to stop vandalism and disrespect for persons, or to the practical problems of setting up religious education programs. No quick rules or guidelines are given for parents baffled by forms of adolescent rebellion, social defiance, or religious apathy.

But what *is* given is, in our view, a more essential background of understanding and research concerning the modes of moral and religious development in persons, a background which should deepen and support any particular efforts to teach and nourish people in their growth toward more mature religious and moral life.

We attempt in these pages to lay out something of what we are learning about *how* people develop—from the earliest infancy through adulthood—and how in that development the questions of meaning and morality get shaped, dissolved, transformed, and regenerated at potentially deeper levels. The question of how this occurs has previously been asked. and to some extent answered, by diverse and, to a large extent, discontinuous investigators: human developmentalists, educators, personality psychologists, psychoanalysts, ministers, cognitive theorists, theologians, ethicists, and multitudes of simply concerned persons. But what is unique and important about this volume is that it brings a number of these diverse investigations together and puts them in conversation with each other. The result is not a perfect blending or a new super-theory, but it *is* a deepened and enriched view of a number of perspectives that should be seen together, along with some effective suggestions for how these might be interrelated.

Also, while the essays are not "programmatic" in the narrow sense, there are significant guidelines given in each essay for those concerned with educational programs—whether they be in the schools, the churches, families, or some other setting. These suggestions of educational implications should serve as "transitional" links between the larger theoretical discussions and the development of specific programs of moral and religious importance.

While this book includes contributions from psychologists, theologians, and educators, the organization of the book does not cluster individual contributors along disciplinary lines. Many of

{4}

the psychological contributors also have theological training and interests, as do the educators. Similarly, to an unusual degree, the theologians in the group exhibit an informed receptivity to the psychologists' studies of moral and religious development.

Each author has provided a brief description of the work he or she has done for this volume. The reader may turn directly to these, which are found at the beginning of each chapter. Here we simply want to give an introduction to the organization of the volume as a whole and to suggest some ways different readers might approach it.

Conceptual Frameworks

The first section of this book, Conceptual Frameworks, includes two papers that set forth the wide boundaries for the "playing field" of the conversation. The first chapter (Rogers) gives a comprehensive overview of the variety of empirical and reflective studies of moral and religious development. Giving particular attention to issues of method, this introductory paper sets forth a bold vision and some important guidelines for a program of integrated inquiry in religion and psychology. The second chapter (Fowler) provides an introduction to a new theoretical approach that seeks to integrate aspects of personality and of religious and moral growth under the category of faith development. With antecedent sources in the works of theologian H. Richard Niebuhr and psychologists Erik Erikson, Jean Piaget, and Lawrence Kohlberg, it represents one significant beginning toward the broad, inclusive program of research and theory building called for in the first chapter.

Processes in Religious and Moral Development

After the presentation of these initial theoretical perspectives, it seemed best to carry the reader into the rich data of some studies that examine more closely the processes of moral and religious development and transformation. Section II includes several research papers that grow out of psychoanalytic starting points (Vergote, Rizzuto, Jaspard, and Loder). These tend to emphasize the primally powerful influences of the child's affective relation- {5} ships with parental figures on his or her composing of repre- sentations of God and forming of the moral disposition. From the same broadly psychoanalytic background, there are empirical studies focusing on the process of "identification" with parental and other referent figures as a decisive aspect of moral and religious development (Hutsebaut) and on the interplay of liturgi- cal innovation and the development of social critique and reform (Lombaerts).

Juxtaposed with the psychoanalytic studies—and offering good examples of both the complementarity and the significant differences between these perspectives—are two reports of re- search and theory building that derive from the structural- developmental approaches of Piaget and Kohlberg (Gilligan, Oser). Focusing upon the genesis of structures of cognition and their evolution, these theorists attend to the ways persons at different "stages" construct, interpret, and respond to situations of religious and moral choice.

The papers in Section II represent an interesting variety of research methods and provide the reader with an instructive opportunity to compare the similarities and differences of these two major theoretical orientations. They also present some very promising new avenues of research.

Theology and Psychology in Dialogue

Section III of the book brings together studies that address both the domains of theology and theological ethics and of psychologi- cal approaches to moral and religious development. Alternating between theological ethicists and psychologists, this section rep- resents perhaps the fullest dialogue to date between moral theology and the structural-developmental approach to moral development. With an eye to mutual enrichment and critique, the three theological ethicists (McDonagh, O'Donohoe, and Hauer- was) draw lines of connection between traditional theological

{6}

approaches and psychological research and theory. In various ways they emphasize the importance of extending Kohlberg's work in the direction of including the social context of moral development, of taking seriously the necessity of religious expression and conversion, the ongoing "life-story" of the moral agent, and the critical importance of the stories, images, and symbols provided by communities of faith as sources of moral motivation and direction. Power and Kolberg contribute a chapter in which a rich examination of the relations between religious faith and morality receive both theoretical and empirical clarification. The chapter by Kegan represents a significant advance toward a nonreductionistic integration of theological and psychological perspectives on personality development. Kegan opens the way for a fundamentally new extension of the structural-developmental paradigm that encompasses the whole person.

Moral and Religious Education

The concluding section of each chapter deals with educational implications; in addition, the final section of the book directly addresses aims, methods, contexts, and contents of moral and religious education. These studies include a very comprehensive look at the shape of moral education in Catholic high schools (Bulckens) and a programmatic approach to education for democratic cooperation in elementary schools (Lickona). The final study is an analysis and critique of the powerful latent impact of television and other mass media on the moral sensibilities of today's children and adults (Sullivan).

This book does not claim to have reached firm conclusions or tight synthetic integrations of the various positions of its authors. The participants were surprised and gladdened, however, by the many points of common engagement and complementary insights that emerged as they read and discussed each other's papers. In our revisions we have tried to alert the reader to places in our colleagues' chapters when related issues are addressed.

As we launch this collection of studies, we hope it will find a wide audience. We believe that educators at many levels will find it useful. It should be valuable in graduate seminars on personality or moral and religious development. It will serve as a text both in university courses and in professional schools of theology and education. Teacher education programs in moral and religious education will find virtually all parts of the book useful. Ministers, teachers, and other practitioners of moral and religious education should find chapters in each of the sections stimulating. Perhaps especially instructive will be the studies contained in Sections II and IV. Researchers and theorists of moral and religious development—as well as of ego and personality change—should find Sections I, II, and III particularly engaging.

We are aware that, frequently, the essays unapologetically employ a somewhat technical language. Nonetheless, we hope that for general readers the difficulty of interpreting these passages will be balanced by the excitement of encountering fresh insights and inspiring directions for our common challenge to develop the moral and religious maturity required for citizenship in a truly global community. And beyond this we hope that the insights, including the understanding of those more puzzling times when growth brings pain and disequilibrium, will be useful to many people troubled, and yet somehow hopeful, about the perilous pilgrimage we are on.

{7}

CONCEPTUAL
FRAMEWORKS

Interdisciplinary Approaches to Moral and Religious Development: A Critical Overview

WILLIAM R. ROGERS

Introduction

{12} Exciting new theories are being developed to bring together previously disparate areas of research, interpretation, and education. This chapter addresses the disarray and fragmentation of current ideas and methods. How can we have a more profound, coherent, true, and relevant understanding of how people develop individually, in familial and social interaction, and within the utlimate context?

The goal of this chapter is to lay out a structure, a map as it were, of the various approaches that can be taken to moral and religious development, and to set forth a paradigm in which they can be most constructively related. Is there any relationship, for instance, between "psychoanalytic" views and "structural-developmental" views? between "moral theology" and "faith development"? between empirical studies of "image formation" and theoretical notions of "character" and "will"?

The teasing out of such an integrative paradigm is not easy. But it is made more accessible by looking briefly at the logic of the debates that have led to formulating new perspectives. These perspectives are examined both as they view each other, and as they focus on the central task of deepening our understanding of the nature of moral and religious development. As Sherlock Holmes once said: "It is only by proceeding with many lines of evidence, my dear Watson, that we shall find the truth somewhere in between."

A Multiperspectival View of Truth

It is said that John Dewey, in an effort to describe the problems of epistemology, developed an example of how various people might analyze a penny. A metallurgist might define it in terms of the dominant copper alloy content. An economist would be interested in its value as one one-hundredth of a dollar and its (marginal) purchasing power. A mathematician might regard it as an elementary binary computer, especially useful for making Yes-No random choices. An artist might define it primarily in terms of the miniature bas relief of Lincoln. And one might go on.

The point is that a variety of questions, interests, and conceptual categories may be applied to a single phenomenon and the consequence of those applications will yield an array of conclusions. No one is necessarily more "true" than another, but rather generates information pertinent to the "universe of discourse" from which its dominating question emerged. Furthermore, taken together, the fuller the array of perspectives and subsequent analyses, the more complete will be the knowledge of the phenomenon.

{13}

Our concern is to come to a more complete understanding of the phenomena related to religious and moral development. And to do so, we are immediately made aware of the variety of perspectives which may be taken—which, indeed, have been taken. The problem of understanding is complicated by the fact that we are not analyzing a single object, like a penny, but a complex array of phenomena—beliefs, commitments, values, rituals, ideas, and actions in relation to matters of ultimate concern.

Unlike Dewey's example, each perspective on religious and moral life is not self-contained and isolated in its own universe of discourse. The perspectives that have grown up around the study of religious experience have many similarities in language and approach (though the more subtle differences could also lead to misunderstanding). Further, there is the expectation of mutual self-correction, elaboration, and augmentation among the perspectives. At least I will argue that there *should* be such an expectation—for without it there may be bias, inconsistency, contradiction, and isolation. Our concern is for a more synthetic, multidimensional understanding, which can locate and relate the various contributions which have been made from various disciplines and various approaches within each discipline.

The compelling task of this chapter, then, is to develop a *constructive theory* of the *structure of issues and perspectives* relevant to the study of moral and religious development. We face here a *metatheoretical* task, a task of developing a theory of theory—that will illuminate the design of fields and arguments, their force and their omissions, as they bear on a central effort to clarify the nature of religious life.

I stand in a certain hesitant envy of biologists and physicists who can use sticks and multicolored balls to show the three-dimensional molecular or atomic structure of material entities (like DNA). To give a clear picture of the way ideas or perspectives are integrated, especially in interdisciplinary studies, it is also possible to set forth a series of *models*. That is to say, these are a few relatively typical ways in which people bring diverse perspectives together. And to schematize these into models may show more clearly not only *how* this is done, but also the relative advantage of one model over the others.

{14}

Figure 1 offers a visual scheme of such models. In this figure

FIG. 1. Alternative Models of Interdisciplinary Relationship

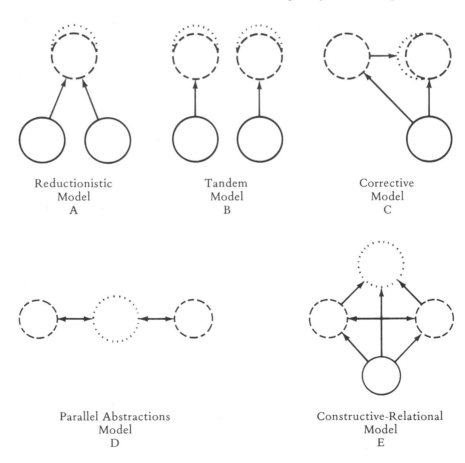

Reductionistic
Model
A

Tandem
Model
B

Corrective
Model
C

Parallel Abstractions
Model
D

Constructive-Relational
Model
E

the black circles represent concrete, lived reality—the "stuff" of experience—the basic phenomena of life (in this case, basic moral and religious life). The lines show connections of observation and reasoning by which the interpretative perspectives, viewpoints, or disciplines—the dashed circles—are formulated. The dotted areas represent essentially new theoretical understanding.

{15}

In the reductionistic model (A), one dominating perspective or discipline assumes that it can interpret within its purview literally any phenomena, although to do so often necessitates a blurring of the richness and particularity of experience or perhaps a negation of self-understandings and alternative explanations given the same experience. Often the interpretative scheme is built from reflection on one dimension of life—for instance, valuing and decision-making or psychopathology and therapy—but its categories are then applied as though exhaustively sufficient to explain other realms of life—for instance, religious belief and practice. The example could, of course, be reversed. There are instances where religious and philosophical perspectives have been assumed to account for all experience, demanding a reductionism of other realms of both experience and interpretation to those philosophical categories.

The difficulty here is twofold: Not only does such reductionism imply an imperialization of one set of interpretations over all others, but it also diminishes rather than enhances our depth of appreciation. The arrogance of such reductionistic judgments is hardly the way to expand genuinely interdisciplinary cooperation in understanding moral and religious development.

One way to guard against such bias or reductionism is to allow for the independent spheres of different disciplines with their own discourse, method, language, and theory—as is represented in the tandem model (B). For instance, psychology could be permitted its own approaches to ordinary life and developmental change, while theology contents itself with interpreting the particular relationships of humanity to the transcendent. Or different forms of psychology, for example, the psychoanalytic and the structural-developmental, might be seen as having their own arenas of investigation—early object relations and dynamic processes, over against stages and transitions in cognitive organization. While such a tandem model allows a certain mutual respect for other positions, it has the serious danger of artificially separating intrinsically unified phenomena, as well as fracturing and compartmentalizing our understanding of what is experienced. For too long we have allowed specializations that do not listen carefully to one another. Especially in the area of moral and religious life, we must seek a unified and more integrated understanding.

Model C, the "corrective" model, would seem to offer such unification. This model represents those attempts, especially in theology (or specifically moral theology), to attend both to the moral or religious experience *and* to the helpful interpretations of that experience coming, for instance, from relevant social scientists. We may see, for instance, how psychological views of narcissism correct and expand some of the understandings of sin. Yet while such interdisciplinary openness is commendable, it leaves out one very important feature. It borrows along a one-way street without taking responsibility for the *mutual* critique and expansion of understanding that would be necessary in a true dialogue. Genuine interdisciplinary engagements entail mutual risk, openness, and willingness for revision. Theories, like persons, are in the process of becoming, and stand in community with one another.

The model of "parallel abstractions" (D) exemplifies something more of this dialogue and mutuality. Here we think of interdisciplinary work about the nature of religious or moral development which appreciates both psychosocial insights and theological interpretations—where there may be mutually descriptive and normative convergence in a newly integrative format. But a major weakness of many such endeavors is that they lose sight of the empirical, living reality which they claim to be understanding. The fascinating and scholarly work may be simply abstraction, removed from the everyday suffering, doubting, wondering, celebrating rhythms of life—especially the life of faith and felt moral responsibility.

Finally the "constructive-relational" model (E) is one which attempts to remain faithful to the primary phenomena, while encouraging relational attention to multiple disciplines of interpretation—moving toward a more constructive and holistic understanding (that cannot be "claimed" or reduced by any *one* of the various approaches). Here there may be both mutual critique and support, empirical attentiveness, and innovative possibilities for integration.

{17}

The overall vision of this volume is one with this constructive-relational intent. But the model must be expanded to indicate the wider variety of disciplines and approaches which orbit as interpretative perspectives. If we could take a "top view" of this model (E), showing the various perspectives (as dashed circles) which come to bear on the central constructive under-standing (dotted circle), it might look like Figure 2.

The following discussion in this chapter attempts to explicate further the logic of relationships among the various perspectives indicated in Figure 2, shown on the following page. The numbers on that figure suggest the sequence of discussion. To some extent they show the history of revisions and critiques which have moved our understanding forward. The discussion enables us to see something of the interesting ferment that brings us to the challenging edge of cooperative and interrelated understandings represented in this volume.

Linkages and Mutual Critique Among Perspectives on Moral . and Religious Development

From Moral Theology to Moral Reasoning

Within the history of Christianity, the discipline of moral theology has represented an attempt to derive principles of right action from the systematic and doctrinal understandings of God's will for humankind. Within a biblical perspective this task has functioned derivatively along three lines of moral discourse: (1) the identification of good ends—the coming of the Kingdom and the enactment of justice; (2) statements of qualities of the good moral agent—as in the Sermon on the Mount; and (3) codifica-

FIG. 2. A Constructive-Relational View of Moral and Religious Development

In this illustration, arrows indicate direction of movement. Dotted arrows indicate directions of needed theoretical attention. Upper areas are more theoretically derivative; lower ones more empirically based.

{18}

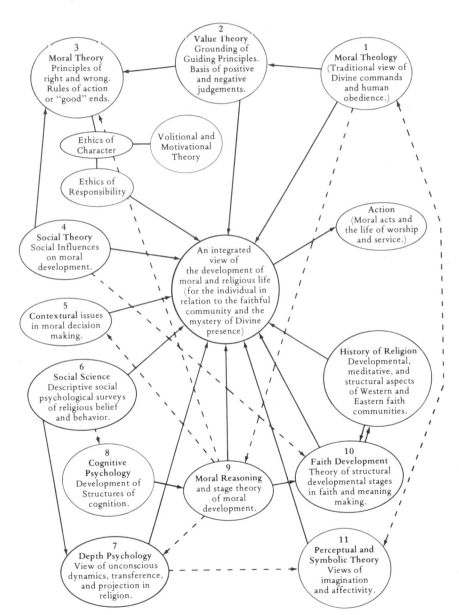

tion of right acts—as in the Decalogue. Through various lines of moral casuistry and interpretation, these understandings of God's commandments were elaborated and taught as guides for moral behavior. The appropriate posture of the believer was understood to be one of obligation and obedience—with appropriate penitential avenues for the restoration of those who inevitably sin.

{19}

This understanding has its counterpart in what appears to be the commonsense view of moral development. Insofar as some actions are deemed correct and others are deemed wrong, we may try to teach our children to differentiate the dos and don'ts both by moral example and by rewards (and punishments) for their obedience (or disobedience). Particularly in periods of history when there seems to be moral decay, insensitivity, untrustworthiness, and violence, the urgency of these moral lessons seems all the more compelling.

But the *job* is not easy:

> Any parent or teacher who has found himself saying to a child "How many times have I told you not to do that?" must wonder whether moral development is as painful to both adults and children as it sometimes appears to be. Assured that the child's hearing is fine, the adult is bewildered by the slowness of the child to assimilate principles and rules of right and wrong and perplexed about the means of assuring consistent application of those principles. Moral education has been equated with the teaching of rules and the development of character, which is expected to manifest itself in behavior that exemplifies the traditionally revered virtues of honesty, self-control, courage, friendliness, and respect. The goal of most programs has been to instill these virtues so that they become internal principles guiding behavior and decision-making. The means of accomplishing this is basically to confront the child repeatedly with examples of adults and older children who exhibit specific virtues by lecturing about these virtues, and by rewarding and punishing their practice or omission.[1]

There are essentially two difficulties with this traditional approach. One is that even if we can teach people to make the "right" moral choices in certain instances, that does not give us

---

[1] R. Duska and M. Whelan, *Moral Development: A Guide to Piaget and Kohlberg* (New York: Paulist Press, 1975), p. 5.

{20} confidence that they will show real maturity in the understanding of reasons for the moral judgment, or that they will be able to generalize to other more complex dilemmas where conflicting principles are at stake. Duska and Whelan give a simple example of this point:

> Take an example of two girls, one fifteen and the other twenty-nine. The girl of fifteen gets invited to a high school prom. It is her first date with this escort, and after a lot of drinking he makes sexual advances. She answers "It's wrong" and refuses. The twenty-nine year old gets invited out by a salesman who came into the office, and after a number of drinks he asks her to go to his hotel room to make love. She refuses. Now, in both cases we have, first, a correct moral judgment and, second, the will to do what is right. Is that sufficient to indicate moral maturity in both cases? The answer is no, because an important factor has been left out—the *reason* for the moral judgment.
>
> Let us continue our supposing for a moment. What if our fifteen year old is challenged by her boyfriend: "Why not?" Probably she would reply: "My mother told me it's wrong." But suppose our twenty-nine year old woman fended off her escort's passes with the same answer. Do we not find such a reason ludicrous coming from a supposedly mature woman? And although we might think our fifteen year old should have a better reason, are we not somewhat more patient with her than with the twenty-nine year old?[2]

The second difficulty is simply that the approach does not work. The principles if only applied deductively and dependent on volitional obedience do not prove to be motivationally effective beyond the earliest stages of behavior, if even there. In the classic and extensive studies by Hartshorne and May, examining injunctions against stealing, cheating, and lying, some startling results were consistently obtained:

1. There is no correlation (relationship) between character training and actual behavior.

2. Moral behavior is not consistent in one person from one situation to another. A person who doesn't cheat in one situation

---

[2]*Ibid*. p. 2.

may cheat in another. The circumstances are the most important factor.

3. There is no necessary relationship between what people say about morality and the way they act. People who express great disapproval of stealing and cheating may actually steal and cheat as much as everyone else.

4. Cheating is normally distributed around a level of moderate cheating—that is, normally everyone cheats a little.[3]

As a number of commentators have pointed out, these findings left considerable question not only about the ineffectiveness of traditional moral education but also about the presuppositions concerning universality and consistency in moral behavior.

In many ways the work of Jean Piaget and Lawrence Kohlberg in cognitive development and moral reasoning has emerged as a more viable alternative for explaining and nurturing moral development. Their ability to demonstrate that the cognitive structures utilized in moral reasoning develop through a series of transitions and definable stage changes led the way to understanding a natural and invariant sequence in which moral development occurs. Furthermore, they also found that the form or style of the next progessive stage was both cognitively accessible and, in some ways, even compelling when persons experienced the challenge and disequilibrium of inadequacy in handling problems within their given stage structures. Though this process could not be rushed or manipulatively induced through the introduction of artificial dilemmas, it did point the way toward a new and apparently more effective view of moral education— one in which discussion and action involving people within a modest range of stages, together with leaders knowledgeable in the components and sequence of stages, could move toward more subtle and responsive moral growth. (A summary of these stages of moral development in Kohlberg's view are found in the Notes on pages 48–50.) Such thinking is amplified in this volume in the work by Power and Kohlberg and by Fowler and in the interesting critiques by Lickona and Hauerwas. Various

---

[3]*Ibid.* pp. 6 and 7. From a study conducted by Hartshorne and May of the University of Chicago.

difficulties have appeared in the Piaget-Kohlberg position, despite its strong appeal as a way of both understanding and facilitating moral development. It does not have a clear way of either studying or interpreting the movement from moral reasoning to moral action; that is, it misses what has been called the cognitive principle related to acting, doing, or striving.

There are research problems in scaling protocols, particularly in the Stage 5 or 6 area. The moral experience of women appears to be insufficiently represented, especially in the Stages 3 and 4 judgments. There is little development of a positive ethic of cooperation or responsibility. And there is criticism of the implied Kantian theory of morality with its dominating focus on a central principle of justice. Using this as the basic organizing question for the interpretation of critical questions in moral reasoning could leave affective components untouched and alternative ethical understandings untapped. From a religious perspective this becomes especially important if we are interested in the moral importance not only of how we think, but of how life and behavior are transformed by the power of a centering *relationship* of faith, fidelity, or religious transformation.[4]

Also of special importance in our analysis of the structural-developmental approach to moral reasoning is the implicity, and until recently unacknowledged, shift from a descriptive and empirically based assessment of stages to a normative evaluation of the virtue, as it were, of progression "up" the stages. On the one hand I wish to argue for the importance and legitimacy of the empirical work that has been done. It is an essential corrective to philosophical and abstract theorizing that characterized much of the earlier moral theory. But on the other hand it is difficult to make moral claims for a descriptive moral theory. Normative justification does not simply spring into being on the basis of a subject matter (particularly in youthful human experience) that involves dilemmas of human choice. Kohlberg deserves credit for

---

[4]See especially Jean Piaget, *The Moral Judgment of the Child*, trans. M. Gabain (New York: Collier Books, 1966): and Lawrence Kohlberg, "Stage and Sequence: The Cognitive Developmental Approach to Socialization," in D. Goslin, ed., *Handbook of Socialization Theory and Research* (New York: Rand McNally, 1969), pp. 347–380; or "Moral Stages and Moralization" in T. Lickona, ed., *Moral Development and Behavior* (New York: Holt, Rinehart and Winston, 1976), pp. 31–53.

coming to address this issue in his interesting essay "From Is to Ought: How to commit the naturalistic fallacy and get away with it in the study of moral development."[5]

Furthermore the emphasis on developmental features of moral reasoning has had difficulty giving sufficient attention to the *social* influences on moral development. There have been some efforts to validate the theory through cross-cultural studies. But there has been little inclusion of work like that of E. Sullivan, W. Schroeder, or V. Obenhaus on the contextual and class features which are expressed in varieties of moral belief and moral behavior, as well as in moral reasoning.[6]

From Value Theory to Will

Perhaps another way of accounting for the ineffectiveness of earlier modes of moral theology and moral education would be to suggest that it was less the guidelines and sense of obligation that were wrong than it was the weakness of human will in carrying out those obligations. Indeed, for centuries the "privations of the will" (Augustine) were seen as instrumental in the sinful turning away from virtuous obedience and the proper love of God. The problem seemed to be in not only knowing the right, but having the will to do the right. "The strengthening of moral fiber" usually meant admonitions, cajolings, lessons from moral exemplars, and veiled or unveiled threats against the weak will.

Yet the undynamic theories of will were also deficient. They often naively assumed a conflict-free cognitive control of volition. It was necessary to see the will in relation both to dissonant affections and to a secure or at best identifiable value base.

More recently there has also been a parallel shift away from abstract or philosophical attempts to state an objective value theory and a movement toward interest in how positive and

---

[5]Cf. T. Mischel, *Cognitive Development and Epistemology* (New York: Academy Press, 1971), pp. 151–235.

[6]See W. Schroeder and V. Obenhaus, *Religion in American Culture* (New York: Free Press of Glencoe, 1964), and the chapters by Sullivan and McDonagh in this volume.

{24}

negative values are comprehended and acted upon in everyday life. The problems in value theory were partially created internally, as the crucial center of confidence in justifiable first principles became undermined after Kant. They were also partially created by a series of convincing arguments from other disciplines: knowledge of the cultural relativity of values (Herskovitz); awareness of the political and economic "mystification" by those who used the idea of an unassailable value theory for their own (elite) ends (K. Marx); and the clinical recognition of unconscious and denied motives connected with the infantile yearning for a secure parent evidenced by forms of "wish-fulfillment" including claims for an absolute moral scheme (S. Freud).

Such arguments raised serious questions about the viability of any absolute value theory. And they seem to have been responsible for at least three intellectual trends related to moral development. One was an accelerated attempt to strengthen our understanding of, and dedication to, a volitional theory that would give more attention to *how* persons become moral whatever the content of the values. It is in this respect that the discoveries of those interested in moral reasoning and cognitive development have been particularly helpful—even though that emphasis has further augmented the shift of attention away from objective moral claims. This trend has been further augmented by process theological attention to the increase of "qualitative meaning" as central to the broadening and deepening of values within the "creative event."[7]

The second trend was a redefinition of "values" on the part of many scholars so that the term now refers most typically to a set or progression of attitudes and preferences which are internally organized by individuals and are very likely to be at least partially ideosyncratic in content. One could think of this as a "psychologizing" of the value questions (a trend which has ironically been fostered by some of the same people who have attempted to draw our social energies toward universal value changes around issues of nonviolence, ecological policy, popula-

---

[7]Henry Weiman, *The Source of Human Good* (Carbondale, Illinois: Southern Illinois University Press, 1973).

tion responsibility, consumer rights, and justice in the distribution of goods and services especially in the Third World).

The third trend has been to dull or obliterate interest in concepts of will. The claims for the significance of social, economic, or psychological determinism seemed so strong to some that even the idea of an autonomous will seemed a figment of the lingering wishful fantasy of self-determination.

Most recently, however, the pendulum has begun to swing back—a fortunate trend in my judgment both for the understanding of moral behavior and for the psychological definition of identity and responsible choice. One evidence of this is the theological work of someone like Lonergan.[8] Another is the reintroduction, especially through phenomenology and existential psychology, of the functions of internal selectivity and direction through processes of perception and choice. Such elements were present in earlier philosopher/psychologists like William James and John Dewey, but only recently have those elements been reemphasized coterminously with attention to unconscious processes. Interestingly in the case of James, one side of his work seems to have stimulated the American penchant for experimentalism in psychology; another was related to originating interests in the unconscious; and a third, his interest in volition and perception, seems to have influenced European thought, especially Husserl. Only now do these divergent streams seem to be reconnecting in work such as that represented in this volume. A further evidence of the renewed interest in what I would like to call a "postanalytic" view of will is found in explicit studies of the psychological and religious nature of will as in the work of James Lapsley.[9] All of these interests in the redefinition of will have a bearing on the possibility of agency and responsibility in moral decision making. They represent an attempt to move beyond the theories of determinism (and overdetermination) that would stifle any genuinely moral life (or for that matter, human initiative generally).

---

[8]Bernard Lonergan, *Insight "A Study of Human Understanding"* (New York: Harper & Row, 1977).

[9]James Lapsley, *The Concept of Willing* (Nashville: Abingdon Press, 1967).

From Will to Character

Even the postanalytic theories of will, however, have serious difficulties on both the psychological and the theological sides. Psychologically they do little to account for the origin or maintenance of those goals toward which the will might organize personal energy. Do such goals come from the social matrix, or are they understood as matters of an emerging internal identity? What are the functions of language and the social construction of reality versus the internal attempts at meaning-making and directional intentionality? If a volitional psychology does not deal with such issues, it is in danger of falling back into a predynamic shallowness in which goals or ends are thought of as freely chosen and then pursued to the degree that the will remains "strong." Any view that fails to deal with the subtlety of "mixed" motivations, unconscious denial and resistance, or changes in the developmental possibilities of self-direction and moral reasoning cannot do justice to the reality of the human condition.

Theologically there is a related but slightly different set of problems. Notions of the will are most frequently connected with a view of religious obligation in response to the priority of divine command. This position, when it functions like the derivative moral theology discussed earlier, also recognizes the inevitable failure of will. But with appropriate contrition, confession, and absolution, one is assured of God's justification and the possibility of personal forgiveness and renewal. The serious difficulty with this construction of the religious life is that it points almost exclusively to the individualistic nature of human moral effort, and it makes the human dilemma "discontinuous" with the need for God's grace.

Stanley Hauerwas, in his study of theological ethics, carefully contrasts this view based on obligation and justification with the more typical Catholic view of growth and sanctification. The latter emphasizes more the features of internal development, and moves the view of the self beyond the image of atomistic compliance with a series of obligations. Hauerwas's view reestablishes the importance of a broader understanding of "character" which treats life more holistically, and in many ways bridges the traditional Protestant and Catholic perspectives on justification and sanctification.[10]

    In particular, a view of religious character alters the primary {27} question of the moral life. Rather than asking "What shall I do and how can I have the will to do it?", it asks "What shall I be?" The concern is with how in the Christian life there can be unity and self-consistency, not how one must reach a specific and atomistic decision about moral dilemmas. The broader issues of character appear to be more typical of the real struggles and growth of the life and faith. And they reflect a fuller religious concern with the normative quality of being—a quality which of course is also thought of as determinative of action, but broadly so, in that its attention is less to rules than to the appreciation of one's own "horizon" (Lonergan)—the maximum field of vision from which all life issues (not just those identified as "moral problems") are perceived more accurately, fully, and compassionately.[11]

    The strength of this understanding of character is somewhat offset, however, by several other omissions in the theory. Though in one sense it attempts to address the real life of faith, it tends to develop its argument at a methodological level which I would call "parallel abstractions." That is, it links philosophy, theology, and psychology in interesting theoretical ways, but shows little empirical attentiveness to the way such character and moral life really develop. Furthermore, aside from a few general references to psychologists like Skinner and Erikson, there is little specific content articulating the dynamics of the psyche in the formation of "character." There is only the broadest statement of "development," with no attention to the influence of progressive stages of cognitive or moral reasoning. Most significantly, there is a ten-

---

[10]Stanley Hauerwas, *Character and the Christian Life: A Study in Theological Ethics* (San Antonio: Trinity University Press, 1975). See also his chapter in this volume.

[11]This understanding has some interesting similarities to the final projects of Nietzsche regarding the development of character. His question after *Gay Science* is one of how we come to love and "be," after points of despair in human effort and will. His suggestions that we need to rid ourselves of resentment imply at one level a critique of the Christian employment of resentment in the hatred of evil; but at another level a support for the more basic insight that love overflows in response to our having been sustained, even in tragedy, much more than when we willfully try to meet the admonition to love.

dency to reintroduce an unqualified view of will and agency which again overlooks the effects of experiences of profound helplessness and the power of unconscious determinants. Statements like "Men are beings who, because they can envisage, describe, and intend their action, initiate change in themselves and the world around them in such a way that they can claim to be the cause of the change" certainly give a sense of potency to human constructions, but come dangerously close to being discontinuous with social reality, egocentric, and potentially blasphemous.[12] Such a view needs to be tempered both theologically and empirically.

From Social Surveys to Depth Psychology

Beginning with the work of Starbuck and Hall in 1900 and 1908,[13] there has been an attempt to collect the sort of empirical data on moral and religious development which would form something of the corrective which I am suggesting is necessary in balancing the more theoretical views of character, will, and value. Though beginning with particular attention to conversion experience and adolescents, the empirical studies have sampled an increasing variety of persons of different ages, religious persuasions, and social settings. The surveys have utilized several methods of data collection—anecdotal observations, personal documents, questionnaires, semiclinical interviews, semantic instruments,[14] word association procedures, and graphic or pictorial methods. The findings from such procedures are perhaps most amply reviewed and discussed in the compendium on *Research on Religious Development*, edited by Merton Strommen.[15] In general they have focused on types of conversion, characteristics of particular "religious experiences," conceptions of God, patterns of religious

---

[12]Hauerwas, *op. cit.* p. 88.

[13]E.D. Starbuck, *The Psychology of Religion* (New York: Scribner, 1900); and G.S. Hall, *Adolescence* (New York: Appleton, 1908).

[14]See Osgood *et al.*, *The Measurement of Meaning* (Urbana: University of Illinois Press, 1957).

[15]M. P. Strommen, ed., *Research on Religious Development: A Comprehensive Handbook* (New York: Hawthorn Books, 1971). See especially ch. 17 and 20.

institutional participation, the formation of religious "identity," and ways of handling intellectual paradox or historical and scriptural contradiction.

Attempts to evaluate and extend this type of research have led to the formation of several major research institutes, most especially the Search Institute, Minneapolis, and the Religious Experience Research Unit, Oxford.[16] Some of the more recent studies have included comprehensive (n = 5000) surveys of religious attitudes and practices across generations,[17] and an extended investigation of a broad taxonomy of religious beliefs in America, funded by the National Endowment for the Humanities.[18] Studies in Catholic religious development have been recently summarized in publications of the Office of Research, Policy, and Program Development in the Department of Education of the U.S. Catholic Conference.[19]

The weakness of such studies, in spite of their efforts to be objective and descriptive, is that they start out with the most conventional definitions of what constitutes the "religious" object of investigation, and in many cases a somewhat provincial and uniform sample. Some would criticize these studies on the grounds that religion is conceived as essentially a human activity (rather than as a bipolar or relational interaction with the Transcendent). I believe the studies are equally suspect on the grounds that they do not delve deeply enough into the fundamental dilemmas, strivings, unconscious yearnings, authentic affirmations, ambiguities, and suffering that constitute the most profound and generic wrestling with ultimate issues of meaning, trust, devotion, and worship.

What is at stake here is perhaps the very definition of religion and morality. And I would want to state clearly that my critique of many of the present survey studies is that they define religion too

---

[16]Search Institute, 122 West Franklin Avenue, Minneapolis, MN 55404: and Religious Experience Research Unit, Manchester College, Oxford, Great Britain.

[17]*A Study of Generations* (Minneapolis: Augsburg Publishing, 1972).

[18]A Search Institute project.

[19]See especially Hart M. Nelson *et al.*, "The Religion of Children"; and Raymond Botvin *et al.*, "Religion and American Youth," U.S. Catholic Conference, 1312 Massachusetts Avenue, N.W., Washington, DC 20005.

narrowly as formal institutional participation or as having to do with what one *says* explicitly about God. In a more comprehensive view of religion, we need to look beneath the surface of what is explicitly expressed and analyze the implicit forms of devotion embedded in the "deep structure" of one's willingness to organize life around something believed to be ultimately trustworthy, or around tacit interests and commitments—those constituting a functional or implicit affirmation of religious significance. To observe the operations of such implicit, functionally religious claims of significance does not mean that we have to judge such organizing concerns as *ultimately* significant. That would take us into the further arena of normative and theological adjudication. But what *is* suggested here is that we take seriously these deeper centers of commitment in studying religious issues in human life, not stopping with the surface phenomena of commonly defined "religious" ideas and behavior.

Obviously, a powerful intellectual influence on the emerging understanding of "depth" structures in human motivation and the underlying organization (or disorganization) of experience has been psychoanalysis. Psychoanalysis might be viewed variously as a mode of psychiatric clinical procedure, as a method in the study of the human situation, or as a set of ideas and presuppositions about the nature of persons, and by extension (intentionally in the case of Freud) as the basis of a theory and critique of culture. It is in this latter sense as a theory of persons and culture that it deserves our attention here. Gathering strength, like the empirical psychology of religion, shortly after the turn of the century, this form of analysis has given us conceptual tools for unraveling some of the dynamic tensions and paradoxical reversals of unconscious intent that lie beneath various manifestations of religious belief and practice.

Perhaps it goes without saying that the original thrust of the psychoanalytic propositions with regard to religious and moral development assigned a strong unconscious pathological skew to such motivation and practice. Beginning with his essay on "Obsessive Acts and Religious Practices" in 1907, Freud identified a whole series of potentially neurotic functions symptomized in religious life, most having their origins in psychosexual develop-

{31}

ment. Religion from this perspective was seen as potentially obsessive-compulsive in its ritual dimensions, a return of repressed guilt or repressed fear of death, a neurotic "wish" for a longed-for father correlative with unresolved Oedipal strivings, a projection onto the cosmic screen of unacknowledged fears and longings for omnipotence, a regression to infantile forms of helplessness and dependence, or perhaps above all an illusory self-deception by which people imagine the security and solace of a loving God, a purposive history, and a stable moral base to protect them from the inevitable suffering, anguish, and death experienced in a hostile reality.[20]

The criticisms of psychoanalysis, philosophically, scientifically, and clinically, have been extensive. The most telling challenge has come in the recognition of the "psychogenic fallacy" in Freud's descriptions of religion; *viz.*, the logical insistence that the possibility of psychologically unconscious motivations related to fear or longing or any other unacknowledged need does not constitute a valid judgment about the existence or nonexistence, the reality or unreality, of that object or force which is desired (or found to be meeting that need). Any truth claims for objective reality have to be determined on grounds other than the subjective wish, or the psychogenesis of the claim itself. Furthermore, Freud hardly based his claims on a broad or representative sample of real experience in religious development, especially given the range and history of religious phenomena. And there was no accounting for the whole prophetic dimension of that history, a dimension which clearly could never be identified with false solace or easy security.

In spite of such criticisms, however, we are deeply indebted to Freud and his followers for developing sensitivities and methodologies that would take us beneath the surface of psychological life into an examination of dynamic, motivational, and symbolic elements at times active in religious development. Especially Carl Jung (whose debate and disaffection with Freud can be read as centering largely on religious issues), Alfred Adler, and Otto

---

[20]See Freud's arguments especially in the *Collected Papers, Totem and Taboo, Civilization and Its Discontents, Moses and Monotheism, Beyond the Pleasure Principle, New Introductory Lectures,* and *The Future of an Illusion.*

Rank in the early period, and later figures like Erich Fromm and Erik Erikson, broadened the understanding of depth psychological dimensions of religious development. Such an understanding has been incorporated directly into the mainstream of theological discussion by writers like David Roberts[21] or, more recently, Paul Pruyser and others.[22] No serious and comprehensive theory of religious and moral development can afford to omit such analyses, especially as they bear on the necessity for differentiations precisely in the areas of unconscious determinants and the origins of distortion versus health (or clarity) in the perception and symbolization of religious forms of devotion. The essays of Vergote and Rizzuto included in this volume illustrate this very well.

Yet concomitant with the sense of importance of this "depth" perspective comes a qualifying sense of its limitations, especially in relation to structural-developmental theory. Other than broad suggestive schemes of early development given especially by Freud, alternatively by Melanie Klein, and revisionally by Erik Erikson, little has been done to link a specific understanding of cognitive and religious development to the unfolding of dynamic conflict or even psychosexual issues. The avenues for such integration may now be available in ways which I shall suggest below.

From Cognitive Theory to Phenomenology and Perception

Our discussion at this point "thickens" considerably, for we begin to deal with simultaneous movements which, as we shall see, all converge in an expanded image of the integrative task to which I just alluded. This and the following sections are in no way neatly sequential—rather they are layered and intermeshed with one another as we move toward the richly textured fabric of this theoretical construction of religious development.

---

[21]David Roberts, *Psychotherapy and a Christian View of Man* (New York: Charles Scribner's Sons, 1953).

[22]Paul Pruyser, *A Dynamic Psychology of Religion* (New York: Harper & Row, 1968); Heiji Faber, *Psychology of Religion* (Philadelphia: Westminster Press, 1975); and Antoine Vergote, *The Religious Man* (Dublin: Gil and MacMillan, 1969).

In the earlier discussion of cognitive theory, we dealt with the movement from moral theology to moral reasoning. Of particular importance in that movement has been the work of Piaget. What I wish to suggest here is that there are two distinguishable trends involving cognitive theories which bear further on the critical task of detailing religious development theory. One trend continues to draw on Piaget and the related moral development theory of Kohlberg in establishing a richly detailed view of stages in the process of "faith development." The other is a movement which is not directly related to the work of Piaget but is more of an outgrowth of philosophical, particularly epistemological, concerns with cognition. And in this latter case, the discourse has proceeded more by way of critique and contrast with earlier epistemological theories than by appreciation, incorporation, and expansion (which is more the case with faith development theory).

Let us begin by focusing on the phenomenological and symbolic approaches. Specifically, there have been both philosophical and psychological critiques of a previous view of knowledge, including religious understanding, insofar as they rested on the primacy of intellective capabilities and a confidence in conceptual categorizations of experience. The earlier view, often identified as Cartesian because of the "cogito" so exactly stated by Descartes, has given way under the pressure of two related forces. One has been the phenomenological movement with its insistence on the primacy of lived experience—on the "facticity," the relationality, the "intentional arc" of experience, which is always rooted in the body. I have in mind here particularly the later work of Husserl, Marcel, and the bulk of the influential work of Merleau-Ponty.[23]

The second influence has been the attention to symbolic and imaginative processes which complement, but are by no means exhausted by, conceptual categories. The power of images and symbols in human consciousness, especially religious consciousness, has been apparent for centuries—indeed the history of that awareness is tragically interwined with some of the most painful

---

[23]See especially Merleau-Ponty, *The Phenomenology of Perception* (London: Routledge & Kegan Paul, 1962).

and divisive controversies in Christendom including the separation of Eastern and Western orthodoxy. But in more recent times, the debate has been newly framed in a psychological/ philosophical way that draws together imagination, affection, and symbolization with cognition. Ernst Cassirer, Suzanne Langer, and Rudolf Arnheim have been particularly important in this connection.[24]

Both of these influences come together around the issue of perception, in particular around the structure and force of internal processes of organization which do not simply await sensory input, or even social values and language, but which anticipate, seek, attend, and evaluate experience in terms of symbolic and synthetic wholes.[25] This interest in perception, and related "perceptiveness," has a direct influence on our understanding of religious development. It points to a way of understanding the functions of image and imagination in faith, including ways in which such images change for individuals (and cultures) over time.[26] It also helps us appreciate the actual symbols which are utilized in the life of worship and teaching.[27] It enables us to understand the power of symbols reappearing across cultures and faith communities. And of particular relevance to our discussion here, it opens up an arena of research concerning the modes of appropriation of symbolic perception in specific stages of religious development.

One creative set of studies which takes this emphasis into account is that of Anne Dumoulin and Jean-Marie Jaspard.[28] These studies give particular attention to the symbolic perceptions of children between the ages of six and twelve as theoreti-

---

[24]Perhaps the most fruitful, though difficult, work putting this position forward is that of Langer, *Mind* (Baltimore: Johns Hopkins Press, 1972).

[25]This position also stands over against the ideas of "structuralism," which as a literary critical position holds that the structure of language shapes "texts," including social interaction, without regard to internal perceptual organization.

[26]See especially W.F. Lynch, *Images of Faith* (Notre Dame: University of Notre Dame Press, 1973).

[27]See especially F. David Martin, *Art and the Religious Experience: The "Language" of the Sacred* (Lewisburg: Bucknell University Press, 1972).

[28]Anne Dumoulin and Jean-Marie Jaspard, *Les Mediations Religieuses dans la perception du divin et l'attitude religieuse de 6 a 12 ans* (Bruxelles: Lumen Vitae, 1972).

cally distinguishable from intellectual conceptualizations. This is achieved largely through an imaginative methodology which draws to some extent on open-ended questions but builds these around stories and photographic images which serve as a stimulus to the imagination and internal narrative of the child. The images in their studies are specifically religious in content—Dumoulin's work being addressed to the image, role, and functions of the priest; Jaspard's focusing more on aspects of the Eucharist—both giving rise to symbolic forms of reflection about the mediating rites that are important particularly within the Catholic perception of the Divine-human relationship. The studies are oriented both toward the phenomenological understanding of the lived experience of childhood and toward a history of religion's perspective which concerns itself with an analysis of the complexity and diversity of religion mediated through particular symbols and practices. This work is particularly important to our understanding here because it builds from an integrative notion of "symbolic perception"—an aspect of religious development which is understood to rest at the intersection of a sense of affective presence, the initiation of effective action, the interiorization of ethical conscience, and the development of a sense of law and work. In this way the theoretical commitments which have guided the research locate themselves in relation both to traditional ritual and ethical activity and to the imaginative ways in which that is both appropriated and expanded by individuals. This is one important way of moving toward an integration of developmental and normative concerns, by a perceptual rather than strictly cognitive formulation. Jaspard's studies of two-to-seven-year-olds, contained in this volume, further this work and enrich it with additional psychoanalytic interpretation.

The difficulties with such studies, however, pertain to the scope and generalizability of findings which are possible when one works with a relatively limited sample population. Specifically, it leaves open questions about the nature of symbolic perception outside the specific age range and developmental processes of the subjects investigated. In addition, it does not examine possible limitations created by the relative uniformity of images in which the particular symbols under investigation (priest, the Eucharist, and God), as well as the familial settings, stem from a single, regional, and religious context. While it is important to start from such a context, it would be valuable to broaden our understanding of religious development as we investigate further aspects of the plurality of religious symbol systems and their functions in relation to imagination as well as cognition.

From Cognitive and Moral Development to Faith Development

The second major way in which cognitive theory has been influential on understandings of religious development, as we suggested above, is through the emergence of "faith development" research. Drawing on the structural-developmental work of both Piaget and Kohlberg, as well as on earlier theological work concerning faith as a way of knowing and being,[29] James Fowler has developed a significant and comprehensive theory of the stages of faith development. In common with the structural-developmental approaches to moral reasoning as well as with Erik Erikson's theories of stage and crisis, Fowler finds a consistent structure of qualitative, irreversible changes in a universally recognizable sequence involving the transformation of previous structures of knowing and their incorporation to new, more comprehensive and differentiated modes of knowing. The definition of faith in these studies (as differentiated explicitly from broader conceptions of religion within institutional and historic structures) points to that process or quality of participation in which knowing, construing, and valuing come to take on a focused significance for an individual's being-in-the-world. There is an attempt to integrate the rational and passional elements within the self and to include as well the relational (tripolar) characteristics of self, community, and the ultimate sources of

[29]See especially H. Richard Niebuhr, *The Responsible Self: An Essay in Christian Moral Philosophy* (New York: Harper & Row, 1963); and Don Browning, "Faith and the Dynamics of Knowing," in Peter Homans, *The Dialogue between Theology and Psychology* (Chicago: University of Chicago Press, 1978), pp. 111–134.

reality. The activity of faith has a direct bearing on the construction of meaning by which forms of "world maintenance" and "world coherence" come profoundly to shape an individual's life and intention.[30]

Part of the importance of this approach is that it already moves toward an integration of a number of divergent strains which we have been examining. It includes within itself ideas about forms of logic and moral reasoning, modes of theological responsiveness, questions of the locus of authority, and some recognition of the emotional attachments which are related to the structure of meaning. Furthermore, the clarity by which both the stages and the transitions between stages are presented gives a refreshing and useful source for those whose educational task is to help facilitate moral and religious education. Without such an understanding of the sequence of the stages, it would be very easy to form global, unrealistic, and unworkable approaches out of reach of the cognitive and relational capabilities of individuals at their particular level of development. Fowler sets forth the components of this theory very clearly in the following chapter. There are important parallels between his stages of faith development and other developmental theories. And these are suggested in his paper.

In spite of the usefulness and clarity of Fowler's theory, there have been several criticisms. Some have objected that there are no essential criteria for establishing the normative object of faith— the transcendent God—whose existence might be said to be a prerequisite for any experience of faith. While such an objection is reasonable on some absolutistic theological grounds, it is not responsive to the lived experience of faith insofar as all definitions, affirmations, or appropriations of Divine reality are, so far as our finite limits demand, from the inevitable perspective of human apprehension or personal knowing.

There has also been criticism of the social science methodology in faith development research. Rather than an adequate product of developmental psychology, it has been termed "a

---

[30]J. Fowler and S. Keen, *Life Maps: Conversations on the Journey of Faith* (Waco, Texas: Word Books, 1978).

rather well-informed hunch, articulated into a broad series of unproven assumptions, a veritable library of a priori's that have not been deeply tested in any usual sense of that word."[31] This is an unnecessarily harsh judgment in my view, since there have, in fact, been significant empirical samples from which this stage theory has arisen. The more serious methodological problem is that the research incorporates a mixed inductive and deductive procedure—inductive in the sense of a patient and open willingness for new categories to emerge through a content analysis of salient features of the open-ended quasi-clinical interviews; and deductive in the sense of utilization of categories, principles, and variables generated by previous social scientists or theologians. It is unfair, however, to charge that these categories are simply imposed on experience. They tend to be used honestly and self-critically, open to refinement and the emergence of new propositions where they do not account for the data. Important revisions of this sort have been suggested, for instance, by Carol Gilligan, primarily in reference to moral development, as she analyzed the experience of women, finding material that did not fit the existing model.[32]

Two other criticisms that emerge in the light of our schema in this chapter are the following. The links to perceptual and symbolic theory are not made clear in the faith development research. Even though there is a general appreciation of the functions of imagination, the dominant attention to variables having to do with ways of knowing does not take into account a discussion of the processes of perception, or the modes by which visual form and anecdotal narrative give an organizing focus to one's meaning of the constructions. Secondly, the contributions of depth psychology while again viewed appreciatively are not incorporated directly into the faith development materials. Aspects of unconscious conflict or paradoxical intention, more specifically areas of self-deception, anxiety and fear of loss of

[31]Alfred McBride, "Reaction to Fowler: Fears about Procedure," in T. Hennessey, ed., *Values and Moral Development,* (New York; Paulist Press, 1976), p. 214.

[32]Carol Gilligan, "In a Different Voice," *Harvard Educational Review,* Vol. 47, No. 4 (Fall 1977), pp. 481–517.

self-esteem, grief and despair, might (and I believe do) confound the apparent statements of meaning and value which are given in quasi-clinical interviews. Indeed, the very term "quasi-clinical" may be misleading insofar as most research interviews done within the structural-developmental perspective follow a format designed to elicit material relevant to the stage analysis or, at least, to the resolution of particular dilemmas imposed by the interviewer, rather than focusing attention strictly on the clinical well-being of the individual. On the other hand, there does appear to be a therapeutic dimension to these interviews, and there certainly is an honest attempt to understand the internal categories, feelings, and meanings intended by the subjects in their own terms. In Section III of this volume, Robert Kegan identifies such sensitivity as a significant point of convergence between structural-developmental, pscyhoanalytic, existential, and moral approaches to persons.

From West to East

Much of the work discussed thus far has arisen exclusively from the Western and primarily Christian understandings of religious and moral development. And although it may seem like a difficult complication, I would suggest that the most comprehensive view of religious development will have to take account of the pluralism of traditions in various faith communities. This appears especially true insofar as a number of Eastern traditions place specific emphasis on just these questions of stage development in faith which we have been discussing. They do so, however, with a symbolic or metaphoric language that at first seems nonsynchronous with the terms of cognitive or moral development in Western psychology.

Recently, however, several careful scholars working with original texts and interpretations of stages obtained with the meditative traditions have made just such correlations. In one study by Daniel Brown, the form of cognitive theory which has seemed most useful is the information-processing model of K.

Pribram.[33] The integrative work has shown similar forms of attention to perceptual processes, cognitive organization, attitude formation, affective interaction, and universalizing comprehension. This research assesses the Mahamudra tradition of Tibetan Buddhism in relation to cognitive psychology. Similar work on a variety of traditions, although with less attention to the original texts, has been done by Mary Jo Meadow.[34]

But the missing element of comparative work, at least in the case of Brown, is that it does not specifically address the issues of moral and value theory in the West, nor does it draw lines of complementarity or comparison with meditative traditions in Western Christianity. Furthermore there are serious difficulties when handling what might be called "teleological counterclaims." For instance, even though there may be important similarities in the stages along the path of development as perceived by both cognitive psychological and Buddhist traditions, there may be, indeed are, some very divergent views of the proper ends. Whereas cognitive information theorists envision goals that are constructionist, synthetic, accurate in pattern recognition, and complex in conceptualization, there are contrasting goals within Buddhism which are deconstructionist, breaking down patterns, relinquishing conception, and permitting the central soteriological end of relief from suffering. To simply say that both views may be right in terms of their own differing internal structures may be valuable but insufficient. It is hoped that the new work of Wilfred Cantwell Smith, *Faith and Belief,*[35] also in comparative religions, will establish a frame for understanding these complementary traditions in a universalizing but particular fashion, aiding our integrative task.

[33]Daniel Brown, Unpublished doctoral dissertation, University of Chicago, 1978, p. 00.

[34]Mary Jo Meadow, "Personal Growth: An Eastern Spiritual and Western Ego Approach." Paper for the Psychosocial Interpretations in Theology Section of American Academy of Religion, New Orleans, Louisiana, November 1978.

[35]Wilfred Cantwell Smith, *Faith and Belief* (Princeton, NJ: Princeton University Press, 1979).

From Faith Development to Moral Theology

In a similar way, then, both comparative religion studies and faith {41} development research leave open the important question of how to relate most effectively to the substantive understandings of Christian theology. This brings us full circle, back to the recognition that while moral theology may have needed correction in the direction of moral reasoning, faith development also needs modification in the direction of a revised moral theology if it is not to be simply relativistic, or naive in its assumption of an implicit norm of progression. This question is both methodological and theological. When we start with empirical studies, either semiclinical interviews with individuals or observations of religious rituals or, for that matter, the analysis of texts, a series of careful steps must be followed to assure validity in the lifting up conceptually of the most salient features of the data at hand. But even with the greatest care, such studies generally remain descriptive. When they are considered normative it is only in the sense of statistical averaging, not valuational superiority.

On the other hand, the difficulty with earlier forms of moral theology was that they remained oblivious to the descriptive task of observing how moral or faith development actually occurred experientially. Hence, the authority of their normative stance was diluted by its potential obtuseness, nonutility, and irrelevance.

What is obviously needed is a mode of interaction which can remain faithful simultaneously to the data of experience (both developmentally and within its social embeddedness) and to the normative affirmation of rootedness in Divine presence and creativity. As long as static, deistic, and absolutistic views of God remained dominant, this meeting was difficult, if not impossible. But as moral theology becomes more responsive to the implications of a living God, and more appreciative of the embodiment and historicity of revelation, that discontinuous dichotomy is transcended. Process, relationship, and development may be seen as characterizing both the divine and human realms *and* their essential interaction.

Furthermore the territories of the descriptive and normative may not be as discontinuous as had been argued. Even norms in the sense of the valuationally desirable must be acknowledged as conceptions articulated within the human community. And insofar as creation is celebrated and valued as an aspect of Ultimate Presence in time, the very possibilities and actualities of life and growth become manifestations of that Presence. Within a naturalistic theological and moral perspective, the very place to look for the normative compassion and judgment of God is in the reality of that development of character which, under the optimal conditions of nourishment, actualizes the divine creativity and responds with gratitude and deepened perception. To understand the processes by which that development unfolds is to see something of the profound intention of our very being. That, indeed, is a normative sensitivity.

Refining Our Interdisciplinary Theory

In painting this series of theoretical relationships, I have attempted to portray something of the shimmering flow of streams and eddies that move toward deeper convergence in a more "oceanic" understanding of religious and moral development. Consistently, the critical reservations that have been expressed regarding each separate theoretical stream have pointed explicitly to the need for inclusion of data or sensitivities important within the vitality of other streams. Appreciation of the power of further complementarity and interaction surely energizes our mutual effort.

Perhaps what is most needed in this effort is a metaphor or conceptual model to organize such interaction. I began by suggesting a multiperspectival model related to Dewey's analogy of the penny. But I believe we must be cautious lest we end up with what I have termed a set of parallel abstractions (Model D)—that is, a number of theoretical dialogues, all interesting and related to their own presuppositions, but incongruent with one another and out of touch with the lived reality of religious and moral experience.

Our task is perhaps more difficult, but certainly more adequate, if we strive for the *constructive-relational* model (E). This suggests an attempt to retain respect for divergent perspectives and traditions, understood in their own historic contexts and internal thematic development, but at the same time to seek a broader sense of the relationships and interactions among these perspectives, and with the phenomena they seek to understand. Beyond simple relationships, either of complementarity or of contrast, there should also be the intent of a constructive burgeoning toward novelty and unity of understanding at a new level. Such a model is integritive and integrative; it respects the integrity of intact streams of concern and it attempts to see them as a more integrative whole. It is hoped such concerns can be very close theoretically, as well as semantically.

The principles which should govern a constructive-relational model could be spelled out more carefully. Let me suggest the following:

1. Focal flexibility—attention to molecular as well as molar issues in the interaction; that is, bringing together not only broad schema of, for instance, psychoanalytic and structural-developmental thought, but also particular points like "identification" and "role-taking."

2. Ontogenetic fidelity—respect for the integrity of viewpoints in terms of their tradition, context, and originating intention; that is, maintaining of other perspectives, either psychological or theological.

3. Cognate selectivity—attention across perspectives to the comparable levels of particular substrata as well as to comparable cognate levels of abstraction; that is, not making unfair comparisons or criticisms by taking a major point from one tradition and judging it against a more minor point from a different cognate level in another tradition.

4. Interfield relativity—structural awareness of the interdependence of every part of a perspective on every other part, and of the manner in which influences across perspectival fields at one level affect interactions at other levels; that is,

recognizing that the entire "gestalt" shifts when one part is reconceived or responds to a different set of evidence.

5. Observational authenticity—attention to given features in object description, and a quest for implicit order and process relationships rather than the imposition of order in the interests of theoretical coherence; that is, looking honestly and anew at events, for instance, the early life of the child in response to religious images, without predetermination of structures or interpretations. Interpretative issues may guide one's questions, and may be a second step in the analysis. But in between we must observe accurately and authentically the lived phenomena.

6. Nonhierarchical mutuality—cross-perspectival interaction without imperializing the categories and methodological demands of one discipline or perspective over another; that is, a commitment to cooperative interaction, free from the reductionism discussed in Model A.

7. Investigative inclusivity—appreciation of a relatively enduring and overarching structure of being in which particular perspectives and processes are contained (though not exhausted); essentially a theological grounding; that is, an awareness of the more ultimate process of reality in which our interests in how people become moral and religious are most profoundly held. Research and theory, as all of life, are sustained and tested by their inclusion in this larger whole.

Specifically in the formation of a constructive-relational view of religious and moral development, we need to give attention to the variety of perspectives discussed in the preceding sections. That would include relational attention to at least the following factors: modes of cognitive development, patterns of symbolization, forms of experienced identity, affirmations of fundamental trust, areas of dynamic tension, dimension of social, intellectual, and linguistic context, structures of meaning-making ("forms of world coherence"), forms of moral reasoning, styles of transformation from egocentrism to mutual interdependence, changes in perceptual acuity, modes of conceptualization of the Transcendent, and forms of relationship and devotion to that which is understood as Ultimate.

Fortunately, several of the perspectives we have looked at, {45} especially Fowler's faith development theory, already take a number of these variables into account. Therefore, the task is not quite as awesome as it might appear. Furthermore, there are several theorists who are already suggesting ways of carrying out the constructive-relational task. One is Robert Kegan whose work, as presented in this volume, shows theoretical and clinical ways of integrating depth psychological, structural-developmental, and existentialist thought around the Piagetian principles of assimilation and accommodation.[36] Others are William Boyce and Larry Jensen, who bring together moral philosophy and cognitive approaches to moral reasoning in an integrative and research model.[37]

Clearly the task of seeing how these streams come together is a large one. It is unlikely that the wisdom of any single theoretical genius will be sufficient to comprehend the whole. It is hoped that the outline here gives some glimpse of the character of the waterfront presented in this book. But only together can groups of concerned, knowledgeable, and insightful scholars and teachers attend to the constructive-relational challenge. Fortunately, we have such groups. Fortunately, the task is as exciting as it is significant. And fortunately, the benefits are not reserved for obtuse hypertheoretical purists but will be directly helpful in constructing more nurturant environments for the moral and religious development of persons.

Educational Implications

In one sense this chapter has given a theory of theory—an approach to the question of how all the succeeding chapters

---

[36]See chapter by Kegan in this volume, and also his edition of *The Counseling Psychologist,* Summer 1979.

[37]William D. Boyce and Larry C. Jensen, *Moral Reasoning: A Psychological-Philosophical Integration* (Lincoln: University of Nebraska Press, 1979).

might be seen to fit together in a fuller view of moral and religious development. But even within this discussion there are implications for moral and religious education which could be lifted up.

{46}

1. The clearest implication is that any educational program, whether within the school, the church, the family, or some alternative setting, should be based on similar multiple perspectives. It must give attention not only to moral guidelines, or religious precepts and symbols as the case may be, but also to the patterns of identification, the stages of reasoning, the modes of personal attachment, the forms of effective authority, the language and influence of the social context, the felt dilemmas and questions, and the inherent anxieties and yearnings of the person. In a sense it is exactly such multiple sensitivities that correspond to the various theoretical perspectives we have been examining.

2. We must attend to the fact that moral and religious life is not just a matter of *specific* decisions about dilemmas or specific sacred acts of devotion; but that both realms involve highly integrated sensitivities, responsibilities, attitudes—matters of character, will, thought, and affection—that run through all of life. Hence the style of education, the qualities of relationships it fosters, and the total life involvement with persons may be just as important as the *content* "taught."

3. Just as there is a *communal* and *cooperative* element necessary in developmental paradigm construction, there is an important communal element within moral and faith development itself. Our educational activity should optimally include peers, parents, and persons with differing social and moral perspectives, so that in the meeting of felt concerns, together with the resources of a normative tradition, we may develop the maximal benefit of mutual support in the process of growth.

4. Just as we must be attentive to the exactness of different originating questions and languages (of other theoretical perspectives so as not to do them an injustice—what I have called "ontogenetic fidelity"), so we must be attentive to the varying questions and assumptions of those for whom we have educational responsibility. We must be similarly careful

about the use of language, respecting the forms of the other, and attempting to work from where they are—even if in our original judgment they seem coarse or uniformed. Even as we may try to exert influence, we must be careful not to fall into the trap of an arrogant reductionism by which we pretend that our view is the *only* view. There is always mutual learning to be done!

5. We must be careful about the tendency toward provincialism in moral and religious education. Especially when we think about non-Western approaches to moral development, we see the particularity of our own approach. And it is hoped that one of our goals can be to help bring new respect for other *world* traditions in the context of mutual understanding.

6. We must guard against capitulating to mere "relativism." As some of the following essays show, there are differences between acknowledging relativity and condoning the relativism of self-justification and self-interest (an issue which is also developmentally important). Our constructive-relational model does not imply that any one perspective is sufficient (or "better"), but rather that in viewing the whole we are led to appreciate a wider variety of concerns which often come to focus on a more centering unity. Stated educationally, our goal might be one of congruently appreciating a breadth of persons and positions, relative to their particular concerns; and a focusing on a position which "brings us home" as it were—that brings us to a place appropriate to our faith community, situation, and cognitive capability. Put quite simply, we need not feel guilty about the importance of such a resting place, a place of affirmation, even while recognizing that there are other perspectives. It is analogous to the religious awareness of, and respect for, pluralism, while at the same time acknowledging a particular confession and community of meaning. Such a balance can be very important to the tension/support of the individual and the communal in education as well.

7. Finally, moral and religious education has sometimes floundered on the horns of a dilemma between a form of ab-

{48}

solutism and a form of relativism. The choice for educators has sometimes seemed to be one between giving the absolute norms and dogmas of the Church versus allowing exclusive freedom to the recognition and fulfillment of individual needs. In its classic form this has pitted demands of conformity and authority over against antinomianism and relativity. Yet neither alternative is satisfactory—either to the subtleties of moral choice or to the fostering of significant human, let alone transcendent, relationships. It is hoped that the preceding theoretical discussion will help us move beyond that bipolar dilemma. It does so in two ways. First, it shows that the full range of considerations in moral education must include a number of other facets (character, value, social critique, cognitive development, depth structures of personality, etc.) as well as traditional moral concerns and human feelings in relation to one another. Only taken together do these enable people meaningfully to "construe the world." And second, it shows that the very predicament of authoritarianism and relativism is developmentally concluded. It is hoped that, within knowledgeable and supportive educational settings, the leaders will be nourished in their movement beyond dependent authoritarianism or instrumental relativism toward a place of maturity, inclusiveness, and creativity. Mature creativity within education, as within individuals, is always marked by both affirmation of commitment and mutuality of exploration; by both centeredness and openness.

NOTES

DEFINITION OF MORAL STAGES*

I. Preconventional level
At this level, the child is responsive to cultural rules and labels of good and bad, right or wrong, but interprets these labels either in terms of the physical or the hedonistic consequences of action (punishment, reward,

---

* Kohlberg's "Stages of Moral Growth" in Hennessy, Thomas C., ed., *Values and Moral Development*, (New York; Paulist Press, 1976), pp. 2 and 3.

exchange of favors) or in terms of the physical power of those who enunciate the rules and labels. The level is divided into the following two stages:

Stage 1: The punishment-and-obedience orientation. The physical consequences of action determine its goodness or badness, regardless of the human meaning or value of these consequences. Avoidance of punishment and unquestioning deference to power are valued in their own right, not in terms of respect for an underlying moral order supported by punishment and authority (the latter being Stage 4).

Stage 2: The instrumental-relativist orientation. Right action consists of that which instrumentally satisfies one's own needs and occasionally the needs of others. Human relations are viewed in terms like those of the marketplace. Elements of fairness, of reciprocity, and of equal sharing are present, but they are always interpreted in a physical or pragmatic way. Reciprocity is a matter of "you scratch my back and I'll scratch yours," not of loyalty, gratitude, or justice.

II. Conventional level

At this level, maintaining the expectations of the individual's family, group, or nation is perceived as valuable in its own right, regardless of immediate and obvious consequences. The attitude is not only one of *conformity* to personal expectations and social order, but of loyalty to it, of actively *maintaining*, supporting, and justifying the order, and of identifying with the persons or group involved in it. At this level, there are the following two stages:

Stage 3: The interpersonal concordance or "good boy–nice girl" orientation. Good behavior is that which pleases or helps others and is approved by them. There is much conformity to stereotypical images of what is majority or "natural" behavior. Behavior is frequently judged by intention—"he means well" becomes important for the first time. One earns approval by being "nice."

Stage 4: The "law and order" orientation. There is orientation toward authority, fixed rules, and the maintenance of the social order. Right behavior consists of doing one's duty, showing respect for authority, and maintaining the given social order for its own sake.

III. Postconventional, autonomous, or principled level

At this level, there is a clear effort to define moral values and principles that have validity and application apart from the authority of the groups or persons holding these principles and apart from the individual's own identification with these groups. This level also has two stages:

Stage 5: The social contract, legalistic orientation (generally with utiliturian overtones).   Right action tends to be defined in terms of general individual rights and standards which have been critically examined and agreed upon by the whole society. There is a clear awareness of the relativism of personal values and opinions and a corresponding emphasis upon procedural rules for reaching consensus. Aside from what is constitutionally and "democratically" agreed upon, the right is a matter of personal "values" and "opinion." The result is an emphasis upon the "legal point of view," but with an emphasis upon the possibility of changing law in terms of rational considerations of social unity (rather than freezing it in terms of Stage 4 "law and order"). Outside the legal realm, free agreement and contract is the binding element of obligation. This is the "official" morality of the American government and constitution.

Stage 6: The universal-ethical-principle orientation.   Right is defined by the decision of conscience in accord with self-chosen *ethical principles* appealing to logical comprehensiveness, universality, and consistency. These principles are abstract and ethical (the Golden Rule, the categorical imperative); they are not concrete moral rules like the Ten Commandments. At heart, these are universal principles of *justice,* of the *reciprocity* and *equality* of human *rights,* and of respect for the dignity of human beings as *individual persons*.

ABOUT THE AUTHOR

Dr. William Rogers is Parkman Professor of Divinity/Religion and Psychology at Harvard University and serves on both the Divinity and Education faculties. His courses at Harvard include Dynamics of Religion and Psychology, Theology of Perception, Psychotherapy, and Methodoloy in Cross-disciplinary Research: Religion and Human Sciences. Among Dr. Roger's publications are The Alienated Student; Nourishing the Humanistic in Medicine: Interactions with the Social Sciences; "Order and Chaos in Psychopathology and Ontology," *in* Dialogue Between Theology and Psychology: *and* Project Listening.

In addition to his work as an educator and a psychologist, Dr. Rogers has exhibited as a sculptor and painter. He sings with the Tanglewood Festival Chorus and the Boston Orchestra and is a member of the Society of Friends.

Faith and the Structuring of Meaning

JAMES W. FOWLER

Introduction

{52} To get a grasp of what this chapter is about, let me ask you to reflect for a few moments on the following questions:

If you divided your life into chapters like a book, how would you name the chapters so as to suggest what each was really about?

What relationships and experiences have most affected the way you see life?

What becomes of us when we die?

Are we accountable to anyone or anything beyond ourselves for the ways we use our lives?

Do you consider yourself to be a religious person?

In the last seven years I and my associates and students have asked those questions and many more like them in long interviews with about 380 persons. Our respondents are men and women, boys and girls; Protestants, Catholics, Jews, agnostics and atheists, homemakers, professors, business people, and blue-collar workers. Their ages range from four to eighty-four. Their responses give us vivid windows into those lives in progress. As they speak—sometimes with difficulty, and often bringing important things to speech for the first time—we get access to how they are making and maintaining meaning in their lives. We learn something about whom and what they trust. We see something of their life-values and commitments. We see something of the shape and direction of their *faith*.

From analyzing and comparing these interviews we have found seven different major "styles" of faith. We believe these seven "stages" are developmentally related. We believe they describe a faith pilgrimage which is generic—a kind of "Everyman's Story"—though not everyone completes the journey. The stages describe "forms" of faith which underlie the great variety of our values, beliefs, and life-styles.

This chapter presents this understanding of faith development. I believe this work has important implications for parenting, for counseling, and for religious education. Some of these implications are suggested at the end of the chapter.

Faith: An Overview

"The meanest man must have his canvas, and it must be one which reflects somehow, his own sense of significance in a world that is significant. Above all, it must be integral, unified, even if it should suffer from being pale." So writes Ernest Becker in the conclusion of one of the most insightful chapters of *The Structure of Evil*.[1] The chapter is about *Homo Poeta*, man the meaning-maker, the singular animal burdened with the challenge of composing a meaningful world. *Faith* has to do with the making, maintenance, and transformation of human meaning. It is a mode of knowing and being. In faith we shape our lives in relation to more or less comprehensive convictions or assumptions about reality. Faith composes a felt sense of the world as having character, pattern, and unity. In the midst of the many powers and demands pressing upon us, enlarging and diminishing us, it orients us toward centers of power and value which promise to sustain our lives, and to guarantee "more-being."[2]

Although it is by no means fully conscious, and is often largely unreflective and tacit, I believe faith to be a human universal. Most often it comes to expression and accountability through the symbols, rituals, and beliefs of particular religious traditions. The major religious communities are the living repositories of the faith—expressions of countless peoples in the past and present. These elements form traditions. They can serve to awaken and express the faith of people in the present.[3] But faith is not always religious in the cultural or institutional sense. Many persons in our time weave and paint their meaning-canvases in communities other than religious, and often with media which have no direct relationship to traditions of group piety or religious worship.

Faith is an extremely complex phenomenon to try to operationalize for empirical investigation. It has more dimensions than any one perspective can contain. An examination of two

{53}

---

[1] Ernest Becker, *The Structure of Evil* (New York: Macmillan, 1968), p. 210.

[2] H. Richard Niebuhr, *Experimental Religion* (New York: Harper and Row, 1972).

[3] See Wilfred Cantwell Smith, *The Meaning and End of Religion* (New York: Mentor Books), especially ch. 7.

major dimensions of faith's dynamic may help us to appreciate that complexity and to be clearer about faith. In this approach I aim to treat faith as a generic *human* phenomenon—a way of leaning into or meeting life, whether traditionally religious, or Christian, or not.

Faith as Relational

Faith begins in relationship. Faith implies trust in another, reliance upon another, a counting upon or dependence upon another. The other side of faith as trust is faith as attachment, as commitment, as loyalty. Erik Erikson points to the developmental foundations of faith when he observes that the first major task faced by the child's infant ego is that of achieving mutuality in a relationship marked by trust with the primary giver of care (usually the mother).[4] As the infant comes to trust and rely upon the consistency and care of the parent it also comes to feel a sense of trustworthiness, of *rely*-ability in the self, which becomes the anticipation of a later ability to commit the self and to invest loyalty. Writers such as Martin Buber, George Herbert Mead, Harry Stack Sullivan, in addition to Erikson, have clarified how imperative for the devleopment of the self is this fundamental "faithfulness" in the relation of the child to primal others.

But I turn to the philosopher Josiah Royce[5] and to the theologian H. Richard Niebuhr[6] for the most helpful clarifications of the foundational quality of faith as relational in human life. Royce and Niebuhr show us that all viable and lasting human communities have either a tacit or an explicit faith structure which is triangular in form. In communities a self (S) is bound to others (O) by shared trust and loyalty:

S ⟷ O

4Erik H. Erikson, *Childhood and Society*, 2nd ed. (New York: W. W. Norton, 1963), ch 7.

5Josiah Royce, *The Sources of Religious Insight* (New York: 1912), ch. V.

6H. Richard Niebuhr, *Radical Monotheism and Western Culture.* (New York: Harper and Row, 1960); *The Responsible Self* (New York: Harper and Row, 1963).

But our ties to others are mediated, formed, and deepened by our shared or common trusts in and loyalties to centers of supraordinate value (CSV). Thus: {55}

Consider a few examples: Although I will never know personally more than a few hundred other citizens of my nation, I am bound to them all in some quality of trust and loyalty through a shared commitment to the principles of justice and right which inform the Constitution and Declaration of Independence. In another context, the faith structure of the university centers in free inquiry and a commitment to truth. Though I may never know personally many of my colleagues in other schools or departments of the university, I presume—until proven otherwise—that they share with me a loyalty to and trust in the central values underlying the university. Other examples could be offered endlessly: the tacit covenant to truth required in the use of language; the covenantal aspect of marriage; the presumption of fidelity to duty and to standards of excellence in the professions and business; and so on and on. The interesting thing is that this triangle of faith, which is the hallmark of viable and lasting human relationships at every level, is made visible to us as much in its breakdowns or failures as when it is in good, working order. Theodore White's book on Watergate is aptly titled *Breach of Faith*. When we fail the public trust in politics, are unfaithful in marriage, or fail to live up to the standards of our profession, not only do we betray our covenanting partners—tacit or explicit—but we also betray the center(s) of supraordinate value to which we are presumably loyal.

A moment's reflection will show that each of us belongs to a number of faith-relational triangles. In each of the roles we have assumed, in each institutional context in which we work, in each significant relationship we enjoy, we "keep faith" with some others and with the value commitments we share with them. Certainly, in examining this triangular faith structure of relationships, we are in touch with a major source of the forms and colors with which we paint on the canvas of meaning which nurtures *Homo Poeta*.

As a culmination of our look at faith as relational, let me point to the broadest and most inclusive relationship in faith. This is the faith triangle that includes—when it is intact—all the others of which we are part. This is that most inclusive triangle in which the self relates to the canvas of meaning itself. In other writings I have referred to this largest canvas of meaning as our sense of an *ultimate environment*. In Jewish and Christian terms, the ultimate environment is expressed with the symbol "Kingdom of God." In this way of seeing, *God* is the center of power and value which unifies and gives character to the ultimate environment.[7]

We have not come to terms with faith as relational until we have examined it as an activity of knowing and being in which the self makes a bid for relationship to a center of value and power adequate to ground, unify, and order the whole force-field of life. In the study of faith development we recognize, of course, many moments—some of which may last the remainder of a lifetime— in which persons do *not* feel themselves related to any value or power adequate to unify and order their experience. For some persons the images they form to express a unity and order in the ultimate environment are at best neutral toward their lives and human events generally, or at worst they are hostile, and destructive. Nonetheless, even as negativity or as void, a person's unconscious assumptions or conscious convictions regarding power and value in the ultimate environment have important implications for the character and quality of the relational commitments in the range of his or her other triangular relationships.

An important double action is at work here: In the weaving and painting of our meaning-canvases, the materials, forms, and colors often come directly from our experiences of faith and unfaith in the more everyday relationships of our lives. Conversely, our commitments in these smaller faith triangles have

---

[7]See J. Fowler and S. Keen, *Life Maps* (Waco, Texas: Word Books, 1978). For a theological examination of the vision of the Kingdom of God, see James Fowler, *To See the Kingdom* (Nashville: Abingdon Press, 1974), especially ch. 3 and 4.

everything to do with the way we see them in relation to larger and more comprehensive frames of felt meaning.[8]

Faith, we have seen, is an irreducibly *relational* phenomenon. It is an active mode of knowing and being in which we relate to others, and form communities with whom we share common loyalties to supraordinate centers of value and power. Faith is an active mode of knowing and being in which we grasp our relatedness to others and to our shared causes as all related to and grounded in a relatedness to power(s) and value(s) which unify and give character to an ultimate environment.

Faith as a Knowing

Faith is a way of being, arising out of a way of *seeing* and *knowing*. The attentive reader will have caught our use of such verbs as "compose," "construct," "maintain," "form," "attach," "invest," "commit" to characterize aspects of the dynamic relationships involved in faith. In this approach to faith we stand in the structural-developmental tradition pioneered by J. Mark Baldwin and John Dewey, and brought to heightened clarity by Jean Piaget, Lawrence Kohlberg, and their associates. In this tradition, *knowing* means an acting upon and "composing" of the known.[9] Knowing occurs when an active knower interacts with an active world of persons and objects, meeting its unshaped or unorganized stimuli with the ordering, organizing power of the knower's mind. Knowing is adequate or "true" when the mental ordering of the elements of reality correspond to their relationships as experienced and known by other reliable knowers. When the "object" of knowing is thus accurately known, when it is not "subjectively" distorted, we speak of "objectivity."[10] Piaget, in

---

[8]For example, a man who experienced a profound disturbance in the relationship with his mother in infancy will likely have either a deep-going inability to trust others at all levels in later life, or a powerful religious experience which opens a relationship with God which transforms his ability to trust and make commitments to other persons. See the chapters by Loder, Vergote, Rizzuto, and Jaspard in this volume.

[9]William F. Lynch, S. J., *Images of Faith*. (Notre Dame, Indiana: University of Notre Dame Press, 1973).

[10]Jean Piaget, *To Understand Is to Invent* (New York: Viking Press, 1974).

the latter part of his career, has focused with special acumen on the child's and adolescent's way of composing the reality of the world of objects and of relationships between objects. His work has disclosed integrated patterns of thought, formally describable, which characterize a sequence of increasingly more adequate mental systems of knowing ("stages"). Armed with this Piagetian theoretical approach, Kohlberg[11] and later Selman[12] have renewed the constructivist approach in a more thorough reworking of Piaget's earlier investigations. Kohlberg has investigated the child's, adolescent's, and adult's ways of constructing situations of moral dilemma and choice, and of forming solutional approaches to them.

An important aspect of moral thinking and knowing is the capacity to construct the point of view of other persons and groups. Kohlberg and Flavell[13] did pioneering work, extending Piaget's investigations of perspective-taking. But it is Robert Selman who has developed the best theoretical work, based on empirical studies, on social perspective-taking.

Recently, Robert Kegan has made a new extension of the Piaget and Kohlberg paradigms. In an impressive doctoral dissertation, Kegan[14] rigorously sought to extend Piaget's primary focus on knowing as an active structuring or organizing to account for the dynamics of personality or ego development. The ego, Kegan argues, is to be understood as the total *constitutive activity of knowing* (with its evolving characteristic patterns) by which the self constitutes and therefore knows other persons and the self as related to others. Ego, he insists, is the construal of the self and others in relationship. In an approach that seeks to unify

---

[11]Lawrence Kohlberg, "Stage and Sequence: The Cognitive Developmental Approach to Socialization", in D. Goslin, ed., *Handbook of Socialization Theory and Research*. (New York: Rand McNally, 1969), pp. 347–480.

[12]Robert L. Selman, *The Development of Conceptions of Interpersonal Relations*, Vols. I & II. Publication of the Harvard-Judge Baker Social Reasoning Project.

[13]John H. Flavell, *The Development of Role-Taking and Communication Skills in Children* (New York: John Wiley & Sons, 1968).

[14]Robert G. Kegan, *Ego and Truth: Personality and the Piaget Paradigm*, Unpublished doctoral dissertation, Harvard University, 1977. See Kegan's chapter in this volume, which builds on and further develops Kegan's position. My dialogue with Kegan here is based primarily on the earlier work.

an understanding of the ego's total constitutive activity (including even the "dynamic unconscious" of depth psychologies), Kegan throughout points to the ways we construct both the "world" and ourselves in the "knowing" that is ego. [15]

{59}

Later in this chapter, we will return to an assessment of aspects of Kegan's bold thesis. Our purpose now is to show that *faith itself is a powerful expression of constructive knowing*. Here we have in view the composition (constitution) and interpretation of the *persons, values, communities,* and *images of ultimate environments* to which we are related in trust (or mistrust) and loyalty (or disloyalty) in faith.

In the previous section we traced the relational character of faith at several levels. We spoke of interpersonal faith, of faith as involved in the relation of person and group or groups. We noted a triangular faith structure in all viable social institutions or associations. And finally we sought to evoke an awareness of one's relatedness to an "environment of environments," a unifying, integrating vision centering in an image or images of supraordinate value and power, that can unify one's experiences in the confusing welter of the force-field of life. From a constructivist (structural-developmental) standpoint, *each* of these levels of relationship involves *constitutive-knowing* (the knowing that composes or establishes both the known and the knower in relation to the known).

Up to a point the structural features of constitutive-knowing disclosed to us by Piaget, Kohlberg, Selman, and now Kegan, for each of their respective domains, serve us well in understanding the constitutive-knowing that is faith. Faith does involve knowing the world of physical objects and the laws of their relatedness, movement, and change. Faith does involve constructions of the self and others, in perspective-taking, in moral analysis and judgment, and in the constitutions of self as related to others which we call ego.

But when we conceptually address the last relational step of faith—that of relatedness to an ultimate environment—certain

---

[15]This point finds resonance, though in quite another frame of reference, in the papers of McDonagh and Hauerwas in this volume.

decisive problems emerge for the effort to extend the Piagetian approach to constitutive-knowing so as to encompass the domain of faith.

At one time, I would have named three such problems. The first of these I would have seen as arising from the fateful way Piaget (and following him, Kohlberg) separates *cognition* (the "structural aspect of knowing") and *affection* (the "energetics or emotional dimension of knowing"). Clearly, from what we have said about faith, it is a knowing which involves both reason and feeling: both rationality and passionality. While Piaget and Kohlberg acknowledge the inextricable unity of cognition and affection in actual behavior and choice, neither of them has dealt adequately in his theory with that unity. Kegan's thesis, however, has helped me reformulate the cognitive-affective problem. He argues that the problem we confront here is not one of how theoretically to integrate thought and feeling. Rather the challenge is to recognize that meaning-making, as a constructive movement, is prior to and generative of both reason and emotion. We must, Kegan asserts, see meaning-making as the self's total constitutive-knowing activity, an activity in which there is no thought without feeling and no feeling without thought. So long as we widen and deepen our understanding of cognition (and the structures of constitutive-knowing) in this broader sense, then this problem of the Piagetian bifurcation of cognition and affection is, in principle, overcome.

But there remain two other significant sets of issues which any adequate accounting for the character of faith as a "knowing" in structural-developmental terms must address. Neither Piaget nor Kohlberg intends to provide a theory of ego or personality development. Both, therefore, have approached the task of identifying the forms of reason or logic characteristic of different "stages" in human thought without making a critically important distinction: They have not attended to the differences between constitutive-knowing in which *the identity or worth of the person is not directly at stake* and constitutive-knowing in which it is. This has meant that Kohlberg has avoided developing a theory of the moral self, of character, or of conscience. Strictly speaking, his stages describe a succession of integrated structurers of moral logic. He has given very little attention to the fact that we "build" ourselves through choices and moral (self-defining) commit-ments. His theory, for understandable theoretical and historical-practical reasons, has not explicated the dynamics of the inner dialogue in moral choice between actual and possible selves.[16]

There is a problem involved in Kegan's 1977 proposal that we extend Piaget's structural paradigm to include *all* the self's constitutive-knowing. It arises from a lack of clarity about how he makes the move from a theory of knowing which strives for *objectivity* and rational certainty in knowing to one in which the self's identity and worth and more—its very constitution—are at stake. Kegan does in fact call attention to two parallel phi-losophics of knowing in recent European thought: the objec-tifying, technical reason which has as its ideal the elimination of all subjectivity (positivism), and the kind of knowing which emphasizes subjective freedom, risk, and passionate choice (exis-tentialism). And he acknowledges Piaget's primary focus of attention on the former. But then he moves toward an inclusion of the second with the first without adequately accounting for how various subfunctions of knowing, such as perception, feeling, imagination, and rational judgment, are related and are to be distinguished from one another.

In both faith-knowing and the kind of moral-knowing which gives rise to choice and action, the constitution or modification of the self is always an issue. In these kinds of constitutive-knowing not only is the "known" being constructed, but there is also a simultaneous extension, modification, or reconstitution of the *knower in relation to the known*. To introduce this freedom, risk, passion, and subjectivity into the the Piaget-Kohlberg paradigm (as we must in faith development) requires that we examine the relationship of what we may call a *logic or rational certainty* (Piaget's major concern) to what we may call a *logic of conviction*. (I use the term "logic" here in a metaphorical sense, designating two major kinds of structuring activity which interact in the constitutive-knowing that is faith.) This relationship between these two "logics" is not one of choice between alternatives. A logic of conviction does not

---

[16]See chapters by McDonagh and Hauerwas in this volume.

negate a logic of rational certainty. But the former, being more inclusive, does contextualize, qualify, and anchor the latter. Recognition of a more comprehensive "logic of conviction" does lead us to see that the logic of rational certainty is part of a larger epistemological structuring activity, and is not to be confused with the whole.

This focus on the logic of conviction as a more comprehensive knowing, transcending while including the logic of rational certainty, brings the recognition of another layer of problems. Faith, as a generative knowing, "reasons" holistically—it composes "wholes." In faith the self "knows" itself and the neighbor in relation to an ultimate environment. A spread of meaning, a canopy of significance is composed to backdrop or fund more immediate, everyday action. The Piaget paradigm took form and has been refined as a logic of objects and of relations between objects. To be sure, Piagetian formal operational logic does involve the construction of nonempirical, imaginative constructs some of which (say, in theoretical physics) operate with the same remoteness from the possibility of direct empirical validation as do faith constructions. But we must recognize a critical distinction between the "fictive" or "imaginative" constructions of theoretical physics and those of faith and theology. This distinction arises primarily from our earlier point about the degree to which the identity and value of a self or selves are at stake in our acts of constitutive-knowing. I can live with curiosity and intrigue about the question of the nature and character of "black holes" in space. But in my unknowing, I am not paralyzed in my choices of life-style and commitments. At certain points in my life, and in the lives of all of us, however, situations arise in very practical contexts, and with fateful life-defining potential, that are of another sort. These are situations in which rational analysis and systemic mapping yield clarification of options, but provide no criteria for highly consequential value choices. In these situations we choose and act (and/or find explanations and rationales for our acts) with reference to our assumptions or convictions about the character of power and value in an ultimate environment. Our choices and explanations of choices in these situations reflect operative attachments to meaning-giving images and centers of value and power.

This latter domain—the domain of faith and of logic of conviction—involves recognizing the role played in faith of modes of knowing we call ecstatic[17] and imaginative.[18] As is becoming generally recognized, the mind employs the more aesthetically oriented right hemisphere of the brain in these kinds of knowing.[19] To my knowledge none of the Piagetian cognitive-constructivists, including Kegan, have given any significant attention to the bihemispheric, bimodal forms of thought involved in the constitutive-knowing that is faith. To move in this direction requires coming to terms with modes of thought that employ images, symbols, and synesthetic fusions of sense and feeling. It means taking account of so-called "regressive" movements in which the psyche returns to preconceptual, prelinguistic modes and memories, and to primitive sources of energizing imagery, bringing them into consciousness with resultant reconstruals of the experience world.[20] To deal adequately with faith and with faith's dynamic role in the total self-constitutive activity of ego means trying to give theoretical attention to the transformation in consciousness—rapid and dramatic in sudden conversion, more gradual and incremental in faith growth—which results from the *re*-cognition of self-others-world in light of knowing the self as constituted by a center of value powerful enough to require or enable recentering one's ultimate environment.[21]

We must underscore that the effort to attend to these more effective, imaginative, and holistic modes of knowing does not *negate* the part played by the operations of the logic of rational certainty. It does not mean a capitulation to unbridled fantasy or subjectivity, nor does it mean a relinquishing in faith of the critical role of rational reflection. Rather the challenge is to see how

---

[17]Andrew Greeley, *Ecstasy: A Way of Knowing* (Englewood Cliffs, New Jersey: Prentice Hall, 1974).

[18]Lynch, *op. cit.*; Ray Hart, *Unfinished Man and the Imagination* (New York: Herder & Herder, 1968).

[19]Robert E. Ornstein, *The Psychology of Consciousness* (San Francisco: W.H. Freeman, 1972); Julian Jaynes, *The Origin of Consciousness in the Breakdown at the Bicameral Mind* (Boston: Houghton Mifflin, 1976); see especially chapter by Loder in this volume.

[20]W.W. Meissner, S.J., "Notes on the Psychology of Faith," *Journal of Religion and Health* (1969), pp. 47–75.

[21]See chapter by Loder in this volume.

rational knowing plays the crucial role of conceptualizing, questioning, and evaluating the products of other modes of imaginal and generative knowing. As Lynch writes: "And for what shall we be held more accountable than for our images?"[22] We are trying to grasp the inner dialectic of rational logic in the dynamics of a larger, more comprehensive logic of convictional orientation.

Our discussion of faith as a knowing has led us on a somewhat circuitous route: Faith, we have claimed, is a mode of knowing and construing. It is that part of the total constitutive-knowing of selves in which we compose a holistic sense or image of an ultimate environment. Our compositions of an ultimate environment derive unity and coherence by virtue of our attachments, our convictional investments, in power(s) and value(s) of supraordinate significance.

Going beyond Piaget and Kohlberg, and building on Kegan, we have claimed that the constitutive-knowing by which self-other relationships are constituted does not involve just an *extension* of the logic of rational certainty. Instead, it involves a transformation in which a logic constitutive of objects must be seen as integrated with and contextualized by a logic of conviction. This means that what we are calling faith is a core process in the total self-constitutive activity that is ego. Ego development so understood must take account of the integration of and interplay between a logic of rational certainty and a logic of conviction that characterizes the epistemology of faith.

Inquiry into Faith Development: The Search for Structures

A summary, composite definition of faith as we are discussing it might go this way. Faith is:

The process of constitutive-knowing

Underlying a person's composition and maintenance of a comprehensive frame (or frames) of meaning

---

[22]Lynch, *op. cit.* p. 18.

Generated from the person's attachments or commitments to centers of supraordinate value which have power to unify his or her experiences of the world

Thereby endowing the relationships, contexts, and patterns of everyday life, past and future, with significance.

So understood, faith is an aspect of the total constitutive activity of the *ego*. It functions to provide orientation, hope, and courage. It grounds sustaining strength, purpose, and experiences of shared commitment which bind the self and others in community.

In a constructivist perspective, faith is understood to have its own structural characteristics. That is to say, underlying the wide variety of *contents* which come to be expressive of the faith of persons, there are formally describable *patterns* or *structures* of thought, of valuing, and of constitutive-knowing. In seven years of research we have generated a provisional constructivist theory of faith development in which structural "stages" are characterized by relatively equilibrated integrations of such patterns. In the course of faith development periods of equilibration alternate with transitional phases in which, under the impact of new experiences, of changed environments, and of new ways of knowing in other domains, the structural patterns of faith-knowing undergo relinquishment and transformation. We believe that the sequence of equilibrated stage-like positions we have identified is developmentally related. We believe that the order of appearance is sequential and that the sequence will prove to be invariant. Each new stage builds on and incorporates into its more elaborate structures the operations of previous stages. An eventual aim of our research is to test whether further refinements of our descriptions of these stages, through the analysis of future longitudinal and cross-cultural research, can demonstrate the salience of generic or universal structuring potentials of the human psyche.[23]

---

[23]See Richard Anthony, "A Phenomenological Structuralist Approach to the Scientific Study of Religion," Unpublished paper presented at an American Psychological Association symposium on Methodological Issues in the Psychology of Religion (1976).

Our research procedure has been described in detail else-where.[24] Briefly, we employ a semi-clinical, open-ended inter-view of one to three hours (somewhat briefer with children) in which the respondent is asked to share aspects of his or her life-history and to express in detail his or her feelings and attitudes regarding a cluster of universal life-issues with which faith must deal.* This list is uniformly pursued in each interview. Respondents are encouraged to share concrete experiences and crises out of their own lives, and to address the faith issues experientially whenever possible. Though respondents often vol-untarily answer in specifically religious terms, religion as an issue and context is not explicitly introduced until the last quarter of the interview. An effort is made to test espoused beliefs, values, and attitudes against self-reports of performance and choice in actual situations.

These interviews are then transcribed. Analysis for structural features is carried out by trained scorers. The formulations of position and outlook *vis à vis* the faith issues are regarded as the *contents* of the person's faith. A thematic or content analysis can be carried out and systematized in order to understand the person's faith or belief system. Structural analysis, however, aims to go "under" the content elements to "liberate" the deeper structural operations of knowing and valuing which underlie, ground, and organize the thematic content.

We have conducted and analyzed more than 380 interviews of the type just described.** The sample has been cross-sectionally balanced for age from four to eighty. It includes slightly more females than males, includes Protestants, Catholics,

---

[24]"Stages in Faith: The Structural-Developmental Approach," in Thomas Hennessey, ed., *Values and Moral Education* (New York: Paulist Press, 1976).

*The list of issues: Death and afterlife: the limits of knowledge; causation and effectance in personal and historical life; evil and suffering; freedom and determinism; power and agency; meaning of life; ideal manhood or womanhood; the future; grounding of ethical and moral imperatives; communal identifications and belonging; bases of guilt and shame; loyalties and commitments; locus of transcendent beauty, value, or power; objects of reverence or awe; grounds of terror or dread; sin and violation; religious experiences, religious beliefs and practice; specific meaningful religious symbols.

**The "we" refers to the present author, a number of research associates in the Research Project on Faith Development and Religious Education, my graduate students at Harvard Divinity School, Boston College, and Emory University, two professorial colleagues, and several master's and doctoral candidates in other universities.

Jews, atheists, and agnostics in representative numbers, several Western adherents of Eastern traditions, and has a reasonable range of educational, social class, and ethnic variations. A select longitudinal sampling is being followed at five-year intervals.

Based on the research procedures and data base described here, we have formulated seven structurally distinct faith stages. As with other constructivist theories, movement from one of these stages to the next is not an automatic function of biological maturation, chronological age, psychological development, or mental age. While each of these factors plays a significant role in the "readiness" for stage transition, transition itself occurs when the equilibrium of a given stage is upset by encounters with crises, novelties, and experiences of disclosure and challenge, which threaten the limits of the person's present patterns of constitutive-knowing. A change of social, political, or economic environment can contribute to stage change. Of course, a person can overdefend existing faith structures by screening out and "not-knowing" dissonant data. In extreme forms this becomes the "closed" or "authoritarian" mindset. But when there is sufficient ego strength and faith to sustain a vulnerability to the threats to one's meanings, through constructive accommodation new patterns of constituting and maintaining a meaningful world can emerge. The role of supporting communities, usable models, revelations of and ecstatic experiences with the powerful lure which religionists call "grace" in this process can only be alluded to here.[25]

Structural Stages in Faith Development

In *Life Maps*[26] I have given a detailed description of the stages, with illustrative passages from interviews scored at each stage. I refer the interested reader to that account and to my earlier "Stages in Faith: The Structural-Developmental Approach"[27] for

---

[25]See the papers included in Part II of this volume for many examples.

[26]Fowler and Keen, *Life Maps*, pp. 25–97.

[27]"Stages in Faith: The Structural-Developmental Approach," in Thomas Hennessey, ed., *Values and Moral Education* (New York: Paulist Press, 1976).

comprehensive introductions to this theory. In this context I will limit myself to a necessarily schematic presentation. First, let's examine an overview of the stages. The description of each stage will include a general characterization. This will be followed by a somewhat more detailed elaboration. Then, briefly, we will suggest some of the signs of transition to the next stage.

Undifferentiated Faith

The preconceptual, largely prelinguistic stage in which the infant unconsciously forms a disposition toward its world.

> *Trust, courage, hope, and love are fused in an undifferentiated way and contend with sensed threats of abandonment, inconsistencies, and deprivations in its environment. Though really a prestage, and largely inaccessible to empirical inquiry of the kind we pursue, the quality of mutuality and the strength of trust, autonomy, hope, and courage (or their opposites) developed in this phase underlie (or undermine) all that comes later in faith development.*

Transition to Stage 1 begins with the convergence of thought and language, opening up the use of symbols in speech and ritual-play.

Stage 1. Intuitive-Projective Faith

The fantasy-filled, imitative phase in which the child can be powerfully and permanently influenced by the examples, moods, actions, and language of the visible faith of primal adults.

> *The stage most typical of the child of three to seven, it is marked by a relative fluidity of thought patterns. The child is continually encountering novelties for which no stable operations of knowing have been formed. The imaginative processes underlying fantasy are unrestrained and uninhibited by logical thought. In league with forms of knowing dominated by perception, imagination in this stage is extremely productive of long-lasting images and feelings*

(positive and negative) which, later, more stable and self-reflective valuing and thinking will have to order and sort out. This is the stage of first self-awareness. The "self-aware" child is egocentric as regards the perspectives of others. Here we find first awarenesses of death and sex, and of the strong taboos by which cultures and families insulate those powerful areas.

The emergence of Concrete Operational thinking underlies the transition to Stage 2. Affectively, the resolution of Oedipal issues or their submersion in latency are important accompanying factors.[28] At the heart of the transition is the child's growing concern to *know* how things are and to clarify for himself or herself the bases of distinctions between what is real and what only seems to be.

Stage 2. Mythic-Literal Faith

The stage in which the person begins to take on for himself or herself the stories, beliefs, and observances which symbolize belonging to his or her community. Beliefs are appropriated with literal interpretations, as are moral rules and attitudes. Symbols are taken as one-dimensional and literal in meaning.

In this stage the rise of Concrete Operations leads to the curbing and ordering of the previous stage's imaginative composing of the world. The episodic quality of Intuitive-Projective Faith gives way to a more linear, narrative construction of coherence and meaning. Story becomes the major way of giving unity and value to experience.[29] This is the faith stage of the school child (though we sometimes find its structures dominant in adolescents and in adults). Marked by increased accuracy in taking the perspective of other persons, Stage 2 composes a world based on reciprocal fairness and an immanent justice based on reciprocity. The actors in its cosmic stories are full-fledged anthropomorphic "personalities." It

---

[28]See the chapter by Jaspard in this volume.

[29]The chapter by Hauerwas in this volume points to the continuing power of narrative to organize and express our meanings in this stage and continuing into the later stages.

can be affected deeply and powerfully by symbolic and dramatic materials, and can describe in endlessly detailed narrative what has occurred. Stage 2 does not, however, step back from the flow of its stories to formulate reflective, conceptual meanings. For this stage the meaning is both carried and "trapped" in the narrative.

The implicit clash or contradiction of stories leads to reflection on meanings. The transition to Formal Operational thought makes such reflection possible and necessary. Previous literalism breaks down; new "cognitive conceit" (Elkind) leads to disillusionment with previous teachers and teachings. Conflicts between authoritative stories (i.e., Genesis on creation vs. evolutionary theory) must be faced. The emergence of mutual interpersonal perspective-taking ("I see you seeing me; I see me as you see me; I see you seeing me seeing you.") creates the need for a more personal relationship with the unifying power of the Ultimate Environment.

Stage 3. Synthetic-Conventional Faith

The person's experience of the world now extends beyond the family. A number of spheres demand attention: family, school or work, peers, street society and media, and perhaps religion. Faith must provide a coherent orientation in the midst of that more complex and diverse range of involvements. Faith must synthesize values and information; it must provide a unifying basis for identity and outlook.

Stage 3 typically has its rise and ascendency in adolescence, but for many adults it becomes a permanent equilibration. It structures the ultimate environment in interpersonal terms. Its images of unifying value and power derive from the extension of qualities experienced in personal relationships. It is a "conformist" stage in the sense that it is acutely tuned to the expectations and judgments of significant others, and as yet does not have a sure enough grasp on its own identity and autonomous judgment to construct and maintain an independent perspective. While beliefs and values are deeply felt, they typically are tacitly held—the person "dwells" in them and the meaning world they mediate. But there has not been occasion reflectively to step outside them to examine them explicitly or systematically. At Stage 3 a person has an "ideology," a more or less consistent clustering of values and beliefs, but he or she has not objectified it for examination, and in a sense is unaware of having it. Differences of outlook with others are experienced as differences in "kind" of person. Authority is located in the incumbents of traditional authority-roles (if perceived as personally worthy) or in the concensus of a valued, face-to-face group.

Factors contributing to the breakdown of Stage 3 and to readiness for transition may include any one or more of the following: serious clashes or contradictions between valued authority sources; marked changes, by officially sanctioned leaders, of policies or practices previously deemed sacred and unbreachable (i.e., in the Catholic Church changing the Mass from Latin to the vernacular, or no longer requiring abstinence from meat on Friday); the encounter with experiences or perspectives that lead to critical reflection on how one's beliefs and values have formed and changed, and on how "relative" they are to one's particular group or background.

Stage 4. Individuative-Reflective Faith

The movement from Stage 3 to Stage 4 is particularly critical, for it is in this transition that the late adolescent or adult must begin to take seriously the burden of responsibility for his or her own commitments, life-style, beliefs, and attitudes. Where genuine movement toward Stage 4 is under way, the person must face certain unavoidable tensions: Individuality versus being defined by a group or group membership; Subjectivity and the power of one's strongly felt but unexamined feelings versus Objectivity and the requirement of critical reflection; Self-fulfillment or self-actualization as a primary concern versus Service to and being for others; the question of being committed to Relative versus Struggle with the possibility of an absolute.

This stage most appropriately takes form in young adulthood (but let us remember that many adults do not construct it and that for a significant group it emerges only in the mid-thirties or forties). This stage is marked by a double development. The self, previously sustained in its identity and faith compositions by an interpersonal circle of significant others, now claims an identity no longer defined by the composite of one's roles or meanings to others. To sustain that new identity, it composes a meaning frame conscious of its own boundaries and inner connections, and aware of itself as a "world view." Self (identity) and outlook (world view) are differentiated from those of others, and become acknowledged factors in the reactions, interpretations, and judgments one makes on the actions of the self and others. It expresses its intuitions of coherence in an ultimate environment in terms of an explicit system of meanings. Stage 4 typically translates symbols into conceptual meanings. This is a "demythologizing" stage. It is likely to attend minimally to unconscious factors influencing its judgments and behavior.

Restless with the self-images and outlook maintained by Stage 4, the person ready for transition finds himself or herself attending to what may feel like anarchic and disturbing inner voices. Elements from a childish past, images and energies from a deeper self, a gnawing sense of the sterility and flatness of the meanings one serves—any or all of these may signal readiness for something new. Stories, symbols, myths, paradoxes from one's own or other traditions may insist on breaking in upon the neatness of the previous faith. Disillusionment with one's compromises, and recognition that life is more complex than Stage 4's logic of clear distinctions and abstract concepts can comprehend, press one toward a more dialectical and multileveled approach to life-truth.

Stage 5. *Paradoxical-Consolidative Faith*

This stage involves the integration into self and outlook of much that was suppressed or evaded in the interest of Stage 4's self-certainty and conscious cognitive and affective adaptation to reality. This stage develops a "second naivete" (Ricoeur) in which symbolic power is reunited with conceptual meanings. Here there must also be a new reclaiming and reworking of one's past. There must be an opening to the voices of one's "deeper self." Importantly, this involves a critical recognition of one's *social* unconscious—the myths, ideal images, and prejudices built deeply into the self-system by virtue of one's nurture within a particular social class, religious tradition, ethnic group, or the like.

> *Unusual before midlife, Stage 5 knows the sacrament of defeat and the reality of irrevocable commitments and acts. What the previous stage struggled to clarify, in terms of the boundaries of self and outlook, this stage now makes porous and permeable. Alive to paradox and the truth in apparent contradictions, this stage strives to unify opposites in mind and experience. It generates and maintains vulnerability to the strange truths of those who are "other." Ready for closeness to that which is different and threatening to self and outlook (including new depths of experience in spirituality and religious revelation), this stage has a commitment to justice that is freed from the confines of tribe, class, religious community, or nation. And with the seriousness that can arise when life is more than half over, this stage is ready to spend and be spent for the cause of conserving and cultivating the possibility of others' generating identity and meaning.*

Stage 5 can appreciate symbols, myths, and rituals (its own and others') because it has been grasped, in some measure, by the depth of reality to which they refer. It also sees the divisions of the human family vividly because it has been apprehended by the possibility (and imperative) of an inclusive community of being. But this stage remains divided. It lives and acts between an untransformed world and a transforming vision and loyalties. In some few cases this division yields to the call of the radical actualization that we call Stage 6.

Stage 6. Universalizing Faith

This stage is exceedingly rare. The persons best described by this stage have generated faith compositions in which their felt sense of an Ultimate Environment is inclusive of all being. They become

{74}

incarnators and actualizers of the spirit of a fulfilled human community.

> *They are "contagious" in the sense that they create zones of liberation from the social, political, economic, and ideological shackles we place and endure on human futurity. Living with felt participation in a Power that unifies and transforms the world, Universalizers are often experienced as subversive of the structures (including religious structures) by which we sustain our individual and corporate survival, security and significance. Many persons in this stage die at the hands of those whom they hope to change. Universalizers are often more honored and revered after death than during their lives. The rare persons who may be described by this stage have a special grace that makes them seem more lucid, more simple, and yet somehow more fully human than the rest of us. Their community is universal in extent. Particularities are cherished because they are vessels of the universal, and are thereby valuable apart from any utilitarian considerations. Life is both loved and held too loosely. Such persons are ready for fellowship with persons at any of the other stages and from any other faith tradition.*

What's in a Faith Stage?

Following Piaget and Kohlberg, we think of a stage as an integrated system of operations (structures) of thought and valuing, which makes for an equilibrated constitutive-knowing of a person's relevant environment. A stage, as a "structural whole" is organismic, i.e., it is a dynamic unity constituted by internal connections among its differentiated aspects. In constructivist theories, successive stages are thought of as manifesting qualitative transformations issuing in more complex inner differentiations, more elaborate operations (operations upon operations), wider comprehensiveness, and greater overall flexibility of functioning.

At its present level of elaboration, the faith stage theory can be schematically presented in terms of seven operational aspects which are integrated and reintegrated at each of the six levels or stages. Figure 1 presents a graphic suggestion of the transformations each aspect undergoes in the transitions of faith development and of the organismic interconnectedness of the aspects in each stage.*

As will become plain, we are indebted to the pioneering constructivist theorists for elaborating the stages and structural transformations of Aspects A, B, and C. The inclusion of Piaget's,

FIG. 1. (A-G represent structural aspects of faith in each stage.)

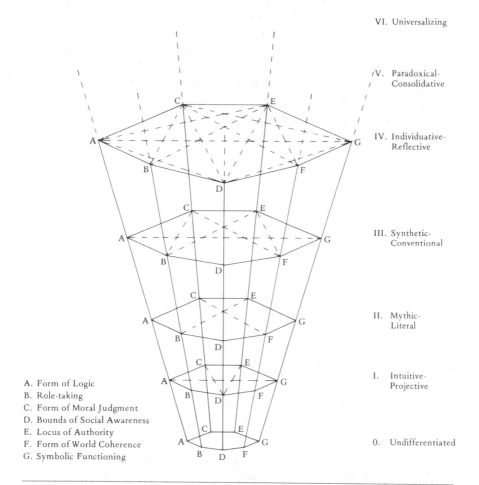

A. Form of Logic
B. Role-taking
C. Form of Moral Judgment
D. Bounds of Social Awareness
E. Locus of Authority
F. Form of World Coherence
G. Symbolic Functioning

VI. Universalizing

V. Paradoxical-Consolidative

IV. Individuative-Reflective

III. Synthetic-Conventional

II. Mythic-Literal

I. Intuitive-Projective

0. Undifferentiated

*The lines connecting the aspects at each stage are merely suggestive and are not to be taken as representations of empirically established relations.

Selman's, and Kohlberg's stages here show the correlations we find empirically between them and the other aspects we investigate. Moving from left to right (from A to G in Figure 1), we are trying to suggest how, in the knowing that is faith, the "logic of rational certainty" (A) and its derivatives (B and C) are contextualized by and integrated with aspects of a logic of conviction (D, E, F, and G). If, as our data suggest, something like the integrated operational system depicted here can be demonstrated at each stage, then of course the actual process of transition from one stage to another will *not* necessarily occur either in a movement from A to G, or in an even and simultaneous transformation of all the aspects. Rather transition will be uneven and ragged, with first one sector leading and then another catching up or creating "drag" on the total process.

Starting now with *Aspect A*, the "Form of Logic," let us characterize briefly each of the elements indicated in Figure 1. Our descriptions of the "Form of Logic" build upon Piaget's theory of cognitive stages. This aspect focuses upon the patterns of reasoning and judgment available to the developing person at each cognitive stage. For the equilibrated operational pattern of a given faith stage *fully* to emerge, the correlated level of Piagetian cognitive operations must have been developed. This underscores again that the holistic knowing that is faith must not be understood as irrational or arational. Kohlberg and Selman (whose stage theories of perspective-taking and moral judgment are Aspects C and B respectively) claim that the Piaget cognitive levels are *necessary but not sufficient* for the correlated levels of perspective-taking and moral judgment. This is true in faith stages as well, though we must qualify the assumption of temporal priority implied in this claim. Because of faith's qualification of the logic of rational certainty within a logic of conviction, it would be a mistake to assume that cognitive development, as Piaget understands it, always leads temporally in faith stage transitions.[30] When examining charted descriptions of faith

---

[30]By extension at this point we can see why Kohlberg's claim that moral stage transition would "logically" occur prior to, and as a necessary condition for, faith stage transition is theoretically mistaken. See Kohlberg, "Education, Moral Development, and Faith," *Journal*

Stages 4 through 6, readers knowledgeable of Piaget's theory will find that we have identified further adult substages in formal operational thought, suggesting ongoing cognitive development. These stylistic variants or substages of formal operations we find necessary in the description of stage-typical patterns in the construction of and reflection upon comprehensive frames of meaning.

Aspect B, "Role-Taking," owes most to the previously mentioned research of Robert Selman on social perspective-taking. In the faith stage theory we rely explicitly upon Selman's account of structural stages in perspective-taking up to and through our Stage 3. Beyond Stage 3 we have found it possible and necessary to extend Selman's approach, applying it to persons' abilities to construct the perspectives of their own chosen groups or classes (Stage 4), and then of groups, classes, or ideological and convictional traditions other than their own.

Aspect C, the "Form of Moral Judgment," represents an inclusion, with slight modifications based on our data, of Kohlberg's stages of moral reasoning. As will become apparent below, there are significant parallels between moral judgment stages and faith stages.

Aspect D, "Bounds of Social Awareness," focuses on the extent of inclusiveness and accuracy of construal of the reference groups in relation to which persons ground their identity and define their moral responsibility. Parallel in some ways to role-taking, this aspect differs in that it attempts to account for the typical range of persons and groups "who count" in one's composition and maintenance of identity and of a meaningful world at each stage.

Aspect E, "Locus of Authority," centers on the patterns of constitutive-knowing and commitment by which persons, ideas, institutions, experiences, and processes of one's own judgment are invested with meaning-sanctioning authority. To whom or what does a person look for validation or legitimation of his or her

of Moral Education, Vol. 4, No. 1 (1974), pp. 5–16. For my response, see Fowler, "Moral Stages and the Development of Faith," in Brenda M. Mapel, ed., *Kohlberg and Moral Education*, Religious Education Press (on press).

most significant felt meanings? How is that "locus" constituted? How is it justified? With this aspect we are well into the elements of a logic of conviction. In the domain where the construction and worth of the self are at stake, trust in and loyalty to sources of authorization cannot be accounted for solely within a logic of rational certainty. In fact, trust in and loyalty to the logic of rational certainty as a comprehensive principle of authority may *itself* involve a faith commitment involving risk, judgment, and conviction.

We have pointed out that faith reasons in "wholes." *Aspect F*, the "Form of World Coherence," represents a focus on each stage's particular way of composing and holding a comprehensive sense of unified meanings. This aspect describes a sequence of stage-typical *genres* employed by persons to conceive or represent patterns of coherence in their ultimate environment. In the movement through its successive stages we see in this aspect, in a sensitive way, the reconciliation or integration of the logics of rational certainty and of conviction.

Much work remains to be done with *Aspect G*, "Symbolic Functioning." It is in this aspect, particularly, that we must take account of the bihemispheric functioning of thought and imagination in faith. It is with reference to this aspect that "regression in the service of faith development," illumined by psychoanalytic investigators,[31] and the integration of unconscious elements into consciousness described by Jungian students of faith and individuation,[32] must be incorporated faithfully. In this aspect particularly, the dynamics of a logic of conviction must be seen as operative with powerful transforming potential for the orientation and functioning of the total psyche. The theoretical and empirical engagement with this aspect at present constitutes one of the most vital yet difficult growing edges of this project.

---

[31]See Meissner, *op. cit.;* and Erik H. Erikson, *Young Man Luther* (New York: W.W. Norton, 1958).

[32]Lawrence Cunningham, "Stages of Faith in Relation to Jung's Theory of Individualization," Unpublished paper in private circulation, 1975; and Gregg Raduka, "Fowler's Stages of Faith Development from the Perspective Taken by Carl Jung in His Published Works," Prospectus for a doctoral dissertation, University of Maryland, College Park, 1977.

A detailed and comprehensive presentation of the stage-by-stage transformation of these aspects and of their integration in each stage must await the completion of the author's book in progress on the faith development theory. As a promissory note, let us give a brief overview of the aspect transformations. Table 1 presents a summary of the stage sequence of transformations found in Aspects A through G. Remember to see these aspects interrelated, as in Figure 1.

Reflection on Sponsorship for Faith Development

To conclude this chapter, I want to share some very general implications of this perspective for religious education. In order to do so, I shift somewhat from the role of theorist and empirical investigator and speak as a theologian and educator.

1. The theory presented here stimulates us to look at faith development in a life-span perspective. Some of the most interesting and powerful faith stage transitions occur only in adulthood. Faith, as seen here, involves an ongoing process, of forming and re-forming our ways of being in and seeing the world. One who becomes Christian in childhood may indeed remain Christian all of his or her life. But one's *way* of being Christian will need to deepen, expand, and be reconstituted several times in the pilgrimage of faith. Churches, synagogues, and other communities of faith need to expect and provide support for ongoing adult development in faith. I am convinced that the faith community which sponsors ongoing adult development will find it quite natural to nurture its children and newcomers in developmentally appropriate and dynamic ways.

2. To our initial surprise, my associates and I found that something on the order of 90 percent of our interviews with adults ended with the respondent—following 2½ hours of intense conversation—saying something like this: "I really appreciate this experience; I *never* get an opportunity to talk about these things." We have found that the faith develop-

TABLE I ·

Aspect Stage	A. Form Of Logic (Piaget)	B. Role-Taking (Selman)	C. Form of Moral Judgment (Kohlberg)	D. Bounds of Social Awareness
0	*	*	*	*
I	Preoperational	Rudimentary Empathy (Egocentric)	Punishment— Reward	Family, primal others
II	Concrete Operational	Simple Perspective-taking	Instrumental Hedonism (Reciprocal Fairness)	"Those like us" (in familial, ethnic, racial, class and religious terms)
III	Early Formal Operations	Mutual Interpersonal	Interpersonal expectations and concordance	Composite of groups in which one has interpersonal relationships
IV	Formal Operation. (Dichotomizing)	Mutual, with self-selected group or class—(Societal)	Societal Perspective Reflective Relativism or Class-biased Universalism	Ideologically compatible communities with congruence to self-chosen norms and insights
V	Formal Operations. (Dialectical)	Mutual with groups, classes and traditions "other" than one's own	Prior to Society, Principled Higher Law (Universal and Critical)	Extends beyond class norms and interests. Disciplined ideological vulnerability to "truths" and "claims" of outgroups and other traditions
VI	Formal Operations. (Synthetic)	Mutual, with the Commonwealth of Being	Loyalty to Being	Identification with the species. Transnarcissistic love of being

*Undifferentiated combination of basic trust, organismic courage, premonitory hope with admixtures of their opposites—preconceptual, prelinguistic mutuality.

E. Locus of Authority	F. Form of World Coherence	G. Role of Symbols

{81}

*	*	*
Attachment/dependence relationships. Size, power, visible symbols of authority	Episodic	Magical-Numinous
Incumbents of authority roles, salience increased by personal relatedness	Narrative-Dramatic	One-dimensional; literal
Consensus of valued groups and in personally worthy representatives of belief-value traditions	Tacit system, felt meanings symbolic- ally mediated, glo- bally held	Symbols multidimen- sional; evocative power inheres in symbol
One's own judgment as informed by a self- ratified ideological per- spective. Authorities and norms must be con- gruent with this.	Explicit system, conceptually medi- ated, clarity about boundaries and inner connections of system	Symbols separated from symbolized. Translated (reduced) to ideations. Evocative power inheres in *meaning* conveyed by symbols
Dialectical joining of judgment-experience processes with reflec- tive claims of others and of various expres- sions of cumulative human wisdom.	Multisystemic sym- bolic and concep- tual mediation	Postcritical rejoining of irreducible symbolic power and ideational meaning. Evocative power inherent in the reality in and beyond symbol *and* in the power of unconscious pro- cesses in the self
In a personal judgment informed by the ex- periences and truths of previous stages, purified of egoic striving, and linked by disciplined intuition to the principle of being	Unitive actuality felt and participated unity of "One beyond the many"	Evocative power of symbols actualized through unification of reality mediated by symbols and the self

ment interview, especially with adolescents and adults, is already an intervention. In the course of the interview, people become involved in the important work of bringing their faith to words. Sometimes they are doing this for the very first time. On other occasions they engage in a process of critically reformulating their faith and values outlook. From this experience I have come to believe that it is most important to provide occasions for people to express in words, in action, in contemplation, "the faith that is in them." Articulation means bringing experience and commitment to word and act. It enables persons to be more responsive and intentional in their own faith growth. It alerts them to unrecognized conflicts, indicating readiness for growth, and enables them to attend to experiences of revelation and disclosure. Commitments are consolidated, integrated, and evaluated in the process of articulation. And if this articulation is carried out in groups, there is a mutually strengthening impact among the members.

3. Faith development sponsorship must avoid viewing the stages as constituting an achievement scale or a program by which to rush people to the next stage. The potential fullness of each stage needs to be recognized and realized. Each stage has a potential wholeness, grace, and integrity. Yet a strong nurturing environment will provide persons with support in facing those challenges of faith in life and action—as well as in reflection—which keep persons open toward new horizons of faith growth. I believe that we are genetically potentiated for growth in faith throughout the life-cycle. And I also believe that each stage represents genuine growth toward wider and more accurate response to God, and toward more consistently humane care for other human beings. We stand under an imperative toward ongoing growth.

4. The language, ritual, and teachings of particular communities of faith are of critical importance for faith development. As Santayana says somewhere, "You can't be religious in general." This theory helps us see that "transmissive" models of

education never succeed in transferring the knowledge and faith of the teacher into the mind and the heart of the child. The child's faith always depends upon his or her own constructions of images and insights. But religious language, ritual and ethical teachings do *awaken* the child to the domain of faith; they channel her or his attention toward the transcendent. They provide experiences of shared attention to and celebration of the actuality of the Holy. As such, to use Horace Bushnell's beautiful language, they are "gifts to the imagination."[33] Therefore, the stories, language, and liturgy of our particular faith communities must be made available and tangible for the child's participation and constructive appropriation. The young child does not, of course, develop conceptual mastery of these things. Rather, he or she encounters images which awaken and form the faith imagination of the child, providing affective, volitional, and conceptual directions by which to grow in faith.

5. Respecting an individual's present "place" of faith, the faith development theory helps us avoid trying to provide comprehensive answers for questions he or she is not yet asking. It helps us avoid playing broken records when he is ready to compose and sing new songs. It helps us understand the power of predictable conflicts and tensions she experiences in the midst of particular stage transitions. It should enable us to allow space to struggle and to provide models which may help in his or her constructions of the next place in faith.

6. Faith development theory helps us overcome the tendency to think of faith as separate from everyday life. The seven aspects of the faith stage, as set forth in Table I, help make explicit the recognition that faith serves to organize the totality of our lives and gives rise to our most comprehensive frames of meaning. We can see that faith development, understood in this way, involves what Martin Buber calls the "sacralization of all life." It stands against the compartmentalizing of a person's or community's life.

---

[33]Horace Bushnell, *Building Eras in Religion*, (New York, 1869).

7. Alfred North Whitehead wrote in *Religion in the Making* that religion involves the transition from God the Void to God the Enemy, and from God the Enemy to God the Companion. Faith development theory helps us recognize that there are times in faith when God seems to approach us as Nothingness or as Slayer. We do not make the transition from one stage of faith to another without disruption, pain, confusion, and a sense of loss. All growth involves pain. To see this does not mean that we can avoid the pain of growth. But it does suggest that we can reimage faith growth so as to embrace the necessary pain and disruption as essential elements in it, thus diminishing the anxiety and fear pain brings.

Saint Augustine in his *Confessions* wrote, "Thou hast made us for Thyself, and our hearts are restless until they find their rest in Thee." The restlessness which so characterizes our frantic and frenzied lives of work and consumption has a source deeper than can be cured by our ambitious activities. The disparate hunger and search for intimacy and sensation in contemporary cultures bespeak a loneliness deeper than even our closest ties of friendship and love can overcome. Faith development theory, for all its technical language and abstract concepts, is an expression of the story of our search for communion with Saint Augustine's "Thou." Faith communities must discover anew how to meet people as *whole* beings, embracing their hearts as well as their minds, their bodies as well as their souls. We must enable people to name and recognize their hungers and their real depth. Forms of spirituality, community celebration, testimony, and shared action in faith can then emerge which will sustain a humanizing common life. Such faith communities are indispensable for the human family's well-being. Our restlessness for divine companionship, if denied, ignored, or distorted, dehumanizes us and we destroy each other. Recognized and nurtured, it brings us into that companionship with God which frees us for genuine partnership with our sisters and brothers, and for friendship with creation.

ABOUT THE AUTHOR

Dr. James Fowler *completed his doctoral studies at Harvard University and is currently Associate Professor of Theology and Human Development at Emory University in Atlanta, Georgia. Prior to joining the staff at Emory, Dr. Fowler taught at the Harvard Divinity School and at Boston College. For the past six years he has directed the Research Program on Faith Development and Religious Education.*

Dr. Fowler's interests lie in focusing the mutually enriching perspectives of theology and life-span psychology toward the work of ministry and religious education. He is best known for his writing and lecturing on faith development. To See the Kingdom *and* Life Maps *are among the books he has authored. A new book,* Trajectories in Faith, *is scheduled for publication in 1980. Dr. Fowler has also written numerous articles for collections on moral and religious development.*

Among his many interests, he includes vocal music, charcoal drawing, and tennis. Dr. Fowler is a minister of the United Methodist Church.

PROCESSES
IN RELIGIOUS
AND MORAL
DEVELOPMENT

The Dynamics of the Family and Its Significance for Moral and Religious Development

ANTOINE VERGOTE

Introduction

Cultural anthropology and clinical psychology—especially psychoanalysis—have shown that the child is humanized by the cultural environment it enters. If it is true to say the human being creates culture, it is also, if not more so, true to say that culture makes the human being. Moral and religious education actualizes the moral and religious potentialities of humans. Is this to be thought of as authoritarian conditioning? Is education not rather an ongoing process of promoting the language, proposing the models, presenting the guiding ideas, and evoking the truths which the person in becoming can personally appropriate, to which he or she can react, and which he or she can try to experience actively?

The first cultural environment in which humanization takes place is the family (or its substitute in cases I think are rather unhappy). It is therefore important to examine the influence of the family on humanization. What ethical formation is achieved by the structured relationships that compose the family constellation? What is the significance of the mother and the father figures for the possible development of a lived, religious relationship with God? How are morality and religious belief interwoven? Can the analysis of the first and fundamental becoming of the person within the dynamics of the family illumine the question of the connection between morality and religion?

The intent of this study is not to examine the moral and religious learning that takes place within the family. The focus is rather on the different processes that structure human identity by reason of the differentiated relations that generally constitute the family as we could study it in different cultural areas. The results of this study shed light on the symbolic meaning the parental figures have for the representation of God, the relational pole of religious faith. The reader will be struck by the nature of the connection between morality and faith among believers. In brief, as the differentiated family relations bring forth the deep structure of the human person in becoming, they implant the sense of moral values as a second spontaneity, and they develop the symbolic figures that underlie religious representations and attitudes.

Overview

I would first situate the focus of this chapter. Leaving aside the {91}
question of the developmental stages of moral conscience and of
religious belief, it focuses on their fundamental psychological
constituents as we can observe them in the becoming of a moral
and religious person. In other words, what are the necessary
psychological conditions for the formation of the moral and
religious personality? Of course, cognitive structures have a
bearing on moral decisions and religious belief. But moral and
religious development involves the whole person. It is more a
question of being in relation than of reasoning.

Moral development gives behavior the quality of spontaneity. And even in conflict situations, when the ethical position
is based on conscious consideration, the moral values appealed to
are applied spontaneously. Let me give an illustration. Consider
an individual who has been raised in the spirit of helpfulness for
people in need. While returning home with friends after a concert
on a cold winter evening, this person sees an old man sleeping in
the street with only cardboard boxes to keep him warm. Our
subject expresses his sympathy and even hesitates a moment and
thinks about calling for help. But then, so as not to disturb the
esthetic pleasure of the evening of music, he goes on his way. The
next day, he feels guilty. The parable of the Good Samaritan
occurs to him and he understands still more clearly that he acted
in an immoral and non-Christian manner.

The situation is thus immediately recognized as one that
demands help, without there being a reasoned passage from
general principles to a practical application. Normally, a moral
judgment consists of just such an immediate recognition of the
meaning of a situation. We could compare making a moral
judgment to recognizing a photograph: "This is Peter." In this
recognition, there is no reasoning process involved, as some
would say: "I make a comparison between the traits of the photo
and my memory image of Peter." Comparisons are made only
when deviant traits complicate recognition.

So, too, it is the conflict between the spontaneous moral
value judgment and a strongly opposing tendency that stimulates
the conscious consideration of moral principles. But, as is clear

from the example, this often takes place later on when it is stimulated by a spontaneous consciousness of guilt. The spontaneity of guilt feelings is the negative side of the spontaneity of moral judgments.

The problem of moral development is, to a large degree, knowing how this spontaneous moral judgment comes about. In other words, it is knowing what factors contribute to it and according to which psychic processes the ethical attitude is formed.

To say that the moral attitude has the quality of acquired spontaneity does not mean that it is conventional in the sense of Kohlberg's use of this term. Moral evaluation is spontaneous because it is a practical judgment with reference to internalized values. A conventional attitude refers directly to the opinion of the milieu, whereas the spontaneity we have in mind refers to values that transcend this opinion. The internalization of values is a very complex process involving different factors: affective experiences and appropriation of norms; a dynamic tension between attachment and affirmation of autonomy; the reference to models and the critical evaluation of them; the tension between self-identity and the freedom to change, between the capacity of enjoyment and the sense of duty. The dynamic tensions between these components are also essential for the development of the religious faith-attitude. Even if there are stages, these processes are going on during our whole existence. And clinical experience shows that everybody has to work through these tensions time and again.

Now it seems to me that the elements that underlie moral attitude and religious faith are basically formed within the complex field of relations that constitute the family. Therefore it is my intention to examine the fundamental influence of the parental figures for the constitution of the moral and religious personality. And by this I mean the experiences and the processes that form and transform, basically and almost definitively, the person coming into existence.

The moral attitude is the expression of the entire personality in its relationship to itself, to others, and to the world. That a person is normally situated on various levels of ethical development does not contradict this, for psychology has adequately demonstrated that a personality manifests harmonious unity only very rarely. Indeed, besides the milieu influences and the learning process, the personality is also created through a variety of identification processes with reference to different and partially successive ideal models. The two parental figures, other family members, teachers, comrades and friends, prestigious people, religious figures—these are all models with whom the developing person more or less identifies and from whom he or she appropriates, to a certain extent, some of their admired characteristics. It is normal, therefore, that there be more than one personality present in one person. Only slowly and seldom or never are they fully integrated into a unity. In different circumstances, the person will often manifest somewhat different spontaneous ethical attitudes according to which identification model is being directly addressed. This seems to me to be one of the main reasons why one can observe a person being situated on two or three levels of moral development.

I shall first clarify the meaning of the parental figures for moral development, and then see how religion can be based on them. I am proceeding from an extensive study we made of parental figures, using a semantic differential scale. This same scale was also applied to the representation of God, thus providing a comparison between the parental figures and that representation.[1] This was not a study in developmental psychology, since the scale is only applicable to adolescents and older subjects. But the data, when interpreted with the aid of psychological insights derived elsewhere, can justify inferences relative to the meaning that parental figures have for moral development. These inferences acquire more force since we were able to establish a significant difference between a group of delinquents and the normal population.

---

[1]This study is soon to be published by the Leuven University Press (Leuven, Belgium) under the title: *Parental Figures and the Representation of God*.

The Parental Figures

In normal populations, the mother figure is characterized primarily by affective availability. Factor analysis showed this to be the main maternal factor. The mother is, in the first place: the one who welcomes me with open arms, the one to whom one feels close at home, the one who expresses tenderness, who is always ready, the one who is most patient, self-giving love, who will sympathize with the child's sorrows, a warm-hearted refuge, sensitive, who takes loving care of me, who is always there when needed, who gives comfort. All these items can be summarized in one phrase: unconditional love.

Factor analyses place the mother second as far as authority is concerned. Interviews with a portion of our research subjects showed that the mother exercises authority with reference to the father. It is by virture of her function as wife in the family constellation that she represents law and exercises authority. These results apply for all normal groups, both of adolescents and of adults, from various cultural milieus. I am abstracting here from the secondary factors that, according to the statistical analysis, supplement these two primary factors in various ways for various populations.

The same two primary factors also determine the father figure, but in reverse. In our populations, chosen in different cultures (U.S.A., Colombia, Belgium, and so on), the father is principally characterized by law and authority: firmness, authority, who gives directions, the one who maintains order, judge, who is the principle, the rule, who gives the law. Strikingly, from the interviews, authority is seen as the proper function of the father, that is, his authority does not derive from the mother. Secondarily, the father is characterized by the typical maternal factor of affective availability. Here, too, I shall omit discussion of the secondary factors.

The group of delinquents and the group of schizophrenics did not attribute this fundamental structure to the parental figures. For them, the predominant factor in the mother figure is initiative, a characteristic that is normally considered to be typically paternal, while the affective components were ascribed to this figure to a much lesser degree. In the father figure, the factor of law and authority is absent.

I am presuming that delinquency expresses a disturbance or deficiency in the formation of the moral attitude. Certainly, environmental circumstances can promote delinquent behavior or can, as during war or revolutions, provide opportunities favorable for the activation of a delinquent disposition. And, of course, delinquency is a relative notion since it can be expressed in various value realms. Nevertheless, it remains true that delinquency is an indication of the absence of an ethical disposition. From our observations, it seems clear that a deficiency in the normal formation of the parental images accompanies a disturbance in moral development. And even when the statistical correlations do not prove a causal relationship, these data indicate the influence of the differentiated parent-child relationship on moral development. In the light of everyday, as well as clinical observations and taking into account the peculiar nature of the moral attitude, I would also contend that the structured family relations form the basis for moral development. The process of acquisition that contributes to moral formation can only develop this foundation. In the absence of the parents, other people such as adoptive parents can provide this formative function.

{95}

Let us now turn to how the two primary factors specifically represented by the two parents form the basis of moral formation.

The Affective Bond with the Mother

Let us reflect on these data and see what they mean for the structuring of a moral personality. The unconditional love that primarily characterizes the mother has a twofold influence on moral formation. In the first place, it is a fundamental condition for the realization of an adequate personal identity. By identity, I mean that particular awareness of being a person that has the possibility and the destiny of self-realization in a specific life project characterized by affective bonds and by the assumption of social tasks. For such a personal identity to develop, it is necessary that the child know that it is loved unconditionally. Confidence of the parents awakens self-confidence in the child. Second, affective availability, primarily on the part of the mother, enables the child to attach itself with pleasure to the first object of attachment, which is the mother. Parental tenderness allows feelings of tenderness to develop in the child. These positive dispositions are implanted in the child by both parents. Nevertheless, our comparative study indicated that the mother is the figure that preeminently contributes to this affective formation. This fundamental maternal availability is all the more important because the child, by its very nature and through the original bio-affective bond with the mother as it has evolved culturally, expects this constellation of qualities from her. When she does not meet this expectation, she drastically disturbs the child's affectivity. An interior opposition then develops between expectation and effective response, which is a typical pathogenic double bind.

When these constellations of self-confidence and capacity for affective bonding are not developed, the person becomes demanding and distrustful and has difficulty in establishing sympathy. He feels as though he is always being treated unfairly and being oppressed. Feelings of hate will be stronger than those of love; revenge is constantly pondered because of the ideas of rejection and injustice that are projected on everything and everyone.

By the way of confirmation of this analysis, I refer to Abraham Maslow.[2] Subjects who can achieve a peak experience see the world and other people as fundamentally good; their experience allows them to realize that life is meaningful. Consequently, they can adopt a more selfless and benevolent attitude toward others. They see others not just as useful pawns on the chessboard of the project with which they would satisfy their own deficiencies.

The positive feelings that are thus developed in the child are amplified by the identification process, because boys as well as girls identify themselves fundamentally with both parents, even though sexual differentiation leads to stronger identification with

---

[2]Abraham Maslow, *Toward a Psychology of Being* (New York: Van Nostrand Reinhold, 1968), pp. 92–93.

the like-sexed parent, particularly in the development of typical sexual feelings and behavior. The parents, and in the first place the mother, not only awaken feelings of tenderness and sympathy, they also are models of identification. Now identification means the interior appropriation of how one person relates to another. To identify is to incorporate in oneself a relational model. Thus, for example, Oedipal identification is the interiorization of the sexual and love relation of the mother with the father or vice versa. The fundamental identification with the mother is the incorporating within oneself of the typical maternal constellations of tenderness, acceptance, and warm sympathy. As the child perceives the mother relating to it, so will it become with respect to others—to a certain degree, of course.

{97}

I am also convinced of the truth of the psychoanalytic theory, supported by clinical observation, that identification is the process by which mourning is worked through. Every child must work through a certain mourning process because it cannot attach itself as completely to the mother as it desires. The intermittent absence of the mother, her bond with her husband, the presence of other children, and so on, arouse normal feelings of jealousy and hate with respect to the partially lost love-object. This loss is compensated for psychologically by incorporating in oneself, as a mode of being, the object that one wants to possess in love. "To be like" partially takes the place of having; one has the other in oneself.

This identification process, in my opinion, forms the personality in a more thoroughgoing way than does the identification that consists of the imitation of a behavior model. In itself, imitation can still be an exterior adaptation, based on strategic calculations, to the behavior of A with respect to B. Identification is an interior transformation of the personality. In identification, X transforms himself so that he incorporates the disposition of A as a source of behavior modes. The identification schema proceeds according to two movements: X incorporates in himself the constellation of A (the mother) with respect to X; X incorporates in himself the constellation of A (the mother) with respect to B (the others).

This positive affective constellation is a source of spontaneous moral conduct because it is peculiar to this form of affectivity to put oneself in the place of the other and to want to treat the other as one experiences that that one has been treated, with love and justice. This is empathy. "Love your neighbor as yourself" very adequately expresses the structure of empathy. The child who is accepted by the mother in receptive love can love itself and put itself in the place of the other. It can have the relation to the other that it has received and that it has for itself. A cognitive capacity for role-taking cannot replace this fundamental empathy but only extend it to those with whom no spontaneous affective bond exists or toward whom prejudice (social or racial) begets feelings of strangeness and aversion. Whoever feels, via empathy, that the other is injured by injustice will not so easily do him an injustice. Whoever is capable of compassion for the other will not easily cause him suffering, at least when that suffering is experienced as the opposite of the desired happiness and pleasure that one has one-self. But someone who experiences himself as a tormented victim can take pleasure in suffering with the suffering of the other, as is indicated in the phenomenon of sadism.

To corroborate this analysis, I can refer to clinical psychology. A child who is afflicted with the tendency to lie or steal, and this in contradiction with the prevailing principles of childraising, acts unwillingly from mostly unconscious affective frustrations. These symptoms indicate *a contrario* that moral development is necessarily based on positive affective relations. Moreover, because of a deficient mother-child relation, the capacity for empathy is absent among delinquents. In place of a positive identification with an affectively available mother, there is, I think, a continuous feeling of frustration that leads to cravings for retribution and vindication and also an identification with the negative constellation of the mother.

My discussion of the results of the research could give rise to a double misunderstanding. First, it could be observed that the mother is not only unconditional love and even that she may not be. She also has expectations of her child. I do not think that our subjects deny this. Indeed, there were mothers among them who entertained such expectations. It is a matter of emphasis. The primary characteristic of the mother, as she should be according to our subjects, is serene acceptance in such a way that the child has the certainty of being accepted by her. As far as this love is concerned, the fortunes, successes and failures, and faults of the child are secondary.

{99}

In terms of this unconditional love of the mother, it could also be thought that she has to meet all the wishes of the child—even when they are unreasonable. To present such un-conditionality as the ideal would, of course, give many mothers guilt feelings. It would also hinder the child's learning to accept reality: the demands of an ordered family community, the mother's own professional responsibilities, her life with her husband, and so on. Unconditionality is indeed a quality of the maternal relationship, but it does not imply that the child can or must demand that the mother-child relationship be the only bond the mother has and that this relationship be exclusive.

Law and Authority in Moral Formation

In our study of parental figures, the giving of the law and the exercise of authority were universally attributed to the father as the statistically first factor by both the male and the female subjects. This observation contradicts the oversimplified psychoanalytic theory that places the origin of the moral conscience in an Oedipus complex that would manifest the same though reversed structure for girls as for boys. According to this psychoanalytic theory, the moral conscience would originate in the Oedipal rivalry and in the prohibition by the same-sexed parent of the incestuous relationship. Thus for a girl, the father would be the libidinal object pole and the mother the prohibiting authority. Our observation that the father represents law and authority for both sexes indicates that these functions must be understood in their opposition to the maternal values as such, that is, to the mother figure as it applies for both sexes. Therefore, I shall interpret the figure of the father, as agent of authority, by situating it in its polarity with the mother figure.

First, however, I want to note that the observed mother-father polarity has nothing to do with the social problem of sexual equality. It would be a false application of ideology to conclude to an equivalence of functions in the family from equality in the economic, political, and social order. For in the family, as I have noted, the parental images are polarized in function of the person-in-becoming. That this differentiation responds to a fundamental requirement is shown by the conformity of our subjects' answers, even those subjects whose parents both exercise a profession and share household tasks. Personally qualified relations are involved here, relations in which the sex of the individual parent is clearly significant.

I think that we must proceed from the fact that the mother, because of her natural bio-affective bond with the child, is the first object of attachment and that she, therefore, remains the figure that primarily represents unconditional and confident love. This fundamental fact implies that the father, as the third pole in the family constellation, enters the field of family relations from the outside, psychologically speaking, and thus, for more than one reason, performs the polar opposite function.

What concerns us here is the understanding of how the specific paternal function contributes to moral formation. It is clear that the father figure is characterized by its direct moral significance. The terms "law" and "authority" are of themselves moral qualifiers. But they are still formal principles. We must now consider how they are psychologically active in the becoming of the mature person. Three elements are important in this regard.

First, the person-in-becoming needs law and authority, for his own tendencies are disordered, full of conflicts, directed to the immediate satisfaction of spontaneous desires. Law and authority bring order to the psychic life. Law is thus a gift that corresponds to a psychological necessity, even when it runs counter to spontaneous impulses and thereby gives rise to conflict. The absence of law and authority generates a feeling of fundamental insecurity. For the acquisition of a feeling of security and of a personal identity, therefore, two conditions, which in a sense oppose each other but which also supplement and correct each other, are necessary: unconditional acceptance and law and authority. These requirements are essentially fulfilled by the two differentiated parental figures.

Second, the father, as the representative of law and authority, must also be situated within the triangular relationship of the family as the child experiences it. The primal attachment to the mother responds to the desire for the experience of unity. This experience, in itself, attaches the child to the past. I do not want to place any negative connotations on this. Still, to become independent, it is necessary that the person be detached from the mother and directed toward the future. The person acquires personal identity by developing within the tension between two poles: attachment and detachment, being rooted in the past and being open to the future.

Third, the father represents the extra-familial community. Here again, I must warn against a simplifying misinterpretation. It is evident that the mother also takes on this function to a certain degree, especially when she has extra-familial responsibilities. According to our study, however, this is not perceived as being specific to the mother figure. And when she combines two functions, the more important is still within the field of familial relations, her making present of the typical maternal values. It is precisely in polar opposition to this that the father has his typical function of introducing the demands of the extra-familial community. Thus he, more specifically than the mother, directs the child to the more general law of society at large. As the bridge between the family and the community, he breaks open the self-directedness and closedness of the family and subjects it to the demands of the relatively universal human community.

In comparison with the unconditional love of the mother, the love of the father is conditional. Let there be no misunderstanding here: It pertains to the essence of his love that it poses demands. His love is dependent on the fulfillment of these demands. Therefore, a father who makes no demands is experienced as a father who does not care for what the child will become. "I didn't have a *real* father" is the spontaneous expression of the contradiction between the physical presence of the father and the absence of the paternal function. Law and authority, therefore, may not be understood as a disciplinary exercise of power. It is a form that paternal love takes, for in the paternal figure the function of law is balanced by love.

The second factor that characterizes the father in our study, that of affective availability, gives, in conjunction with the first factor, the authority function its typical paternal character, just as the first factor determines the meaning of the second. The authority function receives its proper significance on the basis of a personal affective bond. But this is also realized by the demanding character of authority. In a study with children, we also observed that, from the age of seven on, this is clearly formulated in that way: The father *must* be strict. Otherwise he is not a real father. Among the late adolescents and adults, however, the item "strictness" only received low scores for the father image. I think that, for them, strictness signifies the authoritarian manner in which the authority of the father is exercised, whereas for the children the word "strict" expresses the authority function as such as opposed to the tenderness of the child-mother relationship.

Being able to control impulses, to detach oneself from the bond with the mother, to direct oneself toward the extra-familial community—these are conditions necessary for the feeling of security and responsibility with respect to others and thus they pertain to the formation of morality. Law and authority, however, also imply that principles of conduct are impressed. In their polar differentiation the parental figures both contribute to moral formation. Together with the affective development of the ability to share in the emotions of others, the interiorization of principles of authority forms the moral attitude. We see now how this interiorization occurs psychologically. One could possibly think that this is a matter of cognitive development and of systematic acquisition of general rules of conduct applicable to all people. This element is certainly important. I think, however, that while the process of moral learning is important, it presupposes a basis in personality development, and that this basis is provided by the father and mother who exercise effectively the functions expected of them. I see a confirmation of this, *a contrario*, in the lack of the generally applicable father image among the delinquents. It is difficult for me to conceive that this deficient father image could result from only a defective cognitive moral upbringing.

{*103*}

The Ego Ideal

The general moral principles that are learned become sources of moral conduct when they are interiorized. Otherwise they remain exterior rules of conduct that one obeys in order to adapt oneself to the requirements of a particular situation. Not taken up into the identity of the personality, they remain on the surface of the person and are obeyed only insofar as they are *useful* rules of the game. Now, rules of conduct are interiorized when they are taken up into the ego ideal. This term comes from psychoanalysis, and I am convinced that the psychoanalytic doctrine of the ego ideal makes an essential contribution to the understanding of moral development. The ego ideal is the interior representation the subject has of himself as he desires to be in accordance with the expectations of the people with whom he wants to have an affective bond. We are concerned here with the formation of the ego ideal in relation to the mother and to the father. By his claims, the father, and with him and in reference to him the mother, proposes an image of the child as they wish that child to become. Certainly, the parents love the child as it is, but they love it too as it must become in order to be a responsible person. The ideal image is, in this sense, the result of an implantation of maternal love and an inoculation of paternal authority. Now that ideal image belongs to the identity of the person himself. The child, and also the adult, identifies itself with its ego ideal, and this identification is active: One strives to become what one wishes to see oneself as. In other words, one transfers a good deal of one's self-love to the ideal image. On the other hand, this ego ideal is a way of being human that transcends the immediate egocentric passions: It represents within the person the expectations that humanity poses in order for it to recognize someone as a worthy human being. The ego ideal thus forms the bridge between the self-love of the subject and the moral demands of the society. The acquired rules of conduct fulfill, broaden, and give new content to

{104}

the ideal image. But it is only when they are taken up into the ideal image that they are interiorized into the person as his own disposition.

The moral contribution of the parents thus consists primarily of their standing at the origin of the ego ideal with its moral contents by virtue of the dual quality of authority and affective availability. The development of the ego ideal takes place through specific identifications with the parents. It consists of the child constructing its personal identity in conformity with the attitudes of the mother and with directive wishes of the father. The parents impress upon the child an image of conduct to which the child tries to conform.

It is obvious that the personal moral attitude of the parents is more important than the directives they impress with authority. When there is an explicit contradiction between what they demand and the manner in which they act, then they send a contradictory message that makes the formation of a moral ego ideal impossible or very difficult. The moral demands of the parents are then perceived as being in the service of their self-interest, thus losing their moral significance. Moral principles are only perceived as moral when they can be seen as being generally valid and thus also as applying to the behavior of the parents themselves. The same can in fact be observed in the area of religious upbringing, which only has formative power when the parents, by their conduct, show that they are the same as the child with respect to God. What is called "giving an example" thus consists of reflecting in one's own behavior the fact that the impressed truths and rules of conduct are universally applicable to the person as person, to the parents as much as to the child. Before the generality of the principles are conceptualized, it is brought to the consciousness in the identification process described above.

Nowadays, the authority function of the father is often criticized on ideological grounds. It has been asked whether, in a "fraternal society" the father image has not been fundamentally altered. Or, based on psychological conceptions, the opinion is held that the child must be allowed to experiment in freedom and thus, spontaneously and through experience, come to an insight into moral values. I shall respond to this very briefly: First, a fraternal society of adults presumes that the person-in-becoming develops a fraternal disposition precisely through the influence of a paternal authority and a maternal love that represent in the family the moral demands of the fraternal society. Second, it is erroneous psychologically to hold that a person is free by nature. On the contrary, he is originally in the power of all kinds of instinctual impulses. The person can become free when personal development allows him sufficient control of his instinctual impulses to direct them toward a higher, culturally valuable goal. Upbringing, naturally, presumes a certain freedom since it draws on it. But it is upbringing that makes real the possibility of free actions. Third, one must distinguish between the manner in which paternal authority is exercised and the authority function itself. As I have already mentioned, the item "strict" was scored low by our subjects, while authority and law were scored high.

{105}

A Note on Moral Attitude and Moral Judgment

The formation of the moral attitude also includes the formation of moral judgment. By moral judgment, I mean the articulation of principles according to which one takes a decision and according to which one justifies one's behavior to oneself and to others. Clearly, I have not dealt with this aspect. I limit myself to the consideration of the respective influences and characteristics of the interpersonal relations with the parents as they compose the family constellation with their bipolar differences. It is evident that the processes I have analyzed develop progressively and that the transformations in personal life are moments when the processes are repeated and confirmed. Puberty, the entrance to young adulthood, and the adult assumption of family respon-sibilities are important steps where the fundamental orientations are more or less objects of examination and, from then on, more personal choices. It seems to me that it would be difficult to mark off these steps with any amount of precision. In any event, I do not consider them as steps in the sense that they would be moments of transformation of the contents and the guiding

{*106*} principles. It is clearly otherwise for moral judgment in the restricted sense in which I have defined it. The intellectually conceived motivations of moral judgments and behavior certainly are transformed by successive steps. The concept of law as principle of morality, for example, is established at a certain moment, transformed, and more or less universalized. However, the moral attitude may not by identified with moral judgment, which is consciously articulated and intellectually justified. Consider Adolf Eichmann, the architect of the Nazi extermination camps. At his trial, he could articulate perfectly the philosophical principles of Kantian morality, thus placing himself on a superior level of moral judgment that states the principle of the rights of all men. The moral attitude comprises, to be sure, the capacity to express the principles and to refer oneself to them as to critical norms for one's own decisions and for the retrospective evaluation of one's behavior. But it remains that, as a practical judgment, the moral judgment is more essentially a spontaneous taking of a postion in virtue of the models and rules that the subject has interiorized in the course of his identifications.

The Significance of Religion for Moral Development and, Inversely, of Moral Development for Religious Belief

Using empirical studies (tests, questionnaires, and so on), it is very difficult to discern the influence of religion on moral development. This is because of the relation between religion and morality. Thus, the studies that have been done on this subject must be approached cautiously.

Let us consider first the content of morality. Humanist morality is not different from the morality proposed by the Christian religion. There are, of course, limited cases where religion is stricter than humanist morality such as, for example, the prohibition of divorce in Catholicism. But as far as the essentials are concerned, the rules of conduct are the same. This is to be expected, certainly as far as Christianity is concerned, to which I limit myself here. Indeed, the fundamental human relations that are controlled by morality are not abolished by

Christianity. And even when the Gospel presents a perfection of morality, the unbeliever can still consider it to be a consequence of general human principles. Forgiveness, for example, can be seen as a refinement of respect and good will toward one's fellowman.

Therefore, one must approach indirectly the empirical study of the effective influence of religion on moral development. For example, one could investigate the correlation between observed moral conduct and the degree of faith conviction, the representation of God of the subjects, or the components of the lived religious relationship. The observation of recurrent and significantly different correlations could be interpreted as an indication of an influence of religion on moral development. Indeed, one can argue that the emphasis that religion places on its moral laws as conditions for a relation with God has an influence, so that one may conclude from this principle to the probability of a certain causal influence, even though it is not demonstrated by the statistical correlations themselves.

As in the preceding section of this paper, I shall start here with the representation of God as derived from our empirical research, and then I shall consider its importance for moral development. Again, I shall infer this influence from the representation of God. In this case, we are concerned as well with the fundamental constellations that support the moral disposition.

First, I want to mention a study on the representation of God conducted with adults who had received a Catholic upbringing and had gone through higher education.[3] The items used in this study did not express specific dogmatic belief content, such as belief in the Resurrection, but rather various aspects of the lived relation with God as this can be conceived as being generally religious. From factor analysis of the answers, it turned out that the most important factor in the representation of God is the personal relationship with a personal God. The second most important factor is more intellectual: God as the answer to man's ultimate questions. The third factor is God as a rather impersonal dynamism in the cosmos and in the depth of existence. Within the

---

[3]G. Vercruysse, "The Meaning of God: A Factoranalytic Study," *Social Compass*, 1972, 19, pp. 347–364.

first factor, three subfactors could be distinguished: (1) God as a help in need, which was scored the lowest; (2) the personal presence of God as a relationship experienced as meaningful in itself; (3) the highest scored, responsibility to God and confidence that God will perfect what man accomplishes in this world. It can be seen here clearly that the faith position, as experienced in Christianity, involves an immediate appeal for moral responsibility. Naturally, this does not define the content of the moral principles. Nor does it determine the degree to which the believer is consistent with the moral demands of his faith.

Thus it is not the human need for protection or help that determines the relationship to God and gives content to the representation of God. In the I-thou relationship, which constitutes the most important core of the representation of God, the dominant notion is that God holds man responsible for his conduct. For adult believers, at least, religion clearly provides a strong motive for moral disposition. I am not saying that this motive replaces human moral principles. What I am saying is that the belief motive is an accompanying motive that does not so much give content to moral principles as it embraces and supports them. One can distinguish between material principles and a formal principle with the understanding that "formal" means to know that one is accountable to a person both for moral rules and for actual behavior. And although this was not directly proven by this study, one can presume that this notion of responsibility to a personal God is already present to a certain degree when one is brought up to believe in God.

The study on the parental figures also dealt with the representation of God as it is mediated by the parental figures. The subjects also applied the semantic scales with the maternal and paternal qualities to God, using the same seven-step scale. Let us turn now to the representation of God that emerged and its meaning for moral development.

The two principal factors of the father and mother images form, in a very general way, the core of the representation of God. Authority and law, the paternal factors, apply to God in such a way that the specific items (gives the law, judges) are ascribed to God much more than to the father. But the representation of God also includes the maternal factor of unconditional love and this to a higher degree than does the father image. The religious relationship with God is sustained by that essential polarity. This was not the case for the Hindu population, however, where God is seen practically exclusively as lawgiver and judge. It is also striking that firmly believing Christians saw God as paternal to a significantly higher degree than did the doubting believers. The latter saw God more as an inner dynamism, thus as a rather impersonal divinity. Convinced belief implies the awareness of being responsible to God as personal lawgiver and judge and therefore reinforces the consciousness of moral responsibility. Here, too, the belief of being bound to a personal God consists, to a very important degree, of an ethical conception of life. But that this is not felt as repressive and a source of anxiety appears from the strong presence of a personal bond of trust with God, as is shown by the high score of the maternal dimension. This trustful attitude is stronger among the firm believers than among the doubting believers, the latter placing more emphasis on an anonymous affective experience of unity that corresponds to their individual wishes. We may then conclude that the two components that join in the formation of the ethical attitude are also developed and reinforced by religion. And, conversely, that the moral formation prepares and nourishes religious belief.

On the basis of this, we understand that Christian morality is fundamentally humanistic, that humanistic morality is not specifically Christian, and that the explicit motivation of the moral dispositon is seldom specifically religious. Moreover, it would be a falsification of morality as well as of religious faith to conduct oneself morally because of divine commandments as distinct from the fellowman toward whom the conduct is directed. To be just because of God's law and not because of the right the other person has to be treated honestly reduces to acting morally only out of fear of divine punishment. Religious motives, when they are authentic, thus mainly operate indirectly, and not as principles of moral action explicitly appealed to.

However, in the whole of the culture, religion remains important as factor of morality. Faith in God is, in principle, the basis for a universalist morality. From the very nature of faith in

God in a universal religion, it follows that all people, irrespective of national, class, or racial distinctions, are unique persons before God with the same destiny and the same rights. As the universal father figure, in balance with a very maternal unconditional love, God conforms the moral judgment to the universality of principles. It is not by chance that the insight into the universal rights of man as the basic principle of morality developed in the Western culture, which has obviously been formed by Christianity. Of course, this universalist vision was not always or effectively applied by the Christian culture. The believer, too, is not free of racism or nationalism that places him or her, often unconsciously, in contradiction with the principled morality of his or her religion. Nevertheless, to the extent that the content of faith in God is consistently and explicitly recognized, it is a source of energy for a humanistic morality and a norm for a vigilant critique of the closed morality that serves a group's self-interest. True religious faith is a powerful element for promoting the higher stage of development. The formal intellectual principles of this stage are sustained and nourished by the belief-content.

A Note on Awareness of Sin

One may presume that the strong sense of personal responsibility with respect to God as lawgiver and judge necessarily affects the awareness of sin. I want to discuss this element, although it was not included in the scope of the empirical study by Vercruysse.

The sense of sin can develop in two directions, and its influence on moral development is ambiguous. The awareness of sin can lead to rejection, out of distrust of the pulsions: pleasure, sexuality, aggressivity. The accent is then placed on personal asceticism and purity. As religious ideals, the passive virtues of obedience, humility, and self-denial are valued. In this disposition, the person turns in upon himself in a narcissistic striving for perfection. This sort of awareness of sin takes on a masochistic quality of self-accusation, and easily leads to an attitude of despair and even of condemnation of others. I think that this is the case when God is seen predominantly as lawgiver and judge.

{111}

Such an awareness of sin reinforces a legalistic morality and does not promote a dynamic morality.

When, on the contrary, the emphasis of religion lies on responsibility for the community, then the awareness of sin promotes a positive and dynamic morality. First of all, it is a stimulus to make amends by constructive initiatives for one's own unfaithfulness with respect to God. With a trustful attitude toward a fundamentally beneficent God, the believer seeks to fulfill God's commands by identifying himself with the self-giving goodness of God. What I have said about the identification with the disposition of the mother also applies to the faith bond with a God who is seen as positively promoting the welfare of mankind. The awareness of sin is, in this case, the recognition of one's own deficiencies in the disposition that ought to conform to God's dynamic will in order to bring humanity to peace and happiness.

Second, in this attitude, the sense of sin promotes the moral disposition since it occasions generosity and forgiveness. The basic attitude of the proper awareness of sin is expressed in the prayer: "Forgive us our debts as we forgive our debtors." We do not condemn the other person when we know that we ourselves are not free of guilt. This disposition is not of itself a specific moral principle, but it is a basic attitude that keeps the moral disposition sound and active. It also guards against the unconscious projection of one's own culpability in an attitude of accusational distrust: Projection of guilt is one of the greatest hindrances to dynamic moral development.[4]

Conclusions

An intellectualistic view of moral development is inadequate. It has been stressed that one should take into account the affective and conative functions. Now affectivity is not naked energy, and the will is not just the faculty of abstract decision-making.

---

[4]I have considered the question of true and morbid culpability more extensively in *Dette et désir. Deux axes chretiens et la dérive pathologique*. Editions du Seuil, 1978, 317 pp.; and "Dieu notre Pére," *Concilium. Revue Internationale de Théologie*, 130, 1977, pp. 15–24.

{112}

Affectivity is an active disposition toward others as a result of the transformation of the human pulsion. This transformation involves the permanent polarity between norms and experiences, which together form what we call values. Therefore, morality is autonomous and heteronomous. I explain.

Norms are the principles that transcend contradictory passions, fluctuating emotions, changing impressions and feelings. Therefore, norms form the basis for autonomy, which means *autos*, a self-*identity*, a faithfulness to the self, the self as it is the ideal of itself.

Authorities, concrete laws, commandments are the concretization of the guiding norms (justice, respect, loyalty, and so on). Therefore, as Thomas Aquinas already stated, one had to obey first one's own conscience and only secondarily the authorities, insofar as they actualize concretely the norms of the communal life. To be human is to be responsible: to be capable of responding of oneself to the authority of the norms.

Experience is the other side of autonomy and it belongs to the moral transformation of the person-in-becoming. Experience means the inner appropriation of norms so that they become the *second spontaneity* that characterizes the really moral person. The same is true for religion. Experience is first the receiving of the moral attitude of the others so that one can identify with it. In the same way the belief experience is first the gift of God's presence and of God's faith in us. Through human mediation, the invisible God gives us signs and makes himself present to us, so that we can bring forth our creative answer: to believe in Him, and to accommodate our behavior to our belief. Moral experience has the structure of *parole*: Because we were addressed and recognized as a "you," we become an "I" who can answer and respond, saying "you," and recognize the other as an "I," as a person who is unique and who, at the same time, shares a universal human dignity. The experience, moral and religious, which can be at the origin of our moral and religious attitude, is bipolar. It is the experience of unconditional acceptance and recognition of myself by the other. It is also the consciousness of a conditional acceptance: the other desires that I should become fully myself as a human being with reference to the guiding norms that determine human dignity.

In this respect the significance of the structured family relationship is clear. The parental figures not only develop the first humanizing moral formation, they also remain paradigmatic for the whole structure of the moral and religious attitude. Therefore, their influence is profound and determinative. Because the parental figures are by their very nature the concrete symbolic mediations of universal existential and moral values, their influence is not to be conceived of as the imposition of mere conventional standards of behavior. And when they really correspond to their symbolic functions, rather than maintaining the growing person in infantile dependence, they promote inner freedom and autonomy in harmony with attachment and with the normative authority of universal values.

The theoretical questions concerning morality, its development, its stages, the importance of cognitive structures, are not touched upon in this limited chapter. Nevertheless, it is my conviction that they can only be clarified if we refer them to the basic structure of humanization as it is brought forth within the polarities of the family structure.

Educational Consequences

Educational work with parents is important. The changing status of women, the cultural oscillation between stressing freedom for the child and the necessity of norms and authority, the divergence of ideologies, and, not the least, some unhappy memories of the parents' own childhoods often make it difficult for parents to situate themselves with respect to their parental functions.

Educators should be aware that learning is secondary to the deeper processes that structure affectivity as a complex and multidimensional relational form. The contribution of the school differs from the primordial education achieved within the family. In the school itself as a micro-society, however, the basic bipolarity that characterizes the family should also be realized in its own way.

The recognition of necessary authority must go together with a respectful tolerance for the tensions and even the conflicts that

{114}

have to be worked through during moral and religious development. An insight into the deep structuring processes as they occur as an open-ended achievement of the sane family can give the educator confidence in the outcome of conflict, revolt, and autonomy-affirmation as opposed to bondage.

The formation of the ego ideal seems to be the most important factor in education. Its significance is that it is a powerful motivation and the most important foundation for the moral attitude. An egoistic tendency is not at all implied here: The problem is to promote an ego ideal that comprises the social interest as well as the enjoyment of gratuitous, self-enlarging experiences (art, religion). It is the task of the educator to promote an ideal of humanity for the student to identify with.

ABOUT THE AUTHOR

Dr. Antoine Vergote *is Ordinary Professor at the Katholieke Universiteit Leuven and Extraordinary Professor at the Université Catholique de Louvain. After obtaining doctoral degrees in philosophy and theology at the University of Louvain, Belgium, he studied psychology and anthropology in Paris where he received his psychoanalytic training in the "Société francaise de Psychanalyse." He founded the Center of Religious Psychology under the aegis of the Faculty of Psychology and Educational Sciences at the University of Louvain. He teaches psychology of religion, philosophy of religion, and philosophical anthropology.*

Dr. Vergote is a co-founder of the "Ecole Belge de Psychanalyse" (1965) and has been, at various times, its president and vice president. He considers the interaction between his research as a university scholar and his clinical work to be of primary importance.

His major interests in the field of religion are to detect the structure and multidimensionality of religious faith, to examine the connection between belief content and the lived faith relationship, and to analyze the mediation of natural and cultural symbols in the personal appropriation of religious faith. Among the investigations he has conducted over the years are the following: the relation between religious experience and faith; the components of the religious attitude; and the content of the representation of God in different populations and age groups.

The Psychological Foundations
of Belief in God

ANA-MARIA RIZZUTO

Introduction

{116}   If none of us have ever met God in person, how do we "know" about God's feelings or personal characteristics? How did Einstein know that "God is subtle but not malicious"? When does a child begin to form the representation of God? What are the factors that affect people's belief or lack of belief in God? What are the indisputable psychological conditions and antecedents for believing in God?

In the last fifteen years I have been recording the answers to these questions. I first studied fifteen patients and five normal individuals in a pilot research project to determine my methodology. The research results presented in this chapter emerged from the study of 123 individuals admitted as patients in a private hospital. Twenty of those patients' life histories, family histories, and present situations and beliefs were studied in great detail. The purpose of the study was to trace the psychological antecedents in their lives for their present states of belief or unbelief. This chapter describes those findings.

This work brings new insights into the process of becoming a believer. It also provides a deeper understanding of the role of parents and educators in their task of guiding the child through the process of becoming a religious individual.*

What Is Belief?

The *Oxford Dictionary* defines *belief* as "the mental action, condition, or habit, of trusting to or confiding in a person or thing." The dictionary indicates that *"belief* was the earlier word for what is now commonly called *faith."* In tracing the evolution of meaning of the word *faith*, it indicates that it "originally meant in English (as in Old French) 'loyalty to a person to whom one is bound by promise or duty, or to one's promise or duty itself,' as in 'to keep faith, to break faith,' and the derivatives *faithful,*

---

*A more complete report of my method, theoretical assumptions, and findings appears in my book *The Birth of the Living God*.

faithless, in which there is no reference to 'belief'; i.e. 'faith' was = fidelity, fealty.''

In this chapter, I shall attempt to demonstrate that the psychological foundations of belief in God coincide with the original meaning of the words *belief* and *faith*. Departing from a contemporary psychoanalytic understanding of human development, I will show that to believe or not to believe is always an act of fidelity to oneself and to our mental representations of those to whom we owe our past and present existence. Faith or lack of it is our way of keeping ourselves psychologically alive in the context of our historical life by extending our roots toward those private streams that gave us life and which now carry living water for us.

{117}

My specific area of research is belief in God. I propose that belief in God or lack of it is an act of fidelity (in the sense of being bound) to oneself and our primary love objects as they are experienced in the present in the privacy of subjective living. By an act of fidelity I mean that at the moment of belief, in the act of believing, the individual finds himself or herself psychologically "bound"[1] to believe in or to reject a God with whom there has been a prolonged private relation. I further propose that in the contemporary theistic[2] world no faith can exist without a conscious, preconscious, or unconscious bind to an experiential relation with a human object psychologically transformed into a God, nature, the universe, or simply a system of beliefs or a way of organizing meaningfully. This is what the dictionary calls "loyalty to a person" or "a promise itself." In most individuals both aspects, a personal God representation and some transformations of it, are simultaneously present. An example may bring some light to the point I am trying to make. My first experience with this type of process occurred when I was a young internist.

A mature parish priest came to my consulting room complaining of chronic fatigue, insomnia, and a persistent feeling of constraint that burdened his entire life, including his ability to be more available to his parishioners. He was a kind and gentle man,

---

[1]"Bound" here refers to the subjective feeling of the believer, not to a compelling extrinsic process.

[2]Theistic in the sense that the word God is part of language and culture.

rather timid but capable of deep moral commitment. I examined him physically and psychically. The physical examination was entirely normal. In examining his personal history I noticed that he spoke of his father (dead by now) with fear in his voice, while describing him with certain admiration as stern and punitive. To my amazement some of his words about his father coincided with his earlier description of his God. However, as a well-educated priest, he spoke of God as loving, caring and as having all the attributes ascribed to him by Roman Catholic theology as a good father. I realized that my unusual patient was caught between two contradictory representations of his God. The God of the priest was loving, patient, and gentle. The God of the man was critical, stern, and demanding. The God of the theologian, however, I reasoned, was updated, but the God of the man was anachronistic and disturbing. I proposed to him, without sharing my reasoning, that he come to talk with me about his health and his life (as I said, I was an internist in those days) and see how I could help him.

Soon, we were involved in a fascinating process of describing the father, as felt by him in his childhood, as the God of his worries and insomnia and contrasting it with the God of his prayers and his preaching. In a few weeks we were wrestling quite vigorously with the contradictory sides of his God. We pitted the stern God against the loving God. We struggled with them. We argued with the criticism of one side of God while we questioned God's love. It was like Jacob wrestling with the angel. At the end he also said, "I have seen God face to face, and yet my life is preserved." (Genesis 32:30) What he had seen was that the God of his theology also had an antecedent in the kinder and more loving side of his father. His fear of him had obstructed his vision.

After such an unusual medical treatment his symptoms disappeared, he experienced an upsurge of energy and felt more at peace with himself. The improvement lasted up to the last time I saw him, a good fifteen years after the event. He had improved and I, as a young physician, had learned an extraordinary lesson about physical and mental distress and about man and his God. I realized that what I had done, without even knowing my frame of reference, was to update his God representation to the level of his theological convictions. I learned later on, from my research and clinical practice, that he was suffering from a common ailment among believers who have been unable to synthesize the various sources of their composite God representation. Diagnostically, his suffering related to the level of development when the young adult cannot leave his father behind and accept that he has entered full maturity and has the right to see his own father too, face to face, accepting his defects, his failures, and his limitations and acknowledging that that father must humbly rank second after the godly father he has chosen to serve. In other words, for him to be able to sleep he had to give full command to the God of his theology and let go of his anachronistic father-god.

If as a personal representation God causes distress and pain, the individual may repress the conscious representation of a God and transform it through many of the normally acting mechanisms of defense into any of the derivative transformations I just mentioned.

The relation to God finds its primary affectual source in the objects of early life which provide the sensory, subjective, and interpersonal experiences to form the representation of a (for the subject) living God. For God (as a representation) has as much of a developmental history as the historical individual who believes in him or who denies his existence.

Whether the child may or may not come to the world with some innate notion about God, it is not demonstrable. However, developmental studies from many sources (Piaget and Gessel provide the most comprehensive research) reveal that the child's elaboration of his or her representation of God is the result of a developmental process that they have traced at the descriptive level.

The Psychoanalytic Point of View

My study focuses on the developmental process of creating a God representation and its significance for the growing child as well as the conditions for belief in it at each level of development. My methodology and point of view are psychoanalytic. In studying any psychic phenomenon, psychoanalysis takes into consideration its origins and development (genetic point of view) and its participation in the formation of a given type of personality (structural point of view). It also observes the phenomenon from the perspective of the type of internal (dynamic point of view) and environmental (adaptive) equilibrium the person attempts to achieve. In considering the internal and environmental equilibrium of the individual, the psychoanalytic approach pays specific attention to the mental processes (wishes, fantasies, thoughts and the defenses against them) which permit the individual to experience conscious awareness or prompt him to protect himself with repressive unconsciousness. All these processes *are at the service of creating a private sense of safety where the individual feels he is at least minimally deserving to exist and that somewhere, someplace there is somebody who could love him*. In that private world of thoughts, wishes, fantasies (tender, aggressive, lustful, self-aggrandizing, and so on), fears, and imaginary beings, idiosyncratic beliefs acquire a very specific psychic reality which makes them existentially as real and as potentially life-giving or suffocating as the air we breathe.

In brief, the psychoanalytic point of view proposes that *the core of human life is not located in the visible reality of everyday living but in the private psychic life of each individual*.

Freud's View of The Origins Of "God"—A Partial Insight

When Freud applied his psychoanalytic notions to belief in God, he felt that such a belief was the result of an unresolved childish attachment to parental objects, "exalted" into Godhead at the time of the Oedipal resolution. Freud thought that the God of the adult was in fact his childhood father[3] now disguised as Godhead. He proposed that the affectual attachment to the father

---

[3]Ana-Maria Rizzuto, "Freud, God, the Devil and the Theory of Object Representation," *International Review of Psycho-Analysis*, Vol. 3, Part 2, (1976).

and God now desexualized after the Oedipal resolution was one and the same for both.

Freud talked only about the father as the person who provides a source for the God representation. He did not reflect about the role of the mother and obtained his conclusions exclusively from the study of boys and men. Limited by that double restriction, Freud's insight carried, however, a genial discovery: The source of the representation of an individual's God must be traced to primary objects. God is not a given in mental life, but, Freud suggested, a creation of the human mind.

In evaluating Freud's work, I first agreed with his premise: The God of everyday man could not be just a rational idea but the representational creation of a living being, originating in the child's experiences with those who interacted with him at the beginning of life. I also disagree with Freud. If God had such origins, the significance for human life, particularly for the meaning of a person's life, must be more than a regressive attachment to the parents of childhood. In fact, the God representation *must have the same ceaseless potential for new meanings in the long process of life as the parental representations have for us until we die*. Further, both the father *and* the mother provide the experiences for a later formation of a God representation.

We are historical beings whose physic roots and basic personality stem from the early enmeshment with our primary caretakers. If life is developmental process which ceases only with death, then a God created from such substances (parental representations) cannot be easily dispensed with as an outgrown piece of childhood clothing. In fact, two unavoidable consequences must follow from Freud's premises: (1) All persons in the Western world have an unconscious or conscious God representation; (2) all persons must wrestle, until they die, through each stage of development with their God as they do with their parental representations and sometimes their parents.

At that point of my thinking I found myself in the middle, between the classic psychoanalytic view (of religion and the God representation—an affectual fixation to an early representation of the father, a psychological fossil) and an extensive literature on religion based on "explanatory concepts which function only at the highest level of psychic organization and in terms of a more-or-less idealized schema."[4]

My Own Research

The research I did was intended to elucidate the developmental creation of a God representation and its transformations in the course of life. Changes brought about by epigenetic transformation of functions and structures at all levels (physical, intellectual, emotional), environmental influences, and historical events had to have an impact on the individual's need to update, modify, transform, or repress his available God representation.

While I was devising my methodology, I studied normal individuals and psychiatric patients. I found that there were no essential differences in the processes that lead both groups to form, use, transform, or reject their God representation. Psychopathology does not affect the *type* of processes utilized in the creation and transformation of the God representation. Psychopathological events as well as most causal coincidental factors do affect, however, the specific characteristics of a given God representation and, more to the point, *the type of private relation* the individual has with his God. It should be clear at this point that I do not address myself to public religion, or public representation of the Godhead, but to the private, conscious, preconscious, and unconscious traits of a person's representation of God and that person's most intimate dealings with it, from love to total rejection.

When I talk about "representation," I do not refer to a mental content, an idea, or a feeling. I refer to the totality of experiential levels obtained from the life of an individual, which under the aegis of the human capacity to symbolize *are gathered by a person under the name God*. The representation always includes visceral, propioceptive, sensorimotor, perceptual, eidetic, and conceptual

---

[4]See William Meissner, "Psychoanalysis and Religion," *The Annual of Psychoanalysis*, Vol. 7, (1979); and Harry Guntrip, "Religion in Relation to Personal Integration." *The British Journal of Medical Psychology*, Vol. 42, (1969).

components which need not even be hierarchically or experientially synthesized even when, subjectively, they feel related to God and his "personality" in the individual's experience.

An example of these is the vague total body sensation of being "looked after" by God or being in God's hands with a vague preconscious fantasy of being physically held, either as a baby, a child, or a beloved adult. Another example is the actual feeling of an almost eidetic nature of the eye of God scrutinizing our actions and motives. Or, the conceptual conviction with its esthetic expansive feeling that the universe is a harmonious reality under the provident orchestration of a wise God. In fact, a representation of God usually includes most of the representational levels available to the individual, consciously or, most frequently, preconsciously. Not all the representational levels, however, are equally utilized. In most individuals one level prevails over the others, for example, the "feeling" of God's hands or the internal feeling of being "fulfilled" by his invisible presence.

My thesis is that, properly investigated under detailed and careful historical reconstruction, God's representational characteristics can be traced to experiences in reality, wish, or fantasy with primary caretakers in the course of development. These characteristics of the God of childhood, like those of any other nonexperiential characters (monsters, witches, fairy godmothers, idealized heroes, and so on), remain as the basic elements of the God representation of that particular individual for the rest of his life. He will have to reelaborate that representation over and over if he is to keep it up to date with his own epigenetically and historically changing personality. The child "creates" his God as a representation and, once created, the traits attributed to God during that creative process will remain. During the many transformations of the life-cycle, the individual may review and correct some of God's "personal traits," reject and repress others, enhance yet others, but he can no longer "believe" that his God is not as he created it the last time he updated his God representation. To change that belief he will have to change himself and go to a period of religious agitation, soul-searching or, conversely, experience some new exchanges with the relevant objects of childhood (parents, siblings, relatives) or their contemporary representatives (authorities, friends) which will permit him to modify simultaneously his representation of them, himself, and God. Obviously, as Dr. Kegan suggests, he will need structural changes as a condition for this modification.[5] However, the presence of that condition, a new structural level, though necessary does not suffice. It is only, I propose, the subjective modification of the emotional experience in one's private world with God as a felt reality, and therefore of oneself in relation to God, that permits a change in the characteristics consciously or unconsciously attributed to God.[6]

The process of the creation and re-creation of a God representation available for belief or rejection follows orderly psychic rules which can be investigated scientifically. I have given a detailed account of that process in the concluding chapter of my book.[7] The study showed that in creating their God representation and their relation to God all the individuals studied had used their experiences with the people of their childhood. Some individuals had created and kept a God representation directly related to the mother or father. Others had a God with maternal and paternal traits. Some had included another important relative, for example, a grandmother or grandfather, to attribute some character traits to their Gods.

In most individuals the available God representation had well-defined traits. "God does not like liars"; "God is good"; "God has a beard!" In others it was a composite of several people, and the characteristics of the God the individual experienced varied according to the aspects of the composite representation the person was attending to at the moment. The God characteristics seem also influenced by the level of development that prevailed at the time of the last and most significant updating of

[5]Robert Kegan, *The Evolving Self: A Process Conception for Ego Psychology*, 1978. Private copy, graciously provided by the author.

[6]The parish priest changed the emotional balance of his private world in three respects: (1) He compared the God of his theology with the God of his fears; (2) He looked at his stern father and his stern God face-to-face; and (3) He lost his fear of both by remembering that his father, too, was kind.

[7]Ana-Maria Rizzuto, *The Birth of the Living God*. (Chicago and London: University of Chicago Press, 1979).

the representation. "God moves the clouds," said a thirty-year-old woman. Obviously, she was still thinking like a child.

Describing God was an easy task for all individuals. They {125} had no difficulty in detailing many of God's wishes, feelings, attitudes, and actions, whether they believed or not. The question emerges: How can they know and have such conviction about the way God is when none of them have ever seen God? How and from where do we know—to quote Einstein—that "Raffiniert ist der Herrgott, aber boshaft ist er nicht" (God is subtle but he is not malicious)? How did Einstein know that? How did one of my subjects know that "God watches over us"? Obviously, this is the language of the "logic of conviction" Fowler talks about. Fowler says: "Recognition of a more comprehensive 'logic of conviction' does lead us to see that the logic of rational certainty is part of a larger epistemological structuring activity."

I propose that the larger epistemological structuring activity out of which God and religion (a bind to him, as indicated by the Latin origin of the word) emerge is the psychic process of creating ourselves as meaningful human beings in the context of the people to whom we were born and all those who along our historical journey accompany us. The mediatory mental function that permits and contributes to regulating this process is the specifically human capacity to represent and symbolize.

To acquire meaning we create *an epistemology of human relatedness* in the context of the visible reality of the world. That epistemology of meaning, however, is not of the visible and verifiable but of the invisible, the barely perceptible, the domain of private thought and interpersonal events. It is an epistemology of the not measurable whose quantification ("How much do you love me?") paradoxically enough makes a difference. The invisible "substances" which are the essences to be known (in the Thomistic sense of the word) are love, appreciation, acceptance, rejection, subjective worth, and the not less elusive passive action of being known by the other or the active action of knowing the other. The context of these invisible substances is a "background of safety"[8] in which the surrounding environment provides

---

[8]Joseph Sandler, "The Background of Safety," *International Journal of Psycho-Analysis*, Vol. 41, (1960).

{126}

enough protection for survival and psychological time to develop and grow. At each age of development, according to his intellectual and symbolic maturity, the child attempts to integrate all these experiences into a meaningful and comprehensive "ultimate environment" as Fowler says, whose characteristics depend on the type of processes, from mythological to abstract, the child is utilizing to organize his experiences at the level which in psychoanalysis we call secondary process. The epistemology of this knowledge, indispensable for life and conviction alike, is the essence of the developmental process that leads to the simultaneous creation and re-creation of oneself, God, meaning, and religion in the course of the life-cycle.

In this context, *faith in God as a conscious activity takes place when the God whose traits we "know" coincides in the present with whom we feel ourselves to be.* That faith is that unity of experience in which we and the God we believe in feel "bound"[9] to each other. The bind does not need to be a positive one. It may, in fact, be a most painful one, but in it one knows that one is known, even if it is as a bad person. For the essence of interpersonal meaning and conviction is to be known by those we need, and to hide from those we do not need. It is also to be known as we find ourselves acceptable, hiding from those whose love we need what we feel is unacceptable to them. Freud called this process repression.

God is the "invisible being" created by the child in a theistic culture at the moment when the child's wishes and demands must be hidden from his parents and repressed because they are not acceptable. A classic example is the child's wish to be the first and only one in the parent's affection. The God who "sees everything" and is "everywhere" exists now simultaneously with the parents who are not to see and know the private world of the child. To be sure, God is created from parental representations, though once created it becomes relatively independent of them.[10] It is this God, thus created, in the context of the total relation of the child to his parents and the childhood environment that

---

[9]In the sense of the *Oxford Dictionary*.

[10]An illustration of this is the case of a girl of seven, raised by militant atheistic parents. She had already formed her God representation and in her conjectural situations would touch her bedroom door and pray, saying "Please, let it be a God."

constitutes the source for all later religious experiences with the Godhead.

Fowler, using a different theoretical approach and method-
ology, reached the same conclusion: "Our interviews with older persons and our biographical studies of outstanding religious and cultural leaders alert us to the fact that these intuitive-projective constructions, and the deep sentiments both of love and dread that are attached to them, frequently constitute a powerful bedrock of conviction on which later, more adult forms of faith may be grounded."[11] Fowler is referring to his first stage, which he called intuitive-projective and locates from ages three to seven.

It is worth remembering that after the illusory period of early childhood, when the child feels known and "read" by his mother, no human relation can afford to satisfy the wish to be fully known. In the privacy of our experience we are alone. It is interesting to notice that one of God's persistent attributes in the Judeo-Christian tradition is his or her capacity to know the heart of man. The believer knows he or she is never alone. The nonbeliever cannot feel or does not want to feel there is a God who knows him or her internally all the time. In either case, the "presence" of God—so important for the mystics—colors a person's life through the conscious efforts either to make it more real or conversely to deny it is there. Most of the people studied who did, in fact, believe in God obtained great satisfaction out of their conviction that "God is always there."

God Representation's Developmental History: The Influence of Early Experiences[12]

The creation of a God representation is a process which starts very early. The child certainly does not have a representation until he has reached the developmental moment when he is able

---

[11]J. Fowler and S. Keen, *Life Maps: Conversations on the Journey of Faith* (Waco, Texas: Word Books, 1976), p.48.

[12]My methodology does not permit me to conclude about the existence of God. The discipline of psychoanalysis permits me to talk only about the indispensable psychological conditions for actual belief in God. The existence of God must be proved by another discipline.

to form a certain representation of "something" the people around him call God. The child has been experiencing through this lengthy preparatory period of eighteen months of development an intense relation with his mother and—nowadays—his father. Intense experiences of eye contact, bodily care, feeding, affectionate vocalizations and games, shared laughter, crying and soothing, or their converse experiences of neglect and rejection, have provided the child with a wealth of experiences with his or her caretakers. These experiences are to become the very essence of his way of relating to himself and others. Of all the experiences, eye contact is to remain for the rest of his days one of the most important means of establishing meaningful contact with others. The face of the mother becomes a critical organizer of experience for the child. Winnicott has shown (through careful observation of mothers and children and clinical cases) that the face of the mother is the child's first mirror, where he can find and recognize himself. [13]

This modality of relatedness seems prevalent in the Judeo-Christian tradition where God is described as creating man in his own image. We find the "face of God" throughout the Bible, for example; Genesis 32:30: "I have seen God face to face. . ." says Jacob after he had wrestled in the night with his unknown visitor; Numbers 6:25: "May the Lord make his face to shine upon thee, and be gracious unto thee"; Job 41:14: "Who can open the doors of his face?" (In this respect, read the case of Douglas O'Duffy I reported in my book.) Psalm 4:6 illuminates the effect of the face of God, "There be many that say, who will shew us any good? Lord, lift up the light of Thy countenance upon us." Any person who has prayed using these words knows the power of the subjective experience invoked in us by using the metaphor of the face of God. *I propose that the maternal face is the first traceable component of the child's relation with his mother that becomes integrated into the representation of God.* Later he or she would include many other experiences along the line. I mean to say that to form his God representation the child utilizes first his exchanges with his mother, most specifically her face, and then all other exchanges

---

[13]D.W. Winnicott, *Playing and Reality* (New York: Basic Books, 1971).

with his father and mother or other caretakers because they are the only meaningful adults the young child has available for the creation of his God representation. One must remember that God is that particular being that the child can neither see nor hear and that he has to strive creatively to give concrete shape to that being.

When the child arrives at that developmental moment, God is not the only invisible, nonexperiential character he creates. On the contrary, God arrives surrounded by a large company of characters, all of them nonexistent. At first God, for the very young child, is in the company of innumerable monsters, human and nonhuman, imaginary companions, and other animated creatures from imaginary animals to ghostly beings.

Chronologically, God's company is soon joined by his well-known enemy, the Devil, with his classic "forked tail, trident and penetrating penis with which to accomplish his mischief."[14] At this moment, developmentally the child is concerned with the mysteries of urination, defecation, and the sexual organs and the making of babies, and, in reflecting about God, the child includes God and the Devil in his thinking about all these concerns. Aggression and bad sexual behavior go to the Devil. Care, love, and ruling power to God. The universe of the child under his organizing effort is neatly divided between the goodness of God and the badness of the Devil. However, many children do not manage to make this neat separation and although the Devil does obtain all the badness, God frequently cannot be purified of his frightful, threatening, rejecting, or unresponsive traits, which he may have obtained from the child's exchanges with his primary objects.

At this point all children whose parents mention God are believers. They are not atheistic children. The question arises: Why, if God comes together with so many unusual characters, do all the others sooner or later fade away and God remains? To be sure, the others, as does God himself, obtain their repre-

---

[14]Herbert Goldings, "Themes of the Phallic Stage: Repair and Consolidation of Narcissism in the Psychoanalysis of a Six-and-one-half-year-old Hyperactive Boy." *First Annual Beata Rank Memorial Lecture in Child Analysis*, Presented at The Boston Psychoanalytic Society and Institute, Inc., May 27, 1970.

{130}

sentational traits from the child's representational creativity using his images, experiences, and fantasies related to wishes and fears in connection with the adults in the child's world and, also, himself or herself.

God's privileged survival depends on two factors: One is the adult's affirmation that there is a God, and the entire sociocultural system supporting such a belief; the other, psychologically more relevant, is that when the child becomes able to hide some aspects of himself from his parents, he still needs the company of an adult in the privacy of his world. This need has always been recognized, and in the Western world children have been offered a guardian angel to mitigate the fears of separation from the adult. God, however, is the supreme being whose constant presence is available to the child in case of need: God knows the child internally and is a constant witness of his experiences, a witness that can always be resorted to either to confess badness or to request help to be good, to beg for protection or to pray to for the satisfaction of private wishes. Therefore, the creative process of transforming the parental representation into a God is an adaptive process that provides continuation of the parental function[15] through the transmutation of parents into a Godhead or, in more intellectually elaborated systems of beliefs, that in the course of development provides a modulator of the lonely experience of being a thinking human in a complex universe.

Transformations of the God Representation in Later Life

During the course of life, the representation of God may be unconsciously used as a continuation at a magnified level of the relationship to parents: It may be used as an object for displacement of anger, frustration, or hope related to primary objects; it may be used as an organizer of an incomprehensible and chaotically perceived world; it may be attributed the characteristics of being the only invariable person among objects who reject and frustrate. In summary, any of the psychic maneuvers we utilize

---

[15]The parental function in this respect is understood as the need to remain related to a personal reality experienced as larger than oneself. I do not refer to the concrete function of parents.

constantly to relate to ourselves and others in an effort to keep our psychic equilibrium and our relatedness to those we need and love are applicable to the God representation and the felt relation a person has with his God and people with whom he lives.

The epigenetic and developmental process of the life-cycle strain the existing God representation each time a new psychic synthesis occurs, or a new human relation calls for revision of our past experiences with people in our lives. The individual may or may not include his God in the process of updating his private reality under the aegis of new functions, experiences, or relations. If the God representation is not simultaneously updated, the individual may quietly drop his belief or go through a religious crisis. To update his God representation the person must, out of necessity, go through a period of soul-searching, questioning, and renewal until his God coincides with his present felt experience, so as to permit him to feel bound by fidelity to his God and his promises to himself.

The treatment of the parish priest, mentioned earlier, illustrates this point. His case was simple and rewarding because his level of pathology was minimal. Other human beings, however, are caught in more tragic and painful predicaments, whether it is in their unshakable belief in a God who cannot possibly love them or in their inability to believe in a God that may harm them. I have provided two extensive illustrations of one of each of these predicaments in my book. There are the other people, too, those who have made temporary peace with their God and enjoy his company until a new crisis of development puts them and their God to the test.

A predicament with the God whose representation we have created may depend on unresolved issues at any level of development. These unresolved issues are not indicators of general pathology but of a specific conflictual situation between the primary object (who provided their representational sources for the present God representation) and the needs and wishes of the individual. In this respect, belief in God or lack of it is not an indicator of psychic health. It is only an indicator of a historical relation with a primary object developmentally utilized to shape a God. I have provided extensive illustration of this point in my book, and the space allotted to me in this volume does not permit me to demonstrate all the possible variations of the entanglements between the individual and his God. In the book I present Douglas O'Duffy who refused to acknowledge the existence of a God who would pay no attention to him. I also mention Bernandine Fisher who cannot help believing that God hates her, but who keeps on hoping against all realistic evidence that one day her mother will love her. In her case, God is an object of displacement of maternal hatred at the service of keeping indispensable hope. On the other hand, I show how Daniel Miller does not even want to ask the question about whether there is a God because he is so afraid of being humiliated or destroyed by a revengeful God. Among these people filled with genuine human suffering I found a peaceful and joyful believer, Fiorella Domenico, who is in love with a God who is "great" and who "watches over us." When the tragedies of life confronted her naive enthusiasm about her God, she solved the dilemma by developing a phobia—a church phobia—that protected her God, her love for him, and also her need to update her girlish representation of God to a God capable of handling contradiction and suffering.

Not all nonbelievers have a conflict with their God representation. Many have a representation so unobtrusive and quiet that it is there in waiting if the occasion comes when the individual may need it. Others have been busy with people and affairs of everyday life and have not experienced the need to wrestle with a God that may bring them into crisis. Their God is there, in the back of their minds so to speak, neither disturbing them nor providing anything special. Then one day a major or a minimal event may awaken a dormant God. A Paul Claudel, who has lost his faith to rationalism during his days at the lycée Louis-le Grand, may casually go to Christmas services and be a part of a large group of worshipers at Notre Dame and suddenly be awakened to belief by the powerful notes of the Magnificat. At that point his life suddenly changed: "In an instant my heart was touched and I believed," he declared. He then talked about the experience saying that it was as though he had become a new person and that he had been introduced to "a presence in ourselves," a "revealing God." For this conversion, Claudel needed an instantaneous transformation of a preexisting God representation now suitable for belief: a God, in Claudel's case, that awakens the believer and himself under the notes of the Magnificat—perhaps, a jubilant maternal God.

Conclusions

1. Belief-faith is a psychic process by means of which in a given cross section of life an individual finds himself bound to his private representation of God as the result of his conscious, preconscious, and unconscious way of organizing the intangibles of his relatedness to others and the world. He is guided by a private logic of conviction subjectively experienced[16] (as in Claudel's case) as something that is happening to him that he does not control. In this sense it is well known that no rational logic has ever given faith to anybody, that the process of belief and the logic of convictions are events that we feel happen to us even when the conditions for the appearance of belief are the result of our personal creative synthesis.

2. Faith is then always a developmental event. The fact that we believe today does not guarantee that we believe tomorrow. Faith is never a final state.[17] Its presence depends on the quality of the synthesis we are capable of making with the objects of the past, the people in the present, our own personal history, and our expectations of what kind of environment the world should be for us. When we feel that any of those have failed us beyond endurance or beyond our capacity to rearrange ourselves to adapt to the change, our faith may be dropped. For religion to exist as a subjective experience, the subject must have an antecedent in his past experience to create the link between himself and the content of his belief. In this respect, I fully agree with Freud's conclusion that all belief is the result of conviction about "historical truth."[18]

---

[16]See chapter by Vergote in this volume.

[17]See chapter by Vergote in this volume.

[18]Sigmund Freud, *Moses and Monotheism*.

3. The conditions of belief and faith are the result of a complex developmental process that takes the whole personality into account. The creation of the representation of God precedes the child's formal attendance to religious education and, therefore, as I have said before, all children "arrive at the house of God with their own God under their arm."

4. Faith and belief are based on the logic of conviction of interpersonal relatedness organized, when the developmental moment comes, under a more conceptual frame of reference. However, the vicissitudes of any given individual's belief do not depend primarily on his intellectual capacity to synthesize and to organize the world, but mostly *on his psychic ability to convince himself of the meaning of his relatedness to others and the world*. Dr. Fowler has reached similar conclusions departing from his own frame of reference.

5. The psychic process that makes belief in God—and religion—so relevant to human life is what Winnicott calls "silent communication" with our objects of the past and the present. It is that communication that provides the depth of conviction to all faiths.

6. *The "ultimate environment" of man is always all the other human beings from our parents to our present friends* transformed either into a God representation, a trusting feeling about the universe at large, or a conceptual reelaboration about the Divinity. This ultimate environment is there to be organized, if we wish to do so, into our intellectual understanding of the world.

Educational Implications

I have described how the child's creation of his God representation occurs as a private and barely noticeable process out of the exchanges between himself or herself and his parents or caretakers. After them, educators, pastors, and authority figures will contribute their share to the shape of the God representation. The God representation requires continuous reshaping to remain updated to the needs of the growing child. The process is subtle and delicate and requires that the adult provide exquisite attention and respect for the subjective experience of the child.

Religious education must take into consideration the nature of the process of creating a God representation. That process occurs at the core of the child's capacity to relate to himself, to others, and to the world. If the child's religious development appears unusual, understanding of the child's confusions and predicaments, his wishes and his suffering is the shortest way to helping him resolve his "difficulties" with God.

Parents and religious educators might find useful emotional awareness in their own retracing of the evolution of their God representation. That experience may give them a firsthand understanding of the private history of their own God representation. Furthermore, it would enhance their understanding of experiences of the children they are to teach.

ABOUT THE AUTHOR

Dr. Ana-Maria Rizzuto is a Clinical Professor of Psychiatry at Tufts Medical School in Boston and on the faculty of the Psychoanalytic Institute of New England. A native of Argentina, Dr. Rizzuto completed her studies at the University of Cordoba, where she studied medicine and philosophy.

In addition to her work as an internist, specializing in blood diseases, Dr. Rizzuto taught child and adolescent development in the Catholic University of Cordoba and at the Institute for Advanced Education "Domingo F. Cahret." In 1963, she accepted an invitation to teach Pastoral Anthropology to the theology students of the Pontifical Seminary in Cordoba. As part of her activities at Tufts, Dr. Rizzuto conducted a year-long seminar on pastoral care for all the pastors of South Boston. Among Dr. Rizzuto's publications are: madurez y laicado; "Object Relations and the Formation of the Image of God"; "Freud, God, the Devil, and the Theory of Object Representation"; *and* The Birth of the Living God.

The Relation to God
and the Moral Development
of the Young Child

JEAN-MARIE JASPARD

Introduction

Often, and especially in the Catholic Church, adolescents reproach educators for having conditioned them into a religion that essentially served to have them adopt moral attitudes and behavior according to outmoded systems of values. They sometimes accuse their parents of having used religion to buttress parental authority. The educators of these young people are often disturbed by such reactions. They do not understand the psychological significance in the framework of adolescence. They let themselves be impressed by the spokesman for social change and feel guilty or protest their innocence.

The research that is presented in this chapter allows educators to look at some of the psychological aspects at stake in the articulation of the moral and religious awakening of the young child and at the manner in which the parents (particularly the mother) are involved. My contribution to this volume is relatively restricted in the sense that it certainly will not introduce any new elements into the systematization of the stages of the moral development of the child. In the report of the observations, however, psychologists will be able to perceive the action of the dynamic processes that render the individuals both unique and recognizable in the common stages of their growth.

This chapter presents some of the results of a longitudinal study of young children and places in relief, on the level of motivational psychology, some of the dynamisms that conjointly and reciprocally form the basis for the relationship the child has with God and the formation of its moral attitudes.

The material for this study was gathered by members of the Center for Religious Psychology at the University of Leuven who asked practicing Christian parents among their acquaintances to note systematically and in detail the spontaneous remarks of their children concerning religion and the fundamental realities of existence. This observation was carried out over two and a half to three years. It began at different ages for the various families and thus we have data from children from two to seven years old. For this discussion, I have chosen two kinds of notations from a sample of thirty French-speaking Belgian children (15 boys and 15 girls):

1. All the notations that manifest something about the mode of the relationship with the divine figures, who are called God, Jesus, or Lord.

2. All the observations where moral behavior is involved in the context of the religious life of the child. (It must be noted that the directions given to the parents were to note the expressions, questions, or actions that related to the *religious life* of the child. Moral behavior outside this context, therefore, was not recorded.)

I have analyzed these two series of notations separately in order to extricate the characteristics of each and to search for the psycho-affective and motivational dynamisms that underlie the two problem areas and illuminate their psychological coherence. Space limitations imposed by this volume do not permit exploration of these two approaches in full. Therefore, I shall summarize the results regarding the modes of the relationship to God and then present in detail the analysis of the observations regarding the moral factors. Finally, I shall try, by way of a conclusion, to show the connection and the psychological coherence between the two sets of results.

The Structure of the Attachment to God

The statements were collected mostly by the mothers of the children. Thus, it is in the context of the maternal relationship that the analysis reveals the way in which the child experiences its introduction into the "Christian life." The content of the discourse and the observed behavior depends as much on the interests of the child as on the maternal initiative. I shall show in this synthesis how the mode of the relationship to God is structurally dependent on the sex of the people involved: the child, its mother, and the divine person or persons who are almost always perceived as being male.

The Boys: From the Attachment to the Mother's Friend to the Attachment to an Identification Model

The data clearly reveal that the formation of the bond of the boys with God or Jesus is strongly colored by the Oedipal attachment to the mother and by the evolution of this attachment. Before the age of four, one may say that Jesus and God are perceived as being friends of the mother. And if the boys like to adopt and repeat religious acts or to manifest an interest in Jesus, it is largely because they know this pleases their mothers, which fact they do not neglect to confirm repeatedly (Fig. 1).

FIG. 1. FIG. 2.

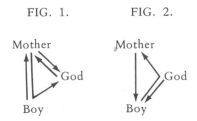

Between the ages of four and six, this motivation for attachment to God, nourished by the attachment to the mother, seems to reach its highest point. But the attachment to the mother becomes more active and the boy searches to aggrandize himself in her eyes as a worthy partner. Correlatively, there is a transformation of the attachment of the boy to the divine person (Fig. 2). He tries to enlist the divine figure as an ally in the service of that which pleases the mother and develops a sometimes very intense identification with the divine figure. The religious statements from this period therefore proclaim a divine omnipotence that is fantasized very concretely and that contributes to the formation of an inflated ideal of the self. In the same way, the prayers manifest an absolute confidence in this divine ally that engenders the most marvelous projects.

After the age of six, the attachment to the mother diminishes. Some of the boys have a parallel loss of interest in God and religious practice, while others submit the image of the omnipotent God to the harsh test of the confrontation with the limits of reality. Numerous doubts occur about the capabilities of

God or Jesus and about the perfection of their works. The agreement of a new catechesis provided by the school is necessary to render new and nonmaternal motivational supports for the boys' faith.

The Girls: From Mother's Friend to Personal Friend

The religious initiation of the girls resembles that of the boys rather closely at the beginning. God—Jesus, the Lord—is, in the first place, perceived as a privileged friend of the mother and their families (Fig. 3).

But it clearly appears that this person very soon becomes their personal friend in a relationship that becomes more and more autonomous with regard to their mothers (Fig. 4).

FIG. 3.   FIG. 4.

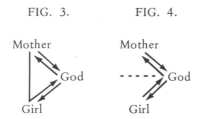

From the age of two to three years and after, the family ritual gestures, imitated with the mother, are rapidly personalized into affectionate greetings and, during the fourth year, an ingenuous familiarity develops that is expressed in a series of small signs (putting on a pretty dress for Jesus, giving him light with a candle, offering him flowers, and so on) and by confidences (telling Jesus all about her day and her encounters).

Toward four to five years, the affective tone rises and there are a large number of declarations of friendship ("Jesus is my friend, you know") along with a demand for affectionate reciprocity from Jesus. Some manage to fantasize the presence of the divine partner very concretely (feeling him caress her, seeing him saying hello, being suddenly cured by him). Others do not experience these "sensations" and therefore become indignant (one girl refused to pray for several months as she thought it was

Jesus' turn to take the initiative). The problem of "having a baby" is not a rare occurrence in this warm relationship with Jesus. After six years old, a certain realism develops and it is in the liturgy, and in the Eucharist in particular, that the girls seem to find the surest way to guarantee the proximity of the Lord.

As regards whether Jesus becomes the Oedipal partner of the girl, this probably does occur for some. But it is certainly not always the case even if the attachment is very strong and the admiration great. Indeed, the father remains very much present in the preoccupations of some of them (like Martha, who accepted God as her friend but refused to say the "Our Father" since she did not want to have a second daddy). Others had no qualms about presenting their "boy friends" to Jesus and thanking Jesus for them.

Ethical Behavior and Its Religious Reference

It is well to stress before I begin the analysis that the observations used did not derive from systematic observation of the children's moral conduct. The parents noted what they interpreted as being conduct or remarks having a religious reference. Obviously, this restricts what can be derived from them as far as moral conduct is concerned.

I have assembled all the observations that explicitly denote a moral problem or moral behavior, that is, everything that touches on actions toward another person when this action is called good or evil, either in the expression of a desire or in the evaluation of fact or principle. In all, I have compiled 181 notations, 125 for the boys and 56 for the girls.

Four major problem areas, each having two or more subcategories, can be distinguished:

1. The problem of trying to do good
   a. When it involves directly pleasing Jesus or God
   b. When it involves concern for others by sharing, rendering a service, forgiving, and so on

2. The problem of an ethical model
   a. God, or Jesus, taken as an example or saying what is good[1]
   b. Fascination for bad people
3. The problem of behavioral development[1]
   a. Self-evaluation: positive, negative, indulgent
   b. Evaluation of others
4. The problem of the issue of moral behavior
   a. Rewards, punishment, the problem of heaven
   b. Future without constraints. The feeling of some children that moral obligations do not endure beyond childhood or terrestrial life.

The Quantitative Data

Inspection of Table I yields several interesting observations:

There are clearly more observations noted for the boys than for the girls: 125 out of 593 for the boys, or 21 percent; 56 out of 440 for the girls, or 12.1 percent. This signifies that, when one observes the religious behavior of children, moral problems occur significantly more often among boys than among the girls.[2]

Concerning the evolution with age of this proportion of moral problems relative to the total number of observations,[3] there is a clear decrease for the boys (from 30.4 percent at three years old to 17.2 percent at six years old) and there is a slight increase for the girls between three and five (13.5 percent to 17.7 percent). Before three years and after six, the proportion is negligible for the girls.

---

[1]When the child referred to a rule established by God or Jesus in the context of self-evaluation or evaluation of others, the statement is classified under 3. Only statements made outside of a direct evaluational context are placed under 2a.

[2]$X^2 = 12.084$ (df $= 1$) $P < 0.001$

[3]To calculate this proportion, use Table I where the total number of observations are listed by sex and age.

TABLE 1

BOYS:

AGES	1.6 to 2.11	3.0 to 3.11	4.0 to 4.11	5.0 to 5.11	6.0 to 6.11	Total
Number of children	3	8	13	11	10	15
Number of observations	30	69	169	220	105	593
Attachment to the divine statements	1	13	29	48	17	108
Moral conduct statements	4	21	38	44	18	125

GIRLS:

AGES	1.6 to 2.11	3.0 to 3.11	4.0 to 4.11	5.0 to 5.11	6.0 to 6.11	Total
Number of children	8	11	15	13	3	15
Number of observations	66	118	125	109	22	440
Attachment to the divine statements	14	31	38	24	3	110
Moral conduct statements	2	16	18	19	1	56

Classification of the Observations

It must be noted, although I could not indicate it in table format, that the individual differences are very great for both sexes. In each of the sexes, five children out of fifteen furnished more than two thirds of the observations with ethical content. Five boys and ten girls had less than five notations with an ethical content during the entire observational period. This indicates directly that for some, particularly the girls, the religious reference is not involved in moral problems while for others the involvement is considerable. This is dependent on the global religious orientation of the family that certainly influences the mother's observations. This hypothesis is only partially verified in our sample, since it does not account for the difference between the boys and the girls. In addition, in five families, two children were observed (brother and sister): in two families, the boy and the girl both had a high frequency, in two families the boy had a

TABLE 2. · FREQUENCY DISTRIBUTION ACCORDING TO AGE AND SEX

AGES	B 1.6 to 2.11	B 3.0 to 3.11	B 4.0 to 4.11	B 5.0 to 5.11	B 6.0 to 6.11	TB	TB %	TG %	TG	G 1.6 to 2.11	G 3.0 to 3.11	G 4.0 to 4.11	G 5.0 to 5.11	G 6.0 to 6.11
CATEGORIES														
1. Effort to do good														
a. *For Jesus*		3	4	4	1	12	9.6	12.5	7		4	2	1	
b. *For others*	1	2	11	7	9	30	24.0	8.9	5		1	1	3	
2. Model/Law														
a. *God, Jesus*		2	6	5	3	16	12.8	7.1	4	1			2	1
b. *Bad people*	1	4	5	3		13	10.4							
3. Evaluation														
a. *Self—positive*		4	2	3		9	7.2	12.5	7		3	1	3	
negative	2	1	2	2		7	5.6	7.1	4			3	1	
indulgent			3	2		5	4.0	5.4	3			2	1	
b. *Others*		3	3	10	3	19	15.2	17.8	10	1	3	2	4	
4. Issue														
a. *Reward—heaven*			2	7	2	11	8.3	28.6	16		5	7	4	
b. *No constraints*	2			1		3	2.4							
Total observations	4	21	38	44	18	125	100	100	56	2	16	18	19	1
Total children observed	3	8	13	11	10	15			15	8	11	15	13	3

high frequency and the girl a low one, and in the fifth family both children had low frequencies. Thus, it is difficult to conclude about family influence alone unless one admits a difference between the religious education for boys and that for girls.

Regarding the distribution of the observation over the four categories, it is obvious that it is much simpler for the girls than for the boys. For the girls, 43 percent of the notations retained consist either of an evaluation of the girl herself or of a judgment of other persons. Note that these judgments rest on a religious reference. Their content will be dealt with later on. An effort to do good is indicated in 21 percent of the notations, and in more than half of these it is a matter of pleasing Jesus or God. Declarations of divine principles or valorization of Jesus as a model for moral behavior attract the girls' attention to a very minor degree. On the other hand, the problem of rewards from God seems to loom very large between the ages of three and six (28.6 percent).

The observations for the boys, however, are situated in all of the categories. Trying to do good is as important for them as behavior evaluation. And it is the effort to do good "for others" that predominates. We shall see how later on. As regards self-evaluation on the basis of a divine reference, the boys are as ambivalent as the girls. Some look instead for divine indulgence, thus showing that they are less confident in their good conduct. One also finds a good proportion who take Jesus as a moral model or who state divine precepts, or who are fascinated by those who do evil, which we do not find at all among girls. Finally, there is little indication of concern for rewards coming from God, and three statements by children who dream of a time when they can live without any moral constraints.

Some Characteristics of the Religious Reference of Moral Conduct for Boys

The Problem of the Effort to Do Good

We encounter the problem of the effort to do good in all age groups and it is recurrent for several boys. This involves doing good either for Jesus himself or for others but out of religious motives.

¶ *To Please Jesus.* Among boys we note two kinds of behavior to please Jesus. In the first type, the child tries to please Jesus or the Lord by the rectitude of his conduct (like François who "thinks about what we cannot say because the Lord is his friend") or by gratuitous gestures like sharing ("I am learning to share, so the Lord is happy"), or nonobligatory prayer ("I don't have to pray, but to please Jesus, I tell him good night all the same"). This behavior is observed at three and at five to six years. The second type is different and is very close to the problem of the attraction of bad people. It occurs with boys four and five years old. They feel sorry for the poverty of Jesus at his birth or his suffering that was caused by cruel men during his passion. Various movements of aggressiveness arise (François wanted to kill the evil men) or protestations of innocence ("You say sometimes I'm naughty, but I don't want to kill Jesus," said Etienne), or manifestations of benevolence (Vincent was ready to give his little sister's cradle to Mary and Joseph and wanted to play something nice to compensate for those who killed Jesus).

¶ *To Please Others.* The religiously motivated efforts of which the beneficiary is the other were generally suggested by the parents for Lent in particular, as well as to prepare for Christmas or for first communion. These are occasions for the mother to motivate the child to accept modes of behavior that she wants from it more often, like obedience, keeping its room in order, kindness toward others, receptivity, and, particularly, sharing (with those around it or with the poor). In fact, the religious motivation is here in the background; it motivates the moment of the effort in a ritual way. The true motivation derives from the persuasive capacity of the mother and, in general, there are two moments in the child's conduct: (1) when it is touched by the poor who are hungry, by the pain caused when one is not nice, and so on, and promises to share, be good, be agreeable, be neat, and so on; and (2) the moment when the promise is to be kept. In general, the enthusiasm of the impulsive promise is directly proportional to the desire to please the mother and inversely proportional to the realization of the promise. There is also a clear evolution with age. At four years old, there are many instances of the boys letting themselves be convinced, and they even add to the motives provided by the mother since they see clearly that this pleases her. But they balk when it becomes a matter of actually doing something, especially when it concerns giving up candy or sharing pocket money. From five years old on and still more after six, the number of promises decreases but more of them are kept. Some children even take the initiative and take care to announce to anyone who will listen what they will do ("Today, I am going to 'love each other' and be nicer to Cateline," said Olivier to his mother). But the motive of the six-year-old is as much to do the act as to please his mother—unless this has become the main way to please his mother!

The Problem of the Models of Good and Evil

Two groups obviously share the attraction of the boys in all age categories: those who represent good, the prototypes being Jesus or God; and those who represent aggressiveness and naughtiness.

¶ *God-Jesus, Model and Author of Law.* The divine figures are already taken as identification models for behavior, as we have seen, particularly around the age of four or five. We note that here they are taken as models of kindness, principally at three to four years old. The identification is clearly stated by the child in a manifest movement of seduction of the mother: "Look, Momma, I'm like a baby Jesus," said Vincent when he did not fight with his brother; "Today, Momma, I'm going to be like God when he was little" (François). François also discovered one day how God let his law be known: "He told it to the heart of Momma and then she told us." But the fact that God is the author of the law and "judges everything" is used, most often after five years old, to decide disputes with others. And, as chance would have it, God almost always decides in favor of the protagonist. It happens too that the rule of love of others supports a true moral effort as with Olivier who, at five, experienced a greal deal of difficulty in accepting the birth of a little sister. He repeated over and over again to himself that God said to love others. At six years old, too, he said that it was important that Jesus said, "Love one another." We see here something that is typical of six-year-olds, the frequent reference to passages of the Gospel learned at catechism.

¶ *The Fascinating World of Evil People.*   After the age of five, the world of evil has become very distinct to the point of being personified by the devil.[4] But the attraction begins much earlier for slightly more than one third of the boys. From three to four years old on, they manifest the atraction in about the same way: a great fascination with the details of the way in which the evil men made Jesus suffer and killed him. Good Friday is a particularly interesting day. Bernard drew a picture of the crucified Jesus with enormous nails in his hands; François counted down the hours until three o'clock with a great interest in the blood that would flow; Vincent asked to hear the story of Judas and the passion again. Three months later, he asked for it again and, at five years old, it was still his favorite story, along with the massacre of the Holy Innocents by Herod. He experienced this as a horrible tale from which Jesus emerges as the victor. "They were caught, huh, the bad men who killed him. He came to life again and he is stronger than they are!"

It is probably necessary to understand this fascination in the sense of an attraction for stories where the hero faces terrible dangers before emerging victorious. At the same time, it canalizes all the aggressive force of these boys and delivers them from the fear of being killed by the aggressiveness of others. The Gospel narrative serves to exorcise the projected aggressiveness and reinforces the act of being "good," that is, of being nonaggressive, which is also expressed in other statements we have heard.

{149}

---

[4]In general, the mothers denied having told their children of the existence of the devil. They attributed this information to the nursery school instructor or to other children. See a similar reference to the emergence of interest in evil beings in Rizzuto's paper in this volume.

The Problem of Evaluation of Behavior

¶ *Self-Evaluation.* Self-evaluation was very rarely noted among the boys in comparison with the girls (hardly 17%). They prefer to speak of their future behavior in terms of promises or in terms of the divine identification model, unless it is in terms of rewards in the future. When they are led to evaluate their behavior (usually when they are caught, scolded, or punished for any number of reasons), their reaction uses the reference to God or to Jesus in three ways that are more or less characteristic of the different ages:

- At two to three years old, the child readily accepts the inevitability of punishment and, seeing its mother angry, attributes the same negative sentiments to Jesus or the Lord ("Jesus mad"). But, for all of that, the child is not distressed. For the child, probably, all adults have the same feelings at the same time, but negative sentiment never lasts very long.

- At three to four years old, the boy has the tendency to deny the negative divine judgment of an act more often by saying that Jesus cannot see or hear it. Among all the observations, these are the only times when the boys deny this possibility to the divine figures.

- At four years old, this attitude disappears, probably because the omniscience of God has become an achievement and thus can no longer be denied. From then on, God's negative judgments give way to indulgence, and even as a countermand. The reply, "It doesn't matter, Jesus loves me all the same" serves to neutralize the anger of the mother and perhaps even threatens her with a bit of emotional coercion by indicating that the identification object could become more interesting than the Oedipal love object. The mother of François noted this one day when she wanted him to return a toy stolen at school. François pretended to pray and then told her very clearly: "Jesus said that I don't have to take it back."

- At five, the boys are the most uncomfortable when they did something wrong. Some blame themselves spontaneously, like Bernard who believed that he did not pray well because the prayer was not granted, or like Vincent who was very sad because "my heart makes me not like Jesus," or like François who was very happy to know that his mother also could commit faults and to learn that it was only in heaven that one will always be good. From this time on, it seems, while there is still a way to escape the notice of Saint Nicholas, one does not escape that of God, who decides about everything. But the effort is sometimes too much to make or the reproach too hard to bear and this releases a proclamation of indulgence that is also out of proportion. One day François could no longer stand his mother saying that Jesus was not happy with him and replied violently: "It's true, he loves me, even when I kill everybody!" One gets the impression that the narcissistic ideal is sensitive and fragile at this termination of the Oedipus complex: it cannot tolerate a negative judgment.

{151}

Only once was the self-evaluation frankly positive: Olivier proudly declared to his little sister after getting along for 15 minutes: "You see, Cateline, God is close to us now." Thus, one can say that the mode of self-evaluation and of defense against negative judgments correlates both to the state of the relationship to the mother and to the position of the divine figure with respect to her or to the child. As far as God is solely the ally of the mother, his presence in the judgment is accepted or rejected according to the perceived importance of the withdrawal of affection. As soon as God also becomes the ideal of the self, the boy can temporarily manipulate God's indulgence, but then he finds himself stymied by the narcissistic guilt due to belief in the performative omniscience of the omnipotent model. Is this the reason why, at six years old, we find no self-evaluations at all among the observations of the boys?

¶ *Evaluation of Others.* Evaluation of the conduct of others takes two different forms according to whether it concerns the boy's parents or his peers. When a brother or sister provoked displeasure by arguing or refusing to share, they were attacked with the same religious argumentation the boy heard his mother use with him, but translated in terms of the problem at hand. Thus, at four years old: "Jesus isn't happy," "Jesus doesn't like greedy people"; at five years old: "The Lord would give me that toy right away"; and at six years old, the reference is still clearer: "You don't do it because you don't want to slap Jesus," said Pierre when his sister threatened to slap him.

The parental behavior the boys judged is essentially the same for which they themselves are punished or scolded. Thus, according to age again, one hears: "Momma, I don't love you any more, you hurt me, you aren't making Jesus happy" (four years old) and "You neither, you aren't always good and besides there aren't any saints around here" (five years old). At six, we have only one quarrel between Stéphane and his mother who punished him. As if by chance, the reply is situated on the constitutional level of identity and it is not God who is taken to task for the bad constitution, as it were, but his own parents who have only to look to themselves: "If I am naughty, it is because you made me with bad material. If Papa had used good material, I would be good." And once a mother was violently condemned by her five-year-old son for a nonpunitive act. She had pretended to exchange her baby for the baby of a visiting friend. This gesture roused a very high degree of anxiety in Pierre which made him furious: "If you give Vincent away, you'll never have another baby again. The Lord won't give you any more." Does not any unworthy mother who abandons her child merit the supreme punishment? But the tone reveals, as well, the fear that the punishment would be applied.

The Problem of the Issue of Moral Behavior

¶ *The Reward in Heaven.* Beyond "pleasing Jesus," which can be an immediate effect that is not negligible, the motivation to do good and the effort to accomplish it only involve personal religious gratification in the very distant future: heaven, paradise. Such a motivational perspective seems particularly attractive to five-year-old boys. Before this age, only Emmanual at four agreed to go to heaven one day on the condition that this mother would be there too and because she had promised him that in heaven there would be no more pain. But this perspective captivates the five-year-olds and Vincent, for example, assessed his chances ("Hey, Momma, I'll go to heaven with Jesus because I make you happy"). When he was punished, he comforted himself with the thought of paradise and became impatient to go and see what it was like. Benoit talked about the conditions of heaven and tried to locate the place of this alternative to hell.

At six, two statements show skepticism instead. Pierre doubted that the devils could take his brother to hell, and Olivier no longer believed very strongly that something interesting could happen after death. At the very most, he conceded more enthusiastically to his mother, after death "it is kindness that goes to heaven."

One could perhaps say that at five, the prospect of going to join the Lord and being with him "physically" exercises more attraction for boys than identification with him. The skepticism of the two six-year-old boys matches that already encountered with others of this age concerning the omnipotence of the divine model.

¶ *The Prospect of a Future Without Constraints.* I shall only mention three statements of two children to indicate the possible existence of this idea in the mind of the child. Vincent, at three years old, when he had just torn a tablecloth and his mother had scolded him, cried: "When I'm grown up, I'll be able to do everything, I'll be able to make holes in the tablecloth." Six months later, it was when he was dead that he would be able to do everything. This dream of omnipotence without constraint is deferred into the ever more distant future. We have already seen the difficulty François (five-year-old) had in containing his aggressiveness and his insisting on Jesus' love, even if he killed everyone. Two months previously he had asserted to his mother, obviously in order to intimidate her, that when he dies and goes to heaven he will be able to do everything, even kill. When his mother told him that then he would not want to kill, he replied: "But if I want to!"

Some Characteristics of the Religious Reference of Moral Conduct for Girls

{154}

The Problem of the Effort to Do Good

¶ *To Please Jesus.*   Except for the younger, the girls set out to please Jesus, not so much by trying to behave correctly but by making spontaneous gestures and by the little considerations they invent themselves. At three years old, probably encouraged by their mothers, they try "to be good for God and for Jesus." Bénédicte one day offered him her piece of candy. Cateline, at four, thought that Jesus was tired so she did not make any noise. Cécile, at five, made up a song for which, to please Jesus, she had to put on her best clothes.

Manuela, at four years, after having heard the narrative of the passion, turned pleadingly and proudly to her father and two brothers: "If you had been there, you would have beaten up the evil men who killed Jesus." Again a very spontaneous reaction, and she was the only girl who was fascinated by the action of evil men. As if by chance, she appealed the aggressiveness of the men of the family to defend Jesus.

¶ *To Please Others.*   Religiously motivated efforts to do good were rarely observed among girls. Most often, the mothers noted failure after having tried to motivate their daughters to share during Lent. When deprived of food or candy, they submitted passively and reluctantly. Bénédicte (four years) gave away the half of a sandwich she did not like, and Christine (five years) gave her piggy bank, in which the rewards for her sacrifices were to be put, back to her mother. She declared that she preferred to eat her dessert.

The Problem of Models

The problem of imitating Jesus is almost totally absent from the conscious preoccupations of the girls. Cécile, at two years old,

after having done something silly, immediately exclaimed: "Jesus doesn't act like a monkey, Jesus doesn't do stupid things . . . Jesus loves everybody," and Mireille, when she was five, pro-
claimed a precept for the whole family by stating that Jesus demanded that everybody should always be nice. At five years, Marthe expressed instead a kind of disappointment when her mother told her about the gifts of Jesus at Christmas. She replied: "Jesus only says what I have to do—share and tell the truth." And Manuela found advice for her mother in the Gospel when she complained that the guests who were invited for dinner did not come: "You just have to do like the Lord, invite the poor and the crippled." It would certainly not be going too far to state here that the girls have a more object-like relationship with Jesus than one of identification. As far as the fascination of evil is concerned, this is completely absent among the girls.

The Problem of Evaluation

¶ *Self-Evaluation.*   One fourth of the observations of the girls that consist of moral references concern self-evaluation. As for the boys, we find three orientations but with slightly different age references.

- At three years, it concerns defense reactions against a judgment of their bad conduct, by Jesus. They deny that Jesus can see them: "Jesus doesn't know it, he doesn't see it."

- At four years, the involvement of Jesus increases and the girls struggle with it in various and sometimes amusing ways. Christine would hide under the cover so Jesus could not see her. One day, Manuela's mother asked her to be nice like Jesus to her little brother whom she detested. Manuela flatly refused the identification: "Jesus was smart. He didn't have a brother"—the implication being, "you can't compare me to Jesus to judge me." But her guilt was not diminished and, while daydreaming or playing, she revealed a fear that Herod would come to kill her if she were not good. Bénédicte defended herself against the admonishments of her mother by retorting that God is stronger and nicer than she is and that he is the only who will decide everything.

• At five years, Christine continued to play hide-and-seek with Jesus so she could keep pilfering and being disobedient without worrying about it: "But, Momma, I don't see his eyes so he can't see me." There seems to be no sense of guilt involved in this exchange. It is not a question of a fault in herself, what matters is that Jesus does not see it. Anne-Catherine recognized that when she was not good at home, she was not being nice to Jesus. Sophie rejected comparison with the devil and Cécile, who already learned some Gospel stories, succeeded in using them to defend herself. One day, she was scolded by her mother for being late to dinner: "It doesn't matter, . . . the first will be last. Jesus said so."

At the end of this series of observations on self-evaluation, it may be hypothesized that the girls do not experience much guilt with regard to their mothers. In their struggle with their mothers to maintain their right to do what they want to do, including not being good, they rejected definitively any intervention of Jesus' judgment, which, perhaps, could make them feel guilty. They try to keep Jesus out of these "quarrels between women."

¶*Evaluation of Others.*   Only four girls used Jesus to support their judgment of the behavior of others. As for the boys, it was most often a negative judgment, but the style depended more on the individual girl than on the person to whom the reproach was addressed—the mother or peers. Thus, Christine and Bénédicte seemed to tend to threaten being seen by Jesus: "Jesus doesn't like it. Look, he is there and he sees you." Cécile, instead, tended to insist on the displeasure given to Jesus ("He will cry") or on the bad act being a proof that one does not love him. At five years, the statements take on a new tone that seems to stress the source of the inspiration of the behavior. So Mireille and Bénédicte invoked the devil to account for the naughtiness of their brother ("The devil told him to quarrel") while Bénédicte once considered Jesus to be in her aunt's heart because she was nice enough to give her a lot of candy.

The Problem of the Issue of Moral Behavior

Proportionally, the problem of moral behavior appears much more often among the girls than among the boys, constituting almost 30 percent of the observations. We recall that what is involved is an issue with religious content or caused by a religious figure. Contrary to the boys, with whom we only found the prospect of an ultimate reward in heaven, the girls looked for very immediate consequences for their behavior both as concerns punishment and the hope of reward. Thus, a suitable reward—if one is good, if one is nice, if one shares—could be that one will receive presents from Saint Nicholas or Jesus, or that one may go to mass, or (more from four years on) that "Jesus will love me a lot." Punishment bears on the same reality. Cécile discovered a new punishment that she wanted to inflict on her sister who had her clean up the room: "Her Jesus (the crucifix) will be taken away." Catherine tried to imagine what happened to adults who did bad things: "They have to go to confession and there they are punished and have to kneel a long time." Finally, Manuela and Christine found the most severe punishment that God could inflict on a little girl, which was also the best gift he could give her if she were good: "If you're good, then he'll give you a baby." The conduct of others can even influence Jesus on this subject. I shall conclude by reporting a statement of Christine that shows the primordial importance of what is at stake for the child. When she was four years old, she was riding with her mother in an automobile. At an intersection, she saw a blind man who wanted to cross the street. She cried out in panic: "Quick, Momma, stop and go help him. Otherwise Jesus will see it and he won't send *me* a baby in my belly and someone else will get the baby."

{157}

As far as heaven is concerned, it seemed perfectly natural to Cécile, at three years, to wonder why people were mourning her dead aunt, "since she is with Jesus." Bénédicte affirmed one day that good people go to heaven (four years old). At five years, Manuela and Catherine were less enthusiastic and raised questions about the real profit of going there. They wondered if, at least, there would be toys so that one would not get bored.

It appears that the girls never acquired perspective other than to live the relationship to the divine in the here and now of

{158} their daily lives. Analysis of their mode of attachment shows that they largely succeed in rendering it present in a nonconflictual model. It is not surprising, therefore, that rewards are situated essentially in the immediate present and in the reaffirmation of a positive relationship with Jesus.

Conclusions

It is time now to draw some conclusions and to see what can be retained from this analysis for the subject of our concern.

The longitudinal observation of thirty children, which concerned essentially the remarks they made concerning religious realities, does not teach us very much about moral behavior. The moral themes are evoked in a vague and natural way. One can only see that it is essentially a matter of controlling family relationships—the parent-child and the interpeer relationships. The moral problems that arise are stated in terms of being nice, obedient, good, of telling the truth, not fighting, sharing, and so on. It is not possible to determine an evolution in the actual behavior between the ages of three and six with regard to the different problems or to specify if some children evolve more rapidly than others.

What we can learn, however, is something about the way the child struggles with the limitations imposed on its desires either by others or by its own personal motivations. In addition, we can see rather clearly how much the structure of the relationship of the child with its mother and also with its father (though our data are less clear in this respect) is involved in this moral debate and determines its evolutionary and differential character. The relationship to the divine figure that is introduced into the life of the child by the witness of the parents—the mother in particular—is also structured in close reference to this position of the child in its family, as the child experiences it. God and Jesus are clearly apprehended as masculine figures who are omnipotent and who can be likened to an adult or a child. These figures are presented to the child as living in a real and positive relationship with its mother and secondarily, but not always, with its father. On the basis of these data, the child more or less confidently develops its relationship to the divine. Its interest in Jesus, its altercations with God, as well as the new things it learns about the divine are directly related to family problems and to the problems in relation to its sex and age.

{159}

I should like to bring this out briefly by reviewing the four problem areas isolated on the moral level and by showing their involvement with the relationship to the mother and the subsequent mode of attachment to the divine.

The Girls [5]

First, the moral problem appears relatively rarely in the observations of the religious behavior of the little girls. When the mother's notations allude to it, it is to mention that the religious argument did not have any effect on the girl as far as getting her to behave altruistically is concerned or to note that the girl rejected the interference of Jesus in the judgment of her quarrels or other acts of disobedience. We have even interpreted this rejection as a barrier placed by the girls between the girl-with-her-mother and the girl-with-Jesus, as a protection against any guilt that would be felt with regard to Jesus while it was not felt with regard to the mother. On the other hand, the effort to do good is motivated, when it is motivated, rather by pleasing Jesus or God under the form of "little gestures." In the same way, the proximity of Jesus, the fact of being loved by him, being able to visit him at church during mass, receiving gifts from him or Saint Nicholas, and the supreme gift, a baby from him, are rewards very highly prized by the girls and are expected in the rather near future. The reward of heaven seems to have much less interest for them. Finally, we have noted that the girls are not very concerned with taking Jesus, or God, as a model or to look to him for what they must do.

---

[5]For convenience, I list here the numbers of the problem areas: 1. problem of the effort to do good (a) for Jesus, (b) for others; 2. problem of models (a) divine, (b) evil; 3. problem of evaluation (a) of self, (b) of others; 4. problem of the issue of behavior (a) reward-punishment, (b) liberty.

All these closely related observations can easily be reconciled when we recall that the relationship the girls establish with Jesus is of an objective nature. Such a relationship explains the motivation to please Jesus. It allows one to understand how the presence or the manifestation of Jesus is experienced as having the value of a reward. It explains, too, how guilt is incurred when the girl is observed by Jesus in the act of being naughty. On another level, the rivalry with the mother, which is explained by the Oedipal situation of the girl, does not account for the absence of guilt with regard to the mother and for the attempts of the girls to keep their relationship to Jesus separate from the conflicts they experience with their mothers. This rivalry was not observed in connection with the positive manifestations of the attachment to the divine. Probably, it would appear here when it is a matter of resolving a conflict arising from the girl's behavior. To accept Jesus as a witness (he sees you, he will be sad) in such a case is to exercise a form of coercion that dissolves resistance. The girl cannot defend herself against it because, contrary to the boys, she has no great interest in pleasing her mother at any cost. And if she has an interest in pleasing Jesus, it is easier for her to believe that he responds unconditionally to her admiration for him and her gestures of affection than to have to prove her love by obeying her mother or by sharing with others. Who else besides the real father could obtain such an effort from her?

The Boys

Contrary to the moral problem of the girls, we note that the moral problem is much more present in the religious life of the boys. There are even more observations on this subject than with regard to the manifestations of their mode of attachment to the divine. As we have seen, all the problem areas are encountered. There is an effort, albeit erratic, to do good, and this effort is more often motivated by altruism sustained by the mother than by a desire to please Jesus. When the latter case arose, the boy revealed his belief that the rectitude of his conduct really pleased Jesus, at least when he was not preoccupied with showing his aggressive virility in helping Jesus against the evil ones or against adversity. The boy is equally attracted by models: the model of good behavior which is imposed by Jesus-adult, which was adopted by Jesus when he was little, so that the boy can imagine that he conforms to it; and also a model of bad behavior, that of the evil men who killed Jesus, so that the boy can affirm that he is innocent and good. As regards self-evaluation, the boys become more and more uncomfortable with the prospect of being found in fault before God or Jesus. The shame is the greatest at age five, and certain reactions betray a particular sensitivity peculiar to the narcissistic ideal, which does not tolerate negative judgments and which generates guilt. The evaluation of others differs according to whether it involves reactions to the mother's behavior or to that of his peers. For the former, the reproaches tend to become emotional coercion, and for the latter, they are expressed in terms of nonconformity to the norms of Jesus. Finally, the problem of the issue of moral behavior lacks religious content, except for the prospect of a final reward in paradise after death. The effort to respect moral rules seems difficult at certain ages and one sees some children begin to dream of total liberty, allowing them to do everything and particularly to manifest their aggressiveness (make holes in tablecloths, realize their desires to kill).

{161}

The double fact that the mother is the Oedipal partner of the boy and that she invites him to construct a positive relationship with God or Jesus and, before God, harmonious relationships with others explains many of the observations to a large extent. The immediate gratification for the little Oedipus is that his mother is pleased with, and proud of, him. All of his altruistic behavior—even if it is sporadic or only promised—will indeed be observed and this suffices for him to be attentive to it. Since Jesus is a friend of the mother, the boy has a direct interest in being his friend and an indirect interest in doing what he does. This, at least, is what happens in the initial period with the boys up until the moment when the identification process begins to function, around five to six years of age. Then Jesus, God omnipotent, becomes the reflection of an ideal of the incomparable self that permits the boy to dream that he is omnipotent and capable of fulfilling all promises. But it also engenders its correlative of

{162} narcissistic guilt that causes the fear of a negative judgment or an appeal for indulgence. This identification movement probably ought to promote, like the relationship with the father, a moving away from the mother. But, like the girls who could escape in a certain way from the obligation of proving their love for Jesus by an effective love for others, the boys can escape the strict obligation of confronting their limitations and their lack of om- nipotence by transposing the paternal model (limited) to the divine being. Three indices lead me to believe that the debate is opened on this level within the six-year-old boy: the fact that he can hardly tolerate the "weakness" of God; the fact that no self-evaluation with religious content was observed at this age; and the fact that the promises of, and efforts toward, moral rectitude are repeated to the mother. Ultimately, it is from her that the immediate reward will come while awaiting the hypothet- ical arrival of heaven, promised for much later to good boys who will have accepted on this earth the heavy burden of passing on to the love of others. It is well to note this evocation of the religious promise and of the vast screen of projection that it offers to the omnipotence of the self in order to allow every son of man to find the courage to continue the effort of growing according to the model ordained by the Father, provided that he still finds somewhere a "Mother" to give him the concrete motivation.

Reflections on Moral and Religious Education

Parents often wonder a great deal about what they must do or not do to succeed in the moral and religious education of their children. Parents may be helped in a number of ways:

1. By helping them discover that religious and moral attitudes are not the automatic results of formal teaching, even though it be of the best theology. Thus, when one wants to evaluate the quality of an educational milieu— the family or the school—one must consider the witness quality of the

educators as well as the dogmatic correspondence of the teaching they provide.

2. By helping them discover that the formation of moral and {*163*} religious attitudes is always a part of the concrete mediation of the relations of the child with its environment, that is, with its love objects, its identification models, its rivals, and so on, and that, consequently, these attitudes are essentially evolutionary. Therefore, it is normal that they differ from one individual to the other, from one sex to the other, from one age to the other. And it is advisable to respect these differences.

3. By helping them understand that they are themselves involved in the moral and religious orientation of their child by virtue of the personal requirements and aspirations they present to the child and that, to a certain extent, this involvement escapes any possible control on their part. If they blame themselves, which often happens, should their child adopt a different orientation, is this not an occasion to help them understand that this does not depend on them and to rework what constitutes their own faith and their own moral values?

4. By having them understand that, apart from the witness that he or she bears by his or her life, the true role of the educator is to be present to the child during its moments of crises, doubt, and so on, in order to help it to understand itself and to grasp the new values it becomes capable of integrating.

5. By having them understand that the differences observed in this study between the evolution of the boys and that of the girls does not mean there is reason to give a different religious message according to sex. It does mean, however, that one must expect that the same message will be received differently and will be integrated into the attitudes that are proper to the individual. During adolescence, certainly, and perhaps during childhood, the sharing of religious experiences and moral aspirations can help individuals of each sex to understand each other better and to qualify their own tendencies.

ABOUT THE AUTHOR

{164}   Dr. Jean-Marie Jaspard *has studied both philosophy and theology and currently lectures at the Faculty of Psychology and Educational Sciences at Louvain-la-Neuve in Belgium. He is director of the Center for Religious Psychology and teaches Religious Psychology of the Child and the Adolescent. His empirical research is focused essentially on the process of the development of the child and the adolescent.*

Dr. Jaspard is also President of the Institue of Family Sciences and Sexology at the Catholic University of Louvain, where he gives courses in family and sexual education. In addition, he is a founding member of the Center for the Formation of Psychological Intervention at Brussels.

Dr. Jaspard has authored many articles. Among them are "La représentation de la présence eucharistique chez l'enfant de 6 à 12 ans"; "Loi rituelle et structuration de l'attitude religieuse chez l'enfant"; "Composantes psychologiques d'une maturation de la foi chrétienne"; and "Avons-nous donc raté leur éducation religieuse?"

Negation and Transformation: A Study in Theology and Human Development

JAMES E. LODER

Introduction

So far as sheerly empirical development is concerned, it might be ...
accurate to say that language and the negative 'invented' man. [1]
My God, my God, why have you abandoned me? [2]

The first theme of this chapter concerns the experience of negation. For most of us, some near-death experience is the most negative imaginable. Negative experiences are not all violent episodes, nightmares, or traumas, but a long, dark thread of lesser negative periods—such as loneliness, rejection, embarrassment, disorientation, or meaninglessness—that stretches through our lives. Beginning with the earliest separation of the newborn child from its mother, through the successive stages of life, and from the highly abstract negations of the mind to the concrete personal losses, we are repeatedly thrown into negative experiences of varying magnitudes.

How does negation get hold of our lives? What *are* the various magnitudes of negation? How is the life of the developing person constructed to negate negation for the sake of transformation? These questions shape the first theme.

The second theme reverses the first to notice that some experiences are so good that they are negative in their impact upon the ordinary. We say of such extraordinary experiences that they are too good to be true. Many people experience God with such power that they believe themselves almost insane. What does one do with such an experience? What role does it play *in* human development, and what do such experiences reveal *about* human development? Does their power lie in their capacity to negate negations of the highest magnitude? If so, how can such a notion be structured and understood? These questions shape the second theme of this chapter and leave us with certain implications regarding the personal integrity of the ethical life.

A central notion of this chapter is "negation of negation" as the key to transformation. By this is meant the fashion in which

---

[1] K. Burke, *Language As a Symbolic Action*.

[2] Mark 15:34

problematic times, periods of infinite difficulty and void, are met by an integrative power of sufficient magnitude to bring the fragments of the original brokenness into a new and higher state of wholeness. Christ's redemptive action upon the sinful condition of human nature is the paradigm case of such a transformation. This chapter attempts to demonstrate the inherent logic of transformation, both as it participates in and effects a corrective of the so-called "normal" course of human development. In a sense, this corrective takes the "norm" out of normal and frees the study of human development to be as descriptive as it claims to be.

The Four Negations

Recognizing that negation is an extremely elusive notion to pursue, this study begins with the premise that negation is always negation *of something*. Types of negation will be determined, then, by *what* is negated. In other words, negation will be given its experiential shape by that upon which it works a limitation, refutation, contradiction, diminution, denial, perversion or annihilation (to mention a few of the ways in which negation operates). Negation is taken to be fundamentally derivative and qualifying; as such it may be divided into four general types: methodological, functional, existential, and transformational. Although subtypes might be constructed, they would add unnecessary complexity to this study.

Methodological Negation

Methodological negation is generally a cognitive and intellectual matter, applied, as a matter of principle, in grammatical, propositional, critical and/or systematic contexts. Methodological negation articulates and preserves objectivity and refers primarily to the negation of subjective or egocentric distortions of presumably objective or universal truths.

Functional Negation

Functional negation is negation of psychological functions, including both intrapsychic and interpersonal relationships. Repression is the most common form of intrapsychic functional negation. In interpersonal terms, E. Erikson's description of shame may be understood as the functional negation of autonomy within the second stage of ego maturation. Correlatively, autonomy may be seen as the functional negation of shame.

Existential Negation

Existential negation refers to the negation of one's own being. The "experience of Nothingness" as that which forcibly confronts one with his or her own nonexistence is as close as one can come to existential negation. Existential negation may also be understood as the ultimate negation of the capacity of the ego to construct its world, sometimes called "ego shock."

Transformational Negation

Transformational negation refers to the negation of negation such that a new integration emerges, establishing a gain over the original negated state or condition.[3] Double negation establishes a new state of being which includes the first negation as an essential element of the gain. Transformational negation, though a distinct form of negation, will occur only in relation to one of the other three types. *Methodological transformation* occurs in scientific discovery when new insight negates a problematic situation by reintegrating the elements of the problem so as to establish an integration of higher complexity than has hitherto existed. Here the imaginative insight provides a double negation by mapping a new situation in the context of the old one.

---

[3]See *Notes* at the end of this paper for an elaboration on transformational negation.

Functional transformation occurs regularly as the stage transition process which begins as a given stage of ego formation or one of its part-processes (for example, language or intelligence) proves to be dysfunctional in meeting the demands of a problematic situation. New competencies (such as grammar) emerge, drawing together the elements of the frustrated or dysfunctional condition around a new, emergent structural configuration, thus multiplying the capacities of that function manyfold. It is by functional transformation that stage transitions are accomplished; discontinuity and continuity are dialectically interrelated so as to bring forward the latent competencies of development. *Existential transformation* refers to the negation of the "experience of Nothingness"; one's potentiality for nonbeing is ultimately negated. This is most common in a religious experience, but the form and substance of such experiences vary widely.

In the last section of this study, Christ crucified and resurrected is taken as a paradigm of the mediator of transformation at the level of existential negation. Christ becomes the adequate "grammar" for existential transformation because in his crucifixion he takes ultimate annihilation into himself and in his resurrection existential negation is negated. The Christ even thus creates an ontological gain for those whose essential existence is defined by his nature. The crucifixion is a *sine qua non* of the new being in Christ; hence the gain is a transformation, not an aberration from or elevation of one's human existence.

Developmental Perspectives on Negation

The main argument of this section is that the prototype of religious experience, potentially available to a three-month-old child, sets up in subsequent human life a cosmic loneliness. Human development beyond this period is to be understood as a series of circumambulations of this longing for a religious recentering of the personality. What follows is a developmental account of the source of this loneliness and the reason it is so difficult to satisfy.

For purposes of setting forth this position, a psychoanalytic view regarding the origins of life and its negation will be assumed. The "birth trauma,"[4] so-called partly because in the normal course of a birth the child comes near to suffocation, is the primal *existential negation*. This experience of negation ramifies through the whole organism and lays down the foundation for interpreting subsequent experiences of negation. If this psychoanalytic type of assertion is correct, then, ontogenetically, existential negation precedes all other forms of negation.

The effect of this original existential negation is that a series of apparently random activities are set in motion as the newborn child seeks postnatal equilibrium. These activities such as sucking, grasping, focusing, and a variety of "primary circular reactions" (Piaget) all contribute to the adaptational struggle. However, what the child is seeking instinctively (as opposed to consciously) is a center around which to integrate this multiplicity of new activities and emerging competencies. The child is looking for an inclusive alternative to living in the random uncertainty of the postnatal world. Ultimately, of course, the solution to this existential negation cannot be met by any emerging functional competence.

Rene Spitz in *The First Year of Life* has made a series of observations regarding this search for a centering of the child's personality. The search goes through four phases. The first is the oral stage in which the *mouth* serves as "the cradle of perception" and the receptive cavity by which the child learns to incorporate his or her world. This standard psychoanalytic observation is considerably elaborated by Spitz, but then he goes on to show that the center shifts toward the love object, a *person* present. The standard indication of this focus (some even say "imprint") of the child upon persons is that at three months he or she seeks and learns to respond to the presence of a human face—even a schematic design of a face will do—and give a smile. So regular is this *smiling recognition of the face* and so marked is the shift from a

---

[4]The emphasis here is not upon "trauma" as such but upon the existential negation implied in the radical transition from the life-supporting dependency of intrauterine existence to the independence of postnatal life. That this is an existential negation without necessarily being a "trauma" should be self-evident.

physiological center to an interpersonal one that Spitz calls this facial mirroring the primary organizer of the personality.[5] This capacity is obviously not as instinctively inevitable as vision or sucking, but it is more like language, a developmentally innate structure which, if it is presented in appropriate environment, will be learned and used as a decisive, formative power for future growth.

Translating this observation into Erikson's terms, this would be the nucleus of trust as it begins to emerge and establish itself in the child by from twelve to eighteen months of age. The face, then, may be the personal center which is innately sought by a child and the focus of the earliest sense of one's humanity. The smiling response focuses primal wholeness. Perhaps wholeness is experienced most primitively at the fetal level, but here the undifferentiated "cosmos" of the child becomes interpersonal and focuses upon the face.[6]

This cosmic integration of self and world focused upon the face-to-face interaction, is short-lived, however. At about six months the child begins to differentiate the mother's face and to react regularly with anxiety and tears to her absence and to strangers who appear at the crib. This reaction is so regular that from six to eight months an anxiety reaction to the *sense of the absence* of the mother's face becomes the second organizer of the personality. During this same period the child is learning to respond to "No!" in verbal, gestural, and affective form so that during this time he or she is sensing an inner absence together with an increasing awareness of external interdiction. It is as if the primal, integrative experience of fetal existence, which is lost in the separation of birth, were now being relived in the interper-

---

[5]For further information and discussion regarding this phenomenon, see the chapter by Rizzuto in this volume; D. W. Winnicott, *Playing and Reality* (New York: Basic Books, 1971); and Ana-Maria Rizzuto, *The Birth of the Living God: A Psychoanalytic Study* (Chicago: University of Chicago Press, 1979).

[6]"Face" here is to be taken as an interpersonal reality and as a primal symbol of wholeness. Many varied studies have pointed to the unique physiological, personal, and interpersonal significance of the face. This view partially reflects a Jungian notion that the face represents an archetype of wholeness since it is generally round and its center bears a cross. Jolande Jacobi quotes Justin Martyr as follows; "The Cross is imprinted upon man, even upon his face." (*Apologia*) The cross in the face represents man in his contradiction unified by the circumference of the face.

sonal outer world. By nine months after birth the child has relived the integration and separation that took place during the first nine months of life before and during birth.

The developmental solution to this return of existential negation shifts personality centeredness from an integrative to a defensive posture. The solution is functional and adaptational, but it splits the psychic world of the child in a way that gives rise to an enduring cosmic loneliness. As the child moves into his or her fourteenth month, the emergent center of the personality becomes a *determined use of negation* in affect, gesture, and word. As the child's inner sense of anxiety and absence is repeatedly reengaged by the outward "No" saying of the parent (in gesture, word, and affect), he or she incorporates negation and inflicts it upon the environment so as to carve out and defend an emerging autonomy against the incursions of negation. This is a primitive form of what may later be called a reaction formation in which one does just the opposite of what he or she would like to do with all the energy (and more) than he or she wanted to do the first thing. The child says "No" with all the energy he or she would like to say "Yes" to self, world, and the loving other.

This *functional negation* of the existential sense of the lost face is an attempt at transformation which is only partially effective. It attempts to make a functional competence deal with an existential condition, but functional negation does not work transformationally with respect to existential negation. As a result, not only is the emergent autonomy built upon a defensive maneuver designed to secure survival against the threat of abandonment, but it leaves the developing personality with an abiding sense of cosmic loneliness. This is not to ignore or to diminish the constructive capacities of the ego which emerge at this time, but in the existential sense, the center of the personality is lost when ontogenesis turns in the direction of autonomy.

The functional negation of autonomy in "shame" (to use Erikson's conception) is a reflection of the "mistrust" engendered by the chronic absence of the face. The psychic split here does not mean that there is a good and a bad side, constructive and destructive side forming an antithesis-in-synthesis. This would imply that we should work for as favorable a balance as possible, eliminating the negative wherever possible. This misses the deeper problem of human development. The problem is not the functional antithesis between autonomy and shame; it is the incomplete transformation implied in the developmental tendency to attempt to make a functional maneuver deal with an existential dilemma. Functional negation is not sufficient to negate the experience of Nothingness; so, transformation is incomplete. This is the developmental reason why J. P. Sartre's dictum rings true, "Nothingness haunts being." However, development seems to say more; namely, the personality longs for the double negation that will negate Nothingness and transform the face-to-face relationship, the human prototype of religious experience, into an Eternal Presence.

If this description is generally accurate, then the longing for the Eternal Presence through an adequate double negation is not based solely on the absence or loss of the face, but upon the hope engendered by the original emergence of the face as a transformation of the existential negation of birth. The face-to-face relation is prototypical because it embodies both the process and the ontology of religious experience. That is, the *transformational process* is affected by a *cosmic ordering, self-confirming impact from the presence of a loving other*. "Rebirth" follows essentially this prototypical pattern regardless of the age of the person.

In spite of its decentering the personality, the emphasis upon functional negation, which reaches a certain peak at about fourteen months, lays the foundation for the subsequent triumphs of culture, including the capacity for *methodological negation*. Spitz writes:

> The acquisition of "No" is the indicator of a new level of autonomy, of the awareness of the "other" and of the awareness of the self; it is the beginning of a restructuration of mentation on a higher level of complexity; it initiates an extensive ego development, in the framework of which the dominance of the reality principle over the pleasure principle becomes increasingly established. [7]

---

[7] Rene Spitz, *No and Yes* (New York: International Universities Press, 1957), p. 129. See also *The First Year of Life* (New York: International Universities Press, 1965).

Obviously the foregoing interpretation of Spitz's findings had departed somewhat from his optimism regarding the dominance of the reality principle. The reality principle as Spitz (and Freud) interpret it is fundamentally defensive, and therefore resists transformational negation. However, Spitz makes evident the connection between functional negation, as it emerges in the first year of life, and subsequent development of the capacity for methodological negation. The movement out of egocentrism in thought, language, and moral judgment is centered in and depends upon the emergent capacity for intentionally establishing "object" relations; "objectivity" (admittedly a somewhat different use of the term) as a constructive work of mentation develops alongside and in dependence upon the maturation of object relations. It should simply be noted that any capacity for the consistent use of methodological negation appears last in course of development.

By Spitz's dictum the formal capacity for the objective formulation of propositions and universal principles would be the highest refinement of the developmental tendency which begins with autonomous self-assertion. However, even highly refined objective, universally valid propositions have not escaped cosmic longing; they have transposed into the abstractions of mathematics an empirically demonstrable thesis, the human nostalgia for a self-secured place in a universal order. The methodological negation of subjectivity comes last in the ontogenetic scheme of things, but even this supreme achievement of mentation directly reflects its subjective origins.

Methodological transformation makes the connection between conceptualization and one's subjective life very evident. The most clear-cut case is Einstein's discovery of relativity, as recounted by Michael Polanyi in *Personal Knowledge*. Einstein sensed very early (late adolescence) that the Newtonian world view was deficient; its inherent negation in the form of a dependency upon a principle of absolute rest Einstein sought to negate with a new, more adequate view. Einstein trusted intuitions, bodily feelings, and hunches as well as his highly developed capacities for abstract thought. The result was an intellectual vision of the universe that contradicted the objective facts, particularly those supplied by the Michaelson-Morley experiment, but the vision was so "beautiful," it was presumed that the facts—not the theory—were in error. When the Michaelson-Morley experiment was repeated, it was corrected and found to confirm Einstein's general theory of relativity. The result was a transformation of the Newtonian world view. It is not that Newton's work became irrelevant but its inherent problems, negated by the new theory, left its assertions to be accounted for in a more adequate way by relativity.

Polanyi's point with regard to methodological negation is the one I want to stress; namely, in this case the theory creates the facts because there is already latent in the person the resources for intuiting a cosmic order that exceeds the order embodied in any purely objective or "factual" account of things. From this case (and countless others) Polanyi wants to insist upon a postcritical philosophy of science in which commitment, subjective passion, and one's trust of intuition become as essential as one's duty to submit to the intellectual canons of the community in which one works. This insistence is generally consistent with the assumption of this chapter: (1) Methodological negation issuing in conceptual objectivity needs repeated transformation; and (2) transformation comes not initially from increasing objectivity, but by reaching back into the subjective sources of one's thought in order to allow personal resources and sensitivities (abandoned early by the developmental drive toward autonomy and objectivity) to inform intelligence regarding the nature of cosmic order.

The developmental history of the capacity for methodological negation is documented thoroughly by Piaget and his followers in their studies of the development of language and intelligence. However, it should be evident that Polanyi's view, and the position taken here, is doubtful about the unqualified affirmation of objectivating intelligence over imagination (including intuition) which Piaget presumes. More likely, the sense of cosmic order rooted in the personality and tacitly present even in the most objective studies already holds the secrets of cosmic order. This dimension of personal knowledge must first be believed if understanding of cosmic order is to be fathomed through successive transformations of methodological negation.

Thus intelligence makes its contribution to the alleviation of cosmic loneliness.

{176}   The case of Einstein's discovery provides us with a basis for introducing a chart of parallel transformational processes, all following essentially the same inherent logic. The stage-transition process, which takes place more or less automatically, is transposed to the level of intentional behavior in the process of creative thought (for example, Einstein's case). A third level of transformation is also intentional but it is dyadic and occurs in therapeutic contexts. It should be clear that the essential sequence is a linear gestalt, that is, it drives toward completion regardless of when one consciously enters the sequence. This derives from the continuous repetition of the process as stage transition or developmental level. When the process is transposed, it continues to seek closure, making the discoverer or client-therapist restless until closure is reached.

It should be evident from the chart and illustrations that intentional sequences are not rigid. All steps are necessary for the completion of the sequence. A back-and-forth movement among the steps is par for the course, as is entering the sequence at any stage (for example, knowing the answer—in sight—before one knows the question is part of Einstein's story, since he had a hunch that he knew the answer to the problem posed by the Newtonian world even before he had formulated it). Similarly, many religious experiences, as will be discussed below, appear first as solutions that exceed any then known problem. Regardless of the magnitude of the insight or when one enters, the continuity of the sequence remains binding, even if the order of the steps does not.

Existential Transformation

The particular problem to which we now turn is transformational negation at the level of existence. We have said that the dilemma of development is that the personality loses its centeredness when the ontology of the face is obscured by a series of functional adaptations in the struggle for survival. The result is the formation of an adaptationally competent ego that functions as if it were

CHART I · PARALLEL PROCESSES FOLLOWING
TRANSFORMATIONAL LOGIC

Stage-Transition Based on Orthogenetic Model	*Creative Discovery* E.g., Einstein	*Therapeutic* E.g., Freud's Case of Little Hans[8]
1. *Global organic* state.	1. *Conflict-free.*	1. *Conflict-free* 3-year-old child.
2. *Differentiation* of the organism.	2. *Conflict* borne in the context of *rapport:* Einstein senses problem in Newtonian world.	2. *Conflict:* threatened with castration; phobic child counseled by father under Freud's guidance.
3. *Specification* of the differentiated parts.	3. *Interlude* for *scanning:* years spent in focusing the issue and searching for key to solution.	3. Focused conflict yielded to *unconscious:* Little Hans acknowledged his conflict and slept.
4. New *integration* emerges.	4. *Insight:* A bisociation between two or more otherwise unassociated frames of reference: $E = MC^2$ as intuition.	4. *Unconscious* produces a solution to conflict as focused in an *insightful image:* Hans has two *fantasies* that restore his masculinity and his potency as a young man (age 5).
5. *Energy* is *released by the integration* and freed for investment in. . . .	5. *The release of energy:* Repeated moments of assurance, and final confidence when speed of light was set as the constant.	5. *Release of tension* bound up in the conflict. Little Hans says, "My nonsense is gone."

[8]Sigmund Freud, *The Phobia in a Five-Year-Old Boy.*

CHART I (continued)

Stage-Transition Based on Orthogenetic Model	*Creative Discovery* E.g., Einstein	*Therapeutic* E.g., Freud's Case of Little Hans
6. Higher level of *functional compe-tence*.	**6.** *Interpretation:* The insight is formu-lated and checked for *congruence* with the conflict and for *correspondence* with the people. Einstein did the first, but others did the second.	**6.** The *reality* list: Subsequent inter-views showed that Hans then entered latency normally.

the center of the personality, when in fact it depends for its own integrity upon the denial of that center to maintain its autonomy. Thus, the ego may be seen as a kind of tragic hero or a truth-producing error since it brings all the subject's competencies into a working unit, but cannot itself suffice as the center of that integration.

Transformational negation at the level of existence occurs when the personality is recentered by a sense of the Divine Presence. In order to examine this phenomenon, I will focus upon certain dramatic experiences. However, it should be clear that such a transformation may take place over a long period of time, in stages, or in an accumulation of experiences. The advantage of looking at the extreme cases is that so much is encapsulated in such brief compass.

Sudden experiences of God are not as far removed from everyday experience as one might think. Andrew Greeley in the *Sociology of the Paranormal*[9] and a recent study of the Presbyterian Church, U.S.A., seem to agree. Slightly less than half

---

[9]A. Greeley, *Sociology of the Paranormal* (Beverly Hills, CA: Sage Publications, Inc., 1975).

(4/10) of the general population of American society, as well as slightly less than half (47%) of the Presbyterian constituency, have had religious experience which turned their lives around. About 75 percent of the Presbyterian clergy have had such experiences.[10] In a similar study done in England, Sir Alistair Hardy, broadcasting on BBC, asked the listening public to send him accounts of religious experiences. Today over 6,000 experiences have been collected at Manchester College, Oxford, and are being studied by the Religious Experience Research Unit of the college. One striking thing about these reports is that 15 percent were experiences reported by adults about events of religious significance which occurred in childhood.

Before moving into the method and cases of this section, a brief comment regarding the ego health of such a transformation is in order. As Carl Jung has pointed out, ego transformation is the key to religious experience and personal wholeness. Ego transformation may then be understood not as destruction to the ego, but as a clear-cut recentering of the personality around a transcendental reality that points to the invisible God. The net effect enhances ego functioning, since the ego has less need to control or limit perceptions or understandings of self, world, or others. Ordinarily, the autonomous ego would constrict its vision lest the underlying existential negation come into view and the centripetal force of development draw it back through Nothingness toward the true center. However, once the center is invested in God's Presence, the ego's anguish at absence and abandonment is dissipated and its defensive energies can now be poured into its competencies. In effect, decentering the ego liberates and empowers its functioning even though and precisely because it is no longer the presumed center of the personality.

As to method, what this section proposes is that the therapeutic process described by Freud for neurosis be made the human analogue for the fashion in which religious experiences work to remove the "normal" resistance we have—just as a result of development—to the transformation of the ego. It will be

---

[10] *The Presbyterian Panel* (New York: The United Presbyterian Church).

evident that this follows the logic of transformation described above.

{180} The analogy proposed is as follows: (1) Let the original condition of neurosis be seen in terms of its double bind character such that no matter what the neurotic *does* to extricate himself from his neurosis he further entrenches it because the neurosis is precisely a pathology of choosing and of doing. The double bind in the ego is the same, since it cannot discover the primal face without undoing itself as ego: it cannot embrace its own annihilation. (2) The mediating factor in therapy is the therapist, who on the one hand works analytically to expose the basis of the neurosis, but on the other supplies the personal reality to which the neurotic may relate constructively as the neurosis abates. The key to successful mediation is sufficient externalization of the causes of the neurosis through the cooperative effort of therapist and patient. Externalization is a matter of both affect and understanding, but once "out there" rather than embedded in one's own system of choice and action, one can choose against it and for the reality represented by the therapist. The mediating factor in religious experience is the event, image, or experience itself. Usually such experiences have a numinous quality that makes them unique, so one has no trouble seeing where they begin and where they end. The work of the mediating event is to externalize for the personal ego the underlying threat of death or annihilation and at the same time supply a new context of meaning which embraces and transcends it. (3) The outcome of therapeutic mediation is a new confidence in the process of self-understanding, self-acceptance and self-affirmation—in effect, confidence in the dynamics of the therapeutic process. Confidence is not supposed to rest in the therapist per se, otherwise the therapist has made the client dependent, and the client is not well but merely identified with the therapist. Accordingly, the outcome of religious transformation is not that one worships the experience but that the transforming process be trusted, that is, what the transformed person will most likely call "the Spirit," or the on-going transformation that takes place under the aegis of such experiences.

The following cases from my practice of pastoral counseling

and research on transforming experiences will provide substance to the claim that transformational negation may occur at the level of existence and effectively raise the ontology of the Face to the level of a living presence.

The Case of Willa

Willa, a middle-aged woman, came from a home in which she had always lived as an intruder. She was the child that forced her mother and father to marry. She was chronically neglected and mistreated, and after her second year in college suffered a schizophrenic breakdown. While getting treatment in a state hospital and not making any progress, she was, as she described it, "too depressed to make myself distinguish between dreams and reality." Her head nurse told me that the staff was resigned to Willa's never leaving the hospital. She would sit for hours, hold her stuffed doll, and wish for death. One day, after being in the hospital for some time, she felt a Presence come up behind her, embrace her, and "tell" her: "The silence is not empty. There is a purpose for your life." When she turned around there was no one there but the silence remained full of affirmation for her. The event was remarkably effective in motivating her back into life. The results of health were not instantaneous, but whenever she felt stronger in her ego functioning she felt more convinced about this experience. Moreover, she said the experience "made people appear as people" and established meaningful boundaries for subsequent relationships. The experience clearly had intervened to establish the center of the personality at a level deeper than ego functioning but consistent with it. For Willa this was the Presence of a loving Other, giving her a place in the world and affirming her worth; the latent symbolic power of the Face had been given life in a Divine Presence.

Interpreting this case, it is evident that Willa's ego had already collapsed into abandonment. She had fallen into what the ego dreads most; she had surrendered the boundaries of the ego to the experience of Nothingness. The religious experience had a transforming effect because the mystical presence of a loving

Other did the work of mediation. The silence was simultaneously negated and filled; her sense of absence or abandonment was simply canceled. At the same time she was implicitly told what she should choose if she wanted help; namely, the reality represented by that Presence and the ego strength that came with it.

In both this case and the one which follows, it is especially remarkable how the experience opened up the repressed past history. Horrendous stories of her childhood came pouring forth in her newfound capacities to "put things together." The point is that the ego had surrendered itself in the schizophrenic break, but was not liberated for seeing things from the past and piecing together her story until the primal longing to be centered in God had been satisfied. Once the defensive structure of the autonomous ego had been negated, it was free to cooperate with the integration which recentering promised.

Another way of saying this is that a reciprocal relationship between the ego and the Divine center of her personality was instituted. By "reciprocity" I mean the figure/ground reversal whereby the ego and the Divine Presence are alternately the center of action, but the center of identification remains the Divine Presence. Thus, the Old Testament prophets said in effect, "I, not I, But JHWH . . .," Jesus said, "I, not I, but the Father . . .," and Paul said, "I, not I, but Christ. . . ." Recentering the personality means that identity ceases to be irreversibly univocal and becomes instead reversible and reciprocal. This case is important not only for the sharp focus it gives to the reciprocal character of this woman's identity but also because she would say she lives increasingly "in the Spirit," that is, in the ongoing transformational process that so suddenly altered the center of her life.

The Case of Norma

Norma was a counselee of mine who chronically passes out at the end of our sessions. My response had been simply to leave her to pull herself together while I took the next client in another office. I tended to assume that she was suffering from some separation anxiety and that her behavior was manipulative. Finally when, in a moment of inspiration, I told her I wanted to work spiritually rather than in a more conventional way, she said she was relieved to hear that. Now she said she could really tell me why she passed out like that. "You see when we start going back into my personal history that way, I get all confused, the world turns to cardboard, and I start to hear screaming in the back of my head. It gets so loud I can't stand it, so that's when I pass out."

We talked about this a bit, then I suggested that I put my hands on her head and pray for her. This I did sitting on the arm of the sofa beside her. I prayed quietly, asking Christ's Spirit to enter her life and take the screaming out of her head. Suddenly as I prayed, she turned and hit me again and again as hard as she could. Fortunately, owing to my position, the blows fell on my shoulder and back, so I could continue to pray. At last she stopped and began to cry, sobbing deeply as if she were totally abandoned. Then she began to laugh. Her tears up to now had been practically nonexistent and her laughter very strained, but this laughter was free and full of relief. She got up, picked up her things, and said, "I am not going to see you anymore!" and *she* left *me*. She went home and began to read the Bible and "pray in the spirit," without any prompting or earlier experience of such a thing.

The voices never returned. However, she came back and told me of a dream she had following her experience in the office. It recalled an episode in her childhood after her grandmother, the dearest person in her life, had died. As a young child she went to the crematorium where the grandmother's body was to be cremated. Sensing the austerity, gloom, and threat of the place she had tried to run outside, but she was suddenly pulled back and a huge door slammed to secure her in the room.

Up to the time of this dream, even though she was a practicing minister, she had dreaded funerals and had never done one—always managing to get someone else on the staff to cover for her. After the history prompted by this dream had been worked through, she was able not only to live through the long, cancerous death of a dear friend of hers, but even to do her funeral with a sense of confidence and spiritual integrity. When I last heard from her she was serving as part-time chaplain in a hospital working regularly with the terminally ill.

The mediatorial role is clearer here than in the first case, since the double negation implied in continuing to pray while receiving the externalized attack (a result of grace, not good management) is what finally makes the positive claims of Christ's Spirit a real choice for her. Her sense of having had existential negation negatived, powerful as it was at this point, was sufficient to change the course of her development, but repeated return to the source of that change was required in order to foster the remedial work necessary for restoration of the crippled ego.

The psychodynamics of this case reveal an unresolved grief process in which Norma came to struggle not only with the loss of the grandmother, but also with the larger existential question of death's meaning and personal nonbeing. The screaming voices represent a thinly veiled attack by an unincorporated sense of separation and annihilation upon her conscious life. When the defensive work of the ego is weakened or damaged, then the negation which it usually enlists in support of the autonomy splits off into demonic forms. Christ is the key to Norma's dealing with grief and the existential despair it produced not only because he provides care in the context of rapport, but also because he is able to deal with the demonic in a way that no human agency can.

Further observations may be made here: (1) Graciously, my role in this is parabolic with respect to Christ who is perceived as the true mediator. This suggests that the mediatorial role may have both a proximate and an alternate form. The following case demonstrates that an imaginative construct provides the proximate form, but the ultimate impact is essentially the same: negation of existential negation. (2) The double negation also has both a proximate and an ultimate form since the dream revealed an experience in which the infants' primal fear of abandonment was brought forward into the grandmother's death. Here the ultimate is experienced first, namely, abandonment is abandoned through Christ's intervention, so that the proximate abandonment inherent in the grandmother's death could also be abandoned as a subsequent and derivative consequence. (3) The gain which results from this existential transformation is that, in spite of some arrested ego development, the personality is centered in such a way that all remedial efforts of the ego may be made in a reciprocal (rather than defensive) relationship to the center, Christ's Presence.

The Case of Gary

Gary, a young black man in his early twenties, had been imprisoned several times for theft and armed robbery. The original episode from which his transformation derived was a childhood dream of Jesus that apparently had the force of a vision. At the age of three he dreamed Jesus was suffering in agony on the cross, and the officials of the church were walking by in indifference. The cross was hanging in a room that had tables and chairs, so the little boy climbed upon the table and tried to pull out the nails. Finally, he fell back on the table and wept bitterly because he could not extract them. He remembered Jesus' words to him, "You will survive!"

As he grew up, he was forced to leave his home and was passed from one orphanage and foster home to the next. Outer cruelty conspired with deepening grief over continual loss of love to compel him repeatedly toward attempts to negate his existential depravity with violence and revenge. He had "misunderstood," as he later put it, "what 'survival' meant." He had thought it meant that he would survive by his own wits and aggressive determination to repay evil for evil.

Over the course of his life, he got some revenge but was caught several times. Recently, serving his last parole, he found himself overtaken by the demonic desire to go out and kill several people and kill himself. His devoted friend and counselor, a seminary student, was sharing his room with Gary at the time. The student, alone with Gary when this desire overtook him, tried every way to stop him, from slapping his face (a dangerous thing to do) to recalling good times from the past. At last in a moment of ecstatic prayer, crying out to Jesus for help, he felt spiritually compelled to stand up before Gary and portray the dream he knew had meant so much to the young criminal when he was a little boy. "Take the nails out of my hands, Gary," he said with his palms open and his arms outstretched. The air was so charged with aggression and inspiration that the young black man fell back in silence, stunned as if he had been overtaken by God himself. In a few moments he was sound asleep on the sofa and in the night underwent a change of personality that seemingly continues with him. He became responsible to and for himself, for his work and to the woman he loved, but above all to the Christ, who appeared to him in that dream and its reenactment. Now he says he realizes that he could not get the nails out because "Christ had to die," so that he could "survive," meaning that salvation for him and for the world depended on Christ's death, not on Gary's effort. Here, through the proximate mediation of his vision enacted by his counselor and friend, the ultimate mediation of Christ's Presence is effected. Of course, the effect of Christ's crucifixion is so powerful because Gary succeeds in sensing a mystical connection between what was destroying him inwardly and what was making Christ suffer on the cross. This means that what Christ takes into himself is the externalization (for Gary) of what Gary was doing to destroy himself. At the same time, Christ was supplying the notion of the reality for which to choose, namely for the sacrificial love of God on Gary's (and the world's) behalf.

Let me pause here to focus about personal transformation for Christian theology. Regardless of what theory of the atonement one holds, the personal appropriation of Christ as mediator depends upon the mystical connection between the ego's underlying self-defeating nature and the suffering and abandonment which Christ experiences on the cross. When Jesus cries, "My God, my God, why have you abandoned me?" he is quoting the opening verse of Psalm 22. Thus, he identifies simultaneously with total abandonment and with the fundamental confidence that beneath the most complete void is the Face of God. Once Christ's sufferings become an externalization of what the suffering observer is doing in and to himself, then the response or choice for the nature of Christ as the self-confirming, cosmic-ordering Presence of love becomes possible.

An important developmental observation is that the decisive experience of Gary's life came before he completed his third
year of life. We can argue with several of the childhood religious
experiences recorded at Manchester College by saying they were
confabulations of later years. However, Gary's case proves that
the early story was not only real but able to be brought forward
and used with transformational power. Had the story not been
true and deeply buried in his personal history, it is doubtful that
its reenactment could have had such a total impact upon his
personality. Thus it may be possible to have an ego-transforming
experience even before there is much of an ego to transform, just
as it is possible to have a fully developed and complex ego
without transformation.

{187}

Finally the ethical significance of Gary's vision should be at
least briefly noted. The power and health of the vision for him
depend upon its faithfulness to the transformational structure,
specifically its capacity to negate existential negation. The whole
range of Gary's activities and relationships began to fit into an
integrated picture for him after this episode, as he increasingly
trusted the vision and its implications. It may be that all ethical
conflict goes in search of a vision that simultaneously unites the
universal and the particular in the way that Gary's view of Christ
put the universe and his personal worth together. This is not to
disregard the content and the context of such visions; indeed,
visions go in search of a context for interpretation of their content.
However, the transformational vision may be what grants integrity in ethical action.

In general, these cases reveal by their very extremity the
personality's structural potential for being transformed and recentered
on an effective vision of God. When the experience of Nothingness, felt as a threat to the developing ego, is embraced by God's
own being, then even cases of extreme abandonment may
undergo transformation. Thus, the sense of cosmic loneliness
may be satisfied by existential transformation.

The emergence of this structural potential is not confined to
any particular developmental stage (since stages are defined by
the ego's development, not by its transformation). Erikson's
treatment of *Young Man Luther* makes much of the same point but

Erikson tends to interpret the religious transformation as if it were recovery from a psychotic episode rather than the expression of a built-in structural possibility. C. G. Jung recognizes the built-in structural potential but does not relate the structure directly to patterns in human development. Kohlberg's concern for "stage 7" in which the individual undergoes a figure/ground shift that answers the question "Why be moral?" points in this direction. However, it is difficult to see from his work where this insight might occur in the course of development. Also James Fowler's cases and interpretations applied to his Stages 5 and 6 suggest that after a person suffers irreversible losses (usually age thirty or over) he or she begins to undergo a shift of perspective similar to that described by Jung and Kohlberg. This looks like a natural progression in Fowler's view; so it may be important to determine whether the fundamental recentering personality that seems most likely to occur in the middle years is not a healthy structural potential that could occur much earlier. Surely adolescence is a likely stage, but so is early childhood, according to the Manchester College studies.

Finally the effect of such a transformation is not only to restore development to a centered course and to reduce states of arrested ego development, but also to initiate a process of deepening at the center of the religious life. That is, strengthening and maturing in relation to the Divine Center also has a developmental history. Saint Augustine seems to describe stages in the deepening of God's love as does Saint Frances de Sales. Elaboration of this aspect of religious development would take us far afield into the lives of the saints. Nevertheless, in consideration of the reciprocal relationship between the ego and the Divine Center that is established by existential transformation, deepening into the center should be taken as seriously as expanding ego competencies.

Conclusions and Educational Implications

The following conclusions are, of course, not final but hypotheses based on the substance of this chapter, and they are to be taken in this context.

Theological Conclusions

1. The parallel, paternal processes, all of which describe the {189}
essentials of the transformation process, describe different
versions of what we may call the human spirit. If the same
transformational logic applies when one appropriates his
redemption in Christ as when the person develops, discovers, and heals, then we have here the foundations for
understanding as analogy between the human spirit and the
Holy Spirit. The process is structured the same way in all
cases, but the key difference is that while the origin and
destiny of the human spirit is the self, the origin and destiny
of the Hóly Spirit is God.[11]

3. It should be evident that views of moral and faith development, such as James Fowler's and Larry Kohlberg's, are
deficient until they include negation, or void, as a basic
dimension of the on-going process. The developmental
history of negation is an integral part of the developmental
history of faith and morality.[12]

3. In keeping with the first conclusion, extraordinary experiences
of God are to be taken not as aberrations but as potential
evidence of the enormous freedom of God.

Developmental Conclusions

1. Apparently there is an underlying structure of transformation,
in particular the transformation of the ego, which may erupt
at almost any time in human life. However, there is a central
tendency in human development to climax transformation in
the middle years.

2. Apparently the experiences of God, which appear even in
early childhood, have enduring power to influence the

---

[11]This analogy is developed at considerable length in "Creativity in and Beyond Human
Development," a chapter in *Aesthetic Dimensions of Christian Education*, published by Paulist
Press.
[12]For a similar observation, see the chapter by Kegan in this volume.

{*190*}

subsequent development of the ego in favor of maximizing its potentials, even though the ego is decentered by such experience.

Educational Conclusions

A premise of all three educational conclusions is that education for responsible, ethical decision-making should not focus exclusively on any one aspect of the personality (that is, moral judgment, interpersonal sensitivity, or religious formulation). Rather, it should be education of and for the integrative processes which we have called the human spirit. Such an education is implicitly, if not also explicitly, education for participation in the Spirit of God.

1. Ethical education would do well to place a positive value on awareness of an engagement in *value conflicts* which engage multidimensional ethical situations. This study, particularly the case of Gary, suggests that all moral and ethical struggles go in search of an adequate, integrative vision. The dynamics by which such an integrative vision emerges are given with the creativity paradigm.

2. Ethical education should attend to a delicate balance of *authorities*. A student in any discipline must learn to trust the authority of his or her own hunches, formulations, and judgments within the context of established disciplinary practices and within the community of learners and experts in that discipline.

3. The learning context for ethical behavior should stress those qualities which foster *creative* behavior: namely, (a) an emphasis upon complexity rather than simplicity, or an emphasis upon those simplicities that master wide ranges of complexity, is to be preferred to a simplistic or prefabricated answer; (b) a sustained tension between the functions of the right and left hemispheres of the brain, especially the rational and the imaginative, should be integral to any discussion or eventual determination of an ethical course of action; (c) recognition and acceptance of personal differ-

ences, person/group differences, and group/group differences are to be supported and sustained for the sake of their creative potential, rather than decried or evaded for their failure to yield to immediate unity and conformity; and (d) a positive self-regard is to be prized as a major personal premise for embracing and sustaining conflict (for example, ethical dilemmas and relational ambiguity) with persistence and expectance.

NOTES

The structure of transformational negation is informed by Claude Levi-Strauss' formula (picture or design might be more accurate) for the construction and analysis of myth. The formula, $f_x A : f_y B :: f_x B : f_{A-1} Y$, is dependent upon a mediator (B) which has a dual function, one positive or constructive (f_y) and one negative or destructive (f_x). The key factor in this structure is a built-in double negation ($f_x 1B$ negates an original negative situation $f_x A$). The f_x of B must be of the same or sufficient magnitude as the f_x of A if the double negation is to be effective in freeing the redeemed state ($A-$) to live in and become a function of the positive function of the mediator ($f_{A-1} Y$). Double negation by the mediator is the condition for establishing not only a redemption of but a gain over the original situation. The extremity of Levi-Strauss' structuralism is to be avoided since for him there is no meaning beyond the structural patterns that govern life synchronically. The formula helps us to focus on certain essential variables in a transformation process, but this study will take diachronic meaning seriously as well. See Levi-Strauss, *Structural Anthropology* (New York: Doubleday Anchor Books, 1967), Ch. XI, esp. p. 225. Also see Maranda, E. and Maranda, P., *Structural Models in Folklore and Transformational Essays* (The Hague: Mouton and Co., 1971), p. 30 ff.

An example of how the formula is being applied in the context of this paper is as follows:

$f_x A$ represents the double-bind condition of original sin (A), whereby even effort (f_x) to extricate oneself only intensifies the condition.

$f_y B$ represents the redemptive activity (f_y) of Christ (B).

$f_x B$ represents Christ's (B) "becoming sin."

$f_{A-1} Y$ represents the forever-canceling sin ($A-1$) function (f) of the redeeming activity (y) of Christ.

This may be taken as the deep structure which underlies the diachronic patterns of transformation, as well as the structure by which we comprehend the work of the Holy Spirit as "Spiritus Creator."

ABOUT THE AUTHOR

Dr. James Loder *is Professor of Christian Education at Princeton Theological Seminary. He completed postgraduate studies at Princeton Seminary and Harvard Divinity School. He received his doctorate from the Harvard Graduate School of Arts and Sciences. In addition, Dr. Loder undertook postdoctoral studies as a Danforth Fellow in Theology and Psychiatric Theory at The Menninger Foundation and at The Institut J. T. Rousseau in Geneva.*

Among Dr. Loder's publications are Religious Pathology and Christian Faith; Aesthetic Dimensions of Christian Education, *and* The Transforming Moment. *Dr. Loder was ordained as a Presbyterian minister in 1978. His ordination, he says, "was an outgrowth of a transforming experience" similar to those noted in this chapter.*

Reference Figures
in Moral Development

DIRK HUTSEBAUT

Introduction

{194}   As parents, we often ask ourselves whether we have any control over what our children find to be good or bad. What is our role in their moral attitudes and conduct? These questions are also asked by others concerned with children, such as ecclesiastical and public authorities. And there are some young people who wonder about their responsibility for each other. Are we all, as people living together, involved in the moral growth of children and adolescents?

In this chapter, this question is approached from the standpoint of adolescents between fifteen and eighteen years old. First, they were asked what they considered good and what bad—not only in the world around them, but also as they themselves were involved in it. We let them talk and we listened. In the second phase of the study, we investigated the question of to whom the adolescents refer in the judgment of their own moral actions. Who are the important figures in such a judgment: themselves, perhaps, or also others; primarily their parents; or their contemporaries?

We also asked them whether they considered themselves believers and investigated whether this had an influence on the references in the judgment of the moral act. Another question we delved into was whether the strictness and the quality of their relationships with their parents had an influence on these references.

Initial answers are offered to these questions. It is our hope that the reader will recognize himself or herself in these situations so that a better understanding of his or her relationship with adolescents can result.

Theoretical Orientations

Like every other science, psychology searches for conceptual schemata, in which concrete research data can be placed, that can lead to and stimulate further research. In the field of moral thought, the model proposed by Kohlberg, which is a continuation of Piaget's, is certainly the best known and the most fruitful as regards research. In genetic psychology, there is a model of Erikson, who places identity central. Although I cannot develop these schemata fully in this introduction, I should like to mention some elements of them that can help situate the concrete research I shall discuss.

{195}

Briefly, Erikson's idea of identity can be described as a feeling of being and remaining the same in spite of the various situations in which one finds oneself. It is via this particular life-style that one wants to be known and recognized by others. The acquisition of an identity, which Erikson situates in adolescence, proceeds by means of a number of crises, which ought not to be considered as unavoidable disasters but rather as moments of imbalance that are necessary for progress to a new equilibrium. The development of the identity passes through a number of identifications that are more or less conscious choices made during the adolescent period. One chooses, to a degree, the persons and behavior styles that one will follow. These are integrated in a unique interplay of identifications that determines the individual life-style, the identity of a person. Of course, it is necessary that there be people present with whom one can identify.

Who are these persons and what is their relative importance? Kohlberg discusses these various figures in dealing with the important question of how moral development is possible, of what causes moral development and moral progress. In order to be able to progress morally, one must be capable of role-taking, of putting oneself in the place of another, of making another's standpoint one's own. Kohlberg sees three basic groups in which the role-taking primarily occurs: the family, the peer group, and all institutional forms, which he sees concretized mainly in social status.

In this chapter, I shall deal with the problem of the figures, or referents, that play roles in the attainment of what I would call moral identity, that is, the figures that contribute to the development of moral attitudes. I shall consider first the concrete content of the adolescent's notion of morality in order to investigate the

{196}

influence of the various figures that the adolescent finds important and to determine whether these figures promote the development of moral identity.

Collection of the Material

The basic material for this study was gathered in group discussions with Catholic adolescents. There were two groups. The first consisted of seven boys from a secondary (college-preparatory) school. The average age was sixteen. They were accustomed to meeting for the purpose of discussing religious subjects. For this study, they met four times, each time for somewhat more than two hours. Altogether, there were ten hours of discussions spread out over two months. The second group consisted of six boys, also with an average age of sixteen, from a secondary technical school. They were volunteers who were invited to discuss this theme. The six discussions of two hours each were taped and subjected to content analysis in two phases. The themes that arose in the discussions were examined, and particular attention was given to the concepts that were employed, that is, the psychic structures involved in dealing with the themes. Each discussion session ended with fifteen minutes of brainstorming in response to the following request: Name as many moral faults as you can. The results of this brainstorming were classified. All discussions were led by someone known to the boys and were observed by the researcher.

Analysis of the Discussions

Themes

The following themes arose in the discussions. I shall only list them since I am concerned here primarily with the reactions to these themes and how morality was introduced. I want to focus mainly on the more underlying elements.

Group 1

First discussion: What does morality mean? What is a moral   {197}
problem? The problem of freedom, the problem of premarital
intercourse.
Second discussion: What does responsibility for one's conduct
mean? The problem of juvenile delinquency.
Third discussion: Informing on a friend.
Fourth discussion: Eroticization of society by advertising. What is
your position on nakedness of parents? The problem of shame.

Group 2

First discussion: The marriage of Jacqueline Kennedy and Aristo-
tle Onassis. The pilot who dropped the bomb on Hiroshima.
Second discussion: An accident with a borrowed automobile. The
problems of guilt and responsibility.
Third discussion: A woman who steals from a store. The prob-
lems of compunction and anxiety.
Fourth discussion: What does it mean to be punished by God?
The problem of premarital intercourse.
Fifth discussion: Again, premarital intercourse. The problem of
love and fidelity.
Sixth discussion: Difference between morality and religion, con-
science and morality.
This summary is, admittedly, very restricted, its purpose being
only to give a general idea of what was discussed.

Underlying Structures in the Moral Thinking of Adolescents

I turn now to the underlying elements, the various psychic
structures that emerged in the discussions. This analysis of the
data formed the basis of Sections II and III of the questionnaire
(see below). Here I shall concentrate on the various referents that
arise in moral behavior. In the concrete formulation of the
questions, I shall discuss mainly the terminology, some of which

was also used by the adolescents themselves. The data were placed in a number of categories, which appeared repeatedly throughout the discussions. The sequence of presentation here reflects no particular hierarchical structure and thus gives no indication of the relative importance of the categories.

God as a Referent

God is the ultimate referent, especially for the Group 1 subjects, who were accustomed to discussing religious topics. Positively, God is seen to be the sign of the law of love, as the call to happiness among men. Negatively, God is the sign of the prohibition to transgress the law. They arrived at this, the most fundamental referent, however, only after a discussion of a series of oppositions: good and evil, inborn and acquired, universal and particular, Christian and non-Christian. Some expressed the importance of God as a referent very strongly: one can feel authentic guilt only with respect to God. Somewhat more moderately, this was also expressed as fear and shame with respect to an almighty being after doing something felt to be wrong.

Moral Faults

Three types of moral faults can be distinguished: to harm someone, to disregard the social contract, to violate sexual taboos. Three elements can always be perceived: it is a transgression of a law, it is a fault with respect to oneself, it is a fault with respect to others. In the discussion of moral faults, continual reference was made to a number of authorities: a repressive authority, society and its law; an expansive authority, the self, which is strongly marked by the narcissism of the ideal self; the authority of upbringing, with the central place being occupied by the parents.

Authorities and Referents

I shall briefly describe the various authorities and referents by indicating some of their content. The referent "God" could also be treated here but since this referent is of another order—and is so stressed by the adolescents themselves—I have dealt with it separately.

Society is seen as the most repressive authority. If an opposition is felt between society and the individual, which is expressed in terms of personal conscience and public morality, the choice is not difficult. Personal conscience is always and clearly given priority.

The self is very much in the center of the experience, and it is conceived in terms of the ideal self. One wants to move toward the ideal good, and it was clearly stated that one knows in oneself what that good is. A sort of *a priori* lucid conscience was posited that specifies what is good and what is evil. Thus, aggression directed against others is always blameworthy since it is done consciously and because it is known, on the basis of one's conscience, that aggression is not good. The shame felt after a moral transgression was also referred directly to the self. It is with respect to the ideal self that an act is to be weighed and evaluated, which results in the self being ashamed after an infraction.

The parents constitute the third significant referent. In the course of the discussions they were referred to with a very high degree of regularity, which may be an indication of the importance that is attributed to the parental role. The tension between dependence on, and independence from, the parents emerged clearly. Some of the boys stated that the dependence relationship must be eliminated; others considered the parents to be a limit and a sanction for the wishes of the adolescent. The tension between dependence and trust is almost palpably present in the texts. With total independence from the parents, there is a fear of one's own impulses and a high degree of culpability. This was very clearly present in the discussions on sexual conduct. Some said that the parents must know of and permit sexual conduct, otherwise it would be a sign of weakness and not of mutual love; others, on the contrary, said that sexual conduct is precisely the most important sign of mutual love and for this reason it must not be referred to the parents. Support is sought from the parents: one wants to know what one must do. Parental law is to be integrated and made one's own, because moral conduct is seen as an integration of a set of rules that are learned during upbringing and operate as one's moral consciousness. It seems, however, that the parental law is not yet fully integrated in the sense that, upon infractions, the reference is not to self-judgment but to a judgment by others, generally the parents themselves. It is as if one would prefer to be judged by others than to judge oneself.

The parents participate, as it were, in two facets of morality: interiorly, one wants to integrate the parental law; exteriorly, they are the authority that re-arouses feelings of dependence, with which the adolescents have difficulty coping. We could almost say that there is a search for a pure moment of independence in full knowledge that one is not and cannot be free of external influences. What it seems to be is a search for control of one's own impulses under the guise of a search for independence of external influences.

In the discussions, the subjects did not refer very often to their contemporaries, and when they did it was a matter of the search for peer group identification. Concord with one's peers is a value to be defended because it provides a feeling of security to know that others also think and act in the same way. This is expressed in, among other things, references to one's own norms, which are perceived as being similar to the norms of the peer group rather than to the norms of the authority, with which they well may conflict.

Moral Transgressions

The various moments in the experience of morality are crystallized very clearly in reaction to an infraction, namely, in the feelings that adolescents have after an act that they consider to be a moral fault. How does the adolescent feel after a transgression of a law or an ideal that he has posed for himself? I have already mentioned that three moral faults were primarily stressed: doing evil, not respecting the social contract, and violation of a sexual taboo.

Three forms of transgression were repeatedly noted: against the law, against oneself, against other people. Morally good acts were rarely mentioned in the discussions. Data on them must be derived from data on moral transgressions. Of course, this is partially due to the themes that were discussed. What is central is the feeling of having been seen, of being judged by another, together with the guilt feeling aroused by the infraction and the fear of its consequences. One is thus afraid of the sanction and of having been seen. This is crystallized in the questions about eroticism and sexuality. One defends oneself against this by "wanting" to resist and by the experience of public censure. The problem of the sexualized body arises here: one is seen or lets oneself be seen. Shame and guilt appear together: shame at having been seen and guilt for not having achieved the norm, and here clear reference was made to the upbringing, especially to the paternal role. The father was again appealed to for the resolution of the conflict. I have the impression that the tension that arises after a transgression is primarily situated in the relation between the self—the nonfulfillment of the presented ideals and the guilt feelings thus aroused—and the other referents by which or by whom one feels watched and judged. There is also the tension between the individual and the society: one judges oneself or is judged.

A questionnaire was constructed on the basis of these data—the references on the one hand and the modalities of the relationship on the other—in order to investigate further with a larger sample the feelings that are aroused by an act that is evaluated as good or evil.

In the further discussion of the construction of the questionnaire, I shall also treat the concrete modalities and terminology that the subjects used.

Analysis of the Brainstorming Sessions

The purpose of the brainstorming sessions was to discover what the adolescents understand as a moral fault. The two groups produced 152 different answers. These answers were classified according to an internal criterion, namely, the meaning of the moral fault in relation to the referents, and criteria that arose in the course of the group discussions.

The following are the categories:

1. Answers reflecting aggression toward another or a lack of respect for what that person is, for example, murder, mockery, cruelty, threatening, hate.

2. Answers with direct sexual overtones or referring to transgression of sexual taboos, for example, masturbation, rape, premarital intercourse, arousing someone.

3. Transgressions of rules made by society, which control involvement with other people and which protect relationships with them, and also violations of the norms of religion and upbringing, for example, stealing, fraud, lying, cursing, nonrespect for the Eucharist.

4. Deviations from the ideal image that one has of oneself, for example, gluttony, smoking too much, sloth, using drugs, boastfulness, needlessly risking one's life.

5. Moral faults that imply individual responsibility, one knows oneself to be responsible for others, for example, giving bad example, selling a dangerous product, professional incompetence, capitalism.

6. A special category, which covers the relations with one's parents, for example, quarreling with one's parents, cheating one's parents.

The categories that occurred most often are aggression (21.7%), the seeking of sexual pleasure (17.1%), transgression of a social law (22.4%), nonrespect for the ideal self (19%). The answers from the brainstorming sessions were used in constructing Section III of the questionnaire.

Concrete Elaboration of the Questionnaire

The questionnaire consists of three major sections: the first section is intended to discern what morality means for the adolescent; the second section is concerned with the role of the various referents after a morally good or bad act; the third section is designed to investigate the manner in which specific referents relate to specific moral faults. I shall deal with each of these sections in turn.

The Meaning of the Moral Reality for the Adolescent

Six open questions were formulated. Asking for strictly personal experiences was precluded because of the danger of refusal to answer. Thus the questions were posed indirectly.

"Give an example of an act—from life, a film, or a book—that you consider to be CLEARLY morally good." This same question was also presented for an act that is clearly morally bad. The word "clearly" was emphasized in the hope that ideal typical examples would be given that could indicate the individual's own moral criteria. The following four questions relate more to the psychological reality of the individual: "Which moral qualities would you like to have and which moral acts would you like to perform?" And the reverse: "Which moral weaknesses would you not like to have and which moral faults would you not like to commit?" Thus, the ideal criteria are sought on the one hand, and, on the other, the attempt is made to bring the data down to the personal level. These questions constitute Section I of the questionnaire.

The Referent and the Morally Good or Bad Act

Here the intention is to discern to whom and how one refers after a morally good or bad act. In the group discussions, some referents were introduced, which we can divide into two groups: *People or groups of people (dealt with in Section II).* The persons were God, oneself, parents, society. These four referents express a relation of inequality or asymmetry. Since reference was also made in the discussions to contemporaries, especially as regards solidarity, this was added as the fifth referent. Included in "contemporaries" are brothers, sisters, friends, and peers. A rather symmetric relationship is suggested with this. *Referents of a more legalistic or functional nature (dealt with in Section III).* These referents were apprehended as rather restrictive of freedom, though still as criteria for moral conduct. These are upbringing, religion, courtesy, the laws of society, personal ideals, respect for one's fellowman.

As regards interpersonal relations, two things must be taken into account:

1. One person need not exclude the other. It is possible that more than one personal referent contributes to, or has an interest in, the evaluation of a moral act. One can feel pleased with oneself after a morally good act with regard to God, parents, and contemporaries. Therefore, a seven-stage, unipolar scale was used to evaluate the importance of each referent separately.

2. The modality of the relationship to the referent can vary a great deal. On the basis of the group discussions, four modalities were chosen, each divided into two forms, for moral conduct.

   a. Expectation and disappointment: the referent expects this behavior of me or is disappointed if I act in a particular manner.

   b. Demands and prohibitions: a dependence relationship is suggested here.

   c. Appreciation or the lack thereof: the other has something valuable to offer me or the inverse.

   d. Giving example or encouraging that something not be done: a rather complex relational form that, nevertheless, was introduced into the discussions and is presented as such. Its complexity derives from the inclusion of the referent.

In Section II, where reference is made to persons or groups of persons after the performance of a moral act, the items are grouped by modality among the referents (contemporaries, parents, society, God, oneself). Twenty items were distributed over five subsections of four each. A final item was added to cover something that came up repeatedly in the group discussions: after doing something morally good, I feel bigger, and after doing something morally bad, I feel smaller. This expresses more than a reference to the self as the referent: it is an indication of a more general feeling of having fulfilled oneself or not.

Schematically, this can be presented as follows:

After doing

something good	something bad
I feel happy because	I feel ashamed because

my contemporaries, parents, society, God, myself

expect it	are disappointed
demand it	prohibit it
appreciate it	do not appreciate it
give a good example	encourage not to do
I feel bigger	I feel smaller

Relations of the Adolescent to the Normative System

What normative systems does the adolescent use in judging moral faults? Six normative systems were derived from the group discussions:

1. Received upbringing: the entire upbringing provided by parents and school.
2. Religion: the set of moral norms and acquired religious attitudes.
3. Courtesy: the set of socially approved and accepted behavior patterns.
4. Laws of society: the laws imposed by the society with which one is not always in agreement and of which one does not always see the significance.
5. Respect for one's fellowman: this is a sort of universal imperative indispensable for human life.
6. Personal ideals: the set of norms, values, and sanction patterns that one has accepted for oneself and that have a binding character.

A number of moral faults that represent these normative systems were chosen from the brainstorming sessions:

1. Use of drugs: a moral fault that implies no respect for oneself, for one's own body.
2. Being dishonest: not respecting the property of others.
3. Being cruel: being intentionally aggressive to another, taking pleasure in the destruction of another.
4. Seeing sex films in order to satisfy the sexual urge, in this case it is voyeurism.
5. Holding others in contempt: not respecting the otherness of the other in comparison with oneself.
6. Cheating someone: having no respect for social rules.

These moral faults can be presented schematically as follows: Using drugs, being dishonest, being cruel, seeing sex films, holding others in contempt, cheating someone is

against one's upbringing
against religion
against courtesy
against the laws of society
against respect for one's fellowman
against one's personal ideal

Here, too, a unipolar, seven-stage scale was used on which the subject could indicate his evaluation.

To summarize, the questionnaire consists of three major portions:

Section I: the inquiry into what the adolescent considers morally good or bad;

Section II: the inquiry into the moral referent and its various modalities;

Section III: the inquiry into the importance of the normative system in the judgment of moral faults.

In addition to the data from the three major sections, other information was also assembled. The classic personal data such as age, sex, type of school, and father's profession were requested. The degree of belief of the subject was also sought via a self-rating five-stage scale on belief in the existence of God (absolute belief,

belief with questions, doubt, tendency to nonbelief, nonbelief). Sunday mass attendance was also measured with a four-stage rating scale (every Sunday, generally, sometimes, never).

Some questions were also added to evaluate the relationship with the parents: strictness of the father and the mother on a seven-stage scale, a question about the quality of the relationship with the parents (best with the father or the mother or no difference). Finally, the position of the child in the family was asked (oldest, youngest, in between, or only child).

I have gone into the construction of the questionnaire at some length to emphasize that it was drawn up on a purely empirical basis, using the material obtained from the group discussions with the adolescents. A discussion of the application of the questionnaire appears below.

A Concrete Study

Information About the Sample

The study was done with 215 Dutch-speaking, male adolescents between fifteen and eighteen years old from Catholic schools. Regarding age, they fell mainly into two groups: 15–16 years old (41.9%) and 17–18 years old (53.5%). These two groups are distinguished because the difference within each group is less than one year. Most of the boys came from medium-size families (62.3% came from families with two to four children) but many came from large families (28.4% came from families with five or more children). Just 6 percent of the subjects in the study were only children in the family; 18.6 percent were the youngest child in the family; and 34.4 percent were the oldest.

It is important to note that 90 percent of the subjects came from families where the father exercised a profession that presumed university or other higher education. Thus there is virtually no representation of the milieu of the common laborer.

Among the subjects, 19.5 percent said that they got along best with the father and 47.5 percent with the mother. A large percentage, 31.2 percent, made no distinction between mother and father. In terms of strictness, 18 percent considered their fathers to be very strict (6 and 7 scores); 18 percent considered him not to be strict (1 and 2 scores). Only 7 percent found their mothers to be very strict and 21 percent found mothers not strict.

When questioned about the existence of God, 13 percent of the subjects said they believe absolutely in the existence of God; 42.8 percent believed but still had questions; 29.8 percent had doubts; 7.4 percent admitted a tendency not to believe; and 4.2 percent said they did not believe in God. There were more sixteen- and seventeen-year-olds among the religious doubters and nonbelievers than the others.

Seventy percent of the subjects went to mass every Sunday; 11.2 percent generally went; 12.6 percent went irregularly or never. The division for Sunday practice for the subjects is very similiar to that of the parents, although the mother went more regularly than either the son or the father.

Data Interrelationships

Those who were the youngest in the family considered their parents clearly less strict than did the oldest children or those in between. If they considered the father as the stricter parent, then they got along somewhat better with the mother. It was much more obvious, however, that they got along better with the father if they perceived the mother as being the stricter.

Processing the Data*

¶ *Section I* The concrete content the adolescents gave to the notion of morality is approached from two viewpoints:

1. Who is the actor and who the object of the moral act? We can distinguish between the others (fellowmen, friends, teachers), society, a religious figure, the family (parents, brothers, sisters), oneself.

*Only significant differences on the 5 percent level are discussed.

2. What is the content of these acts? Classification of the answers yielded the following categories: to offer resistance to aggression or sexual passions, not to want to be like or act like, internal or external motivation of an act, reference to some fundamental value area (honesty, helpfulness, self-sacrifice, to save someone, trust, not to bear resentment).

{209}

¶*Morally Good Acts.* *As actors,* the subjects named primarily the fellowman, oneself, and the peer group. It is striking that few concrete figures were named, only about fifteen in all. For example, Thomas More, Martin Luther King, Jesus Christ. *The helping of others* is clearly in the foreground together with the internal motivation of an act and the trust one must have in others. I am reminded here of Kohlberg's category: concern in the act for the welfare of others. Clearly, for adolescents, morally good conduct is equivalent to altruistic conduct. This applies to all of the age groups and all of the belief groups. The believers, therefore, see morality no differently than do the unbelievers or the doubters. For the description of moral conduct, the subjects relied principally on books and films for examples. The actual persons whom they encounter daily do not seem to offer much inspiration, with the possible exception of the father and the mother and this mostly for the fifteen- and sixteen-year-olds. This could well have been the result of an idealization of their answers, which pressed them to provide clear descriptions. They sought obvious examples that clearly expressed what they wanted to say. This kind of example is found more in books and films where the figures and their actions are more clearly delineated than in daily life.

¶*Morally Bad Acts.* In morally bad acts, as with the morally good act, the actors are primarily the self, the fellowman, and the peer group. The fellowman was given greater priority than was the case for the morally good act. The content of the acts cited concerned mostly manifestation of aggression, being insolent, sexual faults, dishonesty, not being attentive to others, and not helping others. The categories that were formed include 75 percent of all the answers. In terms of Kohlberg's categories, what is primarily involved here is the description of rules and norms. The relation of the person to these rules also appears in the foreground.

The more important piece of data here is certainly dynamic orientation to the others—self-commitment to, and attention and respect for, one's fellowman—with, again, a clear altruistic quality. The life attitude of directedness to others involves for the adolescent a strong promise of becoming himself. The self-realization, self-unfolding, is thus for him, in his concrete experience, very much related to the other.

What is considered to be morally bad is the lack of a sense of responsibility for the other (not helping, not saving), and especially aggressiveness and letting oneself go sexually (for example, the themes of the group discussions). This, according to the adolescents, does not belong to the ideal image toward which they want to evolve.

Not helping is emphasized particularly by the fifteen- and sixteen-year-olds, and aggressiveness and sexual matters mostly by the seventeen- and eighteen-year-olds. Belief or nonbelief in God seems to have little influence on the evaluation of morally good or bad behavior. Thus the adolescent assigns no different content to morality when he considers himself a believer or a nonbeliever. It must be noted that all the boys came from believing environments and that they go to a Catholic school. Thus, nothing can be said about adolescents who have little or no contact with religion or who do not go to a Catholic school.

The further questions regarding desired or undesired qualities and conduct offer little or no new information. They only confirm the preceding, which could indicate that the first two questions required sufficient personal involvement. These questions will probably not be used in the future.

Results from Sections II and III

First, I shall discuss the relative importance of the various referents in Sections II and III, and the modalities of the referents in Section II. Then I shall consider if the various referents, taken from the complete set of answers to Sections II and III, are stressed to a greater or lesser degree in function of the different variables.

Referent and Modality in the Morally Good Acts

After performing a morally good act, the adolescent feels pleased with himself and fulfilled with respect to himself, primarily, but also with respect to his parents and to God. After them, come the others and society. The modalities toward the referent are, in order of appreciation, giving an example, expectation, and re-quirement. The last plays a very small role except with respect to the self. Combining these two elements, the referent and the modality, the following appears: I expect this from myself, I value this conduct for myself, I require this from myself, my parents and others value this conduct. After this follows the religious referent in its various modalities.

The reason the adolescent feels content with himself lies only partially outside of himself, that is, with regard to his parents, God, and the others. It makes him happy largely because he expects this conduct of himself, values it for himself, or demands it of himself. This seems to be important because it indicates a presence and realization of an ideal self. The accent on expecta-tion seems to be the most important: the adolescent is concerned with himself, and the meeting of the expectations he has for himself affirms this self-respect and independence. The other referents are not absent, however, the importance of the parents being particularly stressed. They have significantly contributed and are still contributing to the value system that the adolescent delineates for himself.

Referent and Modality of Morally Bad Acts

After performing a morally bad act, the adolescent is ashamed, particularly with respect to himself, the parents, and God. The self and the parents are rated relatively higher, and God relatively lower than for the morally good act. This adds a nuance to the statement of some during the group discussions that one can feel truly guilty only with respect to God. The others and society are less involved here. It is also important to note that the scores of the self and the parents are very close to each other, which could indicate that the norms of the parents are very similar to the norms of the self.

The modalities in the relationship to the referent are being disappointed, not valuing, encouraging not to do, and prohibiting. Prohibition, as the counterpart of demand, is here also clearly less important except in relation to the self.

Combining these two pieces of data, we see: I am disappointed in myself, I do not appreciate this in myself, I remind myself not to do this, my parents will be disappointed, my parents do not like it. After these comes the religious referent in its various modalities.

The same observations can be made here as were made with respect to the morally good acts. Neither society nor the others are truly important. The self, the parents, and God are the most important. Here, too, and to the same degree, God seems to be an ultimate referential framework, which one can always fall back upon.

The Referents and the Judgment of a Moral Fault

Six moral faults were offered for judgment. If we abstract from the specific referents, the subjects reject them in the following decreasing order: acting cruelly, dishonesty, deceit, contempt for someone, drug usage, and seeing sex films. Aggressiveness and lack of respect for the possessions of one's fellowman were thus rejected the most strongly. This rank order holds for all age groups. The eighteen-year-olds deviate slightly on two points: seeing sex films and having contempt for others are rejected more strongly by them than by the others. Thus sexuality and aggression were rejected more by them although they were somewhat more lenient in their judgment of other faults than the other groups, without this difference being very significant.

As regards the rank order of the referents as reflected in the faults, we find, in order of importance, personal ideals, respect for one's fellowman, upbringing, religion, courtesy, and the laws of society. Here, too, the self is the most important referent. The laws of society and courtesy were given low scores. This can be related to the modality of demanding and prohibiting, which also played only a small role.

Religion was scored much lower than God, and seems to be an extension of courtesy. For the youngest subjects, the upbringing (parents) is more important than the fellowman, and for the subjects older than sixteen, this sequence is reversed. Thus the impact of upbringing seems to decline with age.

Influence of Some Variables

We have seen that the referents vary in importance in the evaluation of moral conduct. I turn now to the relative importance of the respective referents in function of a number of variables: age, getting along with the parents, strictness of the parents, and belief. For this purpose, the 78 items were reduced by factor analysis to 7 dimensions: peers, parents, society, religion (God), self (ideal), courtesy, and fellowman. The interpretation of these factors was done after varimax rotation.

The Influence of Age

The parents, society, God, and courtesy are more important referents for the fifteen-year-olds than for the seventeen- and eighteen-year-olds. The rank orders for the various referents for all the age groups, however, are very similar, and thus also similar to the rank order of the total group. The older adolescents referred less to the parents, probably because they have become more self-sufficient and feel less the need to refer to their parents in their moral conduct. The younger adolescents have more need of the parents as a reference point. That the younger subjects also referred more to God can be explained by the fact that more of them are among the believers: God is present in their experience with greater intensity.

Society and courtesy—an entire set of general behavorial norms—are also more important for the younger subjects. However, we may not forget that these two referents are rather unimportant with respect to the full set of the data. This was also noted by P. Mulligan, who has stated that society and its laws are not a source of morality for youth. The adolescents perceive a certain ambiguity in society, a hypocrisy, and a depreciation of human relations. That society is more important for the youngest subjects can be attributed, perhaps, to a less developed critical spirit, the older adolescents having had more experience with society and thus being more critically oriented.

Influence of Relations with the Parents

Three groups can be distinguished here: those who get along better with the father or with the mother—a choice thus having been made—or those who indicate no differences in their parental relations. When a choice was made between the father and mother, there are few differences worth mentioning, which qualifies the statements from the group discussion that have the father playing the major role. There are, however, interesting differences between the subjects who make a choice and those who do not, who express no preference.

The self, the parents, and courtesy are more important for the subjects who made no choice than for those who did. The making of a choice between the father and the mother also means that there is a slight rejection of the other parental figure, here, generally, the father. What is the significance of no choice being made? Apparently there is a rather harmonious relationship with both parental figures, which is confirmed by the higher scores given to the parents as referent. This has some consequences. The courtesy norms of the society, which are primarily transmitted by the parents, become more important. Here the scores are exceptionally high.

Taken by itself, this could indicate a rather passive, dependent attitude toward the parents and society. But there is a second fact to be considered: the self also becomes more important. The ideal self plays a greater role. I would go so far as to say that the ideal self has been clarified more in this situation than when a choice is made between the two parents. When one gets along equally well with both parents, no conficts are perceived in the values they propose. The self, which partially assumes these values, can function as a kind of radar, seeing clearly and choosing between the proposed values. One is more confident in the self and one can dare to place more trust in others.

Influence of the Strictness of the Parents

When the father is strict, more emphasis is placed on the self and on the fellowman than when the father is not strict. When the mother is strict, one refers more to God and religion and to society than when the mother is not strict.

That one refers more to the self and to the fellowman when the father is strict could support the presumption that the bond between the ideal self and the father is stronger than the bond between the ideal self and the mother. With a strict mother, no differences were found with regard to the self. As has been noted, moral conduct, which is postulated as an ideal by adolescents, must be understood as altruistic conduct. The achievement of this altruistic attitude to life is a project to be realized for the self, it is an ideal to be achieved.

The strictness of the father, however, can have two meanings: first, it can mean that the father is a man who knows what he wants and who can communicate this very clearly to the adolescent. In itself, therefore, this strictness does not constitute a threat to adolescent striving for independence. Indeed, clarity can help the self to realize its ideal. But the strictness of the father can also mean that the father is very demanding and thus he does constitute a threat to the self-affirmation of the adolescent. The stronger emphasis on the self can then be a sign of a sort of inhibited self-affirmation. In my opinion, however, the first interpretation is the more likely because of the greater emphasis that the same subjects placed on the reference to the fellowman, the central pole of an altruistic attitude to life.

Society is more important when the mother is strict. The strictness of the father has no influence on this. This could mean that society bears connotations of decorum and courtesy and that these values are primarily appreciated and instilled by the mother. Religion also becomes more important when the mother is perceived as being strict. I have already noted that religion seems to be associated with courtesy, so perhaps the same interpretation as above can be maintained. One can also accept that religious values are socialized more via the mother than via the father.

Influence of the Belief Rating

In processing the data, three groups were distinguished: those who believe that God exists, including those with questions (56%), those who doubt the existence of God (30%), and those who do not believe in the existence of God (12%). Ostensibly, we would only expect differences regarding the referent God in function of these belief groups, but it turns out that the other referents are also strongly affected by the admission of whether or not one believes in God. I should say that the belief rating indicates more about the subjects than just whether or not they believe in God. Three groups of referents can be distinguished in function of the belief groups:

1. The peers: there are no statistically significant distinctions between the belief groups in this regard. But, relatively within each belief group, we note that this referent is in the next to the last place for the believers, and fourth (of seven) for the unbelievers. Thus, this referent is more important for the unbelievers than for the believers.

2. Parents, society, God (religion), courtesy, and fellowman: here we note that there are clear distinctions between the three

groups. The believers score higher than the doubters who in turn score higher than the unbelievers.

3. The self: this clearly constitutes another situation. There is no difference between believers and unbelievers, but both score higher than the group of doubters. I want to point out that the self is the most important referent for the unbelievers and especially that the difference in the scores between the two most important referents for the unbelievers is clearly larger than for the other belief groups. The self is thus separated from the other referents much more sharply by the nonbelievers.

It is particularly striking that the nonbelievers scored everything very low, except for the self and relatively less for the peers. One could speak of a monopolar affirmation of the self, an affirmation of individual autonomy. But it is an autonomy that is sought for itself by a radical liberation from any tutelage, from that of the parents, of society, and of God—to name only the most important. The self is stressed extraordinarily, but I wonder if this is not a rather rigid self-structure since there is an almost complete lack of positive identification. Only the peers, with whom a relation of equality is possible, are still accepted to a degree. The fellowman also receives a higher score, but this clearly corresponds to the idea that morality is equated to altruism.

I think that there are some similarities here with the concept of negative identity as developed by Erikson, although with reservations since the present study concerns adolescents from Catholic schools. The general expectation pattern of the school is that the boys are believers, but these subjects describe themselves as nonbelievers, thus as not fulfilling the expectations. In a certain sense, they live more or less in a conscious conflict situation. The reaction to this conflict situation is a hardening, a certain polarization of the individual's standpoint, and for the time being this can only be expressed in an attitude of opposition.

The doubters clearly manifest another schema. They are situated everywhere between the believers and the nonbelievers, except for the self where they score clearly lower than the other two belief groups. Doubt in the existence of God thus has a broader effect, as has been shown by other studies using this belief rating scale. The doubters are clearly more hesitant, which is manifest in the lesser degree of emphasis on the reference to the self. It may also be affirmed that the belief rating measures something in addition to the belief in the existence of God. It gives an indication of how one situates oneself with respect to the reality that offers itself. The doubting group is largely made up of the younger subjects. With the fuller development of formal-operational thought techniques and by belonging more to extra-family groups, they gradually have discovered that there are other values than those that had always been imposed on them. They question themselves and lose their certainties, which also endangers the certainty of the individual self. It is aggravated when the adolescent discovers that his parents themselves do not live up to the imposed norms and that society presents a great distance between norms and actions. Doubt, and thus also religious doubt, seems to me to be characteristic of a development that will, to a certain extent, be overcome. As far as religion is concerned, this means a choice between belief and nonbelief, as has been indicated by such authors as J.P. Deconchy. When nonbelief is chosen, the self becomes very important.

For the believers, all the referents are important. God is more important for them than for the other groups, but the remaining referents are not overshadowed. This can mean two things: Either there is a good integration of everything, or everything is affirmed, which can indicate that criticism and doubt have yet to be overcome. Further research is necessary to determine which alternative applies.

Conclusions

In all exploratory research, the various explanatory hypotheses ought to point the way to further research. Therefore, I want to present a few points that I think are important in this regard.

For the content of morality, we have clearly seen that moral conduct is considered equivalent to altruistic conduct, and this both for good and bad actions. The relationship to his peers seems to be essential for the adolescent and has a central place in his self-realization. He wants to develop toward an ideal self, a process in which other people are very much involved.

{219}

On the basis of the group discussions, a number of referents are introduced that play a role in the judgment of, and the feelings regarding, moral action. I have distinguished, as does Kohlberg, between more personal and more institutional referents. It was already clear from the group discussions, and it was confirmed by the research data, that principally and almost exclusively the personal referents were significant. The more institutional referents were involved very little in the judgment of a moral act. This piece of data accords very well with the altruistic nature of moral conduct. The dominance of personal over institutional referents is also present in the religious referents. For most of the subjects, except for the nonbelievers, God is presented as an important referent, but religion has little importance in the judgment of moral faults. Religion seems to be associated more with the less important referents such as courtesy and society. Here I would note a tension, which has also been shown by other studies done among adolescents, between belief in a personal God and religion, which is the specific and limited form in which this belief in God is presented. It is a tension between the institutional and the personal. Adolescents have the tendency to opt for the personal, which can also be observed in the great emphasis they place on the individual self. Moral development seems to be a personal matter for them, which they have to work through themselves. But this has to be done always in reference to a number of figures, which we can call models, that help them to arrive at an identity. This identity is an individual life-style, which is recognized as such by others.

Pedagogical Implications

1. It would be interesting to use this research model as a teaching model. The first phase would be to investigate specific themes with the students. The second would be to establish

together which underlying structures were determinative so that, in the third phase, these underlying structures could be discussed. Thus the students could be made to realize that the discussion of moral conduct does not just happen, but that it is guided by a number of more directive principles that determine why one sometimes speaks in this specific manner about this subject. Attention could also be drawn to the evolution of the group itself. We find that students become more involved in the subject as one moves toward a more personal discussion of the themes. What is the role of the leader and is it possible to initiate this process? I would refer here to the chapter by Lickona in this volume.

2. In this study, we have seen that some of the students consider themselves unbelievers and that as such they occupy a particular place in the whole. Two points seem important to me here. First, it must be realized and accepted that there are unbelievers—or those who consider themselves such—in Christian schools. Second, belief and unbelief do not distinguish groups primarily. They are present in each of us. To be a believer—or better, to become a believer—is a movement within ourselves between belief and unbelief. Those of us who work with young people sometimes react in more believing and sometimes in more unbelieving ways. I think this plays an important role in the process of working with young people.

3. As regards the more specific content of morality and certainly of religion, I would point to the tension between dependence and independence. This seems to me to be a central piece of data that young people must be able to discuss among themselves and that was obviously present in the discussion reported above. Resolving this tension means that one can experience both simultaneously in dynamic tension. This is, I think, a basic condition for religious and moral maturity. There is often difficulty, however, in discussing them both together. Dependence alone leads to stress passivity and, in extreme cases, to a loss of self. But to stress only independence leads to an absolute determination of the self that

can ultimately result in rejection of relationships with others. The experience of this tension is particularly difficult for young people because they are striving for independence— one of the developmental tasks crucial for this period in their lives—while they feel that they are still bound to others and feel, deep within themselves, the need for these bonds.

{221}

ABOUT THE AUTHOR

Dirk Hutsebaut *is currently assistant at the Center for Religious Psychology at the Katholieke Universiteit Leuven, and lecturer in the religious psychology of adolescents at the Faculty of Theology of the same university. He studied philosophy at Leuven-Hervelee and psychology at the Katholieke Universiteit Leuven. His licentiate thesis was entitled "The Experience of Loneliness among Religious" and his doctoral thesis, "Belief as a Lived Relationship."*

His primary interest is in the religious psychology of adolescents, and more specifically in the role of parents, peers, and other reference figures in the religious becoming of the adolescent. What role, for example, do these figures play in the inception and resolution of religious conflicts? What is the significance and function of religion in the experience of young people, what do they call religious, and when do they consider themselves as believing? He believes answers to such questions can help parents begin their dialogue with their older children.

Justice and Responsibility: Thinking About Real Dilemmas of Moral Conflict and Choice

CAROL GILLIGAN

Introduction

Kohlberg, in his study of reasoning about hypothetical moral dilemmas, articulated the development of the concept of justice, focusing on the rationality of the moral conception rather than on the actual consequences of choice. Given his focus on the ethical ideal of a morality of universal rights, he ignored the problem of special obligations as well as the problem of unlimited obligation that arises when duties are correlative to rights.[1] His concern centered on considerations of equality necessary for freedom in a democratic society rather than on considerations of generosity and love, which he placed in a higher, religious domain.

The study of reasoning about actual dilemmas of moral conflict and choice provides a complement to Kohlberg's work through the elaboration of the conception of moral responsibility and the development of an ethic of care. The concern with the actual consequences of choice and the recognition of the disparity between intention and consequence changes the parameters of moral judgment and expands the nature of moral concern. This expansion takes place through a process of decentering that proceeds from the discovery of the relativity of truth to contextual understanding of the legitimacy of different points of view. Thus the integrity of moral respect comes to include responsibility for the knowledge of self and other gained through the experience of relationship that leads to psychological and social understanding.

> The matter does not appear to be so desperate if one does not ask too exclusively (as the Baumgartens, now as often, do): "Who is morally right and who is morally wrong?" But if one rather asks: "Given the existing conflict, how can I solve it with the least internal and external damage for all concerned?"
>
> Max Weber, *Jugendbriefe*

At the end of his lecture on "Politics as a Vocation," Weber turns to consider the place of politics as a calling, "within the total

---

[1]K. Daffner, "Special obligations and Kohlberg's theory of moral development." Undergraduate honors thesis, Harvard University, 1978.

ethical economy of human conduct."[2] Here, in the arena of human action where power legitimizes access to violence, "ultimate Weltanschauungen clash, world views among which, in the end, one has to make a choice."[3] This choice involves not only a problem of justification regarding the relation of means to ends but also a problem of accountability, given the disparity of intention and consequence. Thus ethical principles when put into practice tangle with the facts of human experience, resulting in two maxims of conduct, "fundamentally differing and irreconcilably opposed."[4] In Weber's distinction, these maxims are the ethic of ultimate ends that appears in the gospel of the Sermon on the Mount and the ethic of responsibility that instead takes care of the sins of the world.

Conduct derived from an absolute ethic, which if not trivial must be all or nothing—"not a cab which one can have stopped at one's pleasure,"[5]—is kindled by "the flame of pure intentions,"[6] generating acts of exemplary value regardless of their actual consequence. In contrast, the ethic of responsibility, informed by "the experience of the irrationality of the world,"[7] demands "an account of the foreseeable results of one's action"[8] whatever the purity of its intention. Thus, while an ethic of ultimate ends relies on the principles of moral philosophy, an ethic of responsibility depends on knowledge of psychological and social reality.

In the psychological study of moral development, the tension between these two orientations appears in actual situations of conflict and choice where "these ethical paradoxes" arise.[9] As long as judgment is hypothetical, this tension can remain in the background, but it readily comes to the fore in the joining of ideal

---

[2] M. Weber, "Politics as a vocation," in H.H. Gerth and C. W. Mills, eds., *From Max Weber: Essays in Sociology* (New York: Oxford University Press, 1946) p. 117.

[3] *Ibid.*

[4] *Ibid.* p. 120.

[5] *Ibid.* p. 119.

[6] *Ibid.* p. 121.

[7] *Ibid.* p. 122.

[8] *Ibid.* p. 120.

[9] *Ibid.* p. 125.

and real. Since the formulation of moral ideals is a development of adolescence, this joining has been considered to mark the transition from adolescence to adulthood.[10] Then the metaphysics of justice and truth come together with an awareness of "the reality of things,"[11] initiating the shift that Erikson describes from the ideological morality of adolescence to the adult ethic of taking care.[12] This shift depends on the ego's capacity to deal with the realities of consequence and choice as well as on an expanded awareness of the realm of moral possibility. This expansion, as it comes to center on the themes of justice and responsibility, has been the subject of my research.

In the past several years I have been engaged in two separate studies that focus in common on the development of thinking about real dilemmas of moral conflict and choice. The first study is an ongoing longitudinal investigation of moral and ego development in late adolescence and adulthood.[13] The study began in 1970 with a sample of college students selected on the basis of their interest as sophomores in taking a course on moral and political choice. The men and women in this sample, when interviewed at the end of their senior year and then again by Murphy[14] at age 26, were asked about their personal experiences of moral conflict and choice. The second study was an experiment in nature designed around an ongoing event, the decision being made by women considering whether to continue or abort a

---

[10]See J. Piaget, *Six Psychological Studies* (New York: Random House, 1940/1967); R. Inhelder and J. Piaget, *The Growth of Logical Thinking From Childhood to Adolescence* (New York: Basic Books, 1958): E. Erikson, *Insight and Responsibility* (New York: W. W. Norton & Co., 1964); and C. Gilligan and L. Kohlberg, "From Adolescence to Adulthood: The rediscovery of reality in a post-conventional world," *Proceedings of Jean Piaget Society Annual Meeting*, 1973.

[11]J. Piaget, *Six Psychological Studies* (New York: Random House, 1940/1967), p. 68.

[12]E. Erikson, *Insight and Responsibility* (New York: W.W. Norton & Co., 1964).

[13]C. Gilligan and J. M. Murphy, "Development from Adolescence to Adulthood: The Philosopher and the Dilemma of the Fact," in D. Kuhn, ed. *Intellectual Development Beyond Childhood* (San Francisco: Jossey-Bass, on press): and J.M. Murphy and C. Gilligan, "Moral Development in Late Adolescence and Adulthood: A Critique and Reconstruction of Kohlberg's Theory" *Human Development*, (on press).

[14]J.M. Murphy, "The Development of Moral Reasoning from Adolescence to Adulthood." Unpublished manuscript, Harvard University, 1979.

pregnancy.[15] Since the women were interviewed at the time they were pregnant and again at the end of the following year, the study traces the natural history of thinking as it traverses the bounds between judgment and action.

Together these studies represent a departure from the procedure that Kohlberg followed in deriving his six stages of moral development. While Kohlberg analyzed the judgment and resolution of hypothetical dilemmas that he had constructed, I sought instead to discover the experiences that people construed as moral problems, and to describe the moral constructions they imposed on the ongoing events of their lives. Thus in my studies the participants defined as well as resolved the moral dilemmas. In addition, by focusing on actual experiences of moral conflict and choice, I sought to trace the process of developmental transition and to describe the actual life contexts in which changes in understanding take place. Consequently, my research not only elaborates the moral constructs brought to bear on the interpretation of social experience, but also elucidates the role that experience plays in the process of moral development.

When the analysis of thinking about real dilemmas of moral conflict and choice is combined with Kohlberg's analysis of judgments of hypothetical moral dilemmas, two different moral orientations arise along the lines that Weber describes. The conception of an ethical ideal emerges more clearly in hypothetical judgments which delineate actions of exemplary value regardless of their actual consequence. In contrast, the judgment of real dilemmas pertains more to the actualities of consequence and choice, so that the context in which action occurs becomes central to its ethical consideration.

However, while the tension between hypothetical and real is, in general, a characteristic of thought, the reflective capacity of adolescent reasoning coupled with the greater consequence of

---

[15]C. Gilligan, "In a Different Voice: Women's Conceptions of Self and of Morality" *Harvard Educational Review*, 1977, 47, 4, pp. 481–517.

M. Belenky, "Conflict and Development: A Longitudinal Study of the Impact of Abortion Decisions on the Moral Judgments of Adolescent and Adult Women." Unpublished doctoral dissertation, Harvard University, 1978; and C. Gilligan and M. Belenky, "Crisis and Transition." Unpublished manuscript, Harvard University, 1979.

adult choice engages this tension in a particular way. The dialectic of assimilation (the fitting of experience to the structures of thought) and accommodation (the modification of thought to fit experience) expands when the structures of thought encompass the full universe of logical possibility and when experience comes to include a wider range of human activity. In this expansion of mature understanding, the interplay of moral judgment and action brings the formal structures of logical thinking together with the contextual understanding of choice and consequence. The resulting transformation in moral judgment that Gilligan and Murphy have described[16] suggests a recapitulation in late adolescence and adulthood of the fusion between the ethics of justice and love that Piaget witnessed on a less reflective plane in *The Moral Development of the Child*.[17]

I will begin with a review of the course of moral development as it has been described in the work of Piaget and Kohlberg and has come to focus on the concept of justice. Then I will turn to the concept of responsibility, considered by Loevinger and Blasi to provide the bridge between moral judgment and action, linking the domains of thought and behavior. However, the understanding of responsibility has also been cited by Erikson[18] and Perry[19] as the distinguishing feature of mature ethic and by Niebuhr[20] as central to the understanding of moral agency. Thus the development of the conception of responsibility would appear critical in the evolution of mature moral thought, particularly as it reflects upon action and the activities of commitment and choice. Following the review of the literature on justice and responsibility, I will turn to the findings of my research, which describe the evolution of an ethic of responsibility as a complement to the justice approach. Through excerpts from interviews with people about their actual dilemmas of moral conflict and choice, I will delineate

---

[16]Gilligan and Murphy, *op. cit.*

[17]J. Piaget, *The Moral Development of the Child*. (New York: Free Press, 1932/1965).

[18]Erikson, *op. cit.*

[19]W. G. Perry, Jr., *Form of Intellectual and Ethical Development in the College Years* (New York: Holt, Rinehart and Winston, 1970).

[20]H.R. Niebuhr, *The Responsible Self* (New York: Harper and Row, 1963).

the discovery of moral responsibility and show how the changing conception of responsibility articulates the development of an ethic of care.

Moral Development in Childhood and Adolescence

The empirical study of morality as a matter of cognitive development began with Piaget's interest in the origins of intelligence, which led him to investigate children's conceptions of both the physical and social world. Just as he observed children's understanding of causality to govern their explanation of natural events, so too did he find that their conception of morality structured their social understanding. Tracing the development of this understanding in his descriptive account of *The Moral Development of the Child*, Piaget considered his work as a "scaffolding" upon which a psychology of moral development could later be built.

In outlining the dimensions of that psychology, Piaget traced with the broadest of brushstrokes the lines of connection between judgment and action, tracing the origin of "the two moralities of childhood," the heteronomous and autonomous conception of rules, in the social experiences of constraint and cooperation that characterized the life of the growing child. In the brilliant simplicity of his naturalistic study of children's consciousness and practice of the rules of the game, Piaget discovered in the microcosm of children's play the paradox of childhood egocentrism, the coexistence of an almost mystical respect for rules with an almost complete disregard for their practical application. Children who considered rules sacred and obligatory were observed to play "more or less as they choose," untroubled by the most serious infractions and "pay[ing] no attention to [their] neighbor."[21]

Piaget then described how the advent of cooperation in the activity of children's play brought with it a change in moral understanding that centered on the concept of justice as fairness.

---

[21]Piaget, *op. cit.* pp. 60–61.

As the authoritarianism of revenge and retribution gave way to the distributive equality of democratic fairness, moral judgment progressed toward the "rational ideal" of full reciprocity. Piaget saw the realization of this ideal as occurring at around the age of ten, when

> the consciousness of rules undergoes a complete transformation . . . [and]the rule of the game appears to the child no longer as an external law, sacred insofar as it has been laid down by adults; but as the outcome of free decision and worthy of respect in the measure that it has enlisted mutual consent.[22]

Thus in childhood moral judgment begins with the concept of fairness as equal retribution (an eye for an eye) and develops through the understanding of distributive justice that guides a "progressive equalitarianism," until, toward the ages of 11 and 12, equality is "tempered by considerations of equity" that refine it "in the direction of relativity." Then,

> without leaving the sphere of reciprocity—generosity, the characteristic of our third stage—allies itself to justice pure and simple, and between the more refined forms of justice, such as equity, and love, properly so called, there is no longer any real conflict.[23]

In this fusion of justice and love, the cognitive and affective aspects of morality merge as mutual respect supercedes unilateral respect and in turn is followed by generosity. In the process of this final transformation, judgment becomes contextually relative, so that "instead of looking for equality in identity, the child no longer thinks of the equal rights of individuals except in relation to the particular situation of each."[24] This expansion in the understanding of reciprocity that enables the child to take into account the reality of psychological and social difference enlarges the understanding of respect and leads to the activity of care.

When Kohlberg took up and extended Piaget's work by studying the responses of adolescent boys to hypothetical dilem-

---

[22]*Ibid*. p. 65.

[23]*Ibid*. p. 324.

[24]*Ibid*. p. 317.

mas of conflicting rights (e.g., the right to life versus the right to property) he discerned in their responses to these dilemmas a progressive realization of the rationality of justice and fairness. Following his sample at three-year intervals, he discovered that the changes in their judgments over time followed an invariant sequence of six stages that described a developmental progression. This progression depicted the transformation and reconstruction of the concept of justice through three levels of social understanding, describing the shift from an egocentric to a societal to a universal perspective on the fair resolution of moral dilemmas.

In the process of development, the moral egocentrism of the simplistic equation of "would" and "should" gave way to a conventional understanding of morality as inhering in the shared norms and values that sustained social relationships and institutions. This conception then was superceded by a principled understanding of justice as the rational equilibration of individual equality and social reciprocity. However, while thus wedding Piaget's genetic epistemology, striving toward structures of equilibrated adaptation, to a Socratic conception of virtue as justice, redefined as democratic fairness, Kohlberg also separated judgment from action and made moral development a matter of cognition alone. He traced this development through the re-balancing processes of assimilation and accommodation as a progression in judgment toward the democratic ideal of individual and social equality. Basing his notion of equality on the concept of natural rights, he balanced these rights as competing claims and attached to them the correlative duty of respect.

Given the utopian and metaphysical penchant of the thinking of his adolescent male subjects, Kohlberg found that the capacity for formal operational thought and the reflective separation of self from society allowed the construction of a hypothetical "prior-to-society" position from which reality could be realigned in accordance with principles of fairness. Thus tracing the development of moral judgment through the adolescent flowering of formal reasoning, Kohlberg showed how thought came to transcend the bounds of a conventional moral understanding and allowed the adolescent to envision the possibility of a world more just. At the same time, he demonstrated how the concept of justice engaged the adolescent's preoccupation with fairness and freedom, indicating how these concerns could be incorporated in a principled moral philosophy.

However, while this philosophy represented a powerful articulation between the adolescent's psychological concerns with issues of separation and his social concerns with injustices that result from the infringement of human rights, it did not address dilemmas of conflicting obligations that arise from these, obligations to the responsibilities that choice entails. Since such dilemmas pertain to experiences of commitment involving irreversible choice and sustained responsibility for the welfare of others, they lie for the most part beyond the bounds of the adolescent's domain. These experiences, however, engender a universe of problems which have to do with the particularity of commitment and the ethics of special obligations rather than with the universality of rights that is embodied in the ethic of justice. This conflict between the universal and the particular is discussed by Freud (1929) and also by Erikson (1964) in examining the disparity between the psychology of love and the prescription of The Golden Rule. Thus the paradoxical truths of human experience, the tension between separation and attachment that divides the ethics of justice and love, emerge in the experiences of commitment that mark the transition from adolescence to adulthood.

In concluding their discussion of *The Growth of Logical Thinking from Childhood to Adolescence*, Inhelder and Piaget observe that the transformations of adolescent thought contribute to the development of personality through "the moral autonomy finally achieved by the adolescent who judges himself the equal of adults."[25] I begin by asking whether the transformations of personality that occur through the adult experiences of commitment and responsibility contribute to the growth of thought by relativizing the conceptions of justice and truth and generating a more compassionate understanding. In order to understand the transformations that occur when the philosopher becomes the

---

[25]Inhelder and Piaget, *op. cit.* p. 350.

king, engaged in the actual exercise of power and thus in the politics of everyday life, it is necessary to broaden the conception of moral development to include both justice and responsibility.

The Development of Responsibility

While Piaget and Kohlberg have illuminated in rich detail the development of the concept of justice, the growth in the understanding of moral responsibility has only begun to be systematically explored. Niebuhr in the essays compiled in the volume on *The Responsible Self* sees the "rise of the new symbolism of responsibility"[26] as "an alternative or an additional way of conceiving and defining this existence of ours that is the material of our own actions."[27] To the image of man-as-maker that informs a teleological ethic and the image of man-as-citizen that underlies a deontological morality, Niebuhr adds the image of man-as-answerer in defining an ethic of responsibility. This image of the responsive and responding self incorporates the discoveries of the natural and social sciences that "have taught us to regard ourselves as beings in the midst of a field of natural and social forces, acted upon and reacting."[28] Thus Niebuhr brings an interactionist epistemology to bear on the understanding of moral agency, so that the understanding of responsibility can take into account

> the way in which opportunity on the one hand, (and) limiting events on the other, form the matrix in which the self defines itself by the nature of its responses.[29]

In outlining an approach to "man's self-conduct that begins with neither purposes nor laws but with responses; that begins with the question, not about the self as it is in itself, but as it is in

---

[26]Niebuhr, *op. cit.* p. 56.

[27]*Ibid.*

[28]*Ibid.*

[29]*Ibid.* p. 59.

{234}

its response-relations to what is given with it and to it,"[30] Neibuhr indicates how this approach implies a new question for moral inquiry. This question asks "What is going on?" It can be answered only in a context of interaction, and the knowledge it generates thus reflects the social construction of reality. Summarizing his argument, Niebuhr concludes that . . .

> purposiveness seeks to answer the question: "What shall I do?" by raising as prior the question: "What is my goal, ideal, or telos?" Deontology tries to answer the moral query by asking, first of all: "What is the law and what is the first law of my life?" Responsibility, however, proceeds in every moment of decision and choice to inquire: "What is going on?" If we may use value terms then the differences among the three approaches may be indicated by the terms the *good*, the *right*, and the *fitting*; for teleology is concerned always with the highest good to which it subordinates the right; consistent deontology is concerned with the right, no matter what may happen to our goods; but for the ethics of responsibility the *fitting* action, the one that fits into a total interaction as response and as anticipation of further response, is alone conducive to the good and alone is right.[31]

Within this insistently contextual understanding, Niebuhr restores the narrative to moral discussion, locating accountability in the interchange of interpretation and response, placing moral inquiry in a context of historical time and place, and tying responsibility to the social solidarity of ongoing community. Relying on Mead for "the recognition that the self is fundamentally social . . . a being which not only knows itself in relation to others but exists as self only in that relation,"[32] Niebuhr rejects the primacy of the individual and the society of social contract. While Kohlberg builds his just society on a universal respect for natural rights, Niebuhr's ideal lies instead in "a life of responsibility in a universal community."

Thus the self that is the center of Niebuhr's ethic of responsibility comes to understand that "in my responsive relations with

---

[30]*Ibid*. p. 60.

[31]*Ibid*. pp. 60–61.

[32]*Ibid*. pp. 71–72.

others, I am dealing not with laws but with men, though with men who are not atoms but members of a system of interaction."[33] Since the discovery of the constancies of that interaction allows responses to be interpreted in "anticipated and predictable ways," a knowledge of social psychology underlies the development of an ethic of responsibility. In defining the moral life as the responsible life with the self as the responsive and responsible moral agent, Neibuhr establishes a fundamental link as well between the concepts of identity and morality. To him the moral question "To whom or what am I responsible?" is joined to the question of identity, "In What community of interaction am I myself?" By insisting that morality be understood in a context of human interaction, Niebuhr goes beyond both a deontological and teleological ethic and argues instead for a more psychological understanding in which self and morality are joined.

In this respect Niebuhr's ethics are very closely tied to the work of Loevinger and Blasi[34] who suggest that "since responsibility, by definition, consists in establishing relations of consistency between self and action," its study may give rise to a theory that links the domains of mental structures and behavior.[35] The study of the development of responsibility, in providing the bridge between judgment and action, would also elucidate the relation of moral and ego development, as separately conceived by Loevinger and Kohlberg.

Since changes in the conceptions of self and other alter the understanding of social relationship, these conceptions centrally shape the understanding of moral problems. This understanding becomes of particular importance when, in the transition from adolescence to adulthood, thought begins to reflect upon actions of increasing social power and consequence. Thus the understanding and uses of power become central to the depiction of moral development, both in the context of personal relationships

---

[33]*Ibid*. p. 73.

[34]J. Loevinger with the assistance of A. Blasi, *Ego Development* (San Francisco: Jossey-Bass, 1976).

[35]*Ibid*. p. 446.

and in the more public societal domain. Kohlberg[36] pointed toward this distinction between childhood and adult moral development by considering moral experience in childhood to be largely cognitive and symbolic while describing it in adulthood as becoming in some sense more real. Thus he speculated that "personal experiences of choice involving questioning and commitment in some sort of integration with stimulation to cognitive-moral reflection"[37] may be necessary for the development of a mature moral understanding. However, for Kohlberg, as for Piaget,[38] the question remained open as to whether adult experiences of commitment and responsibility gave rise to new structures of thought or whether such experiences were best understood as leading to the accommodation of formal thought or as a matter of ego development.

Blasi directly addresses this question in his study of children's conceptions of responsibility, which he measured by their responses to hypothetical story dilemmas.[39] Defining responsibility as "that relation of necessity that an individual establishes or recognizes between himself and his own action,"[40] Blasi considers a judgment of obligation to be interposed between moral judgment and action and a judgment of accountability to mediate the effects of action on thought.

In his study he found that children's judgments of both obligation and accountability progress through an order of increasing maturity that follows the same lines of structural differentiation described by Loevinger and Kohlberg's stages. However, Blasi also observed a gap between the understanding of

---

[36]L. Kohlberg, "Continuities in Childhood and Adult Moral Development Revisited," in P. Baltes and W. Schaie, eds., *Life-span Developmental Psychology*, 2nd ed. (New York: Academic Press, 1973).

[37]*Ibid*. p. 41.

[38]J. Piaget, "Intellectual evolution from adolescence to adulthood," *Human Development*, 1972, *15*, 1, pp. 1–12.

[39]A. Blasi, "A development approach to responsibility training." Unpublished doctoral dissertation, Washington University, 1971; and A. Blasi, "Personal responsibility and ego development," in R. de Charms, ed., *They Need Not be Pawns: Toward Self-direction in the Urban Classroom.* (New York: Irvington Publishers, 1976).

[40]Loevinger, *op. cit.* p. 446.

morality and of responsibility, in that the criteria children applied to decisions of right and wrong were not always applied to decisions of responsibility. In both instances, though, the criteria followed the same developmental progression, beginning with a concern about punishment and physical consequences and developing through considerations of social relationships to an understanding of contract and commitment which to Blasi signifies a mature approach.

However, the ways in which differing ethical commitments can be associated with different understanding of responsibility is described by Weber's contrast between an ethic of ultimate ends in which,

> If an action of good intent leads to bad results, then in the actor's eyes, not he but the world, or the stupidity of other men, or God's will who made them thus, is responsible for the evil. However, a man who believes in an ethic of responsibility takes account of precisely the average deficiencies of people. . . . He does not feel in a position to burden others with the results of his own actions so far as he was able to foresee them; he will say: these results are ascribed to my action.[41]

Since Blasi's studies centered on children's responses to the Responsibility Story Test, he did not find the divergences in ethical orientations or the conflicts in commitment that Weber describes.

Empirical evidence for such a divergence in ethical orientations comes, instead, from the work of Perry who, like Kohlberg, followed intellectual and ethical development in the college years. However, where Kohlberg speaks of the order of reason and the conception of the moral ideal, Perry talks of the disorder of experience, the realization that life itself is unfair. How thought comes to account for experiences that demonstrate the limits of both knowledge and choice is the problem that Perry sets out to address. In doing so, he describes a revolution in thinking that leads to the reperception of all knowledge as contextually relative, a radical "180° shift in orientation" that follows from the discovery that,

---

[41]Weber, *op. cit.* p. 121.

{238}

In even its farthest reaches, reason alone will leave the thinker with several legitimate contexts and no way of choosing among them—no way, at least that he can justify through reason alone. If he then throws away reason entirely, he retreats to the irresponsible in Multiplicity ("Anyone has a right to his opinion"). If he is still to honor reason, he must now also transcend it.[42]

Because "the ultimate welding of epistemological and moral issues" makes the act of knowing an act of commitment for which one bears personal responsibility, Perry centers the drama of late adolescent development of the theme of responsibility which enters first as a new figure on the familiar ground of logical justification. However, because the understanding of responsibility demands a contextual mode of thought, the concern with responsibility signifies a fundamental shift in ethical orientation that ushers in what Perry calls "the period of responsibility." Following this shift, judgment "is always qualified by the nature of the context in which one stands back to observe," so that the interpretation of the moral problem determines the way in which it is judged and resolved. Thus principles once seen as absolute are reconsidered within a contextual interpretation. As a result, moral problems formerly seen in philosophical terms as problems of justification come to be considered in psychological terms as problems of commitment and choice.

Thinking About Real Dilemmas of Moral Conflict and Choice

In my research on people's judgment and resolution of actual experiences of moral conflict and choice, these experiences were often described as precipitating a crisis in moral understanding. The awareness of contradictions between judgment and action or of a disparity between intention and consequence led to a period of questioning and doubt which had the hallmarks of stage transition. My interest in the role that life experience played in late adolescent and adult moral development was initially spurred

---

[42]Perry, *op. cit*. pp. 135–136.

by the retrospective reports of students in the college sample who identified their confrontation with real moral dilemmas as turning points in their conceptions of self and morality.

A college senior when asked how she would describe herself to herself spoke of the changes in her self-concept that resulted from her becoming pregnant and deciding to have an abortion. Prior to this experience, she "had never really seen the importance of decision-making and for the first time I wanted to take control and responsibility for my decisions in life." She described "the whole month or so I spent waiting and thinking" about this decision as a time that led to:

> a change in self-image because now that you are going to take control of your life, you don't feel like you are a pawn in other people's hands. . . . You have to accept the fact that you have done something wrong, and it also gives you a little more integrity because you are not fighting off these things in yourself all the time. A lot of conflicts are resolved, and you have a sense of a new beginning.

Thus, the awareness of moral agency was tied to a new sense of identity and an ethic of responsibility, a willingness to be accountable. The moral judgment that led her to consider that "what I had done . . . was so wrong," had initially led her to expect blame and condemnation from other people. When instead her friends offered understanding and help, their response contradicted her assumptions and provoked a reassessment of her own behavior as a failure of responsibility rather than a fall from innocence. This reassessment then "brought to light things in myself, like feelings about myself, my feelings about the world."

> It came to light to me that I was not taking responsibility [and that] I could have gone on like I was, not taking responsibility. So the seriousness of the situation brings the questions right up in front of your face; you see them very clearly . . . in a way that you can't just keep going through school or even going through that course [on moral and political choice].

In taking responsibility for serious choice, she begins to take responsibility for judgment as well, having learned through experience the meaning of respect ("how important it was to have somebody acknowledge your feelings and not condemn you"). Just as she has gained a greater sense of integrity through accepting responsibility for herself, she also has developed a new understanding of others, a "sympathy for people having trouble." Morality, she says, "is not separate from life."

As she locates morality in the activities of everyday interaction and response ("Are you going to take advantage of this person or not?") rather than in the abstraction of absolutes, she begins by defining it negatively as "almost not making moral judgments at times . . . not impinging on somebody else." She then goes on to criticize this position, saying that a concern with noninterference

> is one of the easier ways to look at [morality]. That is somewhat how the system of rights works—as long as you do not impinge on somebody else's rights—that isn't a very complete definition. I keep on wanting to look for a system of thought that has what I want to say and I really can't [find one]. I guess that I look at [morality] more as concern. Morality shows concern in the sense that concern itself comes from an awareness of the importance of life and an awareness of death and being able to empathize with another person's situation. Otherwise you would not really care. So morality starts with a sense of concern for not only what happens to you, but what happens to somebody else.

Her emergent conception of morality as an active care and concern, arising from feelings of connection with others and manifest in the activity of taking care, vies with her old moral judgment which led to her "great personal feeling of being very evil" because of a pregnancy that was "at least in the eyes of society, if not my own, a moral sin." In taking responsibility for the pregnancy and recognizing the seriousness of the abortion decision, she begins to consider the consequences of choice, the actual legacy of moral decisions rather than their justification. In her judgment of Kohlberg's dilemma of whether a husband should steal a drug to save the life of his wife when he can do so in no other way, she says that he should "because of the memories." She goes on to say that the druggist who refuses to sell the drug for less than ten times its cost "does not stand to lose a whole lot and what the other person stands to gain is so much more," but goes beyond this utilitarian formulation to reconstruct the dilemma as a problem of responsibility. The action of stealing then is seen to arise out of a relationship of care, and this action is deemed necessary because of the failure of responsibility and care on the part of the druggist and society at large.

{241}

Her adoption of a responsibility construction of the moral problem in Kohlberg's dilemma follows from her recognition of the limitations of the justice approach. Realizing that while deriving obligations from rights would solve this particular hypothetical dilemma, she also sees the limits of this formulation by realizing its actual implications:

> You can take that principle and expand on it [only] so far because that would get back to if you had enough money to alleviate the ills of the world or you had some kind of power to do that, would you devote your life to that?

Thus her resolution of Kohlberg's dilemma ultimately turns not on principles of human rights but on the psychology of human relationships that has come to center her moral concern.

The discovery of moral agency and responsibility appeared repeatedly to be at the center of the crises reported by the students who traveled beyond the bounds of their adolescent reason to discover the actual constraints and consequences of choice. These students often reported their discovery that principles of justice did not encompass the complexity of the moral problems they faced. Such principles, in fact, were often found to coexist with feelings of intolerance that limited knowledge of both self and others. One student concluded that his claim to an objectively principled moral truth had distanced him in a relationship with a woman and blinded him to the realization of what—from her perspective—was going on. Then the claims to an absolute moral judgment was seen to depend on "staying really far apart from people" or "hardening yourself to people you are really close to" and ignoring the reality of more distant suffering. Consequently it was often in the experience of relationship that moral judgment came to be transformed.

Just as Piaget observed that the experience of cooperative

play overcame the egocentrism of childhood morality and led to the development of the concept of justice, so too did the intimacy of adult relationships appear to overcome the egocentrism of adolescent morality and give rise to an ethic of care. This new understanding of moral responsibility overrode the objectivity of moral truth and made moral judgments contextually relative, matters of commitment and responsibility. Moral understanding, opened to context, could include the different logic of feelings and the considerations of time and place that shaped the consequences of choice. Thus moral development beyond adolescence engaged the dialectic of justice and responsibility through the actual experiences of moral conflict and choice, which demonstrated the tension between ideal and real.

While the discovery of moral responsibility appeared repeatedly to be at the center of the crises reported by students as turning points in their moral development, the understanding of responsibility has a developmental history of its own. This history is delineated by the pregnancy decision study which focused on an actual choice and indicated the different ways in which responsibility could be understood.

While the different constructions of the concepts of self, justice, and responsibility that were manifest in thinking about the abortion decision recapitulate the structural progression in thinking described by the stages of Kohlberg, Loevinger, and Blasi,[43] the study itself goes beyond that work in addressing the relationship of judgment and action in the naturalistic context of an actual choice. The experience of turning judgment into action often led to a change in understanding both of the parameters of moral judgment and of the moral consequences of choice. These changes centered on the concept of responsibility whose rediscovery at different levels of understanding articulated a process of development in which the conception of social relationship came to be transfomed.

Within the single perspective of an egocentric understanding bounded by individual need, the pregnancy decision revolved around the woman's sense of how best to get what she wanted.

[43]Gilligan, "In a Different Voice," and Belenky, *op. cit*.

These wants were centered on issues of survival, seen as precarious in the absence of power. Thus the abortion choice in its simplest construction was considered only from the woman's perspective with others seen as either enhancing or impeding her ability to meet her own needs. Having a baby might offer a way of leaving home or having someone to keep you company while having an abortion might preserve the freedom to go out every night or finish school.

{243}

In the transition to conventional understanding, the word *responsibility* appeared to signal an emerging contrast between moral decision and the "selfishness" of willful choice. As the separation of "would" from "should" was embodied in the counterpoint of selfishness and responsibility, the pregnancy decision was reconstructed as a problem of human relationship. The consideration of the perspective of others and the ability to differentiate the needs of parent and child began to inform an understanding of relationship which centered on issues of responsibility and care. Then the woman began to ask whether she was or could be a responsible person, capable of caring for a child and thus worthy of societal recognition and respect.

In its conventional understanding, responsibility was defined by the shared norms and values that underlie social relationships and institutions. Responsibility was both prescribed and limited by social roles and rules which for women included prominently the role of the mother as the responsible, caring, and ultimately good person. As conventional concepts of feminine goodness came to anchor identity and define security, these concepts replaced the former image of self as embattled and struggling alone for survival. Now security was seen to lie in the continuation of social relationship, with the result that a concern with sustaining relationships replaced the preoccupation with individual needs. With membership in community, moral responsibility was shared and danger lay in the ostracism that followed the violation of social norms and values. In this context, the legalization of abortion presented women with a confusing situation since the act itself was legally approved but violated the norms of feminine goodness. Since the good woman sacrificed herself to others and never caused anyone harm, the abortion decision could only be justified when having a child appeared to be selfish or having an abortion could be construed as an expression of love and care. Within this construction, the notion of moral agency readily became hopelessly confused, since women, acting in others' behalf, held others responsible for what they did. ("He was my life. . . . I would do anything for him. . . . He made me feel that I had to make a choice and there was only one choice to make . . . that [abortion] was my choice, I had to do it.")

When the contradictions in this understanding pierce the strategies of evasion and disguise, then the second transition begins in the shift from goodness to truth. Once again the issue of responsibility is raised, but this time with respect to the knowledge of what is actually going on. The concern with the actualities and consequences of choice, whatever the conventions of its judgment, follow from the woman's realization that she will be left with the memories of abortion or with the responsibility for deciding to continue the pregnancy and have the child. Thus the recognition of her own agency, that in the end she makes this decision, as well as of her accountability for the consequences of this choice, leads to a reexamination of what this choice means apart from its conventional constructions. While the good woman had taken responsibility for others, for helping and pleasing and meeting their needs, the recognition of moral agency extends responsibility to the self as well.

The recognition of moral agency, however, not only leads to a differentiation between self and others but also fosters the extension of care to include both self and others. In this context, the abortion decision comes to involve not only an ethic of respect for life, but the recognition that life itself depends on a context of social relationship. Thus both the choice to have an abortion and the choice to have a child come to be considered in terms of their actual consequences as well as in terms of their moral possibility.

The salience of the abortion dilemma to some of the students in the college study came in part from the fact that it highlighted so clearly the inadequacy of moral absolutes. Within a principled rights conception of morality, given the logical priority of the right to life, abortion is clearly wrong unless the fetus does not have rights, in which case the moral problem disappears. However, in this context the rights which otherwise had seemed to be natural come to appear as arbitrary instead, in that the discussion of whether the fetus has rights leads eventually to the question of how to decide. However, when construed as a problem of responsibility, the morality of abortion becomes contextually relative, and dependent on the contingencies that will affect the actual consequences of this choice. Thus the tension between an ultimate ethic and an ethic of responsibility erupts in a reflective understanding of the abortion decision since on the one hand abortion is clearly wrong in ending a developing human life while in another sense it may be "the right thing to do" given the likely consequences of bearing the child. When women's thinking about the abortion choice comes to center on these considerations, then they no longer speak of a right solution but rather of choosing "the lesser of two evils." However, in abandoning the search for goodness, the wish to be above blame and reproach, they begin to take responsibility for choice and to develop a greater capacity for compassion and care.

The collision of two different ethical orientations around the morality of abortion is addressed by Daniel Callahan.[44] Describing the progression in his own thinking from an initial moral absolute, a belief that abortion was morally wrong in that it violated a respect for life, he goes on to indicate how his thinking changed through experiences which led him to see the actual consequences of this choice. Thus while abortion is wrong when considered in terms of an ethic of ultimate ends based on an absolute respect for life, within an ethic of responsibility, it may be the better decision. Callahan in the end reaches the conclusion that the morality of abortion resides in an ethic of "personal responsibility" that recognizes the reality and the seriousness of the choice to end a developing life, but also the necessity for that choice in situations where it is not possible either for the individual or for the community to provide adequate love for the child.

---

[44]D. Callahan, *Abortion: Law, Choice and Morality* (London: MacMillan, 1970).

Callahan's conclusion is essentially the same as that of a woman in the college study who said that her experience of working as a counselor in an abortion clinic led to a state of "moral turmoil" in which she was "just constantly torn." Caught between the two orientations of an ultimate respect for life and a recognition of the responsibilities that raising a child entailed, she came to the realization that the morality of abortion began in the recognition that it posed a moral dilemma to which there was no easy solution; "It is so easy to say, well, either/or and it just isn't like that. And I had to be able to say, yes, this is killing, there is no way around it, but I am willing to accept that." Realizing that "there are times when killing like that is necessary, but [it shouldn't] become too easy," she considers the morality of abortion to depend on the recognition of what is entailed both in terminating and in continuing the pregnancy and the willingness, in light of that knowledge, to accept responsibility for choice. Thus she relinquishes the purity of an absolute ethic for an ethic of responsibility, dependent on a full recognition of what is going on and on the ability to understand the foreseeable consequences of choice.

In coming full circle back to Weber's distinction between an absolute ethic and an ethic of responsibility, his insistence on the necessity for "a trained relentlessness in viewing the realities of life"[45] is echoed by Niebuhr's belief that responsibility is manifest in the inquiry as to "What is going on?"[46] The significance of experiences of actual choice in the process of moral development lies in the fact that these experiences generate the knowledge of psychological and social reality on which the ethic of responsibility depends. When the reality of consequence brings this knowledge to bear on moral judgment and choice, moral understanding changes from a formal to a contextual mode. Then the passion of moral commitment is tied to a responsiveness to the actualities of choice so that, in the end, Weber's opposition becomes two

---

[45]M. Weber, *op. cit.* p. 127.
[46]H.R. Niebuhr, *op. cit.* p. 60.

complementary orientations which "only in unison constitute the genuine man, the man who *can* have 'the calling for politics.'"[47]

> Reflecting on the condition of moral maturity, Weber finds it immensely moving when a *mature* man—no matter whether old or young in years—is aware of a responsibility for the consequences of his conduct and really feels such responsibility with heart and soul. He then acts by following an ethic of responsibility and somewhere he reaches the point where he says: "Here I stand; I can do no other." That is something genuinely human and moving. And everyone of us who is not spiritually dead must realize the possibility of finding himself at some time in that position.[48]

Given the power that adulthood brings in the cycle of human life and the potential for exercising power in a way that does violence to others, moral development in adulthood depends on the dialectic of justice and responsibility. Only then can moral understanding encompass the actualities of choice and the moral possibilities that inhere in the uses of power, both for good and for evil.

Educational Implications

The educational implications of the foregoing discussion reside in the recognition that moral development extends beyond the ability to conceive an ethical ideal and pertains to the actual exercise of power, the actualities of consequence and choice. The study of thinking about real dilemmas of moral conflict and choice brought the concept of moral agency into the center of moral development. When judgment was tied to action, thinking shifted to issues of responsibility and care, and the understanding of what these activities entailed also followed a developmental progression. Thus this work represents an expansion of Kohlberg's research in two directions which have important

---

[47]M. Weber, *op. cit.* p. 127.

[48]*Ibid.*

educational ramifications. First it ties moral and ego development together by showing how the concept of self includes an understanding of moral agency which informs the conception of moral responsibility and changes the nature of moral concern. Secondly, it adds to Kohlberg's focus on justice a complementary ethic of care. These ethics together delineate the developmental progression of differentiation and integration in the moral domain, with the concept of justice charting the progression in the understanding of individual equality and the concept of care marking the realization of the interdependence of the human community.

In this expanded conception of moral development, moral education which aims to foster development would focus on developing the understanding of both justice and responsibility, the former through the experience of equality gained through participating in a democratic society, the latter through the experience of care gained by membership in a responsible community. Then the concepts of equality and reciprocity would be joined to the activities of generosity and love, bringing the cognitive and affective bases of morality together and preparing for an adulthood of justice and care. Thus the knowledge of the function of rules in adjudicating disputes according to an order of justice and fairness rather than personal preference or brute strength is complemented by the knowledge of self and other, of the contextual fabric of intention and the consequence that sustains the narrative of human relationship and brings individuals together into community.

ABOUT THE AUTHOR

Dr. Carol Gilligan *is Associate Professor of Education at the Harvard Graduate School of Education. She is a member of the Laboratory of Human Development and is engaged in research on moral and ego development. Dr. Gilligan received a graduate degree in clinical psychology from Radcliffe College and a doctorate in social psychology from Harvard University. She has taught at the University of Chicago and Harvard University.*

Dr. Gilligan has written with Lawrence Kohlberg on moral development in adolescence and is currently working on expanding the conception of human development to include the experiences of women and of adult life. Her publications include: "In a Different Voice: Women's Conceptions of Self and of Morality" and two articles that she authored with J.M. Murphy: "Development from Adolescence to Adulthood: The Philosopher and the Dilemma of the Fact" and "Moral Development in Late Adolescence and Adulthood: A Critique and Reconstruction of Kohlberg's Theory."

Reciprocal Relationships Between Moral Commitment and Faith Profession in Worship

HERMAN LOMBAERTS

Introduction

Does the liturgical experience preserve its credibility in the face of the promises and possibilities of modern society? Is social and political commitment to a new society a more convincing witness of evangelical inspiration than ritual religious practice? Is conversion to individual religious experience the only way to surpass human finiteness?

Many people, and particularly the members of the younger generation, often experience these questions as dilemmas. And the enormous effort expended in the adaptation of the liturgy has made us still more conscious of the vulnerability of our faith confession with respect to the autonomous, ethically, socially, and politically divided society.

In this chapter, I tell the story of a group of young people who dared to respond to this vulnerability and conflict of society in the context of a Eucharistic celebration they designed themselves. Then, on the basis of a psychological analysis of the celebrations, the pattern of the religious symbolization process is sketched as a key moment in the development of the belief attitude and the liturgical experience. Third, I show how social and political involvement forms a real foundation for the deepening of faith involvement. This leads to a number of practical conclusions for moral and religious formation.

This study on the relationship between moral involvement and faith expression is based on material assembled through participant observation of a liturgical experiment. The point of departure for this initiative, which was designed by the young people themselves, is on the pastoral-pedagogical level. In modern society, is it still worthwhile to take the faith experience seriously and to express it in sacramental, ritual form? And, if so, what liturgical expressions can take up and orient daily life?

These questions have many facets. To the extent that it was primarily older adolescents who formulated the problem and reacted to it, the aspect of the development of faith in this life phase comes strongly to the fore. The entire problematic is very much involved in the interplay and intermingling of human and religious realities, which are very difficult to disentangle. Ethical

awakening and involvement are, in such a context, inevitable. A
liturgical experiment offers the possibility of tracing the structural
regularity of their mutual influence.

{253}

But before beginning the report of the systematic research, it
is well to present first what happened. So, I begin with a history.

Worship and Faith: Room for Experimentation

The observational material at my disposal concerns the celebration of the Eucharist. The subjects were a group of young people
and adults who, between 1968 and 1974, participated in an
"alternative" celebration of the Eucharist in Brussels each Sunday. After an initial period of moderate attendance, there were
often four to five hundred participants.

The initiative arose among a few young people who had
agreed among themselves that they wanted to get away from the
normal practice of the Sunday Mass. In their eyes, it represented
an unreasoned and dependent form of religious and moral
behavior which they had acquired in their formal Catholic education. The Sunday Mass was experienced as not being operational
in their real lives. It was also the expression of a kind of test: Are
the Eucharist and the faith able to be defended and integrated in
their sociocultural context? In what form is this possible, and
what would this involve? In addition, participation in the
Eucharist was seen as compromising with regard to their peers; it
put them in a vulnerable position with respect to the accepted
hierarchy of values and patterns of behavior.

This decision to leave the usual Eucharistic places was
important. Because of their upbringing as Catholics, their initiative could easily be interpreted as a transgression or as infidelity.
Initially, no one could predict whether anything positive would
come out of their "rebellion."

But their withdrawal from institutional liturgy forced them
back on themselves: What are, then, our concerns? What are we
working for? What is normative for our existence, and where does
it come from? In such a context, the problem of God soon arises.
They retained the faith and the Christian experience as recog-

nized values. But what are these values? In addition, they raised questions of ethical action and moral conduct with respect to themselves, the world, the society, and other people.

In this way, these young people were posing their questions regarding the faith and Christian life in terms of self-decision and of individual responsibility. They wanted to contribute to the decision-making process and to design a space where all this could be explored with the necessary margin of freedom. Working together, they soon found this space and thus opened the door to a reintegration of the rite of the Eucharist into their concrete aspirations and to a new recognition of its value. In their eyes, the atmosphere of friendship and respect for difference in personal opinion and life-styles necessarily had to influence the evolution of the celebrations.

The Eucharist of the experiment differed from normal Eucharist in exterior form: place, role division, progress of the celebration, interactional forms, objectives, prayers of the faithful, and so forth. In addition, it differed from the classical Eucharistic celebration by the concern that was given to involving concrete human realities and the manner in which they were taken up into the liturgical sacramental event.

To make it operational, the group gradually developed a number of norms to control the initiative in function of the questions raised and the objectives intended. Here are five of them, which are the most important:

1. A Eucharistic celebration was to be designed and the responsibility for it shared. This implied that they, in their own "profane" space, could gradually desacralize and destructure the classical liturgical space in order to contact more directly the dynamic forces that their coming together ought to make possible.

2. Interpersonal relations were considered vital: mutual acquaintance, community formation, receptivity, encounter, openness, friendship were pillars without which, for them, the Eucharist was unthinkable. In that climate, personal expression, more spontaneous participation, discussion, and greater mobility were striven for and valued.

3. By varying their contact with each other, they wanted to make experiential moments possible so that the celebration would take on a strong experiential character and the "here and now" become meaningful to them, the participants.

4. There was an obvious concern for concrete life, facts, situations, people, and the world and for the collection of information about society, along with involvement in social needs, the development of solidarity, and care for people.

5. There was a consciously expressed intention to celebrate the Eucharist together and to form a community that seriously reflected together and wanted to deepen the experience of the uniqueness of the Christian faith.

These norms were considered by the group to be vital and decisive for the success of their initiative. Over the years, three distinct and successive ways of handling them emerged. From 1969 until the end of 1972, they contributed to the identity of the group and controlled the celebrations. In 1973, the emphasis gradually shifted to a style proper to the meetings of a "prayer group," where the mediating interpersonal relationships and the human realities were less predominant. From October 1973 on, there occurred a rather authoritarian attempt to change the rules. The group was told to take the charismatic movement as the only valid model for the shaping of the Eucharistic celebration. This was the source of a great deal of conflict and finally led to the group's demise.

The Pattern of a Celebration

Each celebration consisted of two parts and lasted for about two hours. The atmosphere of the first part was joyful and welcoming with singing, the development of a theme, discussion of events, experiences, ideas, and so on. The second part consisted of the celebration of the Eucharist itself and integrated the different moments of the first part. For example, the following celebration centered on the theme of solidarity:

The First Sequence

In the first sequence, the participants were reminded of situations of need in the world. Reactions were offered. One cannot remain indifferent. With sympathy and material contributions, one will try to ameliorate these situations. A discussion develops in which the effectiveness of such actions is called into doubt. Then someone tells how he worked in developing countries and how he still continues to work for the betterment of these countries now that he is back in Europe.
(A song is sung)

The Second Sequence

In the second sequence, attention is drawn to the "poor." The way in which some deal with the poor in the city, specifically with regard to housing, is discussed. The political implications of granting assistance to the poor are stressed. Some begin to understand that the problem of poverty and solidarity must be seen in a broader context than the short term mitigation of immediate needs.
(A song is sung)

The Third Sequence

In the third sequence, the participants again offer examples that reflect how they experience their solidarity with the poor in a concrete way. The participants are then urged to actually set to work. The moderator observes how acting in concert actually accomplishes things, as is shown by the examples.

Accomplishments are only possible when people help each other to see things. It is essential to be involved together in the resolution of these problems. This attitude provides another conception of the purpose of coming together in the youth mass. The quality of the open solidarity with human situations gives meaning to the Eucharistic gathering.
(The next song reiterates this idea.)

The Fourth Sequence

In the fourth sequence, concrete proposals are made: Who will {257} help? In the discussion, the emphasis is placed on the encounter. The spectacular is to be avoided. A complaint is registered about the lack of follow-up on the promises made in the youth mass. Further discussion occurs on the realization of the concrete proposals.

After another song, the first part is synthesized. Two scriptural texts are read: the Parable of the Good Samaritan and the Pauline text on the unity and diversity of the body. These various elements are taken up in the second part of the Eucharistic prayer.

The Structure of the Celebrations

The structure of the celebrations was characterized, in this first period, by a great deal of inventiveness and variation in style and procedure. Both the group dynamic and the content aspects were centers of interest. Out of all the things that were created, I want to deal in particular with socio-ethical commitment. Obviously, this is a dimension that is explicit in the framework of the Eucharist but that is not experienced in the same way by everyone, nor accepted by everyone as being essential to the Christian faith. This became a major source of conflict from 1973 on because a subgroup advocating the charismatic approach gradually gained more and more influence. The data from the first period—before 1973—will be used to clarify the problem I am concerned with here. What happened afterward gradually divorced the sociopolitical reality from the Eucharist.

Moral Commitment: An Inevitable Concern

Identifying the Challenge

The socioethical dimension occurred on two levels in the course of the experiment. First, this dimension appeared in the themes that were chosen for the celebrations. Of the 133 celebrations registered, 61 were built around an explicit anthropological theme. These themes can be classified under three headings: subjective (friendship, loneliness, hope, joy), psychosocial (interpersonal relations, celebrations, encounter), and sociopolitical or society-related. Twenty-six of the celebrations came under this last thematic category and treated subjects such as violence and nonviolence, political involvement, leprosy, immigrants, justice and injustice, labor, revolution, environmental protection, and homes for delinquents. The remaining 72 celebrations were related more to explicit religious themes such as God, Christ, the Church, Church and society, faith and prayer, and the Eucharist itself.

The celebrations, organized around explicit anthropological themes, stimulated the posing of moral problems and the introduction of the problem of moral involvement. The sociopolitical and society-related themes were direct occasions for the mobilization of the participants and for perceiving a direct relationship between the socioethical dimension and commitment on the one hand, and faith on the other.

Second, the participants in the youth mass tried to meet specific, local, and well-defined social needs; they tried to challenge the policies of civil authorities and the relations between various population groups in the city, especially as regards social justice and interpersonal relations (prejudice, racism, exclusive groupings); and they wanted to participate in protests against particular international situations.

A number of these intentions were implemented. For example:

1. Language courses and cultural and manual activities for the children of foreigners;
2. Language courses for foreigners and help with the governmental administrative apparatus;
3. A club for socially handicapped youths;
4. Participation in demonstrations and actions with regard to property condemnation and property polarization in the neighborhood;

5. Demonstrations and actions for the acquisition of civil voting rights for foreigners and to draw the attention of the public to specific situations of social injustice in the world;

6. Initiatives designed to provide occasions for the blind and the handicapped to participate in cultural activities and in social life;

7. Assistance to people in temporary and acute material difficulties;

8. Demonstrations and consciousness-raising activities with regard to conscientious objection, environmental protection, violence, and nonviolence;

9. Critical reactions to, and critical participation in, programs assisting developing countries.

Thus, the ethical or moral involvement was expressed, in the first instance, in social terms, focusing on the sociopolitical aspects of concrete situations, often from the immediate vicinity of the group. The development of sensitivity to social realities, the collection of information, the critical approach to organizations and social structures, and the active concern to change these situations, insofar as this was possible, were considered to be an important element of the Christian personality and an ethical task for a faith community.

Initiatives were taken by members of the Eucharistic community. These initiatives originated in the Eucharistic assembly and were reviewed in the same context. It must be noted that the adults present often played an important role in the realization of these initiatives. The experiment, consequently, offers data relevant to the mutual relationship between ethical involvement and a Eucharistic assembly explicitly oriented to the expression of faith.

An Impossible Task?

Keeping in mind the specific psychology of youth that characterizes the experiment (Is the youth mass a moratorium?)[1], there is

---

[1] E.H. Erikson, *Identity, Youth & Crisis*, (London: Faber & Faber, 1968), p. 236.

still the problem of the conflictual relationship between concretely involved praxis and the contemplative quality and actions proper to the liturgical celebration. On the one hand, the participants were concerned with a critical approach to reality in its historical specificity, its potential for further development, its contradictions, and its disproportion between groups and individuals. From a militant point of view, activities were planned to change the actual situation to which they had direct access. The arguments and atmosphere of conflict represented an absorbing concern and ceaseless involvement. On the other hand, the religious attitude rests on a radical transcendence of the directly accessible human world to a reality recognized in faith so that the believer, by interiorization and reflection, can give form to his recognition of God in a doxological-ritual expression.

The question rises, therefore, of whether it is possible to sustain both in the context of the liturgy of this youth mass. It was not just a matter of tensions between realities, of differences in language and action, of differences in thought categories. The people who gathered in this liturgical space also lived in conflict with each other within their actual social relationships and opposed each other when designing specific projects. There was also the tension between people who wanted to concern themselves with the socioethical dimension and those who did not. The latter had a not unreasonable fear that the Eucharist would be manipulated to direct conflicts to a specific resolution. If it was possible to relate moral commitment and the liturgy, was it also possible to articulate the person-related conflicts within the Eucharistic celebration, to work them out, and to take them up into the sacramental experience?

What technique or model can a believing community use to carry out such a task? Obviously, these questions must be approached from many different angles for any clarity to be achieved. The very posing of the problem seems to me to be important, since it never would have arisen from the participants in a normal liturgical celebration because of the ahistorical and apolitical character of the language and ritual schema. This led some to a radical rejection of the standard liturgy and the intentional construction of a "militant" liturgy. It also raised questions about the reciprocal relation between moral commit-ment and faith expression, about the rite as such.

However, I am interested here primarily in the data that {*261*} were assembled from actual observation. How does the subject come to a profession of faith in God, in Christ, as a radically other dimension which, because of this radical otherness, acquires its own authority and becomes a norm for the approach to human reality? How does the believer reconcile in himself the conflict inherent in the autonomous construction of social relationships and moral action and in the confession of dependence on God?

Analogous questions arise in the development of Christian involvement in highly controversial social situations such as occur, for example, in developing countries. There are reports of other occasions where similar questions were central and where the Eucharist provided the opportunity for a local faith commu-nity to integrate socioethical commitment.[2]

Screening the Process: The Focus

Only the first portion of the celebration is relevant to our concern here. At this time, the participants could contribute to the content of the liturgy and interactions occurred within the group with regard to the treatment of the themes. Within the established framework of these gatherings, the first part provided rather spontaneous and often unexpected approaches to the themes. Thus it is possible to take into account what the participants did in their treatment of specific themes and how their mutual interac-tion polarized qua content. Often, this part of the liturgy was ended with a scriptural text that served as the terminal point of an evolution, as a confrontation with the standpoints taken by the participants.

Generally speaking, this part could be compared with the "Liturgy of the Word." Its interior dynamic and structure, how-ever, differed markedly from the classical schema. The movement

---

[2] I. Berten, "Il est mort pour nous . . . il vit," *Lumen Vitae*, XXXIII (1978), pp. 265–296.

was reversed. Instead of listening to the Word of God and then, via a homily, searching for its applicability to life, here the concrete situation was postulated and brought into confrontation with the biblical Word, which then invited the participants to personal and collective deepening.

To make our study possible, it was not sufficient to limit it to descriptive observation and then to derive conclusions on the basis of intuitive insights. Therefore a theoretical analysis of religious symbolism was used.[3] The symbolization process seems to be the most fundamental nucleus of the problem.

Theoretical References

According to the theoretical concept of the religious symbol that was used, there is a dynamic tension between the anthropological components and the religious, invisible reality connected to them. In the structuring association of these poles, the symbolic order is constituted and the religious dimension becomes a faith reality for the subject.

An important piece of data here is the place that is ascribed to experience, with its peculiar and irreplaceable status as a source for consciousness-raising and knowledge. Experience forms the anthropological point of departure for, and the substructure of, the religious symbol: the anthropological, visible elements are interwoven with the sensory-affective experiential moments, which are characterized by immediacy. It is proper for man to transcend this character of immediacy by a distancing through which the experiential moment and its first meaning are lost. Specific elements of the experience are thus available, as mediating factors, to engender a new meaning, to function as signifiers, and to be taken up in an association with other, invisible religious signifiers.

This process occurs via language which is oriented by a socialization in which religious tradition has normative value.

---

[3]A. Vergote, "Dimensions anthropologiques de l'Eucharistie" in *L'Eucharistie, Symbole et Realite*, (Gembloux, Duculot, 1970), pp. 7–56.

Through being involved in reciprocal interactions in such a process, a bond of solidarity is created within a group, and a collective faith identity structure is made possible.

In order for this process to occur, it is presumed that the subjects can experience its distinct dynamic moments and can deal with them in a personal manner (experiential moments, memories, associations, language and expression, reflection, interpersonal interactions, contact with a historical tradition, and so on).

Content Analysis

Using this theoretical base, a system of categories was designed to facilitate the analysis of the content of the celebrations. Seventy celebrations that took place between 1971 and 1974 were taped and subjected to content analysis. On the basis of general observation while participating and the initial review of the tapes, it could be expected that various factors are present in the youth mass that would permit the community to be actively involved in the symbolization process.

The problem may be formulated as follows: What do the speaking participants do with the tension between the anthropological and the religious dimensions? Does the community bring them together in a structuring relationship peculiar to the religious symbolic order? Three things were examined in the transcripts of the tapes in this regard:

1. Identification of elements as introduced by the participants, thereby distinguishing between anthropological and religious elements on the one hand, and elements that form a specific, recognizable bond between them on the other.

2. Identification of the social field with which the introduced elements are concerned, thereby distinguishing between elements situated outside the context of the group and the youth mass and elements having to do with the life of the group and with the Eucharistic celebration as such.

3. Identification of the speech acts used by the participants to place themselves in relationship to these elements: an event is evoked, the community is requested to take a position or to do something, a particular reality is explained, and finally, a position is taken regarding the reality under discussion or such a position is articulated.

Results of the Content Analysis

The first general observation is that anthropological realities were discussed virtually as often as explicitly religious ones. When the participants spoke freely and interacted with each other through the introduction of data, situations, and so on, they were concerned with both poles to the same degree. Second, the participants brought up elements that were related to facts, situations, and realities *outside* the group context and the celebration to the same extent as they brought up elements that were directly related to the experience and the reality of the group and of the Eucharistic celebrations as such. Thus the group was not predominantly centered upon itself nor was it overly preoccupied with its own group experience. Real-life situations from the world beyond the group also contributed systematically to the evolution of the content of the celebrations

The second general observation is that there was a striking shift of emphasis in this regard. When the participants spoke about something from outside the celebrating group—thus about subjects to which each could contribute out of his own personal experiences and observations—then, in 75 percent of the cases, they spoke about anthropological realities without any reference to a religious dimension. Religious facts and religion in the society—as the participants perceived it—from outside the context of the youth mass were referred to in only 25 percent of the cases. But when the participants introduced facts, situations, considerations, and so on, that were directly related to the group and the celebration as such, then reference was made to the religious dimension 75 percent of the time.

In other words, attention to the religious dimension was most frequently given when reality was being discussed that concerned the "here and now"; that is, when the subjects were situations that almost everyone was aware of and in which everyone, to a greater or lesser degree, was involved. This is to be expected since we are dealing with a liturgical celebration, a religious reality. But it still may be asked why the religious realities from outside the group were not discussed in the same proportion.

I presume that this may not be attributed simply to the fact that a Eucharistic celebration is involved. I think another factor is present, namely, the conditions or circumstances under which these gatherings were held and which almost always concerned anthropological aspects and involved clear experiential elements. These are the circumstances that made it possible for the participants to focus on the religious pole in such an explicit manner, namely, in reference to the concrete situation that they had built together.

Considering the distribution of the content and the interrelations of the content categories, I think a dynamic assimilation process can be indicated. Moreover, when the nature of the speech acts—or the relationship the speakers experience with regard to the content evoked—is taken into account, then it seems that they were personally affected by the facts and situations proper to the life of the group and the celebration, and that they, from a position that has emotional overtones, can speak about them—more than is the case when a situation or event from "outside" the group was discussed.

I would argue that the strong experiential character of the gatherings (character of immediacy, the "here and now" aspect, the affective implications) is one of the determinative reasons for the religious dimension being so frequently referred to in connection with the group situation and the celebration. However, it is still a question whether the participants formed a structuring symbolization process with their speech acts and their mutual relations. This is affirmed on the one hand by a relatively small number of expressions that explicitly articulate the structuring movement. This occurred in two ways: in an ascending movement when a participant expressed how a concrete experience or interiorization formed a basis for a new understanding and appreciation of faith in God and in Jesus Christ and its meaningfulness; and in a descending movement when a participant expressed how faith had an inspirational effect on the experience of a concrete relationship to another person and the world.

The formation of a structuring symbolization process is also affirmed by a structuring bond that runs in a less direct but still constant manner throughout the entire experiment. Both movements, the ascending and the descending, are clearly and complementarily recognizable in more than 50 percent of the celebrations studied. There is a clear indication of the involvement of the group in a symbolization process. In other words, the anthropological reality and the faith dimension are related in a structuring manner and therein a profession of faith is made possible for the participants.

Content analysis clarified the components of the religious symbol as well as the dynamic structure bond in the evolution of the celebrations. It is important to note, however, that not everyone was involved in this process in the same manner. The participants primarily introduced anthropological data and rendered value judgments on them, while it was mainly the preparatory group, the leader, or the celebrant who developed the structuring bond between the anthropological and the religious poles. When, however, the global experience of the youth mass was discussed, then the participants could establish this same bond from their own experience and could specify its meaning.

Interpretation of the Observations

As has been mentioned, the choice of the themes and the evocation of facts and experiences were largely determined by interest in well-determined social, ethical, and political situations. This was the case with respect to the neighborhood where the gatherings took place, concrete situations in the city, national, and international events. The concrete activities that were undertaken reinforced this interest. The association of the Eucharist with concrete activities for the benefit of other people was considered a necessity by many. The consequences of such socioethical involvement were often mentioned in the course of the gatherings and seem to have had a decisive influence on those who were directly involved in such activities.

{267}

The content analysis provided a valuable framework that permits further interpretation of how the bond between the socioethical involvement and the faith expression was experienced in the course of the brief history of the youth mass. I would like to indicate some aspects of this.

Personal and Shared Involvement

First, the content profile is significant. Many participants mentioned facts, situations, and events as they experienced, noticed, and observed them in the general context of their lives. Many of these facts were connected with their experiences and represented specific values for the speaker. But such experiences were necessarily unique to the speaker and could not be shared completely. The experiential background as such is difficult to determine as it was not common. Only the context of the celebration, where the facts were described, was common to all.

The fact that these situations from outside the group were mentioned is important in itself. They thus took on value within the group. This appears from the numerous expressions used by the participants to indicate a position with respect to these situations. But they had little attractive power and did not readily lead the participants to become personally involved and to act on them. This reality stayed at a distance.

When facts or situations were brought up in which the participants—or at least some of them—were directly involved because of a direct relationship to the celebration and the group, then there was a common experiential base. This made the content discussable in another manner. Among other things, this was the case when several of the participants were involved in a concrete initiative that they wanted to accomplish somewhere in the city.

Contact with social reality provided and initiated a variety of experiences. Relationships were formed with other people. Material data were assimilated, reflection and analysis took place, and a broadening awareness of a more general social structure in society developed. On this basis, those involved proceeded to take initiatives and to engage in activities.

Precisely this being involved in communal action created a cycle of new experiential moments, of reflection, of broadening, and so on. This had a profound effect on those involved. Afterward, this was often described as something decisive, as a definitive acquisition that changed their attitude with respect to social reality, and that oriented their sensitivity for concrete actions in new directions. Enriched by this "experience" of being taken up into the cycle and later specifying how one had been influenced, the participants came to the celebration, that is, to a well-defined "context." Thereupon, a new kind of distancing and interaction occurred.

Those involved developed a relation between their involvement and the context of the liturgy and proceeded to examine it more consciously. Ultimately, when they had the occasion to speak about this and to formulate their experiences and reflections, they often came to a reformulation of their faith in, and insight into, the person of Christ. In addition, the belonging to the group and the participation in the celebration, where the specific circumstances of coming together and interacting continued to be central, seem to have a stimulating and motivating influence on their further involvement in social reality.

In other words, we can recognize an interaction between the ascending and the descending movements: the quality of the involvement with other people contributed to another kind of sensitivity to the religious dimension, as this was approached in the context of the celebration. Moreover, this new kind of relationship with the Eucharistic celebration permitted another kind of approach to the social reality and gave it signifiance. This became apparent on the occasion of a television report on a project that some of the participants were carrying out among foreigners. When the (unbelieving) reporter noted how much the participants felt that they were motivated by the youth mass, he found it incomprehensible.

{*269*}

Conflicting Matters

The second dimension that this interaction between socioethical involvement and the liturgy brings out clearly is the attention that was given to the conflictual aspects, the ambiguities, and the contradictions inherent in each actual situation in society. They formed objects of critical reflection through which the subgroup concerned found a complementary reaction in the community. In the discussions, reference was often made to scriptural texts that reflected analogous aspects in order to examine the various positions and to test them against the actions and fundamental inspiration of Jesus of Nazareth.

A Home Base

Third, I want to point out once again the importance of the context of the Eucharist in which the moral involvement of the participants was taken up. This context was strongly tied to experience. The conditions that determined the form of the celebration were focused to a large degree on experience in the "here and now" in which the participants were able to feel that they were directly involved. The tension between this experience and the unavoidable distancing was typical for this youth mass and can be seen to have formed a background that certainly played a role. The participants constantly fell back on it. In other words, the fact that there existed an open community that was concerned with the faith reality and searched for a possible confession of faith provided a context in which the various aspects of socioethical involvement were taken up and developed to more explicit self-consciousness and restructuring of the faith insight.

Taken by itself, perhaps, socioethical involvement does not

offer sufficient possibilities for the creation of greater sensitivity or any other position with respect to the reality of faith. But the communal experiential context offered by the youth mass and the ultimate praxis expressed in it made it possible for those involved to be able to work through their "experience" with socioethical involvement and to make it an enriching contribution to seeing the faith dimension in another perspective.

Returning to the theoretical point of departure for my analysis, I would contend that, under these conditions, a sequential development of the religious-symbolic order can be recognized. The inclusion of socioethical activities in this specific style of Eucharistic celebration made possible a deepening of faith and formed the point of departure for the fulfillment of the sacramental Eucharist.

A Learning Process

The interplay of socioethical and the liturgical involvement constituted a cycle in which the group was taken up in its search for a personalized restructuring of the faith and for the development of a community. The participants were helped to transcend, or at least to deal with, certain conflicts:

• between the tangible, secular pole, divided and ambiguous as it is, and the invisible, ineffable religious dimension;
• between the concrete involvement in direct needs aiming at concrete results and the radically other God who is confessed in word and prayer;
• between the individual striving for autonomy and wanting to form his or her own life and the relation of dependence inherent in the confession of faith.

The construction of this cycle was a learning process for the group. The concrete resolution of the socioethical involvement did not take place according to ready-made formulas. The community had to confront these concrete situations again and again. The group was also invited to review its relation to this reality in terms of the insights and wisdom that were acquired in the course of the short existence of the group.

The youth mass offered the occasion to experience this {271} learning process. For the participants, the results constituted a test and a criterion to reconfer credibility to the Eucharist as a rite and to the Christian faith as well as bringing them systematically into their daily lives.

The Relevance of This Experiment

The point of departure for the creation of the youth mass was a pastoral-pedagogical problem. The celebrations were analyzed from a religio-psychological standpoint. Let us turn now to the possible pastoral and practical implications of the assembled data.

For the Liturgical Renewal

The possibilities and limits of the liturgical renewal have to be examined critically. Liturgy, the most explicit and gratuitous expression of religious behavior, is related to the mission of the faithful in the world. This is self-evident. Infused with a consciously lived attitude of faith, the faithful want to make the promise of God's Kingdom recognizable and offer it visibly by their commitment in solidarity and by the quality of their life praxis. Religion has an ethical dimension.

In both respects, namely as religious experience with a value in itself and as directed to a mission in the modern secularized society, the role of liturgy is declining. In response to this, Vatican II set out to renew the liturgy so that it would become a meaningful event for the people. By the simplification of the ritual, the promotion of participation, the introduction of the vernacular, the rewriting of texts, and the new organization of the scriptural readings, the Church tried to make the liturgy accessible. Broader, more correct insight would, it was thought, almost automatically contribute to more intense experience.

{272}

1. Very clearly, a fundamental evolution has taken place and Vatican II has fulfilled many important aspirations.

2. On the other hand, the schema of liturgical celebration, as before Vatican II, has remained an institutionalized, codified gathering with very limited participation; the celebrant and his liturgical actions are central; the relation among the participants is only constituted and experienced via the celebrant; the liturgical schema, content, acts, and contributions of the participants are fixed in a uniform and always identical pattern. The faithful are confronted with a liturgical product that is presented as such by the Church to the community.

3. Many of the faithful, even the well-educated, continue to feel equally alienated from this liturgy. In spite of all the translating, rewriting, explanations, and commentaries, the integration of the liturgy into Christian life is still problematic. Taken globally, the liturgy has increasingly lost its function over the last ten years.[4]

4. Because of the translations into the vernacular, it has become apparent that the liturgical prayers and texts are, in fact, ahistorical and have little or no connection with the concrete situations, social circumstances, and current events in which the faithful are involved in their everyday lives. The prayers of the faithful are printed in advance and couched in generalities. In the process of making the liturgy more accessible to the people, a number of contradictions have emerged.

When a current problem—social injustice, for example—is mentioned, it soon becomes clear that it is extraordinarily difficult to speak coherently about it in the liturgical context. Social and political realities are alien to the timeless, calm, codified language of the liturgy.[5]

---

[4]J. Kerkhofs, *De Rooms-Katholieke Kerk en Europa. Enkele Aspecten*, (Brussels, Pro Mundi Vita, 1978), cf. Table 1, p. 7.

[5]F. Houtart, "Le discours homilétique et la dimension politique de la foi," *Lumen Vitae*, XXVIII (1973), 409–414; A. Rousseau & F. Dasseto, "Le discours du 'Careme de Partage,'" *Lumen Vitae*, XXVIII (1973), 415–446.

Through this, the concept of mission has lost its content and it is no longer clear to what in fact it relates. Its translation into terms of concrete historical reality and its realization are best left to the laity.

In other words, under such conditions, the reciprocal relationship between liturgy as the hymnic expression of the praise of God and moral involvement in daily life can indeed be called problematical. On the one hand, the faithful cannot articulate their experience and cannot confront it with the specific implications of the faith attitude. On the other hand, the ecclesiastical aspiration toward the establishment of the Kingdom of God does not penetrate sufficiently to guide the concrete acts of the faithful and to stimulate them creatively.

I contend that the implied hypothesis that the renewal must primarily contribute to better "understanding" of the liturgy so that it can again become functional and meaningful is inadequate and, as such, does not efficiently contribute to the promotion of the integration of the moral involvement of the faithful into the liturgical experience.

With these observations in mind, it is important to stress that the liturgical expression is founded in the historical development of the Judeo-Christian tradition, and it can only find suitable expression in its own code language. This is something that must be assimilated by the upcoming generations. But a too strict and too exclusive tie to the historical background of the mystery of faith and its particular code language together form the cause of the liturgy remaining a closed world for modern man with his own historical specificity and sociocultural sensitivity. I think it necessary that modern man, with his concrete experiential world, be taken up into the context of the liturgy so that the believing tradition and its language can be opened, and so that this tradition can give a dynamic stimulus to the mission of the faithful in the world—for the moral involvement and the profession of faith to be fruitfully related to each other.

In other words, the kind of liturgical renewal that the Church needs—at least for the group I have been discussing, which I consider in many respects to be representative of a broad group of the believing population—requires much more than using the vernacular, simplifying the ritual, rewriting the texts, and supplementing the ritual with commentaries. The faithful that I met in this group needed instead a rethinking of the fundamental psychological structuring process proper to the faith act so that the ritual expression could fulfill its function in a coherent and integrated manner, and so that they could again establish contact with the liturgical tradition as it developed throughout the history of the Church.

The socioethical dimension and the concrete involvement in real situations played a decisive role in this learning process. The "mission" of the Church took on existential content.

For Religious Education

1. The striving for faith deepening and faith formation has to give attention to those moments when believers become conscious of a gap, a conflict, a contradiction, in the value of what they experience and pursue in their lives. They must be able to find support and encouragement in the Church to confront it with their own initiatives and to resolve it effectively in order to evolve their own vision of faith. For adolescents and young adults, this attitude has a decisive influence on their readiness to examine the question of faith in a new way and to recognize the institutional Church as credible. Their positive or negative answer to the offer of faith is not necessarily definitive but the fact that they are able to experience this confrontation in a personal way has profound significance. With this, I would stress the respect for every believer as the author of, and as responsible for, his or her faith confession.

2. The appreciation of the inductive moment in religious education is a necessary basis for the development of the religious symbolization process. This process must be seen as a never complete, an ever dynamic task. Rather than offering purely religious "products," the educator must be concerned with

assisting the evolution of the symbolization process. The biblical-ecclesiastical tradition and the universal church community must be taken up in an open dialogical and invitational confrontation with the inductive human search.

{275}

3. The real human experience, the contacts with the world and society, the socioethical effort, and the responsible concern for the total and local human community within the historical and political evolution of the world offer an irreplaceable dialectical base that guarantees the believer identity and a real force of mission.

4. Religious formation occurs in community, and a community is constructed through concrete interaction and initiatives and through the communal pursuit of circumstances and values that assure the realization of set objectives. In a climate of acknowledgment and confirmation, the life of a community witnesses to the individual member's striving for truth. Belief is proclaimed in a community relationship. People become believers with and through each other. Only within a living community is the confession of faith credible and only there has ritual expression an operational value.

ABOUT THE AUTHOR

Dr. Herman Lombaerts *is a professor of religious education at the Katholieke Universiteit Leuven, where he received his doctorate. He is also a graduate of the International Institute for Religious Studies, Lumen Vitae, in Brussels.*

For the past fifteen years, Dr. Lombaerts's primary concern has been training programs for religion teachers in teachers' colleges and the intercultural study of goal setting, refinement of objectives, and process development for religious education and pastoral work at Lumen Vitae and at various institutes for religious education abroad. Dr. Lombaerts is also a trainer in group dynamics and applies the techniques of mutual cooperation, interpersonal communication, and institutional dynamics in

{276}

professional group settings. Dr. Lombaerts has written many articles for publication. Among them are "Breaking Bread . . . Passing Round the Cup: The Aims of a Catechesis of the Eucharist"; "Toward a New Religious Instruction Syllabus in Belgian Secondary Schools"; and "The Cooperation of Subgroups: Its Importance in the Catechesis of Adolescents."

Stages of Religious Judgment

FRITZ OSER

Introduction*

- How is the God-human relationship seen in specific life situations?
- What do people of different ages think about God's acts in relation to their own actions?
- When faced with real-life or hypothetical problems, how do people make religious judgments?
- Do differences exist between the religious judgments of an atheist and those of a believer?
- How should religious education be shaped if one assumes that addressing emotional dynamics is more important than the mere transmission of knowledge?
- What does it mean to guide someone to a higher stage of religious judgment?

Based on a thorough empirical research, this chapter tries to answer these and similar questions by developing a hierarchical series of cognitive stages of religious judgment and by presenting examples of such stages. This chapter focuses on the so-called "Paul dilemma," a problem story designed to reveal respondents' ways of making religious judgments. The reader should be able to form an understanding of the course of stage development as well as to assess his own religious judgments. The section on the problem of atheism deals with the question of whether the atheist also makes use of religious judgments to legitimate his world view. The last section presents suggestions for a new conception in religious education which stems from the development of the stage concept of religious judgment.

Genetic epistemology holds that all knowing begins with actions. It teaches that these actions are coordinated and integrated into stage-like systems of operations. Genetic epistemology suggests that the conscious ego develops over a considerable time span through a sequence of stages of such processes of

*Dr. Oser has written this chapter in collaboration with Paul Gmuender and Ulrich Fritzsche (University of Fribourg, Switzerland), K. Widmer (University of Zurich), and Clark Power (Harvard University).

coordinated actions of knowing.[1] In this chapter we shall ask if there are specific actions of knowing which one could label as religious in the broadest sense and which, if transformed into operative schemes, could represent the religious judgment of an individual.

{279}

If we ask such a question, we make the assumption that for each human being there exist cognitive-religious structures, just as there are mathematical, logical, moral, and other structures. In other words we assume that religious choices and actions can be formalized and transformed into operative schemes. Whether this assumption is true depends upon which reflective operations we call religious. We begin by clarifying the characteristics of operations of religious judgments.

Features of Religious Operations

Operations of religious thought and choice lie within a frame of reference which may be characterized by the following statements:

1. Realities which may be described and comprehended with the ordinary means of investigating phenomena, of mastering the object (Objektabawältigung), are generally the kinds of thing with which religious knowing and judging are concerned.

2. Realities which, because they transcend description within the methods of "objectifying knowing" (Objektbewältigung), must be approached with other methods and understood in another sort of frame of reference. The religious frame of reference is one in which reality undergoes a transformation.

The religious frame consists of elements which, as far as they are considered in relation to each other, result in a person's cognitive religious judgments. These elements are: (1) meaning; (2) mastering the negative; (3) freedom; (4) causality; (5) tran-

---

[1] *Cf.* F. Kubli, "Introduction," in J. Piaget, *Abriss den genetischen Epistemologie* (Olten, 1974), p. 15.

scendence; (6) personal sense of God's actuality; (7) institu-tionalization; (8) catharsis/change/conversion; and (9) cult, rituali-zation.

Each of these elements can be divided again into subele-ments. Meaning, for instance, is composed of the subelements: reward, unavailability, hope, luck, future, redemption (libera-tion), and so on. So far as these elements are always then associated or combined, where human events must be inter-preted, they are mostly anchored in social perspectives.[2]

The operations of religious knowing, therefore, work with questions, disclosures, interpretations, expectations of events which place the person in relation to a dimension of reality which is experienced as transcendent to man. By the term "religious judgment" we mean to indicate the process of this intellectual activity—the manner in which persons perceive the relation of God (the Divine) to humanity and to being generally through the frame of the nine elements listed above.

Schiblisky[3] holds that religion has its proper range of expres-siveness just beyond the border of the logically certain and defined. By this he does not imply any metaphysical statement but rather intends to describe the actions of thought or interpreta-tion in the frame of reference of the nine structural elements which transcend the mere description of phenomena.

Through this kind of religious knowing, human life is no longer contained within the empirical and logical boundaries of investigable reality, but pushes beyond to a transcending perspective with transforming vision.

In this chapter we intend to show how it is possible to speak of cognitive-religious structures, and how, through empirical research into behavior and the use of language, it is possible to illumine and describe the structures of cognitive-religious know-ing.

---

[2]Cf. J. Habermas's idea of "reciprocal reflexivity of expectations" in Habermas, *Theorie der Gesellschaft oder sozialen Technologie* in Habermas and N. Luckmann, *Theorie der Gesellschaft oder socioligischen Technologie,* (Frankfort, 1971), p. 192.

[3]M. Schiblisky, *Konstitutions bedinquengen religioser Kompetenz,* in W. Fischer and W. Marhold, (Hrsg.) *Religionssoziologie als Wissenssociologie* (Stuttgart, 1978), p. 75.

Previous Research

Three previous research approaches must be emphasized: First {281}
we describe the approach taken in the sociology of knowledge
(Wissenssoziologie); then we consider the approach of concept
research; last we examine the stage model of faith development
offered by Fowler. All three approaches are essentially different
from our model. Whereas the sources of our work are directly
based on the paradigms of Piaget and Kohlberg, the three
research branches mentioned have different theoretical
backgrounds.

The sociology of knowledge, building upon Berger and
Luckmann[4] and Schutz,[5] supposes that the shortcomings of
others are correlatively transformed by religious concepts. In
other words, the cognitive assimilation of the basic doubtfulness
of the You in its continuity and totality is stimulated in such a way
that the external conscience is experienced as a correlate of its
own.

This process is established in the process of giving meaning.
It culminates in the idea of religion, as described by Drehsen and
Helle when they say: "Religiosity is that social power, which
interprets meaningfully and plausibly, but in various ways, the
generally problematic experience of dependence, complexity and
discrepancy with respect to the possible solutions of freedom,
constancy and participation."[6] Consequently religiosity mediates
between experience of the world (Welterfahrung) and its certainty
(Weltgewissheit). This mediation reaches its highest form in its
capacity for transcendence, which, creating meaning, makes it
possible to reach beyond the present. The problem of sociology of
religion as a sociology of knowledge lies, we feel, in that—
perhaps because it does not work empirically—it cannot describe
the essential process of transcendence or the religious modes of

---

[4]P. L. Berger and T. Luckmann, *Die Gesellshaftliche Konstruction der Wirklichkeit* (Frankfort, 1969).

[5]A. Schutz, *Der Sinnhafte Aufbau der sozialen Welt* (Wein, 1960).

[6]V. Drehsen and H. J. Helle, *Religiosital und Bewusstsein,* in U. Fischer and W. Marhold (Hrsg.) *Religionssoziologie als Wissensociologie* (Stuttgart, 1978), p. 44.

{282}

thinking and acting. Just because it is a sociology of knowledge and considers religious processes mainly in a social frame, it is not able to reconstruct the essential religious, reflexively conveyed actions adequately.

We turn now to a second body of theory and research. The development of religious concepts is dealt with in the studies of Goldman, Elkind, and Rosenberg. Goldman writes: "Concepts of God are responses which tie together, or link, or combine discrete sensory experiences such as father is strong, big, all-powerful, cares for me. God is like that and judges and cares for all children." Or "God is a big daddy up in the sky."[7] Concepts have also been studied by the Geneva school; for example, Inhelder has written: "The development of the basic concepts of coincidence and probability in children."[8]

In this tradition we must mention Rosenberg, who investigated concepts of God, angels, priests, and so on, by means of a study of behavior in praying.[9]

In contrast to these studies we are not interested in religious concepts, but rather in the cognitive structures employed in mastering reality as persons face human failure, incompetence, bad luck, and so on. Cognitive-religious structures are ways of judging, valuing, and revealing the meaning of events which can only insufficiently be inferred by the usual means of studying the "mastery of objects" (Objektbewältigung). It is, of course, possible that concepts enter into religious judgments. In our data we found assertions by a twelve-year-old boy of the following kind: "If something bad happens to us, God can preserve us from a much larger evil. He planned it that way in advance." We score this as a Stage 2 statement (or at least Stage 1, see page 292). Conceptually the same boy told us that he imagines God to be an old man with a white beard, which corresponds to Goldman's lowest intuitive stage.

---

[7]R. Goldman, *Religious Thinking from Childhood to Adolescence* (New York, 1964), p. 15.

[8]B. Inhelder, *Die Entwicklung von Zufall und Wahrscheinlichkeit bei Kindern,* in H. & E. Bohr (Hrsg.), *Religionsgesprache Zur Gesellschaftlichen Rolle der Religion* (Darnstadt und Neuwied, 1975), pp. 98ff.

[9]R. Rosenberg, *Die Entwicklung des Gebotsbigriffs bei judischen Kindern in Israel* (Jerusalem, 1977).

Fowler's stage concepts represent a third fundamental approach in the field of religious genetic epistemology. We do not describe Fowler's stages here but we must indicate some differences between his approach and ours. While we wish to capture the generalized religious judgment, that is, some kind of cognitive pattern of religious knowing of reality, Fowler is more interested in faith. He employs a broad definition of the concept of faith: "Faith has to do with making, maintenance, and transformation of human meaning."[10] We think that Fowler, in the final analysis, aims at some category of ego development with all its emotive and empirical components. Thus Fowler's approach illumines some of the conditions necessary for the possibility of the act of faith, always understood as a social, personal-psychological, and existential approach.

In our research we aim at the relationship between transcendence (God) and humanity. We approach this relationship as a cognitive and specifically religious act faced with border situations of life. If Fowler writes: "Faith does involve constructions of the self and others in perspective-taking, in moral analysis and judgment, and in the constructions of self as related to others which we call ego," we would say that religious judgment begins there, where the descriptive categories of self and others, the role-taking and moral interpretation of the world are no longer sufficient. Cognitive-religious patterns are modes of constructing the Divine-human relation within the frame constituted by the nine elements of operation mentioned earlier. These give rise to a construction of reality which results in a participation in systems of transformation, whose product we are. In other words, during this assimilation process we look at life and reality in a religious way, influencing them in an interpretative manner.

There are still other reasons why we think that Fowler's stage concept is different. Instead of emphasizing the specifically religious, he aims at a conglomerate of stage conceptions of different sources (logic, role-taking, moral judgment, meaning of life, locus of authority, symbolic interaction, and so on) which only in

---

[10]For this and following quotes from Fowler's work, see his contribution to this volume, "Faith and the Structuring of Meaning."

combination make it possible to experience the ways of the world based on faith. This is again a consequence of the fact that Fowler basically does not describe cognitive structures, but rather conditions or modes of action which lead to a higher identity.

Comments on the Collection of Data Concerning Religious-Structural Judgments

We took as our basic hypothesis that individuals, faced with border situations, produce religious judgments if either the dilemma situation itself already contains parts of a religious operation, or if the semistandardized questions aim at the religious dimensions of reality.

For this reason we introduced elements of religious content into our dilemmas, e.g., "in this situation he thinks of God and starts to pray." Because of their religious content it does not follow that a certain stage structure is already inherent in the dilemmas, but only a specific demarcation of content. Our experience has shown that this kind of prestructuring with respect to the religious judgment does not hinder but is actually a necessity. We have also found that particularly the persons with higher stages of religious judgment critically questioned and transcended the pattern of thought presented in the dilemma.

Though this approach is strongly based on the findings of Piaget, Kohlberg, and Selman, the decisive difference lies in the fact that in the formulation of our study we must cover a broader spectrum. Whereas Kohlberg studied the cognitive basis of human interaction in the field of moral norms, the development of cognitive stages of religious judgment involves dimensions which transcend the moral domain.

The man-God relation which manifests itself in religious judgment certainly implies moral judgments, but transcends these by including specific religious dimensions such as questions of absolute meaning, transcendence, coping with evil faced with God, and so on.

The table below illustrates this:

Development of intelligence	Social development	Religious development
subject–object relation	subject–subject relation	subject–transcending relation
(Piaget)	*(Kohlberg/Selman)*	*(Oser/Fowler)*

These three reference areas permeate and imply each other. In other words, religious development implies an adequate development of intelligence and socialization, without which a religious development is not conceivable. In spite of this, it is possible to differentiate structural patterns for each relation, for these patterns are correlated structures of formal elements which extend in the same way over various areas.

A religious dilemma then should stimulate the operations explained above. Obviously not every dilemma stimulates all nine of the elements mentioned and, regardless of the richness of the questions related to a dilemma, they will not evoke all of a person's structure of religious judgments.

Digression: The Concept "Theological Mother Structure"

The construction of the dilemmas raised the question of whether we could find stories which universally stimulated the structures of religious knowing at different stages. We found that the more original and the more archetypal the elements of a story and their relations within the overall pattern of the story, the more directly the persons addressed react to the dilemma situation. In the sense of Jung, archetypes activate depth structures which can be experienced by everyone if addressed to their consciousness. In our perspective, these archetypal situations make contact with religious experiences which everyone has had and which stimulate certain patterns of thought and reasoning. Stories which have these archetypal patterns and images may be said to exhibit a "theological mother structure." The story which presents a

{286} "theological mother structure" is recognizable within any religious or cultural situation. This recognition is a support for our hypothesis of universal structures of religious judgment. Stories with "theological mother structure" features also evoke constructions of religious meanings from atheists.

The concept of mother structures was mentioned for the first time by Piaget. He refers to three mother structures in the field of mathematics: mother structures which are not reducible to each other but from which all other structures can be derived. These are algebraic structures, ordering structures, and topological structures. There are then two ways to define substructures: combination and differentiation. Stated in other words, the transition from stronger to weaker structures is revealed by means of these operations. Piaget, however, also states that the genesis of new structures must be considered more within the framework of the coordination of elements of mother structures than within their own framework.

Presumably "theological mother structures" are structures which combine the elements we mentioned above. Although we cannot present a system of "theological mother structures," we do wish to illustrate our understanding as embodied in a particular story. For this purpose we cite the old Russian legend of the farmer Simon:

> Simon was a pious farmer. He had many children and even more stable lads and maids, who all congregated in the farm sitting room. He was sad because he was so seldom alone in order that he could meet God and speak with him. For this reason he left his farm in the search of God. Suddenly he felt that God was very close to him. He was driven forcefully toward a door on which the name of God was written in flaming letters. When he opened it, trembling, he found himself in the middle of his old sitting room, in the midst of his children and servants.

In order to understand this little story it is useful to see through the underlying theological pattern of thinking. It consists of several important elements which are reversibly related to one another. We will try to describe these elements:

First Element: S

This element embodies man's search for peace, happiness, for God. This is a basic dimension which all people share. It is an existential—a universal desire of all persons.

{287}

Second Element: V

Man abandons his everyday involvements and searches for his God outside them.

Third Element: G

God himself approaches man. He is not to be forced to a specific place or to a certain time. For that which meets man, meets also God.

Fourth Element: N

Man finds God in his immediate environment. God is there where man approaches his everyday world in which he knows himself to be enclosed "from back to front" (Psalm 139). This "approaching the world" is at the same time approaching man. It is a liberating interaction. For man then becomes man in his relation to God or rather in God's relation to man.

If we relate these elements to each other, a theological structure of subjects emerges. This structure is very original and can at the same time be developed and applied to many texts and situations.

There probably exist only a few such "theological mother structures." Their degree of complexity is mostly low. They overlap several disciplines, such as dogmatic, christological-soteriological, ecclesiological, moral-theological, and other substructures. They are stimulated or developed in man according to circumstances."[11] For our study it is of importance that the "theological mother structures" are strongly narrative and, finally, that they can be reformulated in the form of a religious dilemma which evokes a religious judgment.

Method of Data Collection

We have tried to develop a number of dilemmas which all stem from the range of experience of subjects covered by our prepilot study. These dilemmas include most of the nine religious issues mentioned above. On the basis of a pilot study (Study I) we performed an item analysis, thereby eliminating those questions which did not yield any new structural aspects.

To begin, we determined the test-retest reliability of our interviews to be $r_{tt} = .84$.

Then four different dilemmas were presented to 120 subjects in the age groups 9, 12, 15, 18, 20–25, 26–35, 66–75 years (cross-sectional study, Study II). The aim of this study was to test the consistency of the dilemmas, to determine possible horizontal decalage, and to demonstrate the expected age trends.

In this chapter we present only one dilemma in order to demonstrate the development of our cognitive-religious stages. It is the so-called Paul dilemma with questions for the semiclinical interview.

Paul Dilemma

Paul, a young medical doctor, has just successfully passed his exams. He is very happy. He has a girl friend, whom he promised to marry. Before this his parents reward him by paying for a visit to England. Paul sets out. No sooner had the plane lifted off, than the captain announces that one engine is damaged and that the

---

[11]See F. Oser, *Theologisch denken lernen* (Olten, 1975), pp. 17–19.

other engine does not function reliably. The plane looses height. All safety measures are immediately taken: oxygen masks, safety vests. First the passengers cry out; now it is deathly still. The plane dives rapidly. Paul's whole life races through his head. Now he knows, it's all over.

In this situation he thinks of God and starts praying. He pledges that he will dedicate the whole of his life for the poor in the Third World if he is saved; that he will give up his girl friend, whom he dearly loves; and will renounce a high income and prestige in our society.

The plane is smashed in the emergency landing in a field. Paul is saved miraculously!

On his return home, a lucrative position is offered to him in a private clinic. He was selected from ninety candidates on the basis of his abilities. Paul recalls his promise toward God. Now he does not know what to do.

Questions

1a. Should Paul keep his promise to God? Why or why not?

1b. Must one really keep a promise to God? Why or why not?

1c. Do you believe that one has duties to God at all? Why or why not?

2. What do you say to this statement: "It is God's will that Paul goes to the Third World" (that is, that he keeps his promise)?

In the foregoing story two demands oppose each other: first, Paul's girl friend and the job offered to him; second, God and his promise to God.

3a. Which of these two demands do you feel to be more significant, or how do you experience the relation between the two demands?

3b. What is more significant in this world: man or God?

Let us suppose Paul tells his (religious) parents of his experiences and of the difficult situation in which he finds himself. They implore him to obey God and keep his promise.

{*290*}

4. Should Paul follow the advice of his parents? Why or why not?

Paul feels duty bound to a religious community (church, sect, etc.) and is strongly committed to it. The spiritual attitude and the precepts of this community require that the call and the will of God must be accepted by man, that Paul should keep his promise unconditionally.

5a. What does this demand mean for Paul? Must he, as a believing person, be led in his decision by the dictums of this community? Why or why not?

5b. Must one be led in one's fundamental decisions by the principles/demands of a religious community? Why or why not?

5c. Which duties does one have vis-à-vis a religious community at all? Why?

5d. May a person oppose the demands of a religious community by his personal freedom? Why or why not?

Let us assume that Paul does not keep his promise, after many sleepless nights and a time of uncertainty and despair as to how he should act, and that he accepts the promising position in the private clinic.

6. Do you believe that this choice will have any consequences for Paul's future life? Why or why not?

Shortly afterward Paul has a frontal collision in his car with another automobile. This accident was disastrous, for it was his fault.

7a. Did this accident have any connection with the fact that Paul did not keep his promise to God? Why or why not?

7b. Do you believe that God punishes Paul for not keeping his promise? Why or why not?

7c. If this is so, will God intervene in this world without fail? If not, does God manifest Himself in this world? In which way?

Suppose Paul acts out as a career-making doctor and decides to donate a tenth of his income every month to charitable organizations.

8. Do you believe that Paul can in his way keep his promise after all? Why or why not?

This dilemma and the corresponding questions evoke the following cognitive-structural elements: responsibility of man in view of the relationship God(the Divine)-man; redemption of God (providence); constitution of man in the face of the reality of God; freedom of decision vis-à-vis the law; relationship of grace and personal deeds. Within the frame of his competence the individual is led to his limits with respect to these elements. The individual need not in this connection explain his comprehension of God or the Divine, but it is a question of God's work with respect to man in a specific problem situation.

On the Development of Cognitive-Religious Stages

Possible stages of cognitive-religious development lie in a continuum between complex (highest) and simple (lowest) patterns of thinking. The simplest patterns can be deduced on the one hand from recent stage concepts of Goldman, Eckensberger, Kohlberg, and Fowler. On the other hand they may be described from studies of primitive religious cultures. [12]

Thus Kohlberg writes: "A considerable portion of a child's orientation to divinity, to the ultimate source, power or being in the universe is a moral orientation. At our moral stage 1, divinity is bound to be an authority who is the ultimate dispenser of punishment and reward. At moral stage 2 one of our children says; 'You be good to God and He will be good to you.' "[13] It is regrettable that this idea has neither been elaborated to further stages, nor been empirically substantiated.

In order to determine the highest stage, we performed on the one hand several interviews with philosophical and theological experts. Our dilemmas were laid before these experts and at the

---

[12]See G. E. Swanson, *The Birth of Gods* (Ann Arbor, 1960).

[13]L. Kohlberg, "Education, Moral Development, and Faith," *Journal of Moral Education*, Vol. 4, No. 1 (1974), p. 13.

same time we discussed our preliminary heuristic notions on a stage concept in the field of religious judgment. On the other hand we analyzed different models of theological reasoning, such as those of Pannenberg and Jüngel, as well as the review of present theological thinking in the anthology of Bitter and Miller, and above all Peukert and Rahner. From the philosophical point of view particularly, the approaches of Habermas and Apel, as well as the transcendental-philosophical approach of Krings, must be noted.[14]

In this area between possible lowest and highest stages our data were arranged in a hierarchical order. In correspondence with this order, generalizations and logical relations were developed, the logic of the lower stages being assimilated in the higher ones and integrated with their appropriate value.

This led to the following stage conceptions of religious judgment.

Outline of Cognitive Stages of Religious Judgment

Stage 1: Orientation on complete determination (deus ex machina)

Man in his actions is at the mercy of God, who is seen as an ultimate power. He cannot grasp God's reasons ("God knows what He does"). Man acts because God forces him to act. Man's reactions to God's acts are one-dimensional and blindly responsive. God's interventions in the world are usually comprehended as reward or punishment. God cannot intervene everywhere at the same time. Conclusion: Everyone has his turn.

Stage 2: Orientation on reciprocity

The relationship God (Ultimate)-man is seen instrumentally as an exchange. Man becomes active in his own interest toward God.

---

[14]The reader is encouraged to read the works of the authors noted in this paragraph.

Preventive function of reward and punishment. Scrutinizing attitude with regard to reciprocal loyalty. Historical causal naiveté. Division into two domains: God and the world, whereby God intervenes in the world only under certain circumstances ("if it is too much for Him," one has to be careful that these circumstances don't occur). God wants the best for man; for this reason man tries to win God's favor.

Stage 3: Orientation on voluntarism

The relationship God-man shifts in the direction of a growing autonomy of man, but stays ambivalent. Everything that exists is seen as contingent ("keep a promise because it is important for *me*, not because of God"). But in the case in which fate rules, man cannot be the cause of his own experience (coincidence). God is in fact here (e.g., as a far-reaching horizon), but human autonomy is not conveyed in him. God examines whether man fulfills His "Will" ("one can, but one need not").

The God-man relationship is constituted in the unquestioned deed of faith ("God may help, if one believes"). Man is only able to solve the conflict between God's acts and his free will if he understands this will as being dependent upon God. Man cannot perform any act of which he is not convinced. Free will and conformity with God remain independent desiderata (tension).

Stage 4: Orientation on autonomy and "Divine Plan"

The relationship God-man is characterized by a still limited but mediated conscientiousness. Life is based on man's own capability for taking decisions. He is responsible for his actions, which he has to judge and to answer for. The God-man relationship is discussed reflexively in the sense of a mutual mediation. It gains a normative-educational accent ("God gives Paul a sign, in order to bring him to reflect"). God is seen as love, goodness, because man shares with Him the idea of what is right, of goodness ("what one considers as right, one can obey, if not, one should not obey"). The God-man relationship comes to pass for the sake of the good of an entirety (plan, system). Human free will unfolds within God's Divine Plan. God wills only man's best, but He only creates the appropriate conditions.

For this reason man must become active toward his fellow-men. This commitment is the means to bring God and man together ("Thou shallst . . . . examination whether one stands the test of faith"). On the one hand God is intrinsically and directly an imparted strength, spirituality, mercy, on the other hand He manifests Himself indirectly in the events, in the encounters between human beings. Distinction between a personal and an obligational level. On the personal level man can create only himself. On the relational level God is rather seen platonically as external and unchangeable. For He is the pure truth, the pure spirit.

Stage 5: Orientation on self-fulfillment in intersubjectivity

The human subject in his autonomous disposition (Verfasstheit) is the focus of this stage. The relationship God-man (transcendence-immanence) is seen in such a way that God is experienced as that reality which makes possible and vouches for man's autonomy in a meaningful way (God as liberation to freedom). Intersubjectivity is here the significant location of God's manifestation and articulation. The true reference to God is conveyed by human deeds, i.e., by the unconditional acknowledgment of others in their freedom (creating the possibility to act and to fulfill actions). The relation God-man then is restricted to interpersonality.

Stage 6: Orientation on universal communication and solidarity

The crucial point of this stage is a communicative practice with a comprehensive demand applied to universal solidarity (communicative practice with God as conveyed through human interaction).

    As in Stage 5, man's own autonomous freedom is considered as being constituted intersubjectively. The God-man relationship is now seen not only as the reason and aim of both my own and the other's existence, but as that of the whole of history and reality. Full consciousness of grace and justification: trust in being accepted by the God of love and in absolute freedom, especially in the case of failures, in pain, in death (the indicative precedes absolutely the imperative). God is experienced as the feasibility of absolute meaning—conveyed through finite freedom in the fragmentary occurrence of impotence and love.

{295}

Examples of the Stages of Cognitive-Religious Judgment

The following excerpts from the records of interviews will illustrate the structural-cognitive stages of religious judgments. The data were collected on the basis of the Paul dilemma by semiclinical interviews. No examples can as yet be given for Stage 6. The interviews have been reproduced verbatim, and the English translation attempts to reproduce the oral statements faithfully.

Stage 1

1. Total heteronomy of the individual.
2. Man in his actions is at the mercy of God, who is seen as an ultimate power.
3. Man acts because God forces him to act. His acts are one-dimensional and blindly responsive.
4. God's interventions are comprehended as reward or punishment.

Boy: 11 years old, Catholic, third school year

2. *What do you say to this statement: "It is God's will that Paul goes to the third world" (that is, that he keeps his promise)?*
"If he made the promise, he must keep it."

7a. *Did this accident have any connection with the fact that Paul did not keep his promise to God? Why or why not?*
"Yes. God has punished him now, in another place."
What did you mean by this?
"People should realize, that God really exists. Perhaps they will mend their ways."

7c. *If this is so, will God intervene in this world without fail?*
"Yes. God wishes that the human beings which He created remain as He wants them; and this sometimes can be achieved only by force."
Always?
"In most cases yes. Of course there are first admonitions, later on he'll be in for it."
What does that mean?
"He will be strictly punished. Perhaps an accident in which he is badly hurt; then he was not so bad as in the case he is killed."

Stage 2

1. God-man relationship is instrumentally seen as an exchange.
2. Man becomes active in his own interest to win God's favor.
3. Preventive function of reward and punishment.
4. Dichotomy between God and the world.
5. Scrutinizing attitude with regard to reciprocal loyalty.
6. Historical-causal naiveté.

Boy: 15 years old, Catholic, high school

1a. *Should Paul keep his promise to God? Why or why not?*
"Yes, I do feel that he should keep his promise, because it is just best to keep your promises. And I myself am rather careful with making promises, because I am also a rather

strong believer in God. If something is wrong I always pray hard, before every exam, etc., and it has already helped often."

Why must promises have to be kept?

". . . a promise, that is as if a workman does a job and he also gets his pay only afterward, and he has to be told how much he earns. I feel that this is a sacrifice and it wouldn't be just if one told this workman afterward: 'The job is done, now you don't get anything for it.' "

3a. *Which of the two demands, (a) Paul's girl friend and the proposed job or (b) God respecting the promise to God, do you feel is more significant?*

"I do feel that it is more significant to work in the Third World. . . . This doctor can practice there also. And if he can heal someone he may receive a pumpkin or something like that . . ."

What is more significant in this world: Man or God?

"That is rather difficult to say. There is the saying: Man proposes, God disposes. But one could not live without people, or only badly, and certainly not without God."

6. *Do you believe that this choice will have any consequences for Paul's future life? Why or why not?*

"God will punish him somehow. Perhaps by an accident, so that for example his girl friend soon dies or something like that. So that he will always be the underdog."

Stage 3

1. God-man relationship: growing autonomy of man though still ambivalent.

2. All existence is seen as contingent.

3. God exists, but human autonomy is not conveyed in him.

4. God-man relationship is constituted in the unquestioned deed of faith.

5. Free will and conformity with God remain independent desiderata (tension).

Woman: 23 years old, Protestant, teacher

1a. *Should Paul keep his promise to God? Why or why not?*
"I find myself in a conflict for I don't know whether I would keep this promise. I don't doubt that God exists, but I do doubt that He has such a strong influence on us human beings that Paul's life would develop in a negative way if he would not keep his promise. Altogether I don't know whether I could and would renounce the good position in the clinic. Neither could I give up marrying my friend."

1b. *Must one really keep a promise to God? Why or why not?*
"On the basis of my personal attitude I would not keep this promise, because I could not abandon all plans I have made. If Paul keeps this promise, he will in any case be dissatisfied with his life because he has to renounce things which would have meant much to him. I would not be prepared to push my life into the background because of such a promise.

"I am *myself* and I want to live my life in the way *I* feel is right. I do not wish to be deflected in my path through life by a power, of whose existence (God) I am not convinced. Perhaps I would keep such a promise if its observance would mean very much to me. However, a promise should be held because it is a promise and not because it was given God."

1c. *Do you believe that one has duties to God at all? Why or why not?*
"No. I somehow believe that some sort of authority exists. But I don't know if this authority is called God or if it has another name and whether this authority exists in the form presented. I imagine God to be an old man with a white beard. I do not know if He exists. But I do believe in some kind of predetermination. Whether this predetermination comes from God or from another authority I don't know. Because everything in life is predetermined, even keeping a promise cannot influence the predetermined path through life."

2. *What do you say to this statement: It is God's will that Paul goes to the third world (that is, that he keeps his promise)?*
   "If it is God's will that Paul goes to the Third World, then he goes even without a promise."

3b. *What is more significant in this world: Man or God?*
   "Man with his free will."

7a. *Did this accident have any connection with the fact that Paul did not keep his promise to God? Why or why not?*
   "If it was predetermined that Paul should have kept his promise, this automobile accident has something to do with his not keeping it. But this accident may have been purely coincidental."

7b. *Do you believe that God punishes Paul for not keeping his promise? Why or why not?*
   "I never have considered God as a punishing power. If there is an authority which guides our path it will have other ways to guide us than by means of punishments."

Stage 4

1. God-man relationship: still limited but mediated autonomous consciousness.
2. Man is responsible for his actions, but this happens within God's "Divine Plan."
3. God is seen as love, goodness, man sharing with him the idea of what is right.
4. God-man relationship is for the sake of the good of an entirety (plan, system).
5. Two-fold mediation of God—directly: as an imparted strength;—indirectly: in the events and encounters of human beings.

Woman: 50 years old, Catholic, housewife

1b. *Must one really keep a promise to God? Why or why not?*
"That is very hard to say. I do not know if it was only an empty promise; if in this situation he only wanted in some way to provocate something. It is the same game we used to play as children: if I succeed, then I'll do such and such. In this case it is essentially an empty promise and I do not feel that one must keep it without fail."

Why should an empty promise not be kept?
"Because the inner conviction is missing and because the words are just words. And then the necessary love and the necessary substance is absent."

What does this inner conviction signify for you?
"Oh, rather much. If one does not have the necessary inner conviction to do something, one will not see it through."

If one does not see it through, is there no reason to keep a promise?
"I believe so. One simply has not enough strength for the whole thing. I feel that if one makes such a big promise then one should also be convinced of it."

Is it justified to make such a big promise in such a panic situation?
"Certainly yes. Again I think that if it is an empty promise which stems from a provocation, then it is not such a sincere promise toward God that one could not give it up."

1c. *Do you believe that one has duties to God at all? Why or why not?*
"I do think so. Yes, how shall I put it. One should live in such a way that one could take the responsibility for life in relation to God. Yes, that's it.

"But if I can answer for something before God then I could also answer it before myself. That's the reason why I should live in such a way that I could accept the responsibility before God and before myself."

Why must we take the responsibility for our actions?

"Because our actions take place in a general framework such that one does not live crosswise, so that one does not become too much of a nuisance to others, that one does not lay too much claim on them. I have the feeling that one could live hand in hand, so as to complement one another, which would lead to a nice community. This is what God basically wanted."

3a. *Which of the two demands, (a) Paul's girl friend and the proposed job or (b) God respecting the promise to God, do you feel is more significant?*
"Essentially it is dependent upon man himself. From our own and our world's point of view, certainly material things, his girl friend, his job are more important. But what counts are more the inner values; perhaps later it would be these values, the less material things."

What is the meaning of God? And what is the meaning of man?
". . . The meaning of man is really the following: he serves as worker before God; man should be here on earth in principal to do the work which God has imposed on him. It is also the burden we have to carry. We are responsible for doing this; essentially we are the working people."

Why?
"God created us; He created the world and He also expects something from the world. I am convinced that we are here to do something for that."

Why do we exist at all?
"I do not know; perhaps it is in order that we can be here for each other, and that we try to live together."

And what is the meaning of God?
"He is surely of great importance for our world. I feel, in the final analysis, that everything does happen in the way He imagined it. I feel that we are, in general, guided by Him. It is our predetermination that God knows more or less where He wants to go with us."

7a. *Did this accident have any connection with the fact that Paul did not keep his promise to God? Why or why not?*

"No. I do not have that impression."

Why?

"I cannot imagine that God always punishes in this way, if He punishes at all, because he (Paul) did not keep his promise. I cannot imagine that this (accident) happened because of his not having kept his promise. I do also feel that God would not punish so quickly. That is not what I would consider as a punishment by God. I could rather imagine that he would have to work for a few years, would have to ponder over it in his inner conflict whether he should have done this or not. It is rather some kind of a stroke of faith. But perhaps it will help him to live in that way he believes he should. It is rather a hint, but I don't think that it is a punishment."

7b. *Do you believe that God punishes Paul for not keeping his promise? Why or why not?*

"I do not believe that He punishes him. I feel He keeps him in suspense, and when God sees that he fulfills that which He expects of a helping fellowman He has no reason to punish him."

Stage 5

1. Focus of this stage: the human subject in his autonomous disposition (Verfasstheit).
2. God is experienced as that reality which makes possible and vouches for man's autonomy in a meaningful way.
3. Intersubjectivity is the significant location of God's manifestation and articulation.
4. The relationship God-man is restricted to interpersonality.

Man: 37 years old, Catholic, university education

1a. *Should Paul keep his promise to God? Why or why not?*

"The question is always, what does God mean; what does it mean this moment of mortal fear when he makes this pledge to God. He tries to find some sort of way out of this situation. Because no mortal being can help, he turns to the highest authority which can help him in his predicament, and this is plainly the Transcendent. For all secular possibilities now fail; there are no technical means left and he himself also can do nothing to help.

"It is natural that he should use the expression God, but this is an irresponsible act in the frame of his relationship to God. To be true, he has no other choice; he is to all intents and purposes being blackmailed. From my point of view and with respect to a Christian apprehension of God such a relationship to God is irresponsible. My belief would lead me to say: of course he should accept the post. I would not comply with this situation because the Love of God destroys love if it becomes a compulsion."

1b. *Must one really keep a promise to God? Why or why not?*
"No one must unconditionally keep a promise. For me a promise is a dedication for the freedom of the other and this act itself lies within the range of freedom between you and me, that is, between two persons. If one says a promise must be held, then it is not a promise any more. A promise is in addition always entrusted to the freedom of the individual. A promise is no contract. A contract must be fulfilled. A promise may be kept or not kept. It is just the same as in a love relation. If one says, you have married me, you have loved me, therefore you must continue to love me, then this will destroy love. You are once more dependent on free acknowledgment; the same in the relationship to God."

1c. *Do you believe that one has duties to God at all? Why or why not?*
"Not duties; he may or he can do something for God in a case in which he is affected by that which for me and for Christian understanding is termed God.

"If he receives the impulse to perceive his recognition, then he may act, then he is authorized to act vis-à-vis God. Of course there is such a thing as a compulsion of love, where one has to act. For instance I must sacrifice my life for my children, if I had the choice. A certain compulsion actually exists. But compulsion in love is not the same as, for example, compulsion in education."

2. *What do you say to this statement: It is God's will that Paul goes to the third world (that is, that he keeps his promise)?*
"Usually the expression 'Will of God' is the claim to power of a community, which can interpret God's Will in history (cf. the Crusades). The Will of God must be established and interpreted in the sense of the Gospel and the great theology and in the framework in which the individual has been placed. The decisive criterion for me would be the need of the others. The Will of God is that which the others need from me, where they lay claim to my freedom. The legal formulation of the Will of God is absolutely inadequate."

3a. *Which of the two demands, (a) Paul's girl friend and the proposed job or (b) God respecting the promise to God, do you feel is more significant?*

3b. *What is more significant in this world: Man or God?*
"The 'either-or' is an impossible alternative. That is a choice which really does not exist.

"The New Testament and the prophets say: 'He who loves God but hates his brother has not really understood anything. He is a liar and a hypocrite.' There is no such a thing as a separation, otherwise one does not know what God signifies. This means that I cannot possibly realize a relationship to God and do God justice if I do not do justice to my girl friend. Of course Paul has realized freedom by entering this love relation which may not be separated from the relationship to God. Here too the interpretation of the Will of God is the interpretation of the situation, of the love for his girl friend and of the love for his profession. The fact that he is the best candidate of all for this clinic is for me—and I have practiced this always in my own life—

indirectly a call of God's Will. Whenever I asked myself what I should become, I always asked others, and when they said: 'You are capable of doing this,' then this is also that which I must do, or at least an important criterion for that which is to be realized in the relationship to God. What is the aim of my life if I wish to live within the Kingdom of God or toward it? For what will I exchange my life? In this connection the needs, criteria, and judgments of others appear, whereby—and this is important—the needs of the oppressed weigh more than those of the dominators.

"The alternative before which Paul sees himself here is false. I cannot conceive my relation to God independently of a reference to my communication and my work, otherwise it would be empty of content and thus an escape. The relationship to God can realize itself only within history—even if it cannot be absorbed therein."

6. *Do you believe that this choice will have any consequences for Paul's future life? Why or why not?*

"Certainly, because these episodes are very dramatic for him and because he has, in his view, been saved in his conception of himself (Selbstverständnis), otherwise he would not have made the promise. This is, however, a mistake; it is objectively false. For there just is no causal connection. Paul here demonstrates that he is unenlightened.

"Through the fact that he has had the courage to acknowledge that something is wrong in his logic; or because, in spite of being so afraid, he did not act on his promise after all, his conception of God becomes confused and this is excellent. I presume that he will go through life in the future with more fear and trembling in his relationship to God. Or at least that he is not so sure any more that the assumptions which he had about himself and about a firm God, to whom one may present wishes and who gives and saves, are not adequate. Instead he has become conscious of his personal responsibility, has been thrown back more strongly onto himself, and I consider this to be benefit."

7a. *Did this accident have any connection with the fact that Paul did not keep his promise to God? Why or why not?*

7b. *Do you believe that God punishes Paul for not keeping his promise? Why or why not?*

"In such a heart-wringing story this cannot be omitted. Psychologically there is a certain chance that he might himself have caused an accident in order to punish himself, perhaps because he has not inwardly digested his autonomy.

"Only if he has really seriously thought over and digested the promise, perhaps in prayer if he is such a religious person, and if he says:

'I have used You, God, through a bribe. This is not worthy of You. You must recognize this, as I recognize it,' and thereby clears things up, then only will the self-punishment cease. But if he says: 'Really, I did promise, but I shall take up my post anyway,' then the self-punishment will not come to an end."

7c. *If this is so, will God intervene in this world without fail? If not, does God manifest Himself in this world? In which way?*

"This description of Paul's life does show what God means, but it does so without proper consideration of his responsibility in or his interpretation of his own life. Here God is depicted as bound in a natural causative (naturkausal) relationship and not in connection with the history of freedom (Freihaitsgeschichte), which is not permissible. For me, the revelation and manifestation of God can only be found within the history of freedom. To begin with, I would reject the thought that God reveals Himself only in wondrous ways, punishing as well as rewarding. On the other hand (I feel that) God reveals Himself to man in the outcome of the event. By the crucifixion and the rising of Christ, in history, He reveals Himself in the world, where men are beaten, where the history of freedom is realized in the most extreme opposition. This for me is an important instance of the manifestation of God.

"An important instance is also love and hate, in which are revealed what kind of being man is and is not, and what he can do. At all events, God reveals Himself in intercommunication and in the interruption of communication. Our whole life can be interpreted as a manifestation of God, and natural history must be seen in this connection.

"I cannot speak of evil without speaking of God. One can, of course, say that evil is good, that the will for power must prevail. Here I ask myself: 'Why should this not be so?' The differentiation between good and evil is only possible if man has been liberated so as to realize something like goodness at all, to assume something as an unconditional claim. Surely one should realize that good without encroaching upon the freedom of the other. This one can only achieve if one is delivered from alien freedom unto oneself."

{307}

Observations on the Problem of Atheism

In the description of stages presented here, as well as in the dilemma stories and the corresponding questions, the term "God" is used as if it were the nucleus of a crystallization of religious judgment. We therefore wish to offer at least some legitimating remarks, acknowledging that the problem of "giving meaning" lies at the root of any decisions, this also in connection with the subsequent reflections on the problem of atheism.

We do not here identify the question of meaning with that of Being as such in its inner precision, or with that of a single being within the total frame of reality. Time and again, beginning with various modern systems and extending to totalitarian historical ideologies or functionalistic system theories, one meets with the tendency to see the meaning of something in the totality of its relationships, in spite of the fact that such a totality remains open and is, in fact, indefinable, while the relationships are basically finite. In consequence, this must lead to mediatizing (Kierkegaard) the individual human being, in order to contest its absolute and therefore irreplaceable significance.

The question as to the meaning, as it is to be understood here, presupposes the question of this totality and that of the general definition of Being, it is true. But it transcends them also, pointing toward the meaning of reality as such and to the absolute meaning of existence, which can be questioned in this way. It goes into the de facto meaning of Being and existence.[15]

The question as to the meaning of reality as such, as an inquiring after absolute meaning, constitutes the specific religious experience in which one inquires after the total interrelatedness of *all* meaning. Such an act of religious experience is therefore a step by the subject beyond his own self, beyond the world of facts and of human control, toward a withdrawing horizon which cannot objectively be defined, and from which it returns de facto to itself. This act of transcending shifts the activity "away from man toward an activity of the comprehended object (the Transcendent), which discloses itself in the recognition of experience and shows itself to be the determining subject. This 'change' of that which is comprehended as object into an independent subject, which acts out of itself, alone permits one to speak of 'God.' "[16]

Thus the term "God" denotes the most far-reaching unity of meaning. The religious act should be a fabric of experience, which is not to be understood in a causal way. And the reality "meaning" should be comprehended as being, to all intents and purposes, not producible by man.

The category "meaning" cannot function as the highest dimension in the religious context. This is because it is a particular feature for no other reason than that it is the peculiarity of cognitive-religious ways of thinking also to digest productively the experiences of meaninglessness in the context of absolute meaning.

"The subjectivity of God, that is, the initiative of the object of religious experience and insight, can only be adequately understood if its specific substance is not mistaken. Precisely in being subject, God is no disconnected individual reality, but rather the undivided all-embracing embodiment of all meaning, the truly

---

[15]T. Pröpper, *Der Jesus der Philosophen und der Jesus des Glaubens* (Mainz, 1976), p. 135.

[16]T. Koch, *Religion und die Erfahrung von Sinn*, in H. and E. Bahr (Hrsg.), *Zur gesellschaftlichen Rolle der Religion* (Darmstadt und Neuwied, 1975), p. 140.

general subject. He embodies, as it were, the dimension of the unconditional *universal* meaning, 'before' which a human being lives his life in such a way that he develops within himself an equivalent dimension.''[17] From the point of view of the sociology of religion, one is led to the same view:

> Because there is not one single point in the immanent existence of man in which the diverse and diverging forces of society could meet, the point of intersection of the forces which aim at an individed consistency are, according to the logic of religion, shifted to the next world. God thus becomes the formula for the 'transcendental site of the group forces' as it were, the 'name for the sociological unity' of a society which, of course, is of consequence also for the ideological interpretation of subareas.[18]

Thus God appears as an authority who promotes meaning and as an inexhaustible embodiment of all meaning, which lays the foundation for the *whole* life-story of a human being with all its eventualities and acts.

A religious judgment, in essence, implies and makes a subject of the relationship between man—God. This means that the problem of meaning must be left aside in order to inquire after the more basic God-man relational structure if one wishes to search for cognitive-religious patterns of thinking.

If we approach the subject of religious stage theories in this way, the problem of atheism is raised imperatively. How may those points of view in which the reality of God is rejected as irrelevant to behavior and thought be assessed within such a theory? We must start from the horizon which is common to atheistic and religious points of view, which quite generally consists in the attempt to establish the ultimate meaning of existence. Thus we do not begin with positive religiosity as an intrinsic constant, but rather with that which lies behind both points of view as plausible positions, namely, with the possibility that human beings can grasp in a unity everything which they

{309}

---

[17]Helle, in W. Fischer/W. Marhold, eds., *Religionssoziologie als Wissenssoziologie* (Stuttgart, 1978), p. 19.

[18]*Cf.* Drehsen/Helle, in W. Fischer/W. Marhold, eds., *Religionssoziologie als Wissenssoziologie* (Stuttgart, 1978), p. 49.

encounter and to which they are related. By this comprehensive grasp, a dimension is attained in which everything which must be can be seen as having value, as being significant, and as being worthwhile. For to the extent that the subject returns to itself, it checks on itself, and having completely reached itself, it arrives also at the whole of reality. The common *structure* of religious and atheistic points of view thus expresses itself in the fact that man can behave in a final way toward himself and toward the whole of reality, toward that which should be of value and should be worthwhile.

The atheistic point of view then describes this relationship to the whole of reality without recourse to God, that is, the totality is thought of without a reason which is distinguished therefrom: but I behave toward everything, toward totality, in such way that I do not establish a reason outside of myself. Rather, only that is valid which is myself, which I myself establish; it is my own potential that I must realize.

The religious point of view on the other hand "designates the reason, which of itself is incomprehensible and which the limited intellect must presuppose as being distinct from himself, when he attempts to ascertain the condition of absolute accountability of his self-completion."[19] It is the religious subject (God) which has penetrated the self and which, after all, cannot be imparted through others without mediation of the self. And, finally, it is also the two human subjects which each impart themselves through the other, but which do not wish to be thus imparted without once more being imparted through God. The difference between the two positions (theistic and atheistic) now lies in the fact that a guarantee of the meaningfulness of freedom exists for the religious subject, whereas, for the atheistic subject, the meaning is limited to an insistence on his own formal freedom or upon intersubjective fulfillment as his achievement.

As already shown above, the fulfillment of absolute meaning forms the constituent for the religious subject, so that the real common denominator or difference between the two positions lies in the question of absolute meaning and in its corresponding

[19]Pröpper, p. 137.

answer. The final intelligence of atheistic potentiality would be that the comprehension of absolute meaning could be attained and that God would not be admitted as argument, that is, that the consciousness of the absolute need for meaning prevails but no answer is given, or the answer is withdrawn to himself. This would be the solution of absurdity. But the concept of absurdity is at the same time a correlate to absolute meaning, for an absurd position presupposes an absolute need for meaning.

With a growing contemplation of that which can be held for meaning, both positions, the possibility of a relationship toward God and the possibility of an atheistic point of view, are increasingly deepened. Thus what both positions have in common from the formal and structural point of view is the radical question as to absolute meaning. Contemplation reaches its limit in the question as to the why of this reality altogether. An answer within the frame of the potential of an atheistic point of view might be to consider meaning to be the personal realization of worldly freedom as such. Man would then find his meaning, or that meaning available to him, in that he makes himself. The concept of absolute meaning appears to the religious subject in its fulfillment only when the relativity of the finite freedom to other freedoms is considered in its full structural depth. "An answer which is appropriate to this extreme question is to be found not alone in the fact that I am, that I assert my freedom in the form of understanding and organization of the world, but rather in that I *shall* be, that I am *permitted* to be, in short, that I am *acknowledged*, in fact *absolutely* and *for nothing*."[20]

The extreme question regarding absolute meaning, which belongs irrevocably to man, would then be the common denominator of these two positions. Nevertheless one may not assume that this question has always been asked by man in this form; rather it has developed by way of historical thought processes. Thus atheism is here not taken simply as the epiphenomenon of religion, that is, it is not merely the negation of theism, but rather theism and atheism arose in mutual reference to each other. In this conception it is therefore problematic to

---

[20]Pröpper, p. 139.

say that man is inescapably religious. Rather man is, above a certain stage, inescapably placed before himself and before totality.

In this way the phenomenon of atheism cannot be taken in on a religious basis and the dignity and the intrinsic value of such a position is preserved. As a result, the potential for a deepened or (stagewise) higher religiosity is directly proportional to the potential for a more conscious, growing atheism. Atheism and theism are thus correlated concepts.[21] Because atheistic responses to the dilemma stories in our study have not yet been evaluated, we are not in a position to present a description of stages which includes the atheistic points of view. In a few words we can say that the potential for a conscious atheism depends upon the achievement of a consciousness of personal identity. In addition, the higher religious stages are indebted to the corresponding atheistic stages in their reverberation and differentiation.

In the lowest stage, atheism and nonatheism are as yet undifferentiated. The potential for a conscious atheism is not yet present because there prevails a direct unity between the world of life and religion. The potential for a conscious atheism is only relevant then with the emergence of a precept in which God appears as a dimension which lays claim to the subject or as an institution (starting with Stage 2).

At this point the possibility arises of rejecting the heteronomous force which hinders and limits one's freedom. Basically the same is true for Stages 3 and 4, in which God is experienced as a sense of demand, a duty or a call on the individual. Here, too, a fundamental refusal is possible, namely in such a way that the subject withdraws in all radicality to its own competence. In the same way an atheistic point of departure may be found in the stage of the determination of the meaning of

---

[21]Perhaps one should, in addition, differentiate between an objective and a historical dependence between atheism and theism. In a certain sense one can say that modern atheism is reactive. It would have to be checked whether this was always so in the whole of history. Considered in the history of the ego, the standpoint of atheism attains a new stage vis-à-vis criticized religion. In this respect later stages of religious consciousness are established through atheistic positions.

personal freedom by means of another freedom (Stage 5). Here the conscious understanding of a matter is considered as our concern and our concern only.

Consequences for Educational Action

The pedagogy of religion of the late sixties launched a vehement attack against inundating the pupil with religious knowledge. The reproaches against those responsible were either that they propagate an old educational method (e.g., the memorizing of catechism) or that they entertain an uncritical superstition regarding the effect of the so-called "preached Gospel." This superstition was also nourished theologically by advocating the thesis: He who hears the Gospel is saved and he who does not hear It is damned. As a reaction to the exaggerated school-like intellectual religious education, we developed, in the early seventies, three different alternative models for the pedagogy of religion.

First there was the "accentuated emotive model," in which the pupil is led by narration into an experience or a profound emotion (inner tension) out of which he or she is enabled to react creatively (dance, music, gestures, prayer).[22] The second model was the "experience-model," in which the pupils became active in the community, consoled the ill, visited prisoners, integrated old people into their families, and so on, afterward interpreting these actions in their faith.[23] The third approach consisted in an attempt to train "religious dispositions." Such dispositions are, for example, to express respect, to sensitize empathy, to utter joy creatively, and so on. Nowadays we return to the question of coping cognitively with religious phenomena; or better, the mastery of reality by means of cognitive-religious structures.

Based on the results of our study we can deduce that an approach solely imparting information is clearly insufficient to

---

[22]See F. Oser, *Kreatives Sprach-und Gebetsverhalten in Schule und Religionsunterricht* (Olten, 1972); and Oser, *Die Jesus-Beziehung* (Olten, 1973).

[23]F. Oser, *Theologisch Denken lernen* (Olten, 1975).

bring the individual to religious maturity. It is evident that information is perceived through the frame of interpretative structures developed by the individual. If these structures correspond, for example, to the Stage 2 pattern of religious judgment, then the individual will gather new information selectively under the aspect of Stage 2 thinking, and in this way no effective change can emerge. It is thus a passive model which leaves the structure of the religious judgment unchanged.

Based on our study, we try to guide pupils to a higher stage of religious judgment by (a) introducing new dilemmas, (b) holding intensive group discussions on these dilemmas, and (c) stimulating higher staged argumentations. For if we accept the notion that a higher stage implies a "better" relation toward God or a higher equilibrium in the God-man relationship as well as greater freedom, and that it is in addition more complex and flexible, then the course indicated is evident: Development must become the aim of education.[24] However, it would be wrong to speak of this approach as involving predominantly an intellectualization of education. On the contrary, the cognitive and emotive poles would once more appear in the person's practical discourse. This practical discourse is optimally realized if the four fields of interaction mentioned in this volume by Lickona are aimed at: (1) social and moral discussion; (2) cooperative learning; (3) building of social community; and (4) participatory decision-making.

Studies Planned

In continuation of Study II, which has been described in this chapter, we plan to perform two additional investigations. In Study III we wish to examine the structures of moral and religious judgments of trade school students from fifteen to eighteen years old. We shall pursue this comparison by giving the test-subjects Kohlberg's Heinz dilemma and our Paul dilemma.

---

[24]See L. Kohlberg and R. Mayer, "Development as the Aim of Education," *Harvard Educational Review,* 42 (1972), pp. 449–496.

For the questioning of atheists (Study IV) we shall use two of our religious dilemmas (Paul, Job, or suicide). In extension of this we plan to analyze the way in which various nonbelievers come to their atheistic viewpoint, using a specially constructed questionnaire to clarify personal life-histories. Following a preliminary data analysis we also plan to try a scale of anxiety and Machiavellianism, as well as the Heinz dilemma with about forty chosen atheists.

As our main hypothesis, we postulate that atheists do not differ from theists in the *structure* of their thinking when they grapple with the problems of meaning. In other words, atheists too may be assigned to our six stages of cognitive-religious judgment.

{315}

ABOUT THE AUTHOR

Dr. Fritz Oser *is Professor of Educational Psychology at the University of Fribourg in Switzerland and Visiting Professor of Religious Education at the Faculty of Theology at Lucerne. He completed his doctoral studies at the University of Zurich and undertook postdoctoral studies at the University of California at Los Angeles and at the Center for Moral Development at Harvard University.*

Among Dr. Oser's many publications are Kreatives Sprach und Gebetsverhatten; Jesus-Beziehung; Den Frieden lerner; Mit dem Kleinkind Gott erfahren; *and* Das Gewissen lerner.

THEOLOGY
AND
PSYCHOLOGY
IN DIALOGUE

Moral Theology and Moral Development

ENDA McDONAGH

Introduction

Is moral development theory a denial or a new development of Natural Law theory? Is Natural Law theory itself and its detailed expression in virtues and vices outmoded in current moral theology? Does an easy optimism about human goodness prevail among theologians, psychologists, and educators without effective sense of evil and sin? And what price a moral theology, moral psychology, or moral education that has nothing to say about the global problems which threaten us such as war, pollution, and starvation? Can an individualist moral theology or theory of development be taken seriously today?

This paper raises and struggles with these questions. If it does not provide definitive answers (and who could?), it may encourage and assist theologians, psychologists, educators, and all others concerned to take some initial steps together in that communal task of promoting a complete moral education within and without a religious context.

Shall We Dance?

For all moral theology's claims, at least in the Roman Catholic tradition, to be concerned with the practical living and growth of the Christian as a person, it has proven remarkably shy in engaging in any kind of dynamic interchange with investigations and theories of moral development. It might have been expected that the pioneering work of Piaget, first published in 1932, might have received some notice in subsequent textbooks whether of the unreformed manual kind or the reformed kind that appeared in the aftermath of Haring's *Law of Christ* (first German Edition 1954). Yet I cannot find any serious notice of such work before Haring's new effort at a textbook, *Free and Faithful in Christ*,[1] published late in 1978. Similar contemporary attempts to produce comprehensive coverage of fundamental moral theology, such as O'Connell's *Principles of Catholic Moral Theology* or Bockle's *Fun-*

---

[1]Haring does not engage in critical dialogue with the work of the developmentalists.

damentalmoral, do not appear to consider such work from Piaget to Kohlberg to be relevant to theological investigation of the basis and structure of morality for Catholic Christians. Of course Catholic educationists and moralists have taken a certain notice as the Duska-Whelan book on *Moral Development*, the Bockle-Pohier (eds.) *Concilium 110 Moral Formation and Christianity*, and, more notably, Paul Philibert's "Lawrence Kohlberg's Use of Virtue in His Theory of Moral Development"[2] testify. It would be difficult to characterize this belated and limited interest as manifesting or achieving the continuous and profound exchange which serious empirical exploration and theoretical interpretation of moral development demand of professional investigators and expositors of morality for Christians, even of the Catholic variety.

The first task of theologians, therefore, is to acknowledge their neglect in this area and accept the kind of collaborative reflection which this volume proposes. Personally, I do not feel equal at this stage to any comprehensive theological or philosophical critique of the methods or results of the people engaged in moral development research in recent years. I have too much to learn to attempt that. Neither do I think it an entirely suitable starting point in any event. My heading for this section was not meant to be simply facetious. The image of the dance, the opportunity to get to know one another and above all the discovery of which steps we both know and approve, and which we find it impossible at present to harmonize, suggests something of the movement, the choice and exchange of partners, the rhythm and, I hope, the enjoyment which may characterize our efforts.

Dancing to the Music of History

If I may be indulged in my image of the dance a little further, it is clear that none of us are actually taking first steps. Morality, moral philosophy, theology, psychology, and education did not begin

---

[2]*International Philosophical Quarterly*, pp. 455–479; *cf.* same author's slighter treatment in "On Kohlberg," *The Living Light*, V. 12, n. 4, pp. 527–534.

with us or indeed with any of the illustrious predecessors we may summon to our aid in defining and defending our own particular dance pattern. As practitioners and theoreticians of morality we join the dance, we don't initiate it. However inventive we may prove to be, the dance has a history which we cannot ignore and a future in which we participate for a time but which we cannot finally determine or predict. The historical character of morality in all its dimensions of living, reflection, and communication not only encourages modesty on our part; much more importantly, it reveals the continuing chain or process within which we work. And it is a chain with many complex links and strands, much too complex to unravel fully here. Yet we cannot simply break the chain; we cannot totally step out of the dance into which we were in some sense precipitated by our entering the human community at a particular time and place, with a particular endowment and environment. The further course of our life and thought has made significant differences to us, we hope, but we have in some sense retained our identity and some of the shaping of that identity in our understanding and practice of morality as it swirls out of the past.

Perhaps the time has come to drop the imagery as it may be obscuring the centrality of history in the development not only of the person, as so many colleagues have recently underlined, but also of the community to which we belong, or more accurately of the communities to which we belong. As Americans and Europeans, as Christians and humanists, as Catholics and Protestants, as academics and people engaged personally in the art of living, as members of particular social and economic classes, even as women and men, we belong to a series of overlapping and yet distinct communities with tangled and intertwining histories. No serious attempt to understand our moral theory and practice can ignore that. A useful attempt may well begin right there. To which communities with moral ballast, as it were, do I belong? Which communities and which aspects of their historical formation have entered influentially into my moral formation in reflection and action?

These communities are for such a diverse group as this so wide-ranging that it would not be fruitful or indeed possible to distinguish and enumerate them. At least it is important that each of us bear in mind their reality and their influence, and that some of us endeavor to spell out more fully how certain influential historical communities enter into the shaping of our thought and behavior. Perhaps the obvious way to confront that challenge is for me to reflect for a moment on the different communities and their traditions which entered into the forming of my moral theology. I am concerned here with my academic formation and not my personal moral formation, although clearly the two are interconnected.

{323}

The Shaping of a Moral Theologian

As a Roman Catholic theologian, I have grown to believe that religious commitment demands and shapes moral living and reflection on moral living. In that community and tradition, I have observed as central the attempt to relate and even integrate the way of life enunciated and above all lived out by Jesus Christ with the wider moral wisdom of the race. From the theological perspective the basis for such relationship was the doctrines of Creation and Incarnation; from the perspective of human wisdom or philosophy it was the doctrine of natural law as developed by Aristotle and reformulated by Thomas Aquinas. I would, however, have to acknowledge that the theological dimension, as found in Scripture and elaborated by patristic and scholastic theologians such as Augustine and Aquinas, reached the twentieth-century student in the very attenuated form of the moral theology manual which has for the most part disappeared in the sweeping revisions of the last twenty years. Its disappearance has not, however, led to any new agreed-upon and comprehensive understanding of moral theology within Catholic theology, although certain distinctive features survive. In philosophical terms also, the intrusion of new analysis and the reduction of influence of the older natural law tradition have changed the dialogue between religious or theological approaches to morality and the fruits of human wisdom. And one of the unexplored dimensions of Catholic moral theology is how far Kant may have indirectly and unconsciously replaced or certainly modified Aristotle and Aquinas in the manuals and later.

Catholic and Protestant traditions of moral reflection cannot be readily translated into Aristotle-Aquinas versus Kant, into teleological versus deontological, or, above all, into absolute versus relative with the various approving or disapproving overtones attached to these. Furthermore, the impact of ecumenical dialogue makes it increasingly difficult to distinguish Catholic and Protestant moralists.

Having sufficiently muddied the streams of Catholic theological tradition which have washed over me, let me turn to a parallel stream which has become more significant with the years, both for me and for the renewal of Catholic moral theology. My early doctoral work dealt with Church-State relations. In the intervening years I have for practical and academic reasons found myself greatly preoccupied with social and political morality, nourished to a limited extent by the encyclical tradition of Catholic social teaching but more deeply and widely by the political tradition and needs of my home country Ireland and by an increasing awareness of, uneasiness about, and commitment to the deprived and exploited countries which constitute a large part of the world. The result of all this has been a series of attempts for my university students and ordinands to articulate an account of moral reflection that did justice to the Catholic-Christian traditions and which still provided critical insight into the meaning and structure of human life, personal and social, and into the fresh insights, structures, and claims which were continually emerging in the world about my students and myself. These attempts have naturally undergone important changes with which I will not bore you here. I believe however that some account of where I find myself now with some of the background reasons may indicate my readiness or unreadiness for joining in dance or dialogue with moral developmentalists. (How I do wish I had a more elegant name to describe them—one more in keeping with the elegance of their own work!) In any event this is all I have to offer as a prospective dancing partner just here.

Content: Structure and Basis

A distinctive feature of the Catholic moral tradition has undoubt-   {325}
edly been its attention to content in describing and prescribing a
way of life for Christians. The origins of this content shared the
complexity already alluded to in the relationship between scriptural and philosophical sources. The manner of presentation
varied enormously through parable or story, direct command,
exhortation and counsel to the system of virtues and vices of the
Aristotle-Aquinas type and to the legal system of commands and
prohibitions which characterized the manuals. In whatever fashion it was presented, it had clear and frequently precise and
detailed directions on what constituted good moral behavior in a
range of areas from sex to trade to war. It would have been
unthinkable in this tradition, therefore, to propose a program of
moral education which did not emphasize content. Catholic
objections to the Piaget-Kohlberg method, fairly or unfairly,
seized on the lack of interest in content which they claim to find
there.[3] This may prove a profitable area in which to practice some
steps together.

Of course, the hard-nosed content of traditional Catholic
morality has not survived unscathed in theory or practice in the
developments which have been taking place. The concessions, as
some read it, to a more flexible or liberal or vague understanding
of content in sexual and other issues are not simply surrender to
the *Zeitgeist*. Serious difficulties in defending the origins or
argumentation or presentation of particular problems have arisen
and not always in the permissive direction. For example, the
arguments justifying war and capital punishment have come
under sustained and cogent criticism. Such difficulties in content
have forced Catholic moralists to examine more critically the basis
for particular ethical positions which for long had been unquestioned. Two of the more notorious of these, illustrating the
precise problems of origin and argumentation and the interrela-

---

[3]Cf. Philibert, *op. cit;* K. Ryan, "Moral Formation: The American Scence," Bockle-Pohier,
op. cit., pp. 100–105.

tion between Scripture and Natural Law, are contraception and divorce. Despite such difficulties it would be a mistake to think that all interest in and practical certainty (as Aquinas might call it) about moral content have disappeared or been undermined by the new search for origins and for coherent defense of clear-cut ethical positions.

In discussing the more formal elements of basis and structure in relation to content, one of the more important items on the agenda for theologians, philosophers, and developmentalists is the meaning and role of virtues and vices. Indeed Professor Kohlberg explicitly rejects what he takes to be traditional virtues approach to moral analysis and education, reducing it, it would appear, to some kind of Skinnerian reinforcement procedure and finding "the bag of virtues" incoherent and arbitrary.[4] As my colleague Professor Hauerwas[5] has some important criticisms to make of that position and as it has already been effectively analyzed and criticized from a more traditional Catholic view-point in the article by Philibert instanced above, I will try a rather different approach.

One of the points on which the defenders of the virtues and their developmentalist critics seem to agree is the goal of morality as development of the self, self-actualization, (self) perfection or personal holiness. However these descriptions may intend impor-tant differences, and they do, they seem to me to focus on the individual person or moral agent as source and term of the development process. This I believe to be only half of the truth. Moral behavior is for me relational and communal as well as personal. Indeed I see the focus for each of us in learning morality and behaving morally as lying equally outside and beyond the self in another person or community. Moral action is always interac-tion. The summons to respond and in my view, developed in more detail elsewhere, the empowerment to do so come in an important sense from the *other*. At its fullest, the summons and

---

[4]L. Kohlberg, "Stages of Moral Development as a Basis for Moral Education," *Moral Education* (Toronto, 1971), pp. 23–92. Other works by Kohlberg as well as Piaget's original volume are taken for granted in this discussion.

[5]S. Hauerwas, "Character, Narrative and Growth in the Christian Life."

response are mutual at least to the point of demanding mutual recognition and response as human beings. This structure applies between groups or communities as well as individuals. It is that continuous interplay of summons and response, which occurs between people at every stage and in every context, which provides some general formal account of the structure of morality.[6]

In this account the virtues describe critical qualities of the responses or rather of the relationships which the responses at once express and create. (It may be that Professor Hauerwas's difficulty with Aristotle's circle may be more intelligible in a relational interpretation of morality.) The classification and enumeration of these virtues may not be as easy or as coherent today as in the time of Aristotle and Aquinas. Yet to dismiss such useful tools of analysis entirely seems foolhardy at this stage. However, my concern is a little different, deriving from a relational view of morality. In recognizing, respecting, and responding to the other (individual or group), the complex reality of self and other calling for such recognition focuses the responder on different aspects, characteristics, and needs of the other in different, recurrent, and typical situations. These responses to typical situations are to some extent categorized by the virtues, for example, to the sexual situation by the virtue of chastity. This categorization applies to the responses and the responder, agent or subject but they are evoked by the other and her or his human endowment and need in the situation. Looking at it from the point of view of the evoking or provoking other, what typifies the situation is a value to be responded to or realized. Virtue and value analysis of morality come together in this way in a relational or interactional structure. Such analysis has the advantage of grounding value in existing human beings even if, like the virtues both in number and kind, they have been created by the community to describe and cope with the complex interactions in which the members of the community find themselves. They both, virtues and values, form part of the complex dance which has

---

[6]My extended version of this occurs in *Gift and Call* (Dublin-New York, 1975). For later developments, *cf. Doing the Truth* (Dublin-Notre dame, 1979).

been in motion since the dawn of history and which seems essential to the survival of human community and human person.

By that I do not mean to suggest that the particular concepts of virtue and value or any particular classification of them is essential to human and moral existence. Other moralists, including Catholics, operate and organize differently. The most obvious alternatives center around duties, laws or rules or principles. It may be the Kantian influence of Catholic moral theology to which I referred previously, but I do not find any ultimate incompatibility between deontological and teleological approaches to morality, although admittedly certain examples of the one might exclude the other. In my earlier analysis, the person(s) of the other(s) are at once goal of my response in a teleological fashion and constitutive of my duty to respond in a deontological way. I find that person comes before me as "is" and "ought" combined, not as puzzle about that relationship. In the universe of moral development and moral education, I should think this fundamental to an understanding and justification of various stages of response as being truly, if incipiently, moral.

Another aspect requires consideration here. If values and virtues are rooted and relative to persons in the way indicated above, then duties, rules, and principles are no less so. Kant may well be invoked in support of such a position with his call to treat persons as ends and not means. The formal nature of this statement should not blind us to its fundamental significance.

Duties, rules, and principles constitute a further way of coping with human moral interactions, identifying, structuring, and classifying them as good or bad morally. Such a procedure has a long and honorable history, including a biblical history, but it is not the only possible procedure or necessarily the best one.

I should, for myself, be inclined to distinguish such rules or principles, however formal (in the sense of lacking material content), which seem to me to be properly based in human person and community from principles such as the universalizability principle or Rawls's original position or adopting the other's role, which seem to me sophisticated hermeneutical devices for illuminating or testing certain ethical positions or rendering them more persuasive, but not for finally grounding or justifying them, still less for excluding others as equally or more central. Or is this the Catholic preoccupation with an ontological foundation for ethical positions rearing its ugly head again? And if it is, must we face those "gory locks" and "ugly head" if we claim a philosophical or theological justification for the morality we espouse in developmental research and moral education?

{329}

Persons, Communities, and the Great Moral Issue[7]

The basis for morality and its structural analysis centers on the person in the account offered so far. However, a little more attention must be paid to personal reality and its community context than has been possible so far. I did emphasize the role of the historical community in one's entering into, understanding, and living morality. The center of call and response might, I pointed out, be individual or group. That this is so is clear from any consideration of the great moral problems of our time from racism and sexism to peace and war to population and starvation to conservation and pollution. These are problems which concern large masses of people. It is from such large groups or communities, varying in size from Three Mile Island and Harrisburg to the subcontinent of India, that the moral call or summons comes. And it comes to and can only be responded to by groups with the necessary resources, organization, and moral commitment. A moral analysis which ignores such demands or a moral education whose contents are confined to one-to-one or small-scale and more manageable problems can hardly be said to be facing the moral needs of the time. It is clear that the problems exist but the "how" of tackling them remains obscure. The "how" includes more adequate analysis of the concepts of group responsibility and response, strategies for exercising that responsibility, and education in understanding these problems precisely as moral for us and in responding to them coherently and effec-

---

[7]A basis for Christian ethics or moral theology giving primacy or equiprimacy to the social is attempted in the author's *Social Ethics and the Christian*, Manchester, 1979; *cf.* Sullivan in this volume.

tively. Too much of our moral analysis and education reduces to rearranging the deck chairs on the *Titanic* precisely because these problems are not faced. A consideration of them would, for instance, radically alter the general character of the dilemmas posed in some moral development exercises.

From the analytic viewpoint, moral philosophy and theology have been greatly impoverished by their concentration on individualist issues and on the moral behavior and development of the individual in isolation from his or her communal existence. The individual can only become a person in and through a community. If one were to accept self-actualization in one of its secular or religious forms as the goal or test of moral development, as so many do, even that is threatened if the close and unbreakable relationship between person and community is not attended to. In their anxiety for the welfare of their children, to take a homely example, parents frequently ignore the kind of community they are preparing or endorsing for their children in pursuit of what seems to them the necessary wealth to give their children a chance to go to college, to have the best possible chance in life. Their chance of fulfillment in life may be much more influenced by the kind of society such pursuit of wealth is promoting than by college education or any other family provision. The socioeconomic structure of the national and international society not only is a source of some of the moral problems listed above, it also enters into how different people perceive and respond to these problems. And it may have an even more inhibiting effect on the conventionally privileged than on the obviously deprived. In the language of the Latin Americans, the deprived and exploited may be loudly or silently calling for liberation and this may be one of the great moral imperatives of our time, even if our moral analysis and educaton don't indicate this. Paradoxically, however, the privileged may also need their liberation from self-centered, consumerist, and trivialized lives which their society offers them. And to be liberated in this way they may need the deprived because only in the new structures and relationships which a new society might offer could both privileged and deprived emerge as liberated and new people and, in the process of interactional morality, operate as mutual liberators.

Without in any way accepting either a collectivist or a positivist version of society and its relation to morality, I believe that adequate moral analysis and education must focus on both poles of person and community. It is important that Kohlberg's postconventional level reveals such a strong social awareness. I do not think that it may or can be bracketed out at earlier levels or that the Kohlberg form reveals the deeper dialectic between person and community which I have been seeking to articulate here. The contractual or liberal versions of society do not take seriously enough its organic character and the destructive divisions of class and race and sex which may exist within it or the destructive relationships such a society may have with other societies. All are issues that must figure prominently on the agenda of moralists and educators.

{*331*}

The basic connecting links between form and content are more fully expressed as persons-in-community and community-of-persons with both their historical concreteness and their capacity to transcend themselves. But that is to anticipate.

Time Past and Time Future: Fulfillment or Destruction

The historical nature of morality enters intimately into its personal-community understanding and expression, as we have seen. The past supplies some of the resources out of which the agent (individual or group) performs moral actions. In doing so he forms or shapes himself. He develops morally, for good or evil. To borrow Hauerwas's word, the agent is building his "character."[8] This way of expressing it overcomes the atomistic emphasis on individual actions which bedeviled the Catholic manuals for example. I am not altogether sure that some accounts of moral education escape it, if exclusive attention is to hypothetical problems as a method of promoting cognitional growth. The holistic development of the person is neglected. Moral development in the perspective of this chapter is not increased moral understanding of particular dilemmas or even the simple transla-

---

[8]This movement in recent moral theology from focusing on actions to focusing on agents or subjects is traced by O'Donohoe in this volume.

{332}

tion of these solutions into action. It is about the growth of person and community through time, of course by activity based on some understanding but set in the appropriate personal and community context.

I say *some* understanding because as moral activity takes one into the future, no one properly understands what he has done until he does it. By this I mean not only that the consequences of his action are not predictable but that the very activity itself is properly understood only in the doing. This element of learning through *praxis*, which reflects the openness and creativity of moral activity, must play a role in any tests devised to explore moral development and in programs designed to promote moral education.[9] Otherwise the creative nature of our moral lives is totally ignored and little more may be at stake than highly sophisticated marble-playing.

The role of the future in relation to moral development of person and community carries its shadow side also. We have seen too many people and communities destroy themselves not to recognize that the moves we make into the future carry a high risk of failure and destruction for self or others. This destructiveness is not usually simply initiated by us. We live in an ambiguous world. The ambiguity of the destructive and the creative characterizes the moral community within which we hope to become moral beings. The ambiguity is deeply rooted in our persons and activity. The best of our moral responses will be predominantly not exclusively good or creative. Moral development consists from this point of view in promoting the creative at the expense of the destructive. Moral philosophers and theologians seem curiously loath to discern and affirm this ambiguity and present their natural law or other moral principles as if they were derived from and intended for a world basically unmarked by evil.[10] True, they measure failure against the virtues or rules or principles they enunciate. But this anaemic failure derives from the weakness or the malice of the particular agent. It is not the rich prevailing failure of seemingly ineradicable evil in person and community

---

[9]*Cf.* Chapters by Lickona and Lombaerts in this volume.

[10]Interesting reflections on this "evil" dimension occur in the chapters by Rizzuto and Loder in this volume.

and which one endorses or augments, but in which one is also trapped. Clearly there is great scope for those engaged with morality as philosophers, theologians, educationists, psychologists, and social scientists to give, if not the devil, at least the evil, its due. Thereby conservatives and progressives might enjoy a more realistic view of a past which the former so easily romanticized and of a future which the latter so readily idealize. Perhaps the point is to change the world rather than understand it, but some developing awareness of the creative resources of person and community and of their destructive limitations seems essential to the task.

{333}

Self-actualization: Transcendence and Conversion

I have already expressed my reservations about an understanding of morality and moral development that centers on the actualization of development of the self on the grounds that morality is relational, interacting with other persons, and communal, understood and exercised in community structures. I wish to pursue a further aspect of that by observing that the call of the other(s) which evokes moral response is first of all their very presence seeking recognition as other(s). The recognition of them as constituting worlds of their own who may not be regarded as extensions of my world, or manipulated by it or incorporated into it, takes me out of myself to be aware of this finally other world and by the very same act of transcending self, as I would call it, enables me to discern and distinguish myself. It is the transcendence to others then that is at the heart of growth of self. Recognition of, respect for, acceptance of others in the mystery of their otherness help achieve at the same time an awareness and acceptance of the mystery of the self. I do not use the word "mystery" here lightly or in any mystifying sense but as calling attention to the inherently rich character of person (self or other), which makes our exploration never-ending and the ultimate meaning and structure inaccessible to our conceptualizing and verbalizing.

It is the presence of the other which calls forth at least the response of recognition. In a true sense that presence not only calls, it enables It is a gift presence which we cannot command or create and which in its gift-character draws us out of ourselves, enables us to transcend ourselves, sets us free to respond. Moral life is, in that sense, gift and not achievement.[11] It is not possible to ignore the achieving and striving dimension of moral response, but it must be balanced by and indeed subordinated to this gift dimension.

A number of obvious connections with Kohlberg's work occur to me here. The line of development, provided it is not interpreted in a too narrow sense, suggests to me growth in our recognition of, respect for, and response to others. The first level of avoiding punishment or seeking reward reveals typical reactions to people by people at very different stages of their chronological development. I would find it, therefore, rather difficult to accept the irreversibility which is claimed, knowing, as I do, how people regress in critical situations and fail to transcend themselves maturely in recognition of and response to others. The rich young man in the New Testament bears thinking about here.

A somewhat different feature, not peculiar to Kohlberg and his colleagues, stresses the value of entering into the roles of the others. As a device for increased understanding of others, particularly in face of the dilemmas presented, I can only approve. However, if it is presumed that one can really probe the mystery of others in this way, even for the purpose of moral response, I would be very wary. I am still more wary of the implied suggestion that there is only one mature response to each dilemma or that responses can be so easily classified as Stage 3 or 5 or indeed that there may be any satisfactory response at all, given the ambiguous world in which we live. This, of course, suggests some connections with later stages and my unwillingness to give the universalization device the critical role which Kant or Kohlberg do. I believe it has considerable value in certain areas which might be traditionally described as dealing with

---

[11]Hauerwas, in this volume.

distributive justice, but it cannot really cope with a great deal of moral life ranging from trust and love to personal vocation. And of course it removes or at least greatly impoverishes any notion of both the creative mystery of the human being and the pervasive reality of evil in its myriad forms.

{335}

The summons of higher stage reasoning which Kohlberg presents so persuasively I would want to anchor also in persons and communities where one is engaged in actual living and not in classroom discussion. It connects with the summons to transcend oneself and one's condition in the awareness of the other. However, the strictly cognitional limits of the experiment prevent this from fully emerging. The change to another level of moral reasoning, which this precipitates, has overtones of intellectual conversion as explored by Lonergan and others. (I could not avoid the impression of close parallels between Kohlberg and Lonergan[12] in the stages, the invariance in sequence and cross-cultural claims. This is an impression which may be unjust to both thinkers.) My view of the transcendence necessarily involves the whole moral agent and again is embodied in his turning to the other. Conversion is to the others, perhaps through the medium of ideals or values but as finally grounded in the others. Conversion then is an apt description of the historical moral life. It is so first of all because we must continuously recognize, know again the others, whether already known or swimming into our ken for the first time. Their mystery summons us again and again, their needs for love or food or education or simply recognition as persons constitute a permanent task. In attempting to fulfill it we are ourselves converted, changed, if not "utterly" at least partially. And that change is as much their gift as our achievement. The conversion I speak of is not first of all provoked by evil or given religious significance. Of course, our need to turn and turn again to the other is rendered the more urgent and the more difficult by our being enmeshed in evil or sin, being entangled in self and in fear of the other. The presence of the other is never merely gift bearing the promise of conversion or liberation. In his ambiguity and mine his presence is also threat or potentially

---

[12]*Cf.* Lonergan, *Method in Theology* (London/New York, 1973).

{336} destructive. Only the predominance of gift over threat in the mutual recognition of gift or the restoration of that recognition where it has been lost can provide the appropriate conversion and liberation. In this evil world I and my brother or the other also carry the mark of Cain. But it is the turning to the other, not some abstract turning from evil, that makes for real conversion. The implications of such transcendence and conversion in social rather than personal terms are even more urgent today, as I suggested earlier. The consciousness such conversion will demand, the political will necessary, and the logistics of carrying it out, even partially, almost induce despair. How moral education will face the problem is not just the concern of moral educationists. The survival as well as the growth of all may be at stake, unless radical conversion through social, political, and economic structures occurs between people now a threat to one another on a nationalist, racial, sexual, or class basis.

Morality, Love, and Faith

The apocalyptic overtones of the previous paragraph are not the main reason for introducing the discussion of faith at this point, as if, to quote Brendan Behan, I were a nighttime Catholic, the fear of the dark inspiring belief in God. I have perhaps sufficiently emphasized the dark side of human living and its relevance to moral analysis. I do not wish to invoke faith or God as literally *Deus ex machina*. For all the secular pattern of my particular dance, I am well aware that this secular pattern cannot be taken in isolation and that much of what we enjoy as purely moral steps in our world has a religious history, played a role in that dance we call Judeo-Christian tradition, and can only be fully understood in its origins and development within the history of that tradition. I do not conceive developing that understanding as my precise role here, although it is a task that may not be ignored in this kind of discussion.

In most human traditions, religion and morality have been in interaction. This is particularly true of Judeo-Christian story. The interaction may be viewed and described in diverse ways. Many view it in an exclusively deductive fashion. From faith in Yahweh or the acceptance of Jesus Christ as historically recorded one can deduce a whole pattern of life or morality. Even if this view is not espoused in an exclusivist fashion, it plays a role in the way most Christians derive and justify their moral stances. On no less solid historical grounds one can say that Jews and Christians have viewed the relationship between their faith and morality in a more dialectical way, with the one challenging, confirming or condemning, and finally transforming the other.[13] From the Decalogue in its Covenant setting to the dialogues of the Book of Job to the moral diatribes of many of the prophets one can discern these dialectical relationships between faith in Yahweh and moral response to the neighbor. The character of your God is revealed by your treatment of your neighbor; commitment to the God of Israel demands very specific responses to the neighbor. The dialectic is no less evident in the New Testament and reaches tragic proportions in failure of the guardians of the faith of Israel to recognize their own God in the person, life, and teaching of Jesus Christ. Unable to break out of their own self-righteousness, they cannot truly recognize the human other and so are blind to the Ultimate Other, the one true God in whom they profess to believe. Moral blindness bespeaks a deeper blindness in faith and they destroy the disturber of their ways lest his light dissipate their now comfortable and comforting darkness. In the subsequent history of Christianity this dialectic has been at work in the entire Christian community and in the individual believer. If, to adapt Aristotle, only the just person can do just acts, only the good can know God. Must we complete the circle and say only the one who knows God can be good? It may be more instructive to cast it in different form, the form beloved by prophets in preaching, by Jesus in his teaching, and by Saint John in his theologizing. Recognition of the neighbor in her mystery, response to her in her need is not only demanded by Jesus, and imitative of him, it is response to Jesus himself as his express teaching in Matthew 25 reveals and as the reflections of the author of the Johannine epistles confirms. In systematic reflection on the

---

[13]See the chapter by Bulckens in this volume.

doctrines of Creation and Incarnation we begin to sense the inner dynamism of response to neighbor as it encounters image of God now transformed into adoptive daughter or son and mediator of the absolute mystery which Jesus called the Father. If recognition of the neighbor is deficient, as in this ambiguous world it will always to some extent be, then recognition of the Father shares that deficiency and ambiguity. Yet the distinction of the two traditions of morality and faith, and the ability of person and community to discern the distinction, provide the challenge to mutual condemnation and correction as well as mutual endorsement and illumination.

For Christian moral educators the distinction and dialectic are of critical importance. How far may they separate what they distinguish? How free are they to embark on moral education programs which abstract entirely from the commitment of faith? How valid are formulas and programs explicitly designed to restrict the moral in a way that does not breach public school policy on religion under United States law, for people for whom such separation is not finally acceptable? I do not pretend to know the answer to these and other questions which might be posed along similar lines. I do believe however that if the work of the moral developmentalists were expanded to take account of what I believe to be a richer although still primarily secular expression of morality, Christians would be considerably more helped in their work of moral education. Indeed it may be that it is the individualist, liberal character of the underlying philosophy rather than the bracketing of the religious which is the greatest obstacle to effective cooperation of Christians with the very remarkable achievements of Kohlberg, his predecessors, and his colleagues. One might illustrate this by recalling the preeminence afforded to justice in this work, practically to the point of the neglect or rejection of the other virtues. How extraordinary that academics should find so little room for discussion of truth as a central social virtue and not as an antidote to cheating at exams but as a dynamic force summoning men to seek, speak, and even die for the truth. In conventional Christian terms the passing over of love or charity seems more remarkable. The rational and liberal thrust of the participants may have made them unduly suspicious of the vagueness and pliability of the term. In the approach to morality outlined here as in many other approaches, love can be a very hardheaded term. The recognition, respect, and concrete response demanded by the presence of the other are at once the test and expression of the love, which takes account of the whole person in appreciative recognition and turns that into service in feeding or clothing or education or whatever. In the larger-scale and more structured relationships operative in local, national, and international society the same appreciative recognition must find expression in the sensitivity of the provisions made and of the people who implement them. Without such human fullness people are degraded by our service rather than enriched and liberated and we in turn fail to break out of our protective, calculating shell, fail to transcend ourselves and be liberated. Perhaps the final rational but to me absurd conclusion of such a situation would be that one would feel called to the supreme expression of loving, by laying down one's life, without in fact having any love at all.

Moral Theology and Moral Education: Notes of a Would-Be Choreographer.

Even if the particular specialist is still unable to say, "I could have danced all night," one may at least try a few hesitant, awkward steps with a cooperative and learning partner. The choreographer's suggestions outlined here derive from the sometimes slow and patient, sometimes fast and furious exchanges which took place as the nightingales sang at the Abbey of Senanque.

1. The continuing tradition of the Natural Law, treasured by moral theology, has clear affinity with the respect for the moral reasoning process and the importance of justice in the work of Kohlberg and others. A broader and deeper understanding of that reasoning process as involving the biological, psychological, social, and spiritual unity called person would provide for richer exchange, and fewer *"faux pas."* The tendency to isolate justice and rights and claims in

{339}

conflict does not convey the sweep of morality in the Natural Law at its best or as incorporated in the Christian tradition of the West. Other issues and attitudes, virtues and values have to form part of any program of moral education and its scientific investigation.

2. Moral philosophy and theology as well as moral education have been predominantly individualist. One becomes a person only in community, thereby changing the community of family, school, neighborhood, city, nation, world. Community is in turn formed and reformed by persons. Moral educators, like moral philosophers and theologians, are faced with the difficulties of maintaining in creative tension the poles of person and community. The experience of Senanque suggests that they try to face them together.

3. The community dimension of all morality assumes almost apocalyptic urgency as one contemplates the global moral problems confronting mankind: war, actual and potential; starvation; waste of diminishing resources; pollution of the atmosphere and beyond. Only community awareness and response can cope with such problems. Only effective moral analyses and education can enable a community to achieve that awareness and response.

4. Analysts and educators cannot ignore the darkness that dogs their steps, the evil that lurks outside or even within the patch of light in which they have chosen to practice their steps. The evil is structured into both person and community, not necessarily as a prevailing force but always as threatening. The moral task involves a struggle that the good may prevail over the evil. The best results will always retain some ambiguity. The struggle is never finally resolved. The threat continues and must be carefully identified in analysis and education.

5. The historical sense, so clear in moral development programs, provides further help for the philosopher and theologian in understanding the moral agent. In the contexts of both community and evil, of moral action as interaction and good action as also overcoming some evil, the development takes

the form of conversion. It is in the traditional senses a conversion *from* (evil + self-centeredness) and a conversion *to* (good and the others). It should be a conversion of person and community.

6. Such conversion is only partly understood in anticipation of moral activity, which at its best and deepest is a creative venturing into the unknown. It is in the doing that full moral understanding is achieved. Programs of moral education require opportunities for such doing by persons in community and by communities of persons.

7. The relationship between morality and religion is perhaps best understood as one creative interaction. Distinct but inseparable for Christians, they provide mutual challenge and correction as well as illumination and confirmation. The conversion to the human other (person and community) which characterizes moral activity encounters also the mystery of the Ultimate Other as mediated by the human. The further reach of moral activity is prayer. The turning to the Ultimate Other demands and empowers the recognition of and response to its incarnate presence in the neighbor-(hood).

Theologians, philosophers, psychologists, and educators have their own patterns and rhythms. They can and must enrich and extend them together, if their efforts are not to resemble some individual *danses macabres*.

ABOUT THE AUTHOR

Dr. Enda McDonagh is a Catholic priest of the Archdiocese of Tuam, Ireland, and Professor of Moral Theology at Maynooth University, Ireland. He is currently on leave of absence as Huisking Professor of Theology at the University of Notre Dame. Dr. McDonagh studied at Maynooth, Rome, and Munich and has degrees in science and philosophy and doctorates in theology and canon law.

Besides his theological work at Maynooth and Notre Dame, he has lectured at universities and theological conferences in Europe, Africa, and

{342}

North America. He has also worked in catechetical institutes, continuing education for the clergy, and adult education groups in many places. His publications include Gift and Call, Doing the Truth, *and* Social Ethics and the Christian. *In preparation is* The Simple Demands of Justice: A Study in Church and Politics with Special Reference to Zimbabwe-Rhodesia.

Despite being a newspaper addict, he prefers for relaxation theater-going, novels and poetry reading.

Religion, Morality, and Ego Development

F. CLARK POWER AND LAWRENCE KOHLBERG

Introduction

In his pioneering work in the areas of moral development and education, Kohlberg has treated moral judgment as a domain distinct from religion. He has defined moral judgment as the way a person resolves conflicting claims between individuals and has found that moral decisions are made on the basis of a developing sense of justice. Furthermore, his articulation of the highest stage of moral judgment (Stage 6) is based on a universal principle of justice, derived from reason and not from religious belief or precept. This separation of morality ·from religion disturbs some people who feel that religious convictions are integral to their sense of being moral. Their discomfort is rooted in a concern that living morally is impossible without God's aid and that the religious life must be informed by a moral dimension. In this paper, we seriously engage this concern and offer a framework for relating religion to morality which respects the integrity of each as interpenetrating aspects of human experience.

Since Plato's *Euthyphro*, philosophers have inquired into the dependence of religion on morality. The lines of debate have classically been drawn around the position of Aquinas, who argues for a natural law morality in which God commands actions because they are right, and the position of Occam, who argues for a morality of divine command in which actions are right because God commands them. In this paper we will take the side of Aquinas and maintain that morality can, in principle, be derived rationally apart from divine revelation. This position is consistent with contemporary Catholic moral theology as the chapters in this volume by Bulckens and O'Donohoe suggest. While we will logically differentiate morality from religion, we will also be concerned with understanding how the two are related. Our central claim is that religion is a response to and an expression of our quest for an ultimate meaning for our moral judging and acting. As such, the main function of religion is not to supply moral prescriptions but to support moral judgment and action as a kind of purposeful human activity.

Religion and the Naturalistic Fallacy

The contemporary formalist philosophical response to Socrates' {345}
question, "Is what is holy holy because the gods approve it or do
the gods approve it because it is holy?" centers around Hume's
dictum, "No ethical conclusions from nonethical premises."
Hume demonstrated that one could not proceed from descriptive
statements about what is to prescriptive statements about what
ought to be. Thus, as Frankena points out,[1] theological statements about God's relationship to man—for example, that God
loves all men—do not imply moral obligations that man ought to
love his fellowman. Moral claims must be justified on their own
merit. In addition to the problem of prescriptivity of an ethic
derived from religious beliefs is the problem of universality.
Religious statements reflect the shared belief of a particular
religious community. Given the diversity of religions, an ethic
based on religion would lead to an arbitrary religious relativism.

Religious Content and Moral Stage Structure.

Kohlberg's longitudinal research on moral judgments[2] indicates
that moral reasoning develops in a hierarchical sequence of
stages. The structure of any given stage is defined in a formal way
according to the social perspective-taking which provides the
basis for the judgment. The developmental sequence described by
Kohlberg is universal—that is, it applies to every individual
regardless of the particularities of personality, religion, and
culture. The longitudinal study of moral development provides
support for the position that morality should be viewed as a
logically independent cognitive realm. While a small percentage
of individuals explicitly appeal to religious concerns in order to
justify their moral judgments, the vast majority do not. It is also

---

[1]W. Frankena, "Is Morality Logically Dependent on Religion?" in G.Outka and J. Reeder,
eds., *Religion and Morality* (Garden City: Anchor, 1973).

[2]L. Kohlberg, "The Meaning and Measurement of Moral Development." Lecture I. Hans
Werner Memorial Lecture, Clark University, April, 1979.

apparent that moral development occurs whether individuals have particular religious beliefs or not, and that individuals at the highest moral stage scored—Stage 5—differ widely in their religious and nonreligious views.

Religion as Reassurance

The intention of moral reasoning is to resolve competing claims among two or more persons on the basis of a norm or principle. Religion has as its primary intention an affirmation of the relatedness of man to the transcendent. The argument for a certain autonomy between morality and religion must be qualified by a proper understanding of how the process of moral judgment points beyond itself to the affirmation of faith. Toulmin[3] demonstrates that there are certain questions which appear to be moral but which turn out upon inspection to be religious. For example, if one asks why a promise should be kept, we may answer with certain norms about keeping contracts and provide a justification according to moral principles. If he probes further, we can respond with an ethical theory to support those principles. If he still presses his inquiry, we may no longer answer within the confines of moral reasoning. We must recognize that he is asking for some ultimate basis for moral action. We have reached the limit of moral reasoning and must appeal to religion.[4]

Questions such as "Why act morally?" are unsettling because they are directed toward the limits of our understanding. Ordinarily we have a prereflective confidence that we should be moral. When we call this confidence into question, we seek a mode of response which offers a reassurance for rational human action. Ogden[5] points out that the religious affirmation in response to the limit question restores a prior confidence in the ultimate significance of moral action. The religious "answer" to the limit question of morality is not the cause of that basic confidence but is its effect.

---

[3]S. Toulmin, *An Examination of the Place of Reason in Ethics* (Cambridge: University Press, 1950).

[4]See *Notes* at the end of this paper.

[5]S. Ogden, *The Reality of God* (New York: Harper and Row, 1966).

Fowler's analysis of faith, presented in this volume, focuses on how human knowing, acting, and relating are informed by this prior, implicit confidence in their meaning and worth. Fowler distinguishes the concept of faith from that of religion, as we have been using it, by defining faith as functioning as "largely unreflective and tacit, a human universal. "He speaks of religion primarily as a cultural and institutional expression of faith, whose symbols, myths, and history can serve to nurture and enrich an individual's faith. In this chapter, we will focus on the more personal dimension of religion as an appropriation of what is available in the culture as well as a response to one's life-experience. Our use of religion is consonant with the term "religious judgment" as studied by Oser, elsewhere in this volume. We thus consider religion to be that part of faith in which there is a conscious reflection on that which provides ultimate reassurance and meaning for life. Through the symbols, concepts, and theo-logic of religion, the concerns of one's faith are openly addressed in a reasonable way. Normally, we do not interrupt the decisions and activities of our lives by questioning life's meaning. We take meaning for granted until the boundaries of our finitude are disclosed and our confidence is shaken. Then what is implied must be brought forth into consciousness. This is the traditional task of theology in relation to faith, *fides quaerens intellectum*.

{347}

In contemporary studies of religious language by such philosophers as Ferre,[6] Ramsey,[7] and Tracey,[8] we see that religious language usually consists of normal language and a qualifier or an unusual juxtaposition of words or phrases. For example, we may speak of man as good but of God as absolutely or infinitely good. Such linguistic devices as analogy, metaphor, and parable serve to jar us out of our ordinary way of thinking and acting to the limits of our experience. They transcend the everyday, for example, by presenting images of *extravagant love*, as in the parable of the forgiving father, or perfect community and harmony with nature, as in the following portrayal of the kingdom of God by Isaias:

---

[6]F. Ferre, *Basic Modern Philosophy of Religion* (New York: Charles Scribner's Sons, 1964).

[7]I. Ramsey, *Religious Language: An Empirical Placing of Theological Phrases* (New York: Macmillan, 1963).

[8]D. Tracey, *Blessed Rage for Order* (New York: Seabury Press, 1976).

Then the wolf shall be a guest of the lamb and the leopard shall lie down with the kid . . . The baby shall play by the cobra's den and the child shall lay his hand on the adder's lair.

The purpose of this language is not to transport us to some supernatural realm of existence but to bring us back to the natural with a new sense of conviction and confidence. In Toulmin's words, "Ethics provides the *reasons* for choosing the 'right' course, religion helps us put our hearts into it."[9]

Knowing as Religious Activity

We never could have asked, "Why be moral?" without having an unrestricted desire to know which leads us beyond questions of particular problems to questions about the whole of life and the universe. Theologians such as Lonergan,[10] Rahner,[11] and Scanlon[12] employ the transcendental argument that the possibility for such questioning must be based on an *a priori* openness of reason to the very ground of existence. In this view, knowing itself presupposed a relatedness to the transcendent or ultimate source of being and meaning. However, in this form of relatedness the transcendent is not known as an object of experience but as a principle of understanding. We may think of this relatedness as we would think of an operative structure in cognitive-developmental psychology. The child at the concrete operational stage can classify objects but is not aware of the logical structure which makes classification possible. Such an awareness comes through reflecting on the necessary cognitive conditions for such action. In a similar way, an explicit awareness of God comes through, reflecting on the necessary ontological conditions for the dynamic of questioning itself.

---

[9]S. Toulmin, *op. cit.* p. 219

[10]B. Lonergan, *Insight: A Study of Human Understanding* (London: Longmans, Green, and Company, 1957).

[11]K. Rahner, *Foundations of Christian Faith*, trans W. Dych (New York: Seabury Press, 1978).

[12]M. Scanlon, "Christian Anthropology: An Overview," *American Ecclesiastical Review* 1970, *162*, pp. 2–10.

Kegan's chapter in this volume calls attention to the importance of the knowing process in cognitive development. It is the process itself which, Kegan points out, "partakes of the numinous, the graceful, the holy, the transcendent." What is most remarkable about the developmental process from this perspective is that it is basically restless, questioning, and struggling. In this continuous knowing process there is an interaction between the knowing subject and the known world such that each particular construction of what is true, right, and meaningful becomes relativized in the light of a later construction and in very pursuit of truth, justice, and meaning itself.

Religion and Ontological Anxiety

While we may raise the religious question by giving full reign to our rational desire for ultimate intelligibility, we turn more commonly to religion when we are existentially confronted by such real and anguishing problems as evil—Why be just in an unjust world?; separation—Why form relationships when our sense of our individuality and subjectivity is such that we can never share ourselves completely with other selves?; and mortality—Why feel that my life has significance when my self, my labor, and my love are doomed to perish at the end of my life or at the end of history?

Tillich[13] makes clear that such problems are not mere psychological or sociological observations which can be resolved by psychotherapy or by membership in a caring community. They are not due to the lack of progress of science, technology, or social institutions; they are rooted in our very being which is both limited and unlimited, finite and infinite. Tillich sums up these problems in his concept of "ontological anxiety." Anxiety differs from fear in that our fears have a definite object which we may analyze and strive to overcome. Anxiety has no definite object—its object is nothingness, ultimate nonbeing, meaninglessness.

---

[13]P. Tillich, *The Courage to Be* (New Haven: Yale University Press, 1952).

The question which religion addresses is fundamentally one of affirmation or negation—courage or submission. Limited as we are by nonbeing, we strive for transcendence in order to be—to act—to bring about justice. We do this naturally without reflecting on it. The courage to confront ontological anxiety is not to be sought as a remedy outside of ourselves. Paradoxically, the courage we seek when we are confronted by the limits of our existence is the courage which animates us even when we are not aware of it.

The Ego

In our deliberations thus far we have related religion to morality through the notion of "limit." Religion is a reflective response to our questioning of the limits of morality, whether that questioning stems from an unrestricted rational inquiry or an existential crisis. A second way of relating morality to religion comes through a consideration of the psychological unity of the two provided by the ego. The same self that asks moral questions asks religious questions, integrating what is known such that it can maintain itself in its enviornment. The ego refers to a more comprehensive domain than the moral, while including the moral as a dimension or an aspect of character.

In our discussion of ontological anxiety we pointed out that it is the self as well as the self's ideals which are threatened. We ask, why must *I* suffer, why must *I* be alone, why must *I* die, why must *I* be moral, because we are concerned about ourselves in relationship to those conditions which threaten our fundamental survival and functioning. Those conditions represent what Loder in this volume calls "existential negation" or "the ultimate negation of the capacity of the ego to construct its own world."

One of the ways in which Fowler distinguishes his theory of faith development from Kegan's theory of ego development is that faith carries with it an emphasis on that knowing in which "the identity or worth of the person is at stake." It is out of this sense of crisis that the self attaches itself to significant others, social institutions, values, ideologies, and so on. Fowler calls our attention to the fact that the ego's struggle for being and meaning is a continuous and essential factor in its development. There are, of course, moments of radical discontinuity, of overwhelming existential anxiety. Religion responds to this ultimate state of ego distress by pointing toward the ego's salvation, what Loder calls "the negation of the negation."

These considerations on the relationship of religion to the ego have implications for our original inquiry into the relationship of religion to morality. Insofar as religion serves to strengthen the self which makes moral decisions, it has an effect, not on the particular formulation of the moral judgment, but on whether any judgment is to be made at all and whether and how, if it is made, that judgment will be carried into action.

Let us illustrate several ways in which religion may be thought of as supporting the self's moral judgment and action by referring to some pertinent material from Fowler's sample of faith interviews.[14] First, a religious interpretation of one's life as a vocation can renew one's sense of moral purpose and commitment. One woman recounted an experience of nearly being killed in an accident and asking herself in the instant when she realized her life had been spared, "Why me?" She answered her own question:

> Maybe there is something I have to do. Now I have to find what that thing is. Ah, you know, maybe I just keep doing the things I am doing . . . Which is, you know . . . I guess I was pretty much involved in doing for people which was enough worth for Someone to say, "Okay, you have to keep on living."

The experience of the utter contingency of her life became an occasion for both a felt sense of self-affirmation as a moral person—"I was involved in doing for people," and a sense of commitment—"you have to keep on living." The sanction for moral action is seen religiously as coming from a will beyond the self.

Second, religion can serve to encourage the self confronted by the abyss between the moral ideals of the self and the injustice

---

[14]See *Notes* at the end of this paper.

of the world. If the ultimate order of the universe is sensed as being lawful or loving, then we feel that we should conform our spirit so as to be at one with all that is. When an "activist" who had spent a considerable portion of her life working on behalf of the poor was asked whether her efforts were not futile in the face of the indifference of society, she conceded, "I could go the way of Sartre and conclude that all is absurd." Yet she went on to speak of her responsibility to struggle for justice because "I believe that's what the kingdom's going to be." The religious symbol of the kingdom spurred on this person's involvement, providing some confidence that she was fighting a winning battle against the forces of human degradation and enslavement. Thus a religious understanding can offer a sense of reassurance that ethical actions in an unjust world are not fruitless, that they have some eternal or eschatological significance.

Third, a religious perspective can heighten one's moral sensitivity by offering a vision of the self as intrinsically related in a familial bond with other selves. Evans speaks of religious language as providing an "onlook" on a moral situation.[15] Onlooks are typically expressed "I look on x as y." In answering affirmatively to one of Kohlberg's moral dilemmas about whether Heinz should steal a drug to save a stranger's life, one man elaborated "we all have the same common Father, therefore we are all brothers and sisters." Thinking of strangers as brothers and sisters had the effect of making what may have been construed as a nonobligatory situation, one in which moral action was obligatory. In addition, the motivation to act was intensified.

Structural and Functional Approaches to the Ego

Having outlined how religious considerations relate generally to the ego, let us turn to how they relate more specifically to two psychological approaches to the development of the ego, the Piagetian logical and the Eriksonian functional.

---

[15]D. Evans, "Does Religious Faith Conflict with Moral Freedom?" in G. Outka and J. Reeder, eds., *Religion and Morality* (Garden City: Anchor, 1973).

The Piagetian approach we term *structural* because it starts by abstracting a structure or form of thinking from the *function* which the thinking is serving or the content of interest of thinking. For Piaget, the same function, moral judgment, is served by successive structures of judgment, each of which displaces or reintegrates prior structures for serving this function. The Erikson model we term functional because it defines stages not by new structures for old functions but by new functions of the self, person or ego or new foci of concern and choice for the person. The distinction is summarized in the table below.

{353}

TABLE 1 · Structural and Functional Stage Approaches

Piaget	*Erikson*
Stages are different for a single function, e.g., moral judgment, logical reasoning. Accordingly, later stages replace earlier stages. Experience leading to development is cognitive experience, especially experiences of cognitive conflict and match.	Stages are choices or uses of new *functions* by an ego—earlier functions or choices remain as background to the new stage. Experience leading to development is personal experience, especially experiences and choice of personal conflict.
The developmental change is primarily a changed perception in the physical, social, and moral world.	The developmental change involved is primarily a self-chosen identification with goals in a choice or a commitment.
Later stages are more cognitively adequate than earlier stages: 1) including the earlier stage pattern, 2) resolving the same problems better, and 3) in being more universally applicable or justifiable, i.e., in the universality and inclusiveness of their ordering of experience.	Later stages are more adequate than earlier stages, not in cognitive inclusiveness, but in virtue of ego strength, i.e., in their ability to order personal experience in a form that is stable, positive, and purposive. Attainment of a stage and adequacy of stage use are distinct, however.[16]

[16]L. Kohlberg, "Continuities and Discontinuities Revisited," in P. E. Baltes and L. R. Goulet, eds., *Lifespan Developmental Psychology*, 2nd ed. (New York: Academic Press, 1973).

While structural stages are hierarchical, Erikson's stages are not. Erikson's stages form a sequence of problems, not of structures of their solution. Regardless of attainment or solution of the problem of generativity, the person moves on to face the problem of integrity versus despair. Erikson believes there is a biological (and/or psychosexual) source for the problems of each stage in the sequence, but biological maturation or change defines the problem, not the form or attainment of its solution. For instance, generativity (or stagnation) represents forms of response to the problem or task given by biological parenthood, integrity (or despair) represents forms of response to the problem given by impending death and senescence.

The religious question is relevant both to a functional and to a logical approach to the ego. The most striking illustration of how the functional approach considers religion is seen as Erikson's ideal man passes through a seventh stage of generativity to become an ethical man. There remains a final task—the resolution of the crisis of integrity versus despair—which is more broadly religious and which defines an eighth stage. The concepts of integrity and despair are related to the awareness of death. In this and in all of the stages, the sense of confidence which religion brings may be seen as supportive of "ego strength."

In the logical approach to the ego, the religious question arises out of fulfillment of the ego's search for ultimate meaning in the universe. Ego developmental stages may be understood as progressive redefinitions of the self in relationship to the world—what is subjective and what is objective. The limit question for the ego is how the dualism of subject and object, self and other, may be overcome, as Kegan so well describes it in his chapter in this volume.

One of the shortcomings of the cognitive-developmental approach to the ego is that because of the expansiveness of the domain, the logical relationships that underlie the unity of stage structure are obscure, as are the hierarchical relationships of the stages to each other. The research approach used for the study of moral development is to treat scientific reasoning, morality, epistemology, aesthetics, and religion as distinct domains each with its own set of logic. If such an approach is taken, then the logical features of the stage sequence of each domain may be elaborated and clarified. Of course, we recognize that these domains are related to each other insofar as they reflect logical-mathematical structures. This provides a basis for treating the ego as having a logical principle of unity as well as a psychological one. Oser and his colleagues have narrowed their research perspective to include only concerns which are specifically religious. We would expect their study to yield a more carefully detailed description of how religious thinking develops than has heretofore been produced. Fowler, on the other hand, has had to sacrifice a detailed exploration of how religious thinking develops in favor of a more holistic description of the faith present in the way a person gives meaning to his or her way of life. His interpretation of the developmental process of meaning-making as faith activity is a bold way of relating traditionally religious concepts to all aspects of knowing.

Moral Judgment as Necessary But Not Sufficient for Religious Reasoning

Having explored some of the theoretical issues concerning the relationship of religion to the ego and morality, we would like to raise empirical questions. Stated simply, we would like to examine the hypothesis made elsewhere by Kohlberg that a stage of moral judgment is a necessary but not sufficient condition for a stage of religion.[17] In order to examine this hypothesis we have adapted Fowler's scoring scheme to focus more exclusively on "religious reasoning"[18] The stages of religious thinking were constructed making use of actual data to logically parallel, as far as possible, the moral stages such that they would reflect the logic of the moral stages but represent something more. This approach is similar to the one undertaken by Kohlberg who assumed a certain stage of Piagetian logic was necessary for a given moral stage, i.e., a Stage 4 social system perspective presupposes Piagetian formal operations.[19]

---

[17]Kohlberg, *op. cit.*

[18]See *Notes* at the end of this paper.

[19]See *Notes* at the end of this paper.

We have discussed how morality and religion represent distinct, but related, domains by exploring the dynamic by which moral questions lead to religious ones. While there may be a functional relationship between morality and religion such that religion answers to the questions beyond faith—this does not mean that they are related in their logical content. This demands an analysis of the moral characteristics of the object of religion—the ultimate—conceived of as the God of revelation or as the whole of nature.

For the theist in the Judeo-Christian tradition, God is symbolized as personal in an idealized way and is seen as establishing as the end point of human history an ideal community of justice—the kingdom of God. Man's relationship with God is viewed from this perspective as fundamentally an interpersonal one. The experience the Hebrew people had of overwhelming justice and care as manifested in their history was integral to their faithfulness and devotion to Yahweh, their God. As the theologian D'Arcy points out, in the biblical tradition, such a God did not command worship out of awesome power but proved himself "worthy of worship" out of just deeds.[20]

From the perspective of the mystical pantheist, such as Spinoza or Santayana—Nature is the whole which encompasses the universal and yet is more than the aggregate. The pantheist's religious experience is marked by a sense of the impassivity of Nature, which, nevertheless, fills us with a sense of overwhelming beauty, awe, and union. In the experience of participating in the beauty of Nature, we experience the beauty of something permanent in spite of our transience. It is the beauty best represented from the mountaintop in which we have that sense of distance in which we seem to share Nature's eternal and inclusive perspective. While Nature does not appear personal in itself, it does answer to our deepest personal longings for eternal justice, beauty, truth, and union. The religious attitude is one in which we know ourselves in mind and body to be one with Nature. Nature sustains morality because morality is part of a larger whole

---

[20]E. D'Arcy, "Worthy of Worship: A Catholic Contribution," in G. Outka and J. Reeder, eds., *Religion and Morality* (Garden City: Anchor, 1973).

which is its source. A love or passion for justice ultimately derives from one's love of Nature, which is in part "just."

Having indicated how religion and morality conceptually overlap such that a moral logic is a necessary condition for a religious one, let us proceed to show how religion is more than morality such that a moral stage cannot be a sufficient condition for a parallel religious stage. We illustrated in our discussion of religious questions as limit questions that they raise problems of meaning which morality cannot solve. Furthermore, in our brief treatment of religious language, we pointed out that religion has a unique logic in which ordinary meanings are qualified in ways which make them extraordinary. Thus to say that God is good requires not only an understanding of the ordinary meaning of "good" as applied to human persons, but also some recognition that good is only being applied analogously to God since God transcends the categories of human personhood.

Now, let us consider the distinguishing characteristics of religious logic which lead us to acknowledge that the domains of religion and morality may fruitfully be studied separately.

A religious logic must be a logic of the whole, such that what Tillich calls the basic polarities of being may be resolved.[21] This means that the gap between ideals of justice, community, and immortality must be reconciled with the realities of suffering, alienation, and death. Not only subjective human experience but all of Nature itself must be integrated in relationship to a whole. A religious view is one in which every part of the world takes on meaning from the perspective of the whole which includes them. This entails a shift from figure to ground in which we identify ourselves with the cosmic or infinite perspective itself; we value life from its standpoint. The holistic logic of religion is one which transcends the distinction between the subjectivity of the knower and the objectivity of what is known—the world is brought into unity through God or Nature. God and Nature are notions which ground and unify both the intelligence of the knower and the unbelievability of the universe.

---

[21]Tillich, *op. cit.*

If we logically construct a sequence of religious stages to depend on a parallel moral stage, what can we learn from collecting empirical data about their relationship? Since we have differentiated the functions of morality and religion, one empirically resolvable question is which stage of reasoning does a person use first. It is entirely possible that a person could use a higher stage of moral reasoning in the context of religious problems than she or he would use for solving a moral dilemma. Of course, what we expect to be the case is that individuals will develop moral and religious stages simultaneously or the moral stage before the faith stage. Empirical data relating to which stage a person uses first would appear to have implications for the question of whether the attainment of one stage is really necessary for the attainment of a parallel one. It is possible, if religious stages are developed prior to the moral stages, that moral judgment does depend on the construction of religious ideas. If the reverse is the case, then we would venture that religious ideas are built in part out of moral judgment.

A qualification is in order. We have followed the approach taken by Kant that religion is a matter for practical reason. However, we could have approached religion as a matter for speculative reason, as well. The underlying religious question for the scientist is what sustains the process of scientific inquiry such that he has confidence that the logical relationships constructed in the human mind can be found to be a part of the world. While we may expect that any adequate construal of God must include both a notion of truth and a notion of justice, it is possible that the religious views of individuals may be incomplete and only depict God according to one or the other notion. Strictly speaking, our necessary-but-not-sufficient argument is applicable when moral qualities are attributed to the ultimate.[22]

In order to examine our necessary-but-not-sufficient hypothesis, interviews from twenty-one subjects were drawn from a large pool of interviews collected by Fowler. Selection was done

---

[22]See *Notes* at the end of this paper.

on the basis of representing each faith stage by at least three interviews. The subjects had a diversity of religious and nonreligious backgrounds. Each subject was orally administered Kohlberg's moral dilemmas and Fowler's faith interview, consisting of three parts: (a) a life history; (b) reasoning about the meaning of life in the face of such boundary conditions as death, suffering, wonder and so on; and (c) thinking about specifically religious topics. Scoring was done according to Kohlberg's standard scoring manual[23] and Fowler's stage descriptions[24] modified such that there was a focus on explicitly religious reasoning.

Stage scores for moral judgment and religious reasoning were obtained by determining the modal stage used by a subject and the next most frequently used stage (if more than 25 percent of a subject's reasoning). Comparing the modal stages of morality and faith there is an 81 percent overall agreement. Through Stage 3 the agreement was 100 percent. The divergencies occurred in Stages 4 and 5. In these stages, moral reasoning was sometimes higher than religious reasoning, although no more than one stage higher.

Our data suggest that moral judgment is a necessary but not sufficient condition for religious reasoning, at least in the higher stages. Moral reasoning appears to provide the basic concepts of justice and care, out of which a theistic notion of God can be fashioned. God is never known directly but is always mediated indirectly through human experience. It is only by being able to form concepts of ordinary socio-moral that we can qualify them in a way to point beyond to the extraordinary—to God.

Now let us turn to our data in order to see how religious conceptions depend on moral structures. First, we will describe each stage of religious reasoning.

---

[23]L. Kohlberg, A. Colby, J. Gibbs, B. Speicher-Dubin, C. Power, and D. Candee, *Assessing moral stages: a manual*. Book in preparation, 1979. (Preliminary edition available from Center for Moral Development and Education, Harvard University Graduate School of Education.)

[24]J. Fowler, "Stages in Faith: The Structural-Developmental Approach," in T. Hennessey, ed., *Values and Moral Development* (New York: Paulist Press, 1976).

TABLE 2 · RELIGIOUS AND MORAL JUDGMENT

Religious Stage Scores	*Moral Stage Scores*
1	1
1	1
1	1
2	2
2	2
2 (3)	2 (3)
3	3
3	3
3	3
4	5
4	4
4	4 (3)
4	4
4	4½ (relativist)
4	4
4	4
4–5	5
4–5	5
5 (4)	5
5 (4)	5 (4)
5	5

Stage 1

The notion of God at this stage is, as Fowler points out, "prean-thropomorphic."[25] God has a mixture of human-like qualities, such as looking like a person, wearing clothes, having hair, and so on, and nonhuman-like qualities, such as going everywhere by "spreading Himself out" or "splitting Himself up." God's powers are limitless, often surpassing the powers of people. God can make dead people alive again and even make Himself again when he dies. In spite of the fact that God is invested with different

---

[25]See Fowler' Chapter in Fowler and Keen, *Life Maps* (Waco, Texas: Word Books, 1978), especially discussions of Stages I and II, pp. 42–60.

powers than people, there is no rigid categorization of divine and human causality. God makes plants and animals as well as houses. God is moral according to the Stage 1 moral criterion that one should not break any rules, for example, "He never tells a lie in his life." Being God does have its drawbacks, however, as one youngster pointed out—"He can't play with kids."

As can be seen, depictions of God utilize the imagery of physical and psychological superiority such as power, size, and wisdom, and qualify it. In this manner God is understood as the ultimate authority and source of nurture in the child's life. The child at this stage does not consider the intentions of God as significant, but thinks of God as whimsically making things, and what is of interest is the supposedly magical way in which God creates—as one child marveled, "He makes things by 'saying their names,'" or "by putting his thumb on them."

Very often the religious language and symbols which the child receives from his religious tradition present a challenge in fathoming their meaning. These symbols and concepts are assimilated to the world as the child knows it; the child supplies his own meanings to these words and symbols which are revered because they are held sacred in the adult world. As an example of this, a five-year-old in this study was asked if people can talk to God. The child responded, "Well God can hear them, but he's in signs. He doesn't talk." When probed about what signs God is in, he responded, "Stop signs and peace signs."

Stage 2

God is a dispenser of good things, both in this life and in the next. However, God, too, puts a price on his merchandise, requesting the performance of moral and religious actions in exchange for his aid. As one person put it, "They preach if you are good you go to heaven, if you are bad you go to hell."

Religious symbols which at Stage 1 were magical now become instruments of manipulation. Superstitious practices appear as ways of knowing and influencing the future. The "ultimate concern" at Stage 2 is the satisfaction of my needs. God

{361}

provides the assurance that one's deepest desires will in fact be met. A typical religious problem at this stage is whether God is fair because those who pray do not always get what they ask for.

> At times when I have had a close call and I've come through it all right, I've been so glad and I've thought God was there . . . but at other times when I don't get pulled through it, why isn't he there, then? I prayed just as hard both times and sometimes he was there and sometimes he wasn't. It never did me any good.

Stage 3.

The image of God invariably evoked at this stage was that of a "personal deity," as described by Fowler,[26] for example, "a buddy," "a caring shepherd," and so on. God was one who could be approached on an interpersonal basis in prayer. He was understanding and one to whom to go when all other efforts to help loved ones have failed. Such a God affirms the "rightness" of helping others even in the limit situation in which ordinary means of help are inaccessible or futile. God's authority is supreme but benign, possessing a wisdom which far surpasses man's. While at Stage 2 God was questioned for not answering prayers, at Stage 3 it was reasonable that God would not answer prayers at times because he knows what is truly best for us. God acts not simply to make man happy, but to make man virtuous.

An illustration of the way in which a religous limit experience can both call the "moral enterprise into question and enhance one's commitment to it" was provided by one subject's poignant account of the death of her brother:

> And there has to be something beyond because here is a person who ten minutes ago was alive, vital and functioning and loving, and yet it's just a cold body there. And what happens to all that spirit that was in that person? There has to be a hereafter. It would be finding all the people you loved and have lost.

---

[26]J. Fowler, "Stages in Faith: The Structural-Developmental Approach" in T. Hennessey, ed., *Values and Moral Development* (New York: Paulist Press, 1976).

We find in this statement how the experience of a limit situation can jar one into a peculiar way of thinking. The death of people that we love threatens the ultimacy of love. The world, taken as a whole, seems callous and indifferent to human love. Why love at all if this is the way things really are? The belief in a hereafter functions as a reassurance not only that love is appropriate, but that love is our destiny.

Stage 4

The nature of God becomes a great problem for theists at this stage. There is an effort to qualify the personalistic qualities found at Stage 4 and more precisely define His nature according to His perfections. Thus, while admitting the usefulness of personalistic language about God, a young man in speaking of God's sorrow qualified himself by saying, "In essence God cannot be grieved." A more controlled, systematic language for God is invented if one's tradition does not provide it. Thus God is conceptualized as "Supreme Being," "a force," or "the sum total of the universe."

At this stage, God does not relate simply in a dialogue with individuals, as at Stage 3, but He relates to the universe as a whole and has a plan for the parts within that nexus. Such thinking can go so far as to negate the worth of the individual as was illustrated in the following:

> There is something that you don't understand and that is con-
> cerned with the whole human condition and mankind as a whole,
> but not concerned in a rather simplistic way by you know, praying
> your car won't get stolen or your kids will be safe. It won't work
> that way . . . It works more generally, and it may turn out very
> well that you personally and your family will be just plowed under.

The moral imperative to do what the system requires is rendered meaningful by faith in that system. When the ground of all that is experienced is orderly, then one can commit oneself to order with the assurance that one is acting in harmony with the universe. Thus, we found the appearance of a civil religion in which the Ten Commandments are justified in light of their beneficial effect on society and society's own laws are felt to be in harmony with God's. For example, Heinz's stealing was condemned as wrong because it was against the law of the state and the law of God.

Stage 5

At this stage, religious symbols are consciously employed to express an acceptance of the fundamental paradoxes in life and, in a way, transcend them. Those at Stage 5 indicated an awareness of the inadequacy of a purely conceptual mode of thinking when addressing the question of God. Their language often faltered and they confessed that they were trying to find words for the inexpressible, for that which Wittgenstein once claimed "can be seen but not said." For example, one subject, when asked what God meant to her, responded:

> Um . . . I don't . . . I don't really like to talk about that. O.K. It's not that I don't like to talk about it. God, to me, is an ultimate, is a, is a transcending of a lot of . . . It's a consciousness beyond us, it's transcending . . .

The limit language of Stage 5 expresses a recognition that to become conscious of God is to become conscious of the ground of one's own subjectivity. To know God as the infinite is to know the self as always directed toward the infinite. Yet the self *is not* infinite. The self experiences itself as finite, as we have seen, and grasping beyond itself to ultimate happiness, justice, unity, and so on.

In contrast to what we found at Stage 4 in which human activity was directed toward the fulfillment of a divinely preordained plan, Stage 5 presents God and man as mutually involved in a "creative" activity which consists of establishing a society in which the dignity and freedom of each man might flourish. In this view, man does not look to God for moral answers but for moral support.

While, generally, religious and moral assertions appeared to be complementary, there were cases of conflict. One young man who exhibited Stage 5 moral reasoning and Stage 4 religious reasoning had great difficulty responding to the Heinz dilemma when he attempted to coordinate his religious and moral views. In answering a moral dilemma, he interspersed his judgments related to the dilemma with religious thinking. Twice when he used his theology as a premise for a moral judgment he lapsed into State 4 moral reasoning. He then recognized his thinking was inadequate. In the first instance, he reasoned that life was valuable because of the contribution one could make by spreading God's word. But then he countered that such a position would imply that the life of an evil person was not worth saving. This was unacceptable because he felt each person has a right to life. In the second instance, he employed a theory of predestination to say that even unjust death was necessary in accordance with God's plan. However, he rejected predestination as an excuse for inaction in order to save a life, although he became flustered at his inability to resolve this inconsistency in his thinking.

{365}

Returning to our necessary-but-not-sufficient hypothesis, the fact that we could find no individuals between Stages 1 and 3 who did not have the same stage of religion as they had of moral judgment leaves the question open of whether one is a necessary condition for the other at the early stages. Our analysis of the interviews indicates that religion and morality are so undifferentiated in people's thinking that there is a real interplay between them. At Stages 4 and 5, moral stages do appear to precede religious stages. The divergence of religious reasoning from moral judgment at the higher stages may be due to the attained cognitive capacity to systematize thinking such that moral and religious beliefs can appear distinguishable.

The claim that moral stages are necessary but not sufficient for religious stages does not imply that religious stages are less important than moral stages, or are in some way reducible to moral stages. Such a claim is compatible with the theistic position that implicit, universal faith grounds the very possibility of making a moral judgment or acting morally. That is, in every moral judgment there is a tacit further judgment that the activity of moral judging is, in fact, necessary. Such a judgment is based not on the fulfillment of moral criteria for an ethically right act but on the fulfillment of "religious" criteria for an ultimately meaningful act.

Toward Further Investigation: Morality, Religion, and the Social Atmosphere

Thus far, we have considered faith and morality from the perspective of Piagetian cognitive-developmental psychology, which views knowledge as the construction of the individual interacting with the environment. This psychological approach obscures the extent to which moral and religious development occurs in a social context made up not only of other individuals, but of collective norms, meanings, and values. Early applications of Kohlberg's moral developmental theory took the form of Socratic moral discussion and largely neglected the dynamics of collective influence. However, Kohlberg's efforts in moral education have shifted decidedly to an approach which seeks to build "Just Communities" through a hybrid of Deweyan democracy and Durkheimian collectivism.[27] A concern for the development of the individual requires a concern for the development of social institutions in which one participates. Our analysis of what we call "the moral atmosphere of the group" makes clear that when members of a group discuss moral problems related to the group, they are involved in representing shared norms and values as well as their own particular points of view.

Continuing research in religious faith development should carefully consider the relationship between the developing individual and the shared beliefs of the community. The typical pattern of religious development is not the construction of a "natural religion" by an individual reflecting on the dynamics of consciousness or on existential boundary situations, but a participation of an individual in a church or synagogue which has a particular religious tradition. The developmentalist must take into account that religious concepts, such as God, salvation, and creation are not, in the Piagetian sense, "spontaneous" constructions but are best described as cultural constructions or, in the

---

[27]L.Kohlberg, "Exploring the Moral Atmosphere of Institutions: A Bridge Between Moral Judgment and Moral Action," Lecture II, Hans Werner Memorial Lecture, Clark University, April 1979; and C. Power and J. Reimer, "Moral Atmosphere: An Educational Bridge Between Moral Judgment and Action" in W. Damon, ed., *New Directions for Child Development*, Vol, II (San Francisco: Josey-Bass, 1978).

terminology of Vygotsky, as "scientific."[28] One does not develop cultural concepts strictly out of direct experience when left to one's own devices, but appropriates the communication of these concepts by others to one's own understanding.

{367}

Given the importance of studying religious communities, we may inquire into the sociological functions of religion, especially with respect to a group's moral interests. We agreed earlier that the psychological function of religion is to provide a reassurance or courage which sustains the ego in confrontation with "ontological anxiety." We now would like to argue that the sociological function of religion is to provide a courage of participation which sustains community in confrontation with privatism and totalitarianism. Durkheim saw that sociological function of religion as the *preservation* of society.[29] He posited that God was a hypostatization of society, and that the religious emotions of respect and attachment were indispensable for secular morality. Society, like God, was greater than the individual and alone capable of inspiring a sense of duty and altruism. Durkheim pointed out how religious rituals served to strengthen collective beliefs and attitudes by symbolically representing them to the group. He noted that an institutional moral process such as trial and punishment may also be seen as a ritual symbolizing the triumph of collective values over deviant impulses and thereby "healing the wounds" caused by the violation of the collective unit.

Durkheim coupled a conservative view of religion as a means of social control and cohesion with a progressive view that the religious experience energized society enabling it to re-create itself through creating new collective details. His analysis that religious transcendence would, in the course of social evolution, be replaced by societal symbols raised important problems which he himself realized. He noted that the secular ceremonies and moral ideals of his day failed to animate society as had religious

[28]L. S. Vygotsky, *Thought and Language*, trans. E. Hanfmann and G. Vakar (Cambridge, Massachusetts: M.I.T. Press, 1962).

[29]E. Durkheim, *The Division of Labor in Society*, trans G. Simpson (New York: Macmillan, 1964) and *The Elementary Forms of the Religious Life*, trans. J. W. Swain (New York: Macmillan, 1965); originally published in 1915.

events in the past. Yet, he predicted, "a day will come when our societies will know again those hours of creative effervescence, in the course of which new ideas arise and new formulae are found."

Following the thrust of Durkheim's thinking that religion (whether secularized or not) is crucial to maintenance of society, we maintain, in agreement with Tillich, that religion supports not only the courage to be an individual self but the courage to be a part of community.[30] How does being a part of a community raise the religious question? We have pointed out that an element of our anxiety is being separate. Having an individuated self-consciousness, we strive for union and accept incomplete association. The quest for union with others—for community—presents two dangers. Without union, we risk loneliness, estrangement, and anomie. In union, we risk total absorption into the other and a loss of self.

The impossible problem for any society is how to meet these conflicting demands of the self—separation and union. Another way of stating the problem is to ask how transcendence—a standing above or apart from—may be reconciled with immanence—a being at one with. Clearly, no finite person can resolve this polarity nor can we expect any social order to fully respond to it. The problems are fundamentally religious. Only with a religious view can we reconcile separation and unity, immanence and transcendence.

Conclusion

Our concern has been to show that religion offers reassurance for those ultimate questions such as "Why be moral?" "Why be social?" and "Why be at all?" Morality offers us a reasonable way of resolving interpersonal conflicts but cannot offer us a reason for being and for purposeful human activity. Religion provides such a reason and in so doing infuses our moral sensibilities with a passion which comes from a consciousness that our moral principles resonate with the very nature of the universe.

---

[30]Tillich, *op. cit.*

Educational Implications

One of the most significant advantages to be gained by distin- {369} guishing the domains of morality and religion has been that such a differentiation allows us to promote moral education in the public schools in the United States in which there is a strict separation of Church and State. Educators, no matter what their religious persuasion, generally recognize the importance of developing in children universal standards of justice. Furthermore, preparing for one's role as a citizen in a democratic society demands that one develop the capacity to make responsible decisions which respect the rights and welfare of all.

Considering morality and religion as distinct domains also can be of help to educators in public and nonpublic schools in designing programs which respond to the particular characteristics of each domain. While, in general, stimulating cognitive conflict appears to be crucial for promoting structural development, development in a given domain of reasoning does depend on the particular kind of problem-solving experience one has had. For example, experience with problems of physics may serve to promote the way one resolves scientific problems, but not necessarily moral problems. If moral and/or religious development is desired, then it is incumbent upon the educator to give specific attention in the curriculum to questions with moral and/or religious implications.

The evidence which we have found for a necessary-but-not-sufficient relationship between morality and religion suggests that one's stage of moral development can place a ceiling on religious development. Therefore, religious educators should see the promotion of moral development not only as an important goal in itself, but also as contributing to further religious development. Religious development, of course, requires more than moral education, and religious educators should attend to those problems and methods endemic to theology and religion.

We have indicated that the problem-solving approach seems best suited for promoting moral and religious development. Such an approach, outlined by Dewey,[31] takes into account that

---

[31]J. Dewey, *Democracy and Education*. (New York: MacMillan, 1966),originally published in 1916.

students are active knowers who must be given the opportunity to integrate that body of knowledge which their school, religion, and society deem important with their own structures of reasoning about the world. This entails, as much as possible, allowing students to think through problems for themselves in collaboration with others rather than to passively memorize the answers which the teacher proffers.

In our work in moral education, we have explored two complementary ways of applying the problem-solving method. The first involves Socratic discussion in which the teacher presents the class with dilemmas or problematic situations which are likely to provoke differing points of view. The teacher's role is to facilitate the discussion and resolution of the conflict by encouraging students to speak thoughtfully, sharpening the points of disagreement, raising unexamined but important issues, and presenting ideas which challenge further inquiry. The second way utilizes not just the curricula but the social atmosphere of the school as an educational resource. Lickona's chapter, in this volume, on cooperative democracy in the classroom is an example of such an approach. We contend that the real-life problems in the school can provide the grist for development. We encourage the democratization of the classroom and school which can enhance student participation. In addition, we advocate that the form of association in the school can be "communal," focusing on an intrinsic valuing of improving the relationships of individuals with each other and the group as a whole, and not simply "pragmatic," focusing on an instrumental valuing of these relationships as a means for individualistic ends.

While our research has only dwelt on the effect the social atmosphere can have on moral development, we believe social and religious atmosphere can have a similar effect on religious development. The chapter by Lombaerts in this volume, while not a cognitive-developmental study, does point to the potential of a democratic religious community to influence moral and religious thinking and action. However, his account of the eventual decline of the group cautions us against a naive appropriation of democracy as itself sufficient to bring about a positive group atmosphere.

Having presented some of the educational implications which we see in this paper and in our experience and research in moral education, we caution educators in reflecting upon our remarks to view them as an invitation to further dialogue. Educational practice cannot simply be deduced from psychological or theological theory. Rather, there must be an interplay between theory and practice such that each can be enriched by the other.

NOTES*

[4]This notion of religion as a response to the limit question of morality, "Why be moral?" is present in Kohlberg's (1973) depiction of a Stage 7. Stage 7 is a metaphorical way of stating that the "Why be moral?" question is related to moral development but is beyond the domain of normative morality as it is strictly defined. While Stage 7 is not a moral stage, since there is no higher way of moral judging than to judge in terms of Stage 6 universal principles of justice, it does respond to a set of problems left over at Stage 6 which Stage 6 cannot answer. At all of the stages prior to Stage 6, the question "Why be moral?" is never fully understood because nonmoral values which contradict the nature of morality may be advanced as answers. At Stage 6, individuals are able to differentiate moral from nonmoral concerns such that the limits of the moral domain become clarified, making the religious question inescapable. The Stage 7 metaphor should not be interpreted to mean that religious concerns do not arise before one is fully developed morally. Religious concerns do have a developmental history, as we will indicate.

[14]These interviews were analyzed as part of the study described later in this paper. We wish to acknowledge our gratitude to James Fowler for making the material available to us and for his help in analyzing it. We also wish to thank the Kennedy Foundation for their grant to James Fowler, which supported the research in this chapter.

[18]The scoring criteria were developed as part of a scoring manual for the assessment of faith stages. We selected issues from the scoring manual that reflected "religious" concerns which could be differentiated from moral and other concerns.

[19]The structural stage descriptions and scoring methods of Kohlberg and Fowler have been developed by relating theoretical

*These references are keyed to footnotes that appear in the body of this chapter.

"hunches" about the logic and sequence of stages to interview data and allowing the data to revise the stage definitions.

[22]Snarey (1976), after analyzing the religious beliefs of over 100 cultures, found that in those cultures having a "high god," depictions of God as moral varied depending on the harshness of environmental conditions. In severe environments with problems of scarcity due to little water or vegetation, the high god was described morally and seen as supportive to human morality. In lush environments with an abundance of food and water, the high god was not described in moral terms nor concerned with human moral behavior. This study shows the impact of salient life experience on the formulation of religious concepts.

ABOUT THE AUTHORS

F.Clark Power *is a doctoral candidate and research assistant at Harvard University Graduate School of Education. He completed graduate studies in systematic theology at Washington Theological University. Mr. Power has taught courses in morality and religion to secondary school students.*

In the last four years he has been involved in moral education research with Lawrence Kohlberg. Last year Mr. Power co-authored "The Moral Atmosphere: An Educational Bridge Between Moral Judgment and Action" *which was published in* New Perspectives in Developmental Psychology.

Dr. Lawrence Kohlberg *is Professor of Education and Director of the Center for Moral Development and Education at Harvard Graduate School of Education. For more than twenty years he has pursued research on the development of moral judgment in persons and groups. His pioneering work has earned him a place as a foremost authority on moral development and moral education. His cross-cultural research has carried him to Yucatán, Taiwan, Turkey, and other places. He and his associates have generated moral education programs in prisons and schools. Most recently the "Just Community Schools" in the public high schools of Cambridge and Brookline, Massachusetts, which Dr. Kohlberg was instrumental in founding, have received widespread attention.*

Dr. Kohlberg has authored many articles on moral development and other topics. His collected writings are appearing now in a three-volume collection.

Moral and Faith Development Theory

JAMES A. O'DONOHOE

INTRODUCTION

{374}   The contributors to this volume were chosen chiefly from the ranks of developmental psychologists, with due representation from both the cognitive and the psychoanalytic schools. I was invited to contribute as a person who has been involved in the teaching of moral theology within the context of a Roman Catholic school of theology over a period of twenty-five years.

I should point out that I am a mere lay person when it comes to knowledge of developmental psychology. Whatever competence I have lies within the context of Roman Catholic moral teaching. For that reason, I envision my principal contribution as that of a person who is in a position to inform a group of developmental psychologists about some contemporary thought and writing in the area of Roman Catholic moral theology.

I was requested to share some insights concerning the possibilities for Roman Catholic moral theology which might be found in the theories of moral development and faith development as recently set forth by Lawrence Kohlberg and James Fowler. To that end, I have divided this chapter into three parts. First, I would like to sketch some basic concepts on the nature and task of Roman Catholic theological ethics. Then, I intend to outline some of the possible implications which the work of both Kohlberg and Fowler might have for Roman Catholic theological ethics. Finally, I would like to share some pertinent reflections on the phenomenon of religious conversion which many contemporary Roman Catholics today see as central to the task of teaching theological ethics, and I would like to suggest that it might be considered as a means of bringing together both the cognitive and the affective not only in the area of moral development but also in the area of faith development.

While I worked with the other contributors to this volume, a number of questions came to mind. Are contemporary Roman Catholics really interested in "moral development" or is their principal preoccupation merely one of "moral indoctrination"? Is the "tradition" of the moral manuals the real Roman Catholic "Tradition" or is it simply a product resulting from conditions peculiar to the Counter-Reformation? Are the theories of moral development, so convincingly proposed by contemporary psychologists, an aid or a detriment to the teaching of Roman Catholic moral theology today? Are the great writings of the Church Fathers and the medieval Scholastics, as well as the classical treatises on the nature of the spiritual life, severely limited in their insights into personal moral development or do they contain material similar to that currently articulated by some of the developmental psychologists? Can Roman Catholic moral theologians really enter into dialogue with developmental psychologists and, if so, can both really profit from the experience?

I hope the material in this chapter can shed some light on these important questions. I hope, too, that it helps the reader formulate some answers.

The Nature and Task of Roman Catholic Theological Ethics

Vatican II and the Teaching of Theological Ethics

For the past fifteen years or more, members of the Roman Communion have witnessed what might be called an unprecedented development in the field of Roman Catholic theological ethics or moral theology. The principal impetus for this phenomenon is often attributed to a simple injunction to be found in a decree issued by the Second Vatican Council entitled *On Priestly Formation* and promulgated by Pope Paul VI on October 28, 1965. It reads as follows: "Special attention needs to be given to the development of moral theology."[1]

For many years prior to the Council, a good deal of impressive writing had been done within the Roman Catholic community on the necessity of taking a critical look at the manner in which moral theology had been approached since the appearance of the *Institutiones Morales* in the sixteenth century.[2] The Council's

---

[1]*Decree on Priestly Formation (Optatam totius)*, n. 16 in W. Abbot & J. Gallagher, *The Documents of Vatican II* (New York: Guild Press, 1966), p. 452.

[2]J. Ford and G. Kelly, *Contemporary Moral Theology: Questions in Fundamental Moral Theology* (New York: Newman Press, 1958), pp. 42–103; J. Leclercq, *L'enseignement de la morale Chretienne* (Paris: Casterman, 1952).

official recognition of the fact that something had to be done about the development of moral theology increased the publication of books and articles and, since that time, a tremendous amount of literature has appeared offering serious suggestions for the implementation of the mandate issued by the Council.[3]

Shortly after the Council, Josef Fuchs, S.J., a professor of moral theology at the prestigious *Gregorianum* in Rome, published an article in which he outlined a method of updating moral theology in accordance with the mandate of the Council.[4] He insisted that what the Council urged was "a scientific exposition" of moral theology and, to that end, he recommended an examination of the data of philosophical and psychological anthropology as well as a corresponding confrontation with other moral theories, both Christian and non-Christian. He felt also that students for the priesthood should be exposed to the probings of contemporary psychological theory, inasmuch as comparison with systems of thought other than those professedly rooted in theology could lead to a better understanding of Roman Catholic moral teaching and provide a more rigorous scrutiny of the reasons so often suggested for its acceptance by members of the Roman Communion.

A Word About Theology

Actually, Fuchs was suggesting nothing new or radical. All theology is concerned with an attempt to articulate in language the content of a religious faith. This is evident from the definition offered by the Scholastics from the time of Anselm, *fides quaerens intellectum*, and by that offered by John Macquarrie in the twentieth century. The latter wrote: "Theology may be defined as the study which, through participation in and reflection upon a religious faith, seeks to express the content of this faith in the

---

[3]One can get some idea of the volume of literature by consulting the "Notes on Moral Theology" which appear at least annually in *Theological Studies*, a journal published for the Theological Faculties of the Society of Jesus in the United States.

[4]J. Fuchs, "Theologia moralis perficienda; votum Concilii Vaticani II," *Periodica de re morali, canonica, liturgica* 55 (1966), pp. 499–548.

clearest and most coherent language available."[5] It goes without saying that any attempt to set forth the content of a religious faith must draw upon many resources: the sacred writings of the specific faith community, its communal wisdom developed down through the ages, its history, the philosophical forms which it adopted, the relevant discoveries of the empirical sciences, and so forth.

{377}

Our day has witnessed remarkable growth in some of the empirical sciences. This has been especially evident in the area of developmental psychology. No theologian worth his or her salt can ignore these findings whenever an attempt is made to set forth the content of a religious faith in contemporary language. In most instances, the theologian is not a psychologist but he or she is bound to attend to what the experts in psychology try to make clear while, of course, subjecting their theories and findings to the rigorous criticism which the specific discipline of theology requires. Insofar as theology talks about faith growth and moral development, it is imperative that it take into account the discoveries which modern developmental psychology has made in these areas.

A Word About Ethics

Every ethical system is concerned with the determination of what is truly humanizing. It searches for what constitutes the human and for what contributes to the growth and development of the human person. The philosopher Vernon Bourke put it well when he described ethics as "the study of voluntary human activity with the purpose of determining what types of activity are good, right, and to be done as opposed to types of activity that are bad, wrong, and to be avoided so that a person may live well."[6] The same sentiments are articulated by theologian William May, who suggested the following definition: "(It is) an inquiry into what is

---

[5]J. Macquarrie, *Principles of Christian Theology* (New York: Charles Scribner's Sons, 1966), p. 1.

[6]V. Bourke, "Ethics," *New Catholic Encyclopedia* 5 (New York: McGraw-Hill, 1967), p. 570.

{378}

needed to make life livable, to provide us with the roots and support we need."[7]

As everyone knows, there are two types of ethics: philosophical and theological. The former attempts to discover that which constitutes the human by the use of reason alone; the latter attempts to discover that which constitutes the human by the use of "reason illumined by a religious faith." For the purposes of this chapter, it is interesting to note that both reason and faith are important elements in the study of theological ethics. The former element plays a predominant role in Kohlberg's theory of moral development and both receive significant scrutiny in Fowler's theory of faith development.

In spite of much discussion on the subject,[8] there is considerable agreement that there exists a specific entity known as Christian theological ethics. Basically, it might be described as an attempt to discover the humanizing by a diligent examination of the meaning and content of the Christian faith commitment. As William May has pointed out, "Christian ethics is continuous with the general moral strivings of mankind with respect to its principal concern and goal: how to make and to keep human life human. It is distinctive in that it offers a specific perspective for assimilating the data and for integrating them into a vision of the meaning of human existence."[9] The same author sees this specific perspective as the manner of being human which Jesus made manifest in his passage from death to life. Irish theologian Enda McDonagh likes to describe Christian theological ethics as a critical reflection on how the Christian community and/or individual ought to behave on the basis of their faith in Jesus Christ.[10]

In particular regard to the question of Christian theological ethics, the biblical scholar Joachim Jeremias makes an interesting point. He writes: "One should avoid in New Testament theology

---

[7]W. May, "Christian Ethics and the Human," *American Ecclesiastical Review* 167 (1973), p. 653.

[8]C. Curran, *Ongoing Revision in Moral Theology* (Notre Dame, Indiana: Fides/Claretian, 1975), pp. 1–36.

[9]W. May, *art. cit.* p. 655.

[10]E. McDonagh, "Moral Theology," *New Catholic Encyclopedia* 16. (New York: McGraw-Hill, 1974), p. 302.

the terms 'Christian morality' and 'Christian ethics' because these expressions are inadequate and liable to misunderstanding. Instead, one should speak of 'lived faith.' Then, it is clearly stated that the gift of God precedes his demands."[11] Every gift makes demands; the gift which is Christian faith is no exception.

{379}

When Catholics are engaged in the doing of Christian ethics, the teaching Church *(Magisterium)* plays an important role in pointing up the nature and content of what constitutes the human. Like their fellow Christian ethicists, Roman Catholic moral theologians strive to discover the ethical implications of the Christian faith commitment but they lay special emphasis on the manner in which it is conceived and expressed by the teaching Church. "Bishops, teaching in communion with the Roman Pontiff, are to be respected by all as witnesses to divine and Catholic truth. In matters of faith and morals, the bishops speak in the name of Christ and the faithful are to accept their teaching and adhere to it with a religious assent of soul. This religious submission of will and of mind must be shown in a special way to the authentic teaching authority of the Roman Pontiff, even when he is not speaking *ex cathedra*. That is, it must be shown in such a way that his supreme *magisterium* is acknowledged with reverence, the judgments made by him are sincerely adhered to, according to his manifest mind and will. His mind and will in the matter may be known chiefly either from the character of the documents, from his frequent repetition of the same doctrine, or from his manner of speaking."[12]

Roman Catholic Methodologies

Within the Roman Communion and especially since the sixteenth century, the doing of theological ethics has taken place within the context of the so-called "Traditional Methodology." It came to full possession in the period of the Counter-Reformation and has

---

[11] J. Jeremias, *The Sermon on the Mount* (Philadelphia: Fortress Press, 1963), p. 35.

[12] *Dogmatic Constitution on the Church (Lumen Gentium)*, n. 25, in W. Abbot and J. Gallagher, *op. cit.* pp. 47–48

been virtually the only officially accepted method for doing theological ethics up to the Second Vatican Council. In its approach, this method is deductive, static, abstract, and universal. It concentrates on order and attempts to place things into a precise system that tends to be conceived in an *a priori* manner. It envisages the moral life as something lived primarily in terms of conformity to preexisting norms and structures and it conceives of human existence as something which consists in a prearranged plan which is spelled out in every minute detail. Its approach is most deontological; it views the moral life almost exclusively in terms of the model of obedience to law and magisterial authority. It must be pointed out, however, that there are some very definite advantages to this system inasmuch as it makes for a certain amount of clarity, security, and simplicity. Nevertheless, these are far outweighed by the possible disadvantages of anti-intellectualism (there is a solution available for every problem and we have it already), authoritarianism (the Church has all the answers), and dogmatism (the Church's answers are final). Popularly, the classic approach is seen as a "laying down of the law" or as a concise presentation of basic objective norms which are to be followed by everyone everywhere and in an unquestioning fashion.

Since the Catholic intellectual revival, dating from the middle of the nineteenth century in Germany, another methodology for the doing of theological ethics within the Roman Communion has been emerging. However, it was never officially recognized until the period immediately following the Second Vatican Council. Since that time, it has gained a lot of publicity through the writings of many contemporary Roman Catholic moral theologians[13] and its influence has been strongly felt in the allied field of catechetics.[14] This approach, sometimes called "the historical

---

[13]A. Jonsen, *Responsibility in Modern Religious Ethics* (Washington, D.C.: Corpus Books, 1968); R. McCormick, "The Moral Theology of Vatican II," R. McCormick, ed., *The Future of Ethics and Moral Theology* (Chicago: Argus, 1968), pp. 7–18; G. Regan, *New Trends in Moral Theology,* (New York: Newman Press, 1971); J. Walgrave, "Is Morality Static or Dynamic?" in F. Boeckle, ed., *Moral Problems and Christian Personalism* (New York: Paulist Press, 1965), pp. 22–28; T. O'Connell, *Principles for a Catholic Morality* (New York: Seabury Press, 1978).

[14]G. Sloyan, "Catechetics," *New Catholic Encyclopedia* 3 (New York: McGraw-Hill, 1974), pp. 220–225.

consciousness method," is dynamic, concrete, particular, and adjustable. It stresses the empirical and works in terms of evolution, growth, change, and history. It reflects the reality of movement and tension as well as being loath to elaborate a system of complete order and categorization. It adopts a method which is *a posteriori* and inductive. The principal stress in this method is placed on the growth and personal responsibility of the moral subject. It has manifest respect for the dignity of the person and for his or her freedom. As is quite obvious, the contemporary methodology focuses almost complete attention on the person acting and therein lies the source of some of its more patent disadvantages: subjectivism (do your own thing), relativism (there are no absolutes), and antinomianism (norms, laws, and principles are irrelevant). In fairness to the methodology, however, it must be pointed out that the above-cited "disadvantages" are to be found only in incidents when those employing the system exaggerate or even corrupt its proper approach.

The presence of two accepted methodologies for the doing of Roman Catholic theological ethics has led to considerable confusion within the ranks of the Roman Communion. A failure to appreciate the strengths and weaknesses of both systems has occasioned the emergence of "naive enthusiasts" and "rigid opponents" on both sides. The two methodologies must not be seen as antithetical and dichotomous. Insofar as possible, they must be seen as complementary. One cannot construct a viable Roman Catholic ethic today if one is not able to keep both approaches in what has been called "a dynamic tension." There is good and bad in both approaches and the moral theologian must always strive to attempt the achievement of a critical balance.

The Manner of Teaching Roman Catholic Theological Ethics Today

One of the principal effects of the presence of two officially accepted methodologies for the doing of Roman Catholic theological ethics is a growing concern relative to the task of teaching morality at this present juncture in the history of the Church. Some continue to insist on the importance of an approach which "lays down the law" while others insist on the importance of "forming a responsible people." This very important question has been explored by several writers,[15] but for our purposes here it might be profitable to investigate the approaches suggested by two contemporary Roman Catholic theologians who are systematicians rather than moralists but whose insights have made considerable impact on the manner of teaching moral theology today. I speak of Karl Rahner, S.J., and Bernard Lonergan, S.J.

Karl Rahner[16] sees the heart of the controversy between Roman Catholic moralists and certain Protestant ethicists as something rooted in the meaning and function of specific moral precepts. As he envisages it, Protestant ethicists sometimes tend to see moral norms as signposts only inasmuch as they mistrust specific moral maxims which, by their universality and externally permanent character, claim to bind men and women in every situation without exception. Roman Catholics, on the other hand, would hold that there are some moral precepts which bind always and everywhere and thus refuse to admit a Christian uniqueness outside these norms.

Rahner points out that several factors in contemporary society are leading Roman Catholics to reconsider their position. First of all, they are beginning to realize that in the complexity of today's world, the moral decision can no longer be just a simple and obvious application of universal principles. Secondly, they are beginning to realize that in today's fluid and changing human milieu, the "nature of things," which seemed so "clearly evident" in the Moral Manuals of the past, is no longer such and this makes the discovery of clear and practicable prescriptions much more difficult than before. For these reasons, Rahner suggests the development of what he terms a "formal existential ethic." To his mind, the Church must learn that by her official teaching and guidance she can accompany the individual to the end of the road (from universal principle to concrete prescription) much less frequently than formerly. As a result, the Church's task is no

---

[15]E. McDonagh, "Teaching Moral Theology Today," *Irish Theological Quarterly* 33 (1966), pp. 195–207; B. Haering, *The Law of Christ*, Vol. 1, (New York: Newman Press, 1961), pp. 35–53.

[16]K. Rahner, *The Christian of the Future* (New York: Herder and Herder, 1967), pp. 39–48.

{383}

longer that of giving concrete answers; rather, she must work to form a moral people. For Rahner, this new approach to moral formation or moral development can be achieved only if the Church devotes herself to a threefold task: (1) she must help her people to deepen the ardor of their personal and ecclesial faith commitment; (2) she must convince them that moral responsibility goes far beyond the mere assimilation of detailed instructions about right and wrong; (3) she must teach her members how to make decisions which do justice to moral principles seen and comprehended in the light of existential situations.

Bernard Lonergan, S.J., offers a theory of moral education which represents a radical reversal of an attitude toward the nature of Christian ethical instruction which has prevailed in the Roman Catholic Church for a long period of time.[17] To his mind, the competence of ethics lies not in the area of determining the morality of specific types of acts but in the area of "self-appropriation." He feels that it is the task of the ethicist to help people to become aware of the elements in themselves which cause them to flee from reasonableness and personal authenticity. As he sees it, the principal interest of the moral theologian is to give people those Christian attitudes which should be operative in evaluating the total complex of rules and regulations which are involved in the human person's response in faith to the initiative of a loving God who has redeemed him or her in Christ.

As a result of the writings of people like Rahner and Lonergan, Roman Catholic theological ethics today is moving from a system which gave almost total attention to the "object pole" of ethics (the total complex of the data to be evaluated in formulating a moral decision) to a system which is very much concerned with the "subject pole" of ethics (the believing person who, prior to his or her decision, must evaluate the data which are placed before him or her). Also, in that connection, considerable attention is given to the manner in which the faith-person is brought to a perception of the data to be evaluated. It seems to me that it is for this reason, among many others, that Roman Catholic ethicists have begun to manifest some interest in the theories of

---

[17]D. Johnson, "Lonergan and the Redoing of Ethics," *Continuum* 5 (1967), pp. 211–220.

Lawrence Kohlberg concerning the phenomenon of moral development[18] and in the probings of James Fowler into the phenomenon of faith development.[19] Roman Catholic moralists today, for the most part, are very much concerned about the person's development of a moral stance over and beyond that of mere conformity to rules and regulations and many of them see this development as something which is allied to, if not deeply rooted in, a development of the faith commitment.

Comment

Personally, I feel that authors like Rahner and Lonergan are on the right track. New insights into the nature and method of Roman Catholic theological ethics require a new look at the means to be employed in doing moral education. In the past, Roman Catholic moral educators were content to teach what Jef Bulckens, talking in continence with the contributors to this volume, called "an assimilation morality." Today, this should give way to what the same author would call "a creative morality." In no way does this mean the elimination of moral content; however, it does mean that the educator must not be satisfied merely to communicate content; he or she must also be concerned with the task of

---

[18]T. Bachmeyer, "The Use of Kohlberg's Theory of Moral Development in Religious Education," *The Living Light* 10 (1973), pp. 341–350; W. Conn, "Postconventional Morality: An Exposition and Critique of Lawrence Kohlberg's Analysis of Moral Development in Adolescent and Adult," *Lumen Vitae* 30 (1975), pp. 213–230; M. Joy, "Kohlberg and Moral Education," *New Catholic World* 215 (1972), pp. 14–16; A. McBride, "Moral Education and Kohlberg's Thesis," *Momentum* 4 (1973), pp. 23–27; P. Philibert, "Some Cautions on Kohlberg," *The Living Light* 12 (1975), pp. 527–534; E. Sullivan, ed., *Moral Learning: Some Findings, Issues and Questions* (New York: Paulist Press, 1975); R. Duska and M. Whelan, *Moral Development: A Guide to Piaget and Kohlberg* (New York: Paulist Press, 1975); J. Youniss, "Kohlberg's Theory: A Commentary," *The Living Light* 10 (1973), pp. 352–358.

[19]P. Brennan-Nichols, "James Fowler: Faith and Development," *Catechist* (1978), pp 22–23; W. Gilmour, "What Does Fowler Have to Say to Adult Educators?" *The Living Light* 13 (1976), pp 524–535; R. Haunz, "Models in Relation to Fowler's Faith Development," *Religious Education* 71 (1978), pp. 640–655; J. Hennessey, "Reaction to Fowler: States in Faith or Stages in Commitment," Hennessey, T., ed., *Values and Moral Development*, (New York: Paulist Press, 1976) pp. 218–223; A. McBride, "Spiritual Education: Fowler's Stages of Faith," *Momentum* 6 (1975), pp. 22–25; A. McBride, "Reaction to Fowler: Fears about Procedure," Hennessey, T., ed., *Values and Moral Development*, pp. 211–218.

communicating to students the means of handling the content in a responsible and creative manner.

As indicated above, Roman Catholic theological ethics today {385} is concerned with "a return to the subject." In the past, it has been perhaps overly concerned with the action performed; at this juncture of history, it must also evidence more concern for the person who does this action. In that connection, however, it must be pointed out that this in no way envisages an individualistic morality which eschews the social and the communal. It must not be forgotten that "human existence is coexistence," that "no man is an island" (John Donne) and that we humans are "solitaries who live in solidarity" (Albert Camus). This dimension of Roman Catholic theological ethics is treated at greater length in this volume by Enda McDonagh, but its importance must also be stressed here lest the comtemporary preoccupation with the moral subject be envisioned in a purely individualistic manner.

Kohlberg's Theory of Moral Development and Its Possible Contribution to Roman Catholic Moral Theology

For the sake of clarity, I will lay out, in the briefest manner, my own comprehension of Kohlberg's theory of moral development. Obviously, it will be a layman's view and hence imperfect since, as I have said before, I am not a developmental psychologist. Much of what I present in this summary, I owe to two works which helped to clarify much of Kohlberg's writing. I refer to the doctoral dissertation of Craig Dykstra[20] and the recent publication by Ronald Duska and Mariellen Whelan.[21]

The Theory

Lawrence Kohlberg is a psychologist who belongs to the cognitive-development school within the tradition of Jean Piaget.

---

[20]C. Dykstra, *Christian Education and the Moral Life: An Evaluation of and Alternative to Kohlberg* (Ann Arbor, Michigan: University Microfilms International, 1978).

[21]R. Duska, and M. Whelan, *op. cit.*

As I understand it, the cognitive school of moral development focuses on the genesis of epistemological structures by which individuals come to understand the world in which they live and places its attention on the act of thinking itself. It exists alongside two other schools of moral development: the psychoanalytic school and the school of social learning. The former sees the acquisition of morality as something existing in the internalization of cultural norms through identification with one's parents; the latter sees the acquisition of morality as a lengthy process of learning social rules through reward and punishment, as well as the imitation of significant others who meet one's biological and social needs.

For Kohlberg, moral maturity does not consist simply in the internalization of rules and norms but in the development of one's ability to differentiate and integrate one's conception of social interaction. For him, moral development is achieved by the stimulation of the natural development of the individual child's own moral judgment and capacities. That is achieved either through the discussion of moral dilemmas which involve a conflict of interests between persons or through the establishment of "just communities" which offer many opportunities for engaging in social interaction and communication as well as modeling principled means of arbitrating social conflicts. For Kohlberg, then, morality is not defined in terms of content but in terms of the formal character of the moral judgment. The moral person is one whose judgments are universal, prescriptive, and overriding. Morality is not something concerned solely with one's attitudes, habits, character, vision of the moral life, or conception of the good. The basic referent of morality is a type of judgment; a person's morality is revealed not necessarily in one's actions but in one's decisions.

Roman Catholics and Kohlberg

Kohlberg's theory of moral development has been given a good deal of attention by Roman Catholic educators, and the depth of their interest has been confirmed by the fact that a few years ago he was asked to be one of the principal speakers at the annual convention of the National Catholic Educational Association.

The actual reception of Kohlberg's theory among Roman Catholic moral educators has been varied. Some have been quite enthusiastic[22]; others have been rather negative;[23] and still others have taken a middle-of-the road position. [24]

Alfred McBride sees Kohlberg's six stages as a useful tool for understanding the growth in moral thinking that is possible for all young people, but he hastens to point out that Kohlberg's typology is just a typology and nothing more. "Like any number of clear outlines it has some value but should not be taken as an absolute comment on moral education. It is part of a larger picture, to be used when needed and useful and laid aside when not. It should not be turned into a new fashion."[25] Nevertheless, McBride feels that Kohlberg does deserve attention inasmuch as he offers a much needed fresh approach to the traditional methodology of moral education.

Even those Roman Catholic educators who are sympathetic to Kohlberg's theory of moral development are quick to point out certain areas of concern: (1) his theory's apparent lack of consideration for specific content; (2) its overemphasis on the role of reason; (3) its failure to appreciate the importance of developing other virtues besides justice.

Lack of Specific Content

Kohlberg's apparent lack of concern for specific content is carefully articulated by Kevin Ryan. In his opinion, Kohlberg closes ranks with other value clarificationists and cognitive-developmentalists who are not concerned with the day-to-day

[22]S. Rowntree, "Faith and Justice, and Kohlberg," P. Scharf, ed., *Readings in Moral Education* (Minneapolis: Winston Press, 1978) pp. 230–247; R. Duska and M. Whelan, *op. cit.*

[23]K. and R. Ryan, "Moral Formation: The American Scene," F. Boeckle and J. M. Pohier, eds., *Moral Formation and Christianity*, (New York: Seabury, 1978), pp. 95–107.

[24]A. McBride, "Moral Education and Kohlberg's Thesis," *Momentum* 4 (1973), pp. 22–27.

[25]A. McBride, *art. cit.* p. 27.

moral decisions of people. Since this seems to be so, Ryan feels that the whole tradition in Western thought which applied reasoned issues of right and wrong is unfortunately ignored. He sees such an approach as casting aside our accumulated intellectual heritage for some "untested and surely incomplete method of helping the young toward moral development."[26] In like manner, the British author M. Haggett is convinced that such a lack of concern for content is entirely unacceptable to the Roman Catholic moralist inasmuch as it would seem to exclude the content which comes with every response of faith.[27]

Overemphasis on Reason

Kohlberg's overemphasis on the role of reason is also severely criticized by several authors who write out of the Christian tradition of moral education. Their objection is put in a cryptic fashion by J. O'Toole, who writes: "I do not believe it is possible to conduct moral education in a completely rational or secular way . . . reason is undoubtedly paramount to morality but it is not the only relevant criterion."[28] The same sentiments are articulated by two other writers who state: "We believe that great issues of human spirit . . . must be dealt with on a level deeper than that suggested by such phrases as 'justification strategies' or 'moral reasoning.' We believe that education should encourage people to examine the relationships of men to their societies or to the universe not only through the rational analysis of 'case studies' but also through the genuine attempt to create and wonder about a profound, perhaps, religious experience."[29]

---

[26]K. Ryan, *art. cit.* p. 104.

[27]M. Haggett, "Do Catholics Need Moral Education," *The Clergy Review* 59 (1974), pp. 681–687.

[28]J. O'Toole, "The Philosophy of Christian Moral Education," *The Clergy Review* 61 (1976), pp. 388–397.

[29]E. Oliver and M. Bane, "Moral Education: Is Reasoning Enough," in C. Beck, B. Crittenden, and E. Sullivan, eds., *Moral Education: Interdisciplinary Approaches* (New York: Newman Press, 1971) pp. 264–265.

Lack of Stress on Virtues Other Than Justice

Kohlberg's failure to insist on the development of virtues other than justice has also been subjected to some very serious critique. This dimension of Kohlberg's theory has been strongly criticized by P. Philibert in two articles. In a piece published in a philosophical journal,[30] he points out that what Kohlberg caricatures as "a bag of virtues" has nothing in common with the classic tradition of the discourse on virtue in the Scholastic and Aristotelian senses. It is his impression that Kohlberg's theory remains further outside the sphere of true intrinsic moral growth than does the Aristotelian position on virtue which sees the latter as a sort of maturation which resides proportionately within all the human faculties. In another article published in a catechetical journal,[31] the same author argues that there are other components to good acts besides good moral reasoning. He sees that Kohlberg is too quick to dismiss the idea of "training for virtue." To Philibert's mind, the latter is too significant a component of moral development to be overlooked and, for that reason, he warns religious educators against a too naive acceptance of Kohlberg's work as a good tool for moral education.

{389}

Protestant Critique

To my mind, the most coherent critiques of Kohlberg's theory of moral development have been done by two writers within the Reformed Tradition. I speak of Craig Dykstra and Ralph Potter. Their observations are right on target and should be taken into serious consideration by Roman Catholic writers who would like to employ Kohlberg's approach in their endeavors to improve the art of moral education.

It is Dykstra's considered opinion[32] that the ethical viewpoint which informs Kohlberg's cognitive-developmental theory

---

[30]P. Philibert, "Lawrence Kohlberg's Use of Virtue in His Theory of Moral Development," *International Philosophical Quarterly* 15 (1975), pp. 455–479.

[31]P. Philibert, "Some Cautions on Kohlberg," *The Living Light* 12 (1975), pp. 527–534.

[32]C. Dykstra, *op. cit.*, especially ch. 2.

is inadequate as a theoretical foundation for moral education within a Christian context. To his mind, the theory restricts unnecessarily the notion of morality to a function which appears to be juridical in its very essence. He sees Kohlberg's concept of morality as unduly restricted to a juridical notion in which moral situations are limited to those in which publicly communicable claims of various persons in a social situation conflict. This approach envisions the morally mature person as a detached, rational agent who makes moral decisions from a disinterested point of view based on an objective understanding of the situation as well as universal and autonomously held moral principles. Dykstra sees morality as something which requires more than a transformation of cognitive structures and he is quite right; it is something which requires the transformation of the entire person. Moral maturity can never be achieved by impersonal moral judgments but only by the gradual acquisition of moral virtues.

While very conscious of the "formidable contribution" which Lawrence Kohlberg has made to the field of moral education, Ralph Potter of Harvard Divinity School points to three major faults in his theory of moral development: (1) there is an oversimplification of the nature and contents of moral deliberation; (2) there is an overemphasis upon the logic of moral reasoning as an influence upon conduct; (3) there is an impoverished view of moral character which, by concentrating exclusively upon justice, neglects all the other virtues.[33]

In regard to the first two faults, Potter points out that to give content to moral reasoning, it is not enough to regard the form of moral logic which is employed; concern must also be given to the subject's capacity for getting the facts straight, for judging whose welfare is at stake, and for interpreting the reality of human existence in some fairly coherent manner. Discussing the nature of the third fault, Potter states that morality has to do with benefits and harms to persons, while justice has to do with the distribution of these to persons in relation to certain criteria. In order to do the latter, one needs to have a definite understanding

---

[33]R. Potter, "Justice and Beyond in Moral Education." An unpublished address given at the Regional Conference on the Moral Development of Youth, Spring Hill Center, Wayzata, Minnesota, June 1, 1977.

of the nature and constitutive elements of the human person. Any system of moral education which relies solely on justice to the extent that it prescinds from the context established by a specific anthropology is seriously deficient. Potter agrees that Kohlberg's program would raise the level of moral logic, but he finds that it is seriously lacking in the presentation of quasi-theological components which can serve to enlighten one's understanding of the ultimate context of human existence.

{391}

Potter brings his remarks to a close by outlining four factors about Kohlberg's system of moral development which must be taken into consideration by people who would be tempted to make his theory the sum and substance of moral education: (1) One cannot be truly just unless one has cultivated the other three moral virtues; (2) in our religious tradition, love and not justice is the highest form of morality; (3) a justice-centered morality does not fulfill the quest for intimacy, community, and friendship that is necessary if personal interactions are to be truly human; (4) the formalism proposed by Kohlberg must be complemented with very specific, concrete, historically and sociologically informed investigation of ways of life and ideals of character that have helped people discover the true manner of acting humanly.

Comment

Is Kohlberg's theory of moral development capable of making a positive contribution to Roman Catholic theological ethics? It is my considered opinion that it has to be handled very carefully. As Louis Monden, S.J., has pointed out,[34] it is certainly true that one can discern various levels of moral development and that it is the task of the moral educator to stimulate students to an ever higher level. However, I am convinced that the almost exclusive use of the rational faculty to accomplish this, coupled with a presentation of justice as the epitome of moral perfection, should raise some serious questions in the minds of Roman Catholic moral educators who otherwise find many other things in Kohlberg's

---

[34]L. Monden, *Sin, Liberty, and Law* (New York: Sheed and Ward, 1965), pp. 4–17.

theory quite acceptable. Moral education within the context of Roman Catholicism has always insisted on the primacy of charity[35] as well as on the necessity of cultivating the virtuous life.[36] Any approach to moral education which would fail to give due consideration to both of these elements would be seriously deficient. Kohlberg has a lot to say to Roman Catholics who are interested in doing theological ethics. However, his theory of moral development must be approached with a critical sense, giving due recognition to what is in accordance with the tradition while being open to confront that which is apparently not.

Kohlberg's work deserves the respectful attention of all Roman Catholics who are interested in moral education. Alfred McBride put it well when he wrote the following: "He [Kohlberg] offers a maturity in our approach to moral education that is needed. His six stages are indeed a fascinating method for organizing some of our thinking about development in moral thinking. He points us beyond relativism and asks for the development of a mature moral consciousness. Few of us now would want to argue with that. Religious education can do much to develop moral consciousness in our time. The Kohlberg insight should be of help."[37]

Fowler's Theory of Faith Devlopment and Its Possible Implications for Roman Catholic Moral Theology

As indicated above, Christian theological ethics may be accurately described as "lived faith."[38] Since that is so, the Christian ethicist must be interested in the nature and growth of the Christian faith commitment. It follows also that faith development can have influence on moral development.

---

[35]G. Gilleman, *The Primacy of Charity in Moral Theology* (New York: Newman Press, 1959).

[36]J. Pieper, *The Four Cardinal Virtues* (Notre Dame, Indiana: University of Notre Dame Press, 1966).

[37]A. McBride, "Moral Education and Kohlberg's Thesis," *Momentum* 4 (1973), p. 27.

[38]J. Jeremias, *op. cit.* p. 35.

Roman Catholics and Faith

Roman Catholic theologians generally understand religious faith as an affirmative response to a God who reveals himself. In other words, they see religious faith as somehow or other involving the acceptance of a divine revelation. Becoming more specific, the same theologians would understand Christian faith as the affirmative acceptance of God's invitation to union with him and hence an acceptance of the Word (revelation) of God who presents himself to us in the person of Jesus of Nazareth. It should also be noted that when they speak of Christian faith, theologians within the Scholastic tradition often make the distinction between *fides qua* (the act of faith) and *fides quae* (the content of faith).

{393}

Faith and Revelation

It seems fair to say that many Roman Catholic authors are of the opinion that one's comprehension of the meaning of faith is in direct proportion to one's comprehension of the meaning of revelation. As Avery Dulles, S.J., pointed out several years ago, there are three basic mentalities which can be distinguished as giving rise to three different understandings of revelation theology.[39] First, there is the positive or factual mind which concentrates on revelation as concrete event generally meaning the crucial events of biblical history, culminating in the death and resurrection of Jesus. Secondly, there is the conceptual or abstract mind which fastens on the "eternal truths" in revelation. For this type of mind, revelation is essentially a body of doctrine. Thirdly, there is the intuitive or mystical approach which tends to depict the divine in either a transcendent or an immanent fashion. In this view, revelation is a highly personal matter and therefore largely incommunicable.

---

[39]A Dulles, *Revelation Theology: A History* (New York: Herder and Herder, 1969), pp. 177–180.

Inasmuch as there are three possible understandings of revelation, and inasmuch as faith is the affirmative acceptance of revelation, there are three possible understandings of religious faith. First of all, there is the positive understanding which sees Christian faith as the acceptance of Jesus in the saving event which is his death and resurrection. Secondly, there is the abstractive understanding which sees it as the acceptance of a body of doctrines about Jesus, God, the world, and the human race. Thirdly, there is the intuitive understanding which sees it as a highly personal acceptance of the divine in either a transcendent or an immanent fashion.

Faith and Ethics

Inasmuch as there are three possible understandings of Christian faith and inasmuch as Christian morality is "lived faith," it could follow that there are three possible understandings of Christian theological ethics. The positive understanding of faith tends to erect an ethic of example. This is especially evident in some of the fundamentalist sects which take the actions of Christ and of the earliest Christians as an exclusive standard of conduct. The abstractive understanding of faith tends to erect an ethic of conformity to laws or abstract rules designed to cover all particular cases. The intuitive understanding of faith tends to erect an ethic which attempts a response to the present leading of the Spirit and therefore embraces a charismatic ethic which can at times lead to a certain antinomianism.

Faith in Contemporary Roman Catholic Theology

As indicated above, throughout history, Christian faith has been regarded as both act *(fides qua creditur)* and as content *(fides quae creditur)*. In the Middle Ages, it was seen as essentially content; at the time of the Reformation, Protestants tended to see it more as a personal encounter (an interpersonal relationship) but Roman Catholics, in a defensive posture over their former position, placed even greater stress on it as content (i.e., a corpus of doctrines to be held). Today, however, Roman Catholics seem to place more emphasis on faith as an act of self-surrender in a radical and unconditional manner to the God who presents himself to human beings in the Christ Event but they continue to insist that such a surrender also entails some definite content. They constantly stress the fact that all forms of "I believe that . . ." are grounded in the form "I believe in you." As many of them are anxious to point out, without concrete content, Christian faith is empty, but without a personal relatedness, Christian faith is impersonal and dead. Most Roman Catholic theologians today insist on the fact that Christian faith entails first and foremost a personal surrender to Jesus in the act of his death. However, they insist that this personal surrender has content. It is their conviction that whoever gives himself or herself totally and unconditionally to Jesus can attain a true understanding of what it means to be human. It is also their opinion that this humanization is found in the manner revealed to us by the act of Jesus in the gift of himself for us even unto death.

Since one's understanding of the nature of faith and the possibility of its development are of significant importance for any purposeful exposition of moral education, it is easy to see why so many Roman Catholic moral theologians are interested in the phenomenon known as faith development. For that reason, the research and publications of James Fowler, even though they are still at an early stage of development themselves, are received with thoughtful consideration. It is interesting to note that the *General Catechetical Directory* recently approved by the National Conference of Catholic Bishops points out that religious education has as its aim making "men's faith become conscious and active through the light of instruction."[40] Since this growth in faith is the aim of religious education, Fowler's attempt to delineate stages in this faith growth or development is certainly something to be picked up and examined by Catholics concerned with moral education. As one author recently pointed out, "the crux of religious education is growth in faith."[41] Fowler's work fits well into this area.

---

[40]*General Catechetical Directory*, n. 17.

[41]W. Gilmour, *art. cit.*, p. 525

Contemporary Roman Catholic moral theology is not only concerned about the communication of rules and regulations; it is also very concerned about the development of a morally responsible people who are capable of internalizing the values behind the rules and are able to act more out of personal conviction than out of fear of punishment or out of desire for the approval of authority. This responsible self-determination seems to be characteristic of the higher levels of faith development and the whole theory seems to envision the assistance of the moral agent as he or she moves toward personal and responsible self-determination. It would seem to me that Fowler's concentration on how faith "knows" does not exclude the matter of religious content. It seems simply to focus in on the manner in which the content is apprehended; it seems to assume that religious content is comprehended at ever deeper levels or stages. Fowler's theory is also useful to determine the nature and extent of the interpersonal relationship with Jesus in the act of his death which is a constitutive element in the Christian understanding of the faith commitment.

Fowler's Theory and Roman Catholics

Inasmuch as Fowler's mode of stages of faith development is still very much in an early period of growth, Roman Catholic moral theologians are still a bit guarded in their enthusiasm. Some of the cautions which have been articulated by them are as follows: (1) It is more a well-informed hunch or a series of *a prioris* that have not been deeply tested in the usual sense of the word as an adequate product of developmental psychology; (2) he seems to identify development with stages far too casually; (3) his perspective on faith is distinctly almost exclusively Tillichian and not sufficiently imbued with the thoughts of others such as Augustine and Aquinas.[42] However, in spite of these reservations, a goodly number of Roman Catholic moral theologians feel that Fowler is in the process of making a fine contribution to the field of moral

---

[42]A. McBride, "Reaction to Fowler . . .", *Momentum* 6, p. 216.

education. As a result of his work, developmental psychology is beginning to come to grips with that most profound manner of knowing what is faith perception.

The Conversion Phenomenon

Moral Development and Conversion

At the present time, Roman Catholic moral theology exists in a period of intense renewal. There is a definite move from the traditional methodology to the historical-consciousness method-ology. As a result of this, both morality itself and the faith in which it is grounded are no longer conceived of in static terms but in dynamic terms. Both morality and faith are envisioned as entities which are capable of growth and development, entities which are in process. For that reason, the theories of both Kohlberg and Fowler have occasioned much interest among a certain number of Roman Catholic moralists and catechists. However, the latter must always remember that both theorists focus their attentions only on the processes and not on the goals of moral judgment and faith development.

The moral-development theory of Kohlberg and the faith-development theory of Fowler seem to place more emphasis on the cognitive than on the effective, even though the latter element is rendered some recognition by each theorist. While giving due recognition to the difficulty of placing proper emphasis on both of these elements within the process of faith development as well as that of moral development, the Roman Catholic moral theologian is more comfortable with holding cognition and affectivity in dynamic tension. The latter approach is becoming quite evident today as a result of the heavy emphasis placed by Roman Catholic moralists on the phenomenon of ongoing personal conversion. Since this is so, it might be of value to include in this chapter a brief sketch of the conversion phenomenon as set forth in the thought and writings of Bernard Lonergan, S.J.[43]

Conversion might be best described phenomenologically as a transformation in a person's manner of acting in reference to any given person, place, or thing. The Hebrew word for conversion (*shuv*) describes the action of a person who comes to a dead stop in his or her tracks and makes a 180-degree turn. In a theological context, conversion implies a spiritual change or transformation, a moral or religious turning in reference to God and his message. In the Christian sense, conversion implies a complete and radical breaking with self-centeredness which marks the human condition since Adam's fall but followed by a total and definitive dedication to that gift-of-self for the sake of others which Jesus manifested in his death on the cross.

Lonergan and Conversion

Lonergan believes conversion is fundamental to all religious living. He sees it as a radical transformation of the individual and his world. It entails a change of direction, an opening of the eyes, and the consequent perception of a new world. Lonergan speaks of three types of conversion: intellectual, moral, and religious. Intellectual conversion is a radical reorientation of the authentic subject from one's own little world to the world of the intelligently understood and reasonably affirmed. It entails a fundamental alteration of the subject's basic stance toward self, others, God, and world. Moral conversion consists in the recognition and choice of oneself as a free and responsible originator of value. It is an overcoming of moral impotence to the extent that the subject is able so to develop his or her will as to break into action which he or she perceives as intelligent and reasonable. It changes the basis of the person's decisions from satisfaction to

---

[43]K. Colleran, "Bernard Lonergan on Conversion," *Dunwoodie Review* 11 (1971), pp. 3–23; W. Conn, "Bernard Lonergan's Analysis of Conversion," *Angelicum* 53 (1976), pp. 362–404; C. Curran, "Christian Conversion in the Writings of Bernard Lonergan," in P. McShane, ed., *Foundations of Theology: Papers from the International Lonergan Congress 1970* (Notre Dame, Indiana: University of Notre Dame Press, 1972), pp. 41–59.

value, from what gives pleasure to what is truly good and worthwhile. Religious conversion is a total being-in-love with ultimate concern as the efficacious ground of all self-transcendence. Central to this is love of God with all one's heart, and all one's mind and strength. Intellectual conversion broadens one's horizons; moral conversion brings with it a new value system; religious conversion consists in a falling in love with love itself.

{399}

A superficial reading of Lonergan's understanding of the phenomenon of conversion could give the impression that the process begins with intellectual conversion and then proceeds through moral conversion to religious conversion. Lonergan strongly insists that the process is in reverse. First of all, there is the acceptance of the gift of God's love; then, the eye of this love reveals values in their true splendor; and finally, among the values discerned by the eye of love is the value of believing the truths taught by the religious tradition. For Lonergan, intellectual and moral conversion are the goals of full religious conversion. He also sees them as implications of the latter but not as prerequisites for, and inevitable results of, the latter.

Some Implications for Religious Education

1. Concern with content should in no way exclude concern with the personal development of the one who receives the content.
2. The Christian moral life is an ongoing process of personal conversion within the context of the community. It begins with the acceptance of Jesus in the act of self-giving which was his death and it is lived out, under grace, in the community of those for whom he gave his life.
3. "Indoctrination" is part and parcel of Christian moral education inasmuch as every moral system has "role expectations" or basic norms which must be communicated. However, the task of the educator does not stop there; he or she must also

supply sufficient information on the values which the norms intend to articulate and he or she must also enable the moral subject to so handle the norms that the values behind them can be best achieved in the light of existential situations.

4. There is an intrinsic connection between Christian moral development and Christian faith development. How the Christian is to act is rooted in what the Christian believes.

Final Comment

The Roman Catholic moral theologian sees Christian morality as "lived faith." To his mind, faith begins with religious conversion which consists in the acceptance of God's love as it is offered to himans through the act of Jesus as he hands himself over to death on the cross. This phenomenon which has as its essence a "falling in love with love" leads to moral and intellectual conversion as well. The whole thing is a continuous and developmental process which entails mind and heart but seems to begin with that "change of heart" which belongs to the essence of religious conversion. The latter is rooted in a definitive "change of heart" but it is something which must grow and develop in a manner parallel to various stages of human development. As it develops, the converted person's intellectual horizons and appreciation of moral values also develop and it is thus that moral development can be seen as something rooted in and parallel to faith development.

ABOUT THE AUTHOR

Father James A. O'Donohoe *is a priest of the Archdiocese of Boston. A graduate of Boston College (A.B.) and Saint John's Seminary (M.Div.), he pursued graduate studies in canon law and moral theology at the Catholic University of Louvain in Belgium, from which he received his degree (J.C.D.) in 1954. Since that date he has been Professor of Moral Theology at Saint James Seminary, where, from 1965 to 1971, he served* as Dean of Students. In 1979 he accepted an associate professorship in the Department of Theology at Boston College.

His long experience in preparing candidates for the priesthood led to considerable engagement in programs of continuing education for the clergy in many dioceses throughout the United States. In 1974, his interest in moral and religious development led to his acceptance of a visiting scholarship at Harvard Divinity School. His proficiency in Church law occasioned his appointment as judge at the Metropolitan Tribunal of Boston and because of his interest in the Church's worship, he has served for almost a decade as the chairperson of Boston's Archdiocesan Liturgical Commission.

Father O'Donohoe's publications have appeared in many journals and he has contributed several articles to the New Catholic Encyclopedia.

{401}

There the Dance Is:
Religious Dimensions
of a Developmental Framework

ROBERT KEGAN

Prologue

At the still point of the turning world. Neither flesh nor fleshless;
Neither from nor towards; at the still point, there the dance is,
But neither arrest nor movement. And do not call it fixity,
Where past and future are gathered. Neither movement from nor
    towards,
Neither ascent nor decline. Except for the point, the still point,
There would be no dance, and there is only the dance.
I can only say, there we have been: but I cannot say where.
And I cannot say, how long, for that is to place it in time.
The inner freedom from the practical desire,
The release from action and suffering, release from the inner
And the outer compulsion, yet surrounded
By a grace of sense, a white light still and moving,
Erhebung without motion, concentration
Without elimination, both a new world
And the old made explicit, understood
In the completion of its partial ecstasy,
The resolution of its partial horror.
Yet the enchainment of past and future
Woven in the weakness of the changing body,
Protects mankind from heaven and damnation
Which flesh cannot endure.

                              Time past and time future
Allow but a little consciousness.
To be conscious is not to be in time
But only in time can the moment in the rose-garden,
The moment in the arbour where the rain beat,
The moment in the draughty church at smokefall
Be remembered; involved with past and future.
Only through time time is conquered.

                              —T. S. Eliot, "Burnt Norton"

Introduction

There is a common paradigm (a framework, a collection of related
theories) which informs the work of many of the American
theorists and practitioners who contributed to this volume. I call
this paradigm the "constructive-developmental" because it attends to the *development* of our *construing* or meaning-making
throughout life. The seeds of this framework are to be found in
the work of American philosopher-psychologists like George
Herbert Mead,[1] James Mark Baldwin,[2] and John Dewey,[3] but it
was necessary that these seeds cross the ocean to heartier,
European soil before they could take root and grow. Here they
found their most influential modern form in the work of Jean
Piaget.[4] Thus the American neo-Piagetians who have just crossed
the same ocean to attend the Senanque conference are already in
debt to their European hosts for having nourished the ideas and
perspectives that they bring with them.

The image of the child as philosopher, which Piaget made
real through a series of studies still breathtaking in their elegant
simplicity, has undergone considerable elaboration in the United
States. The study of the child has been extended to adulthood,
and "natural philosophy" has been articulated into its familiar
parts. In addition to Piaget's stages of "natural logic," we now
think we understand something of the developing person's stages

---

[1]George Herbert Mead, *Mind, Self, and Society* (Chicago: University of Chicago Press, 1934).

[2]James Mark Baldwin, *Social and Ethical Interpretations in Mental Development* (New York: Macmillan, 1902).

[3]John Dewey, *Experience and Education* (New York: Collier, 1938).

[4]Jean Piaget, *The Language and Thought of the Child* (New York: Harcourt Brace Jovanovich, 1926); *The Origins of Intelligence in Children* (New York: International Universities Press, 1936); *The Construction of Reality in the Child* (New York: Basic Books, 1937).

of natural ethics,[5] epistemology,[6] aesthetics,[7] and theology.[8] This understanding has emerged from these theorists' many years of painstaking research; no matter how refined the methodology and measurements have become, there was, and still is, no escape from the careful analysis of what by now are thousands of hours of interview material.

Meaning—Constructive Evolutionary Activity

As much as the constructive-developmental paradigm has grown throughout this century, it is not yet mature. In truth it has perhaps realized only a small portion of its potential stature. Despite the brilliant elaborations upon Piaget's contribution, there are important respects in which the potential depth of the paradigm is no more realized today than it was fifty years ago, when Piaget published *The Language and Thought of the Child*.[9] With very few exceptions, the work of the Piagetians ("neo" or otherwise) must still be characterized as about *cognition*, to the neglect of *emotion*; the *individual*, to the neglect of the *social*; the *epistemological*, to the neglect of the *ontological* (or *concept*, to the neglect of *being*); *stages* of meaning-constitution, to the neglect of meaning-constitutive *process*; and (forgive the awkward expression of this last) what is *new and changed* about a person, to the neglect of *the person who persists through time*.

---

[5]Lawrence Kohlberg, "Stage and Sequence: The Cognitive Developmental Approach to Socialization," in D.A. Goslin, ed., *Handbook of Socialization Theory and Research* (Chicago: Rand McNally, 1969); William G. Perry, *Forms of Intellectual and Ethical Development in the College Years* (New York: Holt Rinehart and Winston, 1979).

[6]John Broughton, "The Development of Natural Epistemology in Adolescence and Early Adulthood," Unpublished doctoral dissertation, Harvard University, 1975; Perry, *op. cit.*

[7]Michael Parsons, "Baldwin and Aesthetic Development," in J.M. Broughton and D.J. Freeman-Moir, ed., *The Foundations of Cognitive Developmental Psychology* (Norwood, N.J.: Ablex Press, in press).

[8]James W. Fowler, see "Faith and the Structuring of Meaning" in this volume; and with Sam Keen, *Life Maps: Conversations on the Journey of Faith* (Waco, Texas: Word Books, 1978).

[9]Piaget, *Language and Thought, op. cit.*

In other places[10] I have tried to demonstrate that these multiple "neglects" are actually unitary, that they are all the result of a single truncation in the attention of the paradigm. Stated somewhat oversimply, I believe (1) that the cognitive/individual/epistemological/concept-/stage-/and present-oriented ·cast to the framework is due to the study of development as a succession of subject-object or self-other differentiations; (2) that this, in fact, *is* one of the most significant, robust, and universal phenomena to be found in nature; and (3) that it forms the "deep structure" in all the constructive-developmental stage theories.[11] But the relation of self to other goes on in a context—and there the dance is. I have suggested there is a context which is prior to the self-other relation, a context which actually gives rise *to* it. I call this context "meaning-constitutive evolutionary activity," by which I mean to refer to something that is more than biology, philosophy, psychology, sociology, or theology, but is that which all of these, in their different ways, have studied. I am referring to the restless creative motion of life itself, which is not first of all "individual" *or* "world," "organism" *or* "environment," but is the source of each. I suggest that when meaning-constitutive evolutionary activity is taken as the basic context of development, then cognition, the individual, the epistemological, the stage, the present organization of the person, all get integrated into a bigger conception which includes the emotions, the social, the ontological, the process, the person who is doing the developing.

Put more simply, I am saying that persons are not their stages of development; persons are a motion, a creative motion, the motion of life itself. Let me, at least, point to the way this extends the focus of study in each of the dimensions I have

{407}

[10]Robert Kegan, "Ego and Truth: Personality and the Piaget Paradigm," Unpublished doctoral dissertation, Harvard University, 1977; "The Evolving Self: A Process Conception for Ego Psychology," *Counseling Psychologist,* Fall, 1979; "A Neo-Piagetian Approach to Object Relations," in *New Approaches to the Self* (Norwood, New Jersey: Ablex Press, in press).

[11]See the section "The Deep Structure of Piagetian Theories," in "The Evolving Self," *op. cit.*

{408}

claimed. The study of the underlying process (of constitutive activity rather than constitutions) moves "stages" from the very ground of our concern, to a figure upon the ground; it makes *process* the ground, and stages a reference point to periods of dynamic stability in that process. What is being kept dynamically stable in such moments is the present distinction between subject and object or self and other. Such constructions are naturally *epistemological*; they *know*; they shape reality. But they shape the "self" as well. The subject-object balance is not just a source of *concepts*, or thoughts, or construing; it is how "I" am at present composed, how I "be," and thus the structures are also naturally *ontological*. Looming over a balance always threatened with evolution is the spectre of not knowing; from the point of view of the present construction of the self, it is the spectre of whether I shall continue to *be*. When the structures are taken as the basic consideration, the framework is unavoidably *cognitive*. When we study the motion which gives rise to these constructions, and the experience of this motion, we discover the very source of our *emotions*. (The word itself suggests something which arises out of a motion.) A change in how we are composed may be experienced as a change in our own composure.

Self-other relating goes on in a prior context, I say, and this context has a *philosophical* meaning (the prior ground to the subject-object relation; the dialectic which continually resolves the subject-object dichotomy), a *biological* meaning (the relative or absolute state of undifferentiation, out of which emerges, through the process of adaptation, an increasingly articulated organization), a *psychological* meaning (the psychologically undifferentiated "culture of embeddedness" out of which the organism emerges in its self-other constructing; for example, in the beginning, the infant differentiating its reflexes, its sensing and moving, from the mother with whom it had been fused during the first nine months of *extrauterine* life[12]); and it also has a *social* meaning. Subject-object relating goes on in a context, and this context, in addition to everything else, is *an actual social arena*.

---

[12]I refer briefly to these "cultures of embeddedness"—the social mediators of undifferentiation at each stage—in the last section of the present chapter; and at length in "A Neo-Piagetian Approach to Object Relations," *op. cit.*

What Margaret Mahler calls "the psychological birth of the human infant"[13] during the first two years of life, referred to a moment ago, goes on in the social context of the infant's undifferentiated relationship with the mother. It is psychologically born out of a social environment. What constructive-developmental theory suggests (and one of the ways it differs from neo-psychoanalytic theorists like Mahler) is that such differentiation, which replays itself in later life, is not fundamentally a matter of infancy, but that the transformation during infancy—and all the transformations that follow—are fundamentally a matter of the lifelong process of evolution.[14] We are born not once but a succession of times, and each time, there is a qualitatively new culture of embeddedness, a qualitatively new social environment in which the motion of life represents itself, and out of which the individual is born.

{409}

It is not my intent here to elaborate in any thorough way the nature of "the affective" or "the social" as we are able to discern them when the constructive-developmental framework makes meaning-constitutive evolutionary activity the ground of investigation.[15] But inevitably I will be dealing with these elaborations in my claims for a religious dimension to this framework; for such claims proceed from this same ground. It should be clear that in suggesting religious, or spiritual, dimensions to the framework, I will not be tacking anything onto the framework, or speaking from its periphery; rather I will be speaking from its heart. I will be suggesting that the *same* reality said to be philosophically real, biologically real, psychologically real, and socially real, is also "religiously" real, that it partakes of the numinous ("a white light still and moving"), the graceful ("a grace of sense"), the holy, the transcendent ("only through time time is conquered"), and the oneness of all life. This underlying motion, especially as it is seen in its spiritual reality, is, I believe, what James Fowler refers to

---

[13]Margaret Mahler, *The Psychological Birth of the Human Infant* (New York: Basic Books, 1975).

[14]See "A Neo-Piagetian Approach," *op. cit.*

[15]Ernest Schachtel, *Metamorphosis* (New York: Basic Books, 1959); Perry, *op. cit.*; Kegan, "Ego and Truth," *op. cit.*

when he speaks, in this volume, [16] of an "ultimate environment." Everything that follows here is really a way of joining Fowler's crucial insight that the framework must not lose sight of "the Third"[17]—that moving ground which roots and regenerates our self-other relating. When the framework includes this fuller dimension, its study of the changing person in time becomes, in addition to everything else, *theological*—especially in the sense Tillich intended when he said, "the criterion of all theology" is its "ability to preserve the absolute tension between the conditional [any given self-other balance] and the unconditional [meaning-constitutive activity]."[18]

This chapter suggests a religious power for the constructive-developmental framework which goes beyond the quasi-religious status of stages of moral judgment or even stages of faith construction; beyond these into the very experiences and phenomena that have been a feature of self-consciously and unself-consciously religious persons, of faith communities and individuals, as long as persons have given expression to the reality of being alive. Any developmental framework, taken as a whole, should be a kind of attention to the human dance—the changing form through time in space. The constructive-developmental perspective has not yet found a way to do justice to what Whitehead called the ultimate reality of the universe—its motion.[19] Much less has it recognized the religious dimension of our relation to this reality, what Buber spoke of both as an inevitable lifelong tension between the I-Thou and the I-It, and as the sacredness of the everyday.[20] Yet of greater magnitude than this neglect is the potential of the same framework to reflect this very motion—there where the dance is—and do it honor.

---

[16]James W. Fowler, "Faith and the Structuring of Meaning," in this volume. All future references to this appear internally.

[17]Vincent Crapanzano, "The Self, the Third, and Desire," in *New Approaches to the Self, op. cit.*; J.P. Sartre, *Huit Clos* (Paris: Gallimard, 1945).

[18]Paul Tillich, *The Protestant Era* (Chicago: University of Chicago Press, 1948), p. 79.

[19]Alfred North Whitehead, *Process and Reality* (New York: The Free Press, 1929).

[20]Martin Buber, *I and Thou* (New York: Scribners', 1958); *The Origin and Meaning of Hasidism* (New York: Horizon Press, 1960).

Beyond Empirical Realities

In his book *Rumor of Angels,* Peter Berger writes of "signals of   {411}
transcendence," "phenomena that are to be found within the
domain of our 'natural' reality but that appear to point beyond
that reality."[21] Berger works from an approach he calls "inductive
faith," by which he means "a religious process of thought that
begins with certain assumptions (notably assumptions about
divine revelation) that cannot be tested by experience. Put simply,
inductive faith moves from human experience to statements
about God, deductive faith from statements about God to interpretations of human experience."[22] I take a somewhat similar
approach in this chapter. Grounding myself in empirical realities,
especially those we have come to see more clearly through
systematic investigations from the constructive-developmental
paradigm, I try to suggest how those realities (and the present
organization of that paradigm) point beyond themselves. Specifically, I consider three phenomena. The first is the apparently
universal tension between the longing to be included, attached,
"a part of," on the one hand, and the longing to be distinct,
separate, autonomous, on the other. The second is the apparently
universal and recurring experience of losing and recovering a
sense of meaning or order. And the third is the apparently
universal need to be recognized. As will become clear, these three
phenomena, addressed in this order, come to expose an ever-
expanding relationship of *logos* to *ousia,* of the meaning-we-
compose to the ground of being which is doing the composing.

Inclusion and Independence

Let us consider two great—perhaps two of the greatest—human
longings. We see their expression everywhere, in ourselves and
in those we know, in small children and in mature adults, in

---

[21]Peter Berger, *A Rumor of Angels* (New York: Anchor Books, 1975), pp. 65–66.
[22]*Ibid.* pp. 71–72.

cultures East and West, modern and traditional. Of the multitude of hopes and yearnings we experience, these two seem to subsume the others. One of these might be called the yearning to be *included*, to be a "part of," "close to," "joined with," to be held, admitted, accompanied. The other might be called the yearning to be *independent* or autonomous, to experience my distinctness, the self-chosenness of my directions, my individual integrity. David Bakan called this "the duality of human experience," the yearnings for "communion" and "agency."[23] Certainly in my experience as a counselor or therapist, a context in which old-fashioned words like "yearn" and "plea" and "long for" and "mourn" have great meaning, it seems to me that I am often listening to one or the other of these yearnings, or to the fear of losing a most precious sense of being included or feeling independent. Nor will it escape those who are religiously oriented that the same old-fashioned language finds its way into prayer, and that much liturgy and scripture are an expression of one or the other of these two longings. I think of Schleiermacher's "ultimate dependence" on the one hand[24]; Luther's "Here I stand" on the other. Or of the fervent communalism of Hasidism, on the one hand[25]; the lonely Job, *talking to* (even cursing) the Lord, on the other.

But what is most striking about these two great human yearnings is that they seem to be in conflict, and it is, in fact, their *relation* that is of greater interest to me at the moment than either by itself. I want to suggest that their relation, a lifelong tension that is in some sense an animating force, is itself a reflection of Whitehead's "fundamental reality," itself our experience of the single, restless, creative motion of life itself. The motion of evolution, in which all living things participate, of which all living things are a part, brings into being an increasingly organized relationship of the part to the whole. Any stable organismic organization, whether it be a period in the life of a person, a panda, or a coleus plant, is a kind of "evolutionary truce,"

[23]David Bakan, *The Duality of Human Existence* (Chicago: Rand McNally, 1966).

[24]Friedrich Schleiermacher, *On Religion: Speeches to Its Cultured Despisers* (New York: Harper and Row, 1958).

[25]Buber, *Origin and Meaning, op. cit.*

maintaining the current extent of *differentiation from*, and *integration with*, the whole. Thus every equilibrated level of adaptation represents a kind of temporary compromise between the move toward differentiation and the move toward integration; every developmental era is a new solution to this universal tension.

{413}

In other words, while "differentiation" and "integration" sound rather far from human experience in the mouth of a biologist talking about adaptation, I am suggesting that they are the biological way of speaking of those same phenomena we experience as the yearnings for autonomy and inclusion; and that their tension is our experience of the single, underlying ground of being which gives rise to, and resolves, the tension in the first place. (This "underlying ground" should not be confused with one's parents, as I believe we find in the thinking of Vergote in this volume. Vergote is concerned with the same tension but places its origins in the experience of one's parents. Mother, it may be argued, can become a representative or archetype of integration; and the father, of differentiation. But to make of the parents themselves the ultimate context is to fall into the classic psychoanalytic reduction of the religious, albeit in a new way.)

Paul Tillich brings these same processes and tensions, of differentiation and integration, to a fuller size.[26] He talks of the developmental era, or stage, as a "uniting center."[27] This acquired centeredness Tillich, himself, refers to as "a structural whole,"[28] just as Piagetians would. The developing individual is "sharply centered," he "reacts as a whole," says Tillich, echoing an axiom of constructive-developmental theory: "Life is a process of going out and returning to itself as long as one lives. One takes in elements of the encountered reality and assimilates them to one's own centered whole, or one rejects them if assimilation is impossible. One pushes ahead into space as far as one's individual structure permits, and one withdraws when one has overstepped this limit. . . . One develops one's parts in balance

---

[26]Paul Tillich, *Systematic Theology: Three Volumes* (Chicago: University of Chicago Press, 1967), Vol. III, p. 30.

[27]*Ibid*, p. 35.

[28]*Ibid*. p. 33, p. 62.

under the uniting center."[29] This balance is between "individuation" and "participation," exactly the tension to which I refer.

Tillich describes "being at a stage," in a way that would, I suspect, be acceptable to the *Centre international d'Epistemologie genetique:*

> I am a centered unity. I try to increase this content by going out, and try to preserve it by returning to the centered unity which I am. In this process I encounter innumerable possibilities, each of which, if accepted, means a self-alteration and consequently a danger of disruption. For the sake of my present reality, I must keep many possibilities outside of my centered self, or I must give up something of what I now am for the sake of something possible which may enlarge and strengthen my centered self. So my life process oscillates between the possible and the real and requires the surrender of the one for the other—the sacrificial character of all life.[30]

Tillich speaks, too, of the risk of resolving the tension between differentiation and integration by excluding one or the other side, in which case one risks either "annihilating narrowness" or "annihilating openness."[31]

"Differentiation" and "integration," thus, can seem like cold, latinate abstraction taken only biologically, but, seen more existentially, their tension is descriptive of the very activity of *hope* itself, which Holmes calls "a dialectic of limit and possibility."[32] Were we all limit (all differentiation, all exclusive), there would be no hope; all possibility (all integration, all inclusive), no need of it. I am suggesting that "the underlying context"—what Tillich calls "the ground of being," what Fowler calls "the ultimate environment," meaning-constitutive evolutionary activity, there where the dance is, reflected in the tensions between differentiation and integration in any organism, between the competing longings for inclusion and distinctness in persons—is the very exercise of hope itself, a hope which living things do not "have" so much as

---

[29]*Ibid.* p. 35.

[30]*Ibid.* p. 42.

[31]*Ibid.* p. 33.

[32]Lincoln Holmes, "The Nature of Hope," Unpublished senior thesis, Harvard College, 1974.

a hope which living things *are*, a hope which all living things do not share so much as it shares them.

In other places I have tried to argue that this ground of being—meaning-constitutive evolutionary activity—should be taken as the prior context upon which all considerations of personality should go.[33] I argue that it is a promising candidate for a grounding phenomenon because it does not seem as vulnerable as other candidates do to the arbitrary partialities of sex, class, culture, or historical period. It is an activity in which we have always partaken and always will. But in this section of the chapter, I am trying to suggest that its universality is not alone a philosophical or an empirical matter; it is also a religious one, in that it offers a vision of the oneness of the universe of which we are a part.

Let me suggest the power of that vision in the explicit context of the tensions between cultures, East and West; and between sexes, male and female. Again, like Berger, I am charting an "inductive faith," moving from the empirical to the religious.

The competing yearnings for agency and communion, for independence and inclusion, for differentiation and integration, are—I have suggested—a fundamental ambivalence of life itself. Like any ambivalence we might try to deal with it by owning one side and denying or projecting the other. In fact, my own reconstruction of the successive evolutionary truces (or stages) of personal development (building largely on Kohlberg, Piaget, Loevinger,[34] and my own empirical work[35]) suggests a moving back and forth between a resolution of this tension in favor of the one side at one stage, the other at the next.[36]

{415}

---

[33]See Note 10 in this chapter.

[34]Kohlberg, *op. cit.*; Piaget, *op. cit.*; Jane Loevinger, *Ego Development* (San Francisco: Jossey Bass, 1977).

[35]"Ego and Truth," *op. cit.*

[36]This can be seen more clearly in the context of Table 1. Put briefly: What everyone refers to as the "undifferentiated" state of infancy is also an "unintegrated" state; thereafter, an imbalance seems to shift back and forth, one way of identifying each truce's vulnerability to growth—i.e., its susceptibility for disequilibrium. The young child's cognitive and emotional lability is due to the "over-integrated" character of the Impulsive balance. The latency-age child, with its "concrete," time-extensive sense of a separate self, is "over-differentiated." The Interpersonal balance opens this system up again, gaining mutuality, risking fusion—an "over-integrated" balance. The internal administrator which the self becomes at the Institutional balance is a shift back to "over-differentiation." This self-containment breaks open again in the Interindividual balance.

{416}

But it can be argued that whole groups of people tend to favor a given pole in this universal tension, even as they move from stage to stage. It has been suggested that males and females differ in this respect, the former tending to be more expressive of the yearnings for differentiation, the latter, of integration; or, put another way, that men tend to be more disowning of their yearning for inclusion, and women of their yearning for agency. Gilligan suggests this distinction when she regards Kohlberg's orientation to morality, with its emphasis on individual rights and abstracted principles, as a male orientation, in contrast to what she discerns as a female orientation to morality, expressed in terms of caring for others, not hurting, and the inextricable contextual nature of life's dilemmas.[37]

Similarly, one finds this same overemphasis of a given side of the balance between Eastern and Western cultures. Cultural anthropologists are particularly helpful in making clear to us that the values of independence, self-assertion, personal achievement and aggrandizement, increasing autonomy and separateness from the family of origin, all so highly valued in the West, are anathema to most Eastern cultures (including the American Indian).[38] We begin to get a sense of a culture's orientation to "integration" rather than "differentiation" if we consider, for example, that the Cheyenne, asked to talk about themselves, typically begin by saying, "My grandfather . . .";[39] or that many Eastern cultures use the word "I" to refer to a collectivity of people of which one is a part;[40] or that the Hopi do not say, "It's a nice day," as if one could separate oneself from the day, but say something that would have to be translated more like, "I am in a

---

[37]Carol Gilligan, "In a Different Voice: Women's Conception of the Self and of Morality," *Harvard Educational Review*, (1978) Vol. 47, No. 4, pp. 481–517.

[38]Robert LeVine, "Psychoanalysis and Other Cultures: An African Perspective" and Raymond Fogelson, "The Anthropology of the Self; Some Retrospects and Prospects"; both in *New Approaches to the Self, op. cit.*

[39]Terry Straus, "The Structure of the Self in Northern Cheyenne Culture," in *New Approaches.*

[40]McKim Marriott, "The Open Hindu Person and the Humane Sciences," in *New Approaches.*

nice day," or "Its nice in front of me, and behind me, and on top of me."[41]

{417}

These differences between cultures and sexes are powerful, probably enduring, and beyond question of noncomparable dignity and stature. There should be no question of one emphasis being any "better" than another, certainly not on developmental grounds (indeed, it is as true to say that each is equally limited and denying, to the extent it excludes the other side). And yet, it is easy for a given group to make its persuasion the standard. The cross-culturalists' claim of ethnocentrism (even the accusation that Western psychology is no less a "folk psychology" than that of any other culture's)[42] is analogous to the feminist psychologists' claim that the definitions of growth developmental psychologists esteem are male-biased.[43] And both claims would seem to be more true than false. Wherever one looks among developmental psychologists, from Freud at one end of a spectrum to Carl Rogers at the other, one finds a similar conception of growth as *increasing autonomy* or *distinctness;* the yearning of equal stature—the yearning for inclusion—tends to be demeaned as a kind of dependency or immature attachment.

But, however real the differences between cultures or sexes, and however vulnerable to imperialization one is by the other, I do not believe, as many cross-culturalists do,[44] that we must rule ourselves out as having any capacity to judge, or even think about, another culture unless we expunge ourselves of our own origins. Nor do I believe that the possibility of profound communication and understanding between the sexes is denied to us. Our differences, we might be helped to see, do not *radically* separate us because there is a single context we all share and from which *both* sides of the tension spring—namely, meaning-constitutive evolutionary activity, the motion of life itself. I

---

[41]Benjamin Lee Whorf, *Language, Thought and Reality* (New York: The Technology Press and John Wiley & Sons, 1956); Edward T. Hall, *The Hidden Dimension* (New York: Doubleday, 1966).

[42]See the anthropologists in *New Approaches, op. cit.*

[43]Gilligan, *op. cit.;* Natalie Low, "The Mother-Daughter Relationship in Adulthood," Paper presented to the Massachusetts Psychological Association, May, 1978.

[44]Levine, *op. cit.;* Folgelson, *op. cit.*

believe East *can* talk to West and West to East, that man can talk to woman and woman to man—if neither makes its particular pole-preference ultimate; if neither forces the other to be known in its language; if each recognizes that its language is only relative to *the ultimate language* they both share. A perspective like the constructive-developmental can help us with this.

The struggle of the sexes to know each other, to see each other, and to communicate deeply—a struggle which may be more a feature of adult life in the West than at any time in the past—may rest in the capacity of men and women to learn the universal language they share, an evolutionary esperanto, the dialectical context in which these two poles are joined; it may rest in their recognition that neither differentiation nor integration are prior, but that each is a part of the reality of being alive, which is experienced as the tension between the two.

But in the midst of the tension between men and women, East and West, we have the opportunity for what I consider a religious experience, to drop back to consider the whole of which we are a part. When we do, something quite beautiful and moving appears, something that takes us from the empirical to the religious (without being any less empirical): a single community of man and woman, of Oriental and Occidental, who together give expression to the full complexity of being alive, of being a living organism; a universality, and, miraculously, one which each of us can find reflected in ourselves (the woman in every man, the Easterner in every Westerner), for each of us reflects these same ambivalences. The individual mirrors the universe and the universe mirrors the individual. I am reminded of the story of the infant Krishna, taken to the beach by his mother who did not yet know he was a god. As infants will, Krishna ate some sand, and when his mother went to him and looked into his mouth, it is said she saw the entire universe. Who among us is not in this way a god?

Evolutionary Truces

I have said that the developmentalists' stages, or evolutionary truces, work out temporary, and dynamically maintained, resolutions between differentiation and integration. And I have suggested that, in developing, we move from one such resolution to the next. But the experience of such movement has not been discussed, and in this section, I seek to suggest that it, too, is an arena in which we might move from the empirical to the religious, and, in doing so, might better understand the empirical.

From developmental theory and research we are informed that an evolutionary truce, maintaining a balance of what is subject and what is object, is a system of *knowing*; that a level of adaptation is itself a construction of reality.[45] We know that when the system meets experiences it cannot make sense of or ignore, it faces its finitude, and the relationship between the present composition of reality and the underlying meaning-constitutive evolutionary activity may change. The disjunction between my "self" (my present balance) and the person who is the activity of creating and maintaining this balance may only be felt in these moments of disequilibrium. Erikson called them moments of "ego chill."[46] Binswanger called them "ontological anxiety."[47] When they are actually happening to us, we are likely to call them neither, but to speak the more eloquent, if colloquial, language of evolutionary threat: "I am not myself," we sometimes say; or "I'm beside myself." From my own research I have suggested, and tried to empirically support the idea, that depression is the phenomenology of balances, the loss of my way of making meaning, and—from the point of view of the present construction of self—a loss of one's very self.[48]

H. Richard Niebuhr and Paul Tillich both help us move from this empirical reality to the religious in their understanding of the tension between the preliminary (the present construction of self and other) and the ultimate (the ground of being in which this construction lives). Put another way, their speculations of forty years ago now have an impressive empirical basis.

What I have called the defensive side of meaning-making[49] Niebuhr takes into the religious realm by considering our experi-

[45]See Broughton, *op. cit.*; Perry, *op. cit.*

[46]Erik Erikson, *Identity: Youth and Crisis* (New York: W.W. Norton, 1968).

[47]Ludwig Binswanger, *Being-in-the-World* (New York: Basic Books, 1963).

[48]"Evolving Self," *op. cit.*

[49]*Ibid.*; see also Peter Marris, "The Conservative Impulse."

ence of the "void" against which we are defending. When we are seeking to maintain our balance (ourselves) in a world become discrepant, become meaning-threatening, we fall prey to what Niebuhr called "the ethics of self-maintenance." This is a stance "against threatening power that is not identifiable with any specific agency we meet, but rather with a movement or law in the interaction of all things. . . . In our ethics of self-defense we act toward the realization of no ideal, unless continuing in existence is an ideal. . . . With our ethics of self-defense or survival we come to each particular occasion with the understanding that the world is full of enemies though it contains some friends, and ultimately the distinction between them has to be made by reference to the way they support or deny our life. . . ."[50]

From our ethics of survival the possibility of our own evolving throws us into a void. (Loder writes powerfully of this experience in this volume.) The underlying context or ultimate ground which we are thrown back upon when we are "just not ourselves" is inimical and hostile. This is a construction of ultimacy Niebuhr calls "God-the-enemy":

> The maker is the slayer; the affirmer is the denier; the creator is the destroyer; the life giver is the death dealer; . . . the creative source, whence comes destruction. Hence the color of lives is anxiety and self-preservation is our first law. Hence we divide our world into the good and the evil, into friends who will assist us to maintain ourselves awhile and foes intent on our reduction to beings of . . . nothingness. . . . The maker is destroyer. In sin man lives before God—unknown as God, unknown as good, unrecognized as love-worthy and loving. . . . This is the body of death, this network of interactions ruled by fear of God the enemy . . . salvation now appears to us as deliverance from that deep distrust of the One in all the many that causes us to interpret everything that happens to us as issuing ultimately from animosity or as happening in the realm of destruction.[51]

At bottom, Niebuhr finds in our balance-maintaining the essence of "sin," which "always involves the idea of disloyalty,

---

[50]H. Richard Niebuhr, *The Responsible Self* (New York: Harper and Row, 1963), pp. 98–99.
[51]*Ibid*. p. 142.

not of disloyalty in general, but of disloyalty to the true God, to the only trustworthy and wholly loveable reality. Sin is the failure to worship God as God."[52] In this sense, any stage theory involves a succession of sinful "henotheisms," to use another of Neibuhr's terms, or what Tillich would call "idolatry"—the taking for ultimate what is only preliminary, the making of any given way of knowing the world, *the* way of knowing. It is the process-orientation to development rather than the stage-orientation, the recognition of the underlying context that gives rise to the stages, which saves the framework from being alone about idolatry or sin. For in those periods where we are forced to experience the disjunction between how we are presently composed and who we are, we make contact with the ultimate ground of which we are a part. As our emergence from the old balance gets further under way, we experience a sense of our own inadequacy, a sense which William James refers to as the essence of religious convcition, "that there is something wrong about me as I now stand."[53] In these movements we may confront our own sinfulness, our own disloyalty, our own idolatry, whether we have religious language for it or not.

Tillich, too, is most eloquent about these earlier moments of meaning-evolution, when the old balance is at risk, when we begin to give it up ("release from the inner/And the outer compulsion") on behalf of the possible creation of a new center ("both a new world/And the old made explicit"). At such moments the (present construction of) self faces what Tillich calls, "the meaning of nonbeing."[54] Nonbeing is that which threatens self-affirmation. "The subject of self-affirmation is the centered self."[55] "Self-affirmation, if it is done in spite of the threat of nonbeing," Tillich says, "is the courage to be."[56] This discovery of the courage to be, between the prior self-affirmation and the future self-affirmation, is probably at the heart of what Tillich

---

[52]H. Richard Niebuhr, "Man the Sinner," *Journal of Religion*, (1935) Vol. 15, pp. 276–77.

[53]Quoted by Peter Bertocci in Merton Strommen, ed., *Research on Religious Development* (New York: Hawthorn, 1971), p. 3.

[54]Paul Tillich, *The Courage to Be* (New Haven: Yale University Press, 1952), p. 32.

[55]*Ibid.* p. 87.

[56]*Ibid.* p. 89.

means when he says, in another place, that the "transcendence of the center makes the cognitive act possible, and such an act is a manifestation of the spirit."[57] The duality of the state of disequilibrium, its pain and its promise of a new creation, is nicely understood by Tillich's analogy with the meaning of "labor": "In English the word 'labor' is used both for the pangs of childbirth and for the toil of tilling the land. Labor as a result of being thrown out of paradise is imposed on the woman and the man . . . . Individualized and separated from the encountered reality, life goes beyond itself to assimilate other life . . . but in order to go out, it must submit to the surrender of a well-preserved self-identity. It must surrender the blessedness of a fulfilled resting in itself; it must toil . . . . It cannot escape the labor of destroying a potential balance for an actual creative imbalance."[58]

This creative imbalance is, literally, an ecstatic experience, an experience of *ex-stasis*, of standing outside one's self. "Ectasy is the act of breaking through the fixed form of our own being," Tillich says.[59] As this by itself implies neither a positive nor a negative result, we should expect that ecstasy might include both dimensions of anxious nonbeing and courage-to-be. The fearful side of ecstasy Tillich calls "shock": "The threat of nonbeing, grasping the mind, produces the 'ontological shock' in which the negative side of the mystery of being—its abysmal element—is experienced. 'Shock' points to a state of mind in which the mind is thrown out of its normal balance, shaken in its structure."[60] In its positive dimension, ecstasy "unites the experience of the abyss to which reason in all its functions is driven with the experience of the ground in which reason is grasped by the mystery of its own depth and of the depth of being generally."[61] This is the stuff of which revelation is made (" . . . yet surrounded/By a grace of sense, a white light still and moving"). As Tillich says: "Ecstasy points to a state of mind which is extraordinary in the sense that

---

[57]Tillich, *Systematic Theology, op. cit.,* p. 27.

[58]*Ibid.* p. 54.

[59]Tillich, *The Protestant Era, op. cit.* p. 79.

[60]Tillich, *Systematic Theology, op. cit.,* p. 113.

[61]*Ibid.*

the mind transcends its ordinary situation. Ecstasy is not a negation of reason; it is the state of mind in which reason is beyond itself, that is, beyond its subject-object structure. In being beyond itself, reason does not deny itself. 'Ecstatic reason' remains reason; it does not receive anything irrational or antirational but it transcends the basic condition of finite rationality, the subject-object structure. . . . The experience of ecstasy is due exclusively to the manifestation of the mystery in a revelatory situation."[62] Tillich is quite clear that our experience of the ground of being, of the meaning-constitutive evolutionary context itself, yields its own kind of "knowledge," which lives with, and through, our ordinary way of knowing:

{423}

> Knowledge of revelation does not increase our knowledge about the structures of nature, history, man. Whenever a claim to knowledge is made on this level, it must be subjected to the experimental tests through which truth is established. For the physicist the revelatory knowledge of creation neither adds to nor substracts from his scientific description of the natural structure of things. For the individual his revelatory knowledge of the *processes of his own growth* neither adds to nor substracts from his content complexifying cognitive apprehension . . . Knowledge of revelation is knowledge about the revelation of the mystery of being to us, not information about the nature of beings and their relation to one another.[63]

What is thus at first non-Being, or the Void, can become, on the other side, our experience of the ultimate mystery in which we live, of which we are. This is Niebuhr's sense, too, that we can move from God-the-enemy to God-the-friend. His words suggest that the Cross is itself a powerful image of these universal, empirically demonstrated "conversions" from the "survival ethics" of our balance-defending to the evolutions of new life. "The cross raises the question," he says, "whether . . . beyond that nothing there is not Being. The new hypothesis: we are being saved. We are indeed coming through disaster, but we will not be lost. The cross does not deny the reality of death. It reinforces it. It

---

[62]*Ibid*. pp. 111–112.
[63]*Ibid*. p. 129.

denies its finality. How are we enabled to move from the first statement ('we are perishing') to this other one, 'we are being saved'? However we explain the transition, this remains the fact, that in our history, the cross has been and is that demonstration of the power of God whereby that conversion . . . is accomplished."[64]

Tillich and Niebuhr both are saying that revelation is not something which occurs outside of life, or beyond the natural processes of growth, but something which may occur again and again in the concrete world and through the natural processes of growth ("only through time time is conquered"). As such they give focus, I believe, to a religious dimension of the constructive-developmental framework's attention. Together they help us to do greater honor to what Hasidic legend calls the "holy sparks" which wait within all things of the universe, trapped until hallowed. This is the holy pregnancy of the everyday. In this volume, Loder writes of its experience in a specifically Christian context. "We are grasped in the experience of faith," Tillich says,

> by the unapproachably holy which is the ground of our being and breaks into our existence and which judges us and heals us. This is 'crisis' and 'grace' at the same time. Crisis in the theological sense is as much a matter of faith as grace is. To describe the crisis as something immanent, open for everybody at any time, and grace as something transcendent, closed to everybody, is bad theology. Neither crisis nor grace is in our reach, neither grace nor crisis is beyond a possible experience. The present situation is always full of 'critical' elements, of forces of disintegration and self-destruction. But it becomes 'crisis' in the religious sense, i.e., judgment, only in unity with the experience of grace. In this way historical realism becomes self-transcendent; historical and self-transcending realism are united.[65]

Tillich and Niebuhr, too, are saying that "revelation" is a fleeting phenomenon, that contact with the ground of being is

---

[64]H. Richard Niebuhr, "The Logic of the Cross." Unpublished sermon, undated, manuscript copy, p. 5.

[65]Tillich, *The Protestant Era, op. cit.*

soon to be replaced by a new idolatry. ("The enchainment of past and future/Woven in the weakness of the changing body/Protects mankind from heaven and damnation/Which flesh cannot endure.") This is what Buber called, "the exalted melancholy of our fate," that *Thou* passes over continually into *It*. This is again an "inductively faithful" apprehension of the empirical phenomena constructive-developmental research exposes.[66]

{425}

Most of all Tillich and Niebuhr, in their constructive-developmental recognition of the *philosophical* (rather than *temporal*) priority of a ground of being, help us to make a theological challenge to the "idolatrous" understanding of infancy. Just as it seems to me *psychologically* wrong to take the separation-attachment phenomena of infancy as the lifelong context within which to consider later separation-attachment phenomena (so that these are seen as reprisals or representations of infancy issues),[67] so it seems *theologically* wrong to consider all postinfant religious experience as re-creations of an infantile state, as Freud suggested.[68] That is, it is psychologically wrong because the separation-attachment phenomena we see in the first years of life may not have anything intrinsically to do with infancy, so much as they are the first expression of the lifelong activity of meaning-evolution which involves issues of separation and attachment continuously. Analogously, is the "oceanic experience" of an adult a throwback to the infantile state (the *temporal* priority), or is it the experience of a prior ground—the ground of Being—which is always present?

Community of Meaning-Making

By "inductive faith," what begins to emerge out of the movement of development is an image of sacred history—not a sacred history separate from the individual, of events in which he or she has had no part, available only in holy writ that one can send to

---

[66]Buber, *I and Thou, op. cit.*

[67]Kegan, "Neo-Piagetian Approach," *op. cit.*

[68]Sigmund Freud, *The Future of an Illusion* (London: Hogarth, 1928).

do one's bidding; but a *personal* sacred history built by each of us out of our own rhythmic relatedness of loyalty and betrayal to that which is ultimately valuable; and further, a personal sacred history that is universally shared, binding human being across ocean and century.

It is especially this *community* of meaning-making I last want to consider. To be sure, a kind of global religious community suggests itself from a theological appropriation of the constructive-developmental framework. We can see that all people are engaged in an activity which is intrinsically religious. We can consider the capacity of particular traditions to give persons access to the religious nature and expression of this activity through ceremony and symbol, for example; and we can consider the capacity of a world community to recognize the unity which binds these particularities.

We live on a turning world and are turning ourselves. We have always needed to get at the depths of these relations of private to public season. When we cannot, time itself is profaned; closed off from the dance of our own development, we live less. In a community worthy of the name there are symbols and celebrations, ritual, even gesture, by which I am known *in the process of my development,* by which I am helped to recognize myself. Intact, sustaining communities have always found ways to recognize that persons grow and change, that this fate can be costly, and that if it is not to cost the community the very loss of its member, then the community must itself be capable of "recognition." It must operate richly at many evolutionary levels dedicating itself less to any evolutionary level than to the process itself.

At this chapter's start I chose three empirical phenomena I thought the constructive-developmental perspective helped us to see; and I thought a *theologically-minded* constructive-developmentalist might, through the route of "inductive faith," see through the empirical to the religious. The order in which I have considered these phenomena is not random. It describes an increasing involvement of the person with the ground of being. The first phenomenon I addressed—the yearnings for agency and inclusion—is a polarity reflective of every evolutionary balance.

{427}

In suggesting the unity that underlies this polarity, I was considering the relation of any balance to the ground of being which sustains it. The second phenomenon—the loss and recovery of meaning and coherence—involves more than a theorist's bid for the recognition of the unity underlying and generating our balance; it involves *each individual's* bid for such recognition. That is, it involves those periods of adaptation in which the relationship between the meaning-constitutive and the meaning constitution (between the underlying process and the stages it gives rise to) is undergoing fundamental reconstruction. Having moved from the presence *behind* the phenomenon to an active partner *in* the phenomenon, the "ultimate environment" is now to be considered the phenomenon itself.

As Fowler suggests in this volume, every stage composes its own "Ultimacy." The process of development, which Piaget called "decentration," always involves a blow to what has been taken for ultimacy. This shift has been spoken of in terms of the whole becoming part on behalf of a new whole; structure becoming content on behalf of a new structure; subject becoming object on behalf of a new subject, and so on. It is also true that what was taken as ultimate becomes relative or preliminary on behalf of a new ultimacy. These "ultimacies" can be spoken of individually, in terms of the personal psychological structure in which the person is embedded. For example, I have suggested an underlying logic which seems to take account of structural developmental stages such as Piaget's, Kohlberg's, Loevinger's, or Fowler's.[69] One sees in Table I on pp. 428–429, which presents this logic, that each balance is characterized by a new subjectivity. For example, the young child is embedded in its "impulses"; it "is" its impulses, and the threat of their nonexpression is "ultimate"; that is, it is costly to the very balance of meaning. When this evolutionary truce is transcended, the child no longer "is" its impulses; rather it "has" impulses; they have become preliminary, and can be contained without ultimate risk to meaning. What contains them is the new balance, which in "having" impulses, creates the "impulse across time," the enduring dispo-

---

[69]"Evolving Self," *op. cit.*

TABLE I

The Evolving "I"	Piaget	Kohlberg	Loevinger	Maslow	McClelland/Murray
Incorporative (Stage Zero)	Sensorimotor		Presocial	Physiological Survival Orientation	
Underlying Structure:		SELF—OTHER:	*Reflexes (Sensing, Moving)—NONE*		
Impulsive (Stage One)	Preoperational	Punishment & Obedience Orientation	Impulsive	Physiological Satisfaction Orientation	
Underlying structure:		SELF—OTHER:	*Impulses Perceptions—(Sensing-Moving)*	*Reflexes (Sensing-Moving)*	
Imperial (Stage Two)	Concrete Operational	Instrumental Orientation	Opportunistic	Safety Orientation	Power Orientation
Underlying structure:		SELF—OTHER:	*Needs, Interests,—Impulses, Perceptions Wishes*		

The Evolving "I"	Piaget	Kohlberg	Loevinger	Maslow	McClelland/Murray
Interpersonal (Stage Three)	Early Formal Operational	Interpersonal Concordance Orientation	Conformist	Love, Affection, Belongingness Orientation	Affiliation Orientation
Underlying structure:		SELF—OTHER:	The Interpersonal,—Needs, Interests, Wishes / Mutuality		
Institutional (Stage Four)	Full Formal Operational	Societal Orientation	Conscientious	Esteem and Self-Esteem Orientation	Achievement Orientation
Underlying structure:		SELF—OTHER:	Authorship, Identity, Psychic Administration — Ideology	The Interpersonal, Mutuality	
Interindividual (Stage Five)	Postformal? Dialectical?	Principled Orientation	Autonomous	Self-actualization	Intimacy Orientation?
Underlying structure:		SELF—OTHER:	Individuality, Interpenetrability — of Self Systems	Authorship, Identity, Psychic Administration, Ideology	

{430}

sition, or "need," which is the hallmark of the less labile, more concrete personality organization of the school-age child. But notice now that "needs" (not as a content, but as a structure) has become the new ultimacy. The school-age child "is" its needs; their exercise is not something the self "does" and would survive not doing; the risk of their nonexercise is an ultimate one. Only when the new evolutionary truce is negotiated and I "have" my needs do they become preliminary—but again, on behalf of the new ultimacy, interpersonalism, which their relativizing brings into being.

But these "ultimacies" go on in a social context. We can think of actual, developmentally appropriate, social arenas in which ultimacy (the ground beyond ground) gets presented and represented in the form of these social contexts. We need to consider what these contexts provide, not only psychologically, but spiritually; and we need to consider the challenge of a faith community to provide and subtend them.

The most considered of these social contexts, which serve as a kind of culture for a given developmental embeddedness and represent the ultimate environment, is the mother, the madonna enfolding the infant, her gaze returning that of her child's. This powerful image reflects the psychological reality of the infant's embeddedness of its reflexes (sensing and moving) in the mothering one (the infant cannot distinguish between itself and another, between deficits and satisfactions that come from within and those that come from without); but it reflects as well the spiritual reality that the relationship is somehow holy, and I would suggest that its holiness lies in its representation, in the form of the mother, of the Ultimate Ground. The psychological function of this culture of embeddedness is at least twofold. First, it must "hold" the child securely (recognize him or her, honor the infant's displays), and second, it must let go; it must not resist, and if possible, even assist, the emergence from embeddedness on behalf of a new one by serving as a transitional bridge and eventually allowing itself to be reknown (recognized) as figure *upon* the new ground. In the absence of these functions—a mothering one who cannot "hold" (for example, a mother who is separated from the child, or too depressed to respond to the child), or a mothering one who cannot "let go" (whose own impoverishment requires that the infant maintain its completely dependent relationship to her, for example), we expect unfortunate consequences in the child's psychological development. But the same environment can be considered to provide spiritual functions as well, and their absence might be considered to have consequences for spirtual development. How good a representative of ultimacy is the given mothering one?—a matter of her or his own relationship to the ground of being. Is she able somehow to provide access presymbolically to ultimate reality? Is she able to let go and become god-the-enemy? Is she able, once the infant has recognized his own betrayal of ultimacy, to become idol having been god? (Rizzuto, in this volume, helps us to think further about these questions.)

But the relationship of madonna and child needs to be considered with the same questions we have brought to Freud's "oceanic experience" and Mahler's issues of differentiation and attachment. Are we witnessing here something intrinsic to *infancy*—so that these phenomena's later manifestations are to be considered representations of *infancy*—or are we witnessing something that is intrinsic to the *ground of being*, to meaning-constitutive activity? If the second is more the case, then it can be seen that these later phenomena—in this case, the later cultures of embeddedness and social representations of ultimacy—are not attempts to re-create an infantile state of sacred maternal recognition, but the creations appropriate to a lifetime of developing, a lifetime of needing to be recognized in this sacred way, a lifetime of participation in the ground of being. (This is a lifetime participation which ultimacy conceived as something more than a lifetime of reworking one's representations of primary objects, the less-than-full image I find in Rizzuto's chapter in this volume.)

If the infant's reflex embeddedness goes on in the culture of the mothering one, its impulse embeddedness goes on in the culture of the family (usually, the culture of a marriage); its needs embeddedness goes on in the culture of the peer gang; its interpersonal embeddedness goes on in the culture of dyadic relations, initially Sullivan's "chums";[70] its institutional embeddedness goes on in the culture of social forms of ideology, tacit or explicit, personal or bureaucratic; and its interindividual embeddedness goes on in the context of intimate human relations. Each of these cultures is a medium of ultimacy, social, and spiritual contexts which re-present the ultimacy each metaevolutionary truce constructs.

The constructive-developmental approach offers a way to think about assessing the nature of a person's psychological supports that moves beyond the quantity of caring others, even beyond the intensity of their care, to consider, in a fairly discriminating way, the structural quality of those supports. Are there others who *know* the person, who can see, recognize, understand? Support is not alone an effective matter, but a matter of *knowing;* a matter of shape, as well as intensity. But a theologically-oriented constructive-developmentalism suggests a means of assessing *spiritual* support as well. Here is where Fowler's developmental delineations of the means by which ultimacy might be conveyed and expressed at different stages becomes so important. Thinking of this sort seems to make clearer the task that lies before a faith community of a "religious education" hoping to provide some initiation into the mystery of existence. Are there symbols, rituals, memories, images, myths, heroes, ceremonies, and celebrations which can actually become a medium in which a ten-year-old child in a peer gang might suspend his or her experience?

But the need of a religious community to respond to *each* of the "ontologics" is no more crucial than its need to recognize *all* of them, to represent the ground beyond ground. It must not lose the fundamental reality of the person (the reality which shares all persons) in its address to the "self" which personality constructs. What developmental theory has paid the least attention to is the person-through-time, the person who persists, and to memory itself; instead it focuses on what is new and different about the person, the new self, integrative and differentiative of the old. But it attends in this one-sided way at just a time in our history when

---

[70]Harry Stack Sullivan, *The Interpersonal Theory of Psychiatry* (New York: Norton, 1953).

we are least likely to be living in social contexts which themselves are available for differentiation and reintegration. We live more often in contexts that are themselves departed when we emerge {433} from a given embeddedness; contexts, that is, that are more identified with a *given* ontologic, than with the continuity of meaning-making across ontologics. If communities cannot recognize the need for their sacred media (symbol, ceremony, and so on) to be reappropriated as persons re-compose themselves (their "selves"), then the community itself can become profane when the old "ontologic" becomes idolatry.

We live in a time when separation is virtually celebrated as a sign of growth—notably in marriage, but also, more subtly, in a host of commitments persons make. The continuity of the adaptive rhythm of repudiation *and recovery* is protected in childhood when the young's need of the parents insures proximity, but the same protections are not so present in adulthood. Particularly living in a time which is so much more promoting of fundamental growth in adulthood for both men and women, we may be faced with a task at the growing edge of a culture's evolution—how to fashion long-term relations, even "long-term communities" (the term should sound redundant) which are the context for fundamental change rather than ended by it. What is the possibility, I am asking, that the separations from real persons and communities which so often accompany fundamental growth are a function of the identification of these persons and communities with a faith now become idolatry, a function of our inability—and that of our companions and communities—to re-know (and be re-known) with the new construction of reality? Our recognition of our disloyalty, our betrayal, our idolatry, our sinfulness, our now impermissible subjectivity can leave us with feelings of shame and anger at those whose "holding" might now seem like deceit. What is the possibility we turn to the new "community" and the new relation with the relief that here only the new me will be known, and that the new others in their not knowing will help me leave my old self behind, help me leave myself behind? Serial relations and serial communities are much in vogue these days, but we might consider at what price we elect this. Long-term relations and life in a community of considerable duration may be essential if we are not to lose ourselves, if we are to be able to recollect ourselves. They may be essential to the human coherence of our lives, a coherence which is not found from looking into the faces of those who relieve us because we can see they know nothing of us when we were less than ourselves, but from looking into the faces of those who relieve us because they reflect our history in their faces, faces which we can look into finally without anger or shame, and which look back at us with love.

An interesting example of the way the constructive-developmental perspective articulates the challenges of a faith community in this respect comes from the Unitarians with whom I have been privileged to work for several years. Nearly 85 percent of Unitarian adults in the United States were not themselves raised as Unitarians; they left other religious traditions for the most part, during their adulthood, and became Unitarians. They did this for many reasons to be sure, but one of the most widespread seemed to be the feeling that the religious communities and traditions in which they grew up were no longer adequate vessels for the nature of their religious faith. More particularly, they often seemed to have come to the limits of their own absolutist appropriation of their faith, an appropriation which had been recognized and confirmed and with which their religion had inevitably become identified. In their repudiation of their own "ontologic" they seemed to have repudiated their religious community as well, most likely because of the felt impossibility of the reconstruction of those same materials in the shape of the new ontologic. (I am not suggesting their original religion *could not be* reappropriated, or that Unitarianism is somehow developmentally beyond Catholicism, Judaism, or whatever. I am only suggesting they came to the limits of their own construction of their original religion.) In this sense their conversion could be understood as the courageous expression of the yearning to have their new *faith* (in just the way Fowler means that word) recognized. The Unitarian faith community recognizes (some might even say celebrates) just this particular developmental move, but in being so largely about this it faces some extremely poignant and interesting problems. Growth is not about differentiation alone; the repudiation and truncating of the past are more features of transition. New balance, won in the re-collecting of my past, now figures on a new ground. "I understand what I remember," as Niebuhr put it, "remember what I forgot, and make familiar what before seemed alien."[71] In what way might it be important for the Unitarian faith community to assist these adults in recollecting what they have left behind? Not doing so would seem to threaten the community with the same hollowness we find in individuals who leave themselves behind.

{435}

Then, too, Unitarian *religious education* faces a task illuminated by this way of thinking. These adults, who were not themselves Unitarians as children, want to provide a Unitarian education for their own young. This means the community must come to recognize all those preliminary constructions of ultimacy which many of the adults neither themselves fashioned *with Unitarian materials*, nor understand Unitarianism to be about. And yet if the community cannot recognize and hallow these earlier representations of ultimacy, it will fail its young in a way exactly like their parents were failed by their community's inability to recognize and hallow their later representations. These are challenges no less spiritual than developmental, no less developmental than spiritual.

The Cultural Symbolic

Phillip Rieff has written about the "cultural symbolic," a centering motif—a mythology, really—yielding up a rich set of images and symbols by which a whole culture might suspend its experience.[72] He considers the Enlightenment, in the past, and Freudianism, in the present, to be examples. I would suggest that Freudianism is but a part of what is emerging as the cultural symbolic of our time. Of the four greatest shapers of the way modern persons experience their experience—Freud, Marx, Darwin, and Einstein—three partook of a developmental "symbolic."

---

[71]H. Richard Niebuhr, *The Meaning of Revelation* (New York: Macmillan, 1941), p. 81.

[72]Phillip Rieff, *The Triumph of the Therapeutic* (New York: Harper and Row, 1966).

(Within Western psychology, itself a secular "religion," the three most seminal contributors are probably Freud, Piaget, and Skinner; two of these are developmental.)[73]

A particular way of studying and recognizing development has flourished throughout this century, enriched by travel between two continents, which the conference at Senanque replays What has been focal to the vision of Jean Piaget is the image of the child as a philosopher. His own research demonstrated that the child is a natural logician. The research that has followed has further articulated this perception of personality as natural philosophy, and it has extended the history of this career throughout the life-cycle. Kohlberg's and Gilligan's work suggest that the person is a natural *ethicist;* Perry's, Selman's, and Broughton's, that he or she is a natural *epistemologist;* Fowler's, a natural *theologian.*[74] Truth is the vocation of the philosopher; for the natural philosopher, it is a natural vocation of the philosopher; for the natural philosopher, it is a natural vocation. That is, the theories do not study the philosophies the self *holds* (and, for example, deliberates *upon*) but the philosophies the self *is;* the stages do not describe the logical, ethical, epistemological, or theological "answer" the individual *has* for the world, but the "answer" he or she has *become, in* the world. The theories look to the sequence of philosophies the person composes.

But what of the person? What of the underlying context which is *doing* this composing? When we study the experience of *being one* who composes philosophies—being an "answer," and, as important, being a "question" at those times when a philosophy *de*composes—the developmental framework is moved to attend not only to cognition but to emotion (the phenomenology of the movement of meaning-constitutive evolutionary activity); not only the individual but the social (the representation of ultimacy in the culture of embeddedness); not only epistemology but ontology (balances of "subject" and "object" are naturally epistemological, but the relation of the subject-object balance to the evolutionary ground which holds it

---

[73]I am indebted to Prof. Norbett Mintz for this insight.

[74]See Notes 5, 6, 7, and 8 in this chapter.

and threatens to transform it raises the question of the self of whether it shall continue to *be*). But most of all the framework becomes not only philosophical but also theological; it studies the tension between the preliminary (any given adaptive truce) and the ultimate (meaning-making as the ground of Being). The making and surrendering of meaning, it is suggested, is a "universal" activity; but not because Someone remembers to make each person this way. It is universal because it is a single activity, there where the dance is, an activity which may itself be the Someone.

If the constructive-developmental paradigm contributes to a new cultural symbolic, it will be because of the careful work of researchers and theorists over these many years. But what I have wanted to suggest in this chapter is that there is a largely unfathomed depth to that paradigm which ought to be a part of its contribution. When the paradigm makes meaning-constitutive *process* its ground of investigation, it not only rescues our nascent cultural symbolic from an ahistorical, asocial individualism (which we have become comfortable decrying), but from the profaning of the deeply mysterious circumstance of our participation in the living world. ("Over against all this behavior of present-day man," I remember Buber saying, "the simple truth is that the wretchedness of our world is grounded in its resistance to the entrance of the holy into lived life."[75])

When the constructive-developmental paradigm makes not the stages the focus but their relation to the process which subtends and creates them, then the paradigm directs us anew to those rhythms of death and rebirth, fall from grace, loss of innocence, eviction from paradise, return and repentance, the leap of faith, saving grace, redemption—those rhythms we find in the hot centers of human history, where men and women have found ways to see beneath the dust of daily life.

I have drawn my sources here perhaps too largely from Christian theologians, so let me conclude on a Hasidic note. (Of course it has been my point all along that these Christian and Jewish "notes" are emanating from a common tune.) The image

---

[75]Martin Buber, *Hasidism and the Modern Man* (New York: Horizon Press, 1958), p. 39.

with which a theologically attuned developmentalism leaves us reminds me of the Hasids, among whom, Buber says, "the spiritual power of Judaism has most made itself felt."[76] The Hasidic vision testifies to a sacredness in the everyday, a spirituality to be found in the concrete world. As I have said in another place,[77] "it is a concrete world *pretending;* but this in the literal, Latin sense, a 'holding forward' of the everyday. Behind, burst-ready, concealed: something wonderful about to take place. This artifice, but Whose?" "Meeting with God," Buber writes, "does not come to man in order that he may concern himself with God, but in order that he may confirm that there is meaning in the world."[78] And finally: "From of old Israel has proclaimed that the world is not God's place, but that God is the place of the world."[79]

Educational Implications

Were I to direct my attention specifically to the implications of my essay for religious education I would make three points.

1. There are qualitatively different systems of meaning-making people grow through in the human journey. A system of meaning-making shapes one's entire reality—cognitive, affective, moral, and religious. An education that matters to a child goes on in a child's home; perhaps it is the experience of a trustworthy presence in my home that makes it safe for me to venture beyond it. Thus, the educator must know about the separate reality of those he or she would teach. Good teachers have always done so; developmental theory can assist in the effort. The teacher's understanding the interpretative system of the student fundamentally alters the

---

[76]Martin Buber, *Jewish Mysticism* (London: J. M. Dent & Sons, 1931), p. xv.

[77]Robert Kegan, *The Sweeter Welcome* (Needham Heights, Mass.: Wexford Press, 1977), p. 136.

[78]Buber, *I and Thou, op. cit.*

[79]Martin Buber, *Mamre: Essays in Religion* (Melbourne: Melbourne University Press, 1946), p. 105.

experience for both the teacher and the student. For the student the learning situation becomes one in which persons and materials address his or her most fundamental experience of making meaning. This creates the possibility of the "burning present," as Buber would say. For the teacher, the essential meaningfulness of the student's efforts and responses can recruit the teacher to an invested concern for and interest in the student. This creates the possibility of a burning present for the teacher, as well. The educational moment is a combustible one, but the holy sparks remain imprisoned without this understanding.

2. Development is costly—for everyone, the developing person and those around him or her. Growth involves a separation from an old system of meaning. In practical terms this can involve both the agony of felt meaninglessness and the repudiation of commitments and investments. To the educator the first can be experienced as frightening, the second as offensive; both as alienating. Developmental theory can heal this alienation and permit the educator to be of assistance at this most important time. It cannot reduce the risk of growing or the risk of being vulnerable to recruitment to those who are in the throes of a new becoming, but it can make these moments less terrifying to a helper and less offensive. Developmental theory gives us a way of thinking about such pain that does not pathologize it; a way of thinking about such repudiation that lets one know it is not he or she who is being repudiated so much as the student's old construction of him or her. For religious educators, especially, these periods of meaning-reconstruction offer the opportunity to meet the student at the level of his ultimate concerns. They challenge the religious community to provide appropriate media (in word, symbol, gesture, ceremony, story, ritual, or whatever) by which one may more publicly (to oneself and to the community) partake of the depth of one's own fundamental experience.

3. Religious educators, and all those who educate in the context of the student's participation in *a community*, need to understand the special challenge that development poses for the

{440}

individual's continued participation in the community—hence, for the very survival of the community itself. The community must be able to serve as a "holding environment" for *each* developmental meaning-system; if it cannot, the repudiation of an old meaning-system will mean the repudiation of the community as well. For a *religious* community, the challenge is to provide a *religious* holding environment, a support for each meaning-system that resonates to, and makes publicly shareable, its own appropriation of ultimacy.

ABOUT THE AUTHOR

Dr. Robert Kegan is a lecturer in human development at Harvard Graduate School of Education, Senior Counselor at the Bureau of Study Counsel (a counseling center at Harvard College), and a member of the faculty of the Massachusetts School of Professional Psychology. He has studied psychology, theology, philosophy, and literature. Among his publications are The Sweeter Welcome: Buber Malamudé Bellow; *and "The Evolving Self: A Process Conception for Ego Psychology."*

In commenting on his varied activities, Dr. Kegan writes: "I am not alone a professional. I have been told it helps to know about me that I am a father; influenced by the Hasidic expression of Judaism; an airplane pilot; a Woody Allen fan; a magician since adolescence; and a pretty fair kite flyer."

*Character, Narrative,
and Growth
in the Christian Life*

STANLEY HAUERWAS

Introduction*

Is the language and concept of "moral development" adequate to describe the kind of growth that should be characteristic of those who seek to form their lives in accordance with Christian convictions? For example, can the Christian conviction that life is a "gift" be expressed morally in terms of "autonomy"? How do the concepts of character and narrative help explicate how we do and/or should grow in the moral life? Can Aristotle's and Aquinas's analysis of how we acquire virtue and character still serve as a significant account of moral development? In particular, what are the limits and possibilities of Aristotle's and Aquinas's account of the "unity" of the virtues for helping us understand how it is possible for us to claim our actions and history as our own? In what manner does the Christian story, and in particular the Christian understanding of our existence as gift, provide the skills necessary for the development of character sufficient to make our actions our own? This chapter attempts to address these questions by providing a constructive account of character and narrative as crucial categories for understanding the moral life and moral growth.

Moral Development and the Christian Life

Recent attention to the nature and process of moral development occasioned by the work of Piaget and Kohlberg is a welcome development. *Philosophers and theologians have for too long left the analysis of moral development to educators and psychologists.* Yet it is important that we not forget that the experience and necessity of moral growth have always been the subjects of philosophical and religious reflection and disciplines. Every community has to provide some account and means to initiate their young into their moral traditions and activities; and it seems every community

---

*The author's footnotes are in commentary form and include valuable insights. The notes are included at the end of this chapter. References to those notes are maintained within this chapter for reader convenience.

finds some way to encourage its members to move from the less good to the better, and from the good to the excellent.

The fact that some sense of moral development is implicit in {443} any account of morality is not, however, sufficient to allow us to make generalizations about what moral development means and how it must always take place.[1] It may be that there are certain biological and social aspects of human nature that allow us to draw some generalizations about moral development,[2] but I remain skeptical that these are sufficient to provide a noncontext-dependent account of moral development.

The phrase "moral development" is seductive as it seems to imply that we know what we mean by "moral." Since the Enlightenment, moreover, powerful philosophical accounts have attempted to provide a foundation necessary to sustain the assumption that moral is a univocal concept. In contrast I assume that the notion of morality has no one meaning and any attempt to talk about morality generally will require analogical control. Correlatively this means that one community's sense of moral development may be quite different from another's.

This is particularly important for trying to understand how and why Christians have been concerned with moral development. While it is certainly true that Christians have emphasized the necessity of moral development, it is equally interesting to note that they have seldom used that kind of language to talk about moral growth. Rather they have talked about the necessity of spiritual growth, growth in holiness, the pilgrimage of the self, being faithful to the way, and the quaint, but I think still significant, notion of perfection. It is quite legitimate, of course, to suggest that these are simply colorful ways to talk about moral development, but such a suggestion fails to do justice to the kind of life Christians have been concerned to promote. For as I will try to suggest, the language of spiritual growth, holiness, and perfection directs attention to the development of the moral self in a manner quite different from the contemporary concern with moral development.[3]

Having said this, however, it is equally true that Christians have failed to develop the conceptual categories necessary to illuminate the kind of morality appropriate to their language.[4]

Because of their lack of conceptual paradigms, Christians have eagerly claimed the language of moral development as their own as it seems to offer the philosophical and empirical accounts necessary to display what seems to be the implications of their religious language. I will try to show, however, that the translation of perfection into the language of development involves a transformation of the language of perfection that robs it of its religious import.

There are a number of ways such a contention might be developed but I will mention only three: (1) The Christian thinks it more important to learn to live in recognition that our life is a gift rather than autonomously; (2) Christian ethics involves learning to imitate another rather than, although not excluding, acting on principles; and (3) the Christian moral life is finally not one of "development" but one of conversion. I can only touch on each of these briefly.

It is often assumed that Christians cannot be wholly satisfied with the language of moral development because they are also concerned with a dimension beyond the moral suggested by the term "faith." So construed, *faith* does not change or add anything to "moral," but rather denotes something beyond the moral or provides a different perspective on the moral.[5] Not only is such a view a misunderstanding of faith, but more significantly it fails to see that the kind of life Christians describe as faithful is substantively at odds with any account of morality that makes autonomy the necessary condition and/or goal of moral behavior. For the Christian seeks neither autonomy nor independence, but rather to be faithful to the way that manifests our conviction that we belong to another. Thus Christians learn to describe their lives as a gift rather than an achievement.

From the perspective of those that assume that morality is an autonomous institution, the idea that life is a gift can only appear heteronomous. For it is assumed that autonomy entails the attempt to free myself from all relations except those I freely choose and the language of gift continues only to encourage dependence.[6] Yet, from the perspective of the Christian, such freedom can only mean slavery to the self and self's desires. In contrast, it is the Christian belief that true freedom comes by learning to be appropriately dependent, that is, to trust the one who wills to have us as his own. In more traditional language, for the Christian to be perfectly free means to be perfectly obedient. True freedom is perfect service.

Yet it may be objected that the contrast between gift and autonomy is overdrawn. For Kant also argued that autonomy depends on doing our duty in accordance with the universal law of our being. However, such an objection fails to appreciate that for Christians freedom is literally a gift. For we do not become free by conforming our actions to the categorical imperative, but by learning to imitate another under the direction of master. Such imitations can only appear heteronomous from the moral point of view, since the one imitated cannot be reduced to or determined by principles known prior to imitation.[7] For the Christian, morality is not chosen and then confirmed by the examples of others, but rather we learn what the moral life entails by imitating another. That this is the case is not accidental to the nature of Christian convictions, but rather reveals the grammatical fact that the Christian life requires a transformation of the self that can be accomplished only through direction from a master. Morality cannot be separated from moral persons so that it can be learned independent of them, but rather requires learning to be as they are. For the problem is not knowing what I must do, but how I am to do it. And the how is learned only by watching and following another.[8]

Finally, to be holy or perfect suggests more radical transformation and continued growth in the Christian life than can be captured by the idea of development. For the convictions that form the background for Christian growth take the form of a narrative that requires conversion, since the self is never fully formed appropriate to the narrative. Thus the story that forms Christian identity trains the self to regard itself under the category of sin,[9] which means we must do more than just develop. Rather, Christians are called to a new way of life that requires nothing less than a transvaluation of their past to reality.

Moreover because of the nature of the reality to which they have been converted, their conversion is something that is never accomplished but remains always in front of them. Thus, growth in the Christian life is required not only because we are morally deficient, but because the God who has called us is infinitely rich.

Therefore, conversion denotes the necessity of a turning of the self that is so fundamental that the self is placed on a path of growth for which there is no end.

Character, Narrative, and the Christian Life

Nevertheless, Christian reflection has largely failed to provide conceptual categories to understand and articulate the kind of moral development appropriate to Christian convictions. As a result, too often claims about the Christian life have appeared to be assertions that certain kinds of behavior or action were to be done simply because "that is the way Christians do things." The relationship between behavior and belief was assumed rather than analyzed.[10]

This has had many *unfortunate consequences* as it has often created the context, if not encouraged the growth, of legalism, self-righteousness, and a refusal to analyze the rationality of Christians' moral convictions. On a more theoretical level the Christian life was divided into internal matters dealing with the spiritual life and external concerns about morality. Indeed in some traditions distinct disciplines developed to deal with each aspect of the Christian life: Thus moral theology dealth with matters of right and wrong abstracted from concern with the agent's moral growth, aesthetic or spiritual theology with the spiritual growth of the inner man.[11]

The Protestant condemnation of moral theology did not help as Protestants did little more than assert that good works "flow" from faith. Concern for moral development from the Protestant perspective was thus seen as a form of work righteousness. And in absence of any way to talk about and form the behavior of Christians, Protestants were left vulnerable to whatever moralities happened to pertain in their culture. Thus, too often being Christian simply became a way to indicate what the society generally regarded as decent.

Because of the lack of conceptual categories, attempts to deal with moral development in the Christian life always seem to call forward irresolvable issues such as the relation between faith and works, and so on. It is my intention to try to avoid these issues by providing conceptual categories that may help us see that they finally represent false alternatives. In particular I will argue that the language of virtue and character is especially helpful to provide the means to elucidate the kind of moral expression appropriate to Christian convictions.[12] Moreover, I hope to show how the concepts of virtue and character help account for the kind of moral development that is required for those who have undertaken to live faithful to the Christian story. Even though it is my view that the language of virtue or character might well be useful to most accounts of moral development, I am content to simply try to make the case here that they are conceptually crucial for articulating the kind of growth commensurate with Christian convictions.

Even though the concepts of virtue and character help situate the appropriate locus for Christian growth, they do not provide a sufficient account for the kind of growth required of those seeking to lead the Christian life. Character is but a reminder that it is the self that is the subject of growth. But the kind of character we develop is a correlative of a narrative that trains the self to be sufficient to negotiate our existence without illusion or deception.[13] For our character is not the result of any one narrative, as the self is made up of or consituted by many different roles or stories. Moral growth involves the constant conversation between our stories that allows us to live appropriate to the character of our existence. By learning to make their lives conform to God's way, Christians claim that they are provided with a self, that is, a story, that enables the conversation to continue in a truthful manner.

Puzzles of Moral Growth and the Ethics of Character

I am acutely aware that the concepts of character and narrative have received scant attention in recent moral theory.[14] In this chapter, I cannot hope to provide an analysis of character and narrative sufficient to defend the significance I have claimed for them. However I can show how the idea of character and narrative provides natural or useful ways to think about moral development by analyzing some of the puzzles that bedevil most theories of moral development, namely: (1) growth as a threat to moral integrity; (2) how someone can be held responsible for acting in a manner that requires moral skills that they have not yet developed; and (3) how moral growth increases our capacity for moral degeneracy. By providing a brief discussion of each of these puzzles, I hope not only to introduce how the concepts of narrative and character may work to help explicate moral growth, but also to introduce themes necessary for the development of the more constructive aspect of this essay.

It is seldom noticed but the general assumption that it is a good thing for anyone to grow morally involves a deep paradox—for how can we grow and yet at the same time remain faithful to ourselves. We have little respect for someone who constantly seems to be "changing," as we are not at all sure we can trust them to be true to themselves. Or even more troubling is the fact that often we find ourselves unable to grow as we perceive we should, as such growth requires a betrayal of relationship dependent on my being "true to my past self." Marriage often provides a particularly intense example of this kind of problem.

I suspect this to be the underlying reason why moral philosophy generally has been so disinclined to analyze the different "stages" of moral growth. *Modern moral philosophy has been written from the perspective of some last stage as if everyone were already at that stage or at least should be working to achieve it.* [15] The problem of moral development is then taken to be—how to reach the last stage of morality where growth morally ceases. Childhood is largely ignored because it is taken to represent a pre- or nonmoral stage of development. [16]

To proceed in this manner seems to assume that there is no way to account for moral integrity and moral growth. Theories of morality are thus constructed to insure grounds for integrity by supplying monistic moral principles that might render coherent all our activities. The two dominant contemporary moral theories, utilitarianism and formalism, share a common presumption that in the absence of any one moral principle our lives cannot help but be chaos. They assume integrity or moral identity to be possible only if we were guided by a single moral principle sufficient to determine every moral situation. The moral self results from or is the product of discrete decisions that have been justified from the moral point of view. The integrity of the self, ironically, results from always acting as if we are a moral judge of our own actions. For we can only claim our actions as ours if everyone could also be justified in acting as we act.[17]

{449}

The concepts of character and narrative provide a means, however, to express the moral significance of integrity without assuming that any one moral principle exists, or that moral development requires that there be a final stage. Indeed the necessity of character for the morally coherent life is a recognition that morally our existence is constituted by a plentitude of values and virtues not all of which can be perfectly embodied in any one life. Integrity, therefore, need not be connected with one final end or one basic moral principle, but is more usefully linked with a narrative sufficient to guide us through the many valid and often incompatible duties and virtues that form ourselves. From such a perspective growth cannot be antithetical to integrity, but essential to it as our character, like the narrative of a good novel, is forged to give a coherence to our activities by claiming them as "my own."

But if our character is always in process, how can we ever attribute responsibility to anyone? The reason deontological theories seem to have much explanatory power is that they account for judgments that we should be held responsible for behavior that we should or should not have done even though we were personally not able to avoid what we did or did not do. Such theories rightly maintain that we grow only because we are held responsible for behavior we are, in a certain sense, not responsible for. Thus, children grow by being held responsible, not by becoming responsible. But there are the more troubling cases such as those like Patty Hearst where we hold someone responsible, though we are not sure *they* were themselves, but think they should have been. Thus Patty Hearst, it is alleged, may not have known how to deal with the SLA, but anyone her age and with her experience should have known how. As a result, we hold her morally and legally responsible for bank robbery.

Such a judgment, though harsh, seems unavoidable. *Public*

morality would be undermined if responsibility were to be relative to each agent's character. But to attribute responsibility to the agent from the perspective of public morality often seems unjust. Recent moral theories have tried to resolve this tension by writing moral philosophy from the perspective of the moral observer. To become moral thus entails that each person learn to describe and judge his or her own behavior from the perspective of anyone. But, as a result, the subject of moral development, the agent, ironically seems to be lost.

By contrast I assume that no moral theory is capable in principle of closing the gap between what I should do and what I can or have to do. What is needed is not a theory that will insure correspondence between public and agent responsibility, but rather an account of how my way of appropriating the convictions of my community contributes to the story of that people. I am suggesting it is useful to think of such an account as a narrative that is more basic, or at least indicates the place and conflicts, than either the agent's or observer's standpoint. To claim responsibility or to attribute responsibility to the agent is a call for the agent to be true to the narrative that provides the conditions for us to be uniquely ourselves.

Finally there is the problem of moral degeneracy. From the perspective of moral development the possibility of degeneracy simply should not exist. For why would anyone backslide if they had reached a higher stage of morality? And yet empirically there simply seems to be the stubborn fact that we do backslide. The only explanation offered by advocates of the moral point of view is that backsliders have yet to form every aspect of their life according to the supreme moral principle.

But such an explanation fails to do justice to the struggle we all feel in learning to lead decent lives. What we need is an account that will help us deal with the "war that is in our members," that requires constant vigilance if growth is to occur. For as soon as we feel we have "made it" we discover that we have lost the skills necessary to sustain the endeavor. Ironically enough, the demand for moral growth requires an account of morality that provides a means to understand that *with every advance comes an equal possibility of degeneracy.*[18] *The greater the integrity of our character, the more we are liable to self-deception and fault.*[19] Moral growth, thus, requires a narrative that offers the skills to recognize the ambiguity of our moral achievements and the necessity of continued growth.

Moral Virtues and the Unity of the Self

So far, I have tried to suggest that the categories of character and narrative offer a promising way to discuss the moral formation of the self, how Christian convictions may or should function to form lives. In the process I have also hinted that the self can have sufficient coherence to deal with the diversity of our moral existence only by recognizing that the self is finally not our own creation, but a gift. In order to supply a more disciplined discussion of these contentions I am going to analyze some of the interesting suggestions and problems found in Aristotle's and Aquinas's ethics.

It is necessary for me to turn to Aristotle and Aquinas for no other reason than that they, more than any other philosophers, were concerned with how the self, through its activity, acquires character. It is obviously not possible, nor is it necessary, for me to provide a complete account of their extremely complex and oftentimes quite different accounts of moral virtue. Rather it is my intention to exploit certain unresolved problems in their accounts as a means to explicate the meaning and necessity of character and the importance of narrative.

In particular I will call particular attention to Aristotle's and Aquinas's insistence that *only behavior that issues from a "firm and unchangeable character," namely, those actions I am able to claim as mine, can constitute moral virtue.* Such a contention appears circular since those capable of claiming their action as their own must already possess "perfect virtue." This is further complicated by Aristotle's and Aquinas's view that to be virtuous requires that one possess all the virtues, since they assumed that the virtues formed a unity. A perspective like theirs seems to pose insoluble problems for moral development, since one must already be morally virtuous to act in a manner that contributes to moral growth.

I shall try to show that Aristotle and Aquinas are right to think that moral growth is dependent on the development of character sufficient to claim our behavior as our own. But they were incorrect to assume that the development of such a self is but the reflection of the prior unity of the virtues. What is required for our moral behavior to contribute to a coherent sense of the self is neither a single moral principle nor a harmony of virtues, but the formation of character by a narrative that provides a sufficiently truthful account of our existence. If I can show this to be the case, then at least I will have found a way to make intelligible the Christian claim that understanding the story of God as found in Israel and Jesus is the necessary basis for any moral development that is significant.

Acting as a Virtuous Man

There are certainly aspects of Aristotle's account of the moral life that might lead one to think that for him "moral character consists of a bag of virtues and vices."[20] And, if that is Aristotle's view, he seems to have no way to avoid the difficulty that "everyone has his own bag. The problem is not only that a virtue like honesty may not be high in everyone's bag, but that my definition of honesty may not be yours. The objection of the psychologist to the bag of virtues should be that virtues and vices are labels by which people award praise or blame to others, but the way people use praise and blame toward others are not the ways in which they think when making moral decisions themselves."[21] The issue thus seems to be that the language of virtue reinforces an unreflective habituation to do the moral thing, thus ignoring the morally central issue—namely, *it is not only important that we do the right thing but that we do it for the right moral reason.*

It is certainly true that Aristotle's resort to the mean fails to give an adequate explanation for the individuation of the various

virtues.[22] Nor does he seem to appreciate the theoretical significance that the meanings of the individual virtues are relative to
different cultural and societal contexts—in the language I used
above he fails to see that the *virtues are narrative dependent.*

{453}

Moreover, Aristotle at times seems to claim that becoming
virtuous is simply a matter of training. Thus "moral excellence is
concerned with pleasure and pain, it is pleasure that makes us do
base actions and pain that prevents us from doing noble actions.
For that reason, as Plato says, men must be brought up from
childhood to feel pleasure and pain at the proper things; for this is
correct education" (*Ethics*, 1104b10-12).[23] Aristotle thinks, therefore, it does little good to argue with people who have not been
"well brought up," for they "do not even have a notion of what is
noble and truly pleasant, since they have never tasted it. What
argument indeed can transform people like that? To change by
argument what has long been ingrained in a character is impossible or, at least, not easy. Argument and teaching, I am afraid, are
not effective in all cases: the soul of the listener must first have
been conditioned by habits to the right kind of likes and dislikes,
just as land must be cultivated before it is able to foster seed. For a
man whose life is guided by emotion will not listen to an
argument that dissuades him, nor will he understand it. And in
general it seems that emotion does not yield to argument but only
to force. Therefore, there must first be a character that somehow
has an affinity for excellence or virtue, a character that loves what
is noble and feels disgust at what is base" (*Ethics*, 1179b15-30).

Of course, Aristotle does not mean to imply that someone
can become virtuous simply by being taught to be virtuous. For
the virtues must be acquired by putting them into action. "For the
things which we have to learn before we can do them, we learn by
doing: Men become builders by building houses, and harpists by
playing the harp. Similarly, we become just by the practice of just
actions, self-controlled by exercising self-control, and courageous
by performing acts of courage . . . In a word, characteristics
develop from corresponding activities. For that reason, we must
see to it that our activities are of a certain kind, since any
variations in them will be reflected in our characteristics. Hence it
is no small matter whether one habit or another is inculcated in us

from early childhood; on the contrary it makes a considerable difference, or rather, all the difference" (*Ethics*, 1103a30-1103b25).[24]

The behavioristic overtones of these passages have led some to misinterpret Aristotle as an early Skinnerian. Yet he was acutely aware that people do not become just simply by doing the just acts. He knows that although some people do what is laid down in the laws, if they do so involuntarily, or through ignorance, or for an ulterior motive, they do not become just. For unless they cannot be just "despite the fact that they act the way they should, and perform all the actions which a morally good man ought to perform" (*Ethics*, 1144a15-17).

Aristotle was no less concerned than Kant (or Kohlberg) that the morally right thing be done for the right reason. Where he differs from Kant is the character of the kind of reason that forms our agency so we are capable not just of acting but of becoming moral through our activity. A formal principle of rationality could not be sufficient, as the self must be formed to desire and act as a man of virtue desires and acts. For even although Kohlberg observes that Aristotle distinguishes between the intellectual and moral virtues,[25] the latter are only formed rightly when they are the result of practical wisdom.

The Circularity Involved in the Acquisition of Virtue

Aristotle notes that we are capable of performing just actions without becoming just, yet "it is possible for a man to be of such a character that he performs each particular act in such a way as to make him a good man—I mean that his acts are due to choice and are performed for the sake of acts themselves" (*Ethics*, 1144a17-20). Or again, "in the case of the virtues an act is not performed justly or with self-control if the act itself is of a certain kind, but only if in addition the agent has certain characteristics as he performs it: first of all, he must know what he is doing; secondly, he must choose to act the way he does, and he must choose it for its own sake; and in the third place, the act must spring from a firm and unchangeable character. In other words, acts are called just and self-controlled when they are the kind of acts which a just or self-controlled man would perform; but the just and self-controlled man is not he who performs these acts, but he who also performs them in the way just and self-controlled men do" (*Ethics*, 1105a30-1105b8).

{455}

Note that this seems clearly to be circular.[26] I cannot be virtuous except as I act as a virtuous man would act, but the only way I can become a virtuous man is by acting virtuous. Aristotle seems to have thought that there was something about the very exercise of practical reason itself that, if rightly used, made us virtuous.[27] Yet, even if there is some truth to that, it cannot be sufficient, since he also argues that without virtue rational choice can be at best cleverness. A man can only have practical wisdom if he is good, for only the good man can know and judge his true end (*Ethics*, 1144a25-36).

The obvious circularity of the arguments did not bother Aristotle. He assumed that if people were just started off rightly they would naturally over time become people of character capable of moral development.[28] At least one of the reasons he felt no reason to explore the issue further was because he assumed we are capable of acting voluntarily—so that we can claim our actions as our own. In Aristotle's language we are capable of choice, that is, "deliberate desire for things within our power" (*Ethics*, 113a10). Therefore the acquisition of virtue is possible because we are capable of acting in a manner that the "initiative lies in ourselves" (*Ethics*, 1113b20).[29]

On Being Responsible for Our Character

Indeed Aristotle even goes so far as to suggest that we must finally be responsible for our character. He notes, for example, that some may object that carelessness is simply part of man's character. "We counter, however, by asserting that a man is himself responsible for becoming careless, because he lives in a loose and carefree manner; he is likewise responsible for being unjust or self-indulgent, if he keeps on doing mischief or spending his time in drinking and the like. For a given kind of activity produces a corresponding character. This is shown by the way in which people train themselves for any kind of contest or performance: they keep on practicing for it. Thus, only a man who is utterly insensitive can be ignorant of the fact that moral characteristics are formed by actively engaging in particular actions." (*Ethics*, 114a4-10). Aristotle is prepared to admit, however, that once an unjust or self-indulgent man has acquired these traits voluntarily "then it is no longer possible for him not to be what he is" (*Ethics*, 114a20).

Finally Aristotle asks what are we to make of the theory put forward by some that the end is not determined by choice of the individual himself, but is natural gift of vision which enables him to make correct judgments and to choose what is truly good. In contrast he argues such a theory cannot be true for how then can "virtue be any more voluntary than vice? Thus whether the end that appears (to be good) to a particular person, whatever it may be, is not simply given to him by nature but is to some extent due to himself; or whether, though the end is given by nature, virtue is voluntary in the sense that a man of high moral standards performs the actions that lead up to that end voluntarily: in either case vice, too, is bound to be no less voluntary than virtue. For, like the good man, the bad man has the requisite *ability to perform actions through his own agency*, even if not to formulate his own ends. If, then, our assertion is correct, viz., that the virtues are voluntary because we share *in some way* the responsibility for our own characteristics and because the ends we set up for ourselves are determined by the kind of person we are, it follows that the vices, too, are voluntary; for the same is true of them" (*Ethics*, 114b14-25; italics mine).

But obviously everything depends on the ambiguous phrase "in some way." Aristotle has suggested we can become virtuous because we have the ability to make our actions our own—that is, to do them in a manner appropriate to our character. Yet our ability to act so seems to depend on our having become a person of virtue. Indeed that is why Aristotle (and Aquinas) is doubtful if a morally weak person can be said to be acting at all since such a person lacks the strength of character to make his actions his own.[30]

From within Aristotle's position I think there is no satisfactory way to deal with the circularity of his position. Yet for our purposes the circularity is extremely instructive as it suggests that the ability to act and to claim my action as my own depends on my "having" a self through which I am able to give an intelligibility to that which I do and to that which happens to me. But Aristotle simply lacked the conceptual means to articulate the nature of such a self, and as a result he finally has no alternative but to assume that the conventions of Greek society will be sufficient to provide the conditions necessary for us to be morally virtuous.

{457}

Aquinas on Acquiring the Virtues

Moreover I suspect that some such circularity will bedevil any account of moral development. For we must all begin somewhere and Aristotle cannot be faulted for insisting that we must develop certain sorts of habits early if we are to learn how to be moral in a more refined and nuanced sense.[31] The question is not whether such habits are necessary, but what kind they should be that would encourage the development of truthful character. Aristotle, and Aquinas, however, too easily assumed that "character" would result if we rightly embodied all the virtues.

This is perhaps more evident in Aquinas than in Aristotle, for Aquinas argued explicitly that all the virtues are united in the virtue of prudence—indeed, every virtue "is a kind of prudence" (I-II, 58, 4 and 2). For like Aristotle, Aquinas emphasized the centrality of practical wisdom since the doing of good deeds is not sufficient to make a man virtuous, as "it matters not only what a man does but also how he does it" (I-II, 57, 5). And the "how" is always determined by prudence.

As a result we find the same kind of circularity in Aquinas that we saw in Aristotle: *The practice of any virtue requires prudence yet prudence cannot be developed without moral virtue.* "The reason for this is prudence's right reason about things to be done, and this not merely in general but also in the particular. Now right reason demands principles from which reason proceeds. And when reason argues about particular cases, it needs not only universal but also particular principles. Consequently, just as one is rightly disposed in regard to the universal principles of action by the natural understanding or by the habit of science, one needs to be perfected by certain habits by which it becomes connatural, as it were, to judge rightly particular ends. This is done by moral virtue; for the virtuous man judges rightly of the end of virtue because 'such as a man is, such does the end seem to him' (Aristotle, *Ethics*, 114a32). Consequently, the right reason about things to be done, namely prudence, requires man to have moral virtue" (I-II, 58, 5).

The Unity of the Virtues

Unlike Aristotle, however, Aquinas tried to provide a rational scheme to suggest why certain virtues were more prominent than others—thus prudence was the perfection of the practical intellect, temperance perfects the concupiscible passions, courage perfects the irascible passions, and justice perfects all operations. These are of course the classic cardinal virtues which Aquinas claims are called such because they "not only confer the power of doing well, but also cause the exercise of the good deed" (I-II, 61, 1).

Even though Aquinas defends the view that each of the virtues is distinct, he also maintains that they "qualify one another by a kind of overflow. For the qualities of prudence overflow on to the other virtues insofar as they are directed by prudence. And each of the others overflows on the rest, for the reason that whoever can do what is harder, can do what is less difficult. Therefore whoever can curb his desires for the pleasures of touch, so that they keep within bounds, which is a very hard thing to do, for this very reason is more able to check his daring in dangers of death, so as not to go too far, which is much easier; and in this sense fortitude is said to be temperate. Again, temperance is said to be brave, by reason of fortitude overflowing into temperance, insofar, namely, as he whose soul is strengthened by fortitude against dangers of death, which is a matter of great difficulty, is more able to stand firm against the onslaught of pleasures" (I-II, 61, 4).[32]

Aquinas, therefore, maintains that if anyone has "perfect moral virtue," that is, a "habit that inclines us to do a good deed well" then he or she has all the virtues. He thus assumes that perfect moral virtue necessarily provides a unity to the self since there is no possibility of the virtues conflicting. However he is able to make such an assumption only because he asserts that all men have a single last end which orders the various virtues appropriately. Aquinas's claim that "charity is but the form of the virtues" (I-II, 24, 8) is but a theological restatement of his assumption that the unity of the virtues (and the self) is a correlative of men having a single "last end."

Before criticizing Aquinas's (and Aristotle's) views on the unity of the virtues, I think it is well to call attention to the strength of their analysis. For by calling attention to the virtues they at least make the question of the self central and an ethical reflection—"the form of an act always follows from a form of the agent" (II-II, 24, 2). Moreover they do not assume that there is any one external or neutral standpoint from which "the various conditioned moralities can be judged. Precisely the force of the Aristotelian good for man is that it does single out, in necessarily vague terms, the perfect life of a man, taking account of his unconditioned powers of mind; and that this abstract ideal constitutes the permanent standard or norm to which the historically conditioned moralities do converge upon a common core and are not so diverse as the relativist claims. Courage, justice, friendship, the power of thought and the exercise of intelligence, are the essential Aristotelian virtues, although the concrete forms that they take greatly vary in the different socially conditioned moralities. The virtues of splendid aristocratic warriors are not the same as the virtues of a Christian monk; but they are not merely different. Each of the two ways of life demands courage, fairness or justice, loyalty, love and friendship, intelligence and skill, and self-control."[33]

The Disunity of the Virtues and the Unity of the Self

But Aristotle and Aquinas were unable to conceive that we live in a world in which we must choose between ways of life that are inherently incompatible. No positing of a single end or good for man is sufficient to provide a solution for that fact. As Stuart Hampshire has observed, "the ways of life which men aspire to and admire and which to enjoy are normally a balance between, and combination of, disparate elements; and this is so, partly because human beings are not so constructed that they have just one overriding end, one overriding desire or interest. They find themselves trying to reconcile, and to assign priorities to widely different and diverging and changing concerns and interest, both within the single life of an individual, and within a single society. They also admire, and pursue, virtues which could not be combined without abridgement in any possible world: for instance, literal honesty and constructive gift of fantasy, spontaneity and scrupulous care, integrity and political skill in maneuver. Serious moral problems typically take the form of balancing strict but conflicting requirements, which Plato dramatized in the *Republic* by representing the man educated to be just as educated to combine and balance gentleness and firmness. As there must be conflicts in society, so there must be conflict in the soul, and it is the same virtue that strikes the right balance in situations of conflict."[34]

Aristotle and Aquinas seemed to assume that no self could bear such conflict. It was necessary, therefore, to assert that there could be no inherent incompatibility between the virtues. Rather the right balance between the virtues could be exercised within a single complete life. As a result *they failed to see that we often find ourselves involved in ways of life that require certain virtues to go undeveloped or to be essentially transformed.* We cannot depend on "the virtues to provide us with the ability to claim our actions as our own." Rather virtues finally depend on our character for direction, not vice versa.

The Narrative Unity of the Self

Aristotle's and Aquinas's difficulty in accounting for the unity of the self helps one to appreciate the way Kohlberg has approached the problem of moral development. For like Aristotle and Aquinas, he is concerned to articulate, or perhaps better discover, the structure of our moral existence necessary to attain the skills to make our actions and our life our own. But, *unlike them, he feels it is hopeless to confuse the issue of "ego development" with moral development.* "For the requirements for consistency in logic and morals are much tighter than those for consistency in personality, which is a psychological, not a logical, unity. Furthermore, there are relatively clear criteria of increased adequacy in logical and moral hierarchies, but not in ego levels."[35]

{461}

This does not mean that Kohlberg is uninterested in "ego development," or character, but rather his assumption seems to be that "consistency" of self depends on our willingness to guide our life from the perspective of a universal moral standpoint. "A more differentiated and integrated moral structure handles more moral problems, conflicts, or points of view in a more stable or self-consistent way. Because conventional morality is not fully universal and prescriptive, it leads to continual self-contradictions, to definitions of right which are different for Republicans and Democrats, for Americans and Vietnamese, for fathers and sons. In contrast, principled morality is directed to resolving conflicts in a stable self-consistent fashion."[36]

Kohlberg is looking for something equivalent to Aristotle's and Aquinas's last end, but no moral principle (not even the most universal) or last end is sufficient to provide the self with the kind of unity he seeks. For even if such a principle existed, any attempt to guide our lives by it would necessarily require the moral confinement of the self. *What we need is not a principle or an end but a narrative that charts a way for us to live coherently amid the diversity and conflicts that circumscribe and shape our moral existence.*

In summary I am suggesting that descriptively the self is best understood as a narrative and normatively we require a narrative that will provide the skills appropriate to the conflicting loyalties and roles we necessarily confront in our existence. *The unity of the self is therefore more like the unity that is exhibited in a good novel—namely, with many subjects and characters that at times are not clearly related to the primary dramatic action of the novel.* But, ironically, without such subplots we cannot achieve the kind of unity necessary to claim our actions as our own.

Yet a narrative that provides the skill to let us claim our actions as our own is not the sort that I can simply "make mine" through a decision. Substantive narratives that promise me a way to make my self my own require me to grow into the narrative by constantly challenging my past achievements. That is what I mean that the narrative must provide skills of discernment and distance. For it is certainly a skill to be able to describe my behavior appropriately and to know how to "step back" from myself so that I might better understand what I am doing. The ability to step back cannot come by trying to discover a moral perspective abstracted from all my endeavors, but rather comes through having a narrative that gives me critical purchase on my own engagements.

Growth in the Christian Life: A Story

As a way of trying to bring the disparate parts of my argument together, I am going to tell a story. It is not a complicated story, but I think it nicely suggests how character and narrative can help us understand how the self can and should be capable of moral growth. Moreover, I hope this story will serve to suggest how the convictions peculiar to the Christian story require the development of certain kinds of skills. The story relates an incident between me and my father that occurred in an instant but has stayed with me for many years. In order to make it intelligible, I need to supply a little background.

My father is a good but simple man. He was born on the frontier and grew up herding cows. Living with a gun was, and is, as natural to him as living with an automobile is for me. He made his living, as his father and five brothers did, by laying brick. He spent his whole life working hard at honest labor. It would have simply been unthinkable for him to have done a job halfway. He is, after all, a craftsman.

I have no doubt that my father loves me deeply, but such love, as is often the case among Westerners, was seldom verbally or physically expressed, It was simply assumed in the day-to-day care involved in surviving. Love meant working hard enough to give me the opportunity to go to college so that I might have more opportunity than my parents had had.

{463}

And go on I did, in abstruse subjects like philosophy and theology. And the further I went, the more unlike my parents I became. I gradually learned to recognize that blacks had been unfairly treated and that the word "nigger" could no longer pass my lips. I also learned that Christianity involved more than a general admonition to live a decent life, which made belief in God at once more difficult and easy. And I learned to appreciate art and music, which simply did not exist for my parents.

Married to a woman my parents would always have difficulty understanding, I then made my way to Yale Divinity School, not to study for the ministry but to study theology. During my second year in Divinity School, every time we called home the primary news was about the gun on which my father was working. During the off months of the winter, my father had undertaken to build a deer rifle. That meant everything from boring the barrel, to setting the sight, and hand-carving the stock. I thought that was fine since it certainly had nothing to do with me.

However, that summer my wife and I made our usual trip home and we had hardly entered the door when my father thrust the now completed gun into my hands. It was indeed a beautiful piece of craftsmanship. And I immediately allowed as such, but I was not content to stop there. Flushed with theories about the importance of truthfulness and the irrationality of our society's gun policy I said, "Of course you realize that it will not be long before we as a society are going to have to take all these things away from you people."

Morally what I said still seems to me to be exactly right as a social policy. But that I made such a statement in that context surely is one of the lowest points of my "moral development." To be sure, there are ready explanations supplied by the Freudians to account for my behavior, but they fail to do justice to the moral failure my response involved. For I was simply not morally mature enough or skillful enough to know how to respond properly when a precious gift was being made.

For what my father was saying, of course, was someday this will be yours and it will be a sign of how much I have cared for you. But all I could see was a gun. In the name of moral righteousness I callously rejected it. I hope that now I would be able to say, "I recognize what this gun means and I admire the workmanship that has gone into it. I want you to know that I will always value it for that and I will see that it is cared for in a manner that others can appreciate its value. "

I have not told this story to give an insight into my family history or because I get some pleasure from revealing my moral shortcomings. Rather I have told it because I have found it illuminating for reflecting generally about moral growth. For the insensitivity of my response to my father did not reflect my failure to grasp some moral principle, or keep the maxim of my action from being universalized, but showed that *I did not yet have sufficient character to provide me with the moral skills to know that I had been given a gift and how to respond appropriately.* On the surface my response was morally exemplary—I was straightforwardly honest and my position was amply justified. But in fact what I did was deeply dishonest, as it revealed a lack of self, the absence of a sustaining narrative, sufficient to bind my past with my future.[37]

For my response was meant only to increase further the alienation between my father and me in the interest of reinforcing "what I had become." But I discovered that the person who responded so insensitively to my father was not "who I was" or at least not what "I wanted to be." I was and am destined to be different from my parents, but not in a manner that means I no longer carry their story with me. But my own self, my story, was not sufficient to know how that might be done.

And I am struck by how little I would have been helped by becoming more sophisticated in ethical theory or even by conforming my life more completely to the best ethical theory of our day. My problem was not that I lacked skill in moral argument and justification, but that I lacked character sufficient to acknowledge all that I owed my parents and yet still see that I am and was independent of them. Indeed it has taken me years to understand that their great gift to me was the permission to go on even though they sensed my "going on" could not help but create a distance between me and them that love itself would be unable to bridge.

Equally interesting to me has been the attempt to explain to myself how I could have been so unbelievably self-righteous. My temptation has always been to think that what I said was not the "real me." Moreover there is some good reason to accept that kind of explanation since I certainly would not have said what I did had I "known better." Therefore I was not responsible for what I did though I clearly did it at the time.

But such an explanation is a "temptation" as it is equally clear to me that my moral growth depends on taking responsibility for what I said as something done by me. Not to take responsibility for my response is to risk remaining the person who made that kind of response. Philosophically that seems to be a puzzle for how am I to explain that I must take responsibility for what "I did 'unknowingly'" in order that I can now claim responsibility for what I am and have become. But as puzzling as the philosophical problem is, the moral intelligibility of claiming such an action as mine is just as sure. For retrospectively all my actions tend to appear more like what "happened to me," than what I did. Yet to claim them as mine is a necessary condition for making my current actions my own. Our ability to make our actions our own—that is, to claim them as crucial to our history—even those we regret, turns out to be a necessary condition for having a coherent sense of self—that is our character. But such coherence requires a narrative that gives us the skill to see that our freedom is as much a gift as it is something we do.

For our freedom is dependent on our having a narrative that gives us skills of interpretation sufficient to allow us to make our past our own through incorporation into our ongoing history. Our ability to so interpret our past may often seem to require nothing less than conversion as we are forced to give up false accounts of ourself. Because of the pain such conversions often entail, the language of discontinuity tends to predominate in our accounts of such reinterpretations. But the freedom acquired through such reinterpretations is dependent on our having a narrative sufficient to "make sense" of our lives by recognizing the continuity between our past and present and our intended future.

Gifts, Sociality, and Growth

These last claims obviously require a defense more elaborate than I can hope to develop here. Indeed I am not sure I even know how to defend such a claim or know what defense would or should look like. In fact I have suggested two related but different points: (1) that the self is a gift; and (2) we need a story that helps us accept it as a gift.[38] It is from the story that we gain the skills to recognize the gift we are, as well as ways of acting appropriate to bring gift. For the language of gift, without an appropriate account of the gift itself, can be just as destructive as the claim that we are our own possession.

Yet the language of gift at least offers us a way to deal with Aristotle's claim that we are responsible for having a careless character. Even though we may intuitively think that to be correct, it remains quite unclear how we can be said to be responsible for our character. For the very condition required to claim responsibility seems to be character itself. Therefore, Aristotle seems right to suggest that it does not just make considerable difference how we are brought up, it makes "all the difference."

And it is certainly true that we need to be trained to acquire certain habits. But it is equally important to be introduced to stories that provide us a way to locate ourselves in relation to others, our society, and the universe. Stories capable of doing that may be thought of as adventures, for there can be no self devoid of adventure. What we crave is not dignity as an end in itself, but the participation in a struggle that is dignifying. Without self-respect, integrity is impossible and self-respect comes from a sense of the possession of a self correlative to our participation in a worthy adventure. Yet my very ability to take on a role in the adventure is dependent on my understanding that there are other roles I am not called on to play or cannot play. But the very existence of these other roles gives me the ability to step back and test my own involvement in the adventure as they provide a standpoint that helps me see the limits and possibilities of my own role. Moral growth comes exactly through the testing of my role amid the other possibilities in the adventure.

Moreover it is through initiation into such a story that I learn to regard others and their difference from me as a gift, as only through their existence do I learn what I am, can, or should be.[39] For, to be sure, the others' very existence necessarily is a threat to me, reminding me that I could have been different than I am. The truthfulness of the adventure tale is thus partly tested by how it helps me negotiate the existence of the other both as a threat and a gift for the existence of my own story.

The necessary existence of the other for my own self is but a reminder that the self is not something we create, but is a gift. Thus we become who we are through the embodiment of the story in the communities in which we are born. What is crucial is not that we find some way to free ourselves from such story or community, but that the story which grasps us through our community is true. And at least one indication of the truthfulness of a community's story is how it forces me to live into it in a manner that gives me the skill to take responsibility for my character. That does not mean that there will ever be a point I can say, "I am now what I have made myself," for the story must help me see that claiming myself as my own is not the same as claiming that I have made or chosen what I am. Rather it means I am able to recognize myself in the story that I have learned to make my own.

This is a particularly foreign perspective for most of us today. For our primary story is that we have no story, or that the stories that we have must be overcome if we are to be free. Thus we demand a universal standpoint so that the self reaches a point from which it can judge and choose objectively between competing particularistic stories; in short, we seek a story that frees us from the adventure. Ironically, the story that we have no story is one that prevents a moral growth. For it provides us with a self-deceptive story that fails to adequately account for the moral necessity of having a story, and of being a self, in the first place.

What we require is not the absence of a story, but a true story. Such a story is one that necessarily provides a pilgrimage with appropriate exercises and disciplines of self-examination. Christians believe scripture offers such a story, as there we find many accounts of a struggle of God with his creation. The story of God does not offer a resolution of life's difficulties but it offers us something better—an adventure and a struggle, for we are possessors of the happy news that God has called people together to live faithful to the reality that he is the Lord of this world. All men have been promised that through the struggle of this people to live faithful to that promise, God will reclaim the world for his Kingdom. By learning their part in this story, Christians claim to have a narrative that can provide the basis for a self appropriate to the unresolved, and often tragic, conflicts of this existence. The unity of the self is not gained by attaining a universal point of view, but by living faithful to a narrative that does not betray the diversity of our existence. No matter how hard, therefore, such people work to stay faithful to such convictions, they never can forget that it is only by a gift that they are what they are.

To argue that what we need is a true story if we are to grow in a morally appropriate way is not to deny the importance of the "universal." But the test of the truthfulness of any story does not reside in its universality, but rather in how its particularity is the necessary condition for our learning what it might mean to think that such a story could be true for anyone. There is no "story of stories," but only particular stories which more or less adequately enable us to know and face the truth of our existence. Thus, there is no universal point of view that does not bear the marks of a particular history. The recognition of that is one of the first indications that we are dealing with a story that should demand our attention for its power to reveal the truth.

How Can We Be Taught and Grow into the Story?

Every account of moral development must necessarily have educational implications. We must be given some exercises appropriate to the kinds of moral growth desired. That is an incontrovertible risk. The various sets of exercises through which Christians learn to understand and live appropriate to the story of God's dealing with them in Israel and Jesus may be called tradition. The formation inherent in the Church's life will form certain kinds of habits, and those reformed will need to learn to readjust and qualify those habits through facing the ambiguity and conflicts inherent in growing up. There is, therefore, every reason to think that Christians have always been prescribing a form of moral development for training in their own community. It may be, however, that the extent and kind of conflicts to which they are willing to expose the "immature" will manifest a different understanding of "how" one should develop.

{469}

Growth in the Christian life may well involve encouraging a greater conflict between the self and wider society than is generally approved. Thus Christians train or should train their children to resist the authority of the state, not in the name of their "rights" as individuals, but because the "justice" of the state is to be judged against God's justice. Such training is "risky" as it separates the young of the Christian community from powerful support necessary to being "a self." To be trained to resist the state, therefore, requires nothing less than an alternative story and society in which the self can find a home.

Such a society can never be satisfied with external compliance with the story. For the story itself demands that only those who are willing to be the story are capable of following it. That is why it has been the brunt of Christian spirituality through the ages to provide exercises and examples through which Christians might better be what they are. What is crucial is not that Christians know the truth, but that they be the truth. "For if the doctrines of Christianity were practiced, they would make a man as different from other people as to all worldly tempers, sensual pleasures, and the pride of life as a wise man is different from a natural; it would be as easy a thing to know a Christian by his outward course of life as it is now difficult to find anybody that lives it."[40]

I suspect that the insistence on learning to live as you are and be as you live is part of the reason that Christians have maintained that the Christian life finally requires attention to masters of that life. For it is from the masters that we learn skills necessary to have lives appropriate to the claim that we are nothing less than God's people. For the most central of Christian convictions is the assumption that no statement or principle of morality can be sufficient to make us moral. Rather to be moral requires constant training, as the story that forms our lives requires nothing less than perfection.

Conclusions

I am acutely aware that the twistings and turnings in this chapter are enough to test the patience of even the most sympathetic reader. Therefore some attempt at summing up seems called for. I began with the claim that Christians have always been concerned with moral development, but that the kind of moral growth they wish to promote is not equivalent to the current theories of moral development. For Christian convictions require that the self be transformed in a manner that befits their conviction that the world is under the lordship of Jesus Christ—that is, that the fundamental character of our life is that of a gift. By exploring some of the puzzles endemic to accounts of moral growth, I suggested that the concepts of character and narrative are particularly important for understanding moral growth and in particular the kind of growth appropriate to Christians.

The exploration of these puzzles also allowed me to suggest some of the difficulties of the more Kantian-inspired theories of moral development. By analyzing the strength and weakness of Aristotle's and Aquinas's understanding of the acquisition of virtue, I tried to suggest how the growth of character, and the corresponding ability to claim our actions as our own, is a correlative of our being initiated into a determinative story. For it is only through a narrative which we learn to "live into" that we acquire a character sufficient to make our history our own.

By telling and analyzing a story from my own experience I sought to suggest in a more concrete manner the rather abstract analysis of Aristotle and Aquinas. The development of character involves more than adherence to principles for their own sake; rather we acquire a narrative that gives us the skill to fit what we do and do not do into a coherent account sufficient to claim any life as our own. Such narratives may of course be false and as a result produce false character. Indeed an indication of a truthful narrative is one that remains open to challenge from new experience. That is why a truthful narrative necessarily must be one that can provide integrity in a manner that does not deny the diversity of our lives and the necessity to claim as mine what I wish I had not done as well as what I have done well.

{471}

By suggesting how the story that Christians tell offers them place in an adventure, I have tried to indicate how such a theory provides a pattern for moral growth. But this suggestion remains enigmatic apart from my few suggestions concerning learning to trust in our existence as a gift. A more detailed account would require how that claim is spelled out through the story of God's dealing with his people and how the struggle that always goes with learning to make that story ours. For internal to the story itself is the claim that we canot know the story simply by hearing it but by learning to imitate those who now are are the continuation of the story.[41]

Educational Implications

Rather than placing an emphasis on the analysis of how decisions involving "moral dilemmas" are or should be justified, I recommend more attention be given to helping us better understand the stories and images through which we live or should live our lives. For example, I suspect it would be a very interesting exercise to have students write a description of someone they admire and why. Reflections on such lives should help them reflect on how their own lives exhibit a narrative. Correlatively I would encourage greater attention to hagiography as a critical tool for moral training. It might be better not to call attention to the process as "hagiography," but rather simply spend some time reading biographies. In particular, however, it might be useful to compare the similarity and differences between the kinds of "saints" different traditions call attention to.

Analyses of "dilemmas," of course, can have an important place in moral training, but how they are analyzed is extremely important. In particular, attention should be directed to the kind of person we are or should be so that certain matters are considered as "dilemmas" at all. A sensitivity for the kind of language used to "describe" the dilemma is particularly important. The use of novels and short stories might be more extensive, as they help remind us that the "dilemma" presupposes a whole context and history.

I would also recommend that a good deal of thinking go into aesthetic and liturgical training. For if the moral life is a matter not just of "deciding" but also of seeing, then it is important that we use those areas that are expressly designed to help us see.

Of course, finally and most importantly, we should involve students in practices that require the development of virtues. Athletic activities certainly should not be overlooked in this respect, as they often require the formation of attitudes and skills crucial for other aspects of our lives. It is particularly important that the young, like any of us, be given the opportunity to do something for someone else and to have someone else do something for them.

NOTES

[1]It is not clear what a theory of "moral development" is meant to do. Is it an attempt to describe how moral development *does* occur? Or is the object to indicate how moral development *should* occur? In much of the recent literature these two issues are often confused. The assumption seems to be if you can learn how development occurs you will be better able to suggest how it "ought" to occur, but that by no means follows. Descriptive "stages" do not in themselves indicate what "ought to be the case."

[2]I have no doubt that there must be some correlation between cognitive development and moral development. But I am less sure that there is or can be any one account sufficient to describe this relationship since what is meant by "moral" will necessarily differ between cultural contexts. Empirical cross-cultural correlations cannot resolve the issue since they presuppose exactly the conceptual point at issue—namely the assumption that "moral" is a univocal term.

³Fowler argues that Kohlberg and his colleagues have "not attended to the differences between constitutive-knowing in which the identity of worth of the person is not directly at stake and constitutive-knowing in which it is. This has meant that Kohlberg has avoided developing a theory of moral self, or character, or of conscience. Strictly speaking, his stages describe a succession of integrated structurers of moral logic. He has given very little attention to the fact that we 'build' ourselves through choices and moral (self-defining) commitments. His theory, for understandable theoretical and historical-practical reasons, has not explicated the dynamics of the inner dialogue in moral choice between actual and possible selves." See "Faith and the Structuring of Meaning" in this volume. Even though I think Fowler is right about this, Kohlberg, like Kant, can and does give an account of moral character. The difficulty is that such accounts lack what we think is crucial for having character—our personal history.

⁴It must not be forgotten, however, that Christians have developed spiritual writings and disciplines that provided means to make their lives conform more perfectly with their language. Their practice was often better than they knew how to say.

⁵Kohlberg simply assumes, for example, that faith denotes our most general attitude toward the world—it is how we answer the question of "the meaning of life." "Faith" is thus understood to be a general epistemological category that characterizes a necessary stance anyone must take vis-à-vis the world. In fairness to Kohlberg it must be admitted that modern theology has often described "faith" in this manner, but such an understanding of faith can do little to advance our understanding of how Christian convictions work and require moral growth. For what Christians are concerned with is not that all people need to assume an ultimate stance toward the universe, but that Christians learn to be faithful to the way of God revealed in the death and resurrection of Christ. *Faith is not an epistemological category, but a way of talking about the kind of faithfulness required of worshipers of the God of Israel.* For Kohlberg's understanding of "faith," see his "Education, Moral Development, and Faith," *Journal of Moral Education,* 4, 1, pp. 5–16.

⁶For a critique of the concept of autonomy, see Gerald Dworkin, "Moral Autonomy," in *Morals, Science and Sociality,* eds. Engelhardt and Callahan (Hastings-on-Hudson: Hastings Center, 1978), pp. 156–170. Dworkin rightly argues that "it is only through a more adequate understanding of notions such as tradition, authority, commitment, and loyalty, and of the forms of human community in which these have their roots, that we shall be able to develop a conception of autonomy free from paradox and worthy of admiration" (p. 170). But the whole force of the modern concept of autonomy has been to make the individual "a law to itself" and thus free from history. See Kant, *Foundations of the Metaphysics of Morals* (New York: Liberal Arts Press, 1959), p. 65.

By questioning the adequacy of Kantian accounts of autonomy, I do not mean to suggest that determinist or behaviorist denials of moral freedom are correct. Rather my intention is to call attention to the false assumptions about moral agency shared equally by the Kantian and the behaviorist. What is required is a language that suggests how our "becoming and being free" is possible by the self's being formed through truthful convictions. I try to do this below by employing the Aristotelian language of virtue and character. For Aristotle rightly saw that the issue is not whether we are "autonomous," but whether we have a character sufficient to claim our actions as our own. The Kantian mistakenly assumes that the ability to claim our actions as our own requires that we be free from our past and all particular commitments by assuming a "universal" point of view.

⁷See for example James McClendon's *Biography As Theology* (Nashville: Abingdon Press, 1974). With his customary clarity, Kant argued that imitation of another, even God or Jesus, would be pathological except as the other is a representative of the moral law known through reason. Thus he says, "The living faith in the archetype of humanity well-pleasing to God (in the Son of God) is bound up, in itself, with a moral idea of reason so far as this serves us not only as a guideline but also as an incentive; hence, it matters not whether I start with it as a rational faith, or with the principle of a good course of life. In contrast, the faith in the self-same archetype in its (phenomenal) appearance (faith in the God-Man), as an empirical (historical) faith, is not interchangeable with the principle of the good course of life (which must be wholly rational), and it would be quite a different matter to wish to start with such a faith (which must base the existence of such a person on historical evidence) and to deduce the good course of life from it. To this extent, there would be a contradiction between the two propositions above. And yet, in the appearance of the God-Man (on earth), it is not that in him which strikes the senses and can be known through experience, but rather the archetype, lying in our reason, that we attribute to him (since, so far as his example can be known, he is found to conform thereto), which is really the object of saving faith, and such a faith does not differ from the principle of a course of life well-pleasing to God." *Religion Within the Limits of Reason Alone*, trans. Theodore Greene (New York: Harper Torchbooks, 1960), pp. 109–110. Of course it was Kant's hope that "in the end religion will gradually be freed from all empirical determining grounds and from all statutes which rest on history and which through the agency of ecclesiastical faith provisionally unite men for the requirements of the good; and thus at last the pure religion of reason will rule over all, 'so that God may be all in all'" (p. 112).

It is extremely instructive to note the contrast in style between Kant's way of doing ethics and works dealing with the spiritual life. For the latter, the use of examples is crucial as they necessarily must invite the reader to imaginatively take the stance of another as the necessary condition for the

{475}

examination of their own life. Thus, for example, in Law's *A Serious Call to a Devout and Holy Life* (New York: Paulist Press, 1978), characters are created and discussed with almost the same detail as in a novel. Indeed, it may be for that reason that the novel remains our most distinctive and powerful form of moral instruction.

[8]I suspect that there are extremely significant theoretical issues why this is the case which reach to the very heart of what morality is about. For if Aristotle is right that ethics deals with those matters that can be otherwise *(Nicomachean Ethics,* trans. Martin Ostwald (Indianapolis: Bobbs-Merrill, 1962), 1904b10–1095a10), then ethics must deal with particular and contingent events and relations. Because Aristotle posited a "final good," it is often overlooked that he maintained that "the good cannot be something universal, common to all cases,and single; for if it were, it would not be applicable in all categories but only in one" (*Ethics*, 1096a26). Or again, "The problem of the good, too, presents a similar kind of irregularity, because in many cases good things bring harmful results. There are instances of men ruined by wealth, and others by courage" (Ethics, 1904b16). To learn to be "moral," therefore, necessarily requires a guide since there are no universal standards that are sufficient to insure our "morality."

[9]At least one curiosity concerning the current enthusiasm among Christians for "moral development" is the complete lack of any sense of sin associated with the process of moral development. From the Christian perspective, growth necessarily entails a heightened sense of sinfulness. For it is only as we are more nearly faithful that we learn the extent of our unfaithfulness. Put differently, "sin" is not a natural category, that is, another way of talking about a failure of "moral development" or immoral behavior, but rather a theological claim about the depth of the self's estrangement from God. That is why we are not just "found" to be sinners, but that we must be "made" to be sinners.

[10]That such is the case is not surprising as most communities are not called upon to articulate the conceptual linkages between what they "believe" and what they do. Such "linkages" are forged through the traditions and customs of a people developed from the interaction of their convictions and experiences. Once such "linkage" is broken, no amount of "conceptual clarification" can restore the "naturalness" of the relationship. Indeed it may be that the development of "ethics" as a distinct discipline that takes as its task the establishment of the "foundation" of morality may denote something decisive has happened to a community's moral convictions that no "foundation" can rectify.

[11]For a fuller discussion of this distinction, see my "Ethics and Ascetical Theology," *Anglican Theological Review,* LXI, 1 (January 1979), pp. 87–98.

[12]For a more complete analysis of the idea of character, see my *Character and the Christian Life* (San Antonio: Trinity University Press, 1975). There I described "character" as "the qualification or determination

of our self-agency, formed by our having certain intentions rather than others'' (p. 115). However, no one-sentence description can do justice to the complexity of a concept such as character. Indeed it is my hope that this essay through the development of the idea of narrative will supplement the insufficiency of my analysis in *Character and the Christian Life* of how character is acquired and the necessary condition for us to be able to "step back" from our engagements.

[13]Tom Ogletree has recently argued that the idea of "narrative" should be more basic than the idea of "character" for my general position. He may well be right though I would argue that unless the significance of "character" for the formation of the self is appreciated, we lack the conceptual tools to make sense of the "narrative" form of our lives. See his "Character and Narrative," *Religious Studies Review* (Forthcoming) and my response, "The Narrative Character of Character," *Journal of Religious Ethics* (Forthcoming).

I am aware that the category of "narrative" will appear foreign to many of the readers of this paper especially as something having to do with ethics. Yet it does not seem appropriate for me to repeat here work I have done elsewhere. See, for example, my *Truthfulness and Tragedy* (Notre Dame: University of Notre Dame Press, 1977), pp. 15–100. I am also aware that most of the suggestions about the meaning and significance of narrative I have developed raise as many questions as they solve. However, it is my conviction that while my analysis may be mistaken in detail, the fundamental claim that narrative is a crucial category for understanding the self is correct. For no other category is able to suggest the contingent yet rational character of the self. For narratives are nothing less than the connected description of actions and sufferings which move to a point that is not detachable from the description itself. Thus narrative is a correlative of the nature of intentional behavior since the latter is purposeful but not necessary. The self requires a narrative and is a narrative exactly to the extent that we are able to claim our behavior and lives as our own. For an extraordinary account of the nature and significance of narrative, see Reynolds Price, *A Palpable God* (New York: Atheneum, 1978), pp. 3–46.

[14]For more detailed critiques of moral philosophy from this perspective, see my *Vision and Virtue* (South Bend: Fides Claretian, 1974) and *Truthfulness and Tragedy.* In particular I criticize recent moral philosophies' assumption that the primary moral question is "What should I do?" rather than "What should I be?" From my perspective the former question masks a deep despair about the possibility of moral growth as it accepts us as we are. The only sign of hope such a view entertains is that we can free ourselves from who we are by making moral decisions from "the moral point of view." Yet the material content of the "moral point of view" assumes the description of the "situation" does not require reference to the self for how the description should be made. In contrast, the question

"What should I be?" demands we live hopeful lives as it holds out the possibility that we are never "captured" by our history, as a truer account of our self, that is, a truer narrative, can provide the means to grow so that we are not determined by past descriptions of "situations." Our freedom comes not in choice but through interpretation.

Interestingly almost all ethical theory since Kant assumes that the moral life is lived primarily prospectively—i.e., our freedom comes only as each new "choice" gives us a new possibility. But as we look back on our "choices" they seldom seem to be something we "choose" for we often feel we would have done differently had we "known what we now know." In contrast I assume that ethics must be concerned with retrospective judgments as we seek the means to make what we have "done" and what has happened to us our own. Moral "principles" cannot do that; what is required is a narrative that gives us the ability to be what we are and yet go on.

[15]Kohlberg's Kantian commitments are commendably explicit, and like most Kantians he seems to assume that there really exist no other moral alternatives. He thus argues that morality must be "autonomous," that is, independent of any community or tradition, and "formal." Yet, like many Kantians he wants to claim that this "formal" understanding of morality provides substantive and material implications for actual moral behavior, i.e., his concern for justice. Yet in fact it remains to be shown that purely formal accounts of morality can generate the kind of commitment to justice Kohlberg desires. In particular, see Kohlberg's "From Is to Ought: How to Commit the Naturalistic Fallacy and Get Away with It in the Study of Moral Development," *Cognitive Development and Epistemology*, ed. T. Mischel (New York: Academic Press, 1971), pp. 215–218. For a perspective on Kant very similar to mine, see Alasdair MacIntyre, *A Short History of Ethics* (New York: Macmillan, 1966), pp. 190–199. MacIntyre helps make clear that the Kantian program is not as free from history as it claims but rather is a moral philosophy written to meet the needs of liberal societies. In other words we should not be surprised to get the kind of theory of moral development we find in Kohlberg as it is an attempt to secure "moral" behavior in a society of strangers. It is questionable, however, that such a "morality" is sufficient to produce good people. Martin Luther King, whom Kohlberg admires, would never have been produced nor would he have been effective if all we had was Kohlberg's sense of "justice." Rather Martin Luther King's vision was formed by the language of black Christianity which gave him the power to seek a "justice" that can come only through the means of "nonresistance." See, for example, McClendon's account of King in *Biography as Theology*, pp. 65–86.

Ralph Potter has documented Kohlberg's impoverished sense of justice in his "Justice and Beyond in Moral Education" (Unpublished manuscript). He suggests that Kohlberg's difficulty involves an attempt to define a program or moral education which can be undertaken within what are assumed to be constitutionally defined limitations of the content suitably treated in public schools. Thus he quotes Kohlberg's claim that "moral development approach restricts value education to that which is moral or, more specifically, to justice. This is for two reasons. First, it is not clear that the whole realm of personal, political, and religious values is a realm which is nonrelative, i.e., in which there are universals and a direction of development. Second, it is not clear that the public school has a right or mandate to develop values in general. In our view, value education in the public schools should be restricted to that which the public school has the right and mandate to develop; an awareness of justice, or of the rights of others in our Constitutional system" (p. 8). That seems to be a nice confirmation of MacIntyre's argument and also explains the current enthusiasm for Kohlberg's work among educators. For it allows them to discuss "moral issues" in the classroom seemingly without substantive moral commitments. The ideological bias of the assumption that a "formal" account of morality is "neutral" vis-à-vis actual moral convictions is overlooked as it is exactly the ideology necessary to sustain a society that shares no goods in common.

[16]For an extremely interesting account that treats "childhood" as an integral moral project, see David Norton, *Personal Destinies: A Philosophy of Ethical Individualism* (Princeton: Princeton University Press, 1976), pp. 170–178. Kohlberg, unfortunately, never analyzes or defends his assumption that the metaphor, stages, is appropriate to describe the process of moral development. One of the reasons for this, I suspect, is that he has not noticed it is, in fact, a "metaphor."

One of the anomalies of Kohlberg's commitment to Kant is Kant was very clear that the development of virtue could not be learned or come through "stages." Thus, in *Religion Within the Limits of Reason Alone*, Kant says, "The ancient moral philosophers, who pretty well exhausted all that can be said about virtue, have not left untouched the two questions mentioned above. The first they expressed thus: Must virtue be learned? (Is man by nature indifferent as regards virtue and vice?) The second they put thus: Is there more than one virtue (so that man might be virtuous in some respects, in others vicious)? Both questions were answered by them, with rigoristic precision, in the negative, and rightly so; for they were considering virtue *as such*, as it is in the idea of reason (that which man ought to be). If, however, we wish to pass moral judgment on this moral being, man *as he appears, i.e., such*, as experience reveals him to us, we can answer both questions in the affirmative; for in this case we judge him not according to the standard of pure reason (at a divine tribunal) but by an empirical standard (before a human judge)" (p. 20).

From Kant's perspective, Kohlberg's attempt to provide a naturalistic account of "autonomy" is a category mistake since the latter must be free from all "natural" causes. Kohlberg's interests are oddly enough Aristotelian in inspiration, but I think his attempt to express them through

Kantian categories has prevented him from having the conceptual tools for a fuller account of moral development.

[17]For a more detailed argument concerning this point, see *Truthfulness and Tragedy*, pp. 15–39.

[18]For example, see that Aquinas maintains the more excellent a man is, the graver his sin. *Summa Theologica,* trans. Fathers of the English Dominican Province (Chicago: Benton, 1952), I-II, 73, 10. Other references to the *Summa* will appear in the text.

[19]"The less integrity, the less is there motive to enter into self-deception. The greater the integrity of the person, and the more powerful the contrary inclination, the greater is the temptation to self-deception (the nearer to saintliness, the more a powerful personality suffers). It is because the movement into self-deception is rooted in a concern for integrity of spirit that we tempt our condemnation of the self-deceiver. We feel he is not a mere cheat. We are moved to a certain comparison in which there is awareness of the self-deceiver's authentic inner dignity as the motive of his self-betrayal." Herbert Fingarette, *Self-Deception* (New York: Humanities Press, 1969), p. 140. See also *Truthfulness and Tragedy,* pp. 82–100.

[20]Kohlberg, "Education for Justice: A Modern Statement of the Platonic View," in *Moral Education,* eds. Nancy and Theodore Sizer, (Cambridge: Harvard University Press, 1970), p. 59. In an interesting manner, Kohlberg rightly seems to see that there is a deep connection between Plato and Kant as each in quite different ways tries to provide a "foundation" for "morality" that makes the acquisition of "habits" secondary. Aristotle's insistence that "morality" must begin with habits simply assumes that there is no "foundation" for "morality" abstracted from historic communities.

[21]Kohlberg, "From Is to Ought," pp. 226–117. Kohlberg's criticism in this respect seems a bit odd since his own commitment to a formal account of morality entails that a moral theory is not required to adjudicate between various accounts of "honesty." Kohlberg assumes far too easily that the "individuation" of "moral situations" is unproblematic. If he delved more deeply into this kind of issue, he might be less sure that he holds a "nonrelative" moral theory. Moreover in this criticism he confuses the issue of the individuation of the virtues with the suggestion that virtues and vices are arbitrary categories of public praise or blame, or he fails to distinguish between them.

[22]Indeed the whole problem of how the various virtues are individuated remains still largely unexamined. It seems that there is a general agreement that honesty, justice, courage, temperance should be recognized as essential, but the fact such "agreement" exists tends to mask the fact that there is little consensus about what "honesty" should entail. For an extremely interesting analysis of this kind of problem, see Alasdair MacIntyre's "How Virtues Become Vices" and "Medicine and Social

Context," in *Evaluation and Explanation in the Biomedical Sciences*, eds. Engelhardt and Spiker (Boston: Reidel, 1975), pp. 97–121. MacIntyre argues that truthfulness, justice, and courage are virtues that are necessary parts of any social structure, but that these "central invariant virtues" are never adequate to constitute "a morality." MacIntyre argues that "to constitute a morality adequate to guide a human life we need a scheme of the virtues which depends in part on further beliefs, beliefs about the true nature of man and his true end" (p. 104). In the absence of such a "scheme" MacIntyre argues that once the traditional virtues are no longer pursued for themselves, they in effect become vices.

MacIntyre's suggestion that certain "central invariant virtues" exist may well be correct, But I think in the article above he fails to see that even their individuation is dependent on the narratives from which they spring. For an argument along these lines, see *Truthfulness and Tragedy*, pp. 57–71.

Helen North nicely documents the various transformations of the meaning and significance of temperance with the social and narrative shifts of Greek and Roman society in "Temperance and the Canon of the Cardinal Virtues," *Dictionary of the History of Ideas*, IV, (New York: Scribners, Sons, 1973), pp. 365–278.

[23]All references to Aristotle's *Ethics* will appear in the text.

[24]It is well known that Aristotle thought "ethics" to be primarily a branch of politics since "becoming good" ultimately depended on the existence of good politics. Yet Aristotle was by no means ready to despair at the possibility of producing morally decent people if such a polity did not exist. Thus he says, "with a few exceptions, Sparta is the only state in which the lawgiver seems to have paid attention to upbringing and pursuits. In most states such matters are utterly neglected, and each man lives as he pleases, 'dealing out law to his children and his wife' as the Cyclopes do. Now, the best thing would be to make the correct care of these matters a common concern. But if the community neglects them, it would seem to be incumbent upon every man to help his children and friends attain virtue. This he will be capable of doing, or at least intend to" (*Ethics* 1180a 26–31). Friendship thus becomes the crucial relationship for Aristotle as, in the absence of good polities, it provides the context necessary for the training of virtue. It is certainly not too farfetched to suggest that Aristotle's description of his social situation is not that different from our own. The ethics of "autonomy" is an attempt to establish the objectivity of "morality" by basing "morality" in "rationality" abstracted from primary relation. Perhaps a more fruitful strategy is for us to try to recover the centrality of friendship for the moral life.

[25]Kohlberg, "Education for Justice," p. 59. For Aristotle practical wisdom is not necessary just to know the good, but to "become just, noble, and good" (*Ethics*, 1143b 29). For a more complete account of Aristotle's understanding of practical wisdom and choice, see my *Character and the Christian Life*, pp. 56–61. R.S. Peters has argued in a very similar

fashion in his critique of Kohlberg, "Moral Development: A Plea for Pluralism," *Cognitive Development and Epistemology* (New York: Academic Press, 1971).

Needless to say I am in agreement with Peters's critique. In particular I think Peters is right that Kohlberg has failed to appreciate the "rational" character of Aristotelian "habits." Moreover, as he suggests, Kohlberg's failure to deal with the class of virtues involving "self-control" is a serious deficiency. I suspect, however, that Kohlberg has not felt compelled to respond to Peters's criticism because he thinks "virtues of self-control" remains too vague. In a sense he is correct about that as obviously more is needed than "virtues of self-control"—namely the self requires a narrative that suggests the kind and how self-control is to function within our project.

James Wallace, in a manner similar to Peters, has recently suggested that virtues are a kind of skill, as the habits that are "virtuous" necessarily are "rationally" formed since they must provide a capacity to do something well. As such, a habit cannot be a technique, as the latter does not provide the kind of flexibility that a skill provides. See his *Virtues and Vices* (Ithaca: Cornell University Press, 1978), pp. 39–59.

[26]There are actually two circles in Aristotle: (1) that only by acting justly can we become just but to act justly seems to require that we be just, and (2) that in order for practical reason to desire and choose the right things rightly it must first be formed by the virtues, but the latter require the right use of right reason to be formed well. The two circles are obviously interrelated, but it is not easy to say how. Aristotle seems to have felt that the first circle, which he was quite aware of, was not vicious since if a people were taught to do the right things rightly and to think about what they were doing they would simply become people of character.

[27]I cannot develop it here, but I suspect it is no accident that Aristotle treats the virtue of courage in the context of his account of the voluntary prior to the virtue of self-control. For to act "voluntarily" is but a way of indicating that a man of practical wisdom must act in a manner that he is "in possession of himself." To act in such a manner requires more than "knowledge," for we must have the "courage" to face the world as it is not as we want it to be. Courage and self-control involve more than restraining the passions, but rather require the kind of self-knowledge that enables man to face reality and renounce delusion. Because he may have been assuming something like this, Aristotle may have thought that the exercise of practical reason in certain aspects of our lives necessarily would have an effect on the self so the other virtue would be formed accordingly.

[28]Aristotle's claim that all men have a "natural" desire for happiness can easily be misleading for interpreting his thought. For the "end" of happiness is not simply given, but rather the "happy life is a life in conformity with virtue" (*Ethics*, 117a1). Moreover it must be the kind of

"happiness" that encompasses a complete span of life *(Ethics, 1177b25)*. Therefore the "end" is simply not given, but correlative of the kind of person we ought to be as a man of virtue or character.

[29]Of course what is tricky about this is that how much the "initiative" resides in us is a correlative of the kind of "character" we have. So "freedom" for Aristotle is not a status prior to our acquisition of character, but exactly dependent on our having become virtuous. It was Kant's great project to make morality dependent on freedom in order that we might be held responsible for our "morality." In contrast Aristotle (and I) assumed that our ability to hold ourselves responsible for our "character" is context dependent on the kind of narratives into which we have been initiated.

[30]To try to analyze Aristotle's theory of moral weakness would simply take us too far afield at this point. However it would provide a fascinating way to attack the issue of "moral development." It is interesting that Aquinas does not discuss the issue of moral weakness in the *Summa.*

[31]Peters's account of different kinds of habits and virtue strikes me as very promising in this respect (pp. 257–262).

[32]It is interesting that though Aquinas argues that the virtues must be connected, sins cannot be. Thus the "goods, to which the sinner's intention is directed when departing from reason, are of various kinds, having no mutual connection; in fact, they are sometimes contrary to one another. Since,therefore, vices and sins take their species from that to which they turn, it is evident that, in respect of that which completes a sin's species, sins are not connected with one another. For sin does not consist in passing from the many to the one, as is the case with virtues, which are connected, but rather in forsaking the one for the many" (I-II, 73, 1).

[33]Stuart Hampshire, *Two Theories of Morality* (Oxford: Oxford University Press, 1977), p. 44.

[34]Hampshire, p. 18.

[35]Kohlberg, "Moral Stages and Moralization" in *Moral Development and Behavior,* ed. Thomas Lickona (New York: Holt, Rinehart and Winston, 1976), p. 52. At least part of the difference between my position and Kohlberg's involves my attempt to show that "personality" can be more than a "psychological" category through the idea of character.

[36]Kohlberg, "From Is to Ought," p. 185. I suspect that there is much to be said for Kohlberg's contention that moral growth occurs through the cognitive dissonance occasioned through our role conflicts. Exercises that help us to anticipate and rehearse such conflicts moreover may well help us to moral maturity. But such "growth" cannot simply be a question of being better able to justify our decisions from a "universal" perspective. For the subject of growth is the self which is obviously more than the sum of principles to which we adhere.

[37]Of course it is equally true that every "binding" requires a "loosing" as we cannot and should not be bound to everything in our past. It may even be true that some inherit a history so destructive we may rightly wonder how we could ever be bound to it. Yet our freedom from such a history cannot come by having "no history" but by acquiring a narrative that helps us have a stance toward our past without resentment. For resentment would continue to bind us to the destructive since the self would still be essentially defined by our assumption that we are primarily creatures of injustice. I suspect that one of the reasons growth in the Christian life is described as conversion is it requires us to learn to live without resentment. And to be able to live in that manner requires us to learn nothing less than that our life, including the destructive past, is nothing less than gift. I wish to thank Mr. Mike Duffey for helping me formulate this point.

[38]Enda McDonagh, *Gift and Call* (St. Meinrad, Indiana: Abbey Press, 1975).

[39]For example, see McDonagh's suggestion that "threat" is always the necessary other side of a "gift," *Gift and Call*, pp. 36–39. That such is the case makes Aristotle's understanding of the centrality of courage for moral wisdom all the more compelling.

[40]Law, *A Serious Call to a Devout and Holy Life*, p. 55. There is a deep intellectualistic bias in much of the literature dealing with moral development. The assumption seems to be that the more "self-conscious" we are of our values and principles, the better chance we have for moral growth. While I suspect any significant moral tradition must develop some who are self-conscious, it is by no means clear that all need to be such. We must remember that the Gospel does not require us to be self-conscious as our first order of business. Rather it requires us to be faithful.

[41]I wish to thank Rev. David Burrell, Mr. Mike Duffey, Rev. Enda McDonagh, Dr. David Solomon, and Rev. Jim Burtchaell for reading and criticizing earlier drafts of this paper.

ABOUT THE AUTHOR

Dr. Stanley Martin Hauerwas *is Associate Professor of Theology at Notre Dame University. He is a graduate of the Yale Divinity School and the Yale Graduate School. Before joining the faculty at Notre Dame, he taught at Augustana College in Illinois.*

Dr. Hauerwas *has authored several books and many essays and reviews. Among his publications are:* Truthfulness and Tragedy;

{484}

Vision and Virtue: Essays in Christian Ethical Reflection; *and* Character and the Christian Life: A Study in Theological Ethics.

Although an ethicist who is primarily concerned with basic methodological issues of the nature of theological ethics, Dr. Hauerwas has published essays on such issues as abortion, euthanasia, the care of the retarded, and political ethics. He is currently working on a book called Story and Rationality: Further Essays in Theological Ethics *and on a book on the theology and ethics of the family.*

MORAL AND RELIGIOUS EDUCATION

Democracy, Cooperation, and Moral Education

THOMAS LICKONA

Introduction*

For the last eight years I have been working with teachers—early childhood, elementary, and secondary—on the theory and practice of moral education. Over the course of that work, thanks largely to the opportunity to interact with teachers, I have developed slowly from thinking (I am embarrassed to admit) that moral education meant discussing hypothetical moral dilemmas to realizing that moral education means something far more inclusive and pervasive—something, indeed, that embraces virtually everything that happens within the walls of the classroom. I have also come to believe that most of what I now think of as moral education can be defined in terms of democracy, broadly construed. Finally, I believe that just about everything that is good about democracy can be understood as some form of cooperation. My goal in this chapter is to lay out what I hope will appear to be a logical chain of ideas linking democracy, cooperation, and moral education. Following that, I will offer a conceptual model of what I call cooperative classroom democracy and share with you some concrete examples of how teachers can implement this model with children.

The Case for Cooperative Democracy

My case for cooperative democracy in the classroom consists of seven interrelated points. Here is the first.

1. Democracy Is Best Understood as a Form of Social Cooperation.

Democracy, like morality, can be viewed as a process of working out or regulating the relationship between the individual and the group or between one group and another. Usually we use a conflict model to think about these relationships. This interest

*Preparation of this manuscript was supported by a grant from the Danforth Foundation.

{*489*}

group wants one thing, this, something else. A union wants to increase its wages; management wants to protect its profits. Minorities want job and admissions quotas as a way of gaining social equality; majorities want the kind of equal justice that is blind to the color of an applicant's skin. Environmentalists want to protect the environment; industrialists, to develop it. And so on. Democracy serves as a system where people can press their interests and where the free and fair interplay of contending forces moves slowly toward the ideal of justice for all.

There is, however, another way of thinking about democracy. One can use a cooperative model. A cooperative model takes a wider, more positive view of human affairs. It recognizes that interests often conflict and that a central function of democracy is to settle such conflicts fairly. But it recognizes that even when people have conflicting goals, they also have common interests that transcend the points of conflict. Everyone, for example, has a stake in clean air and water, decent schools, effective health care, safe and adequate energy, the control of crime, a stable economy, a world without war. Everyone has a stake in maintaining a healthy democracy where interests that do conflict can be heard and justly resolved. From this perspective, even conflict resolution can be viewed as a cooperative act. The question in the cooperative model is no longer "How can I get what I have coming to me?" but rather "How can we help each other achieve our separate and common goals?"

To anchor these abstractions in the life of the classroom, let me present a "democratic dilemma," taken from an instrument that Ralph Mosher, Muffy Paradise, Joe Reimer, and I developed called "The Democratic Reasoning Interview." This interview is part of an effort, sponsored by the Danforth Foundation, to find out how teachers think about three questions: (1) What is democracy? (2) What does it mean to practice democracy in the elementary school classroom? and (3) How does democracy in the classroom foster children's social and moral development?

The first of the two dilemmas in the interview is "The Teacher's Dilemma":

> In a class meeting of fifth graders, several children begin to talk about the behavior of one girl, Karen. With rising anger

they say things like, "You think you're so great!" "You're always sticking your nose in other people's business," and "You're always telling lies about people behind their backs!" The teacher has noticed Karen's haughty and unkind treatment of other children, which has alienated her classmates. She has seen the antagonism toward Karen building and thinks it may be good to get it out into the open. But as she watches Karen grow tense and tight-lipped in the face of her accusers, she wonders whether class meeting is the place to deal with the issue. She says, "I think perhaps it's not quite fair to Karen to discuss this in class meeting."

"*She* doesn't care," a girl says in reply, "do you, Karen?"

"It doesn't bother me," Karen says quickly. "They can say whatever they want to." "Yeah," another student says to the teacher, "you said we could use class meetings to discuss any problems we're having."

After presenting the dilemma to the teacher, we ask, "What should this teacher do? Why?" Next we ask, "Would that be a democratic way to deal with this dilemma? Why or why not?" And finally, "What would be the *most* democratic way of handling this dilemma?"

The model of democracy in the teacher's head is revealed by the way the teacher defines and attempts to resolve this dilemma. The teacher may construe the dilemma as a problem of conflicting rights. That is in fact how one teacher saw it: as a conflict between the class's right to express its feelings and Karen's right to "stop the meeting if she can't handle it." Said this teacher: "I think the other children did have the right (to state their feelings). I also think Karen did have the right not to hear it. I see these as conflicting. I think they are very much even. The question is whether to carry on the meeting. . . ." This teacher came down on the side of Karen's right to stop the meeting if she chose to because "nobody should have to be persecuted or to feel that other people are doing things that they have no control over."

Another teacher took a different tack. He began by asking, "Who are these kids who are now attacking Karen? What's their reasoning? Are they there to attack her or to help her?" Like the first teacher, he is concerned about Karen's welfare. But in contrast to the first teacher, he introduces the idea that the other children have a responsibility for Karen's welfare—a responsibility to help rather than hurt. He continues this theme of responsibility in his explanation of what he would do if he were the teacher. He would begin by asking his students to reflect on the fact "we all have behaviors that bother other people." He would say to his students,

{491}

> What is our reason for informing Karen? We have to be sure we are doing it in a way that will help her and all of us grow, because it could be any of us in that situation. I think it would be beneficial if we sat down tonight and really thought about the behaviors that bother us. What can we do to help Karen or anyone else change? How can we do that in a way that will help us maintain the sense of community that we have worked so hard all year to develop? The truth is we are a community. We are twenty-four people, and we live in close quarters and we have to get along and we have to communicate. How can we do that best?

This teacher clearly sees classroom democracy as a cooperative enterprise. He defines the Karen dilemma not in terms of conflicting rights but in terms of common needs and obligations. He considers it crucial to stress the fact that anyone could be in Karen's shoes, that everyone does things that offend others. And the paramount question he would put before his children is this: How can each person contribute to the solution of the problem in a way that will benefit the class as a whole, the community that they have created together? Significantly, this teacher has in fact worked all year long to develop this kind of cooperative community in his fifth-grade classroom. It was not by accident that his children voted to call their daily class meeting their "Community Conference."

The idea of democracy as a form of cooperation is certainly now new, although it tends to be obscured by the dust of partisan battles. Decades ago, John Dewey wrote that "Democracy is much broader than a special political form, a method of conducting government . . . . It is *a way of life*, social and individual"[1] "The foundation of democracy," Dewey said, "is faith in human intelligence and in *the power of pooled and cooperative experience* . . .

---

[1]J. Dewey, *Problems of Men* (New York: Greenwood Press, 1968).

faith that each individual has something to contribute, whose value can be assessed only as it enters into the final pooled intelligence constituted by the contributions of all."[2] This kind of cooperative participation of "every mature human being" Dewey saw as "the keynote of democracy as a way of life."[3]

2. If Democracy Is Cooperation, Then the Greatest Enemy of Democracy Is Individualism.

In his classic study, *Democracy in America*, Tocqueville observed that democracy fosters individualism. Individualism, he pointed out, first saps the virtues of public life and ends in pure selfishness.[4]

Why does democracy, defined by Dewey as inherently and necessarily cooperative, foster individualism? It does so because it fosters, indeed, cherishes, individual freedom. Freedom, unchecked and unchanneled by an ethic of cooperation, tends naturally toward selfishness. Selfishness these days takes many forms. It appears in the new preoccupation with self-fulfillment as opposed to the old ideal of service to others. It appears in the skyrocketing divorce rate and the self-proclaimed values of what sociologists have identified as a "New Breed" of parents who say that their needs, not those of their children, should come first. And it rears its ugly head with destructive regularity in the forums of national and international affairs. Wrote James Reston in *The New York Times*, "From Toronto to Mexico City, up and down the continent, one hears a rueful lament these days. It is that 'me politics' have taken over; that personal interests and narrow commercial or social concerns are dividing the people and diverting them from the larger questions of the general good."[5]

Reston catalogs the cases: Prime Minister Trudeau appealing in vain for his countrymen to think and act not as French

---

[2] *Ibid.* pp. 59–60 (Italics added).

[3] *Ibid.* p. 58.

[4] A. Tocqueville, *Democracy in America* (New York: Harper & Row 1966); originally published in Paris by M. Levy, 1868.

[5] J. Reston, "A Rueful Lament," *The New York Times*, February 4, 1979, p. 19.

Canadians or as English Canadians but as Canadians; President Carter trying to trim the federal budget to fight the common enemy of inflation and being excoriated by minorities and labor for cutting too much and by business for not cutting enough; even Britain, "which is supposed to have invented team play and democratic responsibility," reduced to turmoil as a result of strikes by truckers and civil servants. Everywhere, Reston grimly concludes, one sees "a tendency to work with factions for limited and often selfish ends. One hears the same refrain over a wide range of free countries—that everybody is out for himself, so why not do the same?"

We are faced, then, with something of a paradox. Democracy both requires cooperation and breeds individualism. We might ask, whence comes the individualism that threatens democracy for the common good? The search for the origins of individualism leads us to the early stages of human development and to the next point in the discussion.

3. Individualism Has Its Roots in Childhood, When It Can Be Best Understood as an Early Stage of Moral Development.

A lack of cooperation in young children does not surprise or dismay us. We understand it to be a spontaneous manifestation of their immature development. Let me offer a personal anecdote to illustrate the natural individualism of the young child.

My wife and I have two sons, Mark, 11, and Matthew, 5. For the last several years we have had a tradition of family meetings, which we use to try to prevent and solve the assorted problems of family living and to strengthen our sense of being a family.

Last September we moved from Cortland, New York, to Boston—from a two-story house with a big yard in a quiet neighborhood to a small, sixth-floor apartment that looks down on the Beacon Street trolley and seven lanes of cars. During the first week in our new environs, we had an inordinate number of family meetings to negotiate the rules of apartment and big-city living: rules about the bunk beds (new for the boys), the building elevator, walking amidst the heavy traffic, the division of chores, and the like.

One night that week, after a series of such discussions, my wife and I were in our bedroom picking up when Matthew, our five-year-old, walked in and presented us with a picture he had drawn of two grown-ups and a child.

"That's very nice," my wife said. "Is that us?"

"No," Matthew said, slightly annoyed, "can't you see that this mother has long, *blonde* hair (my wife's is short and brown) and this kid has *dark* hair (Matthew's is blonde)?" Then he looked away and added in a detached tone, "This is another family. They don't have any problems."

My wife and I exchanged meaningful glances and I said to Matthew, "They don't have any problems, eh? Why don't they have any problems?"

"Because the parents do what they want to do," Matthew replied, "and the kids do what they want to do."

"Oh, Matthew," my wife said, "that would never work."

"It's the *only* way it will work," Matthew said.

"What if the kids want to do one thing," I said, "and the parents want to do the opposite? What if the parents want to go to bed and get some sleep and the kids want to stay up and play and make noise?"

Matthew held his ground. "The parents should go to bed," he shrugged, "and the kids should stay up and play."

Matthew's prescription for a happy family is a good example of the live-and-let-live version of democracy. It is also a classic expression of Kohlberg's Stage 2 of moral reasoning. Kids have their interests, parents have theirs; they should each do their own thing and stay out of each other's way. You can't get much more individualistic than that.

Like the moral philosopher that Piaget and Kohlberg say all children are, Matthew had constructed his individualistic theory of how the world should work on his own. He even advanced and maintained it in the face of our dogged efforts to promote family cooperation. Thus we can attribute the young child's individualistic moral philosophy—and the even more primitive egocentrism of Stages 0 and 1 that precede it—to natural developmental forces at work from within. This is not to say that fostering cooperation is impossible with young children—only that strong environmental supports are needed to compensate for the counter-tendencies of development. (Matthew, I am happy to report, has agreed, however reluctantly, to wash the dishes every other night as one of his contributions to the general family welfare. Teachers of young children, even of kindergarten and preschool age, have been able to cultivate cooperative effort through structured tasks that have children work together toward a single goal.)

{495}

A puzzle remains: Why does self-centered individualism, developmentally natural in young children, persist so long after childhood? Why does narrow self-interest abound even among adults, whose moral reasoning development should have carried them a step or more beyond Stage 2? There are no doubt many explanations, theological as well as psychological. Moral reasoning may be a feeble force when measured against the power of self-interest to determine human behavior. I submit, however, that our natures are not irredeemably selfish and that a good part of the problem lies in the values of the surrounding culture— which brings me to Point 4.

4. Indivdualism Is the Dominant Culture of the School and Influences Older Children and Adolescents to Function at a Level Beneath Their Highest Personal Stage of Moral Development.

Ralph Mosher, in an instructive essay on the evolution of a high school democracy in Brookline, Massachusetts, reports that the jealously guarded "autonomy of the individual" was for a considerable time an impediment to the establishment of a democratic community in which members felt obligations as well as freedoms.[6] It was two years, for example, before this "School-Within-a-School" finally passed a resolution to make the weekly "Town Meeting" a mandatory requirement for all students and staff. This reluctance of students to give up any of their freedom and take on obligations to the group was not due to their lacking the requisite conventional moral reasoning to understand issues

---

[6]R. Mosher, "A Democratic High School," in N. Sprinthall & R. Mosher, eds., *Value Development As the Aim of Education* (Schenectady, New York: Character Research Press, 1978).

of community and responsibility to others. They were largely bright middle- and upper-middle-class kids and they tested Stage 3 or higher on Kohlberg's scale (as, indeed, do most adolescents). Their individualism could not be blamed on immature development. Rather it reflected the prevailing culture of the adolescent peer group.[7] This culture says, "Be cool, do your own thing, hang loose, don't get involved." Stage 2, which was an internal developmental level for children, has for adolescents become a social norm. As such, it has a very powerful effect on the individual person's behavior, even if that individual has available a higher developmental stage of reasoning. This analysis is parallel to what Kohlberg and his colleagues have written about the moral atmosphere of schools and prisons: The perceived ethic of the group can depress the moral functioning of individual members.[8]

It is reasonable to ask why adolescents as a group function at a developmental level that they have individually outgrown. Why in this case is the whole less than the sum of its parts? Schools cannot bear all the blame, but they surely bear some of it. The individualism of the peer group mirrors the individualism that is the dominant culture of the school. Nearly fifty years ago Piaget castigated schools for acting as if their major mission were "the preparation of pupils for competitive examinations rather than for life."[9] The school's determination to "shut the child up in work that is strictly individual," Piaget said, "is contrary to the most obvious requirements of intellectual and moral development."[10] His indictment, sad to say, rings equally true today. It is still very rare to find classrooms where children engage in cooperative learning and help each other on a regular basis. Most

---

[7]The individualism of the adolescent peer group is by no means impervious to social influence. In the School-Within-a-School democracy that Mosher describes, under the press of ongoing discussion of what it means to be a community, there was a steady increase in the willingness of students to take on responsibilities to others, including social action in the community at large.

[8]For example, see C. Power and J. Reimer, "Moral Atmosphere: A Bridge Between Judgment and Action," in W. Damon, ed., *New Directions in Child Development: Moral Development.* (San Francisco: Jossey-Bass, 1979).

[9]J. Piaget, *The Moral Judgment of the Child* (London: Kegan Paul, 1932), p. 405.

[10]*Ibid.*

of what passes for educational reform has served to individualize the curriculum rather than to socialize it. Schools, it seems fair to say, have institutionalized individualism.

That individualism begins as a natural stage of development and gets externalized as a cultural norm and embodied in social institutions like the school—that is the bad news confronting anyone who would educate for cooperative democracy. What is the good news? It is that:

5. *Cooperation Is Natural Human Behavior, with a Long Evolutionary History.*

Having said that human beings have an enormous capacity for individualism and selfishness, I would like now to argue that we have an equally impressive capacity for cooperation. Even in very young children, whom I have portrayed too simplistically as egocentric or individualistic, one can see—in their mutually adaptive play, for example—the beginnings of cooperative behavior. Lois Murphy, in her extensive observations of nursery schoolers, has documented many instances of sympathy and altruism in children, as when one comforts or helps another who is hurt or crying.[11]

That the impulse to cooperate is within us is not surprising when we stand back and consider the behavior of other species. I was prompted to do this by our son, Matthew, who these days is learning eagerly about the animal kingdom. Standing at age five on the threshold of Piaget's concrete operational thinking, he is, like other children at this developmental juncture, intensely interested in things concrete—in the stuff of the real world in all its wonderful and exotic variety. He is exploring the world of animals through a marvelous series of 4" × 4" cards, printed in Japan, each of which provides a stunning color photo of one creature on the front and a short but detailed essay about its characteristics and life habits on the back.

---

[11]L.B. Murphy, *Social Behavior and Child Personality* (New York: Columbia University Press, 1937).

One such card depicts the lowly brown rat. "One of man's most dangerous enemies," the subtitle says ominously. There are—brace yourself—three brown rats for every human being on the face of the earth. Three brown rats consume as much food as one human. The biography of the brown rat goes on to point out that its prominence is no fluke.

> Rat societies are extremely well-organized, and the very close social bonds ensure both survival and security. The different members of such a community work in harmony and will come to one another's aid in times of peril. Thus a rat which is caught in a snare will warn its fellows, and they will avoid approaching the trap. This closeness of communal life makes it almost impossible to eradicate or control the rat population.

So the brown rat survives, at least in part, by cooperating; so too, of course, do dozens of other species. Ants are a marvel of cooperation. Termites are even more astonishing. For a description of how they "throw up columns and beautiful, curving, symmetrical arches," I refer you to Lewis Thomas's elegant little book *The Lives of a Cell: Notes of a Biology Watcher*. [12] Thomas offers many other comparable examples—in bees, fish, birds—of incredibly coordinated behavior.

Like the birds, the bees, and the brown rat, we humans may very well have genes for cooperation. That is what the modern sociobiologists tell us. Cooperation, like aggression, has a very long evolutionary history. It would be surprising if that history were not somehow imprinted on our human nature. But even if that is true, it is abundantly clear that our genes do not work in the same way as the genes of the brown rat. As the already cited evidence of rampant individualism shows, we cannot be counted upon to cooperate. We have to learn and re-learn that no man is an island. Lewis Thomas observes, "Although we are by all odds the most social of all social animals—more interdependent, more attached to each other, more inseparable in our behavior than bees—we do not often feel our conjoined intelligence."[13] With human beings, the interdependence of our species and the

---

[12]L. Thomas, *The Lives of a Cell: Notes of a Biology Watcher* (New York: Viking Press, 1974).
[13]*Ibid*.

consequent need for cooperation must ever be raised into consciousness.

I take it as an encouraging sign that a growing number of {*499*} people—ranging from sociobiologists to psychologists to moral educators—are in fact becoming acutely conscious of the centrality of cooperation to human survival. In this connection, it is noteworthy that the theories of Alfred Adler are enjoying a revival. Adler, as you know, was a contemporary of Freud. He broke with Freud's belief that man is by nature antisocial. Freud saw the individual as pitted against society, in fundamental conflict with it. Civilization meant the repression and inhibition of egotistical, aggressive, and sexual drives. Adler, by contrast, believed that man is first and foremost a social being. Adler coined the term "social interest" to describe the innate capacity within all humans for cooperation and social living. What we call human, Adler argued, is intrinsically social and hinges on the interactions with and connectedness to others. Freud's individualistic model of man fit with Social Darwinism, which held that aggession and ruthless competition—the survival of the fittest—was necessary for human evolution. Adler's cooperative model of man asserted that social interest—altruistic and cooperative acts for the mutual benefit of self and others—was the essential ingredient for humankind's survival.[14]

The discussion thus far has focused on cooperation as crucial for the general welfare. In the face of so much emphasis on working together toward common goals, a question invariably stirs deep within our autonomous hearts: "But what about the individual? Is all this cooperation achieved at the expense of individual development?" I submit that the contrary is true: that cooperation, far from being an obstacle to the full development of the individual person, is in truth essential to it.

6. Cooperation Is Necessary for Individual Development.

Recall the words of the interviewed teacher, quoted earlier, who spoke so strongly about the importance of developing and main-

---

[14]A. Adler, *Social Interest: Challenge to Mankind* (New York: Capricorn Books, 1974).

taining classroom community. He saw a group discussion of Karen's offensive behavior as an opportunity not only to strengthen community but also to "help her and *all of us grow*." His implicit theory is that the growth of the community and the growth of the individuals within it go hand in hand.

He does not stand alone. An impressive roster of theorists have maintained that it is only with and through others that the individual develops his or her full human potential. Adler argued that society, rather than repressing the individual, is the "matrix" in which he develops, functions, reveals himself, and chooses from the available alternatives. Neuroses—indeed, all blocks to healthy functioning and development—were seen by Adler as social problems to be resolved within a social context.[15]

It is not difficult to understand why the "social matrix" is our natural home and such an important support system for our development. We are most fully alive when we are with other people. This is true, I think, of both children and adults. Moments ago, in the middle of these thoughts, I went outside to help Mark, our eleven-year-old son, get his bike tightened up for an expedition with two friends from school, all of them on vacation this week. There was a glow on his face as they all chattered with exaggerated knowledgeability about tightening this bolt or that, taking up the slack in the chain, and the like. He was fully engaged, happier than I've seen him all week. My wife, Judith, has written about the same phenomenon. In the journal of reflections she has kept this year, she records what she regards as an important self-discovery: that without the stimulation of being with a friend—without the playful interaction that friendship affords—an important part of her personality, her sense of humor, remains largely submerged. Other observers have noted the relationship between being with people and having ideas. Ogden Lindsley, a humanistic behaviorist who urges people to count the behaviors that are important to them, once asked his students to make a mark whenever they got an idea and a note about the situation at the time. To their surprise, they found that the great majority of their new ideas came to them when they

---

[15]*Ibid*.

were talking with other people. Social interaction gets the juices flowing.

Social interaction, in the view of Piaget and Kohlberg, is also the principal impetus behind individual moral development. Under the steady pressure of social exchange, Piaget believed, the child's natural egocentrism breaks down. "It is only through contact with the judgments and evaluations of others," he wrote, "that this intellectual and affective anomie will gradually yield to the pressure of collective logical and moral laws."[16]

Development through Kohlberg's stages of moral reasoning can be considered a process of getting better and better at dealing simultaneously and fairly with conflicting perspectives on what is right in any given situation. It is, to use Piaget's term, a process of "decentering," stretching one's thinking to include and structure the relevant viewpoints. Cooperative social interaction demands such decentering; it necessarily involves people in communicating and comparing their ideas and coordinating their actions toward common ends. When students work together on a group project, for example, they must jointly decide what to do and how, and then carry out their plan. They must learn, as an English friend aptly put it, "how to make a mesh of things."

Kohlberg describes the same process in terms of "role-taking opportunities," which his theory regards as crucial for moral stage development. Cooperation requires that I take the role or viewpoint of the others I am cooperating with. Kohlberg finds that environments which are poor in such opportunities—for example, orphanages where there is little stimulation or supervision of peer interaction—produce children who are still at Stage 1 or 2 even in late adolescence. By contrast, environments which are rich in role-taking opportunities—for example, the Israeli kibbutz, where cooperative work and group decision-making are everyday activities—produce children who have reached Stage 4 or even the principled morality of Stage 5 in late adolescence.[17]

Dewey's vision of cooperative democracy spoke of the

---

[16]Piaget, *op. cit.*, p. 401.

[17]L. Kohlberg, "Moral Stages and Moralization." in T. Lickona, ed., *Moral Development and Behavior* (New York: Holt, Rinehart and Winston, 1976), pp. 31–53.

"necessity for the participation of every mature human being in the formation of values that regulate the living of men together." This participation, Dewey believed, "is necessary from the standpoint of both the general social welfare *and the full development of human beings as individuals.*"[18] The development of human potential Dewey saw as democracy's highest calling:

> Democracy has many meanings, but if it has a moral meaning, it is found in resolving that the supreme test of all political institutions and industrial arrangements should be the contribution they make to the all-around growth of every member of society.

Dewey was careful, however, to make it clear that the development of individuals had a larger social purpose. He urged schools to "make ceaseless and intelligently organized effort to develop above all else the will for cooperation" and to help build "a society of free individuals in which all contribute to the liberation and enrichment of the lives of others."[19] He wrote,

> Just as the material of genuine human development is that of human contacts and associations, so the end (of development) is social. The acquisition of skills is not an end in itself. They are things to be put to use, and that use is in their *contribution to a common shared life*. . . . Too often schools, through reliance on the spur of competition and the bestowing of special honors and prizes, only build up and strengthen the disposition that makes an individual, when he leaves school, employ his special talents and superior skills to outwit his fellows without respect for the welfare of others.[20]

In a properly functioning democracy, then, the society cooperates to support the full development of the individual, and the individual cooperates to support the further development of the society. It is truly a case of all for one, and one for all.

Dewey's emphasis on the role of schools in fostering—or

---

[18] Dewey, *op. cit.* p. 58.

[19] J. Dewey, *Reconstruction in Philosophy* (New York: The American Library, 1950), p. 147.

[20] J. Dewey, "The Need for a Philosophy of Education," in *The New Era in Home and School*, 1934, *15*, pp. 211–214. Reprinted in R. Archambault, ed., *John Dewey on Education* (New York: Random House 1964), pp. 12–13.

subverting—a cooperative democratic ethic leads to the last of my propositions about cooperation, democracy, and education:

{503}

7. *In Order to Foster Individual Moral Development and the Development of a Cooperative Democracy in Society, Schools Should Practice Cooperative Democracy in the Classroom.*

The foregoing discussion has sought to establish several points:

a. that democracy is best understood as a cooperative social enterprise where people share the responsibility for the achievement of common social ends; that this system rests on a faith in the power of pooled and cooperative experience (as contrasted with authoritarian systems, which, as Dewey pointed out, rest on the belief that the needed intelligence to manage human affairs is confined to a superior few); and that democracy constitutes what Dewey called "a truly human way of living" because it respects the right and ability of all persons to contribute to the creation and management of their society and its institutions;

b. that individualism—the pursuit of self-interest without regard for the common good—is the antithesis of democracy and its most pernicious enemy;

c. that individualism begins in early childhood as a natural stage of moral development but is perpetuated in the behavior of adolescents and adults at least partly because of individualistic social norms (like that of the peer group) and social institutions (like the school);

d. that cooperation is as natural to human beings as the tendency toward individualism and that cooperation is necessary both for the well-being and survival of humankind and the full development of the individual person.

From all of this it follows that schools, which have an obligation both to society and to the individual, should foster cooperation as a way of promoting both social democracy and individual human development. And the most effective way to do that, I propose, is to create within each classroom the same kind of living cooperative democracy one hopes to establish and sustain in the society at large. That, and nothing short of that, is in my judgment the task of moral education.

The very first step toward realizing such a program of moral education is to see the school as a *social* institution rather than as an atomistic aggregate of individuals each pursuing their own unrelated ends. The school must, as Dewey held, be seen as a "form of community life in which all those agencies are concentrated that will be most effective in bringing the child to share in the inherited resources of the race and to use his own powers for social ends."[21] Much education fails, Dewey said, because it neglects this fundamental principle of the school as a form of community life.

> The best and the deepest moral training is precisely that which one gets by having to enter into proper relations with others in a unity of work and thought. The present educational systems, so far as they destroy or neglect this unity, render it difficult or impossible to get any genuine, regular moral training.[22]

How does one translate the abstract ideal of democratic community into the day-to-day life of the classroom? I have worked out a four-part model that I like to think is a wide enough net to catch the basic meanings of cooperative school democracy. The four overlapping and interlocking spheres of activity included in this model are (1) social and moral discussion; (2) cooperative learning; (3) building of social community; and (4) participatory decision-making.

Social and Moral Discussion

Social and moral discussion involves students in discussing, debating, and sometimes solving various kinds of social and moral problems that are relevant to their interests and appropriate

---

[21]*Ibid*. p. 430

[22]*Ibid*. p. 431.

A Model of Cooperative Classroom Democracy

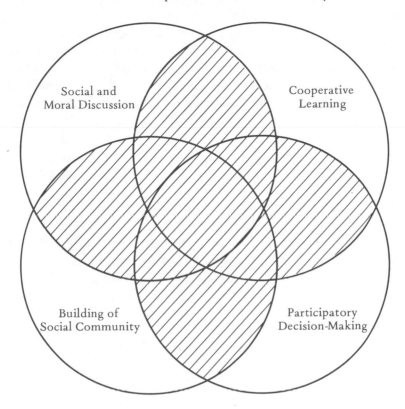

to their developmental level. These include (1) hypothetical moral dilemmas of the kind that Kohlberg made famous; (2) real social and moral problems arising from the life of the classroom; (3) social and moral issues imbedded in the subject areas of the curriculum (such as history, science, and literature); and (4) social and moral problems found in current events in the outside world. Social problems are those which ask the child to be a social psychologist—to understand other people's motives, thoughts, feelings, and behavior. Why, for example, do people develop prejudices? What is it like to be excluded from the group? How does someone feel who has had something stolen? Moral problems are those which ask the child to be a moral philosopher—to make judgments about right and wrong, about what people should and shouldn't do. Why is it wrong to put other people down? What should you do if you see someone stealing? What should be done about nuclear power plants? Even young children may be ready to discuss questions like this last one—ready to begin developing an understanding of the connections between their happening in the society around them. A second-grade teacher told me that her children insisted on discussing the nuclear near-catastrophe at Three-Mile Island. Their discussion ranged over many things: different kinds of energy and the hazards of each; what would happen if there were a nuclear plant meltdown or explosion; how it would affect them; why a new boy in their class who had lived near Three-Mile Island had been sent to live in Boston at the time of the incident by his mother, a hospital radiologist.

How do discussions like these promote both cooperation and democracy? They are cooperative in that they involve a collaborative search for truth and meanings, a sharing of ideas and knowledge about matters of common concern. They are democratic in that no one person has the answer and all are encouraged to contribute their thoughts and feelings in an atmosphere of free exchange and mutual respect. Jef Bulckens (in this volume) speaks in the same spirit when he urges religious educators to develop morality not for but *with* students.

Cooperative Learning

Cooperative learning, the second important sphere of activity in a classroom democracy, clearly goes on during the kind of social-moral discussions I have described. Cooperative learning also defines a pattern of work in the classroom that I think is an essential part of the moral curriculum. Children must not discuss issues as a group, then return to their desks, there to labor for the rest of the time in total isolation. The goal of cooperative learning is that children should frequently work together on their assignments and projects. Elsewhere[23] I have described a dozen teacher

---

[23]T. Lickona, "Beyond Justice: A Curriculum for Cooperation," in D. Cochrane & M. Manley-Casimir, eds., *The Practical Dimensions of Moral Education* (On press).

strategies for structuring cooperative learning in the classroom—including small-group projects, paired learning, peer
teaching, team research, and even team testing. I see cooperative learning as vital to cooperative democracy because it gives
children needed experience in working together toward a common goal. It helps develop both the skills for cooperating and the
will to cooperate. "There is no greater egoism," said Dewey,
"than that of learning when it is treated simply as a mark of
personal distinction to be held and cherished for its own sake."
Cooperative learning helps children come to "the realization that
knowledge is a possession held in trust for the furthering of the
well-being of all."[24]

The Building of a Social Community

The building of a social community is the third major component
of a classroom democracy. I suggest that teachers thinking about
the creation of community in the classroom consider three questions: (1) To what extent do the children know each other as
individual persons? (2) To what extent do they care about each
other? and (3) To what extent are they committed to group values
and goals (for example, the goal of having a democratic community in their classroom)? These three elements—a knowledge of
others, caring about them, and sharing common goals—are the
critical ingredients of human community. Without these social
bonds and shared commitments, the fabric of democracy is
seriously weakened. There is no sense of being part of a larger
whole, no unifying vision or reason for being, no cohesion, no
"glue." Fragmentation, anonymity, alienation—these are the
opposites of community. One might think that twenty children
spending six hours a day together in the same small space would
as an inevitable consequence develop some sense of community.
That, unfortunately, is not the case. Teachers who take over a
class when the regular teacher is absent report that even after two
or three months of the school year, children in many classrooms
do not yet know even the names of all the other children.

---

[24]*Ibid.* p. 12.

There are many ways of building social community, coopera-tive learning and democratic descussion among them. Many of the values-clarification strategies, which encourage students to disclose personally important values, thoughts, feelings, and achievements, are effective in helping them get to know each other as unique, many-dimensional persons. Discussing issues of friendship with children—How do you make a friend? What does it mean to be a good friend? Why do people need friends?—and arranging the life of the classroom to support the development of friendship is another way to build community. Randomly chang-ing children's seating (one teacher had a fish-bowl seat-drawing at the end of each week) and scrambling the composition of learning groups help to maximize children's exposure to each other and prevent the formation of exclusive social cliques. Using a class meeting to foster collective responsibility—by asking, for example, "Who has a problem that we all can help with?"—goes a long way toward developing a group with ties that bind, where members share the value of being concerned about each other's welfare.

Participatory Decision-Making

Participatory decision-making is the fourth sphere of activity that constitutes a cooperative democracy. The goal here is to share with children, even in the elementary school years, the responsi-bility for making decisions about everything that affects life in the classroom. This responsibility is perhaps the most powerful stimulus for their growth both as individuals and as a community. I suggest that teachers, in thinking about how to promote participatory decision-making, consider three areas: (1) *Decisions about the social-moral environment*: Do children help make, revise, and enforce rules for the functioning of the classroom? Do they help solve problems of discipline and social conflict when they arise? (2) *Decisions about the curriculum and learning environment*: Do children have input into what and how they learn? Do they offer their ideas about curriculum projects, room arrangement, work requirements, and other aspects of their learning experience? Do they share the responsibility for creating an environment that is conducive to everyone's learning? and (3) *Decisions about personal behavior*: Does the individual child help to plan how to use his or her time to best advantage? Does he or she help to evaluate his or her progress? To devise a plan, if necessary, for improving his or her academic or social behavior? It should be clear that classroom democracy does not mean the teacher's abandoning his or her responsibility of moral and academic leadership; nor does it mean having the class vote on everything that happens in the classroom. Rather it means a *modus operandi*—a manner of conducting a classroom that includes a wide range of consulting and collaborating between teacher and children. It means helping children learn to participate creatively and actively in their own and each other's development.[25]

I have represented these four spheres of activity—social-moral discussion, cooperative learning, community-building, and participatory decision-making—as overlapping circles in the belief that whenever you are doing one of them, the chances are good that you are doing the others to some extent as well. If, for example, children are engaged in cooperative learning, they may have participated in the decision-making required to plan the project, developed feelings of community by learning about and working with other members of their group, and discussed social or moral problems arising from the need to reach group decisions, divide the work fairly, and so on. Similarly, when children participate in a democratic class meeting to decide rules, they are involved in discussion of a moral issue, learning cooperatively about how to organize their small society, and clarifying the common goals and expectations that will help them build their social community.

If all of this sounds like an ambitious enterprise, it's only because it is. A cooperative democracy, as any teacher who has

---

[25]When considering the prospect of democratic decision-making in the classroom, teachers commonly ask, "How much *time* will it take to do everything democratically? How much time can I afford?" The answer is that the teacher and students should think together about how to preserve the values of efficiency and productivity within a cooperative democracy. If they do not, students and teacher alike will grow weary of their democracy and may even, as one fifth-grade class did, vote democracy out of existence.

attempted it will testify, is no small undertaking. Nor is it built in a day. Let me share with you at this point one of my favorite stories, the tale of a teacher who took four months to unfold a project with her third graders that wove together all of the heretofore described components of a cooperative democracy.

A Democracy Full of Beans

Phyllis Hophan teaches third grade. She has, by choice, the children that other teachers tend not to want: those with learning problems or emotional difficulties, children from stressful home backgrounds.

Teacher Hophan decided that these children would benefit by a project that required close cooperation over a long period of time. She began in February by asking them to work with a partner pursuing answers to a single question: How do you make dried beans sprout without soil?

The project, in truth, began long before that. The teacher had, since the first school days in September, worked with her children to build a caring community. I visited one day as they held one of their frequent circle discussions to share thoughts and feelings. The question that day was, What is something that happened to you that you felt bad about but that you could not change? One boy, his sorrow still keen, spoke of his dog being run over by a car. Another boy spoke of his cat being attacked and killed by a neighbor's dog. A girl, a tiny wisp of a child, told in a small voice of her lingering sadness over the death of her father several months ago, how she still missed him so, how her mother had told her when he died, "Well, Wendy, it's just you and me now." I was deeply touched by the children's disclosures, by the openness with which they shared these painful life events with each other, and by the great respect they showed as they listened with full attention to each child who spoke. I was impressed, too, by the emotional support they seemed to draw from the group, by the climate of understanding and concern that clearly inspired them to share these difficult experiences with their peers.

To launch the children on their bean project, teacher Hophan provided an assortment of dried beans, a book in which to record results, and a "garden corner" filled with various containers, wraps, paper, scales, and calipers. She describes what happened first:

> I was surprised by the children's lack of familiarity with the requirements for growth. Beans were pierced, stomped, smashed, peeled, drowned, and parched. Experimentation was totally haphazard. Some teams chose to do as many as twelve experiments, covering every possible combination of container, light, moisture, and bean variety, rather than pursuing a few experiments in a logical coherent pattern. I decided to allow this scattergun approach and deal with their reasoning as a whole class.[26]

Class meetings were held to share their findings. Lon and Tom reported that "small beans sprout first." "How do you know that?" the teacher asked. "Because," they replied, "our lentils have already sprouted." Others then spoke up: "So has my lima!" and "So has our mung bean!" A look of consternation, the teacher says, passed across Tom and Lon's faces. From discussions like these, the class decided that only agreed-upon findings would be considered "real facts," and these and only these would be entered in a Class Bean Book.

Partners, the teacher found, worked well together. They showed a good ability to divide the labor and to respect each other's abilities and preferences. Said one boy to his teammate: "You write in our record book, okay? You write neater than me. I'll empty the water 'cause I don't care if it smells."

Phase 2 of the project introduced "real planting," using soil. Now the teacher made a significant change in procedure: each team was asked to make a prediction for each experiment they chose to do, to post that prediction on the wall, and to report on the progress of their experiment at class meeting. Soon the wall was dense with children's predictions: for example, "A soybean will push through a wet paper towel," and "A lima bean will push a small stone over as it sprouts."

At this point came an unexpected turn of events. The twin

---

[26]P. Hophan, "Kids, Beans, and Moral Development," in J. Lickona, ed., *Minibook on Moral Development in the Classroom* (Cortland, New York: Project Change, State University of New York at Cortland, 1977), pp. 9–16.

serpents of competition and jealously invaded this Garden of Cooperation. Partners, worried about the growth rate of their plants, blamed each other for over- or under-watering. Teams taunted other teams when their plants grew faster or larger. There were even some cases of sabotage. Some containers were found virtually swamped in water, and a book had been placed squarely on top of a lush crop of soybean plants. One team bitterly blamed the death of their lima bean plant on other children's "talking bad" to it.

In the face of this moral crisis, the teacher turned to the class meeting that had served them so well over the year in developing a sense of community. They talked about competition and jealousy, why people had those feelings, and how they affected their feelings about working together. Several children said they wanted to have their own plant to care for rather than having to work with a partner. Reasons for this were discussed. Wisely, democratically, the teacher allowed the children to make this decision, and half the class decided to go it alone.

But not for long. During the week that followed, slowly but surely, partners who had gone their separate ways got back together of their own accord. The teacher asked Eric and Steve, who had been most unhappy with each other's work, why they had decided to help each other again. Steve replied, "Well, I can't hold this paper (on which he had been recording the plant's growth) and mark it at the same time." Another reunited team explained that apart they forgot to water their plants, but together they could remember.

Phase 3 of the project began with a class visit to the greenhouse of a neighboring university. It was, the teacher says, a delightful trip. "We learned many things—the most important being the benefits of light, heat, and moisture that a greenhouse provided. And as I hoped, everyone clamored to build a greenhouse of our own."

And so they did. They began with careful planning, listing all the necessary steps to go from seeds to garden: selecting the seeds, drawing plans to scale for the greenhouse, constructing the greenhouse, preparing the soil mix and seed trays, reading the planting instructions, sowing the seeds, measuring and selecting outdoor garden sites (they had decided to plant flowers to beautify the school grounds), preparing the soil, and transplanting the plants. Anyone who thinks that moral education must be carried out at the expense of the regular academic curriculum need only consider the formidable range of cognitive tasks involved in this cooperative undertaking.

{513}

And so it went. There were some other bumps along the way; what came to be known as The Peat Moss Disaster occurred when the "soil-mixing crew" added too much water to the peat moss and ended up with 200 pounds of water and soil—a huge, immovable water balloon garbage bag. "It's hard to think when you're doing neat stuff like this!" explained one boy, with a sheepish grin. The teacher, as she had done with other matters, put the responsibility for solving the problem on the shoulders of the children. They came up with the solution of poking a hole in the corner of the bag and letting it drain into a dishpan, emptying the pan as it filled, a process they continued for two days.

At the end of this project in May, the teacher reflected on the children's social and moral growth. She had been greatly pleased by the amount of encouragement, appreciation, and sharing of ideas that she had seen. She observed marked progress in the children's ability to accept group goals and responsibilities. And their self-esteem, she believed, had grown by leaps and bounds, nurtured by all the positive feedback they had given each other. "Many of the children began the year with very negative self-concepts," the teacher says. "I defy anyone to find those children now."

As for the teacher's own growth, she says, "I learned that structure can be an invisible partner." She learned that she could be the careful choreographer of cooperation in the classroom while still allowing children a great deal of freedom and responsibility for charting their own course.[27]

---

[27]Although I have illustrated cooperative democracy with examples from elementary classrooms, I would like to emphasize that the very same processes are applicable to the secondary and post-secondary level. High school teachers, for example, have found cooperative learning and participatory decision-making to be powerful tools. I have found ways to apply the four-part model in the courses I teach and have had a consistently positive response from my university students.

A Parable

I have attempted to make the case for moral education as cooperative democracy and to show how it can work in a classroom. I submit with Dewey that democracy must become part of "the bone and blood" of our daily life if it is to remain healthy and survive. I would like to close my argument that cooperation is the lifeblood of democracy with a parable:

> An old priest was dying. As he prayed for the repose of his soul, he was troubled about Heaven and Hell. What, he wondered, were they really like?
>
> Then, dimly, he saw two figures at the foot of his bed. He recognized one as Moses, the other as Saint Peter. When they beckoned him, he got up and followed, walking through the wall of his bedroom. Silently, they led him through the galaxies of the night sky.
>
> In a far-off place, they stopped before a big house. "The kingdom of God is made of many mansions," Saint Peter explained. "So, too, is Hell. Step inside. We will show you the first room of Satan's palace."
>
> As the priest walked in, his ears were assaulted by a babble of complaints. Many people were seated at a large table. In the center, there was a big pot of the priest's favorite dish, beef stew. Although everyone in Hell had a spoon and could reach the pot, the people were starving. The spoon handles that were attached to their hands were twice as long as their arms. They could catch the stew but they couldn't bring it to their lips. The cries of the starving were so loud that the priest begged to be taken away.
>
> Saint Peter and Moses then took him to another mansion in a distant place. Moses invited the priest to step inside the outer room of Heaven. There the priest saw a similar large table surrounded by many people. In the center, as before, was a huge pot of beef stew. The spoon handles were again too long for human arms, but there were no cries of complaint, for no one was starving. The people were all feeding each other.

The meaning of the parable is clear enough. I am reminded of it each time I enter the campus of Boston University, where I teach. There, in front of Marsh Chapel, stands a sculpture erected in the memory of Martin Luther King, the University's most famous alumnus. Appropriately, the sculpture is a soaring flock of birds, each individual yet one in the unity of their flight. Beneath this stirring symbol, inscribed in the stone base, are King's words, a reminder that the lesson of cooperation was taught to us a very long time ago: "Far from being the pious injunction of a utopian dreamer, the command to love one's enemy is an absolute necessity for our survival."

ABOUT THE AUTHOR

Thomas Lickona is a developmental psychologist currently teaching in the Department of Counselor Education at Boston University. He has also served on the faculties of Harvard University and the State University of New York. From 1976–77 he directed Project Change, a national award-winning program in person-centered teacher education.

His research has studied the growth of children's moral judgment and the development of democratic classrooms. His publications include the edited book Moral Development and Behavior, *and several articles on fostering moral development. He is now at work on two books,* Social and Moral Development in the Classroom *and* Parenting for Moral Development.

Moral Education
in Private Schools:
A Christian Perspective

JEF BULCKENS

Introduction

{518} What are the real possibilities of moral formation in schools? Why is so little account taken of the inherent limitations of moral formation in Catholic schools? Are not the family and the nonschool youth ministry more important for Christian moral formation than the school?

Is there a morality that is specifically Christian? Does moral formation in school in a humanist context differ from moral formation in school in a Christian context? What image of God and Jesus has a dynamic effect on authentic ethical attitudes and conduct of young people?

To what should we give priority: the construction of a creative and possibly new Christian ethic together with the young people; or the deliberate presentation of traditional ecclesiastical norms? What vision of God's revelation determines the choice? Does this choice also have something to do with the deepest human experiences and attitudes of the individual? Why is it that many Christian educators so readily operate on the idealistic level and find it so difficult to take into account the structural background of moral problems?

These questions are treated in this chapter in terms of what is called "didactic analysis." What is *content* of moral formation in a Christian context? What are the *goals* of Christian moral formation in school? What *methods* and *interaction models* are appropriate for this content and these goals?

"A wheel that turns and does not turn anything itself does not actually belong to the machine," so wrote Ludwig Wittgenstein in *Philosophische Untersuchungen.*[1] Is the specifically Christian such a wheel in our world? Or more to the point, is the teaching of the Christian religion such a wheel in moral education in Catholic schools?

---

[1]As cited by A. Auer in *Moraleriziehung im Religionsunterricht* (Freiburg: Herder, 1975), p. 48.

Contemporary Developments in Moral Education

Over the last ten years, the moral pedagogy applied in Christian institutions has been receiving renewed interest in Western Europe and, of late, this interest has heightened considerably.

{519}

Three characteristics are to be noted. First, educators are strongly defending the change from a static to a dynamic, from an assimilating or a conformist to a creative moral formation. Jacques Audinet summarizes this change as follows: (a) from an ethic of the natural order of life to an ethic of the historical, dynamic order of life; (b) from conformity with the social order to creative initiative.[2] In a certain sense, Henri Bergson's famous qualitative distinction between "closed morality" and "open morality" is renewed here. In a closed morality, social pressure, intellectual understanding, and the sense of duty play major roles *(pression sociale)*. They push one from behind, as it were. In an open morality, which finds its dynamism among mystics, saints, and founders and reformers of religions, love *(elan d'amour)* exercises a powerful interior attraction on the person *(émotion)* to surpass himself in a creative manner.[3]

Second, many educators are reconsidering the whole of Christian moral formation in the light of the impressive book by Alfons Auer, *Autonome Moral and christliche Glaube*,[4] which describes in a new way the relation between ethics and (the Christian) religion. These educators wonder about what is specific to Christian moral education, and they often speak about "autonomous moral education in a Christian context."

Finally, more attention has been placed in recent years on a realistic and operational moral education in schools, and this under the influence of the increasing degree of integration of the

---

[2]*Cf.* J. Audinet, "Stratégie d'une éthique chrétienne," in *L'Homme manipulé: Pouvoir de l'homme sur l'homme, ses chances et ses limites* (Strasbourg: Credic-Publications, 1974), pp. 137–165. *Cf.* also Norman J. Bull, *Moral Education* (London: Routledge & Kegan Paul, 1973), pp. 133–137.

[3]*Cf.* Henri Bergson, *Les deux sources de la morale et de la religion*, Paris, P.U.F., 1932; 1976 (216 ed.), pp. 30 100, 102.

[4]A. Auer, *Autonome Moral and christliche Glaube* (Dusseldorf: Patmos, 1971).

empirical findings of Jean Piaget and Lawrence Kohlberg. Noteworthy, too, is the increasing concern for the learning of moral behavior.

{520}

Moral Formation in a Christian Context

The discussion among moral theologians about the nature and contribution of Christian ethics has naturally also influenced the attitude of Christian educators. The following theses have become increasingly common among them.

The Material Autonomy of Morality

There are no specific, exclusively Christian norms: Christianity has not created any new ethical norms. The content of morality is autonomous. Consequently, one cannot distinguish between Christians and non-Christians in this regard. The moral development that has occurred in the Christian religion pertains to the natural human ethic, which is based on reasonableness and which can also be found in other religions and in all sorts of historical movements. The Golden Rule, the commandment of love, and even the bond between God's love and the love of neighbor and the love of one's enemy are also found in Jewish and non-Christian writings. They belong to the secular ethos and do not form a "revealed" morality. For example, it is even possible to show that Seneca, a Roman philosopher from the first century after Christ, was much more radical and "modern" with respect to slavery than was the Apostle Paul.

The Threefold Moral Relevance of the Christian Religion

The original contribution of Judaism and Christianity consists of their bringing the already present secular ethos into their relationship with God. They religiously integrated the experiential wisdom of people and communities, and in doing so, they exposed the deepest meaning of morality: it is an important place of encounter between God and the human person.

It is certain, for example, that the Ten Commandments {521} crystallized the already existing ethos that was interpreted religiously by the people of Israel. In Exodus 20, the Ten Commandments are introduced as follows: "I am the Lord your God, who brought you out of the land of Egypt out of the house of bondage. You shall. . . ." What is specific to Jewish morality lies in the notion that the maintenance of humanly conceived norms becomes an expression of faith in the liberating God.

In the New Testament, the moral life of the Christian—I am thinking of the various catalogs of virtues in the Pauline epistles—becomes an expression of his faith "in the Lord," "in Christ," in the God of Jesus Christ. For the believer, Christ is the foundation and meaning, as well as the guiding motive, of his moral life. If one contends that love is the fundamental ethical principle of the whole of the New Testament, one may not forget that evangelical love is the *divine* virtue of love, theological love (1 Cor. 13), that is, the effective love of neighbor as founded in faith and in the love of God.

Jesus himself did not introduce his own ethos, but he did give a new horizon of meaning, a new faith perspective, to a very high morality. In other words, Jesus integrated high ethical demands into his preaching of God's Kingdom. And Jesus himself is very closely identified with this Kingdom of God.

In addition to its *integrating and motivating* function, the Christian faith also has a *critical* function with regard to the (relatively) autonomous morality. There is no doubt that Jesus directly confronted the prevailing morality of his time. He strongly attacked legalistic rigidity, cultic complacency, hypocritical self-justification, suffocating wealth, and all kinds of social discrimination. Jesus weighed and relativized all existing human attitudes and values in the light of the growing Kingdom of God. His ethos is eschatological. The message of Jesus also had a *stimulating* effect: it included a call for *radical* freedom, love, and responsibility. For example, the preaching of Jesus of the equality of all men before God has had a great influence in history. In short, for the believer, salvific human acts are *ultimately* God's salvific acts. The ultimate and deepest ground of human action is, for the Christian, God.

The Christian Life-Style as the Following of Jesus

The lived ethical conduct of the Christian, who knows he is bound to the God of Jesus Christ, can develop into a particular Christian life-style. In this sense, one can correctly speak of a specifically Christian morality. This Christian life-style colors the entire life of the Christian and not only his individual deeds. It provides the secular ethos with new dimensions and new fields of application, accomplishing a kind of transvaluation, to use Richard Niebuhr's term.

Christian morality is fundamentally a Christian life that is influenced by the imitation of the way Jesus Christ lived. In Jesus, God revealed himself perfectly and gave a blueprint of the definitive *humanum*. The authentic Christian life-style, that is, a way of living characterized by a preference for the values that Jesus concretely and effectively lived, also includes something radical, inexhaustible, infinite, absolute, and universal—in short, something of God himself. "You, therefore, must be perfect, as your heavenly Father is perfect" (Mt. 5:48). At the same time, it can be the guarantee forever new, astonishing, concrete prefer- ences and initiatives that, perhaps, may seem to many to be unattainable. I am thinking here of Jesus' preference in word *and* deed for those who were civically and religiously oppressed, for those on the fringes of society, for all of the "little ones," for forgiving seventy times seven times, for love of enemy, for tolerance of shortcomings, for unconcern for material values because of higher values, and so forth.

The Moral Influencing Mechanism of the Christian Faith

The influence of the Christian faith on everyday life resides in the deepening and protecting insights that are important for concrete actions. This influence is *direct* insofar as the faith can directly influence the value insights that co-determine human conduct. In this sense, Antoine Vergote argues that the divine paternity functions as a moral principle.[5] Faith in a loving God-Father implies treating each person as one's brother or sister in a loving manner. Whoever believes in God as Creator and in man as creature and image of God cannot, on the basis of that faith, tolerate someone being treated as a slave.

{523}

Sharpened by faith insight, human insight into values such as veracity, fidelity, and respect for life is of ultimate importance for concrete moral actions. Moral judgment—a judgment that a specific act is "morally good" or "morally bad"—is impossible without insight into values, for such a judgment is made precisely to protect or to deepen human values. The Christian faith influences this directly, and the Christian message is relevant to the legitimation of fundamental values. In practice, the specifically religious exercises an active force.

But value insights do not of themselves provide an immediate and concrete rule of moral action. The Christian faith only has an *indirect* influence on moral judgments, on the judgment of the moral value of a concrete act, because the concrete act as a whole can only be judged morally (concrete material norms) when account is taken of the "conditions bound to the value, balanced against possible competing values."[6] "Be righteous" is a formal norm that has universal validity, stating how our interior attitude or disposition must always and everywhere be. But with it, one does not yet know concretely what righteous acting involves "here and now," for example, in a country with many large land proprietors or in a country with massive inequality of income levels. In any case, the preference must go to the choice of the greater good or the lesser evil.

Some Consequences for Christian Moral Education

From the foregoing description of autonomous morality in a Christian context, a number of important, though general, conclusions can be drawn for moral formation in Catholic schools.

---

[5]*Cf.* Antoine Vergote, "God, onze vader," in *Concilium*, 1977, nr. 10, pp. 8–16.

[6]F. Boeckle, "Geloof en handelen," in *Concilium*, 1976, nr. 10, p. 53.

Reservations Regarding a Heteronomous Morality
of Commands and Prohibitions

{524}

In contrast to what was done formerly, current moral education in a Christian context has to avoid an announcement of God's commands and prohibitions. The imperative language game of morality differs from the indicative language game for religion in general and the Christian religion in particular. Insight into good and evil logically precedes the knowledge of God and his will. This implies that moral obligations, pedagogically considered, may not be presented directly as God's will. Something is good not because God wills it, but God wills something because it is morally good. Primarily, moral education must teach the students to make moral judgments and to act morally in concrete situations on the basis of human experience and reasonable understanding. An unnuanced presentation of moral demands (the Ten Commandments, for example) as God's demands risks fixing the young student in Kohlberg's Stage 1 of moral development (God as "punisher" or "rewarder").

Integration of Morality into Discipleship

Moral value judgments cannot be derived directly from the Bible or from the tradition of the Church. Actual life experience and intelligent understanding are necessary conditions. Still, the Christian educator will show that morally justified value judgments can also be operative as calls from God and as the following of Jesus Christ or, in other words, as the space within which Christian obedience in faith is realized. For a believer accepts God as the ultimate ground of his autonomous freedom and sees the autonomous construction of the world ultimately as a task from God. Moreover, seriously acquainting the students with Jesus' compelling manner of life can contribute much to the refinement and deepening of the value insights that largely determine value judgments.

Two kinds of programs for Christian moral education are possible. They are relatively autonomous and complementary, each having its own dynamic and method. The first program teaches the student to experience, think, and act in a critical manner with regard to concrete current problems and actual conflict situations. At the appropriate time, by way of integration, reference can be made to Jesus' dealings with men. The second program directly examines with the students Jesus' conduct and personality and also that of the Old Testament prophets. Particular attention is given to Jesus' pattern of values, his preferences, his position in conflict situations, the source of his strength, and so on. Jesus is presented as someone to be followed.

{525}

The Distinction Between Morality and Religion: A Necessity for Creative Morality

Only the distinction between, though not the separation of, morality and religion provides real room for a creative morality, for a morality that develops with and from the students. Therefore, Jean Le Du argues for a "desacralization of the current morality." Until recently, the divine origin of law was taken too much for granted and stressed too directly in Catholic moral formation. I am thinking, for example, of the "naive" treatment of Exodus 19, the proclamation of the Law by God on Mount Sinai. The result was that the divine origin of the law often counted for more than the content of the law itself. The very fact of disobedience seemed to be more important than the violation of this or that precept. *Each* act of disobedience was a sacrilege, it was often reasoned, because it was an act of rebellion against God.

The theological schema, "God gives his law to man," can only lead to an increasing concurrence with, and internalization of, a previously given law (laid down in the nature of man and/or in the Bible), or, in other words, to an "assimilation morality." A more justified creation and incarnation theology today, however, resolutely gives priority to another schema: "God continually creates man, who receives the mission to bring order into his historically conditioned existence via laws." This theological perspective is defended by Jean Le Du, the intention being to construct a creative morality together with the students.[7]

---

[7]Cf. Jean Le Du, *Jusqú où iront-ils? L'éducateor piégé par la morale,* (Paris: Chalet, 1974), p. 71, and *Qui fait la loi?* (Paris: Cerf, 1974), p. 14.

{526} These two differing conceptions of God's revelation, which lead to divergent catechetical approaches to morality, are schematized by Le Du as follows:[8]

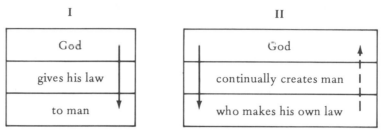

Not unjustly, some humanist authors contend that Christians, and especially Catholics, can achieve Kohlberg's fifth and sixth stages of moral development only with difficulty. Indeed, someone who thinks or teaches predominantly according to the first schema could easily fixate at Stage 4, orientation to law and order, that is, acting as the Church prescribes and because it so prescribes.

On the other hand, someone who approaches God as the Creator of relatively free and autonomous persons will, as Jean Le Du would say it, look on the gift of the law as a gift of a law to be created ("le don de la loi est le don d'une loi á faire"). I have added the ascending arrow to Le Du's Schema II to indicate that God's commissioning of man to construct the world autonomously in freedom and responsibility is an expression of faith. It is an expression, however, that is discovered and deepened often on the basis of a human design of a more just world. The world, or better, the just ordering of the world, can be the place where God is found. This insight was already strongly emphasized by John Henry Newman in the nineteenth century.

Possibilities and Limitations of Christian Moral Formation in Schools

As has been said, there are two ways in which Christian moral influence can be exercised in the classroom. First, there is the

---

[8]Cf. Jean Le Du, *Qui fait la loi?*, p. 41.

rather indirect moral formation accomplished via familiarization with the Christian religion and especially with the Bible. This approach used to take up most of the time and energy of the religion teacher. Religious education was mostly biblical, liturgical, and dogmatic education that had moral implications. The second way focuses more directly on the development of moral judgments, moral dispositions, and the capacity to perform moral acts. This way, which belongs to problem-oriented religious education, has received increasing attention in recent years. It deals with all kinds of real problems such as justice, truth, environmental protection, sexuality, and so on, from a specifically religious point of view. These two ways complement each other.

{527}

Moral Influencing via Bible Education: Religious Development and Moral Development

The Image of God and the Image of Man: Correlatives

The Christian religion is a multidimensional reality: in addition to its experiential dimension, it also has doctrinal, liturgical, social, and moral dimensions. While these dimensions are distinct, they are still closely interrelated. For example, a particular concept of God influences moral conduct and vice versa. Now it seems to me that it is of utmost importance to show *correctly* the mechanism of this mutual influencing in the religion lesson. It is less a matter of speaking abstractly "about God" and "about man" than of concretely clarifying how a particular image of God exercises a functional or dysfunctional influence of liberation on human conduct, and vice versa. The image of God and the image of man and society are correlative. Religious education therefore includes a critique of religions.

In its service of God, Christianity is in service of humanity and society. When Jonah did not want to go to Nineveh with a message of conversion, he had an image of man and an image of God that implied each other. He would not let God be God. In other words, he wanted to impose his will on God because, with

{528}

his limited egocentric vision, he had frozen the people of Nineveh in their sinful past. Jesus himself lashed out sharply against certain legalistic, self-sufficient, and proud attitudes and conduct of the Pharisees and scribes with respect to their fellow religionists because they ultimately obscured the authentic image of God. In a number of parables, Jesus criticized the actual conduct of many Pharisees toward their fellowmen by questioning their image of God and their vision of the Kingdom of God.

Parallelism Between Religious and Moral Development

The image of God and the image of man evoke and mutually determine each other. It may be expected, then, that the development of faith-knowing and the faith attitude on the one hand, and the development of moral thought on the other, could well run parallel and stimulate each other. Lawrence Kohlberg is of the opinion that the six stages of moral development he describes have a considerable degree of formal agreement with the six stages of faith-knowing that J. Fowler has traced.[9]

For example, a child in the second moral stage will perhaps also be situated in a *dou ut des* relationship with God: "If I am good to God, then God will be good to me." Who experiences God primarily as the highest authority that rewards the good and punishes the evil will probably think in the moral area according to the first stage, that is, out of fear of punishment. A statement such as "God won't like you if you do that" not only reflects a narrow and distorted image of God but, at the same time, reinforces the moral thinking of Stage 1. The religious statement of Jesus with reference to concrete situations, "The sabbath was made for man, not man for the sabbath" (Mk. 2:27) shatters a legalistic vision of God and is situated in Kohlberg's sixth stage.

Thus, as far as the *motives* for behavior are concerned, both with respect to God and with respect to man, the roughly parallel stages proposed by Kohlberg and Fowler are very important. But

---

[9]*Cf.* Lawrence Kohlberg, "Stages of Moral Development as a Basis for Moral Education" in *Moral Education: Interdisciplinary Approaches,* (New York, Newman, 1971), pp. 23–92.

in addition, account must also be taken of the content of the behavior itself, with its morally and religiously justified character. As Ronald Duska and Mariellen Whelan state: "If the highest level of moral reasoning is on a principled level, and if the highest principles are justice and love, and if justice and love are to be informed by a free choice, one is hard pressed to find a more consistent statement of such principles than in the New Testament."[10] The problem, however, is whether the content of New Testament morality is, in fact, pedagogically translated in a coherent way in the classroom.

{529}

What requires more empirical investigation is this question: In what degree and how can a specific image of God, reflecting a specific manner of relating to God, stimulate moral development? Concretely, in what degree and how can a continual and coherent approach to God (image of God) and to Jesus as attentive and gratuitous love help bring young people to a higher level of moral disposition? In any event, it is clear that the possible influencing of moral thinking via faith-knowing makes high demands on the religious attitude and image of God of the teacher himself.

Jesus Christ as the "Model" for Imitation

In religious education, and particularly in biblical education, Jesus is regularly presented as the point of reference, as the "model" to be imitated, as the "ur-model" of humanity. In Jesus, the Kingdom of God has broken through in a decisive manner, and in Jesus, too, humanity has given its first and exemplary response to this salvific event. Jesus, however, is not simply an "exemplary" figure in the Christian tradition, but, as François Refoulé has expressed it, he is "an originating and founding figure."[11] In other words, the ethos of Jesus is an ethos of discipleship. What does this imply for Christian moral education?

---

[10]R. Duska and M. Whelan, *Moral Development: A Guide to Piaget and Kohlberg,* (London: Gill and Macmillan, s.d. 1977), p. 99.

[11]François Refoulé, "Jésus comme référence de l'agir des chrétiens," in *Ecriture et pratique chrétienne,* (Paris: Cerf, 1978), p. 202.

From a pedagogical standpoint, it is useful to distinguish as does Dietmar Mieth, between "example" and "model." An example urges faithful imitation of what is done; to follow an example is, as it were, to repeat in an identical manner, to "copy." A model is involved when, from one's own creativity, the formation of an original reality (that is, a person) is evoked. Models invite a realization of the same basic inspiration of the model in an analogous manner in new situations; they evoke freedom and individual responsibility.[12]

The imitation of Jesus, the being a disciple of Jesus, does not consist of "repeating" Jesus, of reproducing him, but rather it consists of imitating him freely and creatively: to do the same in our world that he did in his, to realize the same values in our concrete history that he realized in the midst of his own contemporaries.

In religious education, therefore, it is more important to evoke ethical models—the Old Testament prophets and Jesus—in a narrative way than to present general and abstract virtues or normative systems. When a scribe asked who his neighbor was, Jesus did not answer with an abstract or a normative pronouncement about neighbors and love of neighbor, but with a parable with a concrete model of how one can become the neighbor of others. A teacher makes a substantial contribution to Christian moral formation when he or she succeeds in evoking and discussing with the students the originality of Jesus' manner of life, that is, his interactions with God and people in which his hierarchy of values is expressed.

The classroom verbalization of Jesus' manner of life can only exercise a limited degree of influence, however, even though it may be done in an absorbing manner. An "evoked" model does not have the same attractive power as direct contact with a living model. Moreover, the call to imitate Jesus only has a real chance with the students when the religion teacher himself is recognized as a follower of Jesus in and out of the classroom. But what teacher would dare to say with Saint Paul, "Be imitators of me as I

---

[12]Cf. Gunter Stachel and Dietmar Mieth, *Ethisch handeln lernen* (Zurich: Benziger, 1978), pp. 53, 86–91, 110, 157–158, 171.

am of Christ" (1 Cor. 11:1)? Furthermore, the walls of the classroom usually provide only a limited space for the teacher to be effectively perceived by the students as a follower of Christ. Therefore, other educational situations such as those provided by the family and an extracurricular youth ministry play a much more important role.

{531}

Biblical Narratives and the "Unbelieving" Student

For a number of students, even in Catholic schools, Jesus is without doubt a prominent figure and model though still not an "absolute" revelation of God. For that matter, some students do not believe in God, or at least not very strongly. But let us not forget that belief and unbelief intersect in the heart of every student and teacher.

Therefore, it can be very useful for the religion teacher, when discussing biblical narratives, also to bring out their general human dimension together with the students. The "unbelieving" students can profit from this and also learn the religious and Christian meaning of the biblical texts. The believing students, for their part, can appropriate the full content of Jesus' conduct and person as told in the Bible and, at the same time, find support in the anthropological meaning.

An example can clarify what I mean. [13] The famous parable of the talents (Mt. 25:14-30) can be read on three levels.

The parable focuses primarily on the actions of the third servant who hid his master's money in the ground. This servant is potentially present in all of us. The parable warns the reader against the inactivity of a person who remains passive because of paralyzing anxiety, fearful caution, or self-sufficient certainty. The third servant is merely a shadow of what he could become: he dares not accept his freedom and responsibility, take any risks, or step into the unknown. Consequently, he will be called to account. In short, the general human meaning of the parable of

---

[13]Cf. Jef Bulckens, ed., *Spanning tussen ervaring en verwoording in de huidige schoolcatechese,* (Antwerp: Patmos), pp. 90–128.

the talents is "nothing ventured, nothing gained" or "who gambles, wins."

This meaning matches what Berthold Brecht, the German novelist, recounts in this brief scene:

> A man who had not seen Mr. K. for a long time greeted him with the words:
> "You have not changed at all."
> "Oh," said Mr. K. and turned pale.

For Jesus, however, this parable was primarily directed against the religious leaders of the Jewish people. Out of fear, they had managed poorly the talents entrusted them by the master (God's Covenant and Law). For Jesus, this parable was an urgent warning for, and appeal to, his people and its leaders. Who manages the religious values carelessly will be condemned by God. Man must act as God's co-manager, as being co-responsible with God.

Matthew, the Evangelist, applied the religious meaning of the parable to Jesus himself, and thus it also has a christological meaning. In the final redaction of the parable, the master who entrusts his possessions, the talents, to the three servants when he departs for a foreign country is not God directly but Jesus who, after a long time, will return to judge. For Matthew, the parable is an admonishment for the Christian community of his time. Even though Christ's return be delayed, the community must not be negligent but must remain faithful and vigilant.

From this analysis, it becomes clear that "faith" has human, religious, and Christian dimensions. All students, including those who believe less strongly or who do not believe at all, can be open to the first dimension; the believer will, at the same time, be able to experience this human commission as a divine commission in the spirit of Jesus.

Moral Formation via Problem-Oriented Religious Education

Together with all the other courses, problem-oriented religious education helps the students to grow toward being independent and responsible persons who are prepared to work with others to build a more human world. It does this, however, from a particular angle, a specific standpoint, namely, that of the Christian religion. I shall describe concisely first the content and then the goals of the learning process, and finally I shall deal with some methodological and interactional requirements of problem-oriented religious education, which coincides largely with moral formation.

{533}

The Content of Moral Formation: A Matrix for Moral Education

The human personal identity to be developed within the social culture, the task of all education, is a complex phenomenon. It can be analyzed and structured in various ways. Edward Schillebeeckx distinguishes six essential aspects of human identity, which he calls anthropological constants and which are intertwined and mutually influence each other. The six aspects reveal our enduring human values but do not immediately provide concrete norms according to which a human world must be realized in the here and now. The concrete norms for the protection of human values must be defined and experienced by individuals themselves in a historically situated and inventive manner. Schillebeeckx's six anthropological constants, the sites of values and norms, are as follows:[14]

1. The relation of the human person to his own bodiliness and thereby to nature as a whole and to his ecological milieu forms the first basic existential fact (for example, not only to "control and subject" nature, but also to "cherish and preserve" it).

2. To be a human being is to be with others; one becomes a person only in relation to others. Human personal identity also encompasses a togetherness with people (for example, each human being, including those on the fringes of society, is a person, a goal, and an end in himself, not just a means).

---

[14]*Cf.* E. Schillebeeckx, "Waarden en normen binnen de wetenschappen en de schoolvakken," in *Waarden en normen in het onderwijs*, (Baarn: Ambo, 1977), pp. 9–25 (pp. 16–23).

{534}

3. The third constant is the relation of the individual to social and institutional structures, which must always be at the service of human liberation and which form a value that requires norms (for example, opposition to all forms of oppressive structures).

4. The being situated of the culture and the person in time and space, historically and geographically, is the fourth anthropological constant (tension between nature and history with the attendant consequences, for example, industrialization, poor countries, new social values and norms).

5. The fifth constant is the mutual relationship between theory and praxis, which must assure the durability of the multifaceted history of human culture (for example, against the evolutionary law of the survival of the fittest).

6. The religious and "para-religious" consciousness of man is the last basic human constant. New attempts are always being made to design "cognitive models of reality" or conceptions of totality (religious or secular) that make it possible to give a degree of meaning to or to overcome (Destiny, God, Evolution) the radical finiteness of humanness (suffering, failure, death). These various attempts to provide ultimate meaning (for example, the Christian religion) pertain to the healthy realization of humanness.

These six anthropological constants are dialectically related to each other. They form a kind of system of coordinates for man and his salvation. These large value areas must be introduced along with life experience into education with the view to the communal search for, and discovery of, concrete norms for the realization of a more human existence.

Günter Biemer and Albert Biesinger, for their part, distinguish five fundamental aspects of human existence *(Koexistentialien):* labor, dominance-conflicts, eros-sexuality, death, and play. They further distinguish twelve concrete themes that theoretically and practically supplement each of the five dimensions and indicate relevant moral experiences, attitudes, and conduct:[15]

---

[15]*Cf.* G. Biemer and A. Biesinger, *Theologie im Unterricht,* (Munich: Kösel, 1976), pp. 114–115.

1. Good and evil (freedom as the condition for moral conduct)
2. Responsibility (the conscience of the person)
3. Self-realization in relation to others

4. Success and failure (virtues, guilt, sin)
5. Faith and morals (for example, law and the Gospel)
6. Christian salvific ethos (Sermon on the Mount, faith, hope, and love)
7. Normative forces in the community (for example, authority and self-realization)
8. Right to life and human rights
9. Bodiliness and sexuality
10. Moral responsibility with regard to all communication forms (for example, language, drama, media)
11. Power and justice (for example, politics and science)
12. Conflict and peace (for example, aggression and reconciliation)

The five basic anthropological facts together with the twelve themes form a sort of matrix *(Strukturgitter)* for moral formation in religious education. The twelve themes can, perhaps, be reduced further to five main problems that constitute the actual content of education in moral problems: (1) conscience; (2) how norms are created; (3) the problem of failure; (4) the problem of a Christian aspect of morals; and (5) the social problem.

Content Phases

The treatment of the various moral value areas and problems must be extended through three content phases, each with its own function:

1. Examination and analysis of the concrete situation, for example of poverty, with the aid of the autonomous human sciences, for example, the psychosocial, economic, and political backgrounds of a problem. This examination is often activated by contrast experiences or by a demand for deepen-

ing or fulfillment (the analytical function of the human sciences).

2. Anthropological and theological reflection (evaluation of the situation in function of a specifically Christian human and social image). The search for, and acquisition of, the experience of meaning provide a powerful impetus for this (the integrating function of anthropology and theology).

3. Ethical explicitation, which repeatedly determines provisional priorities for actions inspired by Christianity, often in fact for the transformation of alienated and sinful reality. In this way, the motivation develops to apply value-insights in practice (normative function of morality).

In traditional Catholic education, there is still too little attention given to the first of the three phases. A German study has shown that the predominantly ahistorical and asocial approach to sexual problems taken by the ecclesiastical educational authorities, who generally pronounce absolute value judgments without consideration of the relativizing character of historical, psychological, and social circumstances, appears to many students to be unscientific and alien to real life.[16] For example, in one Portuguese religious handbook that has a chapter on emigration, the lack of a structural analysis is clearly manifest. The following is the way this very important problem for Portugal is developed. The drama of the emigrants:

Using the correspondence of a young Portuguese carpenter in France, the author tries to have the reader identify with the problems of the emigrant: anxiety, loneliness, disillusion, solidarity, and so on. The experience of this young Portuguese man is situated on the national level: There are more than 900,000 Portuguese emigrants throughout the world. Why so many emigrants?

A series of motives are graphically treated: "to improve the personal and family standard of living," "the spirit of adventure," "lack of work locally," "to get away from military service," "to study," "tempting offers from other countries," to name a few.

---

[16]Cf. F. Beffart et al., *Geschlechtserziehung interdisciplinär: Grundlegende Information für Lehrer*, (Dusseldorf, Patmos, 1975), p. 131.

There are human and Christian values at stake: (1) for the emigrants: the freedom to live and work anywhere in the world; (2) for the emigrants among themselves: friendship, solidarity; and (3) for the inhabitants of the country of immigration: welcome, fraternity. All these values are richly illustrated with texts from the Bible and Church documents.

{537}

Antonio Cechin, a Brazilian catechist, reacted as follows to this Portuguese example of catechesis.[17] He faults it for situating the causes of emigration from Portugal only on the level of the individual and not on the level of the structural background. Must one not ask from what part of Portugal the emigrants come? Why? What are the regional, national, and international causes? Is it merely a matter of improving the life situation of the emigrants or is it necessary to commit oneself to changing the structures? And Cechin concludes: "Because of the failure to use proper analytical instruments, the result completely distorts the Gospel and gives religion the image that Marxists assign to it, namely, Christianity as the opium of the people, a bourgeois Christianity for Christians of the developed countries where the emigrants go, and a bourgeois Christianity for the Christians of the country the emigrants leave." Cechin rejects this catechetical project because it is not a "liberation catechesis," because it promotes the current state of society and does not develop a mechanism for liberation.[18]

The Objective of Moral Formation

The objective of moral formation can be broadly stated as follows: "Ultimately, one wants to see developed a supple, insightful, affectively attractive, and operative disposition that helps, as much as possible, assimilate and realize, defend, and if necessary command Christian inspired ethical values and norms in the

---

[17]Cf. A. Cechin, "Révolution dans la catéchèse latino-américaine" in Catéchistes, nr. 85, 1971, Jan., pp. 73–85.

[18]In 1977, a European workgroup for youth catechesis has drawn up a number of important options for the so-called liberation catechesis. These options give concrete content to the abovementioned three phases and can be found in *Bevrijd om te dienen: Bijbelse en eigentijdse bevrijdingstheologie en-catechese*, (Antwerp: Patmos, 1978), pp. 248–260.

various areas of life of the individual personality and of groups."[19]

This general objective of moral formation can be divided into three aspects or components, which evoke each other:

1. Insight components or the cognitive aspect (for example, structural-historical, structural-social insight): the Christian moral formation envisages the development of the capacity to articulate the Christian inspired moral value judgments.

2. Affective relatedness and emotions that stimulate the attitudes and dispositions (affective-dynamic component: moral formation aids the expression of evaluations, approval or disapproval, for a number of objects or situations.

3. Behavioral component: Christian moral formation develops the capacity for appropriate moral conduct for the realization of personal and social values.

The unfolding of these three aspects of the human personality contributes to the formation of independent and responsible personalities and makes possible the growth of young people and adults into moral persons who can be and want to be responsible for their actions and their life projects. The simultaneous realization of these three objectives was always the concern of Jozef Cardijn, the founder of the Young Catholic Workers: "observe, judge, and act."

The learning of the acquisition of values, which influence both attitudes and behavior, ought to stand in the center of moral education. However, it is a fact that the school can fully and directly provide for the cognitive component of moral formation. All the cognitive objectives envisioned by the well-known taxonomy of D. R. Krathwohl and G. S. Bloom can be achieved. On this level, it seems to me that Lawrence Kohlberg's concepts of the stimulation of moral development are very important. The possibilities the school has for affective-dynamic formation with regard to moral attitudes and values are, on the other hand,

---

[19]C. De Keyser, *Mensenrechten en volwassenenvorming*, Brussels, Wereldvakverbond van onderwijzend personeel, 1977, p. 111. (This text has been slightly altered.)

considerably less. The affective objectives, according to Krathwohl and Bloom's taxonomy, can only be achieved via formal education to the second level as a rule, and, exceptionally, to the third level.[20] Affective formation and the preference for and internalization of values have a much better chance of succeeding through contact with living ethical models (imitation and identification) in the family, the parish, or via the school ministry than in the classroom situation.

And as regards action-formation in school, as a rule one can influence the motivations, dispositions, and readiness to act rather than directly the acts themselves. For actions are learned principally by doing, that is, by participating in action groups. It becomes immediately clear that classroom education can pursue real though limited objectives. Its influence occurs mainly via the cognitive aspect, which also is operative in the affective and behavioral domain. Some authors are even of the opinion that formal teaching must limit itself to cognitive mechanisms behind attitudes and values; only under these conditions can intolerable indoctrination and manipulation be avoided. An old Chinese proverb is apropos here: "What I hear, I forget; what I see, I remember; what I do, I know."

Morality as a Learning Process

The uniqueness of religious-moral learning in the classroom is that it is mainly theoretical learning aimed at praxis. The moral learning process presumes an initial life attitude and life praxis aimed at an improvement of this attitude and praxis. The limited academic contribution to moral formation is situated in this process. The moral learning process is specified by a great number of variables that influence the acquisition and alteration of attitudes and value orientations. In addition to sociological determinants (such as the socioeconomic status of the family, the peer group, and the school and the diversity of the sociostructural

---

[20]Cf. B.S. Bloom and D.R. Krathwohl, *Taxonomy of Educational Objectives: Handbook I, Cognitive Domain*, New York, 1956; *Handbook II, Affective Domain*, New York, 1964.

experiential world of the individual) and the psychological determinants (such as the level of cognitive and affective development
and the disposition with respect to the school and the present
beliefs, value structure, and communication competence), there
are also educational-process determinants, which can be divided
into four groups: characteristics of the sender (for example,
credibility, selective exposure), characteristics of the message, in
this case the medium (for example, the nature of the message, the
semantic code, the affective content), characteristics of the re-
ceiver (for example, decoding capacity, degree of identification),
and characteristics of the situation (for example, the nature of the
setting and the number of senders that demand attention).[21]

Much research still needs to be done to trace more exactly the
influence of these different variables on the process of moral
education.

I shall briefly outline some methodological and interactional
aspects of education in values and norms.

Rational Discussion

Values and norms have to be the subject of rational discussion in
general education and also in religious education. The students
may not be left entrenched behind a one-sided appeal to individual conscience. It is thus not enough for the students to
express their feelings and insights regarding all sorts of moral
problems. They also have to confront their feelings and insights in
a faith-critical manner with the experiences, insights, and value
judgments of others in the class and outside of it. Their experiences and insights must at the same time be broadened by being
brought into contact with those of people who have tried in the
past to construct a world worthy of human beings. Students may
not settle into an ideology of self-development and self-
actualization. One can become human only in relation to others.

---

[21]Cf. P.L.M. Jungbluth and C.A.C. Klaassen, *De vorming van waarden en houdingen in socialissatieprocessen: Een voorstudie ten behoeve van onderzoek naar de waardenoverdracht in het ondewijs* (Nijmegan: Instituut voor toegepaste sociologie, 1973), particularly point, 5.2 (pp. 339–354).

To promote rational discussion, the use of conflict situations and "open stories" is very useful. I have had good experiences by having students devise conclusions to an absorbing but un- {541} finished story. After confrontation with the divergent continuations furnished by the students, the conclusion of the author was read and discussed.

A concrete example. In a class of six- and seven-year-old children, the teacher told the following story by the Flemish writer Godelieve Moenssens, but without giving the conclusion the writer had written.

> Very far away, in a tropical country, there once lived a mother giraffe and a father giraffe with their little son, Leo, who was a naughty little fellow but who could still be very lovable. On one beautiful summer day, the little giraffe went for a walk.
> Mother warned him not to go too far away because in the woods there were animals who could well be vicious. Naturally, Leo would be careful, for he was already a big giraffe. But very soon, he forgot the wise advice of his mother.
> There were so many nice things to see in the woods and when Peacock Eye, the butterfly, teasingly flew by him, Leo ran happily after.
> Suddenly a large ape appeared from behind a tree. Fortunately he was not a vicious animal, but he was a teaser. He grabbed the frightened giraffe by his long neck and tied a big knot in it.
> "See here, little brat, that'll teach you to intrude on my domain," said the ape, and, roaring with laughter, he disappeared among the trees of the woods.
> Ashamed, our giraffe slunk home. All the animals he met laughed at him. Such a rare giraffe they had never seen before.

The pupils were then invited to draw a picture of what happened when the giraffe returned home to his mother and father. The answers varied widely. Some pupils commented on their drawings by saying that the young giraffe cried out weeping, "I'll never do it again!" Others said that the parents punished him severely. A number of them suggested that the parents would untie the knot in the neck of their son. They were, apparently, more humanitarian or better child-raisers than the writer herself who finished the story like this:

At home, he got a spanking for his disobedience. The knot stayed in Leo's neck all his life but he was never again disobedient because that one lesson was enough.

Many stories and fables (for example, Little Red Riding Hood) unfortunately resolve very one-sidedly the necessary tension between autonomous exploration and the enjoyment of life and obedience to laws and authority. In other words, they often *moralize*. Therefore, the technique of "open stories" offers many advantages.

Clarification of Emotional Attitudes to Moral Problems and Their Solutions

What occurs in the course of the class discussions is determined not only by "what is said in so many words" (such as the moral concepts regarding abortion, authenticity, money, and so on), but also, if not more so, by the largely unspoken, private, and emotional attitudes that the participants have toward these concepts. Therefore, attention must be given not only to the *meaning*—the significance of the words spoken—but also to the *function* that the words fulfill.

In a class discussion, in addition to what is explicitly stated *(le dit)*, there is often an implicit element *(le non-dit)* of the relationship to a particular concept, both on the part of the teacher and on the part of the students. It is an important, delicate, and difficult task for the teacher to help clarify the attitudes that the students have toward moral concepts and conduct, whatever these may be. And the teacher himself is well-advised to become aware of his relationship to his own moral concepts and attitudes. Concretely, when a forty-year-old teacher and seventeen-year-old students discuss sexuality and marriage, they speak from very different backgrounds, life experiences, structures, value hierarchies, and spheres of interest. Therefore, in all discussions on moral problems, one must listen not only to what the students (and the teacher) *say* about sexuality, drugs, violence, and so on, but also to the emotional way in which it is said, to what *causes* them to say what they say, as well as to what they do not say. Often, indeed, students express something "like this" when they really wanted to say it "like that."

When students between fifteen and sixteen years old ask in religion class for more information about other world religions, this question often implies more than just a desire for knowledge about other religions ("meaning"). In many cases, they probably want to challenge indirectly the sometimes exclusive claims of the Catholic religion and of the Church to absolute truth, which are also defended by their teacher, or to make them points of discussion ("function") and arrive at an expert and honest confrontation between various religions.

An understanding of the large role played by emotions in the living through of moral situations and preferences for certain values will guard the teacher against overestimating the behavior-changing power of theoretical knowledge or yielding to a *Diskussionoptimismus*. Who would treat the problem of drugs in the classroom, for example, has to keep in mind the emotional side of the problem. There are emotions regarding drug usage both on the part of the users and on the part of those who fight against it: curiosity, the struggle against loneliness, the need for real experiences, the lack of courage to see drug use as a symptom rather than the actual evil, irritation toward youth seeking its own way, and so on.

Morality Not for, But Together with and by the Students

It is more important to learn to journey toward a justified vision of, and attitude toward, controversial moral problems together with the students in an atmosphere of power-free communication than to force a specific (even though Catholic) conceptual and normative pattern, or to put such a pattern outside of or above every discussion. Direct exhortation or affective forcing of moral rules and values by the teacher probably produces few lasting results nowadays. Adolescents no longer want to be approached as "objects of moral principles." They want to develop into subjects, into bearers of morality.

This pedagogical approach presumes a great degree of confidence on the part of the teacher in the self-regulating power of the class. In many cases, the class, through open and constructive dialogues, seems capable of defending serious and motivated concepts and values, even though they possibly deviate from some positions of the Catholic Church or do not arrive at the best attitudes and rules of conduct. In the students' discussions, the teacher does not need to stay involved. At appropriate times, he will put his own experiences and insights as well as those of the tradition at the service of the searching of the students. But he must also allow himself to be addressed by the new experiences and value sensitivities of his students.

There is no doubt that tensions can arise between the vision of the religion teacher and that of the ecclesiastical hierarchy. In the letter of the German Bishops, "To All Those Charged by the Church with the Preaching of the Faith" (1967), one can read in §19: "An opinion that is in conflict with the provisional pronouncements of the magisterium of the Church does not, in any case, belong to preaching and catechesis, even though one must, in particular circumstances, inform the faithful of the essence and the limited implications of such a provisional pronouncement of the magisterium." If one wants to proceed from and/or to arrive at the concepts of the ecclesiastical documents with the students, there is a great danger of blocking an enriching and constructive dialogue. Therefore, in my opinion, there is a great *didactic* advantage in the presentation for discussion of the documents of the hierarchy with regard to moral (c.q. sexual) problems—even though one may be in complete agreement with them—as very important pronouncements *alongside* other concepts, and to examine and evaluate them on the basis of their anthropological, social, and theological presuppositions. From a Catholic teacher who, in conscience, cannot agree with the particular Church positions, it may be expected that he will approach the controverted pronouncements (concretely, I have in mind "Humanae vitae" and the declaration "Persona humana") with the necessary knowledge and respect and clarify them while keeping in mind the great concern they have for the securing and promotion of important human values. This attitude will allow him to be completely himself in the classroom, even though he has reserva-tions with respect to specific ecclesiastical pronouncements.

{545}

Education for Realistic and Attainable Interim Solutions[22]

The open discussion of moral questions between students and the teacher can sometimes be seriously disturbed by an (unconscious) idealism. By idealism, I understand here the psychological ten-dency to overvalue and to absolutize ideas, feelings, attitudes, and values. Often a large dose of narcissism is involved, a love for the image that one has of oneself. The craving for the absolutely valid—idealism—is a remnant of infantile impressions and needs. In moral education, an insidious and dangerous relation-ship sometimes develops between the moral idealism of the young person and the moral idealism of the educator, which can arise again in the educational process.

It is not rare for young people in discussions to advocate an "absolute" honesty, and "absolute" transparency with each other, and an "absolute" justice and to have little tolerance for various forms of so-called "interim" solutions. And educators, particularly in Catholic schools, have a ready tendency to defend an "all or nothing morality" or a morality of "doing good *and* avoiding evil."

Under such circumstances, it often happens that the un-avoidable and irradicable ambiguity of concrete life is overlooked. The finite, limited person can generally only progress in a particular direction at the cost of neglect, subordination, or regression in other areas. He can only hope that, taken as a whole, the way to a better future is being opened. And very often, one must even be provisionally satisfied with the least damaging lie, the least harmful presentation of things. This was discovered to her sorrow by an eighteen-year-old girl who wanted to be "absolutely honest" with her fiancé and to have "no secrets" from him.

---

[22]*Cf.* Jean Le Du, *L'idéal en procès*, (Paris: Cerf, 1975).

One day, so Jean Le Du tells in one of his articles,[23] she considered the conditions right to admit to her fiancé very circumspectly that "he was not the first," that she had once given herself, rather casually, to a boy but that this had not had any deep influence on her. Her fiancé was really "the first one," she honestly thought, since she had never truly loved anyone else. And, indeed, for her this was true. She was sorry she had done it, but her guilt was not traumatic.

Her boy friend, however, did not see it that way. He "heard" the confession of her "fault" not as an indication of *her* trust and love, but took it entirely differently: within *his* strict and rigid normative system in which he had been raised. Moved by a high ideal, he had vowed never to marry except with a "true virgin." So he broke off the engagement. The girl, affected more by this rupture than by the fault that had caused it, decided: "Done with sincerity!" and thereby forfeited a part of her spontaneity and openness, of her confidence in life.

During a discussion later on with a couple who were friends of hers, she acquired a great deal of insight and a renewed orientation. She had behaved, she was told, "like a thirteen-year-old schoolgirl" by believing in absolute transparency. The couple explained that although they loved each other heart and soul as man and wife, they still knew very well that not everything could be communicated between them. Moreover, the couple explained, her so-called openness had been an involuntary "lie." What she had said was something entirely different from what her fiancé had understood. And, finally, keeping silent or even lying can sometimes be the only way to help some truth to come about between persons and in institutions.

Jean Le Du had analyzed this phenomenon closely. What he rejects is not the "absolute" but the "absolutizing," the absolute manner in which people relate to their concrete strivings and values. Therefore, Le Du argues for realistic formulations, "interim solutions," that take into account human ambiguity and limitations, the creatureliness of the human being. Certainly, a believer lives bound *(re-ligio)* to the absolute God. But in a limited,

---

[23]*Cf.* Jean Le Du, "La morale dans le conflict des générations," in *Réponses chrétiennes*, nrs. 42–43, 1971, p. 19.

{547}

finite world this bond cannot be experienced in an absolute, divine way. On the contrary, it allows him to experience all "absolute values" concretely in a relative manner. For example, sometimes one cannot communicate everything to one's friend, not even to one's spouse. It would do more harm than good. Whoever accepts the fact that he lives in a relative, limited world thereby creates the condition necessary for the establishment of a hierarchy of values and the application of it in practice, to put one objective above another, to prefer one decision over another. Only in this way do young people learn to act morally, to construct a realistic and attainable but still dynamic morality.

The morality of "all *or* nothing" undermines the dynamics of striving for interim solutions, the only solutions that really exist, and for compromises. So Le Du adds, "a compromise is not necessarily compromising" ("un comprimis n'est pas nécessairement une compromission"): the yielding of an absolute experience of a value (for example, righteousness) does not automatically result in nothing being left over (all *or* nothing). There is always the possibility of a relative and creative experience of the value.

It is noteworthy that a number of governmental authorities and educators all too readily fall back on statements of this form: "If *that* is permitted, where will it all end? A catastrophe will be inevitable." Does this not reflect the fear that someone's brakes will not function as well if a particular transgression is risked? But are there no realistic interim solutions that can be valuable in given circumstances? Concretely, for example, one can long have been a proponent of nonviolence but at a certain moment be forced by circumstances to use violence, or at least a degree of violence, as the only means to prevent even greater violence. Something of the earlier "ideal" remains, since one wants to eliminate the offending violence from the world. But still something is lost in this adventure, namely the absolute character of the earlier ideal. But this never did belong to the concrete practice of actual social reality.

The distance between ideal and reality is often intolerable for students (and teachers). Some want to destroy this distance, to eliminate it by neglecting one of the two poles. In moral formation, however, the only meaningful attitude is to learn to control this distance *(gérer l'écart)* by learning to convert the tension between ideal and reality into a fruitful effort to defend realistic options and to accomplish realistic actions. In other words, in moral formation, it is not a matter of timeless optimization but of reality-conscious meliorization.

ABOUT THE AUTHOR

Dr. Jef Bulckens *is Professor of Catechetics and Religious Education at the Katholicke Universitert Leuven and teaches Fundamental Catechetics, Religious Education in Secondary Schools, and Religious Education in the Family. He has served as a parish priest in Brussels and as a professor at the Major Seminary at Mechelen, where he gave courses in Pastoral Theology and Church History. Dr. Bulckens was also professor at the Higher Institute for Religious Sciences at Leuven.*

Among Dr. Bulcken's publications are "De morele opvoeding volgens Jean Le Du"; Spanning tussen ervaring en verwoording in de huidige schoolcatechese; *and "Verschillende typen van bijbelse catechese."*

The Scandalized Child:
Children, Media,
and Commodity Culture

EDMUND V. SULLIVAN

Prologue[1]

How do we create communities which have moral and religious concerns dealing with the problems posed by our contemporary life (for example, war, racism, ecology)? What can we expect of the schools as moral and religious educators? Is it possible to conceive of moral education as a division of isolated institutions (for example, home, school, family)? Where do we place the social sciences in contemporary life—as sources of enlightenment, as sources of mis-education?

This chapter examines some of these questions in the light of the effects of "mass media" on all contemporary moral and religious questions. It challenges separate disciplinary efforts to deal with these problems effectively.

Introduction

> Anyone who welcomes a little child like this in my name welcomes me. But anyone who is an obstacle to bring down one of these little ones who have faith in me would be better drowned in the depths of the sea with a great millstone around his neck. Alas, for the world, that there should be such obstacles! Obstacles indeed there must be, but alas, for the man who provides them! (Matthew 18:5, 7)[2]

In the International Year of the Child it seems quite appropriate to pursue the issue of giving scandal to children in its various guises. For our purposes here, we will be considering "scandal" as a "structural evil"; by that I mean I will be exploring scandal at the level of institutions. Specifically, our discussion of scandal will focus upon an institutional life that is popularly called commodity culture and one of its most important media, television. The treatment of several dimensions suggested in the title is by no means exhaustive. By treating all of these dimensions in an

---

[1]A note of grateful appreciation is extended to John Broughton, Pat Sullivan, Hank Simons, and Enda McDonagh for editorial suggestions that have improved the material contained in this chapter.

[2]Jerusalem Bible.

interrelated fashion, it is hoped that a certain critical synthesis will be achieved which will suggest the importance of "media literacy" as an important ingredient of contemporary education of our children. Our treatment is divided into several subsections. The first section explores the possible "theological" meaning of giving "scandal to children" in contemporary culture.[3] From there, the treatment of "consumer culture" is established which then moves into how a culture is mediated to its participants. This leads to a discussion of mediating institutions in modern culture which we are calling the "mass media." From there, we explore the effects of "mass media" on some specific aspects of the development of our children which raises serious moral questions tantamount to a "scandal." The concluding section of this chapter explores the wider educational questions within which our present topic is embedded. With that brief introduction accomplished, let us quickly move on to the first dimension to be explored—the "scandalized child."

The Scandalized Child

Let me quickly alert the reader to my use of the "scandalized child" as a concept for discussion. We are not here talking about a particular type of child abuse or a patently atrocious act against children. Rather, our use of the term "scandal" is generic. We are treating scandal as an "institutional evil" with structural ramifications. The scriptural quotation which starts this chapter is a hard saying to scandal givers, be they individuals or social institutions. Our treatment will not point the finger at any specific group of persons, but will be directed toward an "ensemble of persons" called "commodity culture." We will be examining some, but not all, of the specific socialization practices which are the practices

---

[3]The use of specific examples of advertising from North American television in this paper risks the accusation of being parochial in the pejorative sense. My Belgian conferees have made me aware that there is no advertising on Belgian television. This does not mean that Belgian culture is not influenced by advertising through other media. I think that my examples must be seen as particular examples of a moral global phenomena. This thesis deserves argument in another context, since I am not treating my examples as absolute in any sense.

which help reproduce that culture. In short, we will be looking at specific socialization devices in the education of our children.

{552}
    From a theological perspective, to give scandal (that is, scandalon) a social institution must be seen as "setting a trap" or "putting a stone in the path causing someone to stumble." Our treatment here will entertain the idea that our culture, as it is being played out today, is a "scandal" to our children. It will be ventured that "commodity culture" is a "cultural trap" for our children who are growing up in the latter part of the twentieth century. A good trap is always well disguised with attractive bait and, in this sense, the "demonic" must be seen as parading as the "Father of Lights." What we will be considering here will not be socialization processes which are rank and undisguised oppressors of children. We are exploring what German theologian Dorothy Soelle calls the "hidden forms of exploitation":

> Our problem today is no longer the undisguised but the hidden forms of exploitation which themselves are among the apparent freedoms, for example, the freedom to consume whenever, wherever, and whatever quantity possible.[4]

This promiscuous consumption is not related to individuals simply. Rather, it is part of the very structure of contemporary social institution. When considering it as a "scandal," we are therefore looking at it as a "structural evil." In this sense, "sin" or "flaw" is embedded in our social institutions and not specifically in individuals. Therefore, the biblical sense of the "sins of our fathers" being passed on to the next generation brings out the fact that structural flaws of one generation are passed on to the next generation in the process of socialization where a culture attempts to reproduce itself. The Gospel passage shows sound social psychology when it fully expects that "obstacles indeed there must be," since, in our sense, sin is socialization blindness. The question is then, if there is "socialization blindness," why hold humans responsible? Kerans develops the paradox of man being knowingly ignorant.[5] There is a sense in which the person or

[4]D. Soelle, *Political Theology* (Philadelphia: Fortress Press, 1974), p. 69.

[5]P. Kerans, *Sinful Social Structures* (New York: Paulist Press, 1974).

ensemble of persons knowingly remains ignorant or cherishes illusions. Our treatment, being historical, will attempt to bring out the "knowing ignorance" or illusions of capitalism which, in our view, is the underlying mechanism for "consumer culture." Dorothy Soelle gives an interpretation of "original sin" within our historical context which is helpful for our treatment here:

> Natural man is dependent on stimuli; indeed, he understands himself as a function of existing forces. He is—here and now—the man shaped by modern capitalism; he hates God, as the tradition expresses it, because he regards interest in profits and prepared-ness for aggression as unalterable characteristics of man. The basic values of our society (e.g., whoever produces and whoever con-sumes are good) are taken over as self-evident norms. Even when he suffers under these norms and sees what they do to the defenseless members of society who produce nothing, he remains natural man in the theological sense of the word. He is the man who wants to know nothing of sin, since for him the world has been forgiven and is, therefore, to be accepted as is. He cannot understand it as a *laboratorium possibilitis salutis* (Ernst Bloch). His world, from which he has no distance, defines him only in terms of his capacities to produce and to consume. Everything that lies beyond this reality is left in an intangible, fateful darkness, while perceivable reality has already been privately interpreted. The privatization of consciousness and the experience of powerlessness play into each other's hands.

In the above reading, "capitalism" and its by-product "commodity culture" may be meaningfully said to be sinful. Kerans draws this definition out and helps us to focus upon some specific ways in which our social institutions give "scandal":

> A social structure can then be meaningfully said to be sinful. It can be sinful in its source: a social structure emerges as people act out a decision which is biased, narrow and destructive. It can be sinful in its consequences: others confronted with a situation so structured are provoked to react defensively and so to reinforce the destructive characteristics of the situation. Still other people, lacking the power to react defensively, will experience sharp

---

[6]*Op. cit.* p. 86.

limitations on their effective scope of freedom and hence will experience the structures as offensive to their human dignity.[7]

Therefore, "scandalizing children" is setting the "socialization trap" on a population called children who, by definition, are a people "lacking the power to react defensively and who will, as a result, experience sharp limitations on their effective scope of freedom." Our children, when confronted with the "mass media" (in their case, television), are treated to an artistic wasteland whose sole motive is to sell products. As Rose K. Goldsen highlights:

> In the long run, what is "good for children" can only be authentic art and literature and all the other expressive materials children need. They can thrive only on art that captures them without holding them captive, that helps them stretch and reach and grow as they exercise imagination, feeling joy and a sense of accomplishment in the doing of it. Then, no matter how much a child succeeds in grasping, no matter how much a child takes away, there is always more that beckons, spurring him on to reach and stretch and reach again.[8]

This type of educational moment is absent in contemporary culture, as we will presently point out, since it does not serve the purposes of a culture based on commodity production and consumption.

Commodity Culture and the Consumer Society

> Watch, and be on your guard against avarice of any kind, for a man's life is not made secure by what he owns, even when he has more than he needs. (Luke 12:15)

Culture is one of the two or three most complicated words in the English language, having an intricate historical development as well as being used for important concepts in several distinct intellectual disciplines and in distinct incompatible systems of

---

[7]*Op. cit.* p. 79.

[8]R. K. Goldsen, *The Show and Tell Machine* (New York: Delta, 1975), p. 204.

thought.[9] For our present discussion, one of the definitions in Webster suits our purposes and so I offer it here as a provisional definition. Culture is:

> the total pattern of human behavior and its products embodied in thought, speech, action, and artifacts, and dependent on man's capacity for learning and transmitting knowledge to succeeding generations through the use of tools, language, and abstract thought.

The important feature in the above definition is that culture reproduces itself in the natural course of events through symbolic interaction between generations. Even if countervailing forces are present in most instances, they have not reached a critical mass nor are they potent enough to seriously challenge the dominant cultural myth being transmitted. The complexity and apparent diversity of our own culture make one cautious about venturing a definition of a culture as simply "commodity culture." It is true that in all cultures and at all times human groups have displayed an interest in commodities. Usually an interest in commodities was restricted to the class that could afford the luxury of that interest. It is only in modern times, however, that an interest in commodities has crossed over all classes and, in a sense, a whole culture and its mode of production (meaning, capitalist) could be characterized by Marx as being involved with an "obsession with" commodities. When we use the term "commodity culture" we are referring to a dynamic "historical process" which is still in the process of development. William Leiss gives a succinct definition that captures this historical process:

> Modern society represents the first large-scale attempt to found stability and authority not upon earlier patterns of inherited privilege or traditional association, but rather directly on the achievements of economic production and the satisfaction of needs. Naturally this decisive change did not happen all at once; and it is a process that, after many years of development, is not yet completed. This is the tendency which the emergence of capitalism during the early modern era set in motion, however, and it may be

---

[9] R. Williams, *Key Words* (England: Fontana, 1976).

expressed in the following way: the primary social bond is the identification of the self-interest of the individual intent upon maximizing the satisfaction of his needs, with the interests of society as a whole, which is to maximize the whole productive output. In concrete terms, the well-being of every individual is thought to be identical with the steady rise in the Gross National Product.[10]

This type of culture has also been referred to as a postreligious culture since its center of gravity is embedded in self-consciously secular pursuits and away from transcendent values per se.

Let me try now to elaborate on the notion of "commodity culture" by a reflection on one of its cultural artifacts (meaning, artistic creation). I will do this by some anecdotes that are summarized from John Berger's book *Ways of Seeing*.[11] Berger makes an interesting point about an artistic development which became widely known from the fifteenth century to the nineteenth century. I am referring to the "oil painting." Medieval art reflected topics which were clearly pointing toward themes of man's relationship to the transcendent. Earthly pursuits and products were always in the background and man's relationship to God was the dominant motif. With the breakdown of medieval culture and the beginnings of modern secular culture, we see a new emphasis in the art media, reflected specifically in the oil painting, of a secular concern for products. The preoccupation with "objects" and one's ownership of those products is a reflection of a new and different cultural concern. Ownership and possession of objects become an obsession. Berger tries to show some similarities and differences between the "oil painting" and its concerns with modern artistic techniques in publicity advertising. One important contrast between the "oil painting" and modern, publicity artwork is suggested as a certain shift in emphasis about commodities which is characterized by the twentieth century. As Berger puts it:

---

[10]W. Leiss, *The Limits to Satisfaction* (Toronto: University of Toronto Press, 1976), p. 4.

[11]J. Berger, *Ways of Seeing* (Great Britain: Pelican, 1972), pp. 141–142.

Yet despite this continuity of language, the function of publicity is very different from that of the oil painting. The spectator-buyer stands in a very different relation to the world of the spectator-owner.

The oil painting showed what its owner was already enjoying among his possessions and his way of life. It consolidated his own sense of his own value. It enhanced his view of himself as he already was. It began with facts, the facts of life. The paintings embellished the interior in which he actually lived. The purpose of publicity is to make the spectator marginally dissatisfied with his present way of life. Not with the way of life of society, but with his own within it. It suggests that if he buys what it is offering, his life will become better. It offers him an improved alternative to what is.

An ad written in the 1920s for Alpine Sun Lamps and described by Ewen graphically illustrates the latter process:

There are two illustrations in the ad. In the upper-right-hand corner there is an etching of a nude woman, arms outstretched, facing into the sun. The main illustration (at the center of the ad) depicts a woman lounging on the edge of her bathtub, robe open, her nakedness revealed, fondled and nurtured by the "vitally interesting message" of her Alpine Sun Lamp. The text of the ad reads as follows:

"If you were free to live . . . . Were you today to throw off the restraints of social conformity . . . would you, too, first satisfy that inborn craving for Ultraviolet? Would you discard the trappings of civilization to spend strenuous health-brimmed days in the beneficent sunlight?

For most convention-ridden people such action is denied. But the vital Ultraviolet portion of the sunlight can be brought right into the home by means of the justly famous Alpine Sun Lamp."[12]

Advertising is the systematic creation and prolongation of needs with a view to selling commodities. A culture based on the "production of commodities" (mass production) replicates itself by creating commodity needs in all of its members. In "mass culture" as we shall see, the creation of needs for commodities is directed to all; thus, for the first time we see a systematic directing

---

[12]S. Ewen, *Captains of Consciousness* (New York: McGraw-Hill Co., 1976), p. 199.

of commercial life to children's consumption of commodities. Commodity culture, then, is first and foremost a society of "consumers." Consumption becomes the predominant motif of that culture's concerns. Consumption in the pejorative sense is to destroy, to use up, to waste, to exhaust.[13] And why not, since it is an essential mechanism for a "mass production" society? The market mechanism of mass production is incredibly impervious to questions of social justice. Leiss points out that the industrially developed world with a third of the world's population uses up 90 percent of all resource production. The United States, constituting 5 percent of the world's population, takes 27 percent of all materials extracted. Within the United States, the top 20 percent own 76 percent of the total wealth, including 96 percent of the corporate stocks.[14] In addition to the distribution of wealth, the life-style of a "commodity culture" pollutes the "biosphere," exhausts and depletes natural resources to a stage of crisis, and creates working conditions for masses of people all over the world that are alienating and inhumane. It is here that we speak of "scandal" or "setting a trap" when we systematically set out to replicate these cultural mechanisms in new generations. This brings us to some of the mechanisms of cultural transmission.

Media: The Consolidation of Societal Images

Yahweh is slow to anger and rich in graciousness, forgiving faults and transgression,and yet letting nothing go unchecked; punish the father's fault in the sons to the third and fourth generation. (Numbers 14:18,19)

Cultural Mediators

The transmission of culture is a relational activity where the new generation comes into contact with the older generation's cultural

---

[13]Williams, *op. cit.*

[14]*Op. cit.*

myths, values, and so on. The process is a dynamic interchange and in a sense there can be a reciprocity of roles between the generations. The older generation generally attempts to replicate itself (that is, social formation or socialization) and the newer generation tends to force changes in predominant cultural images (that is, transformation or social change). This process is dialectical and it should not be surprising that the valences change. It is safe to say that, in general, the older generation tends to consciously or unconsciously replicate or reproduce some of its dominant accepted myths. The "cultural myths" are the predominant cultural images by which a culture represents itself.

Culture is mediated; that is, its symbols and images are passed on by institutions. Obviously, the most important mediating institution in the socialization of children was the family structure. In simpler cultures, it has been historically the only mediating device for cultural transmission. The second major mediating institution has been the school. Before the advent of the modern era, schools and family were the two main cultural mediators; that is, they carried or mediated the cultural messages to the younger generation. The twentieth century has seen a complete reverse of this process. In our own time, the family has been devastated as a cultural mediating device. Parents essentially relinquish this role to the schools where possible. This cultural transformation is quite complex and I cannot deal with this dramatic change for our present purposes. What I would like to call your attention to is the advent of a new major mediating device for socialization in the twentieth century, that of the "mass media" of communications. We will be focusing upon it in this chapter because it carries, in an unequivocal manner, the message of the central myths of "commodity culture." The "mass media" (that is, newsprint, comics, radio, and television), when compared with parents and schools, are more anonymous and democratic at the same time. As opposed to parents who concentrate their efforts on their own children and possibly their neighbors, mass media are directed to a wider range of people (that is, masses) but with patently more utilitarian motives. In essence, the "mass media" are supported by modern advertising whose main message is to sell products as commodities to people on a large scale (mass production and mass consumption). It can be seen in some of the early advertising journals that the "mass media" were to conflict with the family. The advertising business both welcomed the demise of familial authority and, at the same time, was careful not to demystify all authority:

> Rather it pointed toward the commodity market and its propaganda to replace the father's authority. Business was to provide the source of a life-style, where before the father had been the dictator of family spirit.[15]

The decline of direct parental authority can be seen in all of Disney's comics, where there is a total absence of parental figures which, rather interestingly, goes unnoticed.[16]

Legitimation of Mass Culture

Legitimation can be considered a new word for apologetics. To legitimize an institution is to give it currency and respectability. All cultures have some organs of legitimacy and have used these organs to apologize for a particular social arrangement. For example, the institution of the Church was the organ of legitimacy for the medieval world synthesis. In the twentieth century, the institutions of "legitimation" are more varied. In our century, "legitimation" or apology is technocratic in nature. Technocratic legitimation does not grant any signficance to the beliefs of the citizen or to morality proper. Rather:

> this legitimation grants to political institutions an autonomy and detachment from the public that seem to be as indisputable as the moral principles of traditional legitimacies. Deprived of moral and consensual referents, technocratic legitimation is completely "secularized" and establishes legitimacy either (1) through the manipulation of public opinion, or (2) through the provision of material compensations.[17]

---

[15]Ewen, *op. cit.* pp. 131–132.

[16]A. Dorfman and A. Mattelart, *How to Read Donald Duck* (New York: International General, 1975).

[17]C. Mueller, *The Politics of Communication* (London: Oxford University Press, 1973), p. 135.

Media carry the messages of legitimation and "mass media," as we shall see, help to manipulate public opinion into consumptive patterns of commodity culture. Stuart Ewen gives a current history of the "mass media" and its systematic attempts to manipulate public opinion through advertising.[18] In North America, a significant turn of events took place around 1920. Up to that time there was a considerable amount of "labor unrest" which focused upon both working conditions and wages. Concentrations of wealth (for example, Rockefeller and Ford) increased the resentment against these "captains of industry." By 1920, the North American labor movement was receiving better wages and there were significant attempts to bring the working force in line with industry. One of the carrots was to sell labor on the idea of the necessity of consumption of products. With higher wages, it was found that labor could buy more products and this stimulated industry. The question was, how could the "mass population" come to accept poor working conditions which many industrial jobs have as a natural outcome of "mass production"? The consensus was to draw attention of the public away from the alienating production process and focus upon the attractiveness of the products to be consumed or purchased as the outcome of that process. To this day, it is extremely rare for an advertisement to show a product in the making. This refocusing away from production to products was to be accomplished through advertising. Legitimacy of the capitalist world order would be achieved not by coercion symbolized by the presence of the "captains of industry." Rather, a more anonymous group of people (the ad men) would achieve this through the manipulation of the public's consciousness on a mass scale. Ewen calls advertisers the "captains of consciousness." The message would be common to the population at large. In essence, that message would be in all of its guises the advertising "pitch" for the consumption of products. We seem to take all of this for granted for in advertising we live and move and have our being but one must realize that this is an invention of the twentieth century.

{561}

---

[18]Ewen, *op. cit.*

Children and the Mass Media

> Then the One sitting on the Throne spoke: "Now I am making the whole of creation new." (Revelation 21:5)

Cultural stability is reproduced through the education of our children, yet in a real sense children bring new realities into our world. In one sense, there is a feeling of *hope for the new generation* in our elders. This occurs partly by accident through a certain slippage in the socialization process. As we have already indicated, parents and schooling are partly responsible for the reproductive process of culture, but in the twentieth century, a significant new organ of socialization has, in some significant ways, replaced, or at least encircled, these traditional socializers. That organ is the "mass communications media." In some working families one of these media (probably television) will interact more with the children than even their parents do. Although the school still plays a significant role in the legitimation of culture, it now has a contender in the "mass media." For example, before a child reaches the age of twenty in America, he will have seen 350,000 television commercials. The average American child, it is estimated, will have seen 20,000 commercial messages each year or over three hours of television advertising a week.[19] Television is an "organ of legitimation" and appears quite successful in this role. For example, Marcus Welby, a television doctor (fictitious) serial, received 250,000 letters from viewers, most containing requests for medical advice.[20]

When we are speaking of "mass media," we are essentially talking about newspapers, comics, radio, and television. We will be focusing on television in this chapter because of its saliency in the lives of children. In 1964, television as a medium created the "child market" which specifically pitches its programming at children from three to eleven years of age.[21] Television enters almost every home, rich and poor alike, and makes no literacy

---

[19]Leiss, *op. cit.*

[20]J. Mander, *Four Arguments for the Elimination of Television* (New York: William Morrow Co., 1978).

[21]Goldsen, *op. cit.*

demands (Mander, 1978). It is, if I may be facetious, a very democratic instrument. In their own distinct way, all of the "mass media" serve the cause of "consumer culture." As Dorfman and Mattelart point out about the Disney comics:

> As we have observed, all the relationships in the Disney world are compulsively consumerist; commodities in the marketplace of objects and ideas. The magazine is part of this situation. The Disney industrial empire itself arose to service a society demanding entertainment; it is part of an entertainment whose business it is to feed leisure with more leisure disguised as fantasy. The cultural industry is the sole remaining machine which has purged its contents of society's conflicts, and therefore, is the only means of escape into a future which otherwise is implacably blocked by reality. It is a playground to which all children (and adults) can come, and which very few can leave.[22]

"It is a playground . . . which very few can leave"—that is the "scandal." Let me now briefly look at the "phenomenology of the television experience" to see how the trap is set and how the "scandal" passed by without being noticed.

Television as a Medium

In the Toronto *Globe and Mail*, Monday, January 29, 1979, there is a picture of a 38-year-old woman being arrested. She is being charged for hijacking a plane for the purposes of bringing attention to her plight as a divorced Catholic. Her ransom? Prime time television!

Television as a technological device has been around since 1925.[23] It was not until the 1940s, however, that the advertising industry saw the commercial possibilities that this medium offered.[24] Mander goes so far as to say that television is the invention of modern advertising. By the 1970s, its popularity is so

---

[22]Dorfman and Mattelart, *op. cit.* p. 96.

[23]Mander, *op. cit.*

[24]*Ibid.*

established that its use serves as ransom for a hijacking. Its ubiquity is such that prime time television probably reaches about two thirds of the American population with its messages. It is truly "the mass medium." Of all other "media" mentioned, it is the most active in the creation of "images" while reducing its watchers to a relative state of passivity. For example, in radio you must create your own images since only the audio is supplied. Television does both. Mander, quoting the hypnotist Erikson, tries to indicate the possible "hypnotic effects" that television-watching produces:

> You give the person so much to deal with that you don't give him a chance to do anything on his own. It's fast, continuous, requiring that he try to deal with one thing after another, switching around from focus to focus. The hypnotist might call the patient's attention to any particular thing, it hardly matters what. Eventually, something like overload is reached, the patient shows signs of breaking and then the hypnotist comes in with some clear relief, some simple instruction, and the patient goes immediately into trance.[25]

Mander's experience as an ad man made him conclude that advertising in essence attempts what is tantamount to a hypnotic state. The television, which works best in a dark room with a viewer sitting, aids in the achievement of a passive state. From there, Mander points out that:

> Every advertiser, for example, knows that before you can convince anyone of anything you shatter their existing mental set and then restructure an awareness along lines which are useful to you. You do this with a few simple techniques like fast-moving images, jumping among attention focuses, and switching moods. There's nothing to it.[26]

Our attention in this chapter will be focused, for the most part, on advertising directed toward children, although it is clearly understood that this gives only a partial picture. We are not attempting to focus on the "racist and sexist" images which

---

[25]*Ibid*. p. 197.

[26]*Ibid*.

would be most appropriate for a topic highlighting racist or sexist society. At any rate, the racist and sexist images directed toward children in the programming are carried into the commercial. Our choice of "advertising" as a focus is because it is the "raison d'être" for this medium. Mander contends that esthetically and technically television programming exists for advertising:

{565}

> The fact that advertising contains many more technical events per minute than commercial programming is significant from another, more subtle perspective. Advertising starts with a disadvantage with respect to the programming. It must be *more* technically interesting than the program or it will fail. That is, advertising must itself become a highlighted moment compared with what surrounds it.
>
> If advertising failed to work on television, then advertisers would cease to sponsor the programs, leading, at least as things are presently structured, to the immediate collapse of television's economic base. If the programs ever become too interesting, that will be the end of television. The ideal relationship between program and commercial is that the program should be just interesting enough to keep you interested but not so interesting to dominate the ad.[27]

Before proceeding any further on this topic of advertising, I would first like to consider some of the special constraints that children bring to it as a population of viewers.

The Child

The normative data which we will be using in our discussion are suggestive rather than exhaustive. I have chosen three well-known developmental theories of child development partly because these perspectives inform our present discussion and also because two out of the three theorists to be discussed (that is, Fowler and Kohlberg) contributed to this volume. All of these theories (that is, cognitive—Paiget, moral—Kohlberg, and religious—Fowler) postulate stages or epochs of development which are qualitatively distinct active mediators of the growing

---

[27]*Ibid*. pp. 306–307.

child and his or her environment. All of these theories see the person in "active" interchange with the environment. To talk about the "child and the media" is essentially to talk about a person-environment interaction.[28] From the perspective being developed here, an environment can be educational or mis-educational. An educational environment builds on the child's active strength within a particular epoch or stage. A mis-educational environment preys on the specific vulnerabilities of a specific stage or epoch for ulterior motives which are not related to the child's intrinsic development. It is here that television, and specifically television advertising, can be said to be mis-educational (a scandal) since its sole purpose is to present the child with "images" which will draw his or her attention for the purpose of selling products. The entertainment value of commercials is to sell products and not to educate. Indeed, because of the limitations of children's development and different stages of their development, it is tantamount to deception. It is for this reason that it would be more accurate to say that television is more "reproduction" than "recreation."

Imaging and Children

Every culture produces a set or cluster of images which, in some way, characterizes the important concerns that culture must deal with in order to be called a culture. There are images for social maintenance and social change. Sometimes these images are combined, sometimes they are separate. Either way, these images become part of the symbolic system of the child as he or she moves toward adulthood. The television is a medium par excellence in the presentation of images. Its very business is the production of "images." It is here we would like to say that a society's imaging is fundamentally a "religious" activity. By this, we mean that our "images" reveal our "ultimate concerns." (By their images you will know them.)* Even when an "image" or

---

[28]See D. Hunt and E. V. Sullivan, *Between Psychology and Education* (Hinsdale, Ill.: Dryden, 1974).

*Excuse the play on a biblical text.

symbol appears as "secular" it nevertheless lodges some religious import. Superman is a case in point. Mircea Eliade tries to draw this out in his discussion of myths and the mass media:

> The characters of the comic strips present the modern version of mythological or folklore Heroes. They incarnate the ideal of a large part of society, to such a degree that any change in their typical conduct or, still worse, their death, will bring on veritable crises among their readers; the latter react violently, and protest by sending thousands of telegrams to the authors of the comic strips or the editors of the newspapers in which they appear. A fantastic character, Superman, has become extremely popular, especially because of his double identity; although coming from a planet destroyed by a catastrophe, and possessing prodigious powers, Superman lives on Earth in the modest guise of a journalist, Clark Kent; he is timid, unassertive, dominated by his colleague, Lois Lane. This humiliating camouflage of a Hero whose powers are literally unlimited revives a well-known mythical theme. In the last analysis, the myth of Superman satisfies the secret longings of modern man who, though he knows that he is a fallen, limited creature, dreams of one day proving himself an "exceptional person," a "Hero."[29]

It is interesting to note here how this hero (Superman) is embedded in the process of consumption. With the production of Warner Brothers' new *Superman* movie, there are also the coordinated enterprises of Warner's Superman shirts, Warner's sound track of the movie, Superman suits, and last, but not least, pieces of kryptonite rock. The same can be said for most myth-making movies today (for example, *Star Wars*).

Because we will later discuss the "Television as a Moral Educator," we would like to reiterate its importance in the symbol-making process by one more quote from Rose Goldsen's book, whose subtitle is "How Television Works and Works You Over":

> The power to dominate a culture's symbol-producing apparatus is the power to create the ambience that forms consciousness itself. It is a power we see exercised daily by the television business as it

---

[29]M. Eliade, *Myth and Reality* (New York: Harper Torchbooks, 1963).

penetrates virtually every home with the most massive continuing spectacle human history has ever known. Wittingly and unwittingly, this business and its client industries set the stage for a never ending performance stripping away emotional associations that centuries of cultural experience have linked to patterns of behavior, institutional forms, attitudes, and values that many cultures and subcultures revere and need to keep vigorous if they are to survive. The daily consciousness-raising sessions transmitted by television demonstrate the narrow range of alternatives selected by a handful of people as eminently worthy of attention and collective celebration.[30]

The issue of control over man's symbol-making capacities raises some fundamental religious questions. How, for example, can a Christian be said to be "in the world and not of it" when authentic religious symbols have no foothold in the child's consciousness? How can a child seriously contemplate "the dangers of riches" when his or her consciousness is invaded with "images" to the contrary? Fowler's theory of stages in faith development raises important questions for religious education when the breakdown of the family as a legitimizing institution is taken into consideration. What happens in a person's first two stages of development where parents are considered as the primary "image makers"? It strikes us that these images are completely contaminated today by the images of "commodity culture" which are part and parcel of "mass media." Is it possible to transform "media images" to authentically symbolize religious values? This seems to me to be an important task for religious educators to contemplate in their work. In our view, it would be eminently reasonable to conceive of religious symbols as "counter-cultural" when embedded in the culture of commodities.

Let me close this section by giving a few more examples of advertising directed to children and embedded in children's programs. The examples are given to show how the "advertising images" play into the child's vulnerabilities at particular stages of cognitive and moral development. Looking at Kohlberg's stages

---

[30]Goldsen, *op. cit.* pp. 14–15.

for the moment, one can conclude that the television advertisement consolidates a preconventional morality and plays on the vulnerabilities of interpersonal conventions (Kohlberg's Stage 3[31]). Most children's ads encourage the child to serve his or her own needs and to be preoccupied with them (Stage 2). At the same time, the ad is frequently backed up by some "mythical figure" who is a good person who is to be trusted. Such congenial and authoritative figures as Ronald McDonald and the "Burger-King" are adult models whose ulterior motives are to get the children to the place where hamburgers can be bought. Since the young child is apt to respond positively to these authority figures, they are most effective in selling to children (Stages 3 and 4). If you watch children's commercials carefully, you will notice the ubiquity of these friendly authority figures. The television ads directed toward children prey on the child's "perceptual vulnerabilities." Let me quickly refer you to Piaget's (1970) stages and quote the description for prelogical thought which occurs roughly between the ages of two and five:[32]

> . . . inference is carried on through images and symbols which do not maintain logical relations or invariances with one another. "Magical thinking" in the sense of (a) confusion of apparent or imagined events with real events and objects and (b) confusion of perceptual appearances of qualitative and quantitative change with actual change.

O'Bryan, in an exhaustive analysis of children's commercials, points out in specific ways and with numerous examples how children's ads capitalize on the child's limitations at specific Piagetian stages.[33] Apropos of the preoperational child described above, he alludes to the fact that many children's ads present magical transformations of the product, the characters involved in the product, or the ambience of the setting in which the product is

---

[31]L. Kohlberg, "Moral Stages and Moralization," in T. Lickona, ed., *Moral Development and Behavior* (New York: Holt Rinehart and Winston, 1976), ch. 2.

[32]J. Piaget, "Piaget's Theory," in P.H. Mussen, ed., *Manual of Child Psychology* (New York: Wiley & Co., 1970), ch. 9.

[33]K. O'Bryan, "Advertising: The Science of the Art," Unpublished manuscript, Toronto, 1978.

presented. These can take the form of magical tricks, as in the Burger-King commercials, or manipulations of the settings in which the selling message is presented as in the McDonald's ads. In the McDonald's ads, Ronald McDonald and his friends are able to bring an early dinnertime about, make the sun go down and the stars come out, travel around the world and, in short, do all the necessary things to bring the child magically (through their efforts) to dinnertime at McDonald's. The mix of fantasy and reality in breakfast cereal commercials, such as those for Cookie Crisp and Cornie Snaps, enables the producer to integrate into the children's breakfast-style a loved cartoon or representational elf figures so that the child is literally able to see them bouncing around on the breakfast table. One particular product, Nestle's Quik, employs a cartoon rabbit to interact with a child to illustrate the inability of the child or the rabbit to drink Quik slowly.

Adults, of course, can separate fantasy from reality. The preoperational child often does not. For him, Burger-King *can* pull rabbits from hats, and Ronald McDonald *can* transport the child from the forest to the McDonald's restaurant. The preoperational child is invited to associate Burger-King and McDonald's with magic and wonder, and he will.[34]

The examples given here are only suggestive of some of the ways "mass media" are creating "cultural traps" (that is, scandal) for our children's consumption patterns. I use television and television ads because of the potency of that "medium," but it must be clearly kept in mind that television and all other interrelated "mass media" are cultural creations of a "consumer mentality." They send a message and, as McLuhan says, the "medium is the message." On one Saturday morning (which is prime time children's television), I counted over 50 commercials geared toward children within a period of three hours. Underneath all of the specific messages of the specific products is the metamessage "Consume!" The religious message is "Consume and you shall see the kingdom of heaven."

---

[34]*Ibid.*

A Final Note on Moral and Religious Education

For the past ten years, there has been considerable interest in the areas of moral and religious education. Although much of this work can and should receive critical appraisal, it nevertheless suggests that our own culture is concerned with moral issues. People involved with "Moral Education" have responded to this cultural need. Most of this work has centered on the school as a moral educator. Without attempting to downplay the merits of these efforts, I would nevertheless like to have you consider the "mass media" as a moral educator. It is in this sense that one could consider the "television as a moral educator." The question then comes to mind, "Is a moral education possible in an advanced capitalist consumer society?"[35] As I have developed the issues in this chapter, that question assumes major importance in any efforts at moral education broadly conceived. I have suggested elsewhere that a postcritical approach is necessary for any moral education efforts embedded in a "consumer-oriented" society.[36] A postcritical perspective proceeds on the assumption that values are already assimilated unconsciously and now must be made subject to a "critical awareness." This approach to values proceeds from a frame of reference quite different from *liberal* and *traditional* conceptions of value education. A postcritical perspective starts out with the assumption that our culture is in the grip of a profound "Value Crisis" produced as a by-product of the development of advanced Western capitalism.[37] Moreover, this crisis will not be alleviated to any appreciable extent by "liberal" reforms or a return to the traditional virtues of a previous era. In fact, one can put the development of this problem at the door of liberal institutions and reforms.

It is not a question from a postcritical perspective whether "Values can be taught." The school and media are now and have

{571}

---

[35]M. Welton, "Is a 'Moral' Education Possible in an Advanced Capitalist Consumer Society?" *The History and Social Science Teacher*, Canada, Vol. 13, No. 1 (Fall 1977), pp. 9–22.

[36]E.V. Sullivan, "Can Values Be Taught?" in E. Turiel and M. Windmiller, eds., *New Perspectives in Values* (New York: Allyn and Bacon, 1979).

[37]J. Habermas, *Legitimation Crisis* (Boston: Beacon Press, 1975).

always been institutions immersed in values. In fact, they legitimate current societal values and consolidate and enculturate them for a new generation. If we are facing a value crisis, and that seems clear from this volume, it is a crisis of a legitimacy of the values that our culture holds. It is a crisis of "mass culture," embedded in the values of unending *production* and *consumption*, a set of values which increasingly is failing to merit the allegiance of the young, poor, and disenfranchised. If one considers the school as a legitimizing institution, then it follows from this perspective that the schools and media are currently involved in enculturating the virtues of *consumer capitalism*. One of the functions of education is to provide individual competencies necessary for the adequate performance of social roles; education, therefore, is fundamental to social stability and functioning of any society. In the context of education broadly conceived, the question of whether "values can be taught" must be looked at from at least two perspectives. If education is a process whereby an individual acquires his world view from his society, one must first of all look at the process itself.[38] As to the process, we understand socialization from a theoretical perspective, but there is little knowledge of the particular cultural assimilation that is actually being transmitted from the "media" to the child. There is a "hidden-curriculum" there, and we have little knowledge of the assumptions and myths that are being transmitted in "mass media." Without this understanding of our own assumptions and myths, there is no way of assessing how they influence the psychic and social well-being of the individual who unquestioningly internalizes them.[39] It is frankly difficult for educators to examine the mythic world they live in. The dominant assumptions about work, technology, consumption, success, progress, and so on, are routinely transmitted in schools and "mass media" without any concern about their validity or consequences.[40] I would suggest that one essential component of moral and religious education would be "media literacy." The "television" should be one of the topics for

---

[38]C. A. Bowers, *Cultural Literacy for Freedom* (Eugene, Oregon: Elan, 1974).

[39]*Ibid.*

[40]*Ibid.*

"problem-posing education" in the school and in the home. In that light, this chapter was designed to show how one medium attempts to "name the world" of our children. This is why we see "cultural literacy" as a fundamental process for a truly "liberal education" at this point in our history. In the end, we are ultimately dealing with a religious question which poses the problem of evil in "structural terms."

> For it is not against human enemies that we have to struggle, but against the Sovereignties and the Powers who originate the darkness in this world, the spiritual army of evil in the heavens. (Ephesians 6:12)

Under the massive structural conditions of "monopoly capitalism," the man of faith must be constantly looking out for signals of transcendence. He must be constantly looking for and creating institutions which allow us to experience the "freedom of the Children of God."

> In the world you will have trouble, but be brave: I have conquered the world. (John 16:33).

ABOUT THE AUTHOR

Dr. Edmund V. Sullivan is Joint Professor of Psychology and Philosophy in the Department of Educational Theory at the University of Toronto. From 1968 to 1974 he codirected with Clive Beck a Ministry of Education project on "Moral Education in the Schools." During this period, he carried out extensive research and practical programs in moral education in the elementary and secondary schools of Ontario.

Among Dr. Sullivan's publications are Moral Education: Interdisciplinary Approaches; Moral Learning: Some Findings, Issues, and Questions; Kohlberg's Structuralism: A Critical Appraisal; *and* Between Psychology and Education *(coauthored with Hunt).*

BIBLIOGRAPHY

Adler, A. *Social Interest: Challenge to Mankind.* New York: Capricorn Books, 1974.

Anthony, Richard. "A Phenomenological Structuralist Approach to the Scientific Study of Religion." Unpublished paper presented at an American Psychological Association symposium on Methodological Issues in the Psychology of Religion, 1976.

Audinet, J. "Stratégie d'une éthique chrétienne." In *L'Homme manipulé: Pouvoir de l'homme sur l'homme, ses chances et ses limites.* Strasbourg: Credic-Publications, 1974.

Auer, A. *Autonome Moral und christlicher Glaube.* Dusseldorf: Patmos, 1971.

———. *Moralerziehung im Religionsunterricht.* Freiburg: Herder, 1975.

Bachmeyer, T. "The Use of Kohlberg's Theory of Moral Development in Religious Education." *Living Light,* Vol. 10 (1973).

Bakan, David. *The Duality of Human Existence.* Chicago: Rand McNally, 1966.

Baldwin, James Mark. *Social and Ethical Interpretations in Mental Development.* New York: Macmillan, 1902.

Becker, Ernest. *The Structure of Evil.* New York: Macmillan, 1968.

Beffart, F., et al. *Geschlechtserziehung interdisciplinär: Grundlegende Information für Lehrer.* Dusseldorf: Patmos, 1975.

Belenky, M. "Conflict and Development: A Longitudinal Study of the Impact of Abortion Decisions on the Moral Judgments of Adolescent and Adult Women." Unpublished Ph.D. dissertation, Harvard University, 1978.

Berger, J. *Ways of Seeing.* Drayton, Middlesex, England: Penguin Books, Pelican, 1972.

Berger, Peter L. *A Rumor of Angels: Modern Society and the Rediscovery of the Supernatural.* New York: Doubleday & Co., 1969.

Berger, Peter L., and Thomas Luckmann. *The Social Construction of Reality.* New York: Doubleday & Co., 1966.

Berten, I. "Il est mort pour nous . . . il vit." *Lumen Vitae,* Vol. 33 (1978).

Bergson, Henri. *Les deux sources de la morale et de la religion.* 216th ed. Paris: P.U.F., 1976.

Bevrijd om te dienen: Bijbelse en eigentijdse bevrijdings-theologie en catechese. Antwerp: Patmos, 1978.

Biemer, G., and A. Biesinger. *Theologie im Unterricht.* Munich: Kösel, 1976.

Binswanger, Ludwig. *Being-in-the-World.* New York: Basic Books, 1963.

Blasi, A. "Personal Responsibility and Ego Development." In R. de Charms, ed., *Enhancing Motivation.* New York: Irvington Pubs., 1976. [Formerly entitled *They Need Not Be Pawns: Toward Self-Direction in the Urban Classroom.*]

Bloom, B. S., and D. R. Krathwohl. *Taxonomy of Educational Objectives, Handbook I: Cognitive Domain.* New York: Longman, 1977.

———. *Taxonomy of Educational Objectives, Handbook II: Affective Domain.* New York: Longman, 1977.

Boeckle, F. "Geloof en handelen." *Concilium,* No. 10 (1976).

Botvin, Raymond, et al. *Religion and American Youth.* U.S. Catholic Conference, 1312 Massachusetts Avenue, N.W., Washington, D.C. 20005.

Bourke, V. J. "Ethics." *New Catholic Encyclopedia,* Vol. 5. New York: McGraw-Hill, 1967.

Bowers, C. A. *Cultural Literacy for Freedom.* Eugene, Oreg.: Elan, 1974.

Boyce, William D., and Larry C. Jensen. *Moral Reasoning: A Psychological-Philosophical Integration.* Lincoln: University of Nebraska Press, 1979.

Brennan-Nichols, P. "James Fowler: Faith and Development." *Catechist,* Vol. 11 (1978).

Brown, Daniel. Ph.D. dissertation, University of Chicago, 1978.

Browning, Don. "Faith and the Dynamics of Knowing." In Peter Homans, *The Dialogue Between Theology and Psychology.* Chicago: University of Chicago Press, 1978.

Buber, Martin. *Hasidism and the Modern Man.* New York: Horizon Press, 1958.

———. *I and Thou.* New York: Charles Scribner's Sons, 1958.

———. *Jewish Mysticism.* London: J. M. Dent & Sons, 1931.

———. *Mamre: Essays in Religion.* Melbourne: Melbourne University Press, 1946.

———. *The Origin and Meaning of Hasidism.* New York: Horizon Press, 1960.

Bull, Norman J. *Moral Education.* London: Routledge & Kegan Paul, 1973.

Burke, Kenneth. *Language as a Symbolic Action: Essays on Life, Literature, and Method.* Berkeley: University of California Press, 1966.

Bushnell, Horace. *Building Eras in Religion.* New York: 1869.

Callahan, D. *Abortion: Law, Choice, and Morality.* London: Macmillan, 1970.

Cechin, A. "Révolution dans la catéchèse latino-américaine." *Temps et Paroles* [formerly *Catéchistes*], No. 85 (January 1971).

Colleran, K. "Bernard Lonergan on Conversion." *Dunwoodie Review,* Vol. 11 (1971).

Conn, W. "Bernard Lonergan's Analysis of Conversion." *Angelicum,* Vol. 53 (1976).

———. "Postconventional Morality: An Exposition and Critique of Lawrence Kohlberg's Analysis of Moral Development in Adolescent and Adult." *Lumen Vitae,* Vol. 30 (1975).

Cunningham, Lawrence. "Stages of Faith in Relation to Jung's Theory of Individualization." Unpublished paper in private circulation, 1977.

Curran, C. "Christian Conversion in the Writings of Bernard Lonergan." In P. McShane, ed., *Foundations of Theology: Papers from the International Lonergan Congress, 1970.* Notre Dame, Ind.: University of Notre Dame Press, 1972.

———. *Ongoing Revision in Moral Theology.* Notre Dame, Ind.: Fides/Claretian, 1975.

D'Arcy, E. "Worthy of Worship: A Catholic Contribution." In G. Outka and J. Reeder, eds., *Religion and Morality.* Garden City, N.Y.: Anchor Press, 1973.

"Decree on Priestly Formation." In Abbott, Walter M., S. J., gen. ed., *The Documents of Vatican II.* New York: Guild Press, 1966.

Dewey, John. *Democracy and Education.* 1916. Reprint ed. New York: The Free Press, 1966.

———. *Experience and Education.* New York: Collier, 1938.

———. "The Need for a Philosophy of Education." In R. Archambault, ed., *John Dewey on Education.* New York: Random House, 1964.

———. *Problems of Men.* 1946. Reprint ed. New York: Greenwood Press, 1968.

———. *Reconstruction in Philosophy.* New York: New American Library, 1950.

Dorfman, A., and A. Mattelart. *How to Read Donald Duck: Imperialist Ideology in the Disney Comic,* trans. D. Kunzle. New York: International General, 1975.

Drehsen, V., and H.J. Helle. "Religiosität und Bewusstsein." In W. Fischer and W. Marhold, eds., *Religionssoziologie als Wissenssoziologie* (1978).

Dulles, Avery. *Revelation Theology: A History.* New York: Herder & Herder, 1969.

Dumoulin, Anne, and Jean-Marie Jaspard. "Les Mediations Religieuses dans la perception du divin et l'attitude religieuse de 6 a 12 ans." *Lumen Vitae,* Vol. 27 (1972).

Durkheim, E. *The Division of Labor in Society,* trans. G. Simpson. New York: Macmillan, 1964.

——— *The Elementary Forms of the Religious Life.* 1915. Reprint ed. New York: Macmillan, 1965.

Duska, R., and M. Whelan. *Moral Development: A Guide to Piaget and Kohlberg.* New York: Paulist Press, 1975.

{578}

Dykstra, C. *Christian Education and the Moral Life: An Evaluation of and Alternative to Kohlberg.* Ph.D. dissertation. Ann Arbor, Mich.: University Microfilms International, 1978.

Eliade, Mircea. *Myth and Reality.* New York: Harper & Row Pubs., Harper Torchbooks, 1963.

Erikson, Erik H. *Childhood and Society.* 2nd ed. New York: W. W. Norton & Co., 1963.

————. *Identity: Youth and Crisis.* New York: W. W. Norton & Co., 1968.

————. *Insight and Responsibility.* New York: W. W. Norton & Co., 1964.

————. *Young Man Luther.* New York: W. W. Norton & Co., 1958.

Evans, D. "Does Religious Faith Conflict with Moral Freedom?" In G. Outka and J. Reeder, eds., *Religion and Morality.* Garden City, N.Y.: Anchor Press, 1973.

Ewen, S. *Captains of Consciousness.* New York: McGraw-Hill, 1976.

Faber, Heiji. *Psychology of Religion.* Philadelphia: The Westminster Press, 1975.

Ferre, F. *Basic Modern Philosophy of Religion.* New York: Charles Scribner's Sons, 1964.

Flavell, John H. *The Development of Role-Taking and Communication Skills in Children.* New York: John Wiley & Sons, 1968.

Ford, J., and G. Kelly. *Contemporary Moral Theology: Questions in Fundamental Moral Theology.* New York: Newman Press, 1958.

Fowler, James W. "Stages in Faith: The Structural-Developmental Approach." In Thomas C. Hennessy, ed., *Values and Moral Development.* New York: Paulist Press, 1976.

————. *To See the Kingdom: The Theological Vision of H. Richard Niebuhr.* Nashville, Tenn.: Abingdon Press, 1974.

Fowler, James W., and S. Keen. *Life Maps: Conversations on the Journey of Human Faith.* Waco, Tex.: Word Books, 1978.

Frankena, W. "Is Morality Logically Dependent on Religion?" In G. Outka and J. Reeder, eds., *Religion and Morality.* Garden City, N.Y.: Anchor Press, 1973.

Freud, Sigmund. *The Future of an Illusion.* London: Hogarth, 1928.

Fuchs, J. "Theologia moralis perficienda; votum Concilii Vaticani II." *Periodica de re morali, canonica, liturgica,* Vol. 55 (1966).

Gilleman, G. *The Primacy of Charity in Moral Theology.* New York: Newman Press, 1959.

Gilligan, Carol. "In a Different Voice." *Harvard Educational Review,* Vol. 47 (Fall 1977).

Gilligan, C., and M. Belenky. "Crisis and Transition." Unpublished manuscript, Harvard University, 1979.

Gilligan, C., and L. Kohlberg. "From Adolescence to Adulthood: The Rediscovery of Reality in a Post-Conventional World." *Proceedings of Jean Piaget Society Annual Meeting,* 1973.

Gilmour, W. "What Does Fowler Have to Say to Adult Educators?" *Living Light,* Vol. 13 (1976).

Goldings, Herbert. "Themes of the Phallic Stage: Repair and Consolidation of Narcissism in the Psychoanalysis of a Six-and-One-Half-Year-Old Hyperactive Boy." First Annual Beata Memorial Lecture in Child Analysis, presented at The Boston Psychoanalytic Society and Institute, Inc., May 27, 1970.

Goldman, Ronald. *Religious Thinking from Childhood to Adolescence.* Atlantic Highlands, N.J.: Humanities Press, 1964.

Greeley, Andrew. *Ecstasy: A Way of Knowing.* Englewood Cliffs, N.J.: Prentice-Hall, 1974.

Guntrip, Harry. "Religion in Relation to Personal Integration." *The British Journal of Medical Psychology,* Vol. 42 (1969).

Habermas, J. *Legitimation Crisis.* Boston: Beacon Press, 1975.

———. "Theorie der Gesellschaft oder sozialen Technologie." In J. Habermas and N. Luckmann, *Theorie der Gesellschaft oder soziologischen Technologie.* Frankfurt, 1971.

Haering, B. *The Law of Christ,* Vol. 1. New York: Newman Press, 1961.

Haggett, M. "Do Catholics Need Moral Education?" *The Clergy Review,* Vol. 59 (1974).

Hall, Edward T. *The Hidden Dimension.* New York: Doubleday & Co., 1966.

Hall, G. S. *Adolescence.* New York: Appleton, 1908.

Hauerwas, Stanley. *Character and the Christian Life: A Study in Theological Ethics.* San Antonio, Tex.: Trinity University Press, 1975.

Haunz, R. "Models in Relation to Fowler's Faith Development." *Religious Education,* Vol. 73 (1978).

Hennessey, J. "Reaction to Fowler: States in Faith or Stages in Commitment." In Thomas C. Hennessy, ed., *Values and Moral Development.* New York: Paulist Press, 1976.

Hophan, P. "Kids, Beans, and Moral Development." In T. Lickona, ed., *Minibook on Moral Development in the Classroom.* New York: Project Change, State University of New York at Cortland, 1977.

Houtart, F. "Le discours homilétique et la dimension politique de la foi." *Lumen Vitae,* Vol. 28 (1973).

Hunt, D., and E. V. Sullivan. *Between Psychology and Education.* Hinsdale, Ill.: Dryden, 1974.

Inhelder, Bärbel. "Die Entwicklung von Zufall und Wahrscheinlichkeit bein Kindern." In B. Inhelder and H. Chipman, eds., *Von der Kinderwelt zur Erkenntnis der Welt* (1978).

Inhelder, R., and J. Piaget. *The Growth of Logical Thinking from Childhood to Adolescence.* New York: Basic Books, 1958.

Jaynes, Julian. *The Origin of Consciousness in the Breakdown of the Bicameral Mind.* Boston: Houghton-Mifflin Co., 1977.

Jeremias, J. *The Sermon on the Mount.* Philadelphia: Fortress Press, 1963.

Johnson, D. "Lonergan and the Redoing of Ethics." *Continuum,* Vol. 5 (1967).

Jonsen, A. *Responsibility in Modern Religious Ethics.* Washington, D.C.: Corpus Books, 1968.

Joy, M. "Kohlberg and Moral Education." *New Catholic World,* No. 215 (1972).

Jungbluth, P. L. M., and C. A. C. Klaassen. *De vorming van waarden en houdingen in socialissatieprocessen: Een voorstudie ten behoeve van onderzoek naar de waardenoverdracht in het ondewijs.* Nijmegan: Instituut voor toegepaste sociologie, 1973.

Kegan, Robert G. *Ego and Truth: Personality and the Piaget Paradigm.* Unpublished Ph.D. dissertation, Harvard University, 1977.

—————. *The Sweeter Welcome.* Needham Heights, Mass.: Wexford Press, 1977.

Kerans, P. *Sinful Social Structures.* New York: Paulist Press, 1974.

Kerkhofs, J. "De Rooms-Katholieke Kerk en Europa: Enkele Aspecten." *Pro Mundi Vita* (1978).

Keyser, Cyriel C. de s. Mensenrechten en volwassenenvorming. *Wereldvakverbond van onderwijzend personeel* (1977).

Kohlberg, Lawrence. "Continuities in Childhood and Adult Moral Development Revisited." In P. Baltes and W. Schaie, eds., *Lifespan Developmental Psychology: Personality and Socialization.* 2nd ed. New York: Academic Press, 1973.

—————. "Education, Moral Development, and Faith." *Journal of Moral Education,* Vol. 4 (1974).

—————. "Exploring the Moral Atmosphere of Institutions: A Bridge Between Moral Judgment and Moral Action." Hans Werner Memorial Lecture, Lecture II, Clark University, April 1979.

—————. "The Meaning and Measurement of Moral Development." Hans Werner Memorial Lecture, Lecture I, Clark University, April 1979.

—————. "Moral Stages and Moralization." In T. Lickona et al., *Moral Development and Behavior.* New York: Holt, Rinehart & Winston, 1976.

—————. "Stage and Sequence: The Cognitive Developmental Approach to Socialization." In David A. Goslin, ed., *Handbook of Socialization Theory and Research.* New York: Rand McNally, 1969.

————. "Stages of Moral Development as a Basis for Moral Education." In C. M. Beck et al., eds., *Moral Education: Interdisciplinary Approaches*. New York: Newman Press, 1971.

Kohlberg, L., and R. Mayer. "Development as the Aim of Education." *Harvard Educational Review*, Vol. 42 (1972).

Kubli, F. "Einführung." In Jean Piaget, *Abriss der genetischen Epistemologie*. Hagen: Wilhelm Konemann, 1974.

Langer, Suzanne. *Mind: An Essay on Human Feeling*. Baltimore, Md.: The Johns Hopkins University Press, 1972.

Lapsley, James. *The Concept of Willing*. Nashville, Tenn.: Abingdon Press, 1967.

Leclercq, J. *L'enseignement de la morale chrétienne*. Paris: Casterman, 1952.

Le Du, Jean. *L'idéal en procès*. Paris: Cerf, 1975.

————. *Jusqu' où iront-ils? L'educateur piégé par le morale*. Paris: Chalet, 1974.

————. "La morale dans le conflict des générations." *Résponses chrétiennes*, Nos. 42–43 (1971).

————. *Qui fait la loi?* Paris: Cerf, 1974.

Leiss, W. *The Limits to Satisfaction*. Toronto, Canada: University of Toronto Press, 1976.

Loevinger, J., with A. Blasi. *Ego Development*. San Francisco, Calif.: Jossey-Bass, 1976.

Lonergan, Bernard. *Insight: A Study of Human Understanding*. 1957. Reprint ed. New York: Harper & Row Pubs., 1977.

————. *Method in Theology*. New York: Seabury Press, 1972.

Lynch, W. E. *Images of Faith*. Notre Dame, Ind.: University of Notre Dame Press, 1973.

McBride, Alfred. "Moral Education and Kohlberg's Thesis." *Momentum*, Vol. 4 (1973).

————. "Reaction to Fowler: Fears About Procedure." In Thomas C. Hennessy, ed., *Values and Moral Development*. New York: Paulist Press, 1976.

————. "Spiritual Education: Fowler's Stages of Faith." *Momentum*, Vol. 6 (1975).

McDonagh, Enda. *Doing the Truth: The Quest for Moral Theology*. Notre Dame, Ind.: University of Notre Dame Press, 1979.

————. *Gift and Call*. Notre Dame, Ind.: University of Notre Dame Press, 1975.

————. "Moral Theology." *New Catholic Encyclopedia*, Vol. 16. New York: McGraw-Hill, 1974.

————. "Teaching Moral Theology Today." *Irish Theological Quarterly*, Vol. 33 (1966).

Macquarrie, J. *Principles of Christian Theology*. New York: Charles Scribner's Sons, 1966.

Mahler, Margaret. *The Psychological Birth of the Human Infant.* New York: Basic Books, 1975.

Mander, J. *Four Arguments for the Elimination of Television.* New York: William Morrow & Co., 1978.

Martin, F. David. *Art and the Religious Experience: The "Language" of the Sacred.* Lewisburg, Pa.: Bucknell University Press, 1972.

Maslow, Abraham. *Toward a Psychology of Being.* New York: Van Nostrand Reinhold Co., 1968.

May, W. "Christian Ethics and the Human." *American Ecclesiastical Review,* Vol. 167 (1973).

Mead, George Herbert. *Mind, Self, and Society.* Chicago: University of Chicago Press, 1934.

Meadow, Mary Jo. "Personal Growth: An Eastern Spiritual and Western Ego Approach." Paper for the Psychosocial Interpretations in Theology Section, American Academy of Religion, New Orleans, La., November 1978.

Meissner, W. W., S. J. "Notes on the Psychology of Faith." *Journal of Religion and Health,* Vol. 8 (1969).

———. "Psychoanalysis and Religion." *The Annual of Psychoanalysis,* Vol. 7 (1979).

Merleau-Ponty, Jacques. *The Phenomenology of Perception,* trans. Colin Smith. Atlantic Highlands, N.J.: Humanities Press, 1962.

Mischel, T. *Cognitive Development and Epistemology.* New York: Academy Press, 1971.

Monden, L. *Sin, Liberty, and Law.* New York: Sheed & Ward, 1965.

Mosher, R. "A Democratic High School." In N. Sprinthall and R. Mosher, eds., *Value Development as the Aim of Education.* Schenectady, N.Y.: Character Research Press, 1978.

Mueller, C. *The Politics of Communication.* London: Oxford University Press, 1973.

Murphy, J. M. "The Development of Moral Reasoning from Adolescence to Adulthood." Unpublished manuscript, Harvard University, 1979.

Murphy, L. B. *Social Behavior and Child Personality.* New York: Columbia University Press, 1937.

Nelson, Hart M., et al. *The Religion of Children.* U.S. Catholic Conference, 1312 Massachusetts Avenue, N.W., Washington, D.C. 20005.

Niebuhr, H. Richard. "Man the Sinner." *Journal of Religion,* Vol. 15 (1935).

———. *The Meaning of Revelation.* New York: Macmillan, 1967.

———. *Radical Monotheism and Western Culture.* New York: Harper & Row Pubs., 1960.

———. *The Responsible Self.* New York: Harper & Row Pubs., 1963.

Niebuhr, Richard R. *Experiential Religion.* New York: Harper & Row Pubs., 1972.

O'Connell, T. *Principles for a Catholic Morality.* New York: Seabury Press, 1978.

Ogden, S. *The Reality of God.* New York: Harper & Row Pubs., 1966.

Oliver, E., and M. Bane. "Moral Education: Is Reasoning Enough?" In C. M. Beck et al., eds., *Moral Education: Interdisciplinary Approaches.* Toronto, Canada: University of Toronto Press, 1971.

Ornstein, Robert E. *The Psychology of Consciousness.* San Francisco, Calif.: W. H. Freeman & Co., 1972.

Oser, Fritz. *Die Jesus Beziehung: Werkbuch für den Lehrer.* Stuttgart: Koch, Neff & Oetinger & Co.; and Köln: Koehler & Volckmor, 1975.

————. *Kreatives Sprach-und Gebetsverhalten in Schule und Religionsunterricht.* Stuttgart: Koch, Neff & Oetinger & Co.; and Köln: Koehler & Volckmor, 1972.

————. *Theologisch denken lernen: Ein Beitrag zum Aufbau kognitiver Strukturen im Religionsunterricht.* Stuttgart: Koch, Neff & Oetinger & Co.; and Köln: Koehler & Volckmor, 1975.

Osgood, Charles E., et al. *The Measurement of Meaning.* Urbana: University of Illinois Press, 1957.

O'Toole, J. "The Philosophy of Christian Moral Education." *The Clergy Review,* Vol. 61 (1976).

Perry, William G. *Forms of Intellectual and Ethical Development in the College Years.* New York: Holt, Rinehart & Winston, 1970.

Philibert, P. "Lawrence Kohlberg's Use of Virtue in His Theory of Moral Development." *Living Light,* Vol. 12 (1975).

————. "Some Cautions on Kohlberg." *Living Light,* Vol. 12 (1975).

Piaget, Jean. *The Construction of Reality in the Child.* 1937. Trans. Margaret Cook. New York: Basic Books, 1954.

————. "Intellectual Evolution from Adolescence to Adulthood." *Human Development,* Vol. 15 (1972).

————. *The Language and Thought of the Child.* 3rd ed. Atlantic Highlands, N.J.: Humanities Press, 1962.

————. *The Moral Judgment of the Child.* 1932. Trans. M. Gabain. New York: The Free Press, 1966.

————. *The Origins of Intelligence in Children.* Trans. Margaret Cook. New York: International Universities Press, 1956.

————. "Piaget's Theory." In P. H. Mussen, ed., *Manual of Child Psychology.* New York: John Wiley & Sons, 1970.

————. *Six Psychological Studies.* Edited by David Elkind. New York: Random House, 1968.

————. *To Understand Is to Invent: The Future of Education.* New York: Viking Press, 1974.

Pieper, J. *The Four Cardinal Virtues.* Notre Dame, Ind.: University of Notre Dame Press, 1966.

Power, C., and J. Reimer. "Moral Atmosphere: An Educational Bridge Between Moral Judgment and Action." In William Damon, ed., *New Directions for Child Development*, No. 2, *Moral Development*. San Francisco, Calif.: Jossey-Bass, 1978.

Pruyser, Paul. *A Dynamic Psychology of Religion.* New York: Harper & Row Pubs., 1968.

Rahner, K. *The Christian of the Future.* New York: Herder & Herder, 1967.

————. *Foundations of Christian Faith.* New York: Seabury Press, 1978.

Ramsey, I. *Religious Language: An Empirical Placing of Theological Phrases.* New York: Macmillan, 1963.

Refoulé, François. "Jésus comme référence de l'agir des chrétiens." In *Ecriture et pratique chrétienne.* Paris: Cerf, 1978.

Regan, G. *New Trends in Moral Theology.* New York: Newman Press, 1971.

Reston, J. "A Rueful Lament." *The New York Times,* February 4, 1979.

Rieff, Phillip. *The Triumph of the Therapeutic.* New York: Harper & Row Pubs., 1966.

Rizzuto, Ana-Maria. "Freud, God, the Devil, and the Theory of Object Representation." *International Review of Psychoanalysis,* Vol. 3 (1976).

Roberts, David. *Psychotherapy and a Christian View of Man.* New York: Charles Scribner's Sons, 1953.

Rousseau, A., and F. Dasseto. "Le discours du 'Careme de Partage.' " *Lumen Vitae,* Vol. 28 (1973).

Rowntree, S. "Faith and Justice, and Kohlberg." In P. Scharf, ed., *Readings in Moral Education.* Minneapolis, Minn.: Winston Press, 1978.

Royce, Josiah. *The Sources of Religious Insight.* New York: 1912.

Ryan, K., and R. Ryan. "Moral Formation: The American Scene." In F. Boeckle and J. M. Pohier, eds., *Moral Formation and Christianity.* New York: Seabury Press, 1978.

Sandler, Joseph. "The Background of Safety." *International Journal of Psychoanalysis,* Vol. 41 (1960).

Sartre, J. P. *Huit Clos.* Paris: Gallimard, 1945.

Scanlon, M. "Christian Anthropology: An Overview." *American Ecclesiastical Review,* Vol. 162 (1970).

Schachtel, Ernest. *Metamorphosis.* New York: Basic Books, 1959.

Schiblisky, M. "Konstitutionsbedingungen religiöser Kompetenz." In W. Fischer and W. Marhold, eds., *Religionssoziologie als Wissenssoziologie* (1978).

Schillebeeckx, Edward. "Waarden en normen binnen de wetenschappen en de schoolvakken." In *Waarden en normen in het onderwijs.* Baarn: Ambo BV., 1977.

Schleiermacher, Friedrich. *On Religion: Speeches to Its Cultured Despisers.* New York: Harper & Row Pubs., 1958.

Schroeder, W., and V. Obenhaus. *Religion in American Culture.* New York: The Free Press, 1964.

Sloyan, G. "Catechetics." *New Catholic Encyclopedia,* Vol. 3. New York: McGraw-Hill, 1974.

Smith, Wilfred Cantwell. *Faith and Belief.* Princeton, N.J.: Princeton University Press, 1979.

————. *The Meaning and End of Religion.* New York: Mentor Books, 1964.

Soelle, D. *Political Theology.* Philadelphia: Fortress Press, 1974.

Spitz, Rene. *The First Year of Life.* New York: International Universities Press, 1965.

————. *No and Yes.* New York: International Universities Press, 1957.

Stachel, Günter, and Dietmar Mieth. *Ethisch handeln lernen.* Zurich: Benziger, 1978.

Starbuck, E. D. *The Psychology of Religion.* New York: Charles Scribner's Sons, 1900.

Strommen, Merton P., ed. *Research on Religious Development: A Comprehensive Handbook.* New York: Hawthorn Books, 1971.

Strommen, Merton P., et al. *A Study of Generations.* Minneapolis, Minn.: Augsburg Publishing House, 1972.

Sullivan, Edmund V. "Can Values Be Taught?" In E. Turiel and M. Windmiller, eds., *New Perspectives in Values.* New York: Allyn & Bacon, 1979.

Sullivan, Edmund V., ed., *Moral Learning: Some Findings, Issues, and Questions.* New York: Paulist Press, 1975.

Sullivan, Harry S. *The Interpersonal Theory of Psychiatry.* New York: W. W. Norton & Co., 1953.

Swanson, Guy E. *The Birth of Gods: Origin of Primitive Beliefs.* Ann Arbor: University of Michigan Press, 1960.

Thomas, Lewis. *The Lives of a Cell: Notes of a Biology Watcher.* New York: Viking Press, 1974.

Tillich, Paul. *The Courage To Be.* New Haven, Conn.: Yale University Press, 1952.

————. *The Protestant Era.* Chicago: University of Chicago Press, 1948.

————. *Systematic Theology,* 3 vols. Chicago: University of Chicago Press, 1967.

Tocqueville, Alexis De. *Democracy in America.* 1840. New York: Harper & Row Pubs., Harper Torchbooks, 1966.

Toulmin, S. *An Examination of the Place of Reason in Ethics.* New York: Cambridge University Press, 1950.

Tracey, D. *Blessed Rage for Order.* New York: Seabury Press, 1976.

Vercruysse, G. "The Meaning of God: A Factoranalytic Study." *Social Compass,* Vol. 19 (1972).

Vergote, Antoine. "Dimensions anthropologiques de l'Eucharistie." In *L'Eucharistie, Symbole et Realite.* Gembloux: Duculot, 1970.

{586} ———. "God, onze vader." *Concilium,* Vol. 130 (1977).

———. *The Religious Man.* Dublin: Gil and MacMillan, 1969.

Vygotsky, L. S. *Thought and Language,* trans. E. Hanfmann and G. Vakar. Cambridge, Mass.: The M.I.T. Press, 1962.

Walgrave, J. "Is Morality Static or Dynamic?" In F. Boeckle, ed., *Moral Problems and Christian Personalism.* New York: Paulist Press, 1965.

Weber, M. "Politics as a Vocation." In H. H. Gerth and C. W. Mills, eds., *From Max Weber: Essays in Sociology.* New York: Oxford University Press, 1946.

Weiman, Henry. *The Source of Human Good.* Carbondale, Ill.: Southern Illinois University Press, 1973.

Welton, M. "Is a 'Moral' Education Possible in an Advanced Capitalist Consumer Society?" *The History and Social Science Teacher,* Vol. 13 (Fall 1977).

Whitehead, Alfred North. *Process and Reality.* New York: The Free Press, 1929.

Whorf, Benjamin Lee, and J. B. Carroll. *Language, Thought, and Reality.* New York: John Wiley & Sons, 1956.

Williams, R. *Key Words.* London: Fontana Books, 1976.

Winnicott, D. W. *Playing and Reality.* New York: Basic Books, 1971.

Youniss, J. "Kohlberg's Theory: A Commentary." *Living Light,* Vol. 10 (1973).

1 2 3 4 5 –H– 84 83 82 81 80